The APSAC Handbook on
CHILD
MALTREATMENT
THIRD EDITION

This book is dedicated to two of the most brilliant and influential pioneers in the effort to protect children: Lucy Berliner and David Finkelhor.

The APSAC Handbook on
CHILD
MALTREATMENT
THIRD EDITION

EDITOR

John E. B. Myers
University of the Pacific

*American Professional Society
on the Abuse of Children*

Los Angeles | London | New Delhi
Singapore | Washington DC

For information:

SAGE Publications, Inc.
2455 Teller Road
Thousand Oaks,
  California 91320
E-mail: order@sagepub.com

SAGE Publications India Pvt. Ltd.
B 1/I 1 Mohan Cooperative
  Industrial Area
Mathura Road, New Delhi 110 044
India

SAGE Publications Ltd.
1 Oliver's Yard
55 City Road
London EC1Y 1SP
United Kingdom

SAGE Publications Asia-Pacific Pte. Ltd.
33 Pekin Street #02-01
Far East Square
Singapore 048763

Printed in the United States of America

Library of Congress Cataloging-in-Publication Data

The APSAC handbook on child maltreatment / editor, John E. B. Myers. — 3rd ed.
    p. cm.
Includes bibliographical references and index.
ISBN 978-1-4129-6681-8 (pbk.)
    1. Child abuse—Handbooks, manuals, etc. 2. Child abuse—Prevention—Handbooks, manuals, etc. I. Myers, John E. B.

HV6626.5.A83 2011
362.76—dc22   2009054331

This book is printed on acid-free paper.

10   11   12   13   14   10   9   8   7   6   5   4   3   2   1

Acquisitions Editor:	Kassie Graves
Editorial Assistant:	Veronica Novak
Production Editor:	Catherine M. Chilton
Copy Editor:	Megan Markanich
Typesetter:	C&M Digitals (P) Ltd.
Proofreader:	Annette R. Van Deusen
Indexer:	Molly Hall
Cover Designer:	Gail Buschman
Marketing Manager:	Stephanie Adams

Contents

Preface

My congratulations go out to the editor and authors of this volume. It is an impressive testimony to the refined level of knowledge and practice that are the hard-won fruits of 30 or more years of effort to reduce the toll of child maltreatment.

Child maltreatment scholars and practitioners should feel proud about this cumulate knowledge. It is impressive in its depth and breadth. It is also impressive in representing the work of a really large and diverse corps of contributors—not just a small group of gurus in a few high-profile places. It has also been accumulated in a way that has preserved a coherence and integrity to the field. Some fields in the course of development get riven by deep schisms and bitter controversies. While the child maltreatment field has had its controversies over matters such as ritual abuse, recovered memories, child interviewing techniques, and nurse versus paraprofessional home visitation, these controversies have not led to lasting divisions and alienation. The field—after more than 30 years—looks mature, self-critical, truly multidisciplinary, and broadly based.

The child maltreatment field will look very different in another 30 years, I predict. One large reality that leads me to conclude this is the dynamic of generational transition. The child maltreatment field as we know it is largely a product of the generation coming of professional age in the 1960s and 1970s, activists and policymakers who climbed aboard an accelerating movement and made careers of it. But those with a stake in the founding and nurturing of that field and its institutions will soon be ceding their leadership. Changes in the dominant paradigms in all fields of social activity tend to be associated with generational changes. The field will be much more open for fundamental change as this generational shift occurs.

Among the changes I expect to see in the next 30 years are (1) much more orientation to what is called "evidence-based practice," the use of experimental design and evaluation to decide what and how to act; (2) much more reliance on technology; and (3) the erosion of child protection as a separate institutional structure and its integration into other institutions like education and health care.

The move to evidence-based practice is already well underway. Some see it as an unfortunate straitjacket that excludes from consideration judgments from other forms of expertise besides those of the cold quantitative measurement. But as the knowledge base grows, as evaluation thinking becomes more integral, as ways of using research become more sensitive, and people get more comfortable, the application of evidence-based principles will become more and more routine and accepted. The evidence-based practice revolution will be accompanied by more standardization of practice and a closer relationship between child maltreatment professionals and the research community. It may also be accompanied by new financing and administrative mechanisms, including insurance coverage for some parenting and family interventions. As in the health care field, the evidence-based revolution may eventually move to community-based financing systems that give incentives to providers to keep groups of families healthy (in other words, nonabusive), rather than simply paying for rehabilitation once maltreatment occurs.

A second change will be a greater reliance on technology. It is hard to foresee all the technological developments that may prove useful in child protection, but I would highlight at least three that should see much more widespread utilization. One is expanded use of prescribed drug treatment to assist families and children in dealing with stress, conflict, and dysfunctional modes of relating. Drugs besides those targeted at depression, anxiety, and hyperactivity will probably arise, effective at treating substance abuse, anger, and transient stressors. The child protection field has some entrenched antipathy to drug treatment because it is seen as the medicalization of social work, but the effectiveness of drug treatment will win the argument, and findings will show that drugs are not a substitute for but only an adjunct to behavioral treatments.

Accompanying the use of drug treatments will be the greater use of genetic and biochemical assessments to guide practice. Such assessments will be able to target children who are vulnerable to negative outcomes and parents who may be prone to relapses. These tests may greatly improve the efficiency of interventions.

Another technology that will acquire much greater utilization is communication and surveillance technology. These technologies will be used to improve parenting in the home in real-life situations, provide coaching, monitor risky families, and build effective external support systems for parents and children. All these technologies sound a bit ominous and 1984-ish when taken out of context. But I believe social evolution will find ways to incorporate them in manners that do not clash with accepted notions of individual autonomy and privacy, values whose importance I do not see as lessening to any great extent.

Finally, I think all these changes will occur in the context of child protection practice and its institutions being reconfigured from their current form to be much more integrated into institutional spheres we now think of as health care and education. We can see the seeds of this transformation in the growing emphasis on interventions like home visiting and parenting education for preventing and intervening in child maltreatment. But interventions such as home visiting and parent education are not interventions conceptualized as solely or even primarily targeted at child maltreatment or being the unique province of child protection professionals. They are promoted and adopted in the name of improving a broad range of health and educational outcomes. This convergence among the goals of these various institutions has been apparent for a long time, but the detailed institutional forms for collaborating and coordinating among these institutions have not yet fully emerged. They will emerge, but because health care and education are bigger and broader institutional enterprises I think the resulting institutions will look more like conventional education and health care than like current child protection of our present era. This model already exists in Europe, and I think it will come to be adopted in North America as well.

Predictions about the future are notoriously unreliable, as these will likely be, as well. Among other things, they generally miss developments (like the Internet) that are completely unforeseen from the standpoint of the prognosticators. But they are useful exercises that give us some hints of how to catch and utilize the currents of history and social change. The child maltreatment field has done well as it has navigated these waters up until now. I believe the chances are good that its goals and ambitions and practitioners will continue to thrive and continue to make historic contributions to the improvement of child well-being.

David Finkelhor

Acknowledgments_____

SAGE Publications would like to thank the following reviewers:

Ronald M. Arundell
College of Mount St. Joseph

Caroline Burry
University of Maryland, Baltimore

Alberta Ellett
University of Georgia

Warna Gillies
George Mason University

Michele Gore
Eastern Kentucky University

Sue Green
SUNY Buffalo

Jackie McReynolds
Washington State University Vancouver

Mary Sean O'Halloran
University of Northern Colorado

PART I

The Child Protection System in the United States

Part I of the *APSAC Handbook on Child Maltreatment* describes America's child protection system. Chapter 1 begins the journey with a description of the history of child protection. Chapter 2 describes programs intended to prevent child abuse and neglect. Chapter 3 discusses the agency at the heart of child protection—child protective services (CPS). The juvenile court plays an important role in child protection, and the court is the subject of Chapter 4. Chapter 5 describes foster care and adoption. Part I ends with Chapter 6, an analysis of criminal prosecution of child maltreatment.

1

A Short History of Child Protection in America

John E. B. Myers

The history of child protection in America is divisible into 3 eras. The first era extends from colonial times to 1875 and may be referred to as the era before organized child protection. The second era spans from 1875 to 1962 and witnessed the creation and growth of organized child protection through nongovernmental child protection societies. The third, or modern era—the era of government-sponsored child protective services (CPS)—began in 1962. (For in-depth analysis of the history of child protection in America see Myers, 2004, 2006, 2010.)

Child Protection Prior to 1875

It was not until 1875 that the world's first organization devoted entirely to child protection came into existence—the New York Society for the Prevention of Cruelty to Children (NYSPCC). Prior to 1875, many children went without protection, although there was never a time when children were completely bereft of assistance. Criminal prosecution has long been used to punish egregious abuse. In 1809, for example, a New York shopkeeper was convicted for sadistically assaulting his slave and her 3-year-old daughter (Finkelman, 1988). In 1810, a woman was prosecuted in Schenectady for murdering her newborn child (Finkelman, 1988). Although the woman admitted to several people that she killed the baby, the jury found her not guilty—probably because she was insane. In 1856, the first rape conviction in state history reached the California Supreme Court. The victim was 13 (*People v. Benson*, 1856). From 1856 to 1940, the majority of rape prosecutions in California involved child victims. In 1869, an Illinois father was prosecuted for confining his blind son in a cold cellar in the middle of winter (*Pletcher v. People*, 1869). The father's attorney argued that parents have the right to raise their children as they see fit, but the Illinois Supreme Court disagreed,

3

writing that parental "authority must be exercised within the bounds of reason and humanity. If the parent commits wanton and needless cruelty upon his child, either by imprisonment of this character or by inhuman beating, the law will punish him" (p. 395).

Prosecution was not the only remedy before 1875. As early as 1642, Massachusetts had a law that gave local magistrates authority to remove children from parents who did not "train up" their children properly. In 1735, an orphan girl in Georgia was rescued from a home where she was sexually abused. In 1866, Massachusetts passed a law authorizing judges to intervene in the family when "by reason of orphanage or of the neglect, crime, drunkenness or other vice of parents," a child was "growing up without education or salutary control, and in circumstances exposing said child to an idle and dissolute life." Whether or not a statute authorized intervention, judges had inherent authority to stop abuse. Judge Joseph Story wrote in 1886:

> For although in general parents are intrusted with the custody of . . . their children, yet this is done upon the natural presumption that the children will be properly taken care of. . . . But whenever . . . it is found that a father is guilty of gross ill treatment or cruelty towards his infant children, . . . in every such case the Court . . . will interfere and deprive him of the custody of his children. (pp. 675–676)

Before the spread of nongovernmental child protection societies beginning in 1875, intervention to protect children was sporadic, but intervention occurred. Children were not protected on the scale they are today, but adults were aware of maltreatment and tried to help.

Emergence of Social Work as a Profession

Child protection today is the domain of social work, assisted by law enforcement, mental health, medicine, nursing, law, and education. Prior to the 20th century, however, social work had yet to emerge as a profession. This is not to say that social work was not practiced before the 20th century. In colonial days and throughout the 18th century, local officials—principally overseers of the poor—made arrangements for orphans, protected abused and neglected children, and provided for the poor. The 19th century saw the proliferation of private charitable organizations like the New York Children's Aid Society and associations for improving the condition of the poor. Employees and volunteers of these private societies were not called "social workers," but many of them did wonderful social work.

In 1877, the first Charity Organization Society (COS) was established in Buffalo, New York. Eventually, more than 100 COSs were scattered across the country. The COSs improved the administration of poor relief by coordinating voluntary and public charities and discouraging pauperism. Gradually, COSs hired full-time paid workers and relied less on middle-class volunteers.

Of course, full-time workers need training. At first, training was informal and on-the-job. Eventually, however, more formal training was needed. In 1898, the "New York Charity Organization Society expanded its in-service training program into a more organized effort and established the first school for training social workers in the country. It was called the New York School for Philanthropy, and is now" the School of Social Work at Columbia University (Cohen, 1958, pp. 68–69). COSs and their increasingly full-time staffs contributed substantially to the professionalization of social work.

Another important contributor to the emergence of social work was the settlement movement. The first settlement was established January 10, 1884, in London's East End slums. The settlement was christened Toynbee Hall to honor historian Arnold Toynbee, an advocate for the poor who chose to live in humble surroundings. Toynbee Hall was created by Oxford and Cambridge students working under the guidance of Samuel Barnett, a young clergyman of the Church of England.

Americans visited Toynbee Hall and sailed home to spread the word. Stanton Coit visited Toynbee Hall and returned to New York intent on starting a settlement. Along with Charles Stover, Coit founded the Neighborhood Guild of New York City in 1886, America's first settlement. America's most famous settlement, Hull House in Chicago, was started in 1889 by Ellen Starr and Jane Addams following Addams's visits to Toynbee Hall.

Jane Addams had a tremendous impact on child welfare policy and became the first American woman to receive the Nobel Peace Prize. In 1911, the National Federation of Settlements was founded, with Addams as president, and by 1920 there were 440 settlements in the United States.

Unlike COS workers, who were inclined to blame the poor for their poverty, settlement workers, most of whom were women, saw the roots of poverty in the economic conditions created by industrialization and in the horrible living conditions of the urban poor. Robert Reinders (1982) observed:

> One of the practical implications of a women-dominated staff in [American settlements] was the formation of kindergartens, child-welfare clinics, homemaking programs, handicrafts, play groups, and the involvement of workers in preschool education, juvenile courts, and child and labor legislation. . . . American settlers were at the forefront of the demands for labor legislation, especially for women and children, and they were as much responsible for its passage as any group in the Progressive Period. (pp. 45–46, 49)

Although settlement workers and their colleagues in the COSs did not always see eye to eye, they had similar goals and their mutual need for training contributed to the professionalization of social work. Ralph and Muriel Pumphrey (1961) wrote,

> The COS and the settlement movements were the primary places where an interest in method and education moved workers and the emerging

field of social work toward professionalization. . . . In the forty years between the [economic] panic of the [1890s] and the depression of the [1930s], social work became a recognized profession. (pp. 202, 255)

Murray and Adeline Levine (1992) describe the rise of professional social work:

At first casework was largely handled by untrained volunteers, but little by little the philanthropic agencies began to organize training programs for both the volunteers and the increasing number of full-time, paid workers. Experiments with summer institutes led to full-time social work schools; by 1919 there were seventeen such schools in the country. (p. 155)

By 1930, the number exceeded 30.

In the 1920s and 1930s, social work came under the influence of psychology and psychoanalysis, increasing the focus on individual pathology as opposed to sociopolitical origins of social problems. The Levines wrote,

The need of social work for a methodology, the development of a professional method of casework, the increasing popularity of psychoanalytic thinking—to which psychiatric social workers were exposed from the beginning—work with World War I veterans, and the ultraconservative political climate of the early 1920s all led social work to focus on the individual. (p. 155)

Child Protection From 1875 to 1962

Organized child protection emerged from the rescue in 1874 of 9-year-old Mary Ellen Wilson, who lived with her guardians in one of New York City's worst tenements, Hell's Kitchen. Mary Ellen was routinely beaten and neglected. A religious missionary to the poor named Etta Wheeler learned of the child's plight and determined to rescue her. Wheeler consulted the police, but they declined to investigate. Wheeler sought assistance from child-helping charities, but they lacked authority to intervene in the family. At that time, of course, there was no such thing as CPS, and the juvenile court did not come into existence for another quarter century. Eventually, Wheeler sought advice from Henry Bergh, the influential founder of the American Society for the Prevention of Cruelty to Animals (ASPCA). Bergh asked his lawyer, Elbridge Gerry, to find a legal mechanism to rescue the child. Gerry drew up the necessary papers, and a judge ordered Mary Ellen removed from her guardians.

Following the rescue of Mary Ellen, animal protection advocate Henry Bergh and attorney Elbridge Gerry lamented the fact that no government agency or nongovernmental organization was responsible for child protection. Bergh and Gerry decided to create a nongovernmental charitable society devoted to child protection, and thus was born in 1875 the NYSPCC, the world's first entity devoted entirely to child protection. Gerry became the president of NYSPCC and served in that capacity into the 20th century.

News of the NYSPCC spread, and by 1922 some 300 nongovernmental child protection societies were scattered across America. Although 300 is an impressive number, for much of the 20th century, many cities and nearly all rural areas had little or no access to formal CPS. For most abused and neglected children help came—if it came—from family and neighbors willing to get involved, police, and courts.

As nongovernmental child protection societies sprang up across the country, another important innovation appeared: the juvenile court. The world's first juvenile court was established in Chicago in 1899. Juvenile courts spread quickly, and by 1919, all states but three had juvenile courts. Before long the remaining states fell in line. Although the reformers who created the juvenile court were concerned primarily with delinquent children, juvenile courts from the outset had authority to intervene in cases of abuse and neglect.

As noted previously, in the 19th and early 20th centuries, child protection agencies were nongovernmental. The first few decades of the 20th century witnessed increasing calls to shift child protection from nongovernmental societies for the prevention of cruelty to children (SPCCs) to government agencies. Douglas Falconer wrote in 1935:

> For many years responsibility for child protection was left almost entirely to private agencies. . . . Great sections of child population were untouched by them and in many other places the service rendered was perfunctory and of poor standard. . . . The belief has become increasingly accepted that if children are to be protected from neglect the service must be performed by public agencies. (p. 65)

The call for government child protection coincided with the increasing role of state and federal governments in social services. Prior to the 20th century, there were relatively few state-level departments of social services. The government services that were there were the provinces of local government. During the early 20th century, however, states created or strengthened state departments of welfare, social services, health, and labor.

As for the federal government, prior to 1935, Washington, D.C., played an insignificant role in child welfare policy and funding. Creation of the federal Children's Bureau in 1912 broke the ice, followed by the Sheppard-Towner Act, which provided federal money from 1921 to 1929 for health services for mothers and babies. It was the Great Depression of the 1930s, however, that stimulated the sea change in the federal government's role in social welfare. In 1935, as part of President Roosevelt's economic New Deal to save the nation from ruin, Congress passed the Social Security Act. In addition to old-age pensions, unemployment insurance, and vocational services, the Social Security Act created Aid to Dependent Children, which provided millions of dollars to states to support poor families. Tucked away in the Social Security Act was an obscure provision that authorized the Children's Bureau "to cooperate with State public-welfare agencies in establishing, extending, and strengthening, especially in predominantly rural areas, [child welfare services] for the protection and care of homeless, dependent, and neglected children, and children in danger of becoming delinquent." This provision was an important shot in the arm for the nascent social work specialty of child welfare and a modest step toward what in the 1970s became a central role for the federal government in efforts to protect children from abuse and neglect.

The Great Depression of the 1930s hastened the demise of nongovernmental SPCCs. The charitable contributions that were the lifeblood of SPCCs withered with the economy, and only the heartiest SPCCs weathered the economic drought. In the 1930s and 1940s, many SPCCs merged with other organizations or closed. In some communities child protection was assumed by the juvenile court or the police while in other communities organized protective work ceased.

In 1956, Vincent De Francis, director of the Children's Division of the American Humane Association, and a pioneer in child protection, conducted a national inventory of CPS. De Francis found 84 nongovernmental SPCCs, down from the high of 300 early in the century. Thirty-two states had no nongovernmental CPS. In these states, and in states with SPCCs, government agencies were slowly assuming responsibility. At mid-century, many communities had no agency in charge of this vital service.

A decade after his 1956 survey, De Francis again took the pulse of child protection (De Francis, 1967). By 1967, the number of nongovernmental SPCCs was down to 10. De Francis wrote, "Responsibility for provision of Child Protective Services under voluntary auspices, like the old soldier it is, is slowly fading away" (p. 11). By 1967, nearly all states had laws placing responsibility for child protection in government hands. Yet, De Francis complained, "No state and no community has developed a Child Protective Service program adequate in size to meet the service needs of all reported cases of child neglect, abuse and exploitation" (1967, p. 11). In 1964, Elizabeth Glover and Joseph Reid wrote in a similar vein, "In hundreds of counties in the United States, there is no protective service for children, other than police services" (p. 14). In most states protective services were not available statewide. Most communities lacked 24-hour coverage. Thus, for the first 6 decades of the 20th century, protective services in most communities were inadequate and in some places nonexistent.

The Modern Era of
Child Protection: 1962 to the Present

This section describes the birth of the modern era of child protection.

Child Abuse Becomes a National Issue

The 1960s witnessed an explosion of interest in child abuse, and physicians played a key role in this awakening. Prior to the 1960s, medical schools provided little or no training on child abuse, and medical texts were largely silent on the issue. Even pediatricians were largely uninformed. The spark that eventually ignited medical interest in abuse was an article published in 1946 by pediatric radiologist John Caffey. Caffey described six young children with subdural hematomas and fractures of the legs or arms. Although he did not state that any of the children were abused, Caffey hinted at it. Following Caffey's classic paper, a small but steady stream of physicians drew attention to the abusive origin of some childhood injuries. This trend culminated in the 1962 publication of the blockbuster article "The Battered-Child Syndrome" by pediatrician Henry Kempe and his colleagues. Kempe played a leading role in bringing child abuse to national attention during the 1960s and 1970s.

As the medical profession became interested in child abuse so did the media. Local media had always covered noteworthy cases, as when a child was beaten to death, but coverage by national media was uncommon prior to the 1960s. Following publication of "The Battered-Child Syndrome," national news outlets like *Newsweek*, *Saturday Evening Post*, *Parents* magazine, *Time* magazine, *Good Housekeeping*, and *Life* published emotional stories of abuse, often citing "The Battered-Child Syndrome" and Henry Kempe. A *Newsweek* story from April 1962, for example, was titled "When They're Angry . . ." and quoted Kempe saying,

> One day last November, we had four battered children in our pediatrics ward. Two died in the hospital and one died at home four weeks later. For every child who enters the hospital this badly beaten, there must be hundreds treated by unsuspecting doctors. The battered child syndrome isn't a reportable disease, but it damn well ought to be.

Prior to 1962, there was little professional research and writing about abuse. In 1963, Elizabeth Elmer noted, "The amount of systematic research on the problem of abuse and neglect is conspicuously scant" (p. 180). Following publication of "The Battered-Child Syndrome," a trickle of writing became a torrent that continues to this day.

News stories and journal articles captured public and professional attention. Behind the scenes, Congress placed new emphasis on child protection with amendments to the Social Security Act in 1962. Vincent De Francis (1967) remarked that the 1962 amendments "for the first time, identified Child Protective Services as part of all public child welfare" (p. 4). In addition to sharpening the focus on child protection, the 1962 amendments required states to pledge that by July 1, 1975, they would make child welfare services available statewide. This requirement fueled expansion of government child welfare services, including protective services.

The publication of "The Battered-Child Syndrome" and amendments to the Social Security Act were momentous in 1962, as were two small meetings convened by the Children's Bureau in Washington, D.C. The purpose of the meetings was to advise the bureau on how it could more effectively help states respond to child abuse. Henry Kempe and Vincent De Francis attended along with other early leaders. Among other things, the experts recommended the passage of laws requiring doctors to report suspicions of abuse to police or child welfare. These meetings were the genesis of child abuse reporting laws, the first four of which were enacted in 1963. By 1967, all states had reporting laws.

As reporting laws went into effect, the prevalence of child abuse and neglect came into focus. By 1974, some 60,000 cases were reported. In 1980, the number exceeded 1 million. By 1990, reports topped 2 million; in 2000, reports hovered around 3 million. In the early 21st century, reports declined but remained high.

Turning from reporting laws to another critical component of child protection, the foster care system, during the 19th century children who could not live safely at home were placed in orphanages or almshouses. Nineteenth century reformers like Charles Loring Brace of the New York Children's Aid Society struggled to remove children from institutions and place them in foster homes. Debate over the merits of foster care versus orphanage care raged from the 1850s to the early 20th century. Eventually, proponents of foster care prevailed, and almshouses and orphanages disappeared.

In the early days, foster care was viewed as a major advance and as the best solution for many dependent children. In the last quarter of the 20th century, however, some came to view foster care as a problem rather than a solution. Critics lamented that nearly half a million children are in foster care at any point in time and that too many children get "stuck" in out-of-home care. What's more, children of color, particularly African American children, are sadly overrepresented among foster children. Yet, despite problems, foster care remains a safe haven for many abused and neglected children. Foster care is further discussed in Chapter 5.

The Federal Government Assumes a Leadership Role in Child Protection

Prior to 1974, the federal government played a useful but minor role in child protection. The Children's Bureau was founded in 1912, but the bureau paid little attention to maltreatment until the 1960s. The Social Security Act of 1935, as amended in 1962, provided money to expand child welfare services. Yet, as late as 1973, U.S. Senator Walter Mondale wrote, "Nowhere in the Federal Government could we find one official assigned full time to the prevention, identification and treatment of child abuse and neglect" (Mondale, 1974).

Due in substantial measure to Mondale's efforts, Congress assumed a leadership role with passage of the Child Abuse Prevention and Treatment Act of

1974 (CAPTA). CAPTA authorized federal funds to improve the state response to physical abuse (PA), neglect, and sexual abuse. CAPTA focused attention on improved investigation and reporting. In addition, CAPTA provided funds for training, regional multidisciplinary centers focused on child abuse and neglect, and demonstration projects. Responsibility for administering CAPTA was placed in a new agency, the National Center on Child Abuse and Neglect. The center funded important research on maltreatment. CAPTA played a major role in shaping the nationwide system of governmental CPS in place today. In addition, CAPTA marked the final passing of privately funded, nongovernmental child protection societies. Congress periodically renewed CAPTA, and this important legislation remains in force today.

Prior to 1978, as many as 25% to 35% of Native American children were removed from their parents for alleged neglect or abuse. The majority of these children were placed in non-Indian foster homes, adoptive homes, and institutions. In 1978, Congress enacted the Indian Child Welfare Act (ICWA) to reduce the number of Native American children removed from their homes. ICWA is further discussed in Chapters 4 and 5.

As mentioned previously, children of color, particularly African American children, are overrepresented in foster care, and African American foster children tend to wait longer for adoption than white children. In 1994, Congress passed the Multiethnic Placement Act (MEPA), which prohibited child welfare agencies from delaying or denying adoptive placements on the basis of race (Hawkins-Leon & Bradley, 2002). MEPA is further discussed in Chapter 5.

Child abuse reporting laws, coupled with enhanced awareness of child abuse, produced an increase in intervention. By the late 1970s, the rising number of children in long-term foster care set off alarm bells in Congress, resulting in passage of the Adoption Assistance and Child Welfare Act of 1980. The act required states to make "reasonable efforts" to avoid removing children from maltreating parents. When removal was necessary, reasonable efforts were required to reunite families. Every child in foster care had to have a "permanency plan" to return the child home or move toward termination of parental rights. For children who could not go home, Congress provided financial incentives for adoption. The act also provided financial support for adoptive parents who adopted children with special needs.

The effort to preserve families—family preservation—was a key component of the 1980 act and the dominant paradigm of child protection in the 1980s. In the 1990s, however, critics argued that overreliance on family preservation sometimes led to tragedy. One of the most forceful critics of family preservation was Richard Gelles, who challenged the effectiveness of family preservation in his 1996 book *The Book of David: How Preserving Families Can Cost Children's Lives*. Gelles wrote,

> The essential first step in creating a safe world for children is to abandon the fantasy that child welfare agencies can balance the goals of protecting children and preserving families, adopting instead a child-centered

policy of family services. This is not a new policy, but rather a return to the policy of the early 1960s that established child safety as the overriding goal of the child protection system. It is time to abandon the myth that "the best foster family is not as good as a marginal biological family." The ability to make a baby does not ensure that a couple have, or ever will have, the ability to be adequate parents. The policy of family reunification and family preservation fails because it assumes that *all* biological parents can become fit and acceptable parents if only appropriate and sufficient support is provided. (pp. 148–149)

Although the 1980 Adoption Assistance and Child Welfare Act, with its emphasis on keeping families together, helped many children and parents, the number of children living in foster care did not decline. Moreover, Richard Gelles and others charged that reasonable efforts and family preservation caused social workers and judges to leave children in dangerous homes. Congress responded in 1997 with the Adoption and Safe Families Act (ASFA). Although it did not abandon family preservation, ASFA made child safety the top priority. When children are placed in foster care, ASFA establishes strict timelines for returning them to their parents or terminating parental rights. In cases of sexual abuse and chronic PA, ASFA authorizes states to dispense with efforts to reunify the family and to move directly to termination of parental rights.

Child Sexual Abuse Takes Center Stage

Prior to the late 1970s, many sexually abused children were protected. Yet, recognition of sexual abuse lagged behind recognition of PA. In 1969, Vincent De Francis wrote that social work "literature seems devoid of reference to or content on this subject" (p. 5). In 1975, David Walters wrote, "Virtually no literature exists on the sexual abuse of children." Also in 1975, Suzanne Sgroi wrote, "Although the pioneering efforts of many distinguished professionals and dedicated lay people over the past decade have made child abuse a national issue, the problem of sexual molestation of children remains a taboo topic in many areas" (p. 18). In 1977, Henry Kempe gave a lecture in which he described "sexual abuse of children and adolescents as another hidden pediatric problem and a neglected area" (1978, p. 382).

In the early 1970s, sexual abuse was still largely invisible, but that was about to change. Two related factors launched sexual abuse onto the national stage. First, the child protection system—including reporting laws—expanded significantly in the 1970s. Second, new research shed light on the prevalence and harmful effects of sexual abuse.

By the end of the 1970s, the United States enjoyed for the first time a nationwide system of government-sponsored child protection. The influential CAPTA of 1974 included sexual abuse in its definition of maltreatment. By 1976, all states had reporting laws requiring professionals to report sexual abuse. The expanded child protection system, particularly the reporting laws, wrenched sexual abuse from obscurity.

Prior to the 1970s there was a paucity of research on the prevalence and effects of sexual abuse. Vincent De Francis was one of the first to break new ground. In 1969, De Francis published the results of his study of 250 sexual abuse cases from Brooklyn. De Francis wrote, "The problem of sexual abuse of children is of unknown national dimensions, but the findings strongly point to the probability of an enormous national incidence many times larger than the reported incidence of physical abuse of children" (p. vii). Two thirds of the children in De Francis's study were emotionally damaged by the abuse. De Francis concluded,

> Child victims of adult sex offenders are a community's least protected children. Frequent victims of parental neglect, they are, almost always, also neglected by the community which has consistently failed to recognize the existence of this as a substantial problem. (p. 1)

A decade after De Francis's groundbreaking research, David Finkelhor (1979) published *Sexually Victimized Children*. Much had changed since 1969, when De Francis complained that society ignored sexual abuse. In 1979, Finkelhor wrote,

> Child protection workers from all over the country say they are inundated with cases of sexual abuse. . . . Public outrage, which has for several years focused on stories of bruised and tortured children, is shifting to a concern with sexual exploitation. Between 1977 and 1978 almost every national magazine had run a story highlighting the horrors of children's sexual abuse. (p. 1)

Finkelhor surveyed 796 college students and found that "19.2 percent of the women and 8.6 percent of the men had been sexually victimized as children" (p. 53). Most of the sexual abuse was committed by someone the child knew, and most was not reported.

As Finkelhor was finishing his research, Diana Russell (1983) was working toward similar findings. Russell studied 930 women and found that 16% were sexually abused during childhood by a family member. Thirty-one percent of the women reported sexual abuse by a nonrelative. The pathfinding research of Vincent De Francis, David Finkelhor, Diana Russell, and others exploded any idea that sexual abuse was rare or benign.

Summary of Post-1962 Developments

The period after 1962 witnessed remarkable progress. For the first time, CPS was available across the country—in small towns, rural areas, and cities. The growth of child protection was a boon to thousands of children.

Ironically, however, the expansion of the child protection system, particularly the rapid deployment of laws requiring professionals to report suspected abuse and neglect, carried the seeds of crisis. The reporting laws unleashed a flood of cases that overwhelmed the child protection system. By the 1980s, the system was struggling to keep its head above water.

Conclusion

More than 40 years ago, child protection pioneer Vincent De Francis lamented, "No state and no community has developed a Child Protective Service program adequate in size to meet the service needs of all reported cases of child neglect, abuse and exploitation" (1967, p. 11). What would De Francis say today? I believe he would say that although today's child protection system has many problems today's system is a vast improvement over the incomplete patchwork that existed in the 1960s. Today, CPS is available across America, billions of dollars are devoted to child welfare, and thousands of professionals do their best to help struggling parents and vulnerable children.

References

Caffey, J. (1946). Multiple fractures in the long bones of infants suffering from chronic subdural hematoma. *American Journal of Roentgenology, 56*, 163–173.

Cohen, N. E. (1958). *Social work in the American tradition*. New York: Dryden Press.

De Francis, V. (1956). *Child protective services in the United States: Reporting a nationwide survey*. Denver: American Humane Association.

De Francis, V. (1967). *Child protective services: A national survey*. Denver: American Humane Association.

De Francis, V. (1969). *Protecting the child victim of sex crimes committed by adults*. Denver: American Humane Association.

Elmer, E. (1963). Identification of abused children. *Children, 10*, 180–184.

Falconer, D. P. (1935). Child and youth protection. In F. S. Hall (Ed.), *Social work yearbook* (Vol. 3, pp. 63–66). New York: Russell Sage Foundation.

Finkelhor, D. (1979). *Sexually victimized children*. New York: Free Press.

Finkelman, P. (Ed.). (1988). Slavery, race, and the American legal system: 1700–1872. A sixteen volume facsimile series reproducing over one hundred and seventy rare and important pamphlets. Series VI. (Vol. 1, pp. 179–209). *Free blacks, slaves, and slave owners in civil and criminal courts*. New York: Garland Publishers. (Original pamphlet published 1809 in New York by Henry C. Southwick and covered pages 1–31)

Gelles, R. J. (1996). *The book of David: How preserving families can cost children's lives*. New York: Basic Books.

Glover, E. E., & Reid, J. H. (1964). Unmet and future needs. In Alan Keith-Lucas (Special Ed. of this Volume), Thorsten Sellin (Ed.), Marvin E. Wolfgang (Acting Associate Ed.), *The Annals of the American Academy of Political and Social Science, 355*, 9–19.

Hawkins-Leon, C. G., & Bradley, C. (2002). Race and transracial adoptions: The answer is neither simply black or white nor right or wrong. *Catholic University Law Review, 51*, 1227–1286.

Kempe, C. H. (1978). Sexual abuse, another hidden pediatric problem: The 1977 C. Anderson Aldrich lecture. *Pediatrics, 62*, 382–389.

Kempe, C. H., Silverman, F. N., Steele, B. F., Droegemueller, W., & Silver, H. K. (1962). The battered-child syndrome. *Journal of the American Medical Association, 181*, 17–24.

Levine, M., & Levine, A. (1992). *Helping children: A social history*. New York: Oxford University Press.

Mondale, W. F. (1974, March 15). Letter of transmittal from Walter F. Mondale to Harrison A. Williams. Located at Child Abuse Prevention and Treatment Act, 1974. Public Law 93-247 (S. 1191). Questions and Answers on Children and Youth of the Committee on Labor and Public Welfare, United States Senate. 93rd Congress, 2nd Session. Part VII. April 1974.

Myers, J. E. B. (2004). *A history of child protection in America*. Bloomington, IN: Xlibris.

Myers, J. E. B. (2006). *Child protection in America: Past, present and future*. New York: Oxford University Press.

Myers, J. E. B. (2010). *The history of child protection in America*. Sacramento, CA: University of the Pacific.

When they're angry. . . (1962, April 16). *Newsweek*, p. 74.

People v. Benson, 6 Cal. 221 (1856).

Pletcher v. People, 52 Ill. 395 (1869).

Pumphrey, R. E., & Pumphrey, M. W. (1961). *The heritage of American social work*. New York: Columbia University Press.

Reinders, R. C. (1982). Toynbee Hall and the American settlement movement. *Social Service Review, 56*, 39–54.

Russell, D. E. H. (1983). The incidence and prevalence of intrafamilial and extrafamilial sexual abuse of female children. *Child Abuse and Neglect, 7*, 133–146.

Sgroi, S. M. (1975, May–June). Molestation of children: The last frontier in child abuse. *Children Today, 4*, 18–21.

Story, J. (1886). *Commentaries on equity jurisprudence as administered in England and America* (13th ed.). Boston: Little, Brown.

Walters, D. R. (1975). *Physical and sexual abuse of children: Cases and treatment*. Bloomington: Indiana University Press.

2

Prevention of Child Abuse and Neglect

Deborah Daro

Prevention of child abuse and neglect is fundamentally about strengthening the capacity of parents and communities to care for children's health and well-being. Prevention has three primary goals: (1) reduce the incidence of abuse and neglect, (2) minimize the chance that children who are maltreated will be revictimized, and (3) break the cycle of maltreatment by providing victims the help they need to overcome the negative consequences of abuse or neglect.

The behaviors that constitute abuse and neglect include the physical beating of a child; failure to provide for a child's basic emotional and physical needs; emotional abuse of a child through continuous belittling, inappropriate control, or extreme inconsistency; and the sexual mistreatment of a child or use of a child for sexual pleasure. Ideally, prevention services can help parents and other caregivers avoid these behaviors and offer children the support they need to escape abusive situations.

Some prevention programs provide services to parents, others focus on children, and still others improve the environment in which parents rear their children. Some prevention services are made available to everyone or a large proportion of the population and are referred to as universal or primary prevention services. Examples include public service announcements (PSAs), educational programs delivered through schools, and early intervention and assessment efforts for newborns and parents.

When the factors contributing to abuse or neglect are well defined, prevention services can focus on specific families, children, or communities exhibiting these factors or risk markers. Characteristics commonly associated with an elevated risk for physical abuse (PA) or neglect include young maternal age, single parent status, poverty, an inability to control anger, inadequate information about child development or basic child care, social isolation, and residence in communities with high levels of violence and inadequate services. Prevention programs that focus on specific individuals or communities are referred to as targeted or secondary prevention programs. Examples include support

17

groups for teen parents, family resource centers in high-risk communities, substance abuse treatment programs, and after-school programs.

The objective of both universal and targeted prevention programs is to create a context in which abusive or neglectful behaviors are avoided. Unfortunately, not all abuse and neglect can be prevented. In some instances, abuse occurs because prevention services are not successful in engaging those most in need. In our society, parents who have not abused or neglected their children are free to reject prevention efforts. In some instances, families accept prevention services, but the services are not successful in preventing maltreatment.

Once a child has experienced maltreatment, the focus of prevention shifts to preventing revictimization and reducing the likelihood the child will repeat the cycle of abuse when the child becomes a parent. At this stage, the modes of service delivery—parenting education classes, home visitation services, and support groups—are similar to the services offered in secondary prevention efforts. Following maltreatment, however, the content of interventions becomes more therapeutic and, in many cases, more intense.

Therapeutic intervention for individual victims of maltreatment is discussed in Chapters 12 and 16. The present chapter summarizes the strengths and weaknesses of the most widely available universal and targeted prevention services. The chapter begins by briefly outlining the theoretical frameworks that have shaped the development of child abuse and neglect prevention programming. Following this review, research relating to the relative effectiveness of various service models is outlined.

Overall Prevention Framework

Prevention services are organized within an overarching framework that reflects how abusive and neglectful behaviors develop. Maltreatment often results from a variety of personal, familial, and environmental conditions. Preventing its occurrence, therefore, hinges on the ability of program planners to identify the elements that, if strengthened, will divert parents from maltreating behaviors or empower children to avoid high-risk situations. Efforts to identify these elements generally include an examination of a person's developmental history, personality factors, social interactions or social networks, familial relationships, and child characteristics (Belsky & Vondra, 1990; Sameroff & Chandler, 1975; Sandler, 1979). Broad causal theories are used to explain the relationship between specific individual or environmental conditions and maltreatment. The theories most commonly found in the literature range from interpersonal functioning theories such as psychodynamic and learning theories to systemic and social explanations of maltreatment suggested by theories of stress and poverty (Daro, 1988, 1993).

Since Henry Kempe's work in the 1960s (Kempe, Silverman, Steele, Droegemueller, & Silver, 1962) describing the battered child syndrome (BCS) (see Chapters 1, 11), the dominant theoretical framework for understanding the causal pathway to maltreatment has been ecological theory. Rather than assuming that a single cause triggers abuse or neglect, ecological theory recognizes that most maltreatment stems from a complex web of factors within a person's personality, family history, and community context (Belsky, 1980; Bronfenbrenner, 1979; Cicchetti & Rizley, 1981; Garbarino, 1977). In addition to articulating a nested set of domains governing human behaviors, ecological theory identifies a set of risk factors as well as protective factors. The theory underscores the importance of crafting prevention strategies that seek to reduce the interpersonal and environmental challenges families face and to build a network of protective or supportive factors that help families cope with risks that are not easily eliminated or modified.

The ecological theory has strong heuristic capabilities and is useful in coming to grips with the array of factors that contribute to abuse and neglect. For a number of reasons, however, ecological theory has limited utility as a policy and practice framework. First, although many prevention programs recognize the complex pathways that lead to maltreatment, the more successful efforts are generally those that have clear objectives and a well-stated logic model or theory of change. Interventions that attempt to directly impact too many variables in multiple domains often suffer from mission drift. The idea of focusing on a limited set of outcomes is, in some ways, counter to the multifactorial structure embedded in ecological theories. The second reason it is difficult to translate ecological theory into practice is that the responsibility for health, education, economic well-being, housing, and child protection are distributed across numerous federal, state, and local agencies, each of which defines core outcomes and standards of best practice within its own discipline and sphere of influence. Developing, managing, and sustaining programs that cut across all these areas in the manner suggested by the ecological framework is at best challenging. Third, measuring outcomes is easier at the participant level than at a population level. Because measurement of success or failure is important, prevention efforts have, for the most part, focused on interventions that target distinct populations rather than efforts to alter community context or normative values in the manner suggested by the ecological framework.

In short, we have a theoretical framework that many in the field embrace—the ecological model—but a framework that is at odds with the programmatic initiatives and public policy that currently constitute the child abuse prevention field. Although there have been notable gains in understanding maltreatment, the current prevention system has failed to achieve a deep reach into the at-risk population and has not created the contextual and normative change necessary to maximize the safety and healthy development of the nation's children. These limitations have been particularly acute among prevention strategies targeting very young children; children living in poverty; and children living with caretakers struggling with substance abuse, domestic violence, or mental health issues.

Prevention Services and Their Impacts _____

Although the quantity and quality of prevention efforts vary across communities, the total number of such programs is impressive. One national survey estimated that more than 100,000 groups of parents meet every year in the United States to improve parenting skills, provide mutual support, and advocate for better services and policy options for children (Carter, 1995). The Internet provides myriad opportunities for individuals interested in joining support groups focused on improving parental capacity or child management skills. In addition, numerous home visitation programs are available throughout the United States. Considering only the six most common home visitation models, it is estimated that as many as 550,000 children are reached annually by home visiting programs for pregnant women and for families with young children (Gomby, 2005). Several surveys of children and young adults find that over two thirds received some type of assault prevention education during their early school years (Gibson & Leitenberg, 2000).

The actual and potential ability of prevention services to reduce abuse and neglect remains unclear. Several reviewers suggest that the more universal or broadly targeted prevention efforts have greater success in strengthening a parent's or child's protective factors than they do in eliminating risk factors, particularly for parents or children at highest risk (Harrell, Cavanagh, & Sridharan, 1999; Chaffin, Bonner, & Hill, 2001; MacLeod & Nelson, 2000). Others argue that prevention strategies are most effective when they focus on a clearly defined target population with identifiable risk factors (Guterman, 2001; Olds, Sadler, & Kitzman, 2007). This chapter focuses on prevention services that have demonstrated an ability to reduce child abuse and neglect reports as well as other child safety outcomes such as reported injuries and accidents. The chapter also identifies programs with documented effects on risk factors that correlate with child maltreatment, including parent characteristics, child characteristics, and the parent–child relationship.

Public Education and Awareness Efforts _____

In the years immediately following Kempe's 1962 article on BCS, public awareness campaigns were developed to raise awareness about child abuse and to generate political support for legislation to address the problem. Notably, the nonprofit organization Prevent Child Abuse America (PCA America) (formerly the National Committee to Prevent Child Abuse) joined forces with the Ad Council to develop and distribute nationwide a series of PSAs on TV, radio, print, and billboards. All told, this educational effort garnered $20 to $60 million a year of free media exposure to inform the public about abuse (Cohn Donnelly, 1997).

This early effort, along with efforts by others, increased public awareness of child abuse. Between 1975 and 1985, public recognition that child abuse is a major threat to child safety went from 10% to 90%. These years also witnessed a steady reduction in the use of corporal punishment and verbal forms of aggression in disciplining children (Daro & Gelles, 1992).

In recent years, broadly targeted prevention campaigns have been used to alter parental behavior. For example, the U.S. Public Health Service, in partnership with the American Academy of Pediatrics (AAP) and the Association of SIDS and Infant Mortality Programs, launched its "Back to Sleep" campaign in 1994 designed to educate parents and caretakers about the importance of placing infants on their back to sleep as a strategy to reduce the rate of sudden infant death syndrome (SIDS). Campaign strategies included media coverage; the availability of a nationwide toll-free information and referral hotline; the production of television, radio, and print ads; and the distribution of informational brochures to new parents. As of 2002, the National Center for Health Statistics reported a 50% drop in SIDS deaths and a decrease in stomach sleeping from 70% to 15%. Although the evidence linking the campaign effort to changes in these population level indicators is exploratory, the data are compelling and underscore the viability of public education in changing normative practices (Mitchell, Hutchison, & Stewart, 2007).

One of the most thoroughly examined public awareness and educational campaigns addressing child maltreatment has been the effort to prevent shaken baby syndrome (SBS). SBS is further discussed in Chapter 11. Developing and implementing broad-based programs to educate new parents about the dangers of shaking their infant and about how to deal with the frustration of a crying or "fussy baby" is, in a way, "easier" than tackling other forms of maltreatment. First, the message in shaking prevention programs is clear, and the concepts are easily understood by most parents. Second, virtually all parents deal with a crying infant. As such, coping with crying is an issue well suited to a broadly targeted prevention strategy. Third, there is anecdotal evidence that the programs contribute to parents being more observant of their interactions with their infants and also the interactions between other caretakers and infants. Indeed, many of the programs ask parents to sign agreements to question and educate any person with whom they leave their baby. This type of social surveillance, common in other public health initiatives, may afford children greater protection. Finally, a key element of shaking prevention programs is encouraging parents to identify others in their social network to whom they can turn for relief from the frustration of a fussy baby. The messages are, "You are not alone" and "It is okay to rely on others for support in your effort to be a good parent. Asking for help is not a sign of failure or weakness."

Evaluation of a 1992 federal campaign to educate the public about the dangers of SBS ("Never Shake a Baby") found that one third of those providing feedback on the campaign indicated that they had no prior knowledge of the potential danger of shaking an infant (Showers, 2001).

Moving beyond basic awareness, Dias and colleagues (2005) developed a universal SBS education program and implemented the program in an eight county region in western New York. Dias's program provided information on shaking to parents of all newborns prior to the infants' discharge from the hospital. In the hospital, parents were asked to read a one-page leaflet on SBS and to view an 11-minute video discussing the dangers of violent shaking. The video suggested ways to handle persistent infant crying. Mothers and fathers were asked to sign a statement affirming that they heard and understood the concepts. Ten percent of the parents who completed the forms were contacted 7 months later. Administrative data were used to determine changes in the incidence of abusive head injury in the eight-county region. The New York data were compared to data for the same time period in comparable Pennsylvania communities.

The program obtained signed agreements from 67% of the target parents, suggesting high receptivity on the part of parents, including fathers. The vast majority of parents who were surveyed when their infant was 7 months old recalled the program and the importance of not shaking their baby. Dias suggests that one reason for this high retention of information was attributable to obtaining a signed commitment form from each parent.

The program appears to have reduced injuries. During the 6 years before the program, 40 cases of substantiated abusive head injury were identified in the targeted New York counties. This represented an average of 8.2 cases per year, or 41.5 cases per 100,000 live births. During the 5½ year period of the intervention, 21 cases of substantiated abusive head injury were identified, or 3.8 cases per year (53% reduction) or 22.2 cases per 100,000 live births (47% reduction). In the Pennsylvania comparison communities, there was no change in the number of such cases observed during pre- and post-study periods (Dias et al., 2005).

Another promising public education and awareness program is called the Period of PURPLE Crying. This program focuses on helping parents understand and cope with the stresses of normal infant crying. In 2004, the National Center on Shaken Baby Syndrome (NCSBS), the Harborview Injury Prevention and Research Center of the University of Washington, and the University of British Columbia received a grant from the Doris Duke Charitable Foundation and the George S. and Delores Dore Eccles Foundation to produce materials and an educational film and to test the program.

The Period of PURLE Crying program was tested through four different types of delivery systems: maternity services, pediatric offices, prenatal classes, and nurse home visitor programs. Over 4,200 parents participated in the program. A randomized control trial of the program found that it succeeded in enhancing mothers' knowledge about infant crying. Women who participated in the program were more likely to walk away in a situation where an infant was crying inconsolably compared to control group mothers (Barr et al., 2009).

Videos have been successfully utilized to educate parents about various child health issues including maltreatment (Glascoe, Oberklaid, Dworkin, & Trimm, 1998). Black and Teti (1997) examined the effect of a culturally sensitive video depicting both successful and unsuccessful strategies for parents to employ when feeding infants. Findings from a randomized study of the video's impact on first-time African American teen mothers who viewed the video showed significantly more positive parental attitudes and more parent–child interaction during feedings than mothers who did not see the video. Mothers who viewed the video also received significantly higher ratings on an observational measure of involvement with their baby during a feeding session. Other research corroborates the utility of videos for stimulating behavioral change in parents of children with conduct disorders (Webster-Stratton, 1994).

_____ Child Sexual Assault Prevention Programs

In contrast to efforts designed to alter the behavior of adults who might commit maltreatment, a category of prevention programs emerged in the 1980s designed to alter the behavior of potential victims. Often referred to as child assault prevention or safety education programs, these efforts present children with information on the topic of PA and sexual assault, how to avoid risky situations, and, if abused, how to respond. A key feature of these programs is their universal service delivery systems, often being integrated into school curricula or into primary support opportunities for children (e.g., Boy Scouts, youth groups, recreation programs). Although certain concerns have been raised regarding the appropriateness of these efforts (Reppucci & Haugaard, 1989), the strategy continues to be widely available. A number of programs have adopted a broad focus intended to help children avoid numerous problems, including peer aggression and violence.

Child assault prevention programs provide direct instruction to children on the distinction between good, bad, and questionable touch, as well as the right of children to control who touches them. With older children, prevention classes cover a broader range of concepts such as appropriate dating behavior, gender stereotypes, and nonaggressive conflict resolution strategies. The programs offer children service options or referrals if they have been abused or are involved in an abusive peer relationship.

Most child assault prevention programs include some type of instruction for parents and school personnel. These sessions generally review the materials to be presented in the classroom, discuss the child abuse reporting system, outline what to do if child abuse is suspected, and examine the services available to victims and their families (Finkelhor, 2008).

Meta-analyses and evaluations conducted on assault prevention programs demonstrate that the programs can be effective in conveying safety information to children and providing children with skills to avoid or lower the risk of assault (Berrick & Barth, 1992; Daro, 1994; MacMillan, MacMillan, Offord, Griffith, & MacMillan, 1994; Rispens, Aleman, & Goudena, 1997). Moreover, these programs offer children who have been victimized the language tools and procedures necessary to get help and reduce the risk of subsequent maltreatment (Kolko, Moser, & Hughes, 1989; Hazzard, 1990).

Berrick and Barth's 1992 meta-analysis of assault prevention programs found only modest effect sizes that were limited to knowledge gains. More robust findings emerged from the Rispens et al. 1997 meta-analysis, which revealed significant and large effect sizes at both the post-intervention and follow-up. Variation between the Berrick and Barth and the Rispen studies most likely reflects differences in the pool of evaluations included in the two reviews. The Rispens meta-analysis utilized studies with more rigorous designs, lending greater confidence to Rispens' findings.

Recent years witnessed a significant decline in reported cases of child sexual abuse (CSA). Some attribute this decline in part to the widespread implementation of assault prevention programs, along with greater efforts to screen adults who have direct contact with children and aggressive prosecution of offenders (Finkelhor, 2008). The reduction in reports offers possible evidence of the impact of widespread efforts to inform children and create safe environments.

Parent Education and Support Groups

Educational and support services delivered to parents through center-based programs and group settings are used in a variety of ways to address risk factors associated with child abuse and neglect. Although the primary focus of these interventions is typically the parent, quite a few programs include opportunities for structured parent–child interactions, and many programs incorporate parallel interventions for children. Common features of group-based efforts include weekly discussions for 8 to 14 weeks with parents around topics such as discipline, cognitive development, and parent–child communication. Group-based sessions that include children provide parents and children opportunities to discuss issues and share feelings. Parents have the chance to model the parenting skills they are learning. The programs afford opportunities for participants to share meals and important family celebrations such as birthdays and graduations.

Educational and support services range from education and information sharing to general support to therapeutic interventions. Many of the programs are delivered under the direction of social workers or health care providers. Some programs utilize self-help models. Most programs draw on the family support philosophy, which emphasizes the enhancement of protective factors in addition to the reduction of negative behaviors (Dunst, 1995).

A strength of group-based interventions is the opportunity they provide parents to share experiences, concerns, and solutions. In addition, group-based efforts provide a vehicle for continuing the help-seeking process over time. Parents remain committed and engaged in the intervention because they form a connection to a group of parents—not simply a sense of loyalty to an individual provider (Carter & Harvey, 1996). When these connections are established, parent groups can build the type of reciprocity and mutual support viewed by many as essential to achieving a higher standard of care for children (Melton & Berry, 1994).

Empirical support for the efficacy of parent education in reducing maltreatment is limited but growing (Baker, Piotrkowski, & Brooks-Gunn, 1999; Carter & Harvey, 1996; Chalk & King, 1998; Daro & McCurdy, 2006).

The program called Incredible Years is a multifaceted and developmentally based curricula for parents, teachers, and children delivered in both primary school and early education settings. Significant aspects of the model include group-based parenting skills training; classroom management training for teachers; and peer support groups for parents, children, and teachers. Research on Incredible Years finds that participants demonstrate more positive affective response and a corresponding decrease in the use of harsh discipline, reduced parental depression, improved self-confidence, and better communication and problem solving within the family (Webster-Stratton, Reid, & Hammond, 2001).

Abt Associates conducted a meta-analysis of a broad range of group-based family support services provided to families with children of all ages. The research found that group-based parenting education and support services produced larger effects than home visitation services in impacting children's cognitive outcomes and social–emotional development (Layzer, Goodson, Bernstein, & Price, 2001).

A meta-analysis conducted by the Centers for Disease Control and Prevention on training programs for parents of children ages birth to 7 identified components of programs that have a positive impact on acquiring parenting skills and decreasing children's externalizing behaviors. These components included teaching parents emotional communication skills, helping parents acquire positive parent-child interaction skills, and providing parents opportunities to demonstrate and practice these skills while observed by a service provider (Centers for Disease Control and Prevention, 2009).

The success of parent education and support groups is far from universal (Layzer et al., 2001). Many high-risk families find it difficult to sustain involvement in structured group programs. Barriers to engagement include poor transportation, problems adjusting to a fixed schedule, and limited access to child care (Daro, 1993). As well, group-based services can be difficult to tailor to the individual needs of all participants. If the issue being addressed is general, with broad application across populations, such as how to access a given service or how to anticipate a specific parenting challenge, the inability to personalize the service is less salient. When parents face complex problems, however, the inability to provide personal guidance can reduce effectiveness (Daro & McCurdy, 2006).

Home Visitation Programs for New Parents

Although a plethora of options exist to provide assistance to parents around the time their child is born, home visitation has become the flagship program in the United States for reaching out to new parents. Professionals seeking to prevent child abuse and neglect have promoted home visitation for over two decades, guided by the belief that home visitation can reduce the risk of maltreatment by strengthening early parent–child relationships and linking new parents with needed services (Daro, 2009). When home visitation is employed to prevent maltreatment, the most common population for the intervention is pregnant women and new parents. Services are offered weekly for several months to several years.

Home visitation is an intervention with its own mission and service port-folio. In addition, home visitation programs serve as a gatekeeper to commu-nity resources, including health, therapeutic services, and concrete resources necessary to increase a parent's ability to provide a safe and nurturing envi-ronment for a child.

Some home visitation models extend their outreach to all new parents or pregnant women. Other models target populations presenting specific risk characteristics such as young maternal age, single-parent status, or low income. Finally, some models offer intensive, targeted services for parents facing spe-cific challenges (Daro, 2006).

In addition to a number of national models (e.g., Parents as Teachers, Healthy Families America, Early Head Start, Parent Child Home Program, SafeCare, HIPPY, and the Nurse Family Partnership), more than 40 states have invested in home visitation and the infrastructure necessary to insure that home visitation services are of high quality and are integrated into the broader system of early intervention and support (Johnson, 2009).

Home visitation primarily involves the delivery of services in a partici-pant's home, although a proportion of "visits" with a family may occur in other settings such as parks, recreation centers, restaurants, and other public venues. Services are one-on-one and are provided by staff with professional training (nursing, social work, child development, family support) or by para-professionals who receive training in the model's approach and curricula. The primary issues addressed during visits include the mother's personal health and life choices; child health and development; environmental concerns such as income, housing, and community violence; family functioning, includ-ing adult and child relationships; and access to services. Specific activities include modeling parent–child interactions and child management strategies, providing observation and feedback, offering general parenting and child development information, conducting formal assessments and screenings, and providing structured counseling.

Over the past 15 years, numerous researchers have examined the effects of home visitation programs on parent–child relationships, maternal function-ing, and child development. The research addresses such important issues as cost, program intensity, staff requirements, training and supervision, and the variations in design required to meet the needs of the new-parent population.

The majority of research has focused on programs targeting newborns and their parents. Notable exceptions to the concentration on newborns are the evaluations of Project SafeCare (Gershater-Molko, Lutzker, & Wesch, 2003) and Family Connections (DePanfilis & Dubowitz, 2005). Although both of these programs offer services to parents with young children, SafeCare and Family Connections target their services to high-risk families who often have multiple children of varying ages and a history of child welfare involvement.

Both models have demonstrated improvements in targeted parental behaviors and reduced likelihood of future referral to child welfare.

Efforts to summarize the research on home visitation have reached different conclusions. Some authors conclude that when home visitation is well implemented, it produces significant and meaningful reductions in child maltreatment risk and improves child and family functioning (AAP, Council on Child and Adolescent Health, 1998; Geeraert, Van den Noorgate, Grietens, & Onghena, 2004; Guterman, 2001; Hahn et al., 2003). Other authors reach more sobering conclusions (Chaffin, 2004; Gomby, 2005; Howard & Brooks-Gunn, 2009). To some degree, these disparate conclusions reflect different expectations regarding what constitutes "meaningful" change. In other instances, the differences stem from examining different studies or placing greater emphasis on certain methodological approaches.

The database that is available to assess the impact of home visitation is expanding. Increasingly, researchers are able to measure the effects of programs that are more sophisticated in planning and execution. Sweet and Appelbaum (2004) examined 60 home visiting programs and documented a statistically significant reduction in potential abuse and neglect as measured by emergency room visits and treated injuries, ingestions, or accidents. The effect of home visitation on reported or suspected maltreatment was moderate but not statistically significant.

Geeraert and colleagues (2004) focused their meta-analysis on 43 programs that had an explicit focus on preventing child abuse and neglect in families with children under 3 years of age. Though programs varied in service delivery strategy, 88% of the programs incorporated a home visitation component. Geeraert found a statistically significant, positive overall treatment effect of home visitation on child abuse reports and on injury data.

Whether or not home visitation directly reduces maltreatment, researchers have documented that home visitation can improve child and family functioning. Bull and colleagues concluded that home visiting can produce positive effects on various dimensions of parenting and mother–child interactions (Bull, McCormick, Swann, & Mulvihill, 2004). Sweet and Appelbaum (2004) noted that home visitation produced significant but relatively small effects on mothers' behavior, attitudes, and educational attainment. Geeraert and colleagues (2004) found relatively strong effects of home visitation on indicators of child and parent functioning.

Some of the research on home visitation focuses on models that are frequently included within public service systems for children from birth to age 5. The research is increasingly sophisticated, utilizing larger samples, control groups, more rigorous designs, and stronger measures. Although positive outcomes are not universal, parents enrolled in these home visitation programs report fewer acts of abuse or neglect toward their children (Fergusson, Grant, Horwood, & Ridder, 2005; LeCroy & Milligan Associates, Inc., 2005; DuMont et al., 2008; Williams, Stern & Associates, 2005); more positive health outcomes for infants and mothers (Fergusson et al., 2005); more positive and satisfying interactions with infants (Klagholz, 2005); and a greater number of life choices that create more stable and nurturing environments for children (Anisfeld, Sandy, & Guterman, 2004; LeCroy & Milligan Associates, Inc., 2005; Wagner & Spiker, 2001).

One home visitation model that initiates services during pregnancy found that its infant participants had significantly fewer negative outcomes by the time they were age 15 (e.g., running away, juvenile offenses, and substance abuse) (Olds et al., 1998). A randomized trial of a Brisbane, Australia, nurse home visitation program patterned on the work of Olds found significant reductions in postnatal maternal depression and improved maternal-infant attachment at 6 weeks' postpartum (Armstrong, Fraser, Dadds, & Morris, 1999). The program also reported enhanced parental efficacy and greater acceptance of the child at 4 months' postpartum (Armstrong, Fraser, Dadds, & Morris, 2000).

In addition to documenting the positive impacts of home visitation services, research is contributing to a better understanding of the most effective ways to implement home visitation services. When mothers are enrolled during pregnancy, outcomes are more positive (DuMont et al., 2008). As mentioned above, some home visitation programs use professionals while other programs use paraprofessionals. One study found nurses more effective in achieving program goals than paraprofessionals (Olds et al., 2002). In contrast, a home visitation program in a high-risk community that focused on health promotion used experienced mothers—i.e., paraprofessionals—and found higher immunization rates and more positive parent–child interactions than in a group of women who received health visits by nurses (Johnson, Howell, & Molloy, 1993). Regardless of who does the home visiting, outcomes are enhanced when home visitation is partnered with other early intervention services or specialized support (Anisfeld et al., 2004; Daro & McCurdy, 2006; Klagholz, 2005; Ammerman et al., 2009).

Findings from the initial 2-year follow-up of the Early Head Start National Demonstration Project lend support to the efficacy of home visitation programs with new parents (Love et al., 2009). Early Head Start mothers who received home visitation services were more supportive, more sensitive, less detached, and more likely to extend play to stimulate cognitive development, language, and literacy than were mothers assigned to the control group in this large, randomized trial. Of particular interest for the prevention of child abuse, Early Head Start mothers reported less frequent use of spanking and, in general, described the use of milder forms of discipline in managing their 2-year-olds (Love et al., 2002). These results continued through age 4, with families who received home visits outperforming families enrolled in center-based programs or programs that combined both home-based and center-based services (Love et al., 2009).

Despite continued variation in program objectives and approach, consensus is growing regarding a number of factors that appear to be related to success. These include (1) solid internal consistency that links specific program elements and curriculum content to specific outcomes; (2) establishing a relationship with a family that extends for a sufficient period of time to accomplish meaningful change in a parent's knowledge levels, skills, and ability to form a strong positive attachment to the child; (3) well-trained and competent staff; (4) high-quality supervision that includes observation of the provider and participant; (5) solid organizational capacity in the community-based organizations that are recruited to coordinate and deliver programs; and (6) linkages to other community resources and supports.

Evaluative data indicate that positive outcomes are neither universal for all models nor consistent across all populations. Little evidence exists that home visitation is effective in addressing the needs of families who are at risk due to substance abuse, domestic violence, or serious mental health problems. Moreover, home visitation programs often struggle to connect families to other community resources. What home visitation programs appear to do best is enhance parent–child interaction, improve access to medical care, and, in selected cases, improve a child's developmental trajectory.

Community Prevention Strategies

The strategies previously outlined focus on individual parents and children. Recently, increased attention is being paid to prevention efforts designed to improve the community environment in which children are raised. Among other things, these efforts institute new services, streamline service delivery processes, and foster greater collaboration among local service providers. This emerging generation of "community child abuse prevention strategies" focuses on creating supportive residential communities where neighbors share a belief in collective responsibility to protect children from harm and where professionals work to expand services and support for parents (Chaloupka & Johnson, 2007; Doll, Bonzo, Mercy, Sleet, & Haas, 2007; Farrow, 1997; Mannes, Roehlkepartain, & Benson, 2005). The U.S. Advisory Board on Child Abuse and Neglect noted that these two capacity-building strategies—a focus on community norms and a focus on coordinated, individualized service development—are not mutually exclusive (U.S. Department of Health and Human Services, 1991).

In 2009, Daro and Dodge examined five community child abuse prevention programs that seek to reduce child abuse and neglect—Triple P (Positive Parenting Program); Strengthening Families Through Early Care and Education; the Durham Family Initiative in Durham, North Carolina; Strong Communities in Greenville, South Carolina; and the Community Partnerships for Protecting Children (CPPC). These interventions employ various strategies. In some instances, the primary emphasis is on building service capacity by disseminating new practices (e.g., Triple P and CPPC) or helping managers supervise staff, manage caseloads, and interact with other managers (e.g., Durham Family Initiative, Strengthening Families, and CPPC). All of the initiatives work to increase the odds families will have services available to them either by improving access to existing services or by generating new services. Three of the initiatives (Strong Communities, Strengthening Families, and CPPC) seek to alter the way local residents view the idea of seeking help from "outsiders" to resolve personal and parenting issues. These initiatives attempt to influence attitudes about mutual reciprocity among neighbors and collective responsibility for child protection and safety.

Evaluations of these and similar community child abuse prevention strategies use multiple methodologies to clarify the most promising pathways to achieving community change (theory-of-change analysis and implementation studies) and to more directly use these data in altering their selection of specific strategies and program emphasis (utilization-focused evaluations). Where appropriate, randomization procedures and various quasiexperimental strategies are used to assess outcomes, although in most cases these procedures have been applied to specific elements or components of the initiative rather than capturing the initiative's population-level effects. In addition to the methodological limitations of this research base, few of these strategies have been operational long enough to provide an accurate profile of their potential accomplishments.

Among the community prevention strategies, one of the most widely researched at both the strategy and population-based levels is Triple P. The Triple P program was developed in Australia to assist parents of children with developmental delays or behavioral problems. The program is increasingly viewed as a promising strategy to prevent child abuse (Sanders, in press). Triple P is a behavioral family intervention designed to improve parenting skills and behaviors by changing how parents view and react to their children. Triple P consists of a series of integrated or "scaled" interventions designed to provide a common set of information and parenting practices to parents who face varying degrees of difficulty or challenges in caring for their children. Based on social learning theory, research on child and family behavior therapy, and developmental research on parenting in everyday contexts, each intervention seeks to reduce child behavior problems by teaching healthy parenting practices and how to recognize negative or destructive practices. Parents are taught self-monitoring, self-determination of goals, self-evaluation of performance, and self-selection of change strategies.

These parenting practices are introduced to community residents through the following avenues: (1) a broadly targeted, universal set of strategies to educate the community about the principles of positive parents; (2) offering parents a set of simple techniques for addressing common child care issues (for example, safety, behavior management, discipline strategies, and securing basic health care); and (3) structured individual and group based interventions directed to parents requiring more specific assistance in managing their child's behavior or addressing more complex personal challenges or risk factors. Triple P focuses on enhancing service quality and access to resources by providing training to existing local providers in the model's practice principles rather than developing new service programs.

The broadly targeted strategies—(1) and (2) in the preceding paragraph—include the dissemination of positive parenting principles through the use of radio spots, newspaper articles, newsletters distributed through the schools, mass mailings to local residents, presentations at community forums, and a widely publicized Web site (Universal Triple P); brief parenting advice and contact sessions that are available to parents through various primary care facilities (Selected Triple P); and a short series of skill training workshops to reinforce the concepts presented in the program's written material (Primary Care Triple P). Those families requiring additional assistance can access a 10-session individual skill building intervention (Standard Triple P) or an 8-week group-based intervention (Group Triple P). For families facing the most significant challenges or multiple-risk families, a more intensive behavioral family intervention is provided as needed (Enhanced Triple P).

Research on Triple P indicates impressive achievements helping clients with clinical issues (Sanders, in press). Few studies of Triple P have examined the effects of Triple P's multilayered and universal service approach on population or community-wide outcomes. Prinz and colleagues (2009) randomly assigned 18 counties in South Carolina to either the comprehensive Triple P program or to a "services-as-usual" control group. In the intervention counties, Triple P staff launched an intensive social marketing campaign to raise awareness of Triple P and its related parenting strategies and support services. Staff contacted state and county stakeholders who provide support services for parents of young children, including education, school readiness, child care, mental health, social services, and health. Direct service providers were offered the opportunity to participate in training on Triple P. During the project's first 2 years, 649 service providers received training.

Effects of Triple P were assessed by comparing trends between the intervention and comparison counties on three independently derived population indicators. The comparisons yielded statistically significant, indeed, large positive effects. Between the period just before implementation and 24 months later, intervention counties increased in substantiated child maltreatment rates by just 8%, compared with 35% for control counties. Out-of-home placements decreased in intervention counties 12% but increased 44% in control counties. Hospital admissions for child injuries decreased 18% in intervention counties but increased 20% in control counties. Although these findings are impressive, it remains unclear how the social marketing, universal service offers, and training in the Triple P model might have produced these results. Additional analyses regarding potential variation across the intervention and comparison counties with respect to both implementation efforts and outcomes is needed to understand more fully the mechanisms through which Triple P might affect maltreatment rates.

A nonrandom, matched comparison study of comparable communities in Australia produced similar positive findings (Sanders et al., 2008). Program outcomes in Australia were assessed through a computer-assisted telephone interview of a random sample of households ($N = 3000$) in both intervention and matched communities prior to and after implementation of Triple P. Postintervention interviews found a significant reduction in Triple P communities in the number of children with clinically elevated and borderline behavioral and emotional problems compared to the comparison communities. Parents in Triple P communities reported a greater reduction in the prevalence of depression, stress, and coercive parenting. Although encouraging, preexisting differences between the intervention and comparison communities as well as a low response rate to the telephone survey may have influenced results.

The case for community prevention is promising on both theoretical and empirical levels. Community prevention efforts are well grounded in a strong theory of change and, in some cases, have strong outcomes. At least some of the models reviewed by Daro and Dodge (2009) show the ability to reduce reported rates of child abuse, reduce injury to young children, alter for the better parent–child interactions, reduce parental stress, and improve parental efficacy.

Focusing on community building, such programs can mobilize volunteers and engage diverse sectors within the community, including first responders, the faith community, local businesses, and civic groups. This mobilization exerts a synergistic impact on other desired community outcomes such as economic development and better health care.

There are areas of concern in contemplating community prevention of maltreatment. Effects at the community level explain only a small proportion of the variance in child maltreatment rates, raising questions about the value of investing large sums in changing context over offering direct assistance to parents. Implementing a high-quality, multifaceted community prevention initiative is expensive. As costs increase, policymakers need to consider the trade-offs in investing in diffuse strategies designed to alter community context versus expanding the availability of services for known high-risk individuals.

Conclusion

It is difficult to accept that the best we can do in child protection is offer assistance *after* a child has been harmed. The response to child abuse will always include calls for increased prevention. Fortunately, prevention advocates have responded with a wide range of prevention efforts, and these efforts have measurable impacts. Yet, the utility of prevention efforts remains unclear. Although reports of physical and sexual abuse declined substantially in recent years, one hesitates to attribute the decline solely to prevention efforts. Moreover, during the same period, reports of neglect remained steady. As well, the amount of fatal child maltreatment remains high (U.S. Department of Health and Human Services, 2009).

Despite the absence of uniform progress in reducing maltreatment, empirical evidence suggests the following avenues that can improve prevention impacts: (1) offer families and communities multiple opportunities to match resources and strategies; (2) build strong community partnerships that facilitate the ability of families as well as agencies to draw on a wide range of fiscal resources and technical assistance; (3) initiate prevention services early (at the time a baby is born or a woman is pregnant); (4) augment assistance over time to address the emerging needs of the parent–child relationship and the child's development; (5) follow a clear line of reasoning and target specific individual and systemic issues; (6) hire and train individuals capable of delivering services that are embedded within an overall community service system; and (7) provide ongoing, reflective supervision for staff.

Achieving stronger impacts from investments in prevention will require continued efforts to develop and test a broad array of prevention programs and systemic reforms. No one program or approach guarantees success in all settings, although compelling evidence supports early intervention, beginning when women become pregnant or give birth. In the final analysis, no single model or service will work for all families under all conditions. Protecting children from abuse and neglect is a complex task and one that most certainly will involve changing parental behaviors, creating safer and more supportive communities, and improving the quality and reliability of public institutions.

References

American Academy of Pediatrics (AAP). (1998). The role of home-visitation programs in improving health outcomes for children and families. *Pediatrics, 10*(3), 486–489.

Ammerman, R., Putnam, F., Altaye, M., Chen, L., Holleb, L., Stevens, J., et al. (2009). Changes in depressive symptoms in first time mothers in home visitation. *Child Abuse and Neglect, 33*, 127–138.

Anisfeld, E., Sandy, J., & Guterman, N. (2004, December). *Best beginnings: A randomized controlled trial of a paraprofessional home visiting program.* Final Report submitted to the Smith Richardson Foundation and New York State Office of Children and Family Services. Available at: http://www.healthyfami liesamerica.org/research/index.shtml

Armstrong, K., Fraser, J., Dadds, M., & Morris, J. (1999). A randomized controlled trial of nurse home visiting to vulnerable families with newborns. *Journal of Pediatric Child Health, 35*, 237–244.

Armstrong, K., Fraser, J., Dadds, M., & Morris, J. (2000). Promoting secure attachment, maternal mood and child health in a vulnerable population: A randomized controlled trial. *Journal of Pediatric Child Health, 36*, 555–562.

Baker, A., Piotrkowski, C., & Brooks-Gunn, J. (1999). The Home Instruction Program for Preschool Youngsters (HIPPY). *The Future of Children, 9*(1), 116–133.

Barr, R. G., Barr, M., Fujiwara, T., Conway, J., Catherine, N., & Brant, R. (2009). Do educational materials change knowledge and behaviour about crying and shaken baby syndrome? A randomized controlled trial. *Canadian Medical Association Journal, 180*(7), 727–733.

Belsky, J. (1980). Child maltreatment: An ecological integration. *American Psychologist, 35*, 320–335.

Belsky, J., & Vondra, J. (1990). Lessons for child abuse: The determinants of parenting. In D. Cicchetti & V. Carlson (Eds.), *Child maltreatment: Theory and research on the causes and consequences of child abuse and neglect* (pp. 153–202). Cambridge: Cambridge University Press.

Berrick, J., & Barth, R. (1992). Child sexual abuse prevention: Research review and recommendations. *Social Work Research and Abstracts, 28,* 6–15.

Black, M., & Teti, L. (1997). Promoting meal-time communication between adolescent mothers and their infants through videotape. *Pediatrics, 99,* 432–437.

Bronfenbrenner, U. (1979). *The ecology of human development: Experiments by nature and design.* Cambridge, MA: Harvard University Press.

Bull, J., McCormick, G., Swann, C., & Mulvihill, C. (2004). Ante- and post-natal home visiting programs: A review of reviews. *Evidence Briefing.* Available at: www.hda.nhs.uk/evidence

Carter, N. (1995). *Parenting education in the United States: An investigative report.* Philadelphia: Lew Charitable Trusts.

Carter, N., & Harvey, C. (1996). Gaining perspective on parenting groups. *Zero to Three, 16*(6), 1, 3–8.

Centers for Disease Control and Prevention (CDC). (2009). *Parent training programs: Insight for practitioners.* Atlanta, GA: Centers for Disease Control and Prevention. Available at: http://www.cdc.gov/ViolencePrevention/pdf/Parent_Training_Brief-a.pdf

Chaffin, M. (2004). Is it time to rethink Healthy Start/Healthy Families? *Child Abuse and Neglect, 28,* 589–595.

Chaffin, M., Bonner, B., & Hill, R. (2001). Family preservation and family support programs: Child maltreatment outcomes across client risk levels and program types. *Child Abuse and Neglect, 25*(10), 1269–1289.

Chalk, R., & King, P. (Eds.). (1998). *Violence in families: Assessing prevention and treatment programs.* Washington, DC: National Academy Press.

Chaloupka, F., & Johnson, L. (2007). Bridging the gap: Research informing practice and policy for healthy youth behavior. *American Journal of Prevention Medicine, 33*(4S), 147–161.

Cicchetti, D., & Rizley, R. (1981). Developmental perspectives on the etiology, intergenerational transmission, and sequelae of child maltreatment. *New Directions for Child Development, 11,* 31–55.

Cohn Donnelly, A. (1997). An overview of prevention of physical abuse and neglect. In M. E. Helfer, M. Kempe, & R. Krugman (Eds.), *The battered child* (5th ed., pp. 579–593). Chicago: University of Chicago Press.

Daro, D. (1988). *Confronting child abuse.* New York: The Free Press.

Daro, D. (1993). Child maltreatment research: Implications for program design. In D. Cicchetti & S. Toth (Eds.), *Child abuse, child development, and social policy* (pp. 331–367). Norwood, NJ: Ablex Publishing Corporation.

Daro, D. (1994). Prevention of childhood sexual abuse. *The Future of Children, 4*(2), 198–223.

Daro, D. (2006). *Home visitation: Assessing progress, managing expectations.* Chicago: Chapin Hall Center for Children and the Ounce of Prevention Fund.

Daro, D. (2009). The history of science and child abuse prevention—A reciprocal relationship. In K. Dodge & D. Coleman (Eds.), *Community-based prevention of child maltreatment* (pp. 9–25). New York: Guilford Press.

Daro, D., & Dodge, K. (2009). Creating community responsibility for child protection: Possibilities and challenges. *Future of Children, 19*(2), 67–94.

Daro, D., & Gelles, R. (1992). Public attitudes and behaviors with respect to child abuse prevention. *Journal of Interpersonal Violence, 7*(4), 517–531.

Daro, D. A., & McCurdy, K. P. (2006). Interventions to prevent child maltreatment. In L. S. Doll, S. E. Bonzo, J. A. Mercy, D. A. Sleet, & E. N. Haas (Eds.), *Handbook of injury and violence prevention* (pp. 137–156). New York: Springer.

DePanfilis, D., & Dubowitz, H. (2005). Family Connections: A program for preventing child neglect. *Child Maltreatment, 10*(2), 108–123.

Dias, M., Smith, K., deGuehery, K., Mazur, P., Li, V., & Shaffer, M. (2005). Preventing abusive head trauma among infants and young children: A hospital-based parent education program. *Pediatrics, 115*, e470–e477.

Doll, L. S., Bonzo, S. E., Mercy, J. A., Sleet, D. A., & Haas, E. N. (Eds.). (2007). *Handbook of injury and violence prevention.* New York: Springer.

DuMont, K., Mitchell-Herzfeld, S., Greene, R., Lee, E., Lowenfels, A., Rodriguez, M., et al. (2008). Healthy Families New York (HFNY) randomized trial: Effects on early child abuse and neglect. *Child Abuse and Neglect, 32*, 295–315.

Dunst, C. (1995). *Key characteristics and features of community-based family support programs.* Chicago: Family Resource Coalition.

Farrow, F. (1997). *Child protection: Building community partnerships . . . Getting from here to there.* Cambridge, MA: John F. Kennedy School of Government, Harvard University.

Fergusson, D., Grant, H., Horwood, L. J., & Ridder, E. (2005). Randomized trial of the Early Start Program of home visitation. *Pediatrics, 11*(6), 803–809.

Finkelhor, D. (2008). *Childhood victimization.* New York: Oxford University Press.

Garbarino, J. (1977). The human ecology of child maltreatment: A conceptual model for research. *Journal of Marriage and the Family, 39*, 721–735.

Geeraert, L., Van den Noorgate, W., Grietens, H., & Onghena, P. (2004). The effects of early prevention programs for families with young children at risk for physical child abuse and neglect: A meta-analysis. *Child Maltreatment, 9*(3), 277–291.

Gershater-Molko, R., Lutzker, J., & Wesch, D. (2003). Project SafeCare: Improving health, safety, and parenting skills in families reported for and at-risk of child maltreatment. *Journal of Family Violence, 18*(6), 377–386.

Gibson, L., & Leitenberg, H. (2000). Child sexual abuse prevention programs: Do they decrease the occurrence of child sexual abuse? *Child Abuse and Neglect, 24*(9), 1115–1125.

Glascoe, F., Oberklaid, F., Dworkin, P., & Trimm, F. (1998). Brief approaches to educating patients and parents in primary care. *Pediatrics, 101*(6), 10–18.

Gomby, D. (2005, July). *Home visitation in 2005: Outcomes for children and parents.* Invest in Kids Working Paper No. 7. Committee for Economic Development: Invest in Kids Working Group. Available at: www.ced.org/projects/kids.shtml

Guterman, N. (2001). *Stopping child maltreatment before it starts: Emerging horizons in early home visitation services.* Thousand Oaks, CA: Sage.

Hahn, R., Bilukha, O., Crosby, A., Fullilove, M., Liberman, A., Moscicki, E., et al. (2003). First reports evaluating the effectiveness of strategies for preventing violence: Early childhood home visitation. Findings from the Task Force on Community Prevention Services. *Morbidity and Mortality Weekly Report, 52*(RR-14), 1–9.

Harrell, A., Cavanagh, S., & Sridharan, S. (1999, November). Evaluation of the children at risk program: Results one year after the end of the program. *National Institute of Justice Research Brief.* Washington, DC: U.S. Department of Justice.

Hazzard, A. (1990). Prevention of child sexual abuse. In R. Ammerman & M. Hersen (Eds.), *Treatment of family violence* (pp. 354–384). New York: Wiley.

Howard, K., & Brooks-Gunn, J. (2009). The role of home-visiting programs in preventing child abuse and neglect. *Future of Children, 19*(2), 119–146.

Johnson, K. (2009). *State-based home visiting: Strengthening programs through state leadership.* New York: National Center for Children in Poverty, Columbia University.

Johnson, Z., Howell, F., & Molloy, B. (1993). Community mothers' program: Randomized controlled trial of non-professional intervention in parenting. *British Medical Journal*, 306 (6890), 1449–1452.

Kempe, C. H., Silverman, F. N., Steele, B. F., Droegemueller, W., & Silver, H. K. (1962). The battered-child syndrome. *Journal of the American Medical Association*, 181, 17–24.

Klagholz, D. (2005). *Starting early starting smart: Final report*. Great Falls, VA: Donna D. Klagholz & Associates, LLC. Available at: http://www.healthy familiesamerica.org/research/index.shtml

Kolko, D., Moser, J., & Hughes, J. (1989). Classroom training in sexual victimization awareness and prevention skills: An extension of the Red Flag/Green Flag people program. *Journal of Family Violence*, 4(1), 25-45.

Layzer, J., Goodson, B., Bernstein, L., & Price, C. (2001). *National evaluation of family support programs. Volume A: Meta-analysis*. Prepared for the Department of Health and Human Services, ACYF. Cambridge, MA: Abt Associates.

LeCroy & Milligan Associates, Inc. (2005). *Healthy Families Arizona evaluation report 2005*. Tucson, AZ: Author. Available at: http://www.healthyfamilies america.org/research/index.shtml

Love, J., Kisker, E., Ross, C., Schochet, P., Brooks-Gunn, J., Paulsell, D., et al. (2002). *Making a difference in the lives of infants and toddlers and their families: The impacts of Early Head Start—final technical report*. Princeton, NJ: Mathematica Policy Research, Inc., and New York, NY: Columbia University's Center for Children and Families at Teachers College.

Love, J. et al. (2009). The Early Head Start evaluation: Impacts at the end of the program, two years later, and the context for ongoing research. Poster prepared for the *EHS Poster Symposium, Biennial Meeting of the Society for Research in Child Development*, Denver, CO, April 2.

MacLeod, J., & Nelson, G. (2000). Programs for the promotion of family wellness and the prevention of child maltreatment: A meta-analytic review. *Child Abuse and Neglect*, 24(9), 1127–1149.

MacMillan, H., MacMillan, J., Offord, D., Griffith, L., & MacMillan, A. (1994). Primary prevention of child sexual abuse: A critical review. Part II. *Journal of Child Psychology and Psychiatry*, 35, 857–876.

Mannes, M., Roehlkepartain, E., & Benson, P. (2005). Unleashing the power of community to strengthen the well-being of children, youth and families: An asset-building approach. *Child Welfare*, 84(2), 233–250.

Melton, G., & Berry, E. (1994). *Protecting children from abuse and neglect: Foundations for a new national strategy*. New York: Guilford Press.

Mitchell, E., Hutchison, L., & Stewart, A. (2007). The continuing decline in SIDS mortality. *Archives of Disease in Childhood*, 92, 625–626.

Olds, D., Eckenrode, J., Henderson, C., Cole, R., Kitzman, H., Luckey, D., et al. (1998). Long-term effects of home visitation on maternal life course, child abuse and neglect and children's arrests: Fifteen-year follow-up of a randomized trial. *Journal of the American Medical Association*, 278(8), 637–643.

Olds, D., Robinson, J., O'Brien, R., Luckey, D., Pettitt, L., Henderson, C., et al. (2002). Home visiting by paraprofessionals and by nurses: A randomized, controlled trial. *Pediatrics*, 110(3), 486–496.

Olds, D., Sadler, L., & Kitzman, H. (2007). Programs for parents of infants and toddlers: Recent evidence from randomized trials. *Journal of Child Psychology and Psychiatry*, 48(3/4), 355–391.

Prinz, R., Sanders, M., Shapiro, C., Whitaker, D., & Lutzker, J. (2009). Population-based prevention of child maltreatment: The U.S. Triple P system population trial. *Prevention Science*. Available at: http://www.springerlink.com/content/a737l8k76218j7k2/fulltext.pdf

Reppucci, N., & Haugaard, J. (1989). Prevention of child sexual abuse: Myth or reality. *American Psychologist*, 44(10), 1266–1275.

Rispens, J., Aleman, A., & Goudena, P. (1997). Prevention of child sexual abuse victimization: A meta-analysis of school programs. *Child Abuse and Neglect*, 2, 975–987.

Sameroff, A., & Chandler, M. (1975). Reproductive risk and the continuum of caretaking casualty. In F. Horowitz, M. Hetherington, S. Scarr-Salapatek, & G. Siegal (Eds.), *Review of child development research* (Vol. 4, pp. 187–244). Chicago: University of Chicago Press.

Sanders, M. (in press). The development, evaluation and dissemination of Triple P Positive Parenting Program as a public health approach to strengthening parenting. *Journal of Family Psychology*.

Sanders, M., Ralph, A., Sofronoff, K., Gardiner, P., Thompson, R., Dwyer, S., et al. (2008). Every family: A population approach to reducing behavioral and emotional problems in children making the transition to school. *Journal of Primary Prevention*, 29, 197–222.

Sandler, J. (1979). *Effects of adolescent pregnancy on mother-infant relations: A transactional model*. Report to the Center for Population Research. Bethesda, MD: National Institutes of Health.

Showers, J. (2001). Preventing shaken baby syndrome. *Journal of Aggression, Maltreatment and Trauma*, 5(1), 349–365.

Sweet, M., & Appelbaum, M. (2004). Is home visiting an effective strategy? A meta-analytic review of home visiting programs for families with young children. *Child Development*, 75, 1435–1456.

U.S. Department of Health and Human Services. (1991). *Creating caring communities: Blueprint for an effective federal policy for child abuse and neglect*. Washington, DC: U.S. Government Printing Office.

U.S. Department of Health and Human Services. (2009). *Child maltreatment 2007*. Washington, DC: U.S. Government Printing Office.

Wagner, M., & Spiker, D. (2001). *Multisite parents as teachers evaluation: Experience and outcomes for children and families*. Menlo Park, CA: SRI, International. Available at: www.sri.com/policy/cehs/early/pat.html

Webster-Stratton, C. (1994). Advancing videotape parent training: A comparison study. *Journal of Consulting and Clinical Psychology*, 62, 583–593.

Webster-Stratton, C., Reid, M. J., & Hammond, M. (2001). Preventing conduct problems, promoting social competence: A parent and teacher training partnership in Head Start. *Journal of Clinical Child Psychology*, 30(3), 238–302.

Williams, Stern & Associates. (2005). *Healthy Families Florida: Evaluation report January 1999–December 2003*. Miami, FL: Author. Available at: http://www.healthyfamiliesamerica.org/research/index.shtml

3 Child Protection System

Diane DePanfilis

The child protection system is comprised of the organizations officially charged with responsibility to protect children from abuse and neglect as well as members of the community who care about the safety and well-being of children. Although the child protective services (CPS) program within public child welfare is typically the central agency in a community's child protection system, many professionals have roles to play in reporting suspected abuse and neglect, investigating alleged maltreatment, and providing medical and mental health services to children and families.

This chapter describes the scope of child maltreatment, summarizes the roles of various disciplines, and traces the response of the child protection system from initial report to case closure. Other chapters outline relevant laws and policies, discuss the role of courts, and describe interventions and treatments to address child maltreatment.

_____ Scope of Reported Child Abuse and Neglect[1]

Child maltreatment represents the primary reason children are reported to CPS. In 2008, 3.3 million reports involving the alleged maltreatment of approximately 6.0 million children were made to CPS (U.S. Department of Health and Human Services, 2010). The national rate in 2008 was 10.3 reports per 1,000 children. Of these reports, CPS programs screened in 62.5% for investigation or assessment. In 2008, approximately 772,000 children were confirmed as victims.

---

[1]Portions of this section are adapted from Pecora, P. J., Barth, R. P., Maluccio, A. N., Whittaker, J. K., & DePanfilis, D. (2009). *Child welfare challenge: Policy, practice, and research*. New York: Aldine.

Referral Sources

All professionals working with children have a responsibility to identify and report child abuse and neglect to CPS or law enforcement. See Chapter 21 for discussion of the duty to report suspected child maltreatment. In 2008, more than one-half (57.9%) of all reports of alleged child abuse or neglect were made by professionals (teachers, law enforcement, doctors, nurses, and social services staff). The remaining reports were made by nonprofessionals, including friends, neighbors, and relatives.

Types of Maltreatment Reported

The types of maltreatment reported affect the services required to respond. In 2008, child neglect continued to represent the largest category of child maltreatment confirmed by CPS (U.S. Department of Health and Human Services, 2010). Seventy-one percent of maltreated children experienced neglect, 16.1% were physically abused, 9.1% were sexually abused, 7.3% were psychologically maltreated, 4.2% experienced other types of maltreatment, and 1% were medically neglected (U.S. Department of Health and Human Services, 2010).

Gender and Age of Maltreated Children

For 2008, reports represented roughly equal numbers of boys and girls (48.3% of reports involved boys, 51.3% of reports involved girls). The youngest children (birth to 1 year) had the highest rate of reported victimization (21.7 per 1,000 children). The rate of maltreatment decreased as age increased.

The types of maltreatment reported to CPS nationally varied by the age of children. Of victims medically neglected, 20.4% were younger than 1 year. Of victims sexually abused, 35.2% were in the 12 to 15 year age group.

An analysis of infant child abuse and neglect (Centers for Disease Control and Prevention, 2008) identified 91,278 infant victims under the age of 1 in 2006, most of whom were neglected (68.5%). A large percentage of infant victims were less than 1 month old (38.8%). Of these, 84.3% were less than 1 week old. Understanding the ages at which infants are most at risk is important for targeting prevention efforts.

Race and Ethnicity of Victims

In 2008, African American, American Indian, Alaska Native, and children of multiple races had the highest rates of reported victimization at

16.6, 13.9, and 13.8 per 1,000 children respectively (U.S. Department of Health and Human Services, 2010). White children and Hispanic children had rates of approximately 9.8 and 8.6 per 1,000 children, respectively. Asian children had the lowest rate of 2.9 per 1,000 children. Nearly half of all victims were white (45.1%), one-fifth (21.9%) were African American, and 20.8% were Hispanic.

Perpetrators of Maltreatment

In 2008, 80.1% of children were maltreated by a parent (U.S. Department of Health and Human Services, 2010). Other relatives were responsible for 6.5% of maltreatment. In 2008, 56.2% of perpetrators were women.

Fatalities Due to Abuse and Neglect

During 2008, an estimated 1,740 children died from abuse or neglect— a rate of 2.33 deaths per 100,000 children (U.S. Department of Health and Human Services, 2010). With the exception of 2005, the rate of child maltreatment-related fatalities increased over the last 5 years. Some children who died from maltreatment were already known to child welfare agencies. Children whose families had received family preservation services accounted for 13.1% of child fatalities. Slightly less than 2% of child fatalities occurred in foster care.

Some of the increase in reported child fatalities can be attributed to better reporting and management of data by health departments and fatality review boards. It is unknown whether the increase in child fatalities can be completely accounted for by better reporting.

In 2008, more than 40% of children who died due to child maltreatment were younger than 1 year of age; 15.7% were age 1; 11.2% were age 2; and 7.6% were age 3 (U.S. Department of Health and Human Services, 2010).

Maltreatment in Foster Care

The U.S. Children's Bureau established a national standard for the tolerable level of child abuse or neglect in foster care. To comply with the national standard, a state must be 99.68% free from substantiated abuse and neglect by foster parents or facility staff members. The number of states in compliance with this standard has increased from 16 in 2004 to 24 in 2008 (U.S. Department of Health and Human Services, 2009). The national average during 2008 was 99.4% free from maltreatment in foster care.

Some reports of maltreatment that occur while a child is in foster care are not the result of maltreatment by foster parents or facility staff members, and it is sometimes difficult to determine the perpetrator of maltreatment when multiple caregivers have access to a child (e.g., biological parents during visits, foster parents, or other caregivers during placement) (DePanfilis & Girvin, 2005; U.S. Department of Health and Human Services, 2005a).

Variations in Reporting Trends
Due to CPS Alternative Response Systems

Many states have implemented child welfare reforms that involve responding differentially to reports of child abuse and neglect. Described as dual track, alternative response, or multiple track systems, states adopting this reform changed their practices to accept certain reports of child abuse and neglect without formally logging the report as a CPS report that must go through an investigation and substantiation process (U.S. Department of Health and Human Services, 2005b). Typically, in cases where abuse and neglect are severe, or criminal offenses against children are alleged, an investigation focused on evidence gathering is conducted by CPS alone or in conjunction with law enforcement. (See Chapter 19 for discussion of investigation.) In less serious cases, where the family may benefit from community services, an assessment may be conducted rather than an investigation. In these less serious cases, the facts regarding what happened are obtained, but the intervention emphasizes a comprehensive assessment of family strengths and needs and an appropriate match with community services (Goldman & Salus, 2003).

Alternative response practices have affected child abuse and neglect reporting and substantiation rates. In an effort to explore the impact that this child welfare reform has on child abuse and neglect reporting, the U.S. Department of Health and Human Services contracted for a set of analyses using data from the National Child Abuse and Neglect Data System (NCANDS) (Shusterman, Hollinshead, Fluke, & Yuan, 2005). A review of prior research (Shusterman et al., 2005) suggested wide variations in the percentage of reports diverted to alternative response systems (from 42% to 71%) and in the impact alternative response has on substantiation rates. Based on analysis of NCANDS data from six states in 2002, the number of children who were included in maltreatment reports, as well as the proportion of children who received an alternative response, varied across states. Kentucky, Missouri, New Jersey, and Oklahoma all had large numbers of children who were subjects of a maltreatment report (between 60,000 and 80,000), but in Kentucky and Oklahoma, only 27% and 20%, respectively, were referred to alternative response, whereas in Missouri and New Jersey, 64% and 71%, respectively, were referred to alternative response.

Compared to Kentucky, Missouri, New Jersey, and Oklahoma, the states of Minnesota and Wyoming had much smaller numbers of children who were subjects of a report. In Minnesota, 20% were referred to alternative response, while in Wyoming, 58% were referred (Shusterman et al., 2005).

Findings from the NCANDS analysis found that alternative response was more likely to be used for cases with less immediate safety concerns and that an investigative response (including law enforcement) was much more likely in cases of child sexual abuse (CSA) (Shusterman et al., 2005). No differences in types of responses were found by race or ethnicity.

Recurrence of Child Abuse and Neglect

The recurrence of child maltreatment following a report to CPS is an index of the effectiveness of child protection (Waldfogel, 1998a, 1998b). The Children's Bureau established a national standard for the tolerable level of recurrent maltreatment. To meet the standard, at least 94.6% of children must not have been revictimized during a 6-month period. The number of states in compliance with the standard increased from 17 in 2004 to 24 in 2008. The national average percentage of children without a new substantiated incident of child maltreatment increased from 91.9% during 2004 to 93.3% in 2008.

Roles of Professionals Involved in the Child Protection System

All professionals who come in contact with children have significant roles in the child protection system. CPS, law enforcement, educators, child care providers, health care providers, mental health providers, legal and judicial system professionals, substitute care providers, support service providers, domestic violence victim advocates, substance abuse treatment providers, and concerned community members all play roles in keeping children safe. The roles of the professionals with primary responsibility for child protection are summarized next.

Child Protective Services

CPS is charged with responding to reports of child abuse and neglect and implementing policies, procedures, and practices to support families to adequately meet the needs of their children and to keep children safe from maltreatment. The National Association of Public Child Welfare Administrators (2009) emphasizes child safety as the core mission of CPS:

> Providing for child safety is the core mission of public child welfare agencies. Children are entitled to live in a safe and permanent home with their own families whenever possible. Families of origin have the

right and the responsibility to raise their children. Child welfare agencies have the responsibility to provide a range of preventive and/or supportive services to families having difficulty providing a safe and permanent environment, recognizing that better outcomes for children are achieved by engaging families in the safety assessment process and engaging, strengthening and supporting families to care safely for their own children. When families are unable or unwilling to remedy conditions that threaten the safety of their child(ren), it is the mandate of the designated public child welfare agency to take the necessary action to secure the child(ren)'s safety. (p. ix)

To accomplish these purposes, the responsibilities of CPS are to (1) receive reports of child abuse or neglect; (2) conduct assessments and investigations (as appropriate in collaboration with law enforcement); (3) evaluate child safety and assess risk of future maltreatment; (4) assess family strengths, resources, and needs; (5) develop individualized safety plans and case plans; (6) provide or arrange services to assist families in addressing the problems that led to maltreatment and reduce the risk of subsequent maltreatment; (7) participate in interdisciplinary team meetings; (8) coordinate services provided by other professionals; (9) complete case management functions such as maintaining case records, systematically reviewing case plans, and developing court reports; and (10) testify in court (DePanfilis & Salus, 2003; Goldman & Salus, 2003; National Association of Public Child Welfare Administrators, 2009).

Law Enforcement

The role of law enforcement varies to some degree across states, but in all communities law enforcement investigates reports of child abuse and neglect that meet the definition of a crime. The primary responsibilities of law enforcement include (1) identifying and reporting suspected child maltreatment; (2) receiving reports of child abuse and neglect; (3) investigating reports of child maltreatment (see Chapter 19); (4) gathering and preserving physical evidence; (5) determining whether sufficient evidence exists to arrest and prosecute alleged offenders; (6) participating in multidisciplinary team (MDT) meetings; (7) protecting children from immediate harm (e.g., emergency removal from the home); and (8) providing protection to CPS staff when a caseworker's personal safety may be in jeopardy (Goldman & Salus, 2003).

Health Care Providers

Physicians, nurses, and allied health professionals take steps to (1) identify and report suspected child abuse and neglect; (2) provide diagnostic and treatment services for maltreated children and their families; (3) provide advice and consultation to CPS regarding medical aspects of child abuse and neglect; (4) participate in MDT meetings; (5) provide expert testimony in court; (6) provide information to parents regarding the needs, care, and treatment of children; (7) identify and provide support for families at risk of child maltreatment; and (8) provide training for medical and nonmedical professionals regarding the medical aspects of child abuse and neglect (Goldman & Salus, 2003; Dubowitz, 2000; Leventhal, 2000; Shapiro, 2000).

Mental Health Professionals

Key roles of psychiatrists, psychologists, clinical social workers, and other mental health professionals include (1) identifying and reporting suspected child abuse and neglect; (2) conducting evaluations of abused and neglected children and their families; (3) providing treatment for abused and neglected children and their families; (4) providing clinical consultation to CPS; (5) participating in interdisciplinary teams; and (6) providing expert testimony in court (Goldman & Salus, 2003).

Legal Professionals

Attorneys involved in child protection include attorneys representing the CPS agency, criminal prosecutors, attorneys for children, and defense attorneys. The responsibilities of these professionals are described in Chapters 4 and 6.

Educators, Child Care Providers, and Other Community-Based Providers

School administrators, teachers, school social workers, school counselors, early childhood educators, child care providers, and other community-based professionals play important roles in child protection. Key roles include (1) identifying and reporting suspected child abuse and neglect, (2) providing input related to diagnostic and treatment services for the child and family, (3) providing support services for parents, (4) serving on interdisciplinary teams, and (5) establishing policies related to reporting and responding to maltreatment.

_____ Child Protective Services Case Process

CPS receives reports of suspected child maltreatment, assesses the safety of children, and provides or arranges for services to increase the safety and well-being of children who have been abused or neglected and/or who are deemed unsafe and/or at risk of maltreatment. Each case proceeds through a series of stages: (1) intake and screening, (2) initial assessment/investigation, (3) family assessment, (4) service planning, (5) service provision, (6) evaluation of case progress, and (7) case closure.

Intake and Screening

The first stage of the CPS process involves receiving and responding to reports of suspected child abuse and neglect. Reports may be made to a statewide hotline (in some states) or to the local CPS program. Intake workers question the caller to assess whether the report should be accepted for investigation or assessment. Key decisions at this stage are (1) determining if the reported information meets statutory and agency guidelines for child maltreatment and should result in a face-to-face meeting with the child and family and, if so, (2) determining the urgency with which the agency must respond (DePanfilis & Salus, 2003).

If a report is accepted, states set the amount of time in which a response must occur, ranging from immediately to 24 hours for high-priority cases, and from 24 hours to 14 days for low-priority cases. In 2008, the average response time was 84 hours or approximately 3.3 days (U.S. Department of Health and Human Services, 2010).

Research on screening decision making reveals factors that affect the decision to accept or reject a report. Wells, Fluke, and Brown (1995) conducted a comprehensive study of screening decisions in 12 agencies from five states. The study controlled for maltreatment type, age, referral source, presence of perpetrator in the home, and completeness of information. Wells and colleagues found that the office receiving the referral was the strongest predictor in the decision to investigate. This suggests widespread differences within and across states in decision making about reports. Further research by Wells suggests that organizational factors such as policies, procedures, customs, norms, and worker interpretation predict whether a report is accepted (Wells, 1997). Screening decisions may also depend on the process involved such as relying on an individual worker to make decisions or requiring supervisory or team involvement (Tumlin & Geen, 2000).

Initial Assessment/Investigation

After accepting a report, an initial assessment or investigation is initiated. The assessment or investigation may be completed by a CPS worker alone, a CPS worker and law enforcement working as a team, a CPS worker in conjunction with another service provider, or a community service provider alone when an alternative response system is in place. The initial assessment or investigation includes interviews with the child, siblings, parents or other caregivers, and others who have information concerning the alleged maltreatment and the family (DePanfilis, 2005; DePanfilis & Salus, 2003; Pecora et al., 2009).

In 2008, CPS programs nationally reported conducting 1,996,774 investigations or assessments resulting in some type of disposition (U.S. Department of Health and Human Services, 2010). In approximately 24% of cases, at least one child was determined to be a victim of child abuse or neglect. The remaining cases led to a finding that children were not victims of maltreatment, and the report received one of the following dispositions—unsubstantiated (64.7%), alternative response nonvictim (7.7%), other (1.7%), closed with no finding (1.9%), and intentionally false (0.1%).

CPS programs reported that 63.3% of victims and 28.5% of nonvictims received postinvestigation child welfare services. Slightly more than 20% of victims and 3.8% of nonvictims were placed in foster care.

Key decisions during the initial assessment/investigation stage are to determine the following: (1) Did maltreatment occur as defined by law? (2) If the child's immediate safety is a concern, what intervention will ensure the child's protection? (3) If there is a risk of future maltreatment, what is the level of risk? (4) Are agency services needed to keep the child safe, reduce the risk of future maltreatment, and address any effects of child maltreatment? (5) If safety cannot be managed with an in-home safety plan, should the child be removed from the home? (DePanfilis & Salus, 2003).

Assessment of Child Safety. During the initial stage, a key function is to assess the safety of the child or children. Formal decision-making models to help CPS workers evaluate safety have existed since the 1970s (DePanfilis & Scannapieco, 1994). Decision-making tools came into widespread use following enactment in 1997 of the federal Adoption and Safe Families Act (ASFA), which emphasizes child safety. An early review of 10 safety decision-making models (DePanfilis & Scannapieco, 1994) suggested that although some criteria overlapped in these models, there were wide differences in definitions, purposes, and levels of research support.

Today, consensus exists that the purpose of safety assessment is to determine whether a maltreated or at-risk child is in *immediate* danger of serious harm (Casey Family Programs and American Humane Association, n.d.). A child is deemed safe when all available information leads to the conclusion that the child is not in immediate danger of serious harm. If the child is not safe, immediate steps must be taken to assure the child's safety. Such steps include in-home safety interventions or placement of the child in out-of-home care. Safety interventions are responsive to the immediate danger to the child.

Current conceptualizations of child safety suggest that workers should consider three categories of factors: (1) factors that suggest the potential of serious harm to a child, (2) factors that indicate the family has protective capacities to manage serious threats of harm, and (3) factors that indicate child vulnerability (Morton & Salovitz, 2006). For example, despite the fact that a child was maltreated, safety assessment may suggest that there are no immediate threats of serious harm to the child because the family has protective capacities to keep the child safe.

Assessment of Risk. Safety assessment—discussed previously—focuses on the potential for *immediate* and serious harm. In addition to safety assessment, CPS workers are responsible for assessing the likelihood of future maltreatment—risk assessment. Evaluating the risk of future maltreatment is essential to develop service plans to help families manage and reduce the risk of maltreatment. Risk assessment involves implementing change-oriented services to reduce risk over time.

Assessing risk includes interviewing children, parents, and other family members; gathering information about the child and family; and interpreting information (DePanfilis & Salus, 2003). Although assessing risk has been a responsibility of CPS for a long time, it has only been during the last 25 years that CPS agencies adopted formal risk assessment tools to guide the assessment and management of risk (Mitchell et al., 2005; Rycus & Hughes, 2003).

Family Assessment

For families who are provided continuing services, the responsibility for working with the family usually falls to CPS. A CPS worker conducts a comprehensive family assessment. If an alternative response system is in place, the worker responsible for conducting the family assessment could be a CPS worker or a worker in a community agency.

The family assessment is a comprehensive process for identifying, considering, and weighing factors that affect the child's safety, permanency, and well-being (Schene, 2005). During the assessment, the CPS worker engages the family in an effort to understand their strengths, risks, and needs. The family assessment process may be coordinated with a mental health provider or other professionals who have ongoing roles with the child and family. The family assessment is designed to build on the two previous assessments (safety and risk). Assessment of the family's strengths and needs considers the length of time it will take the family to provide a safe and stable home environment (U.S. Department of Health and Human Services, 2000). Research reveals a connection between the completion of comprehensive family assessments and positive outcomes for children and families (U.S. Department of Health and Human Services, 2007).

Key decisions during the family assessment include the following: (1) Which of the risk factors identified during the initial assessment (e.g., domestic violence, substance abuse, mental health problems) are the most important focus for intervention and services? (2) What protective factors or strengths exist that can be bolstered through supportive services? (3) What effects of maltreatment are observed in the child and/or other family members (e.g., mental health or behavioral problems)? (4) What is the level of motivation of family members to participate in intervention? (DePanfilis & Salus, 2003; DePanfilis, 2005; Pecora et al. 2009).

Service Planning

To be effective, the right mix of services, interventions, and treatments must be tailored to the needs of each child and family. Selecting the right mix of services derives from the family assessment. Key decisions at the service planning stage are to determine (1) outcomes that will be the target of intervention (e.g., enhanced family functioning, behavioral control of emotions, enhanced parent–child interaction); (2) goals that will help family members achieve these outcomes; (3) interventions and services that will support achievement of these goals and outcomes; (4) the best provider of these interventions; and (5) time frames for evaluation of progress (DePanfilis & Salus, 2003).

Service Provision

Following creation of a service plan, it is the responsibility of CPS to arrange for, provide, and/or coordinate the delivery of services to maltreated children and the family. Today, the emphasis is increasingly on evidenced-based practice, which may be defined as the conscientious use of current best evidence in making decisions about clients (Gibbs & Gambrill, 2002; Wells, 2007). States are working to integrate evidence-based practices into services and interventions. Kansas, for example, has a Web-based evidence-based practice tool that guides users to find the latest research on strategies to achieve core child welfare outcomes (University of Kansas School of Social Welfare, 2007). In 2007 in Washington state, the Washington State Institute for Public Policy was tasked to study programs and policies that show evidence of reduced involvement in the child welfare system and to construct reliable estimates of the costs and benefits of evidence-based prevention and intervention programs (Lee, 2008). In California, there are multiple efforts to encourage evidence-based practice as well as evidence-supported practices (i.e., practices with some evidence of effectiveness). The California Evidence-Based Clearinghouse for Child Welfare is an online resource to provide up-to-date information on evidence-based child welfare practices.

Evaluation of Progress

Assessment is an ongoing process that begins with the first client contact and continues throughout the life of the case. Progress toward achieving goals should be formally evaluated at least every 3 months (DePanfilis & Salus, 2003). Key decisions include (1) assessment of the current safety of the child, (2) degree of achievement of family-level outcomes, (3) degree of achievement of goals and tasks in the service plan, (4) assessment of changes in risk and protective factors previously identified, and (5) level of success in addressing the effects of maltreatment on the child.

Case Closure

Ending the relationship between worker and family is itself a process involving a mutual review of progress (DePanfilis & Salus, 2003). Optimally, cases are closed when families have achieved their outcomes and goals, children are safe because the risk of harm has been reduced or eliminated, and effects of maltreatment have been addressed. Some cases close because the client discontinues services and the agency does not have a sufficient legal basis to refer the situation to juvenile court.

Conclusion

This chapter provided an overview of the scope of child maltreatment, the roles of various disciplines in responding to the problem, and the response of the child protection system from initial referral to case closure. At each stage of the process, the CPS worker is responsible for employing assessment skills, analyzing information to make key decisions that will keep children safe, and working with other professionals to coordinate treatment and intervention for maltreated children and their parents. It is extremely difficult and demanding work. At the same time, the job is enormously rewarding and important to children, families, and society.

References

Casey Family Programs & American Humane Association. (n.d.). *A breakthrough series collaborative on safety and risk assessments*. Denver: American Humane Association. Available at: http://www.americanhumane.org/assets/docs/protecting-children/PC-bsc-change-package.pdf

Centers for Disease Control and Prevention (CDC). (2008). Nonfatal maltreatment of infants—United States, October 2005–2006. *Morbidity and Mortality Weekly Report (MMWR), 57*(13), 336–339. Available at: http://www.cdc.gov/mmwr/preview/mmwrhtml/mm5713a2.htm

DePanfilis, D. (2005). Child protection. In G. P. Mallon & P. M. Hess (Eds.), *Child welfare for the 21st century: A handbook of practices, policies, and programs* (pp. 290–301). New York: Columbia University Press.

DePanfilis, D., & Girvin, H. (2005). Investigating child maltreatment in out-of-home care: Barriers to effective decision-making. *Children and Youth Services Review, 27,* 353–374.

DePanfilis, D., & Salus, M. (2003). *Child protective services: A guide for caseworkers.* Washington, DC: U.S. Department of Health and Human Services.

DePanfilis, D., & Scannapieco, M. (1994). Assessing the safety of children at risk for maltreatment: Decision-making models. *Child Welfare, 73,* 229–245.

Dubowitz, H. (2000). What medical evaluation is needed when physical abuse is suspected. In H. Dubowitz & D. DePanfilis (Eds.), *Handbook for child protection practice* (pp. 146–148). Thousand Oaks, CA: Sage.

Gibbs, L., & Gambrill, E. (2002). Evidence-based practice: Counterarguments to objections. *Research on Social Work Practice, 12*, 452–476.

Goldman, J., & Salus, M. K. (2003). *A coordinated response to child abuse and neglect: The foundation for practice.* Washington, DC: U.S. Department of Health and Human Services.

Lee, S. (2008). *Study update: Evidence-based programs to reduce involvement in the child welfare system.* Olympia: Washington State Institute for Public Policy. Available at: http://www.wsipp.wa.gov/pub.asp?docid=08-01-3901

Leventhal, J. M. (2000). How do I interpret medical tests for physical abuse? In H. Dubowitz & D. DePanfilis (Eds.), *Handbook for child protection practice* (pp. 149–153). Thousand Oaks, CA: Sage.

Mitchell, L. B., Barth, R. P., Green, R., Wall, A., Biemer, P., Berrick, J. D., et al. (2005). Child welfare reform in the United States: Findings from a local agency survey. *Child Welfare, 84*, 5–24.

Morton, T. D., & Salovitz, B. (2006). Evolving a theoretical model of child safety in maltreating families. *Child Abuse and Neglect, 30*, 1317–1327.

National Association of Public Child Welfare Administrators (2009). *A framework for safety in child welfare.* Washington, DC: Author. Available at: http://www.napcwa.org/home/docs/FrameworkforSafety.pdf

Pecora, P. J., Barth, R. P., Maluccio, A. N., Whittaker, J. K., & DePanfilis, D. (2009). *Child welfare challenge: Policy, practice, and research.* New York: Aldine.

Rycus, J. S., & Hughes, R. C. (2003). *Issues in risk assessment in child protective services.* Columbus, OH: North American Resource Center for Child Welfare, Center for Child Welfare Policy.

Schene, P. (2005). *Comprehensive family assessment guidelines for child welfare.* Washington, DC: National Resource Center for Family-Centered Practice and Permanency Planning. Available at: http://www.acf.hhs.gov/programs/cb/pubs/family_assessment/family_assessment.pdf

Shapiro, R. A. (2000). The medical evaluation for possible child sexual abuse: When is it needed, who should do it, how should one prepare for it, and what will be done? In H. Dubowitz & D. DePanfilis (Eds.), *Handbook for child protection practice* (pp. 188–192). Thousand Oaks, CA: Sage.

Shusterman, G. R., Hollinshead, D., Fluke, J. D., & Yuan, Y. T. (2005). *Alternative responses to child maltreatment: Findings from NCANDS.* Washington, DC: U.S. Department of Health and Human Services. Available at: http://aspe.hhs.gov/hsp/05/child-maltreat-resp/

Tumlin, K. C., & Geen, R. (2000). The decision to investigate: Understanding state child welfare screening policies and practices. *New Federalism Issues and Options for States, Series A, No. A-38.* Washington, DC: The Urban Institute.

University of Kansas School of Social Welfare. (2007). *Results oriented management in child welfare.* Available at: http://www.rom.ku.edu/EBP_Main.asp

U.S. Department of Health and Human Services. (2000). *Rethinking child welfare practice under the Adoption and Safe Families Act of 1997.* Washington, DC: U.S. Government Printing Office.

U.S. Department of Health and Human Services. (2005a). *General findings from the federal Child and Family Services Review.* Washington, DC: U.S. Government Printing Office.

U.S. Department of Health and Human Services. (2005b). *Alternative responses to child maltreatment: Findings from NCANDS*. Washington, DC: U.S. Government Printing Office.

U.S. Department of Health and Human Services. (2007). Funding opportunity: Using comprehensive family assessment to improve child welfare outcomes [Funding Opportunity Number HHS-2007-ACF-ACYF-CA-0023; CFDA Number 93.670]. Washington, DC: U.S. Government Printing Office.

U.S. Department of Health and Human Services. (2010). *Child maltreatment 2007*. Washington, DC: U.S. Government Printing Office.

Waldfogel, J. (1998a). Rethinking the paradigm for child protection. *The Future of Children: Protecting Children from Abuse and Neglect*, 8, 104–119.

Waldfogel, J. (1998b). *The future of child protection*. Cambridge, MA: Harvard University Press.

Wells, S. J. (1997). Screening for child protective services: Do we accept a report? How do we respond? In T. D. Morton & W. Holder (Eds.), *Decision making in children's protective services* (pp. 94–106). Atlanta: Child Welfare Institute.

Wells, S. J. (2007). Evidence based practice in child welfare. In *Evidence-based practice in child welfare in the context of cultural competence meeting proceedings and findings*. Minneapolis: School of Social Work, College of Education and Human Development, University of Minnesota. Available at: http://www.cehd.umn.edu/SSW/g-s/EBP/

Wells, S. J., Fluke, J. D., & Brown, C. H. (1995). The decision to investigate: CPS practice in twelve local agencies. *Children and Youth Services Review*, 17, 523–546.

4

Juvenile Court

John E. B. Myers

America's juvenile courts play a central role in protecting children from maltreatment. The history of the juvenile court is outlined in Chapter 1. The present chapter describes today's juvenile court. In some states, the juvenile court is called "family court."

The juvenile court in major metropolitan areas differs from the court in rural communities and small cities. Los Angeles, California, for example, has 60 full-time juvenile court courtrooms staffed by more than 500 judges, referees, attorneys, bailiffs, clerks, probation officers, and social workers. In rural areas, there may be one judge for several counties, and this "circuit riding" judge is responsible for all judicial matters, including juvenile court. Although the resources devoted to juvenile court vary from community to community, the philosophy and legal framework of the juvenile court is similar across the country.

Depending on the state, several terms are used to describe the judicial officers working in juvenile court. Judges, of course, work in juvenile court. In addition to judges, many states employ referees or commissioners. A referee or commissioner, like a judge, is trained as a lawyer. Generally, a referee or commissioner is a lower position in the judicial hierarchy than a judge. Thus, a judge is typically the presiding judicial officer of a juvenile court, assisted by one or many referees or commissioners.

The juvenile court has authority (called jurisdiction) over three groups of children: juvenile delinquents, status offenders, and abused and neglected children. Depending on the state, abused and neglected children are referred to as dependent children, children in need of services (CHINS), or simply maltreated children.

Juvenile Delinquency

Juvenile delinquency is illegal conduct by a minor (anyone under 18) that would be a crime if committed by an adult (e.g., theft, burglary, rape, murder, drug offenses). When a minor is suspected of delinquency, the police investigate. The minor may be questioned and searched. If the investigation points to the minor, an arrest may follow. Once arrested on a serious matter, the minor is typically taken to the county juvenile detention center. At the detention center, an intake worker—often a probation officer—interviews the minor, considers the police report, and decides whether the minor should be released or detained. Simultaneously, the intake worker and/or a prosecutor decides whether to file formal delinquency charges against the minor. If charges are filed and the minor is detained, the minor must be taken before a juvenile court judge as soon as possible so the judge can rule on the legality of the detention.

Once a minor is formally charged with delinquency, the minor has the right to an attorney. Because most minors (and their parents) cannot afford to hire private defense attorneys, the judge assigns the public defender's office to represent the minor. The public defender meets with the minor, explains the charges, listens to the minor's side of the story, and helps the minor decide whether to admit or deny guilt. The state is represented by a public prosecutor.

Plea bargaining is a key element of the adult criminal justice system. During plea bargaining in adult criminal cases the defense attorney negotiates with the prosecutor in an effort to get some of the charges against the accused (the defendant) dismissed or reduced in exchange for the defendant's agreement to plead guilty to the reduced charges. As a result of plea bargaining, most defendants plead guilty and do not insist on a trial.

Plea bargaining occurs in juvenile court delinquency proceedings, and here, too, most minors plead guilty in exchange for lighter punishment. Only a small percentage of minors deny guilt and insist on a trial, or, as it is called in many states, an adjudicatory hearing. A juvenile court adjudicatory hearing regarding delinquency looks much like the trial of an adult. The minor is represented by counsel. A prosecutor represents the government. Formal rules of evidence and procedure apply. Witnesses are called and cross-examined. The minor has the right to testify but cannot be compelled to do so.

Adults charged with serious crimes have a right under the U.S. Constitution to trial by jury. In juvenile court, however, the U.S. Supreme Court ruled in 1971 that minors accused of delinquency do not have a constitutional right to jury trial (*McKeiver v. Pennsylvania*, 1971). The Supreme Court reasoned that the constitutional right to a jury trial in criminal cases does not apply in juvenile court because delinquency proceedings are civil not criminal. Because there is no jury in most juvenile courts, the judge fulfills the role of the jury. Judge-only trials are called bench or court trials.

Since the Supreme Court's 1971 decision that the U.S. Constitution does not require juries in delinquency cases, there has been a movement across the country to "get tough" on juvenile delinquents. Adjudicatory hearings for delinquency have more and more in common with criminal trials of adults. As a result, defense attorneys have renewed the argument that minors accused of delinquency should have the right to trial by jury in juvenile court. In 2008, the Kansas Supreme Court agreed, ruling that Kansas minors accused of delinquency have a constitutional right to a jury (In re L. M., 2008). It remains to be seen whether other states will follow suit, although in 2009 the Louisiana Supreme Court rejected the argument that minors accused of delinquency have a constitutional right to a jury trial in juvenile court (In re A. J., 2009).

If a minor pleads guilty or is found guilty following an adjudicatory hearing, the judge decides the appropriate disposition. Unlike criminal prosecutions against adults, where the sentencing judge imposes punishment in the form of incarceration, a fine, or, if the defendant is deserving, probation, the juvenile court judge is concerned less with punishment than with rehabilitation. The judge, aided by a report from the juvenile probation officer, fashions a disposition that is intended to turn the young offender away from crime. Most youth are placed on probation and may be ordered to go to school, obey their parents, perform community service, and stay away from bad influences. If the youth has mental health or substance abuse issues, the disposition may include therapy. To the extent it will teach a lesson, punishment is part of disposition in juvenile court. The goal of disposition is individualized intervention to turn the youth away from the negative influences pulling in the direction of crime.

Some teenagers commit such serious, calculated, callous crimes that they deserve to be punished like adult criminals. Moreover, some teens are already committed to a life of crime and are unlikely to benefit from the therapeutic approach of the juvenile court. The law allows such "hardened" youth to be transferred from juvenile court to criminal court where they are prosecuted as adults. In making the transfer decision, the juvenile court judge considers the minor's age and IQ, the nature and seriousness of the crime, whether the youth is naive or sophisticated in the ways of crime, whether the minor has been in trouble before, and the likelihood the minor can be rehabilitated in juvenile court.

The overarching theory of juvenile court is that youth are malleable. With the right package of individualized services, most can be saved from the downward spiral that leads to crime as a career. Sadly, there are times when the theory of the juvenile court gets lost in crowded court dockets, overworked professionals, and underfunded programs. Today's juvenile court is stretched to the breaking point. Yet, few argue that the juvenile court should be abandoned as a failure. Every day, dedicated judges, probation officers, social workers, and attorneys pour their hearts into turning kids away from crime. Failure is depressingly common, but success stories abound. Thousands of minors benefit from interaction with the professionals of the juvenile court.

Status Offenses

As conceived at the beginning of the 20th century, the juvenile court was intended as a refuge for a broad range of children in difficulty. Thus, the court had jurisdiction over delinquent children, abused and neglected children, and children who were simply poor. In addition, the juvenile court had jurisdiction over so-called status offenders. A status offense is conduct by a minor that is not a crime but that nevertheless justifies intervention by the juvenile court. The traditional status offenses include running away from home, truancy, and smoking and drinking under age. In addition, the juvenile court had authority over so-called "ungovernable children"—that is, older children who refused to obey the "reasonable" demands of their parents. A parent at wits' end with their teenager's disobedience could ask a juvenile court judge to assume control of the child and order the child to behave or face the possibility of commitment to a reform school or some other institution.

The extent to which juvenile courts dealt with status offenses varied from place to place. In the closing decades of the 20th century, expert commissions recommended narrowing or eliminating juvenile court authority over status offenses. In particular, experts called for an end to the practice of placing status offenders in the same institutions with delinquents. Congress responded to the experts in 1974 with passage of the Juvenile Justice and Delinquency Prevention Act. This law required states receiving federal funds to stop institutionalizing status offenders in facilities for juvenile delinquents.

Today, juvenile courts in many states retain authority over status offenses. As before, however, the degree of juvenile court involvement with these children varies. In many communities, juvenile courts are so overwhelmed with delinquency and maltreatment cases that little time and few resources are available to help status-offending youth.

Protecting Children From Abuse and Neglect: Dependency Proceedings in Juvenile Court

The juvenile court has authority to intervene in the family to protect children from abuse and neglect. To this end the juvenile court works in partnership with child protective services (CPS). It must be remembered, however, that although CPS and the juvenile court strive for similar goals, they approach the task as representatives of different branches of government. As members of the judicial branch of government, juvenile court judges are keenly aware of their duty to protect the rights of *all* parties before the court: the child, the government (CPS), and the parents. Although juvenile court judges go out of their way to protect children, the first responsibility of a judge is to the law, even when that means ruling against CPS. Like judges, CPS workers are concerned with the rights and welfare of everyone involved in juvenile court. Unlike the judge, however, whose role requires detached objectivity, CPS workers are concerned primarily with protecting children from maltreatment. CPS workers strive to help parents, but the first goal of child protection is just that—child protection.

Although the different responsibilities of CPS workers and juvenile court judges lead to occasional friction, the relationship is generally harmonious. Moreover, the different perspectives of social work and law engender beneficial checks and balances that temper the tendency toward extremes that are inevitable in complex human endeavors—particularly endeavors involving intense emotion and the exercise of state power over individuals.

The Decision to Involve the Juvenile Court

Cases of possible child abuse and neglect come to official attention when reports of suspected maltreatment are received by CPS or law enforcement. Approximately one third of initial reports are screened out because they do not involve maltreatment (U.S. Department of Health and Human Services, 2008). For cases that are screened in, CPS workers either conduct an investigation or engage the family through alternative response. (See Chapter 3 for discussion of CPS and Chapter 19 for discussion of investigation.) If no maltreatment is detected, the case is closed. On the other hand, if abuse or neglect is substantiated, CPS workers make a series of difficult decisions. How serious is the maltreatment? What is the risk the child will be hurt again? Is it safe to leave the child at home, or must the child be removed and placed with relatives or in a foster home? Can this case be handled safely and effectively without involving the juvenile court? In quite a few cases—particularly neglect cases—CPS workers decide the juvenile court is not needed, and CPS offers services to alleviate the neglect.

The preceding paragraph makes clear that many cases of confirmed maltreatment never reach juvenile court. The paragraph also clarifies that CPS workers are the gatekeepers to juvenile court. For the most part, it is CPS workers who decide when and whether to invoke the authority of the juvenile court.

The juvenile court is needed when maltreatment is serious, when the abused or neglected child—or other children in the home—is at risk, when it is unsafe to leave the child at home, or when maltreating parents increase the risk to the child by refusing to cooperate.

Formal proceedings in juvenile court are commended by filing a legal document called a petition. A petition is what lawyers call a pleading, and all lawsuits—criminal and civil—are started with pleadings. Criminal cases are started with a pleading called an indictment, information, or complaint. Civil cases are started with a complaint or a petition.

The petition that starts proceedings in juvenile court contains a brief description of the facts of the case, including the names and address of the child and the parents, along with an allegation that the child is abused or neglected and in need of the court's protection. A copy of the petition is given to the parents so they are on notice of the proceedings. The parents are informed when and where the juvenile court will conduct hearings on their child's case.

Emergency Removal of the Child From Home

One of the most difficult decisions CPS workers make is whether to remove a child on an emergency basis from an unsafe home (see Chapter 3). Often this decision is made in the middle of the night, in chaotic circumstances, and with less than complete information. Yet, the decision must be made.

CPS agencies have detailed procedures for assessing risk and determining when a child needs to be removed on an emergency basis. In addition to mastering the principles and practice of risk assessment, safety evaluation, and casework, CPS workers should understand that the U.S. Constitution places limits on emergency removal. The Fourteenth Amendment to the Constitution guarantees all citizens due process of law, and the U.S. Supreme Court has interpreted the Fourteenth Amendment to protect parental rights. As one court put it, "Parents and children have a well-established constitutional right to live together without governmental interference" (*Wallis v. Spencer*, 2000, p. 1136).

In addition to the Fourteenth Amendment, the Fourth Amendment protects citizens from unreasonable searches and seizures by the police *and by government social workers*. Removing a child from parents is a "seizure" for Fourth Amendment purposes. Under the Constitution, CPS may not remove a child from the parents unless (1) parents consent to removal or (2) before removal CPS obtains a court order or a warrant authorizing removal or (3) absent a court order or warrant, a genuine emergency exists that necessitates immediate removal to protect the child from serious harm or death. In law, the emergency exception to the requirement of a preremoval warrant is known as the exigent circumstances exception.

When it comes to emergency removal, CPS workers must balance the need for child protection against the right of parents to custody of their children free from unwarranted government intrusion. The Federal Fifth Circuit Court of Appeals discussed the delicate balancing of interests in *Gates v. Texas Department of Protective and Regulatory Services* (2008):

There is no doubt that child abuse is a heinous crime, and the government's interest in stopping abuse and removing children from abusive situations is paramount. . . . Deciding what is reasonable under the Fourth Amendment will require an assessment of the fact that the courts are dealing with a child who likely resides in the same house, and is under the control of, the alleged abuser. The analysis cannot be divorced from that fact, but that fact does not override all other Fourth Amendment considerations.

Therefore, we hold that the government may not seize a child from his or her parents absent a court order, parental consent, or exigent circumstances. Exigent circumstances in this context means that, based on the totality of the circumstances, there is reasonable cause to believe that the child is in imminent danger of physical or sexual abuse if he remains in his home. This is a flexible inquiry that considers all of the facts and circumstances with no one factor being dispositive. . . . Whether there was time to obtain a court order is . . . one factor that informs the reasonableness analysis. . . . Other non-exclusive factors . . . are the nature of the abuse (its severity, duration, and frequency), the strength of the evidence supporting the allegations of abuse, the risk that the parent will flee with the child, the possibility of less extreme solutions to the problem, and any harm to the child that might result from the removal. (p. 429)

On rare occasions, parents whose child was removed file a lawsuit against the removing CPS worker (See, e.g., *Doe v. Kearney*, 2003; *Gates v. Texas Department of Protective and Regulatory Services*, 2008; *Rogers v. County of San Joaquin*, 2007; *Tenenbaum v. Williams*, 1999). In such lawsuits, the parents claim that removal violated their constitutional rights under the Fourteenth and Fourth Amendments. Typically, such lawsuits ask for huge awards of money damages to be paid by the removing CPS worker. Obviously, the thought of being sued—perhaps for millions of dollars—just for doing one's job as a CPS worker is daunting. CPS workers can take solace in the fact that such lawsuits are uncommon, and when they are filed they usually fail. The best way to avoid such suits is to follow the rules governing emergency removal. When CPS workers act within the law, they have nothing to fear.

When a child is removed in an emergency, the law requires CPS to immediately file a petition in juvenile court. Within a short time—often the next day—a hearing is held before a juvenile court judge (or referee or commissioner). The purpose of the hearing is to determine whether the child should remain in out-of-home care or be returned to the parents. At the hearing—which goes by various names, including detention hearing and initial hearing—the judge informs the parents of the nature of the proceedings, including the specific allegations in the petition.

At the detention hearing, CPS is represented by a government attorney. The judge assigns attorneys for the parents and, in many states, for the child. After listening to the attorneys, the CPS worker, and the parents, the judge decides whether CPS made a reasonable effort to avoid removing the child from the home. Assuming reasonable efforts were made, the judge decides whether to "detain" the child in out-of-home care or return the child to the parents. The detention hearing is often surprisingly quick—on the order of a few minutes.

With the detention hearing out of the way, the attorneys get down to the task of resolving the case or preparing for trial. In juvenile court, the trial is often called an adjudicatory hearing. As is true with all types of litigation, few juvenile court cases go all the way to a contested adjudicatory hearing. Most cases settle. The attorney for CPS negotiates with the attorneys for the parents and the child in the effort to reach a solution that is acceptable to all parties. In cases that settle, the parents acknowledge they need help. The parents, CPS, and the child's attorney agree that the child meets one or more of the definitions of maltreatment. The agreement is presented to the judge, who typically approves the agreement and makes a ruling that the child is subject to the juvenile court's authority or jurisdiction. The child is then called a "dependent of the court" or a "child in need of protection."

Once the judge rules that a child is a dependent of the court, the next step is disposition—what is the goal for this child and family? CPS typically prepares a report for the judge outlining the agencies' goals for the family and the services that will be provided to help the parents achieve the goals. In most cases, the goal is reunification of the family.

Adjudication

Cases that do not settle go to contested adjudicatory hearing (trial) before a juvenile court judge, referee, or commissioner. In most states, there is no jury in juvenile court. At the adjudicatory hearing, CPS is represented by its attorney. The parents have the right to hire an attorney of their choosing. Most parents, however, cannot afford to hire an attorney, and the judge appoints an attorney to represent the parents.

Does the child need an attorney? The practice in many states until recently was not to appoint attorneys for children in juvenile court dependency proceedings. Rather, the judge appointed a guardian ad litem to look after the child's interests. A guardian ad litem is an individual—often not an attorney—assigned to safeguard a child's interests in litigation. Today the trend across the country is to appoint an attorney for the child. Although there is some disagreement about the proper role for a child's attorney, in most states the attorney conducts an investigation, communicates with the child, and advocates in court for the position the attorney believes is best for the child.

In addition to an attorney for the child, juvenile courts in many states appoint a court-appointed special advocate (CASA) for children in dependency proceedings. CASAs are nonattorney volunteers—college students, retirees, parents, etc.—who are interested in helping abused and neglected children. CASAs receive training about child maltreatment, the child protection system, and the juvenile court. Typically, each CASA volunteer is assigned only one or two children. The CASA gets to know the child, and in most communities the CASA goes to court when their child's case comes up. Juvenile court judges often place great stock in the opinions of CASA volunteers because it is common for the CASA to know the child better than any of the professionals assigned to the case. CASAs help children's attorneys—who typically have hundreds of cases—from letting children fall through the cracks of the foster care and juvenile court systems.

The Burden of Proof

The issue for the judge to decide at the adjudicatory hearing is whether the child was abused or neglected as alleged in the petition. As the party alleging maltreatment, CPS has the burden of presenting enough evidence to convince the judge that abuse or neglect occurred. In other words, CPS has the burden of proof.

The burden of proof plays a key role in all litigation—civil and criminal. If the party with the burden of proof fails to present enough evidence to meet its burden, the party loses. Which party has the burden of proof? Most of the time, the answer is simple. In criminal cases, the prosecution has the burden of proof of the defendant's guilt. In civil cases, such as a case in which an angry parent sues the CPS worker who removed a child from the home, the parent has the burden of proving that the CPS worker violated the parent's constitutional rights. In a juvenile court adjudicatory hearing regarding maltreatment, CPS has the burden of proof. Unless CPS satisfies its proof burden by presenting enough evidence to convince the judge that maltreatment occurred, the judge rules against CPS and dismisses the petition.

American law uses three burdens of proof: beyond a reasonable doubt, preponderance, and clear and convincing. Proof beyond a reasonable doubt is the most demanding burden of proof—the most difficult to meet. To satisfy the beyond a reasonable doubt standard, evidence does not have to eliminate *all* doubt. Yet, the evidence must be so strong that the judge or jury is *nearly certain* that the evidence is right. Preponderance of the evidence is the least demanding burden of proof—the easiest to meet. The preponderance standard is satisfied when the evidence in favor of a proposition is even slightly greater than the evidence against the proposition. Although percentages do not capture the full flavor of burdens of proof, percentages are a useful way to conceptualize burdens. Proof beyond a reasonable doubt is similar to 95% certainty. Preponderance of the evidence requires only 51% or greater certainty. Clear and convincing evidence lies between beyond a reasonable doubt and a mere preponderance. Think of clear and convincing evidence as 75% certainty.

In criminal trials, the prosecutor must prove the defendant guilty beyond a reasonable doubt. Criminal law imposes the highest burden of proof on the prosecution in order to reduce the likelihood that innocent people are convicted. If the prosecution fails to prove guilt beyond a reasonable doubt, the accused *must* be acquitted. A juvenile delinquency proceeding in juvenile court is essentially a criminal prosecution, and the prosecutor must prove the youngster's delinquency beyond a reasonable doubt.

There are many types of civil litigation, including lawsuits over contracts, property rights, auto accidents, business affairs, divorce, and more. Most civil litigation requires proof by a preponderance of the evidence. Juvenile court adjudicatory hearings regarding abuse and neglect are civil, and in most states the attorney for CPS must prove maltreatment by a preponderance of the evidence.

The clear and convincing evidence burden of proof is used in a narrow range of civil litigation. Thus, before a person can be involuntarily committed to a psychiatric hospital for treatment, the government must prove by clear and convincing evidence that the person is mentally ill and a danger to self or others. In order to permanently sever the parent–child relationship—terminate parental rights—the government must prove parental unfitness by clear and convincing evidence.

For civil litigation, the legislature decides the proper burden of proof and is free to mix and match burdens of proof to meet policy objectives. Thus, as mentioned previously, in most states preponderance of the evidence is the burden of proof in juvenile court adjudicatory hearings regarding maltreatment. Several states, however, require the higher standard of clear and convincing evidence. California has an interesting approach. In California, CPS must prove maltreatment by a preponderance of the evidence. However, if CPS asks the judge to remove the maltreated child from home, CPS must prove the need for removal by clear and convincing evidence. The federal Indian Child Welfare Act (ICWA), which is binding on state courts, is discussed at the end of this chapter. Under ICWA, if CPS asks a juvenile court judge to terminate the parental rights of an Indian child, CPS must prove parental fault by proof beyond a reasonable doubt.

The Adjudicatory Hearing

Juvenile court adjudicatory hearings regarding maltreatment are less formal than criminal trials. Nevertheless, a contested juvenile court adjudicatory hearing is a trial. The rules of evidence apply, although the rules in juvenile court are not identical to the rules in criminal matters. Evidence consists of testimony of witnesses, documents, photographs, and other items that have a bearing on the case (see Chapters 21 and 22).

At the adjudicatory hearing, CPS is the petitioner and the party with the burden of proof. As such, CPS goes first. The attorney for CPS presents the government's case—often called the government's case-in-chief. One or more CPS workers testify and describe their investigation. In addition to CPS workers, the attorney may offer expert testimony from physicians or mental health professionals. In most communities, children seldom testify at juvenile court adjudicatory hearings.

The parents' attorney and the child's attorney have the right to cross-examine the witnesses testifying for CPS. In addition to testimony from witnesses, the CPS attorney is likely to offer into evidence documents and reports prepared by CPS workers, expert consultants, and others. Such reports are hearsay, and the lawyers may argue about the admissibility of hearsay evidence. (Hearsay is discussed in detail in Chapter 21.)

When the CPS attorney finishes presenting the evidence needed to meet the burden of proof, the government's case-in-chief is complete, and the government "rests its case." At this juncture, the parents' attorney typically asks the judge to dismiss the case. The parents' attorney—occasionally joined by the child's attorney—argues that the government failed to present sufficient evidence to meet the burden of proof. Motions to dismiss for insufficient evidence are often made but seldom granted.

After CPS rests its case, it is time for the parents' case-in-chief. The parents have no obligation to put on a case, although the parents may wish to testify or offer other evidence. If parents testify, the attorneys for CPS and the child may cross-examine. Following the parents' case-in-chief, the parents rest their case.

If the child has counsel, the child's attorney may put on a case by calling witnesses, including experts.

After listening to the evidence and considering the opening statements and closing arguments of the attorneys, the judge decides whether CPS proved its case—that is, whether CPS met its burden of proving maltreatment. If not, the judge dismisses the case. If CPS met the burden of proof, the judge sustains the petition and rules that the child comes within the jurisdiction of juvenile court.

The Dispositional Hearing

If the judge sustains the petition and rules the child was maltreated, the next step is disposition. Disposition was discussed earlier in the context of cases that settle, and the same principles apply at disposition following a contested hearing. The judge receives recommendations from CPS, considers the parents' wishes, consults the child if the child is old enough to have a useful opinion, and listens to the attorneys.

If the child can live safely at home then home placement is the preferred disposition. The judge's dispositional order outlines the services the parents will receive to keep the child safe and reduce the likelihood of further maltreatment. The order may provide that the child receive therapy or other intervention.

If the child cannot live safely at home, the dispositional order provides for the child's placement and approves a plan to work toward family reunification. In some cases of severe maltreatment, there is no realistic hope of reunification, and the disposition is to move expeditiously toward termination of parental rights.

Post-Adjudication Placement and Review

Every year, more than half a million children enter America's foster care system. Most children enter foster care following juvenile court adjudication of abuse or neglect. A rural county may have one or two children in out-of-home care while a large urban county has thousands. Keeping track of these children and providing services to the children and their families is one of the greatest challenges facing child welfare. Foster care is discussed in Chapter 5.

CPS workers have myriad rules and regulations to keep kids from falling through cracks in the foster care system. In tandem with efforts by CPS workers, the juvenile court retains authority over the children it adjudicates and the court holds periodic post-adjudication hearings to review progress. The timing of review hearings varies from state to state, but a common approach is to review progress every 3 to 6 months.

To prevent children from languishing in out-of-home care, the federal Adoption and Safe Families Act (ASFA) requires states to consider termination of parental rights for children who have been in foster care 15 of the previous 22 months. ASFA's push toward termination is not required for children in the care of relatives and in cases where termination is not in a child's best interest. ASFA's time limits keep pressure on CPS workers and judges to reunite families or move toward adoption.

Termination of Parental Rights

There is no relationship more revered than the relationship between parent and child. As explained earlier, the U.S. Supreme Court has ruled that the parent–child relationship is protected by the Constitution from unwarranted government interference. Yet, some parents are so thoroughly incompetent, incapable, or abusive that in order to save the child society must sever the parent–child relationship. The solemn responsibility for determining when such severance is necessary is entrusted to judges of the juvenile and family court.

The law of every state has detailed provisions governing termination of parental rights. The party seeking termination—CPS in juvenile court—has the burden of proof and must establish grounds for termination by clear and convincing evidence. To terminate the parent–child relationship, CPS must establish serious parental fault such as abandonment of the child, mental illness, intellectual disability that is incompatible with minimally adequate parenting, or serious maltreatment that is likely to persist. If fault is established, the judge determines whether termination of parental rights is in the child's best interest.

A court judgment terminating parental rights permanently severs the legal parent–child relationship. The "parent" no longer has rights to custody, visitation, or even contact with the child. Severance of the parent–child relationship frees the child for adoption.

Indian Child Welfare Act

Prior to 1978, as many as 25% to 35% of Native American children were removed from their parents for alleged abuse or neglect. The majority of these children were placed in non-Indian foster homes, adoptive homes, and institutions. In 1974, Congress held hearings on the issue. Calvin Isaac, Chief of the Mississippi Band of Choctaw Indians, testified before Congress:

One of the most serious failings of the present system is that Indian children are removed from the custody of their natural parents by non-tribal government authorities who have no basis for intelligently evaluating the cultural and social premises underlying Indian home life and childrearing. Many of the individuals who decide the fate of our children are at best ignorant of our cultural values, and at worst contemptuous of the Indian way and convinced that removal usually to a non-Indian household or institution, can only benefit an Indian child. (Indian Child Welfare Program, 1974, pp. 191–192)

In 1978, Congress enacted the ICWA, designed to reduce the number of Native American children inappropriately removed from their homes. Congress reported, "The wholesale separation of Indian children from their families is perhaps the most tragic and destructive aspect of Indian life today" (Indian Child Welfare Program, 1974, p. 3).

ICWA provides that only tribal courts can decide abuse and neglect cases involving Native American children whose permanent home is a reservation, although state juvenile courts can make emergency orders to protect Indian children found off the reservation. For children who do not live on a reservation, state juvenile courts can make decisions about removal, but the child's tribe must be notified, and the tribe has the right to join in the juvenile court proceedings. A state court judge cannot place a Native American child in foster care unless the need for out-of-home care is established by clear and convincing evidence and is supported by expert testimony.

When a Native American child is removed from parental custody, ICWA requires efforts to place the child with the child's extended family or with foster or adoptive parents approved by the child's tribe. Active efforts must be "made to provide remedial services and rehabilitative programs designed to prevent the breakup of the Indian family" (United States Code Annotated, Title 25, § 1912, 2010).

ICWA brought much-needed attention to the influence of racial bias in child welfare decision making. Progress has been made. Yet, even today, well into the 21st century, American Indian and Alaskan Native children continue to be placed in foster care at a rate that exceeds their proportion of the population (also see Chapter 5) (Carter, 2009).

Conclusion

An effective response to child abuse and neglect requires the combined efforts of numerous professions—social work, law enforcement, judges, medical professionals, lawyers, probation officers, and others. America's juvenile courts play a key role in the response, protecting thousands of children every day. Now more than a century old, the juvenile court remains a mainstay of America's child protection system.

References

Carter, V. B. (2009). Prediction of placement into out-of-home care for American Indian/Alaskan Natives compared to non-Indians. *Children and Youth Services Review, 31,* 840–846.

Doe v. Kearney, 329 F.3d 1286 (11th Cir. 2003).

Gates v. Texas Department of Protective and Regulatory Services, 537 F.3d 404 (5th Cir. 2008).

In re A.J., 2009 Westlaw 4793914 (La. 2009).

In re L.M., 186 P.3d 164 (Kan. 2008).

Indian Child Welfare Program, Hearings before the Subcommittee on Indian Affairs of the Senate Committee on Interior and Insular Affairs, 93d Congress, 2d Session, 1974.

McKeiver v. Pennsylvania, 403 U.S. 528 (1971).

Rogers v. County of San Joaquin, 487 F.3d 1288 (9th Cir. 2007).

Tenenbaum v. Williams, 193 F.3d 581 (2d Cir. 1999).

U.S. Department of Health and Human Services. (2008). *Child maltreatment 2006.* Washington, DC: U.S. Government Printing Office.

United States Code Annotated, Title 25, § 1912 (2010). St. Paul, MN: West.

Wallis v. Spencer, 202 F.3d 1126 (9th Cir. 2000).

5

Foster Care and Adoption

John E. B. Myers

This chapter discusses two vital components of America's child protection system: foster care and adoption. Foster care is intended to be an interim stop, a short layover on the journey to permanence for children removed from home. Most foster children eventually are reunified with their parents. When reunification is impossible, however, the journey takes a different turn, often in the direction of adoption—the creation of a new family.

Foster Care

For the history of foster care, see Chapter 1. Most children enter foster care through the juvenile court. The juvenile court is discussed in Chapter 4.

Foster Care Defined

Children who cannot remain safely at home are placed in out-of-home care. The federal government defines foster care broadly to include "24-hour substitute care for children outside their own homes" (Code of Federal Regulations, Title 45, § 57 [2009]). Under the federal definition, foster care includes children living with relatives, nonrelative foster family homes, group homes, institutions, and preadoptive homes. State definitions of foster care vary.

Number and Characteristics of Children in Foster Care

The number of children in foster care has fluctuated over time. Until recently there were few national statistics on foster care, making it difficult to tell how many children were in care at any given point in time. Examining various data sources, it appears that across the 20th century approximately 1% of American children were in foster care at any given time. The percentage of poor children in foster care always exceeded 1%. L. Pelton (personal communication, April 4, 2005) estimated that in 2001, nearly 5% of poor children were in foster care.

Today, the foster care population hovers around 500,000. Although a half million children is unacceptably high, it is well to remember that foster children make up a tiny fraction of the total child population. Most children are not abused or neglected, and most who are are not in foster care.

According to the U.S. Department of Health and Human Services (2009b), in 2007 approximately 70% of children in foster care were removed from the home due to neglect. Almost 9% were removed due to physical abuse (PA), while just over 3% were removed because of sexual abuse. Roughly 15% were removed due to multiple forms of maltreatment.

Children's Bureau data for 2006 indicate that nearly a quarter of children in out-of-home care were placed with relatives. Less than half of the foster care population lived in nonrelative foster family homes. Ten percent of the children were in institutions. Seven percent lived in group homes. Five percent were living with their parents on a trial basis. Two percent of the children had run away from foster care. Only 3% of the children were living in preadoptive homes.

Of children in foster care in 2006, the goal for half was reunification with parents. For almost a quarter the goal was adoption. Other goals included living with a relative or guardian (8%), long-term foster care (9%), and emancipation (6%).

African American children are overrepresented in the child welfare system. African Americans make up 15% of the U.S. population but 32% of the foster care population. American Indian and Alaskan Natives represent 1% of the U.S. population but 2% of children in foster care (Carter, 2009). In Canada, "40% of children in care are Aboriginal, yet they only make up 5% of the population" (Brown, George, Sintzel, & St. Arnault, 2009, p. 1019). In the United States, whites are 60% of the population but 40% of the foster care population.

It is doubly tragic when a child who has been abused at home is abused again in foster care. Although abuse occurs in some foster homes, it is uncommon. If we assume a rate of abuse in foster care of 1%—a reasonable estimate—then some 5,000 children were abused in foster care in 2009. Although 5,000 is unacceptably high, the fact that the national rate of abuse in foster care is in the neighborhood of 1% is a testament to success not failure and to the hard work of foster parents and the professionals who license and supervise foster homes.

In 2006, approximately 289,000 children left foster care. How long did they stay in out-of-home care? Fifteen percent of the children were away from the home less than a month. Thirty-four percent were in care up to 1 year. Nearly a quarter lived in foster care from 1 to 2 years. Twenty-eight percent were in care more than 2 years.

Unfortunately, some children who are reunified with their parents are reabused and reenter foster care. The following factors are related to return to foster care: (1) prior reports of maltreatment to child protective services (CPS) predict reabuse. Indeed, a history of maltreatment is the best predictor of reabuse. (2) Neglected children appear to be at higher risk of further maltreatment than children suffering physical or sexual abuse. (3) Presence in the home of domestic violence and high parental conflict are correlated with reabuse. (4) Poverty is related to reabuse and reentry into foster care. (5) Substance abuse—alcohol, drugs, or both—is correlated with reabuse. (6) Premature reunification is related to reabuse (Brook & McDonald, 2009; Kimberlin, Anthony, & Austin, 2009).

Aging Out of Foster Care

Every year, approximately 20,000 foster children reach age 18, and "age out" of the child welfare system (Hass & Graydon, 2009). Unfortunately, many of these young people do not fare well (Schneider et al., 2009). Zetlin and Weinberg (2004) observe, "Youth in foster care are twice as likely as the rest of the school-age population to drop out before completing high school" (p. 918). Children who age out of foster care have increased rates of homelessness, incarceration, and mental illness (Hass & Graydon, 2009). Some sell drugs to earn money. Others sell their bodies. In 2005, Courtney and his colleagues described a longitudinal study of former foster youth in Illinois, Iowa, and Wisconsin:

> In summary, youth making the transition from foster care are faring worse than their same-age peers, in many cases much worse, across a number of domains of functioning. They approach the age of majority with significant educational deficits and relatively few of them appear to be on a path that will provide them with the skills necessary to thrive in today's economy. They are less likely to be employed than their peers, and earnings from employment provide few of them with the means to make ends meet. This is reflected in the economic hardships many of them face and the need that many of them have for government assistance. A large number continue to struggle with health and mental health problems. Too many of them have children for whom they cannot provide a home. They are much more likely than their peers to find themselves involved with the criminal justice system. (p. 71)

To help foster youth prepare for adulthood, Congress in 1986 created the Independent Living Program. The program provides federal funds to states to help foster youth achieve independence. In 1999, Congress strengthened the program with the Foster Care Independence Act, including the John H. Chafee Foster Care Independence Program. Under the Chafee program, federal funds allow states to pay educational expenses for foster youth aging out. Additional funds are available to extend Medicaid eligibility to age 21. Money is available to assist former foster youth with housing.

It is important to keep in mind that foster care itself is not responsible for all the difficulties children experience. Berzin (2008) compared outcomes for foster youth and similarly situated youth who were not in care. Berzin's findings

suggest that youth with foster care experience and matched youth do not differ to a statistically significant degree on any of the outcomes measured. This finding differs from the results of previous research, which suggests that many educational and employment outcomes are worse for youth with foster care experience than for other youth. This study does not find such differences. . . . The results challenge the notion that foster care placement is uniquely responsible for negative outcomes. . . . [V]ulnerabilities for foster youth seem to stem from characteristics that existed well before youth's placement in care. (pp. 190–191)

Foster Care Drift

The earliest in-depth research on foster care was Henry Maas and Richard Engler's 1959 classic *Children in Need of Parents*. Maas and Engler studied hundreds of foster children in nine urban and rural communities. Mass and Engler documented that many children live for years in foster care. Mass and Engler wrote,

Of all the children we studied, better than half of them gave promise of living a major part of their childhood years in foster families and institutions. Among them were children likely to leave care only when they came of age, often after having had many homes—and none of their own—for ten or so years. Children who move through a series of families or are reared without close and continuing ties to a responsible adult have more than the usual problems in discovering who they are. They are the children who learn to develop shallow roots in relationships with others, who try to please but cannot trust, or who strike out before they can be let down. (p. 356)

Maas and Engler found low rates of adoption from foster care. When adoption did occur, the child was usually a baby. Older children, children with mental or physical handicaps, and children of color were seldom adopted.

Why did so many children languish so long in foster care? Maas and Engler attributed foster care drift to several factors. First, in the 1950s, the law made it difficult to terminate parental rights so children could be freed for adoption. Second, child welfare agencies did not push adoption. Third, agencies received money for children in out-of-home care, creating incentives to keep children in care. Fourth, in many communities, little effort was made to reunify children with parents. Fifth, many agencies didn't know how many children were in care. Sixth, for children of color, discrimination was a roadblock to adoption.

The second classic study of foster care was David Fanshel and Eugene Shinn's (1978) *Children in Foster Care: A Longitudinal Investigation.* In Fanshel and Shinn's study of 624 foster children, 36% were in care more than 5 years. Of children in long-term care, more than half were not visited by their parents.

How did the children in long-term care fare? Contrary to expectations, Fanshel and Shinn did not find that long-term foster care was inevitably harmful. Indeed, when Fanshel and Shinn compared outcomes for children who remained in foster care with outcomes for children who returned to parents, they found

> Continued tenure in foster care is not demonstrably deleterious with respect to IQ change, school performance, or the measures of emotional adjustment we employed. We do not say that the children are in a condition that is always reassuring—but staying in care as opposed to returning home does not seem to compound the difficulties of the children. (p. 491)

Fanshel and Shinn certainly did not advocate long-term foster care for children. Between 25% and 33% of Fanshel and Shinn's foster children showed signs of emotional impairment. Along with other child welfare experts, Fanshel and Shinn urged greater resources to prevent the problems that lead to out-of-home care. Yet, Fanshel and Shinn remind us that for many abused and neglected children, a good foster home is better than a dysfunctional, drug infested, and abusive biological family.

Unfortunately, many children in long-term foster care are moved from home to home. It is hardly surprising that moving children from one home to another can be detrimental. Fernandez (2009) writes,

> Research into the relationship between placement disruption and children's psychosocial problems notes that children who experience multiple moves tend to develop elevated emotional and behavioral problems which in turn trigger placement breakdown. Children's vulnerability to the loss of significant attachments is also documented. Repeated moves exacerbate the sense of loss they have experienced through separation from birth parents threatening their evolving sense of security and belonging. (p. 1092)

The Journey to Permanence

Finding permanent homes for children in foster care means working toward reuniting children with parents or—when reunification is unwise—moving toward adoption, guardianship, or long-term foster care. For most abused or neglected children in out-of-home care, the plan is to work toward reunifying the family (Pine, Spath, Werrbach, Jenson, & Kerman, 2009). Services are offered to help parents overcome the problems that led to removal. Unfortunately, as mentioned earlier, following reunification, some children are abused again and returned to foster care.

When efforts to reunify a family fail, social workers seek another stable arrangement for the child, with formal adoption the ideal for many children. The federal Adoption Assistance and Child Welfare Act of 1980 established the goal of reducing the time it takes to move foster children to adoption. In 1997, the federal Adoption and Safe Families Act (ASFA) reinforced this goal. ASFA requires states to seek termination of parental rights for foster children who have been abandoned and for children in foster care for 15 of the most recent 22 months.

Since passage of ASFA in 1997, states have worked to speed adoption. Cornelia Ashby (2003) of the U.S. General Accounting Office reported, "The annual number of adoptions have increased by 57 percent from the time ASFA was enacted through fiscal year 2000" (p. 1). The Pew Charitable Trusts (2003) reported, "From 1998 to 2002, states placed over 230,000 children in adoptive homes. More children were adopted during this five-year period than the previous 10 years combined" (p. 1). In 2004, Testa and his colleagues wrote, "The past decade has seen unparalleled success in finding adoptive homes for children in foster care. This achievement—including states' answering the federal challenge to double adoptions out of foster care in five years—was the result of coordinated efforts across multiple fronts" (p. 1).

Guardianship is an increasingly popular option for foster children who cannot return to parents and for whom adoption is unlikely. Often, the guardian is a member of the child's extended family such as a grandparent, aunt, or uncle. Guardianship is a legal relationship established by a judge. A child's guardian receives legal custody of the child, including the decision-making authority normally exercised by parents. Once formal guardianship is established, the child leaves the child welfare system. Guardianship lasts until the child turns 18. The principal advantage of guardianship is that the child has a permanent family. An additional advantage in many cases is that the biological parents can remain part of the child's life because guardianship does not terminate parental rights.

Many family members who are willing to become guardians cannot afford the expense of raising a child. Subsidized guardianship provides an answer. Massachusetts established the first subsidized guardianship program in 1983, and today many states have subsidized guardianship programs.

Is Foster Care a Problem or a Solution?

Foster care is not ideal for children. No one doubts that children are better off with loving biological parents than with substitute caretakers. Yet, there are biological parents who parent in name only: parents who are so incompetent, stoned, drunk, perverted, mentally ill, or violent that they cannot or will not provide what children need. Children in such "families" are better off in foster care.

Some people view foster care as a problem rather than a solution. They lament that a half million children live in foster care. This is a legitimate concern, yet we should not lose sight of the fact that for many abused and neglected children, foster care is better than whence they came. Joseph Reid (1959) observed long ago

> For thousands of children foster care is preferable to their being in their own homes, for there simply is no own home and no possibility for one. . . . The need for foster care programs cannot be eliminated and communities should not blame themselves for this necessity. (pp. 388–389)

Foster care works well for thousands of children. The goal is not elimination of foster care but reducing the number of children who need such care.

Foster Children Speak for Themselves

In the literature on foster care, we seldom hear from children themselves. An early exception was the 1885 *Annual Report* of the Massachusetts Society for the Prevention of Cruelty to Children. A motherless girl was rescued by the society from a brutal and drunken father. Following her placement in a rural foster home, she wrote the society

> I had a lovely time last winter, sliding down hill. I went to private school last winter. I have been may-flowering and got some lovely ones. I sent you a box of them, which I hope you received all right. I think I am a happy girl, and would not exchange for anything of my own accord.

Another little girl was removed from an "intemperate mother," who forced the child to sing in saloons. From her foster home in the country, the child wrote,

> I like my place very much. I love Mr. and Mrs. C. and call them papa and mamma. I have been going to school. The teacher is Miss C. and she is very nice. We spelt for headmarks and I got the second prize. I can play "Sweet By and By" and "Yankee Doodle" on the organ, and mamma is learning me the notes. I had a splendid Christmas and New Years. I have four pets; two pigs, a chicken and a calf.

We would hardly expect the Massachusetts Society to publish children's letters longing for parents or complaining about foster care. Some children weren't happy, and unfortunate placements occurred. Child welfare isn't perfect. Yet, these touching letters attest success.

What do today's foster children say about their circumstances? A report on California's foster care system compiled in 2000 provides insights (Fox, Frasch, & Berrick, 2000). Foster children were asked a series of questions, including "In what ways has your social worker been helpful to you?" Among children's answers we find a 12-year-old saying, "Every Monday she takes me to the library, she takes me shopping, and she came to my graduation." A 7-year-old said, "She helped me because she came to my school and talked to my teacher." A 10-year-old remarked, "She takes me places. She makes sure I get to see my mom, I have what I need, that I'm happy." An 8-year-old stated, "She helps my mommy learn to take care of us better." A 10-year-old said, "She takes care of things when I have a problem. She plays with me and always answers my questions."

Obviously being away from parents is difficult for children. Foster youth were asked, "Is there anything else that you think I should know about what it's like for children who live separate from their birth mother?" An 11-year-old spoke for many when she said, "It's sad. It's not fun. You cry sometimes. You miss them a lot. You want to be with them every day." A 10-year-old remarked, "It's scary, and you don't know what's gonna happen." One child said simply, "I miss my mom."

When asked what they liked about foster care, a 12-year-old said, "They are taking care of me. They treat us right. They do not beat us." An 8-year-old replied, "I have friends. I love my sisters." A 9-year-old's answer was "It has lots of toys and food, and my mom cooks good too." A 13-year-old said, "I like it good. We eat chicken every day. Good house. Clothes on my back." An 8-year-old stated, "My foster mom is the best. She treats me well. When she puts me in the corner I know why. And I like it here a lot." A 13-year-old said, "I feel how it is to have a family that loves you."

Every foster child has a story. Some are happy, some sad. Research tells us that for many foster children the passage into adulthood is stormy. Yet, as we read the quotes from these and other foster children, we see young people who are better off in foster homes than their own homes. We see children who are cared for and in many cases loved by substitute moms and dads. We see children with a future thanks to foster care.

Conclusion

It is sad that some children cannot live safely with their parents. Earlier in our history, such children were indentured or apprenticed. Thousands were consigned to almshouses and orphanages, and thousands lived on the street. Gradually, reformers won the argument that such children deserve something better; they deserve a substitute family, a foster family. The foster care system has faults: Too many children are in care too long, and too many children are shifted from home to home. Despite the problems, we are fortunate that hundreds of thousands of adults open their homes and hearts to abused and neglected children. The great majority of foster parents provide competent, stable homes. Caring for children who have been through so much is stressful (Whenan, Oxlad, & Lushington, 2009), yet foster parents persist and give children the tremendous gift of a "normal" home where a kid can be a kid. Although researchers, policymakers, and legislators must continue efforts to improve foster care, they should devote just as much effort to supporting the existing system. The foster parents, foster children, and professionals in the child welfare system deserve praise and support.

Adoption

Adoption is one of life's most fulfilling experiences for parents and children. Although precise figures are not available, it is estimated that approximately 125,000 children are adopted each year in the United States (Biafora & Esposito, 2007). Roughly 2% of children living in America are adopted.

Adoption has ancient roots, with evidence of adoption in the Bible. In Roman times, adoption was used to ensure that childless couples had an heir. In America, informal adoption was practiced from colonial times forward. In 1851, Massachusetts enacted the first "modern" adoption statute (Freundlich, 2007). Today, all states have detailed laws governing adoption. Although these laws vary, the main themes are the same. Adoption is a court process that creates a new parent–child relationship. In nearly all legal respects, the adoptive-parent adopted-child relationship is identical to the biological parent–child relationship. Thus, adoptive parents enjoy all the rights and responsibilities of biological parents. When an adoptive parent dies, an adopted child has the same inheritance rights as a biological child.

From a psychological point of view, adoption raises complex and far-reaching issues, provocatively outlined by Lifton (2007):

> The time has come to approach the subject of adoption in a new and realistic way: to see where it connects to myth and to plain old life. We have to see the adoptee as a child marked by fate, but not doomed by it. To see birth mothers as women who lost their children as surely as women lose children to accidents, disease, and war. To see adoptive parents as people who have lost their chance for biological continuity, but who have taken other women's children as their own as surely as parents in biblical and mythical times rescued infants found floating on baskets down the river. . . . As an adopted child, I was haunted by the ghosts of the mother and father I was told were deceased, but who proved to be very much alive. As an adoption therapist, I treat ghost-haunted adoptees, birth parents, and adoptive parents. All of them are accompanied by their own ghosts, who are not literally dead, but "as if" dead. (pp. 418–419)

Four Kinds of Adoption

In America, there are four kinds of adoption: (1) stepparent adoption, (2) adult adoption, (3) intercountry adoption, and (4) adoption by one or two adults who are not biologically related to the child.

Stepparent Adoption

Given the high divorce rate and the large number of children born out of wedlock, stepparent adoption is common. Indeed, stepparent adoption is the most common type of adoption. Consider a typical example: Sue and Jim Smith married and had three children. The Smiths divorced, and Sue received custody of the children. Jim got visitation and was ordered by the judge to pay child support. Three years later, Sue fell in love with Ted and they married. Ted has a great relationship with his stepchildren, and after a few years, Ted and Sue decided on stepparent adoption. If Jim consents, the adoption can go forward in the appropriate court. The adoption decree permanently severs Jim's parent-child relationship with the children. Ted is now their father.

If Jim refuses to consent to the adoption of his children by Ted, the adoption cannot proceed unless Jim's parental rights are terminated against his will. In stepparent adoption cases, the most common basis for termination of parental rights is abandonment—that is, the parent who refuses to consent abandoned the children emotionally and financially, thus forfeiting the right to block adoption by the stepparent.

In many stepparent adoptions, child welfare professionals play no role. In some cases, the judge in a stepparent adoption requests a home study.

Adult Adoption

One adult may adopt another adult, typically to create inheritance rights. The social work profession plays no role in the typical adult adoption.

Intercountry Adoption

Around the world, approximately 100 million children have no caretakers. Americans adopt more of these children than any other nation (Meier, 2008). Indeed, "the United States remains, by far, the primary receiving nation of orphaned children, followed distantly by other Western nations, including France, Canada, and Germany" (Biafora & Esposito, 2007, p. 39).

Intercountry adoption is complicated and expensive for the adoptive parents, who must comply with four sets of laws: (1) laws of the country of the child's birth, (2) adoption law of the U.S. state where the adoptive parents live, (3) U.S. immigration law, and (4) in many cases, international law including the Hague Convention on Intercountry Adoption. More than 75 countries have joined the Hague Convention.

Before an American may bring an adopted child home from abroad, U.S. Citizenship and Immigration Services—the immigration service—must determine that the adopting adult is capable of providing a loving home for the child. The immigration service and the U.S. Department of State's Office of Children's Issues have informative publications online to assist prospective adoptive parents.

Some nations require adopting parents to formally adopt the child in the child's birth country. Once the child is brought to America, many experts recommend readopting the child in this country.

Social workers play important roles in intercountry adoptions, advising adoptive parents, conducting home studies, and assisting with the mountains of paperwork involved in this type of adoption.

Adoption by Adults Who Are Not Biologically Related to the Child

This section discusses nonstepparent adoption by adults who are not biologically related to the child.

Agency Adoption

All states allow agency adoption, in which a child's parents relinquish their child—often a baby—to a licensed adoption agency. Adoption agencies are either government or private agencies. Relinquishing the child to an adoption agency has the legal effect of terminating the parent-child relationship. There is seldom any doubt about the identity of the biological mother, and her relinquishment is obtained after the child is born and the mother is appropriately counseled. States generally give the biological mother a limited time to change her mind and reclaim her child from the agency.

The identity of the biological father is not always clear, and states have elaborate procedures for determining paternity. Once paternity is established, the father can relinquish his parental rights or insist that he be given custody of the child. If the father refuses to relinquish his parental rights, adoption can proceed only if the father's parental rights are terminated by a judge.

Under paternity law, not all biological fathers have the right to withhold consent to adoption. A biological father who is not married to the child's mother and who has taken no steps to establish a parent–child relationship has no right to block adoption.

After a child is relinquished to an adoption agency, social workers match the child with prospective adoptive parents who have been carefully vetted by the agency. With many agency adoptions, the biological parents do not meet or even know the identity of the adoptive parents. Following placement in the adoptive home, the adoptive parents file an adoption petition in court, and a judge finalizes the adoption, creating the new family.

Adoption of Children in Foster Care

More than 100,000 foster children are waiting to be adopted (U.S. Department of Health and Human Services, 2009a). Every year, roughly 51,000 of them reach this goal.

Independent Adoption

Independent or private adoption is an alternative to agency adoption and is available in most states. Unlike agency adoption, where the child is relinquished to an adoption agency and the biological parents have no knowledge of the adoptive parents, the hallmark of private adoption is that the biological parents—often just the mother—personally select the adoptive parents and hand over the child to the adoptive parents. In many private adoptions, the mother picks the adoptive parents months before birth, and the adoptive parents receive the child immediately following birth, often at the hospital. The law generally allows the birth parent a limited time (e.g., 30 days) to change her mind and reclaim the child from the adoptive parents.

Although an adoption agency does not place the child in an independent adoption, the law requires an adoption agency to perform a home study following placement with the adoptive parents. The adoptive parents file a petition in court, and the judge considers the home study along with other evidence in deciding whether to approve the adoption.

Independent adoption has critics. First, in agency adoption, adoptive parents are carefully prescreened by an adoption agency. By contrast, in most independent adoptions there is no prescreening by an agency. Second, with independent adoptions the adoptive parents typically pay the mother's living expenses during pregnancy as well as medical expenses related to pregnancy and birth. Critics worry that independent adoption encourages child selling—exchanging a baby for money. Third, critics fear that immature young women are pressured to give up their baby by wealthy adoptive parents and their attorneys.

Defenders of independent adoption argue there is no support for the critics' assertions. Attorneys involved in independent adoptions are experts not only on the law but also on the psychosocial aspects of adoption. The attorney realizes there will be a home study of the adoptive parents, and the attorney will screen out inappropriate parents. Moreover, some states (e.g., California) require involvement of a social worker or mental health professional *before* the birth parent gives up her child. The professional meets with the birth parent, advises her, and ensures that her consent to adoption is fully informed and voluntary. Supporters of independent adoption defend the practice of allowing adoptive parents to provide financial support for the mother while she is pregnant. To ensure that children are not "bought and paid for," the law requires adoptive parents to keep detailed records of the money they spend and to submit a complete accounting to the judge in charge of the adoption. Finally, proponents of independent adoption do not deny that inappropriate pressure could be placed on young, frightened, confused single mothers. The remedy, they argue, is to create procedures that carefully guard against such overreaching—not to outlaw independent adoption.

Criminal Laws Relating to Adoption

States have criminal laws relating to adoption. Thus, it is a crime for an agency (or an individual) not licensed as an adoption agency to place children for adoption or to advertise that it places children for adoption. Of course the birthmother, although not a licensed adoption agency, may place her baby for adoption.

It is a crime for a person to pay to have a child placed with them for adoption, or, to put it bluntly, to buy a baby. It is equally a crime to sell a baby. The law against buying and selling children does not prohibit payment of fees to licensed adoption agencies and attorneys providing adoption-related services. As mentioned previously, in private adoptions, adoptive parents may pay the birthmother's living expenses while she is pregnant as well as her maternity-related medical expenses so long as the payments are not dependent on placement of the child for adoption.

Open Adoption

Until recently, the norm in America was that adoption completely severed any relationship between the child and the birth parents. Indeed, that was the goal: Leave the past behind and begin anew. Yet, for some children, an impenetrable barrier between the past and the future is inappropriate. Some adoptive parents believe their child will benefit from a relationship with birth parents. Today, adoptive parents have the option of so-called open adoption, which allows the adoptive parents to approve a continuing relationship (e.g., visitation) between the child and the birth parents (McRoy, Grotevant, Ayers-Lopez, & Henney, 2007). No state requires open adoption. The decision is left with the adoptive parents.

In recent years, more than half the states passed laws allowing open adoption. In some states, children over a certain age (e.g., 12) must agree to an open adoption. Open adoption laws vary from state to state. Rhode Island, for example, provides that at the time a judge approves an adoption, the judge may grant postadoption visitation for the birth parents if the adoptive and birth parents agree and the judge concludes such visitation is in the child's best interest and there is a "significant emotional attachment between the child and the birth parent" (Rhode Island Statutes § 15-7-14.1, 2003). California law authorizes open adoption—called postadoption contact—and states, "Some adoptive children may benefit from direct or indirect contact with birth relatives, including the birth parent or parents or an

Indian tribe, after being adopted" (California Family Code § 8616.5, 2010). Somit (2008) writes,

> Many forms of post-placement contact are common today. The most common is for pictures, videotapes, or letters to be sent by the adoptive parents on a regular basis. A letter to the child declaring the birth mother's heartfelt love and explaining the reasons for the adoption is given to the adoptive parents, to be read to the child and saved. Adoption contracts are drafted memorializing the understanding, and providing for regular visits, pictures, exchange of information, the right to send letters and give presents. (p. 148).

Policy, law, and practice relating to open adoption are developing rapidly (Javier, Baden, Biafora, & Camacho-Gingerich, 2007).

Adoption Records

For much of the 20th century, adoption records were closed. When a judge approved an adoption, all records of the adoption were sealed. Typically, a new birth certificate was issued, and the old certificate was sealed along with other records of the child's birth and heritage. The idea was that adoption is a fresh start, and it is in the child's best interest to sever all ties to the past—the opposite of open adoption.

Increasingly, states make provision for adopted children to learn their heritage. About half the states have mutual consent registries. These registries differ from state to state. The basic concept is that adoption records can be opened if a birth parent *and* the adoptee consent. Typically, the adoptee must have reached adulthood. Many states ask the birth parent at the time of the adoption if they are willing to have their identity disclosed when the child becomes an adult.

A number of states have laws that authorize "confidential intermediaries" to contact birth parents to see if the parents wish to reveal their identity. Several states allow adult adoptees to request a copy of their original birth certificate.

Single Parent Adoption

The traditional paradigm for adoptive parents was a heterosexual married couple. Today, states allow single persons to adopt. It is estimated that 5% of adoptions are by single parents, and this number is growing. Single parents are particularly likely to adopt older children and children with special needs.

Adoption by Lesbian and Gay Couples

Not long ago, the law forbade gay and lesbian individuals and couples from adopting. Times have changed. Today, nearly all states allow gay and lesbian individuals to adopt.

Adoption Failure, Disruption, and Dissolution—"Wrongful Adoption"

Despite the best efforts of social workers to ensure a good "fit" between a child and adoptive parents, some adoptions do not work. Perhaps the child and the adoptive parents do not bond. Tragically, some abused and neglected children are so damaged that adoptive parents simply cannot nurture and control the child (Adoption of M.S., 2010).

If an agency adoption "fails" before it is legally finalized, the child can be returned to the agency in what is sometimes called "disrupted adoption." The rate of disruption is 10% to 20%.

When an agency adoption breaks down after the adoption is legally finalized, the law generally allows the adoption to be dissolved by a judge, and here, too, the child is returned to the agency. Approximately 1% to 10% of final adoptions are dissolved.

When an independent adoption disrupts, the birthmother often is unwilling or unable to care for the child, and the child may be placed in foster care.

In a small number of cases, adoptive parents sued adoption agencies claiming that social workers did not inform them of their child's medical or psychiatric history (Milks, 1999). The adoptive parents seek monetary damages against the agency to help pay for the child's medical or psychiatric care. In these so-called "wrongful adoption" cases, the adoptive parents do not seek to end the adoption. Rather, they claim that the agency deliberately or carelessly withheld vital information and that if they had known the information they would not have adopted.

The first wrongful adoption case was decided in 1986 by the Ohio Supreme Court (*Burr v. Board of County Commissioners of Stark County*, 1986). Russell and Betty Burr contacted the county adoption agency in 1964, expressing their desire to adopt. A few days later, an adoption worker phoned the Burrs and told them a 17-month-old boy was available for adoption. The caseworker told the Burrs the child was born to an 18-year-old single mother who relinquished the child to the agency. The caseworker told the Burrs the child was "a nice big, healthy baby boy." The Burrs adopted the child. As the years passed, the child developed numerous medical and psychiatric problems, including twitching, a speech impediment, and learning problems. In high school, the child developed hallucinations. Eventually, the child was diagnosed with Huntington's Disease, a genetically inherited disease that damages the nervous system.

In 1982, the Burrs got a court order opening the sealed records of their son's medical history prior to adoption. For the first time, they learned that the things the adoption worker told them were false. The sealed records disclosed that the child's mother was not a healthy 18-year-old but a 31-year-old mental patient at a state psychiatric hospital. The identity of the biological father was unknown, but he was presumed to be a mental patient. The mother was psychotic and mildly mentally retarded. The adoption agency knew this but did not tell the Burrs. As well, the agency knew the child had a fever at birth and was developing slowly. This information, too, was withheld from the Burrs. The adoption worker fabricated the story of the birthmother.

To recoup the more than $80,000 they had already spent on their son's medical care, the Burrs sued the county, the adoption agency, and the caseworker. The jury concluded that the adoption agency committed fraud against the Burrs and awarded them $125,000. On appeal, the Ohio Supreme Court approved the jury's decision.

The Burr case established the precedent that an adoption agency cannot deliberately lie about a child's history. But what about the scenario in which an adoption agency does not intentionally lie but mistakenly fails to tell adoptive parents some detail of a child's medical history? Judges have difficulty deciding whether adoptive parents should be able to sue adoption agencies that try to act responsibly but that make mistakes or act negligently (*Michael J. v. County of Los Angeles, Department of Adoptions*, 1988). The law in this area is developing (Mulligan, 2008).

Interstate Compact on the Placement of Children

Every state and the District of Columbia has adopted the Interstate Compact on the Placement of Children (ICPC). The ICPC is intended to protect the interests of children who are placed across state lines for foster care or adoption. Procedures under the ICPC are complicated but can be summarized as follows: The state *from* which a child is placed is the "sending state," and the state *to* which the child is placed is the "receiving state." An official in the sending state makes sure a proposed interstate transfer complies with law and is in the child's interest. The sending state notifies the receiving state of the pending transfer, and the receiving state has the opportunity to approve or disapprove the transfer. The sending state continues to be financially responsible for the child while the child is in care in the receiving state.

Multiethnic Placement Act

Before the civil rights movement of the 1960s, interracial adoption was uncommon. Several states, including Louisiana and Texas, had outright bans on interracial adoption. Social workers generally believed it was important to place children with adoptive parents of the same ethnic background. During the 1960s, however, courts struck down laws against interracial adoption, and increasing numbers of white parents adopted children of color.

During the 1970s, critics of interracial adoption mounted a spirited campaign against the practice, led by the National Association of Black Social Workers. In 1972, the association issued a position paper based on the premise that America is racist. The position paper stated:

Black children should be placed only with Black families in foster care or for adoption. Black children belong, physically, psychologically and culturally in Black families in order that they receive the total sense of themselves and develop a sound projection of their future. Human beings are products of their environment and develop their sense of values, attitudes and self concept within their family structures. Black children in white homes are cut off from the healthy development of themselves as Black people. (National Association of Black Social Workers, 1972)

Bartholet (1999) wrote that the association's position

found a receptive audience. The establishment forces readily conceded that black and Native American communities had a right to hold onto "their own." . . . The new orthodoxy was quickly established, making the 1960s period of transracial placements seem a brief anomaly in the larger picture. (p. 125)

Hawkins-Leon and Bradley (2002) added, "In an attempt to adhere to the tenets of the [Association's] position paper, adoption agencies began to enact and enforce same-race placement policies. As a result, the number of transracial adoptions dropped drastically nationwide" (p. 1239).

Unfortunately, children of color, particularly African American children, are overrepresented in foster care, and African American foster children tend to wait longer for adoption than white children. The antagonism of the 1970s toward interracial adoption exacerbated the problem of overrepresentation by dissuading whites from adopting African American children. During the 1980s and 1990s, pressure mounted to lower racial barriers to adoption, and in 1994, Congress passed the Multiethnic Placement Act (MEPA). The 1994 MEPA prohibited child welfare agencies from delaying or denying adoptive placements on the basis of race. Yet, the 1994 MEPA allowed race as a factor in placement decisions. Critics argued that allowing race as a factor perpetuated the status quo against interracial adoption. In 1996, Congress amended MEPA to narrow the circumstances in which race may be considered. Under the 1996 amendment, a child's race must normally be considered irrelevant in determining the best placement for a child. Only in narrow circumstances where the needs of a specific child make race important can social workers consider race as a factor.

Transracial adoption remains a challenging issue for professionals, parents, and children. Fortunately, progress is being made in the ongoing effort to help parents and children thrive (Javier et al., 2007).

Indian Child Welfare Act and Adoption

The Indian Child Welfare Act (ICWA) and its impact on foster care are discussed in Chapter 4. In addition to influencing foster care, ICWA regulates adoption and termination of parental rights. Parental rights to a Native American child cannot be terminated against a parent's will unless the state proves the need for termination with proof beyond a reasonable doubt, including "testimony of qualified expert witnesses that the continued custody of the child by the parent . . . is likely to result in serious emotional or physical damage to the child" (United States Code Annotated, Title 25, § 1912[f], 2010).

ICWA establishes special procedures for Native American parents who wish to voluntarily consent to termination of their parental rights and adoption of their child. The parent's consent must be signed before a judge, and the judge must certify that the parent understood they were giving up parental rights (United States Code Annotated, Title 25, § 1913[a], 2010). The consent cannot be signed until at least 10 days after the child's birth, and the parent can withdraw the consent at any time for any reason up until the time a judge finalizes the adoption. Even after an adoption is final, a Native American parent has 2 years to withdraw consent if the consent was obtained by fraud or duress (United States Code Annotated, Title 25, § 1913[d], 2010).

When Native American children are placed for adoption, ICWA establishes an order of preference. The first choice is a member of the child's extended family. Second is a nonrelative member of the child's tribe. The third choice is a member of a different tribe. A judge may depart from these preferences if there is good reason to do so (United States Code Annotated, Title 25, § 1915[a], 2010).

Conclusion

Foster care and adoption are indispensable elements of the child protection system. Foster care is meant to be a temporary stopgap on the path to permanence, and for many children foster care fulfills its mission. Unfortunately, thousands of children languish in foster care, and this sad reality is perhaps the greatest failing of today's child protection system.

Adoption is the creation of a new family. Happily, the past 2 decades witnessed increasing numbers of adoptions, due primarily to the tireless efforts of child welfare professionals. Hopefully, as the 21st century wears on, the trend lines will continue toward more adoptions and fewer children in long-term foster care. These are worthy if difficult goals.

References

Adoption of M.S., 2010 Westlaw 162009 (Cal. Ct. App. 2010).

Ashby, C. M. (2003). *Foster care: States focusing on finding permanent homes for children, but long-standing barriers remain.* Testimony before the Subcommittee on Human Resources, Committee on Ways and Means, U.S. House of Representatives.

Bartholet, E. (1999). *Nobody's children: Abuse and neglect, foster drift, and the adoption alternative.* Boston: Beacon Press.

Berzin, S. C. (2008). Difficulties in the transition to adulthood: Using propensity scoring to understand what makes foster youth vulnerable. *Social Service Review*, 82, 171–196.

Biafora, F. A., & Esposito, D. (2007). Adoption data and statistical trends. In R. A. Javier, A. L. Baden, F. A. Biafora, & A. Camacho-Gingerich (Eds.), *Handbook of adoption* (pp. 32–43). Thousand Oaks, CA: Sage.

Brook, J., & McDonald, T. (2009). The impact of parental substance abuse on the stability of family reunifications from foster care. *Children and Youth Services Review, 31*, 193–198.

Brown, J. D., George, N., Sintzel, J., & St. Arnault, D. (2009). Benefits of cultural matching in foster care. *Children and Youth Services Review, 31*, 1019–1024.

Burr v. Board of County Commissioners of Stark County, 491 N.E.2d 1101 (Ohio 1986).

California Family Code § 8616.5 (2010). St. Paul, MN: West.

Carter, V. B. (2009). Prediction of placement into out-of-home care for American Indian/Alaskan Natives compared to non-Indians. *Children and Youth Services Review, 31*, 840–846.

Code of Federal Regulations, Title 45, § 57 (2009).

Courtney, M. E., Dworsky, A., Ruth, G., Keller, T., Havicek, J., & Bost, N. (2005). Midwest evaluation of the adult functioning of former foster youth: Outcomes at age 19. *Chapin Hall Working Paper*, University of Chicago.

Fanshel, D., & Shinn, E. B. (1978). *Children in foster care: A longitudinal investigation*. New York: Columbia University Press.

Fernandez, E. (2009). Children's wellbeing in care: Evidence from a longitudinal study of outcomes. *Children and Youth Services Review, 31*, 1092–1100.

Fox, A., Frasch, K., & Berrick, J. D. (2000). *Listening to children in foster care*. Berkeley, CA: Child Welfare Research Center.

Freundlich, M. (2007). A legal history of adoption and ongoing legal challenges. In R. A. Javier, A. L. Baden, F. A. Biafora, & A. Camacho-Gingerich (Eds.), *Handbook of adoption* (pp. 44–57). Thousand Oaks, CA: Sage.

Hass, M., & Graydon, K. (2009). Sources of resilience among successful foster youth. *Children and Youth Services Review, 31*, 457–463.

Hawkins-Leon, C., & Bradley, C. (2002). Race and the transracial adoption: The answer is neither simply black or white nor right or wrong. *Catholic University Law Review, 51*, 1227–1286.

Javier, R. A., Baden, A. L., Biafora, F. A., & Camacho-Gingerich, A. (2007). *Handbook of adoption*. Thousand Oaks, CA: Sage.

Kimberlin, S. E., Anthony, E. K., & Austin, M. J. (2009). Re-entering foster care: Trends, evidence, and implications. *Children and Youth Services Review, 31*, 471–481.

Lifton, B. J. (2007). The inner life of the adopted child: Adoption, trauma, loss, fantasy, search, and reunion. In R. A. Javier, A. L. Baden, F. A. Biafora, & A. Camacho-Gingerich (Eds.), *Handbook of adoption* (pp. 418–424). Thousand Oaks, CA: Sage.

Maas, H. S., & Engler, R. E., Jr. (1959). *Children in need of parents*. New York: Columbia University Press.

McRoy, R. G., Grotevant, H. D., Ayers-Lopez, S., & Henney, S. M. (2007). Open adoptions. In R. A. Javier, A. L. Baden, F. A. Biafora, & A. Camacho-Gingerich (Eds.), *Handbook of adoption* (pp. 175–189). Thousand Oaks, CA: Sage.

Meier, P. J. (2008). Small commodities: How child traffickers exploit children and families in intercountry adoption and what the United States must do to stop them. *Journal of Gender, Race and Justice, 12*, 185–224.

Michael J. v. County of Los Angeles, Department of Adoptions, 201 Cal. App. 3rd 859 (1988).

Milks, H. D. (1999). "Wrongful adoption" causes of action against adoption agencies where children have or develop mental or physical problems that are misrepresented or not disclosed to adoptive parents. *American Law Reports* (5th ed.), 74, 1–74.

Mulligan, S. (2008). Inconsistency in Illinois adoption law: Adoption agencies' uncertain duty to disclose, investigate, and inquire. *Loyola University Chicago Law Journal*, 39, 799–846.

National Association of Black Social Workers (1972, April). Position paper developed at the conference of the National Association of Black Social Workers, April 4–9, 1972. Nashville, TN.

Pew Charitable Trusts. (2003, October 9). *Fostering results: Nation doubles adoptions from foster care.* [Press release]. Washington, DC: Author.

Pine, B. A., Spath, R., Werrbach, G. B., Jenson, C. E., & Kerman, B. (2009). A better path to permanency for children in out-of-home care. *Children and Youth Services Review*, 31, 1135–1143.

Reid, J. H. (1959). Next steps: Action called for—Recommendations. In H. S. Mass & R. E. Engler Jr., *Children in need of parents* (pp. 378–397). New York: Columbia University Press.

Rhode Island Statutes § 15-7-14.1 (2003). Newark, NJ: LexisNexis.

Schneider, R., Baumrind, N., Pavao, J., Stockdale, G., Castelli, P., Goodman, G. S., et al. (2009). What happens to youth removed from parental care? Health and economic outcomes for women with a history of out-of-home placement. *Children and Youth Services Review*, 31, 440–444.

Somit, J. (2008). *Adoption law and practice.* Newark, NJ: LexisNexis.

Testa, M., Sidote Salyers, N., & Miller, J. (2004). *Family ties: Supporting permanence for children in safe and stable foster care with relatives and other caregivers.* Champaign, IL: School of Social Work, University of Illinois at Urbana-Champaign.

United States Code Annotated, Title 25, § 1912(f). (2010). St. Paul, MN: West.

United States Code Annotated, Title 25, § 1913(a). (2010). St. Paul, MN: West.

United States Code Annotated, Title 25, § 1913(d). (2010). St. Paul, MN: West.

United States Code Annotated, Title 25, § 1915(a). (2010). St. Paul, MN: West.

U.S. Department of Health and Human Services. (2009a). *The AFCARS report.* Washington, DC: U.S. Government Printing Office.

U.S. Department of Health and Human Services. (2009b). *Foster care statistics.* Washington, DC: U.S. Government Printing Office.

Whenan, R., Oxlad, M., & Lushington, K. (2009). Factors associated with foster care well-being, satisfaction and intention to continue providing out-of-home care. *Children and Youth Services Review*, 31, 752–760.

Zetlin, A. G., & Weinberg, L. A. (2004). Understanding the plight of foster youth and improving their educational opportunities. *Child Abuse and Neglect*, 28, 917–923.

6 Criminal Prosecution of Child Maltreatment

John E. B. Myers

American criminal law is divided into two major branches: criminal procedure and substantive criminal law. Criminal procedure includes the law governing police interrogation of suspects, the right to remain silent, police searches of people and places, and the processes of criminal prosecution. Substantive criminal law defines crimes, defenses, and punishments. Thus, substantive criminal law defines murder, burglary, rape, theft, robbery, child abuse, and other crimes. Substantive criminal law also defines defenses such as self-defense and the insanity defense. This chapter introduces both branches of criminal law.

Purpose and Theory of Criminal Law

Criminal law is as old as civilization. The Ten Commandments, for example, prohibit murder, theft, and perjury. In the United States, the federal and state governments have broad authority to establish and enforce criminal law. This authority is called "police power." The legislative branch of the state and federal governments uses the police power to define crimes and prescribe punishments. Although criminal laws vary slightly from state to state, there are more similarities than differences. As mentioned, the legislative branch of government defines what is criminal. The judicial branch applies the criminal law in individual cases.

Some crimes are more serious than others. Compare murder to driving one mile an hour over the speed limit. The most serious crimes are felonies. The typical punishment for a felony is a number of years in prison. A misdemeanor is a less serious crime. In most states, the penalty for a misdemeanor is a fine and/or commitment to the county jail up to 1 year. An infraction is a minor offense. Simple speeding, for example, is an infraction. With many infractions, the penalty is a fine and no possibility of jail time.

The essential goals of criminal law are to prevent crime and punish those who commit crimes. These goals are advanced through the principles of deterrence, retribution, incapacitation, and rehabilitation. There are two types of deterrence: general and specific. The theory of general deterrence is that people obey the law not only because it is "the right thing to do," but also because they realize they may be punished if they break the law. General deterrence, then, is directed at society at large. Specific deterrence is much narrower. Specific deterrence focuses on a single individual who committed a crime and suffered the consequences. By punishing the criminal, she or he is "specifically" deterred from committing new crimes in the future.

Retribution is based on the belief that someone who commits a crime deserves to be punished. The legitimacy of retribution as a foundation for criminal law is much debated (Dressler, 2009). Most people agree, however, that retribution—just deserts—has a role in criminal law.

Incapacitation is easy to explain. While a criminal is behind bars, she or he cannot commit new crimes in the community. Although some prison inmates, especially gang leaders, orchestrate crimes outside prison, incapacitation constrains many would-be offenders. A serial rapist, for example, cannot assault new victims outside prison so long as he remains behind bars.

Rehabilitation is another controversial underpinning of criminal law. Can criminals be rehabilitated? Should we spend tax dollars trying to reform criminals? Studies of prison rehabilitation programs yield mixed results. Some people believe criminals deserve punishment not rehabilitation, and some go so far as to argue that rehabilitation is "coddling criminals." Others take a different view, arguing that if the goal is preventing crime, the most effective way to accomplish this goal is to provide education, job training, and needed therapy to prisoners. Only by giving inmates hope for a better future do we stand a chance of preventing new crimes.

With the theoretical underpinnings of criminal law in mind, the next section describes the day-to-day operation of the criminal justice system.

The Criminal Justice System in Action

To understand the day-to-day functioning of the criminal justice system, it is useful to compare the system to a funnel. The wide mouth of the funnel represents all cases that are officially reported to police via 911 calls and other means. Of course, many crimes never enter the funnel because they are not reported. The narrow end of the funnel represents the small fraction of cases that go all the way through the criminal justice system and end in a formal trial in court.

As cases work their way through the criminal justice funnel, more and more are resolved. For example, the police do not investigate all reports. Of cases that are investigated, quite a few do not result in the arrest of a suspect—sometimes because no crime occurred and in other cases because there is not enough evidence to make an arrest or because the suspect cannot be found.

If the police make an arrest, the case is turned over to a public prosecutor. Prosecutors have broad discretion (prosecutorial discretion) to decide what cases to prosecute. Depending on the priorities and resources available to the prosecution, some cases are officially charged while others fall by the wayside. One factor prosecutors consider in deciding whether to file charges is the likelihood the accused (the defendant) will be convicted if the case goes all the way to trial. Cases where evidence of guilt is weak are among those that fall out of the funnel. In some child sexual abuse (CSA) cases, for example, the prosecutor believes the child was abused but concludes the case is not "winnable" in court—perhaps because the child is too young to testify, and there is no medical or other evidence. Such cases are frustrating, but prosecutors have an ethical duty not to charge people with crimes they cannot prove.

If a prosecutor decides the defendant should be charged with a crime, the prosecutor takes one of two approaches. First, in some states with some crimes, the prosecutor presents the case to a grand jury. A grand jury is a group of citizens drawn from eligible voters. Do not confuse a grand jury with a petit or trial jury. A trial jury is a group of citizens that sits in judgment on a particular case. A grand jury, by contrast, does not hear individual trials. Rather, the grand jury serves for a number of months and meets regularly with the prosecutor to decide whether criminal charges should be commenced against individuals. The grand jurors listen to the prosecution's evidence and vote on whether individuals should be charged. In most cases, the grand jury agrees with the prosecutor and votes to indict the person. An indictment is a document that the grand jury forwards to the appropriate court and that constitutes the formal charge against the defendant. In unusual cases, the grand jurors disagree with the prosecutor and refuse to issue an indictment. Indeed, the purpose of the grand jury is to serve as a check on the power of prosecutors and to protect citizens from unjust prosecution.

Some states do not use the grand jury system, and even in states that use it, not all criminal charges are commenced by grand jury indictment. When there is no grand jury, the prosecutor files a document in court called a complaint or an information. The complaint or information officially begins the prosecution.

The first court appearance for a defendant is typically an arraignment, at which a judge explains the charges, appoints an attorney to represent the defendant if the defendant cannot afford an attorney, and, if the defendant is in custody, decides whether to release the defendant on bail.

A preliminary hearing is a court proceeding used for many but not all crimes. The purpose of a preliminary hearing is for a judge to decide whether the prosecution has enough evidence to justify requiring the defendant to stand trial. At the preliminary hearing, the prosecutor presents evidence to persuade the judge to "bind the defendant over for trial." In some cases, witnesses, including children, testify at the preliminary hearing. In most cases, the defendant is bound over for trial following the preliminary hearing. In rare instances, however, the judge dismisses the charges because the prosecutor fails to convince the judge that a crime occurred or that the defendant committed it.

Once a defendant is formally charged, the attorneys begin the process of plea bargaining. The goal of plea bargaining is to reach a fair and just resolution of the charges without a trial. The defense attorney negotiates with the prosecutor in an effort to get the best "deal" for the defendant. In a typical plea bargain, the defendant agrees to plead guilty in exchange for the prosecutor's agreement to reduce the charges, drop some of the charges, or ask the judge for a lighter sentence. Many people suspect there is something wrong or unethical about plea bargaining, but this is a mistake. Plea bargaining is ethical and is used with most crimes in most communities. In some especially serious cases, prosecutors refuse to bargain and such cases go to trial. In other cases, the defendant is the one who will not bargain, and again, the case goes to trial. Finally, there are cases where the parties try but fail to reach agreement, and these cases are tried.

A common misunderstanding about plea bargaining is that a defendant who gets a plea bargain somehow "gets away with it." On the contrary, a plea bargain results in a conviction. In a plea bargain, the defendant gives up the right to a trial and pleads guilty to a crime in exchange for the prosecutor's actions. A conviction following a plea bargain is no different than a conviction following a trial.

The vast majority of criminal charges are resolved through plea bargaining. Only a small percentage of cases—on the order of 10%—go to trial. Of cases that go to trial, most end in conviction. If a defendant is convicted, she or he may appeal to a higher court called an appellate court. In the appellate court, the now-convicted defendant claims that the judge who presided at the trial made errors that were sufficiently serious to justify a new trial. Most appeals fail, and the appellate court affirms the conviction. When a defendant is acquitted at trial, the prosecution is not permitted to appeal.

A defendant who pleads guilty or who is convicted after a trial and who is sentenced to prison or jail may ask the judge for probation rather than incarceration. States vary on what crimes are eligible for probation. If probation is a possibility, a probation officer investigates the defendant's past as well as the nature of the crime and gives the judge a recommendation for or against probation. If the judge grants probation, the prison or jail sentence is suspended and the defendant—now a probationer—lives in the community under the supervision of a probation officer. The probationer must comply with a strict set of "conditions of probation" imposed by the judge. If the probationer violates the terms of probation, she or he is arrested, probation is revoked, and the individual is incarcerated.

Criminal Procedure

The founders of our nation lived as colonists under British rule. Many aspects of British colonial law rubbed colonists the wrong way—in particular, colonists chaffed under the power of colonial officials to search and prosecute colonists. When America gained its independence, the individuals who drafted the U.S. Constitution and its first 10 amendments, the Bill of Rights, were acutely aware of the dangers to freedom that lurk in giving too much power to government officials, including police, prosecutors, and judges.

The Constitution and Bill of Rights—especially the Fourth, Fifth, and Sixth Amendments—are designed to protect citizens against unjust conduct by the enforcers of law. The Fourth Amendment provides in part: "The right of the people to be secure in their persons, houses, papers, and effects, against unreasonable searches and seizures, shall not be violated. . . ." It is the Fourth Amendment that requires the police to obtain a warrant before they conduct a search. There are exceptions to the warrant requirement (e.g., emergencies, cars, search following arrest) and the law governing searches is extremely complicated.

The Fourth Amendment limits the authority of child protection workers to remove children from their parents. This aspect of the Fourth Amendment is discussed in Chapter 4.

The Fifth Amendment gives citizens the right to remain silent. The amendment provides, "No person . . . shall be compelled in any criminal case to be a witness against himself." Under the Fifth Amendment, the police cannot legally force us to answer questions. In court, the accused cannot be compelled to testify as witness.

In the famous cases of *Miranda v. Arizona* (1966), the U.S. Supreme Court gave concrete protection to the right to remain silent by requiring police to give *Miranda* warnings before questioning citizens who are in custody. Thus, the police must inform the individual that they have a right to remain silent and that anything they say can be used against them in court. The police do not have to give a *Miranda* warning to people who are not in custody.

The Sixth Amendment gives valuable rights to citizens charged with crimes, including the right to be informed of the charges, the right to an attorney, the right to a speedy and public trial, the right to an impartial jury, and the right to confront and cross-examine prosecution witnesses. Because the defendant has the right to a public trial, the courtroom generally cannot be closed to the public and the press when a child testifies. The judge has limited authority to close the courtroom if a particular child will be traumatized by testifying in public, but in most cases the courtroom remains open (*Waller v. Georgia*, 1984).

Because the Sixth Amendment gives the defendant the right to face-to-face confrontation with prosecution witnesses, children normally must testify in the physical presence of the defendant. The defendant's right to face-to-face confrontation with child witnesses is not absolute (Hall & Sales, 2008). In 1990, the U.S. Supreme Court ruled that a child may testify outside the presence of the defendant if face-to-face confrontation would seriously traumatize the child (*Maryland v. Craig*, 1990). In most cases, however, children testify in open court, just a few feet from the defendant. Fortunately, research and experience teach us that when children are prepared in advance—and when they have emotional support through the process—most testify effectively, and very few experience lasting trauma from testifying (American Academy of Pediatrics, 1999; Goodman et al., 1992; Myers, 2005; Quas et al., 2005). Indeed, some children say they were glad they had the opportunity to tell the judge and jury what happened to them (Henry, 1997).

The U.S. Constitution and state constitutions modeled on it provide an impressive array of rights for the accused. But what about the victim? Do victims have rights? Yes, but not on the scale of the accused (Boland & Butler, 2009; Raeder, 2009). Unlike the accused, for example, the victim is not a "party" to the prosecution. The victim does not have the right to an attorney—nor does the victim have the right to participate in the trial by questioning witnesses or presenting evidence. If the defendant is convicted, many states allow victims to provide input to the judge regarding the appropriate punishment. The victim may appear in court and describe the harm and heartache caused by the defendant.

Child Maltreatment as a Crime

Some forms of child maltreatment are criminal. To understand criminal child abuse and neglect, it is useful to have a degree of familiarity with the basic elements of crimes and with the crimes that play a day-to-day role in child abuse prosecution.

Elements of a Crime

Crimes have two parts: the act (*actus reus*) and the intent (*mens rea*). The *actus reus* is the physical part of the crime—for example, the death of the victim in murder, penetration of the victim in rape, and taking of the victim's property in theft. The *mens rea*, or criminal intent, is the defendant's mental state when the *actus reus* is committed.

To illustrate, theft is traditionally defined as the wrongful (trespassory) taking and carrying away of the personal property of another with the intent to steal. The *actus reus* of theft is the wrongful taking and carrying away of the personal property of another. The *mens rea* is the intent to steal. Rape is traditionally defined as sexual intercourse (penetration) of a woman without her consent and by force. The *actus reus* of rape is sexual intercourse with a woman without her consent and by force. The *mens rea* is the intent to have intercourse by force and without consent.

Murder

The traditional definition of murder is the killing of a human being with malice aforethought. The *actus reus* is simple: the killing of a human being.

The *mens rea*—malice aforethought—is anything but simple. Today, the word *aforethought* is meaningless. The word *malice*, however, is full of meaning. Malice has four meanings in the law of murder.

Before discussing malice in the crime of murder, it is important to understand that in the law of murder, "malice" does not mean ill will or hatred. A person can commit murder without the slightest trace of ill will or dislike for the victim. Suppose, for example, that Wilma and Harry have been happily married for 50 years. They are as much in love today as the day they married. Wilma is dying from a horribly painful disease for which there is no cure. Nothing helps the pain. Wilma begs Harry, "Please let me die, sweetie. I can't stand this pain anymore. I just want to go to heaven and wait for you. Give me an overdose of the medicine. Please do this one last thing for me." Heartbroken and purely out of love for his wife, Harry gives Wilma a fatal dose of medicine, and she passes peacefully away. Harry killed Wilma with malice as that term is defined in the law of murder.

The first meaning of malice is "intent to kill." Intent to kill murder exists when it is the defendant's conscious object to kill. All states have intent to kill murder. Note that Harry killed Wilma with this kind of malice.

The second meaning of malice is called "intent to cause grievous (serious) bodily injury murder." If the defendant injures the victim not with the intent to kill but with the intent to seriously injure the victim, but the victim dies from the wound, the defendant can be prosecuted for intent to cause grievous bodily injury murder even though the defendant did *not* intend to kill. Many but not all states have intent to cause grievous bodily injury murder.

The third meaning of malice goes by the colorful name "depraved heart murder." With depraved heart murder the defendant does not intend to kill or injure anyone. The defendant *does* intend to engage in extremely reckless behavior that has a high risk of killing someone. The defendant is aware of the risk of death but disregards the risk and plunges ahead, accidentally killing the victim. The defendant can be prosecuted for depraved heart murder despite the fact that the defendant did not intend to hurt anyone. All states have some version of depraved heart (reckless) murder.

Two examples help illustrate depraved heart murder. In the first example, the defendant owned a pit bull that he trained to be aggressive and to attack other dogs. The defendant left the pit bull chained up outside his home even though there was no fence separating his yard from the house next door and even though he knew a little boy lived next door. The little boy wandered into the defendant's yard to pet the "nice doggy" and was killed. The defendant did not intend the boy to die, but leaving an aggressive pit bull tied up outside where children could easily approach was extremely reckless behavior that created a high risk of death. The defendant knew the risk but disregarded it and was convicted of depraved heart murder.

A second example of depraved heart murder involves two young men who agree to illegally race their cars through a residential area. The speed limit is 25 mph. The two men start their race and reach speeds of 90 mph when one of them strikes and kills a child playing in the street. Both men may be convicted of depraved heart murder.

The final meaning of malice is "felony murder." Not all states have this controversial form of murder. Felony murder occurs when an accidental death occurs while the defendant is committing a felony. In one case, for example, the defendant entered a convenience store to rob it. The defendant waved a gun in the clerk's face and demanded money. The clerk emptied the cash register, and the defendant ran away with the money. A few minutes later, the clerk died of a heart attack caused by the stress of being robbed at gunpoint. Although the defendant did not intend to hurt the clerk, the accidental death occurred during the commission of the robbery, and the defendant was convicted of felony murder.

States divide murder into degrees. Most states have two degrees of murder; a few have three. First degree murder is reserved for the most egregious killings. In most states, intent to kill murder is either first or second degree murder. What is the difference between first and second degree intent to kill murder? With both types of murder, the defendant intends to kill the victim. The difference between first and second degree intent to kill murder is premeditation and deliberation. If the killer thought about the killing in advance (premeditated and deliberated), the crime is first degree murder. On the other hand, if the killing was intentional but was an instantaneous reaction to some act by the victim, without any kind of premeditation or deliberation, then the crime is second degree intent to kill murder. How much time does it take to premeditate and deliberate? Not much. If the defendant had enough time to turn the idea of killing over in his mind and decide to proceed, that is enough.

States vary on whether intent to cause grievous bodily injury murder, depraved heart murder, and felony murder are first or second degree murder.

Manslaughter

Manslaughter is the killing of a human being without malice. Thus, the difference between murder and manslaughter is malice. There are two types of manslaughter: voluntary and involuntary. Voluntary manslaughter occurs when the deceased victim engaged in extremely provocative behavior that caused the defendant to lose control and lash out in fury, killing the victim. The basic idea of voluntary manslaughter is that certain kinds of provocation are so serious that a normally law-abiding person might temporarily lose control and kill. Voluntary manslaughter is a serious felony, but the punishment for voluntary manslaughter is less severe than the punishment for intent to kill murder. Voluntary manslaughter plays no role in child abuse prosecution. Although children certainly provoke anger, a child's behavior, no matter how provocative, would never cause a law-abiding adult to deliberately kill the child.

Involuntary manslaughter occurs when the defendant lacks the malice required for murder but kills someone due to criminal negligence (also called gross negligence). The details of involuntary manslaughter vary from state to state, but all states have involuntary manslaughter based on criminal negligence.

An example will help clarify involuntary manslaughter based on criminal negligence. Mother and father had a baby whom they dearly loved. Mother and father had very little education and were extremely poor. The baby got sick, could not keep formula down, cried in pain, and was irritable. The parents noticed that the baby's cheek was swollen, but they did not think it was serious. The cheek remained swollen, and after a few days it turned blue. The baby remained ill and would not eat. Again, the parents knew something was wrong, but they did not know the baby's cheek was abscessed and that gangrene had set in. The parents did not take the baby to the hospital because they thought the baby would recover and because they feared child protective services (CPS) would take the baby away from them. After a week, the baby died due to blood poisoning from gangrene. The baby could have been saved if the parents had taken him to the hospital sooner.

Should these parents be charged with murder? They did not intend to kill or injure their child. They loved the baby and were heartbroken when the baby died. Did they act with a depraved heart? Depraved heart murder requires the defendant to be aware of the risk of death. These parents knew their baby was sick, but they did not know how sick. They were not aware that they were endangering their baby's life by not taking the baby to the hospital. This is not a good fit for depraved heart murder. How about felony murder? Did the parents' failure to take the baby to the hospital constitute a felony? Let's assume the answer is no. These parents should not be charged with murder because they did not have the malice required for murder.

How about involuntary manslaughter based on criminal negligence? Were these parents grossly negligent in failing to obtain medical care? They knew for more than a week that their baby was sick. Reasonable minds can differ, but a strong argument can be made that the parents' failure to get help constituted criminal negligence. Thus, if these parents are charged with a crime, the most appropriate crime is involuntary manslaughter based on criminal negligence.

Assault, Battery, and Mayhem

Battery is a harmful or offensive touching of another person without the person's consent. If I push you down or strike you, I commit a battery. A minor battery is a misdemeanor. Aggravated battery, including use of a deadly weapon, is a felony. Mayhem is an aggravated form of battery.

An assault is an attempt to commit a battery. If I walk toward you with a baseball bat raised ominously above my head ready to hit you, and you run away, I can be charged with assault, typically a misdemeanor.

It is common to use the term *assault* to refer to a battery. Indeed, judges and lawyers often refer to the two crimes in one breath, assault and battery.

Specialized Child Abuse Laws

Murder, manslaughter, assault, battery, and mayhem apply regardless of the victim's age. In addition to these crimes, states have specialized child abuse statutes that apply only to child victims and that punish serious physical abuse (PA) and neglect.

Sex Offenses

States have numerous sex crimes. Historically, rape was sexual intercourse with a female without her consent and with force. In many states today, rape is gender neutral. A man can rape another man, and a woman can rape another woman. Statutory rape is consensual sex between a minor and an adult. States criminalize all forms of CSA.

Applying Criminal Law to Real Cases _____

Now that you have a basic understanding of the crimes that apply in child abuse cases, you are ready to make decisions about how the law should be applied in individual cases.

Newborn in a Trash Can

A mother gives birth to a healthy baby in a motel room. The mother thinks to herself, "I can't handle this. I don't want this baby." Within minutes of the baby's birth, the mother puts the newborn in a plastic trash bag, closes the bag, and tosses it in a trash can. The baby dies due to lack of oxygen. You are the prosecutor. Will you charge the mother with a crime? What crime?

I would charge the mother with first degree intent to kill murder, the most serious form of murder. She clearly committed the *actus reus* of murder—she killed her baby. Did she have the *mens rea* for intent to kill murder? Her intent to kill can be inferred from her conduct: stuffing the baby in a plastic bag, closing it so the baby could not get oxygen, and tossing the bag in a trash can, which made it unlikely the baby would be rescued by a passerby. The mother's plan to dispose of the baby constitutes premeditation and deliberation.

I imagine the defense attorney will argue that the mother did not intend to kill her baby. The mother had just gone through the trauma of birth. She wasn't thinking straight. She didn't know what she was doing. She is guilty of bad judgment, but that is not a crime.

What is your opinion?

Shaken Baby

While a mother works, her live-in boyfriend cares for her baby. The boyfriend is not the child's father. One day while the mother is working, the baby won't stop crying. The boyfriend tries a bottle, tries rocking the baby, tries distracting the baby, but nothing works. The crying goes on and on. Eventually, the boyfriend snaps. In a rage, he picks the baby up under her arms, violently shakes her, and throws her against a wall. The boyfriend immediately realizes he has hurt the child and calls 911. The baby is rushed to the hospital but dies of massive bleeding in the brain.

Should the boyfriend be prosecuted? If so, for what crime? I have reviewed hundreds of shaken baby cases, and I am convinced that in most cases the adult does not intend to kill the baby. I would not charge the boyfriend with intent to kill murder. I might charge intent to cause grievous bodily injury murder or depraved heart murder. Shaking a baby is a felony, so I might charge the boyfriend with felony murder. I might consider involuntary manslaughter based on criminal negligence. Finally, I would check the law books to see if my state has a specialized child abuse statute for cases like this.

Beaten and Starved

A father who was divorced had custody of his 8-year-old son Ronnie. The father is over 6 feet tall and weighs more than 300 pounds. Ronnie weighs just 40 pounds. For months, the father used his fists to beat Ronnie. On more than one occasion, the father choked Ronnie. The father starved his son. One day, the father hit Ronnie especially hard in the stomach, and the child stopped breathing. The father drove Ronnie to the hospital, but it was too late. Ronnie was dead. Ronnie's body was covered with fresh and healing bruises inflicted by the father. Ronnie died from loss of blood due to the father's latest blow.

What crime did the father commit, apart from the moral crime of being a horrible human being? Intent to kill murder? Did the father intend to kill his son? Or was his intent to abuse him but not kill him? If not intent to kill murder, this is a good case for intent to cause grievous bodily injury, depraved heart, or felony murder.[1]

Summary

The three cases previously described provide insight into the difficult decisions prosecutors make when children are hurt, killed, or neglected. Has a

---

[1]This is a real case, *Midgett v. State*, 1987. At his trial, the father was convicted of first degree, premeditated, and deliberate intent to kill murder. On appeal, the Arkansas Supreme Court reduced the charge to second degree murder based on the theory of intent to cause grievous bodily injury. The Supreme Court ruled that the father intended not to kill his son but to keep him alive so he could abuse him.

crime been committed? What crime? What was the defendant's intent? Did the defendant intend to kill the child? If there was no intent to kill, was the defendant reckless or negligent? If the child survived, what is the appropriate charge? Attempted murder? Battery? Mayhem? If the defendant is charged, what evidence can be used in court to convict the defendant? What are the chances the jury will convict? If the defendant is convicted, what punishment is called for?

Switching from the prosecutor to the defense attorney, the defender asks, Is the client guilty or has the prosecutor charged the wrong person? If the defendant hurt or killed the child, are there any defenses? If there are no defenses, is there at least some mitigating evidence that can be used in court to portray the defendant in a positive light? Can I reach a plea bargain with the prosecutor in exchange for the defendant's agreement to plead guilty to a lesser crime?

Failure to Protect and Accomplice Liability

Do we have an obligation to help our fellow citizens? More specifically, if someone is in danger, do we have a legal or moral duty to come to their rescue? The moral question has been debated at least since Cain asked God, "Am I my brother's keeper?" In the United States the answer to the legal question is generally no; there is no duty to rescue. Suppose, for example, that an Olympic swimmer is walking past a children's shallow wading pool. The swimmer notices a baby drowning in the pool. The swimmer could easily rescue the baby with no risk to the swimmer, but the swimmer just keeps walking and the baby drowns. Can the swimmer be charged with the baby's death? No, because the swimmer had no legal duty to rescue the child. The swimmer was not even legally required to call 911 or alert nearby adults. Is the swimmer morally culpable? Yes, but morals and law do not always coincide.

Change the facts. Suppose the swimmer is the mother or father of the drowning baby. Can the swimmer/parent ignore the baby's plight without risk of prosecution? No. Parents have a legal as well as a moral duty to protect their children. Failure by a parent to protect their child can be a crime and a basis for CPS intervention.

One of the most difficult dilemmas confronting prosecutors is the case in which a parent—typically a mother—fails to protect her child from physical or sexual abuse inflicted by her husband or paramour. Prosecuting the perpetrator is straightforward. The difficult question is whether to prosecute the mother for failure to protect. The prosecutor considers the circumstances. Did the mother know or only suspect the abuse? Did the mother try to stop the abuse? Was the mother herself a victim of abuse by the perpetrator, making it difficult for her to protect her child? If the mother could and should have protected her child, prosecution is likely.

In rare cases, the nonabusive parent is aware of the abuse and actually takes steps to help the perpetrator. In such cases, the nonabusive parent is an accomplice to the abuse and, in the eyes of the law, is as guilty of the abuse as the perpetrator.

Conclusion

Most child maltreatment is not criminal. In many cases, the intervention of CPS and the juvenile court is all that is needed to protect children and help misguided but well-intentioned parents. In quite a few cases, the courts are not needed at all. Social workers and other professionals help parents do a better job. Make no mistake, however, that there are times when abuse or neglect is so serious, when the harm is so great, and when the perpetrator's mental state is sufficiently culpable that criminal law must step in and punish.

References

American Academy of Pediatrics (AAP). (1999). The child in court: A subject review. *Pediatrics, 104,* 1145–1148.

Boland, M. L., & Butler, R. (2009). Crime victims' rights: From illusion to reality. *Criminal Justice, 24,* 4–10.

Dressler, J. (2009). *Understanding criminal law* (5th ed.). Newark, NJ: LexisNexis.

Goodman, G. S., Taub, E. P., Jones, D. P. H., England, P., Port, L. K., Rudy, L., et al. (1992). Testifying in criminal court. *Monographs of the Society for Research in Child Development, 57,* 1–141.

Hall, S. R., & Sales, B. D. (2008). *Courtroom modifications for child witnesses: Law and science in forensic evaluations.* Washington, DC: American Psychological Association.

Henry, J. (1997). System intervention trauma to child sexual abuse victims following disclosure. *Journal of Interpersonal Violence, 12,* 499–515.

Maryland v. Craig, 497 U.S. 836 (1990).

Midgett v. State, 729 S.W.2d 410 (Ark. 1987).

Miranda v. Arizona, 384 U.S. 436 (1966).

Myers, J. E. B. (2005). *Myers on evidence in child, domestic, and elder abuse cases.* New York: Aspen Law and Business.

Quas, J. A., Goodman, G. S., Ghetti, S., Alexander, K. W., Edelstein, R., Redlich, A. D., et al. (2005). Childhood sexual assault victims: Long-term outcomes after testifying in criminal court. *Monographs of the Society for Research in Child Development, 70,* 1–45.

Raeder, M. S. (2009). Enhancing the legal profession's response to victims of child abuse. *Criminal Justice, 24,* 12–16.

Waller v. Georgia, 467 U.S. 39 (1984).

PART II

Neglect

Part II of the *APSAC Handbook on Child Maltreatment* discusses neglect, the most prevalent form of maltreatment. Chapter 7 defines neglect and describes the harmful effects of this form of maltreatment. Chapter 8 discusses psychological maltreatment (PM). Neglect of children's health occurs less often than other forms of neglect, but medical neglect can have serious consequences. Neglect of children's health is the subject of Chapter 9. Every year, millions of children witness domestic violence. Chapter 10 describes child maltreatment in the context of intimate partner violence (IPV).

7

Child Neglect

Martha Farrell Erickson and Byron Egeland

Although the bruises and scars of physical child abuse are more readily apparent, the quiet assault of neglect often does at least as much damage to its young victims. Neglect is sometimes obvious (e.g., the unkempt appearance of the child who chronically comes to school without a bath or adequate clothing) and sometimes nearly invisible until it is too late. Neglect is often fatal due to inadequate physical protection, nutrition, or health care. In some cases, neglect slowly and persistently eats away at children's spirits until they have little will to connect with others or explore the world.

In this chapter, we present an overview of child neglect. First, we describe the dawning of awareness of neglect as a major problem. Second, we discuss definitions of neglect. Third, we review research on the impact of neglect on children's health and development, including data from our own longitudinal study of the consequences of emotional neglect. Fourth, we offer a brief overview of attachment theory and its relationship to child maltreatment. Fifth, we discuss resilience and protective factors that can shield children from some or all of the damage of maltreatment. Finally, we review what is known about underlying causes and correlates of neglect and discuss how knowledge of those factors can be used to guide preventive intervention and treatment of neglecting families.

Developing Awareness of Neglect

Although children have been abused and neglected for centuries, widespread recognition of maltreatment as an important social problem is relatively recent (see Chapter 1 for discussion of the history of child protection). Kempe's landmark 1962 paper on battered child syndrome (BCS) (Kempe,

Silverman, Steele, Droegemueller, & Silver, 1962) spurred a dramatic increase in public awareness of the impact of physical abuse (PA). Broad recognition of neglect, however, lagged behind despite the fact that neglect is more prevalent than PA (McDonald & Associates, 1999) and has consequences that are just as serious (e.g., Egeland, 1997; Erickson, Egeland, & Pianta, 1989; Greenbaum et al., 2008). Some experts contend neglect (emotional neglect, in particular) is the central feature of all child maltreatment (Brassard, Germain, & Hart, 1987; Claussen & Crittenden, 1991). (See Chapter 8 on psychological maltreatment [PM].) Newberger, for example, wrote as early as 1973, "The essential element in child abuse is not the intention to destroy a child but rather the inability of a parent to nurture [his or her] offspring" (p. 327). In the late 1980s, awareness of neglect expanded to include recognition of the often profound psychological consequences stemming from even the most subtle neglect. In the 21st century, advances in brain imaging technology made it possible to study the impact of neglect on the developing brain, confirming in a very concrete way the harm of maltreatment (Greenbaum et al., 2008).

Definitions of Neglect

Neglect means many things to many people (Black & Dubowitz, 1999; Dubowitz, 1999; Smith & Fong, 2004; Zuravin, 1999). Definitions vary somewhat depending on whether one takes a legal, medical, psychological, social service, or lay perspective. Legally, every state has laws defining neglect. These laws serve different functions, and legal definitions vary slightly from function to function (Dubowitz, 1999; Giovannoni, 1989). Thus, states have laws that require professionals to report suspected neglect to child protective services (CPS), and reporting laws define neglect. In addition to reporting laws, states define neglect for purposes of juvenile court intervention in the family (see Chapter 4 for discussion of juvenile court). Finally, some neglect is so serious that it is a crime, and criminal law has its own definition of neglect (see Chapter 6 for discussion of criminal prosecution). Although legal definitions vary in detail, the core concept remains—neglect is parental failure to meet a child's basic needs (Greenbaum et al., 2008).

There are five subtypes of neglect. First, physical neglect is parental failure to protect a child from harm or to provide the child with basic necessities including adequate food, shelter, and clothing. Second is psychological or emotional neglect. This form of maltreatment is discussed in this chapter and in Chapter 8. In our research on psychological neglect, we use the term *psychologically unavailable* to describe parents who overlook their young children's cues and signals, particularly the children's pleas for warmth and comfort. As discussed later, we found this form of neglect to have serious long-term consequences for children. Third, neglect of children's health—medical neglect—occurs when a parent withholds essential medical care from their child. Medical neglect is addressed in Chapter 9. Fourth is mental health neglect, which occurs when a parent refuses to comply with recommended therapeutic interventions for a child with a serious emotional or behavioral disorder. Mental health neglect is a form of medical neglect. Fifth, educational neglect occurs when a parent fails to comply with laws that require children to attend school.

Outside the legal arena, perspectives on neglect vary. Some professionals, for example, define neglect to include conduct that does not meet the criteria of the law. In an early study of perceptions of neglect, Boehm (1962) asked professionals to respond to vignettes describing various kinds of neglect. Teachers, nurses, social workers, and clergy were more likely to believe cases required intervention than were lawyers. In 1992, David Hamburg, president of the Carnegie Foundation, advocated an expansive view of neglect. Calling attention to the plight of children living in poverty, Hamburg indicted society at large for "collective neglect" in failing to provide adequate health care, child care, preschool education, and policies that support families.

Professionals debate several aspects of neglect. One issue concerns whether parental conduct constitutes neglect if the conduct creates a risk of harm to the child in the future even though the child is not presently symptomatic. In other words, to constitute neglect, must there be evidence of existing harm, or is risk of harm *in the future* sufficient? Most agree that parental actions can be neglectful despite a lack of observable impact on a child's functioning (Greenbaum et al., 2008). Certainly our own research on the long-term consequences of various patterns of maltreatment suggests that the impact of neglect may become apparent later in the child's development, even if it is not immediately obvious. At the 1983 International Conference on Psychological Abuse of Children and Youth, the participants proposed a definition of PM that includes both immediate and ultimate (i.e., manifest at a later point) damage to a child's behavioral, cognitive, affective, or physical functioning (Brassard et al., 1987). Legal definitions of neglect by and large include risk of future harm.

Another debate regarding neglect concerns "intentionality." To constitute neglect, must the parent "intend" to neglect or harm the child? Dubowitz and his colleagues argue for a definition of neglect based on the unmet needs of the child regardless of parental intentions (Dubowitz, Black, Starr, & Zuravin, 1993; Dubowitz, 1999). Harm to a child can be just as serious—even fatal—whether the parent acts intentionally or is simply careless, ignorant, depressed, or overwhelmed (Greenbaum et al., 2008).

In law, the issue of intentionality is complex. Suffice to say that the law allows protective intervention through CPS and the juvenile court whether neglect is a product of intentional acts or mere negligence. Legally, a person acts negligently when the person does not consciously intend to cause harm, but the person's conduct falls below the minimally acceptable level of caution that is exercised by reasonable people in similar circumstances. Intervention through CPS and the juvenile court is proper when a parent's negligence endangers or harms a child. Criminal prosecution for neglect is another matter, but prosecution is allowed when a parent's negligence is so extreme—called gross negligence—that it rises to the level of "criminal negligence." See Chapter 6 for discussion of criminal prosecution.

The Prevalence of Child Neglect

Although physical and sexual abuse garner more media attention than neglect, neglect is the most common type of maltreatment (Greenbaum et al., 2008). Based on reporting data from 2008, of the 3.3 million reports to CPS that year, 71% were for neglect. PA comprised 16% of reports, whereas sexual abuse was 9%. PM made up 7.3% of reports (U.S. Department of Health and Human Services, 2010). These percentages—with neglect the most prevalent—have remained fairly constant over time.

In 2008, an estimated 1,740 children died due to maltreatment, and more than 40% of the fatalities were from neglect (U.S. Department of Health and Human Services, 2010). Young children and babies are particularly susceptible to fatal neglect.

Developmental Consequences of Neglect

The 1970s saw burgeoning interest in the consequences of maltreatment. Early studies focused primarily on children who were physically abused. These studies pointed to a disproportionate number of abused children who performed below average on standardized intelligence tests (e.g., Martin, Beezley, Conway, & Kempe, 1974; Morse, Sahler, & Friedman, 1970; Sandgrund, Gaines, & Green, 1974) and who exhibited varied social and emotional problems, including hostility, aggression, and passive, withdrawn behavior (e.g., Kempe & Kempe, 1978; Martin & Beezley, 1977). In one of the first studies specifically to include neglected children, Steele (1977) found learning problems, low self-esteem, and, as children matured, a high incidence of juvenile delinquency. Reidy (1977) found that both abused and neglected children behaved more aggressively in school than nonmaltreated children, but abused children exhibited more aggression during fantasy and free play than the neglected children. Hoffman-Plotkin and Twentyman (1984) reported that abused children were more aggressive than either neglected or nonmaltreated children, but the neglected children interacted less with peers than either abused or nonmaltreated children. Similarly, Crittenden (1985; Crittenden & Ainsworth, 1989) found that physically abused children had difficult temperaments, became angry under stress, and exhibited mild developmental delays. Neglected children, on the other hand, were passive, tended toward helplessness under stress, and showed significant developmental delays. In a review of studies from 1975 to 1992, Katz (1992) found that both abused and neglected children had language delays or disorders, but the problems of neglected children were more severe. Kendall-Tackett and Eckenrode's (1996) longitudinal study of the school behavior and academic achievement of neglected children documented a notable decline in performance when children entered junior high.

Several 21st century studies further document the link between neglect and aggression. Mersky and Reynolds (2007) found both abuse and neglect to be associated with later violent delinquent behavior. White and Widom (2003) linked both abuse and neglect in childhood to violence against a partner in adulthood, findings that held true for males and females. Raising questions about the relative impact of neglect at different stages of development, a study of more than 1,300 high-risk children showed that neglect in the first 2 years of life predicted later aggression, but neither PA nor neglect at later ages predicted aggression (Kotch et al., 2008).

It is important to consider the consequences of multiple types of maltreatment. Finkelhor (2008) observed,

> It increasingly appears that what professionals should be on the lookout for in children is poly-victimization, not just one type of victimization, even a serious one. Our analyses suggest that poly-victimization is the thing most closely associated with mental health problems and bad outcomes, and that poly-victims are harboring the greatest amount of distress. (p. 36)

It also is critical to consider the severity of maltreatment, age at onset, and a pattern of maltreatment across stages of a child's development (English et al., 2005).

As difficult as it is to draw a clear line separating abused from neglected children, it is even more difficult to distinguish between children who are physically neglected and those who are emotionally neglected. Most, if not all, children who are physically neglected are also emotionally neglected at least to some extent. However, the converse is not always true. We have seen a number of children who were emotionally but not physically neglected (e.g., Egeland & Erickson, 1987). These children were fed adequately, well-clothed, and received proper health care, but their caregivers did not respond to their emotional needs.

The most extreme consequences of emotional neglect are labeled nonorganic failure to thrive (FTT) syndrome, which involves failure to grow (or sometimes even to survive) despite adequate nourishment (Gardner, 1972; Greenbaum et al., 2008; MacCarthy, 1979; Patton & Gardner, 1962). Even after diagnosis and intervention, the psychological consequences of nonorganic FTT persist. In a follow-up of infants diagnosed as FTT, MacCarthy (1979) reported notable attention-seeking behavior and superficial displays of affection after these children were placed out of the home. Later in childhood, the children were described as spiteful and selfish, and they reportedly engaged in stealing. Likewise, Polansky, Chalmers, Buttenwieser, and Williams (1981) chronicled the defiant, hostile behavior of young adolescents who in infancy had been diagnosed as FTT. Hufton and Oates (1977) found that FTT children presented varied academic and behavior problems in the early elementary grades.

Even in cases much less profound than nonorganic FTT, the long-term consequences of emotional neglect are remarkable (Egeland, 1997; Egeland & Erickson, 1987; Egeland, Sroufe, & Erickson, 1983; Erickson, Egeland, & Pianta, 1989; Sroufe, Egeland, Carlson, & Collins, 2005). Our research on children with psychologically unavailable parents, discussed next, provides powerful evidence of the impact of emotional neglect.

The Minnesota Longitudinal Study of High Risk Parents and Children

In 1975, Byron Egeland, one of the authors of this chapter, launched the Minnesota Longitudinal Study of High Risk Parents and Children, originally known as the Minnesota Mother-Child Project. The other chapter author, Martha Farrell Erickson, joined the study three years later. The Minnesota Study is a prospective longitudinal study designed to follow the development of 267 children born to first-time mothers identified as being at risk for parenting problems due to poverty, youth, low education, lack of support, and unstable life circumstances. We recruited mothers through obstetric clinics during the second trimester of pregnancy. The women, their children, and their life circumstances have been assessed regularly using multiple methods including extensive observation, through early adulthood (Egeland, 1997; Erickson, Pianta & Egeland, 1989; Erickson, Egeland, & Pianta, 1989; Sroufe, Egeland, Carlson, & Collins, 2005).

Although this longitudinal study examined the entire range of caregiving, a major focus has been on the antecedents of abuse and neglect, as well as the long-term consequences of maltreatment on children's development. At different points in time, we identified three groups of children who were maltreated. In the period from birth to 4.5 years, we identified physically abused children, neglected children, and children whose mothers were psychologically unavailable, that is, emotionally neglectful. (There was overlap among the groups.)

Of particular interest for this chapter are the neglected children and children with psychologically unavailable caregivers. Mothers in the "neglectful" group did not provide appropriate health care, physical care, or protection for their children—either because of incompetence or irresponsibility. Although these mothers sometimes expressed concern and interest in their children's welfare, their care for their children was inconsistent and inadequate. Mothers who were psychologically unavailable neglected their children emotionally. The mothers appeared detached and unresponsive to their children's bids for care and attention. When psychologically unavailable mothers did interact with their children, it was in a mechanical and perfunctory manner, with no apparent joy or satisfaction in the relationship.

We compared the maltreated children to a group of nonmaltreated children from the same high-risk sample (Egeland & Sroufe, 1981; Egeland, Sroufe, & Erickson, 1983; Erickson, Egeland, & Pianta, 1989). Compared to nonmaltreated children, children in all maltreatment groups functioned poorly in a variety of situations from infancy through the preschool period. For those who were maltreated in infancy, there was a high incidence of anxious attachment compared to the control group. (In a subsequent section of this chapter, we describe attachment theory and its importance to understanding and addressing maltreatment.)

Among neglected children, two thirds were anxiously attached at 1 year of age. At almost 2 years of age, children were videotaped in a problem-solving task with their mothers. Neglected children lacked enthusiasm, were easily frustrated, displayed considerable anger, and were noncompliant. When videotaped with their mothers in a series of teaching tasks, neglected children showed little enthusiasm or persistence, were angry, noncompliant, and often avoidant and unaffectionate toward their mothers, even though they were highly dependent on them for help. At 3.5 years of age, in an independent problem-solving task, neglected children showed poor impulse control, rigidity, a lack of creativity, and more unhappiness than all other groups. At 4.5 years, when observed in a preschool or child care setting, neglected children demonstrated poor impulse control, extreme dependence on teachers, and general adjustment problems in the classroom.

Findings from the Minnesota study show the consequences of emotional neglect (or what we call psychologically unavailable parenting) to be even more profound than physical neglect and other types of maltreatment. At 1.5 years of age, all of the emotionally neglected children were anxiously attached, with the majority classified as anxious-avoidant. In assessments at 2 years and 3.5 years, emotionally neglected children displayed anger, noncompliance, lack of persistence, and little positive affect. The most dramatic finding for these children was their steep decline in performance on the Bayley Scales of Infant Development between 9 months and 2 years. In the preschool classroom, at approximately 4.5 years, these children presented varied and serious behavior problems. They continued to be noncompliant and negativistic, impulsive, highly dependent on teachers, and they sometimes displayed nervous signs, self-abusive behavior, and other behaviors indicative of psychopathology (Egeland et al., 1983). Although the maltreatment experienced by the emotionally neglected children was the most subtle of all the forms of maltreatment, the consequences for the children were very serious.

For children maltreated during the preschool period—3 to 5 years of age—the physically neglected children presented the most problems. In kindergarten, they were inattentive and uninvolved in learning, anxious, aggressive, and unpopular with peers. Their performance on standardized tests of intellectual functioning and academic achievement were the lowest of all the maltreatment groups. Children who experienced emotional neglect (psychologically unavailable parents) at this stage of life (3 to 5 years) also presented significant problems in the classroom. However, the impact was not as dramatic as for the children who experienced emotional neglect during the first 2 years of life.

We assessed the children in our sample during their elementary school years. We gathered information from classroom teachers in Grades 1, 2, 3, and 6. Teachers completed the Child Behavior Checklist (CBCL) on each child (Achenbach & Edelbrock, 1980) and—before teachers knew who the target child was—teachers rank-ordered their students on dimensions of peer acceptance and emotional health. Children were administered the Peabody Individual Achievement Test (Dunn & Markwardt, 1970).

Children who experienced psychologically unavailable parenting in the first 2 years of life continued to have problems throughout the elementary school years. When compared to nonmaltreated children from the same high-risk sample, emotionally neglected children were ranked low by their teachers on peer acceptance and overall emotional health. On the CBCL, emotionally neglected children were rated at all grade levels as being more socially withdrawn, unpopular with peers, and, in general, exhibiting more problems of the internalizing type. In the early grades, they also were rated as more aggressive and less attentive. On the Peabody Individual Achievement Test, emotionally neglected children performed significantly lower at every grade level than the nonmaltreated children. When emotionally neglected children were compared with children who had been physically abused in the early years of life, there were no variables on which the physically abused children did significantly worse than the emotionally neglected children, although the emotionally neglected children were more withdrawn and inattentive than the physically abused children (Erickson & Egeland, 1996; Sroufe et al., 2005). Physically neglected and emotionally neglected children were high on the internalizing and externalizing scores of the Child Behavior Checklist-Teacher (CBCL-T) compared to the control group. Both neglect groups were ranked low on peer acceptance and emotional health compared to the control group. Physically neglected children were low academically and had difficulty organizing themselves to cope with the everyday demands of school. Only one physically neglected child was not receiving special education services in kindergarten through Grade 3. The physically neglected children missed more than 60 days of school between kindergarten and Grade 3 compared to 41 days for the control children. Teachers indicated that maltreating parents seldom had knowledge of or interest in their child's school life.

Clearly, the impact of neglect on children's development is at least as damaging as other more overt types of abuse. Physical neglect, particularly during the preschool and primary grades, seriously impairs children's school behavior. Emotional neglect, especially during the first 2 years of life, has a striking and long-lasting impact on children's adaptation within the family, with peers and teachers, and in regard to learning and problem-solving. The effects of neglect are above and beyond the negative impact of poverty and its correlates on children's development.

When we followed the children during adolescence, those who were maltreated in early life experienced a variety of problems. Children who experienced physical neglect had low achievement scores on an achievement test and had high teacher ratings on the delinquency scale of the CBCL. Teens who were physically neglected earlier had high rates of alcohol use, expulsion from school, and drop out.

Teenagers whose parents had been psychologically unavailable displayed a number of behavior problems. They were high on the social problem, delinquency, and aggression scales of the CBCL-T. More of the psychologically neglected teens attempted suicide than teens in the control group.

At age 17.5, we administered a diagnostic interview for mental illness (Kiddie-Schedule for Affective Disorders and Schizophrenia or K-SADS). The majority of maltreated children (90%) received at least one diagnosis. The highest rate was in the emotional neglect group, where all but one of the children received at least one diagnosis of psychiatric disorder and 73% were comorbid for two disorders or more. Fifty-four percent of the physically neglected children were comorbid compared to 30% for the control group. In sum, both physical and emotional neglect in the early years has devastating consequences for children's achievement, behavior, and mental health in adolescence (Egeland, 1997; Sroufe et al., 2005).

Attachment Theory and Its Relationship to Child Maltreatment

As mentioned in the previous section, one consequence of child maltreatment in general—and neglect specifically—is the development of an insecure attachment between parent and child. But beyond documenting the fact that a child is highly unlikely to develop a secure attachment with a neglectful parent, attachment theory and research also offer a useful framework for understanding the dynamics of maltreatment and why it so often is passed from one generation to the next. Attachment is a complex subject, and a thorough discussion is beyond the scope of this chapter. But we offer here some key findings from attachment research and encourage readers to do further study on this important topic (Gowen & Nebrig, 2002; Sroufe et al., 2005).

Since the 1960s, child development research has yielded a wealth of information about the importance of the quality of parent-infant attachment as a powerful influence on a child's lifelong development. Building gradually and slowly over the first year of a child's life, parent-infant attachment is a child's first close relationship and, to a large extent, a model for all relationships that follow. Although babies almost always become attached to their primary caregiver(s)—mother, father, or whomever is with the baby over time—those attachments vary, with some (about 70% in the United States) being "secure" attachments and about 30% being "insecure" (also referred to as "anxious," with different subtypes depending to a large extent on the particular kind of care the child received from the parent).

Longitudinal observational research using carefully standardized measures of the quality of attachment shows that babies become securely attached when their parents are consistently sensitive and responsive to their needs, comforting them when they are distressed, playing and talking and singing to them when they seek interaction, and allowing quiet time when the baby gives cues that indicate they don't want to be hugged or fed or tickled right now. With sensitive, responsive care, babies learn to trust their caregivers and perceive the world as a safe place (Sroufe et al., 2005).

Babies also learn that they have the power to solicit what they need. When their signals to caregivers bring results, babies have their first experience of competence and what developmental psychologists call "effectance"— discovering that they have an effect on those around them. This is what we want for all children. With that foundation of trust and security, children venture out with confidence and enthusiasm, using their attachment figures as a secure base from which to explore and learn about the world around them. Securely attached children also regulate their emotions more effectively and are more likely to enter into cooperative, caring relationships with other adults and children than children who do not have the firm foundation of a secure attachment (Sroufe et al., 2005).

When parents are inconsistent, unresponsive, and/or insensitive to babies' cues and signals, babies learn that they cannot count on their parents for care and support. Furthermore, these babies feel powerless to solicit the care they need, and they develop an insecure (also called "anxious") attachment. Children who are insecure may manifest their anxiety in one of two patterns: avoidance or resistance and ambivalence.

Avoidantly attached children (who typically have experienced chronic unresponsiveness from their parents) often develop behavior problems (including aggressive or socially withdrawn behavior), are often unpopular with other children, may lack motivation and persistence in learning, and tend to victimize other children.

Resistantly (or ambivalently) attached children (who typically have experienced erratic, unpredictable care) tend to be overly dependent upon teachers for help and attention, lack confidence and self-esteem, are less able to form friendships than other children, and often are the victims of more aggressive peers.

Some parent–infant interactions are so inconsistent, unresponsive, or abusive that a disorganized type of attachment develops. Children showing a disorganized attachment have difficulty coping with emotions and establishing close relationships. They are at high risk for serious psychopathology in adolescence (Sroufe et al., 2005).

Attachment research has addressed the question of what factors most influence a parent's ability to provide the sensitive care that leads to secure attachment. That research points to several critical factors, all of which sound relatively simple and basic, but which often are *not* basic to programs and policies. First, when parents' basic needs for housing, food, clothing, transportation, and health care are met, parents are more likely to have the energy to meet their children's needs. Second, when parents have emotional support for themselves, they are better able to care for their children sensitively and consistently. Third, when parents understand child development, particularly the meaning of certain key child behaviors such as separation anxiety in the infant or negativism in the toddler, they have more realistic behavioral

expectations. Knowledge, understanding, and perspective-taking are fundamental to the sensitive care that facilitates secure attachment. Finally, how a
parent cares for his/her children is strongly influenced by the care the parent
received in his/her own childhood. Of course, we cannot go back and change
a parent's history, but research indicates that what is most important is how a
parent thinks now about his/her own history—facing experiences that were
painful, acknowledging their ongoing influence, and choosing what to repeat
and what not to repeat. In attachment research, how a parent thinks about
his/her childhood experience is referred to as "attachment state of mind"
(Erickson et al., 1989; Erickson, Korfmacher, & Egeland, 1992; Sroufe et al.,
2005). As discussed in a later section of this chapter, these factors and others
are associated with child abuse and neglect. They can provide a useful starting
point for family-focused prevention and intervention with high-risk and/or
maltreating families.

Protective Factors and Resilience

Forty years of research establishes that all forms of child maltreatment are
major risk factors for negative outcomes across the life span. Yet, despite
the link between maltreatment and negative outcomes, some maltreated
children appear to escape relatively unscathed and develop into well-
adjusted, happy adults. Why? Researchers are studying so-called "resilient"
children in an effort to isolate the personality traits and environmental
factors—protective factors—that contribute to good outcomes for maltreated children.

Resilience is the capacity to adapt successfully and to function competently
despite adversity. Resilience does not appear to be an innate attribute that
only a few lucky children possess. Rather, resilience is a dynamic process
whereby particular children use available internal and external resources
to initiate and maintain self-righting tendencies in the face of adversity
(Cicchetti & Valentino, 2006; Egeland, Carlson, & Sroufe, 1993).

We believe resilience is rooted in early competence that grows from a secure
attachment between infant and mother or primary caregiver (Yates, Egeland, &
Sroufe, 2003). As summarized in the earlier section on parent–infant attachment, this early competence (i.e., secure attachment) nurtures healthy development of the self, emotional regulation, and the belief that others can be counted
on. Such competence enables children to cope with adversity.

Tragically, many maltreated children lack the secure attachment that
facilitates competence and that buffers children from the psychological
damage of maltreatment. As a result, many maltreated children develop
negative beliefs and expectations about themselves and about relationships.
Maltreated children often believe others cannot be counted on for support,
love, and guidance. Many of these unfortunate children believe they are not
worthy of nurturance from parents and others. Moreover, maltreated
children often believe they are incapable of solving problems on their own.

Given such beliefs, is it any wonder many maltreated children decline to reach out to relatives, teachers, or other adults for assistance in times of adversity? Is it surprising that maltreated children view themselves as inept and that they give up on school and relationships? No, it is not surprising. What is surprising is that so many maltreated children—nearly always with help from caring adults—pull themselves up and make lemonade when life gave them lemons.

Quality parenting is the most robust protective factor for high-risk children experiencing adversity (Yates et al., 2003; Luthar & Zelazo, 2003). For most maltreated children, however, there is a serious disruption in their relationship with their parents. In situations where the child is fortunate enough to have an alternative caregiver who provides high-quality care, the child's likelihood of resilient adaptation is improved. We found, for example, that adults who were maltreated as children but who nevertheless broke the intergenerational cycle of maltreatment had emotionally supportive care as a child, usually from an alternative caregiver such as a grandparent. As adults, these individuals had a supportive spouse or partner (Egeland, Jacobvitz, & Sroufe, 1988).

Dozier and colleagues (2001) found that maltreated children placed with responsive foster parents are more likely to function in a competent fashion. Positive relationships in many forms serve as a protective factor for high-risk children. Reynolds and Ou (2003) found high-quality day care was a protective factor for a large sample of poor children. Hamre and Pianta (2001) noted the protective functions of supportive relationships with teachers. Elder and Conger (2000) found that positive relationships with peers can serve a protective function for high-risk children. Unfortunately, for many maltreated youth, their negative relationship history increases the likelihood they will associate with deviant peers rather than peers who could provide support and assistance.

Maltreated children with average to above average intelligence are more likely to be resilient (Herrenkohl, Herrenkohl, & Egolf, 1994). Other attributes associated with resilience include an internal locus of control (i.e., believing that one's own choices and behavior influence what happens in life) and good self-esteem (Moran & Eckenrode, 1992). Cicchetti and Rogosch (1997) confirm that the ability to self-regulate, solve problems, and have good self-esteem are associated with resilience. Cicchetti and Rogosch (1997) concluded that interventions for maltreated children should focus on enhancing self-system and promoting self-determination. We would add the need to develop intervention and prevention programs that focus on relationships. In a review of resilience research, Luthar (2006) concluded that the take-home message is clear: "Resilience rests fundamentally on relationships. . . . Whereas some maltreated children will obviously do better in life than others, the likelihood of sustained competence without corrective ameliorative relationship experiences remains compromised at best" (p.780). Interventions with neglected children should center around engaging, caring adults who can provide that corrective experience.

Antecedents and Correlates of Neglect:
_____ Implications for Prevention and Intervention

Similar to the study of resilience, a critical area of research that has important implications for prevention and intervention involves identifying factors that predict—or are characteristic of—families that neglect their children. The more we know about factors associated with neglect, the more precise our attempts will be to identify and support families at risk. Those factors can become targets for intervention in hopes of reducing the potential of harm to the child.

Unfortunately, research rarely points to specific antecedents of neglect. Several studies provide useful information about antecedents and concomitants of maltreatment in general, as well as the way various factors interact to render parents more or less likely to maltreat their children (see Cicchetti & Lynch, 1993).

Parental Characteristics and Attitudes

There are many aspects of how parents perceive and understand their child's behavior, as well as what they expect and believe about behavior. For example, maltreating parents often show a lack of understanding of the emotional complexity of human relationships, especially the parent–child relationship. They have difficulty seeing things from the child's perspective or understanding behavior in terms of the child's developmental level and the context or situation. Maltreating parents tend to think in global, all-or-nothing terms rather than see the shades of gray that more realistically capture human behavior (Brunnquell, Crichton, & Egeland, 1981; Newberger & Cook, 1983; Sameroff & Feil, 1984). Maltreating parents often have unresolved issues of trust, dependency, and autonomy (reflecting their own childhood history) and may seek to meet their own needs through the parent–child relationship (Pianta, Egeland & Erickson, 1989). Attachment theory and research provides a framework for developing intervention and prevention programs designed to promote more positive parenting expectation and realistic beliefs about relationships and their child's behavior.

Maltreating parents have been found to have a high incidence of depression (Lahey, Conger, Atkenson, & Treiber, 1984) and to lack impulse control, particularly when stressed (Altemeier, O'Connor, Vietze, Sandler, & Sherrod, 1982; Wolfe, 1985). In our own longitudinal study of high-risk parents, maltreating mothers presented more mood disturbances. In particular, emotionally neglectful (or what we called "psychologically unavailable") mothers were more tense, depressed, angry, and confused than nonmaltreating mothers. Physically neglectful mothers also were more tense and functioned at a lower level intellectually than mothers who provided adequate care (Pianta et al., 1989).

Environmental Factors

Before discussing several environmental factors that contribute to maltreatment, it is important to consider the role of the child as a "cause" of his/her own maltreatment. Some researchers, particularly in the 1970s, focused on infant irritability and fussiness as factors that could contribute to difficulties in the parent-child relationship (Parke & Collmer, 1975). This idea has remained popular, particularly in the child maltreatment literature. Unfortunately, this early research had methodological shortcomings that make it difficult to interpret the findings (Vaughn, Deinard, & Egeland, 1980). Although few would dispute that some children are more difficult to care for than others, there is strong evidence from observational studies that child characteristics alone do not account for maltreatment or poor quality care. Research taking a transactional view of parent-child relationships demonstrates the power of parental sensitivity and responsiveness in overcoming the child's difficulty (Brachfield, Goldberg, & Sloman, 1980; Sameroff & Chandler, 1975).

At each ecological level, there are numerous risk and protective factors that determine the overall quality of care a child receives. One goal of prevention and intervention should be to increase the balance between risk and protective factors by decreasing risk and increasing protection (Cicchetti & Valentino, 2006). Major risk factors include violence in the marital relationship, parental unemployment, other stressful life events, and the absence of a helpful, supportive social network perhaps especially among single parents who also lack intimate emotional support (Dubowitz, 1999; Pianta et al., 1989). And, of course, poverty plays a role. Research indicates that of all types of maltreatment, physical neglect is most clearly associated with poverty (Sedlak & Broadhurst, 1996).

Not surprisingly, the psychological environment in which a parent grew up is a contributing factor. Our own longitudinal data show that among mothers who were abused or neglected when they were children, 40% maltreated their children in the early years of their children's lives, and an additional 30% provided borderline care. Among mothers who were neglected in childhood, seven out of nine maltreated their own children, and most of those were cases of neglect (Pianta et al., 1989).

Perhaps the most important question of all is what characterizes parents who rise above their own history of abuse or neglect and provide good care for their children? In our research (Egeland, 1988; Egeland & Susman-Stillman, 1996), several major factors distinguish mothers who broke the cycle of maltreatment and those who did not: (1) the presence of a loving, supportive adult during the mother's childhood—someone who gave her a different view of herself and others; (2) a supportive partner at the time she became a parent; and (3) therapeutic intervention that enabled the mother to come to some resolution of her early issues and achieve greater emotional stability and maturity.

Collectively, research on the factors associated with child neglect and other forms of maltreatment indicate that interventions and/or prevention efforts are most likely to be effective when they address both individual and environmental factors. Although families are sure to differ from one another, logical starting points for intervention include building parental knowledge and understanding of child development (including seeing through the eyes of the child), identifying and treating parental mental health problems, strengthening support systems, and supporting parents in reflecting on their own childhood with an eye toward choosing what to repeat and what to leave behind as they build a relationship with their child. These skills are components of the STEEP™ (Steps Toward Effective, Enjoyable Parenting) program, a relationship-based preventive intervention program we developed and evaluated in a randomized, controlled study in the 1980s. We continue to oversee implementation and evaluation of the program with various high-risk populations in the United States and abroad (Egeland & Erickson, 2003; Erickson & Egeland, 1999; Erickson, Egeland, Simon, & Rose, 2002; Erickson et al., 1992). When we developed STEEP, we believed that reaching out to expectant parents before they had a chance to fail—and while they were caught up in the excitement and anxiety around becoming a parent—would be the best opportunity to promote good parent-child relationships and prevent neglect and other forms of maltreatment.

Our research and experience convince us that once neglect occurs (especially emotional neglect), it often is very difficult to secure appropriate intervention services for the family. It is ironic that the impact of emotional neglect is most profound when it is least likely to be detected—when the child is too young to speak out. It is not surprising, however, that early neglect has such a strong negative influence—an infant's whole world revolves around his or her primary caregivers. It also seems ironic that unless the child shows clear physical signs of neglect (e.g., FTT), intervention is not likely to occur. In our longitudinal research, we reached out to prospective parents who had a variety of risk factors in their lives *before* their first child was born. Fortunately, the practice of reaching out early is now the norm in many preventive intervention programs, including Healthy Families America (Harding, Reid, Oshana & Holton, 2004) and the Nurse-Family Partnership (Olds et al., 1997).

It is our experience that it is easy to fall into a catch-22 situation: Neglectful families who may not qualify for mandated intervention also may be the most difficult to engage in voluntary service. Either their lives are extremely disorganized (as is often the case with the physically neglectful) or the parents are distancing and perhaps depressed (as is often the case with the emotionally neglectful). The same factors that make it difficult for parents to connect emotionally with their children also make it difficult for them to connect with service providers or other potential sources of support. If they feel that they are being judged as failures, parents may be even less inclined to connect with service providers.

Our research and experience tell us that the most effective approaches involve empathy and compassion for the parents' experience, even as we hold parents accountable for how they treat their children (Egeland & Erickson, 2003; Erickson et al., 2002). Just as parents need to see through their child's eyes, service providers need to see through the parents' eyes, recognizing what a challenge it is to overcome both current stressors and past relationship history in order to find new ways to parent.

Conclusion

Neglect is a major social problem. Research and experience make clear that neglect damages children's development. Neglected children, if they survive, often fail to develop the confidence, self-esteem, and social skills required to succeed in school and in relationships. Unless someone or something intervenes to make a difference, the behaviors these children bring to the classroom set them up for a continuing cycle of failure and disappointment.

Even subtle forms of emotional neglect can have a dramatic effect on children's development—especially during the early years of life. As discussed earlier, attachment theory provides a useful framework for understanding the impact of neglect. Attachment theory proposes that the infant's relationships with primary caregivers are the prototypes for subsequent relationships. Within those early relationships, children develop expectations about how others will respond and how effective they will be in soliciting the responses they need and want. Children behave in accordance with their expectations, and their behavior perpetuates the kind of relationships they have had. Thus, the child whose mother fails to respond to the child's signals eventually shuts down, no longer seeking or accepting contact with mother. When the child enters school, entrenched expectations and behaviors play out in the classroom, influencing learning, peer relations, and the response of teachers.

Emotionally neglected children expect *not* to get what they need from others, so they do not try to solicit care and warmth. They expect *not* to be effective and successful in tasks, so they do not try to succeed. For some emotionally neglected children, their dependence needs are so overwhelming that they lack the wherewithal to concentrate on other matters. Teachers and peers often are put off by these children's behavior, perpetuating the children's previous relationship experiences and reinforcing their negative expectations of others and self (Erickson & Pianta, 1989; Egeland & Erickson, 1999).

Neither preventive intervention with families at risk for neglect nor intervention with families identified as neglecting have been studied adequately. Although many researchers have seen promise in family support and early intervention programs, particularly programs that are comprehensive, individualized, and relatively long term, researchers point to only modest success even in the best programs (DuMont et al., 2008; Gaudin, 1993; Gessner, 2008; Holden & Nabors, 1999; Macmillan et al., 2005; Wekerle & Wolfe, 1993; Wolfe, 1993; Egeland, Weinfield, Bosquet, & Cheng, 2000). But research on the factors that predict neglect or characterize neglecting families provide useful information to guide and refine prevention and intervention approaches. Attachment theory and research—particularly expanding findings about parents' state of mind about their own attachment history—hold special promise for breaking intergenerational cycles of maltreatment, including neglect. We believe that as researchers and practitioners continue to work together to discover what helps build strong families, we will be increasingly successful in preventing harm not only to today's children but to their children and grandchildren.

References

Achenbach, T., & Edelbrock, C. (1980). *Child behavior checklist: Teacher's report form*. Burlington: University of Vermont.

Altemeier, W., O'Connor, S., Vietze, P., Sandler, H., & Sherrod, K. (1982). Antecedents of child abuse. *Journal of Pediatrics, 100*, 823–829.

Black, M. M., & Dubowitz, H. (1999). Child neglect: Research recommendations and future directions. In H. Dubowitz (Ed.), *Neglected children: Research, practice and policy* (pp. 261–277). Thousand Oaks, CA: Sage.

Boehm, B. (1962). An assessment of family adequacy in protective cases. *Child Welfare, 41*, 10–16.

Brachfield, S., Goldberg, S., & Sloman, J. (1980). Parent-infant interaction in free play at 8 and 12 months: Effects of prematurity and immaturity. *Infant Behavior in Development, 3*, 289–305.

Brassard, M., Germain, R., & Hart, S. (1987). *Psychological maltreatment of children and youth*. Elmsford, NY: Pergamon.

Brunnquell, D., Crichton, L., & Egeland, B. (1981). Maternal personality and attitude in disturbances of child rearing. *American Journal of Orthopsychiatry, 51*, 680–691.

Cicchetti, D., & Lynch, M. (1993). Toward an ecological transactional model of community violence and child maltreatment. *Psychiatry, 56*, 96–118.

Cicchetti, D., & Rogosch, F. A. (1997). The role of self-organization in the promotion of resilience in maltreated children. *Development and Psychopathology, 9*, 799–817.

Cicchetti, D., & Valentino, K. (2006). An ecological-transactional perspective on child maltreatment: Failure of the average expectable environment and its influence on child development. In D. Cicchetti & D. J. Cohen (Eds.), *Developmental psychopathology, Vol. 3: Risk, disorder, and adaptation* (pp. 129–201). New York: Wiley.

Claussen, A. H., & Crittenden, P. M. (1991). Physical and psychological maltreatment: Relations among the types of maltreatment. *Child Abuse and Neglect, 15*(1/2), 5–18.

Crittenden, P. M. (1985). Social networks, quality of child-rearing, and child development. *Child Development, 56*, 1299–1313.

Crittenden, P. M., & Ainsworth, M. D. S. (1989). Child maltreatment and attachment theory. In D. Cicchetti & V. Carlson (Eds.), *Child maltreatment: Theory and research on the causes and consequences of child abuse and neglect* (pp. 432–463). New York: Cambridge University Press.

Dozier, M., Stovall, K. C., Albus, K. E., & Bates, B. (2001). Attachment for infants in foster care: The role of caregiver state of mind. *Child Development, 72*(5), 1467–1477.

Dubowitz, H. (Ed.). (1999). *Neglected children: Research, practice and policy*. Thousand Oaks, CA: Sage.

Dubowitz, H., Black, M., Starr, R. H., & Zuravin, S. (1993). A conceptual definition of child neglect. *Criminal Justice and Behavior, 20*(1), 8–26.

DuMont, K., Mitchell-Herzfeld, S., Greene, R., Lee, E., Lowenfels, A., Rodriguez, M., et al. (2008). Healthy Families New York randomized trial: Effects on early child abuse and neglect. *Child Abuse and Neglect, 32*(3), 295–315.

Dunn, L. M., & Markwardt, F. C. (1970). *Peabody Individual Achievement Test*. Circle Pines, MN: American Guidance Service.

Egeland, B. (1988). Breaking the cycle of abuse: Implications for prediction and intervention. In K. D. Browne, C. Davies, & P. Stratton (Eds.), *Early prediction and prevention of child abuse* (pp. 87–99). New York: Wiley.

Egeland, B. (1997). Mediators of the effects of child maltreatment on developmental adaptation in adolescence. In D. Cicchetti & S. L. Toth (Eds.), *Rochester symposium on developmental psychopathology, Volume VIII: The effects of trauma on the developmental process* (pp. 403–434). Rochester, NY: University of Rochester Press.

Egeland, B., Carlson, E., & Sroufe, L. A. (1993). Resilience as process. *Development and Psychopathology, 5*(4), 517–528.

Egeland, B., & Erickson, M. F. (1987). Psychologically unavailable caregiving. In M. Brassard, B. Germain, & S. Hart (Eds.), *Psychological maltreatment of children and youth* (pp. 110–120). Elmsford, NY: Pergamon.

Egeland, B., & Erickson, M. F. (1999). Findings from the Parent-Child Project and implications for early intervention. *Zero to Three, 20*(2), 3–10.

Egeland, B., & Erickson, M. F. (2003). Lessons from STEEP™: Linking theory, research and practice for the well-being of infants and parents. In A. Sameroff, S. McDonough, & K. Rosenblum (Eds.), *Treating parent-infant relationship problems: Strategies for intervention*. New York: Guilford Press.

Egeland, B., Jacobvitz, D., & Sroufe, L. A. (1988). Breaking the cycle of abuse. *Child Development, 59*(4), 1080–1088.

Egeland, B., & Sroufe, L. A. (1981). Developmental sequelae of maltreatment in infancy. In B. Rizley & D. Cicchetti (Eds.), *New directions for child development: Developmental perspectives in child maltreatment* (pp. 77–92). San Francisco: Jossey-Bass.

Egeland, B., Sroufe, L. A., & Erickson, M. F. (1983). Developmental consequences of different patterns of maltreatment. *Child Abuse and Neglect, 7*(4), 456–469.

Egeland, B., & Susman-Stillman, A. (1996). Disassociation as a mediator of child abuse across generations. *Child Abuse and Neglect, 20*(11), 1123–1132.

Egeland, B., Weinfield, N. S., Bosquet, M., & Cheng, V. K. (2000). Remembering, repeating and working through: Lessons from attachment-based interventions. In J. D. Osofsky & H. E. Fitzgerald (Eds.), *Infant mental health in groups at high risk: WAIMH handbook of infant mental health* (Vol. 4, pp. 35–89). New York: Wiley.

Elder, G. H., & Conger, R. D. (2000). *Children of the land: Adversity and success in rural America*. Chicago: University of Chicago Press.

English, D., Upadhyaya, M., Litrownik, A., Marshall, J., Runyan, D., Graham, J., et al. (2005). Maltreatment's wake: The relationship of maltreatment dimensions to child outcomes. *Child Abuse and Neglect, 29*(5), 597–619.

Erickson, M. F., & Egeland, B. (1996). Child neglect. In J. Briere, L. Berliner, J. Bulkley, C. Jenny, & T. Reid (Eds.), *APSAC handbook on child maltreatment.* Thousand Oaks, CA: Sage.

Erickson, M. F., & Egeland, B. (1999). The STEEP™ program: Linking theory and research to practice. *Zero to Three, 20*(2), 11–16.

Erickson, M. F., Egeland, B., & Pianta, R. C. (1989). The effects of maltreatment on the development of young children. In D. Cicchetti & V. Carlson (Eds.), *Child maltreatment: Theory and research on the causes and consequences of child abuse and neglect* (pp. 647–684). New York: Cambridge University Press.

Erickson, M. F., Egeland, B., Simon, J., & Rose, T. (2002). *STEEP™ Facilitator's Guide.* Minneapolis: Irving B. Harris Training Center, University of Minnesota.

Erickson, M. F., Korfmacher, J., & Egeland, B. (1992). Attachments past and present: Implications for therapeutic intervention with mother-infant dyad. *Development and Psychopathology, 4,* 495–507.

Erickson, M. F., & Pianta, R. C. (1989). New lunchbox, old feelings: What kids bring to school. *Early Education and Development, 1*(1), 29–35.

Finkelhor, D. (2008). *Childhood victimization: Violence, crime, and abuse in the lives of young people.* New York: Oxford University Press.

Gardner, L. I. (1972). Deprivation dwarfism. *Scientific American, 22*(7), 76–82.

Gaudin, J. M. (1993). Effective intervention with neglectful families. *Criminal Justice and Behavior 20*(1), 66–89.

Gessner, B. (2008). The effect of Alaska's home visitation program for high-risk families on trends in abuse and neglect. *Child Abuse and Neglect, 32*(3), 317–333.

Giovannoni, J. (1989). Definitional issues in child maltreatment. In D. Cicchetti & V. Carlson (Eds.), *Child maltreatment: Theory and research on the causes and consequences of child abuse and neglect* (pp. 3–37). New York: Cambridge University Press.

Gowen, J. W., & Nebrig, J. B. (2002). *Enhancing early emotional development: Guiding parents of young children.* Baltimore: Paul H. Brookes Publishing.

Greenbaum, J., Dubowitz, H., Lutzker, J. R., Johnson, K. D., Orn, K., Kenniston, J., et al. (2008). *Practice guidelines: Challenges in the evaluation of child neglect.* Elmhurst, IL: American Professional Society on the Abuse of Children.

Hamburg, D. (1992). *Today's children: Creating a future for a generation in crisis.* New York: Times Books.

Hamre, B. K., & Pianta, R. C. (2001). Early teacher-child relationships and the trajectory of children's school outcomes through eighth grade. *Child Development, 72*(2), 625–638.

Harding, K., Reid, R., Oshana, D., & Holton, J. (2004). *Initial results of the HFA implementation study.* Chicago: National Center on Child Abuse Prevention Research, Prevent Child Abuse America.

Herrenkohl, E. C., Herrenkohl, R. C., & Egolf, M. (1994). Resilient early school-age children from maltreating homes: Outcomes in late adolescence. *American Journal of Orthopsychiatry, 64,* 301–309.

Hoffman-Plotkin, D., & Twentyman, C. T. (1984). A multimodal assessment of behavioral and cognitive deficits in abused and neglected preschoolers. *Child Development, 35,* 794–802.

Holden, E. W., & Nabors, L. (1999). The prevention of child neglect. In H. Dubowitz (Ed.), *Neglected children: Research, practice, and policy* (pp. 174–190). Thousand Oaks, CA: Sage.

Hufton, I. W., & Oates, R. K. (1977). Non-organic failure to thrive: A long-term follow-up. *Pediatrics, 59,* 73–77.

Katz, K. (1992). Communication problems in maltreated children: A tutorial. *Journal of Childhood Communication Disorders, 14*(2), 147–163.

Kempe, R., & Kempe, C. H. (1978). *Child abuse.* London: Lontana/Open Books.

Kempe, C. H., Silverman, F. N., Steele, B. F., Droegemueller, W., & Silver, H. K. (1962). The battered-child syndrome. *Journal of the American Medical Association, 181*(17), 17–24.

Kendall-Tackett, K. A., & Eckenrode, J. (1996, March). The effects of neglect on academic achievement and disciplinary problems: A developmental perspective. *Child Abuse and Neglect, 20*(3), 161–169.

Kotch, J. B., Lewis, T., Hussey, J., English, D., Thompson, R., Litrownik, A. J., et al. (2008). Importance of early neglect for childhood aggression. *Pediatrics, 121*(4), 725–731.

Lahey, B., Conger, R., Atkenson, B., & Treiber, F. (1984). Parenting behavior and emotional status of physically abusive mothers. *Journal of Consulting and Clinical Psychology, 52,* 1062–1071.

Luthar, S. S. (2006). Resilience in development: A synthesis of research across five decades. In D. Cicchetti & D. J. Cohen (Eds.), *Developmental psychopathology: Risk, disorder, and adaptation* (pp. 740–795). New York: Wiley.

Luthar, S. S., & Zelazo, L. B. (2003). Research on resilience: An integrative review. In S. S. Luthar (Ed.), *Resilience and vulnerability: Adaptation in the context of childhood adversitie*s (pp. 510–549). New York: Cambridge University Press.

MacCarthy, D. (1979). Recognition of signs of emotional deprivation: A form of child abuse. *Child Abuse and Neglect, 3,* 423–428.

Macmillan, H., Thomas, B., Jamieson, E., Walsh, C., Boyle, M., Shannon, H., et al. (2005). Effectiveness of home visitation by public-health nurses in prevention of the recurrence of child physical abuse and neglect: A randomized controlled trial. *Lancet, 365*(9473), 1786–1793.

Martin, H. P., & Beezley, P. (1977). Behavioral observations of abused children. *Developmental Medicine in Child Neurology, 19,* 373–387.

Martin, H. P., Beezley, P., Conway, E. F., & Kempe, C. H. (1974). The development of abused children. In I. Schulman (Ed.), *Advances in pediatrics* (Vol. 21, pp. 25–73). Chicago: Year Book.

McDonald, W. R., & Associates (1999). *Child maltreatment 1997: Reports from the states to the national child abuse and neglect data system* (DHHS Publication No. ACF10055951849). Washington, DC: U.S. Government Printing Office.

Mersky, J. P., & Reynolds, A. J. (2007). Child maltreatment and violent delinquency: Disentangling main effects and subgroup effects. *Child Maltreatment, 12*(3), 246–258.

Moran, P. B., & Eckenrode, J. (1992). Protective personality characteristics among adolescent victims of maltreatment. *Child Abuse and Neglect, 16,* 743–754.

Morse, W., Sahler, O. J., & Friedman, S. B. (1970). A three-year follow-up study of abused and neglected children. *American Journal of Diseases of Children, 120,* 439–446.

Newberger, C. M., & Cook, S. J. (1983). Parental awareness and child abuse: A cognitive developmental analysis of urban and rural samples. *American Journal of Orthopsychiatry, 53,* 512–524.

Newberger, E. H. (1973). The myth of the battered child syndrome. *Current Medical Dialog, 40,* 327–330.

Olds, D. L., Eckenrode, J., Henderson, C. R., Kitzman, H., Powers, J., Cole, R., et al. (1997). Long-term effects of home visitation on maternal life course and child abuse and neglect: Fifteen-year follow-up of a randomized trial. *Journal of the American Medical Association, 278*(8), 637–643.

Parke, R. D., & Collmer, C. W. (1975). Child abuse: An interdisciplinary analysis. In F. D. Horowitz (Ed.), *Review of child development research* (pp. 509–590). Chicago: University of Chicago Press.

Patton, R. G., & Gardner, L. I. (1962). Influence of family environment on growth: The syndrome of "maternal deprivation." *Pediatrics, 30*, 957–962.

Pianta, R., Egeland, B., & Erickson, M. F. (1989). The antecedents of maltreatment: Results of the Mother-Child Interaction Research Project. In D. Cicchetti & V. Carlson (Eds.), *Child maltreatment: Theory and research on the causes and consequences of child abuse and neglect* (pp. 203–253). New York: Cambridge University Press.

Polansky, N. A., Chalmers, M. A., Buttenwieser, E., & Williams, D. P. (1981). *Damaged parents: An anatomy of child neglect.* Chicago: University of Chicago Press.

Reidy, T. J. (1977). Aggressive characteristics of abused and neglected children. *Journal of Clinical Psychology, 33*, 1140–1145.

Reynolds, A. J., & Ou, S. (2003). Promoting resilience through early childhood intervention. In S. S. Luthar (Ed.), *Resilience and vulnerability: Adaptation in the context of childhood adversities* (pp. 436–459). New York: Cambridge University Press.

Sameroff, A. J., & Chandler, M. J. (1975). Reproductive risk and the continuum of caretaking casualty. In F. D. Horowitz (Ed.), *Review of child development research* (pp. 187–244). Chicago: University of Chicago Press.

Sameroff, A. J., & Feil, L. A. (1984). Parental concepts of development. In I. Sigel (Ed.), *Parental belief systems: The psychological consequences for children* (pp. 83–105). Hillsdale, NJ: Lawrence Erlbaum.

Sandgrund, A., Gaines, R., & Green, A. H. (1974). Child abuse and mental retardation: A problem of cause and effect. *American Journal of Mental Deficiency, 79*, 327–330.

Sedlak, A. J., & Broadhurst, D. D. (1996). *Executive summary of the third national incidence study of child abuse and neglect* (DHHS Publication No. ACF-105-94-1840). Washington, DC: U.S. Government Printing Office.

Smith, M. G., & Fong, R. (2004). *The children of neglect: When no one cares.* New York: Brunner-Routledge.

Sroufe, L. A., Egeland, B., Carlson, E. A., & Collins, A. (2005). *The development of the person: The Minnesota study of risk and adaptation from birth to adulthood.* New York: Guilford Press.

Steele, B. F. (1977, February). *Psychological dimensions of child abuse.* Paper presented to the American Association for the Advancement of Science, Denver, CO.

U.S. Department of Health and Human Services. (2010). *Child maltreatment 2008.* Washington, DC: U.S. Government Printing Office.

Vaughn, B., Deinard, A., & Egeland, B. (1980). Measuring temperament in pediatric practice. *Journal of Pediatrics, 96*, 510–514.

Wekerle, C., & Wolfe, D. A. (1993). Prevention of child physical abuse and neglect: Promising new directions. *Clinical Psychology Review, 13*(6), 501–540.

White, H., & Widom, C. (2003). Intimate partner violence among abused and neglected children in young adulthood: The mediating effects of early aggression, antisocial personality, hostility and alcohol problems. *Aggressive Behavior, 29*(4), 332–345.

Wolfe, D. A. (1985). Child-abusive parents: An empirical review and analysis. *Psychological Bulletin, 97,* 462–482.

Wolfe, D. A. (1993). Prevention of child neglect: Emerging issues. *Criminal Justice and Behavior, 20*(1), 90–111.

Yates, T. M., Egeland, B., & Sroufe, L. A. (2003). Rethinking resilience: A developmental process perspective. In S. S. Luthar (Ed.), *Resilience and vulnerabilities: Adaptation in the context of childhood adversities* (pp. 243–266). New York: Cambridge University Press.

Zuravin, S. J. (1999). Child neglect: A review of definitions and measurement research. In H. Dubowitz (Ed.), *Neglected children: Research, practice and policy* (pp. 24–46). Thousand Oaks, CA: Sage.

8 Psychological Maltreatment

Stuart N. Hart, Marla R. Brassard, Howard A. Davidson, Erin Rivelis, Vielka Diaz, and Nelson J. Binggeli

Psychological maltreatment (PM) consists of psychological abuse or neglect. PM can occur by itself or in association with physical abuse (PA), sexual abuse, or neglect. Research and experience indicate that the psychological dimension of PA, sexual abuse, and neglect is most damaging to children. Moreover, PM occurring alone is associated with negative effects of a severity equal to and sometimes greater than other forms of maltreatment. PM may be thought of as a unifying concept that embodies the most significant components of all forms of child maltreatment. The more forms of maltreatment children experience, the greater the likely negative consequences (Finkelhor, 2008; Finkelhor, Ormrod, & Turner, 2007; McGee, Wolfe, Yuen, Wilson, & Carnochan, 1995). Chapter 7 on neglect provides additional information on emotional neglect.

During early childhood and adolescence, PM in the forms of denying emotional responsiveness and isolation are the most damaging. In middle childhood, PA accompanied by PM in the form of verbal aggression (spurning) is the most harmful (Brassard & Donovan, 2006; Hart, Binggeli, & Brassard, 1998; see also Goleman, 1995, 2006).

The past quarter century witnessed significant growth in research on PM (Binggeli, Hart, & Brassard, 2000). The American Psychological Association (APA) designated PM a priority for research and public policy (Garrison, 1987). Researchers examined the long-term impact of childhood PM on adult functioning (Wright, 2008), as well as the psychological and health consequences of psychological abuse of adults by intimate partners (O'Leary & Maiuro, 2001). Significant progress has been made in defining PM, understanding its prevalence, and untangling the relationship of PM to various forms of dysfunction (Baker, 2009). Consensus has been achieved among experts on evaluation standards for suspected PM (American Professional Society on the Abuse of Children, 1995). Finally, research in the neurosciences is beginning to shed light on the impact of PM on the developing brain (Greenbaum et al., 2008).

Defining Psychological Maltreatment

Establishing an adequate definition of PM is a significant challenge. In the 1980s, lack of definition was *the* major impediment to progress in this area. To stimulate progress, the International Conference on Psychological Abuse of Children and Youth was held in Indianapolis, Indiana, in 1983. The conference was attended by professionals from eight countries and from virtually all the helping professions. The conferees produced the following definition:

> Psychological maltreatment of children and youth consists of acts of omission and commission, which are judged on the basis of a combination of community standards and professional expertise to be psychologically damaging. Such acts are committed by individuals, singly or collectively; who by their characteristics (*e.g.*, age, status, knowledge, and organizational form) are in a position of differential power that renders a child vulnerable. Such acts damage immediately or ultimately the behavioral, cognitive, affective, or physical functioning of the child. Examples of psychological maltreatment include acts of rejecting, terrorizing, isolating, exploiting, and missocializing. (*Proceedings Summary*, 1983)

Following the 1983 conference, research was undertaken to refine and elaborate the subtypes of PM (Baily & Baily, 1986; Brassard, Hart, & Hardy, 1993; Garbarino, Guttmann, & Seeley, 1986; Glaser, 2002; Hart & Brassard, 1986, 1989–1991; Hart, Germain, & Brassard 1987). This research culminated in the 1995 *Guidelines for Psychosocial Evaluation of Suspected Psychological Maltreatment of Children and Adolescents*, published by the American Professional Society on the Abuse of Children (APSAC). The guidelines begin with a broad definition: "'Psychological maltreatment' means a repeated pattern of caregiver behavior or extreme incident(s) that convey to children that they are worthless, flawed, unloved, unwanted, endangered, or only of value in meeting another's needs" (American Professional Society on the Abuse of Children, 1995, p. 2). The guidelines define six subtypes of PM: (1) spurning, (2) terrorizing, (3) isolating, (4) exploiting/corrupting, (5) denying emotional responsiveness, and (6) mental health, medical, and educational neglect. The APSAC definitions of PM have been subjected to empirical validation (Binggeli et al., 2000; Brassard & Donovan, 2006; Burnett, 1993; English &

LONGSCAN Investigators, 1997; Kairys & Johnson, 2002; Portwood, 1999; Trickett, Mennen, Kim, & Sang, 2009; Wright, 2008).

| **Table 8.1** | Psychological Maltreatment Forms |

A repeated pattern or extreme incident(s) of the conditions described in this list constitute psychological maltreatment (PM). Such conditions convey the message that the child is worthless, flawed, unloved, endangered, or only valuable in meeting someone else's needs.

SPURNING (hostile rejecting/degrading) includes verbal and nonverbal caregiver acts that reject and degrade a child. SPURNING includes

- belittling, degrading and other nonphysical forms of overtly hostile or rejecting treatment;
- shaming and/or ridiculing the child for showing normal emotions such as affection, grief, or sorrow;
- consistently singling out one child to criticize and punish, to perform most of the household chores, or to receive fewer rewards;
- public humiliation.

TERRORIZING includes caregiver behavior that threatens or is likely to physically hurt, kill, abandon, or place the child or child's loved ones/objects in recognizably dangerous situations. TERRORIZING includes

- placing a child in unpredictable or chaotic circumstances;
- placing a child in recognizably dangerous situations;
- setting rigid or unrealistic expectations with threat of loss, harm, or danger if they are not met;
- threatening or perpetrating violence against the child;
- threatening or perpetrating violence against a child's loved ones or objects.

ISOLATING includes caregiver acts that consistently deny the child opportunities to meet needs for interacting/communicating with peers or adults inside or outside the home. ISOLATING includes

- confining the child or placing unreasonable limitations on the child's freedom of movement within his/her environment and
- placing unreasonable limitations or restrictions on social interactions with peers or adults in the community.

EXPLOITING/CORRUPTING includes caregiver acts that encourage the child to develop inappropriate behaviors (self-destructive, antisocial, criminal, deviant, or other maladaptive behaviors) EXPLOITING/CORRUPTING includes

- modeling, permitting, or encouraging antisocial behavior (e.g., prostitution, performance in pornographic media, initiation of criminal activities, substance abuse, violence to or corruption of others);
- modeling, permitting, or encouraging developmentally inappropriate behavior (e.g., parentification, infantilization, living the parent's unfulfilled dreams);

(Continued)

Table 8.1	(Continued)

- encouraging or coercing abandonment of developmentally appropriate autonomy through extreme overinvolvement, intrusiveness, and/or dominance (e.g., allowing little or no opportunity or support for child's views, feelings, and wishes; micromanaging child's life);
- restricting or interfering with cognitive development.

DENYING EMOTIONAL RESPONSIVENESS (ignoring) includes caregiver acts that ignore the child's attempts and needs to interact (failing to express affection, caring, and love for the child) and showing no emotion in interactions with the child. DENYING EMOTIONAL RESPONSIVENESS includes

- being detached and uninvolved through either incapacity or lack of motivation;
- interacting only when absolutely necessary;
- failing to express affection, caring, and love for the child.

MENTAL HEALTH, MEDICAL, AND EDUCATIONAL NEGLECT includes unwarranted caregiver acts that ignore, refuse to allow, or fail to provide the necessary treatment for the mental health, medical, and educational problems or needs for the child. MENTAL HEALTH, MEDICAL, AND EDUCATIONAL NEGLECT includes

- ignoring the need for, failing, or refusing to allow or provide treatment for serious emotional/behavioral problems or needs of the child;
- ignoring the need for, failing, or refusing to allow or provide treatment for serious physical health problems or needs of the child;
- ignoring the need for, failing, or refusing to allow or provide treatment for services for serious educational problems or needs of the child.

Source: Hart, S. N., & Brassard, M. R. (1991, 2001). *Definition of psychological maltreatment.* Indianapolis: Office for the Study of the Psychological Rights of the Child, Indiana University School of Education.

Table 8.1 contains detailed definitions of the six subtypes of PM. To further illustrate the subtypes as they appear in clinical practice, we offer the following examples.

Spurning

Jose's dad publicly humiliated him by coming to soccer games and screaming at him whenever he would fail to get in the correct position, fail to hold on to the ball, fail to kick it accurately to a fellow player, etc. "You clumsy jerk! You poor excuse for a son! Can't you even pass!" he would bellow.

Marcia's mother engaged in spurning behavior when she ridiculed Marcia for showing normal emotions such as anger and sadness. The mother videotaped Marcia when Marcia was upset and forced her to watch the videotapes, pointing out how ridiculous she looked when she was angry or sad. Marcia's mother explained how she was helping Marcia because "good girls don't get angry. Good girls don't lose their composure."

Terrorizing

Lamar's mother knew her son was in the apartment when she fired a shot through the front door in an attempt to kill his father.

Frank's father secretly put tape recorders and surveillance cameras throughout the house. The father told Frank and his siblings when they had gone to the bathroom, who they had talked to on the phone that day, and any "bad things" they had said about him while he was at work. The children came to believe their father was omnipotent. They were terrified of him.

Isolating

Rita was an active baby. Rita's mother kept her strapped in her portable car seat most of the day because she would get underfoot when she was loose.

Detian's family homeschooled her and would not allow her to play with neighborhood children. She could only leave the house with her parents or older sister, and she was strictly forbidden to converse with any adults or children who were not family members. She was told that other people didn't share the family's beliefs and were of the devil.

Exploiting/Corrupting

Tito's mother exploited and corrupted him by keeping him out of school 1 to 2 days a week because she was lonely and wanted someone to keep her company while she drank. Tito would make sure his mother always had a cold beer at her side, would laugh at her boozy jokes, would rub her shoulders to relieve tension, and would make sure she had a comfortable cushion to support her bad back. Over time, Tito's mother encouraged him to drink beer to keep her company.

After Seth's father lost his job and the family home was lost to foreclosure, Seth's parents began a downhill slide into methamphetamine addiction. To help his parents obtain drugs, and to provide income for the family, Seth began selling drugs.

Denying Emotional Responsiveness

Baby Jose was fed and changed on a regular schedule, but his parents rarely interacted with him. When they did, they changed him or bathed him but without any expression of affection. There was no cuddling, little talking, and no eye contact.

Carolyn, age 9, had difficulty adjusting to her parent's divorce. Carolyn's parents agreed to have her seen by the school psychologist after her teacher raised concerns about her deteriorating grades, depressed mood, and her statement that she would be better off dead. Following Carolyn's visit with the psychologist, her parents made extra efforts to pay attention to her. Unfortunately, these efforts were short lived. Both parents fell in love with new partners. Mother took on a work assignment overseas that lasted several months. Carolyn's father's girlfriend dropped Carolyn off at an amusement park and did not pick her up at the arranged time. Carolyn was taken to the police station where her father picked her up later that evening. The father believed the girlfriend's version of events and blamed Carolyn for not being where she was supposed to be to be picked up. On numerous occasions, the girlfriend locked Carolyn out of the house. Once, the girlfriend forced Carolyn out of the car on a highway during an argument and left her standing on the side of a busy road. Carolyn's mother screamed at the father for the girlfriend's poor treatment of Carolyn, but the mother refused to cut short the overseas work assignment. Child protective services (CPS) became involved. To address CPS concerns, the father took control of Carolyn's care, placing her in a camp for the summer. Carolyn was noticeably depressed when school resumed in the fall. She did not want to go home following her after-school program because her mother often did not come home from work until 7:00 or 8:00 at night. Carolyn dreaded weekends with her father and his girlfriend.

Mental Health, Medical, and Educational Neglect

Helena's parents were neglectful of her mental health. She was a 15-year-old cutter with persistent suicidal ideation. Her parents refused both in-school counseling and out-of-school psychiatric treatment, claiming that she was just being manipulative with her behavior.

Leo and Bridget's mother was educationally neglectful. She homeschools them, but this consisted of intense involvement in the arts with no instruction in literacy and math. At age 10, Leo read on a second grade level and his writing was at a kindergarten level. Bridget, age 8, was illiterate. Despite pleas from the grandparents to enroll the children in school to ensure basic educational competencies, the mother was adamant that her schooling was sufficient—and in fact, preferable. The state had no money for monitoring the educational performance of children schooled at home. Educational neglect is also seen in the case of Tito (seen previously), whose mother kept him out of school to keep her company.

Isaac, a 4-year-old and the youngest of five children, was medically neglected by his parents. Despite good health insurance, he never had his required shots and his chronic ear infections were left untreated, giving him intermittent hearing loss and delaying his language development.

Prevalence of Psychological Maltreatment

The true prevalence of PM is unknown because most incidents go unreported. Estimates from the federal government range from a low of 58,577 children psychologically maltreated each year to a high of approximately 532,000 incidents per year (U.S. Department of Health and Human Services, 2008). Binggeli and colleagues (2000) reviewed the literature and estimated that more than one third of American children may experience some form of PM. Clearly, PM is widespread in the United States.

Impact of Psychological Maltreatment

Numerous studies identify adverse effects of PM (Hart et al., 1998; Binggeli et al., 2000; Brassard & Donovan, 2006). PM is related to

(1) problems of intrapersonal thoughts, feelings, and behaviors including anxiety, depression, low self-esteem, negative life views, self-criticism, and other negative cognitive styles that increase vulnerability to depression, immature defenses, and suicidal ideation (Briere & Runtz, 1988, 1990; Caples & Barrera, 2006; Clausen & Crittenden, 1991; Crittenden, Claussen, & Sugarman, 1994; Egeland & Erickson, 1987; Finzi-Dottan & Karu, 2006; Gibb, Chelminski, & Zimmerman, 2007; Gross & Keller, 1992; Herrenkohl, Egolf, & Herrenkohl, 1997; Herrenkohl, Herrenkohl, & Egolf, 1983; Herrenkohl, Herrenkohl, Egolf, & Wu, 1991; Herrenkohl, Herrenkohl, Toedter, & Yanushefski, 1984; Ney, Fung, & Wickett, 1994; Rohner & Rohner, 1980; Sachs-Ericsson, Verona, Joiner, & Preacher, 2006; Steinberg, Gibb, Alloy, & Abramson, 2003);

(2) emotional problem symptoms including emotional instability, impulse control problems, borderline instability, unresponsiveness, substance abuse, eating disorder problems, and more impaired functioning among individuals diagnosed with bipolar disorder (Braver, Bumberry, Green, & Rawson, 1992; Briere & Runtz, 1988; Crittenden et al., 1994; Engels & Moisan, 1994; Garno, Goldberg, Ramirez, & Ritzler, 2005; McCord, 1983; Mullen, Martin, Anderson, Romans, & Herbison, 1996; McLewin & Muller, 2006; Rohner & Rohner, 1980; Rorty, Yager, & Rossotto, 1994);

(3) social competency problems and antisocial functioning including attachment insecurity and disorganization, self-isolating behavior, low social competency, social phobia, low empathy, noncompliance, dependency, sexual maladjustment, aggression and violent behavior, and delinquency or criminality (Briere & Runtz, 1988, 1990; Brown, 1984; Claussen & Crittenden, 1991; Crittenden et al., 1994; Egeland & Erickson, 1987; George & Main, 1979; Glueck & Glueck, 1950; Herrenkohl et al., 1983, 1984, 1991, 1997; Hughes & Graham-Bermann, 1998; Lefkowitz, Eron,

Walder, & Huesman, 1977; Loeber & Stouthamer-Loeber, 1986; Main & George, 1985; Main & Goldwyn, 1984; McCord, 1983; Mullen et al., 1996; Rohner & Rohner, 1980; Rorty et al., 1994; Vissing, Straus, Gelles, & Harrop, 1991);

(4) learning problems including decline in mental competence, lower measured intelligence, noncompliance, lack of impulse control, impaired learning, academic problems and lower achievement test results, and impaired development of moral reasoning (Bilbro, Boni, Johnson, & Roe, 1979; Chan, 1981; Claussen & Crittenden, 1991; Crittenden et al., 1994; Egeland & Erickson, 1987; Erickson, Egeland, & Pianta, 1989; Hart & Brassard, 1991; Hoffman, 1970; Hughes & Graham-Bermann, 1998; Main & George, 1985; Main & Goldwyn, 1984; Manley, 1977; Rohner & Rohner, 1980; Sheintuch & Lewin, 1981; Starkey, 1980). Studies have found rejected children do less well than comparison children on achievement and intelligence tests (Bilbro et al., 1979; Chan, 1981; Manley, 1977);

(5) physical health problems are associated with PM, including allergies, asthma and other respiratory ailments, hypertension, somatic complaints, high infant mortality rates, and delays in almost all areas of physical and behavioral development (see Bowlby, 1951; Burlingham & Freud, 1944; Coleman & Provence, 1957; Goldfarb, 1945; Hughes, 1992; Jacobs, Spilken, & Noeman, 1972; Krugman & Krugman, 1984; McCord, 1983; McGinn, 1963; Miller & Baruch, 1948; Prugh & Harlow, 1962; Puckering et al., 1995; Spitz, 1945).

Theoretical Perspectives

Most of the major theories in psychology contain constructs that shed light on PM. Selected theories are described next (for detailed review see Bingelli et al., 2000).

Human Needs Theory

Human needs theory has particularly strong explanatory value for PM (Barnett, Manly, & Cicchetti, 1991; Binggelli et al., 2000; Hart et al., 1987; Hart, Brassard, & Karlson, 1996). Abraham Maslow (1970) proposed that humans have certain needs that must be met if the individual is to develop properly. The first set is the basic (or deficiency) needs, including physiological needs (food, clothing, and shelter) and the psychological needs of safety, love, belongingness, and esteem. The second set is growth needs, including needs for aesthetic and cognitive knowledge and for what Maslow termed "self-actualization." If a child is thwarted in the efforts to satisfy basic or growth needs, the child may be forced to meet these needs in unhealthy ways that distort development. For example, a child who has joined an antisocial gang to meet safety, belonging, and esteem needs may have done so primarily because those needs were not met in the family and neighborhood where the child was threatened with and subjected to beatings (terrorized), ignored and rejected (denied emotional responsiveness), and told he/she was stupid and worthless (spurned).

Psychosocial Stage Theory

Erik Erikson (1959) proposed that human development proceeds in stages. Each stage has its own tasks and conflicts. From birth to age 2, the young child grapples with trust versus mistrust. From age 2 to 4, the primary issue is autonomy versus shame and doubt. From 5 to 7 the focus is initiative versus guilt. The 8- to 12-year-old comes to grips with industry versus inferiority. During adolescence, the topic is identity versus identity confusion. The degree of success or failure at each stage affects the likelihood of success or failure at subsequent stages. PM can undermine a child's efforts to successfully master the tasks of a developmental stage. Poor resolution at one stage influences the child's ability to successfully complete later stages. For example, when a child's caregivers regularly scream at the child or others in the child's presence (terrorizing) or fail to sooth the child when the child is distressed (denying emotional responsiveness), the child may have difficulty trusting the world and may hesitate to reach out and experience the environment, undermining the child's development of autonomy.

Attachment Theory

The human infant enters the world programmed with a set of behaviors designed to elicit appropriate caregiving (Ainsworth, 1969, 1989; Bowlby, 1973, 1980, 1982, 1988; Sroufe, 1979). The development of attachment with a primary caregiver(s) is a vitally important task for the infant/ toddler period. The quality of that attachment has profound implications for emotional health and interpersonal functioning. A secure attachment with a responsive caretaker provides a "secure base" for the infant to explore the environment. Secure attachment facilitates a sense of trust and helps the young child achieve autonomy. Extensive research shows that infant/toddler attachment patterns are related to specific patterns of caretaker behavior (Ainsworth, Blehar, Waters, & Wall, 1978; Belsky, Rovine, & Taylor, 1984; Crittenden & Ainsworth, 1989; Goldberg, Perrota, Minde, & Corter, 1986; Grossman & Grossman, 1985; Main, 1996; Pearce & Pezzot-Pearce, 1994). Children who experience PM are disproportionately classified as anxiously attached or as experiencing disorganized attachment (e.g., Finzi, Ram, Har-Even, Shnit, & Weizman, 2001). Attachment is discussed in Chapter 7.

Parental Acceptance-Rejection Theory

This theoretical orientation was developed by Rohner and Rohner (1980) to clarify the nature of "emotional maltreatment" and to guide cross-cultural research on rejection. For Rohner and Rohner, "acceptance" means parental warmth and affection whereas "rejection" means emotional abuse, which is embodied in parental hostility, aggression, indifference, and neglect. Rohner and Rohner's research reveals a wide range of developmental problems possibly caused by rejection.

Additional Theories

In Patterson's coercion model (Patterson, 1982, 1986), problems with interpersonal relations arise out of a pattern of escalating negative interactions between individuals. The negative action of one person stimulates a negative response from the other, which, in turn, stimulates an escalating negative response. Through such dynamics, a rejected child may seek attention in irritating and disturbing ways that elicit more rejection. The child may adopt coercive strategies to accomplish goals. A degraded child may take on the identity and behaviors implied by the degrading statements of hostile rejection (e.g., liar, lazy, coward), exacerbating the rejection from significant adults.

The prisoner of war model compares the life of a child who experiences lengthy child abuse to the life of a prisoner of war (Benedek, 1985; Turgi & Hart, 1988). Like the prisoner, the chronically abused child may experience learned helplessness, chronic depressogenic thinking, high baseline physiological arousal, as well as posttraumatic stress disorder (PTSD).

The emotional security hypothesis (Davies, Harold, Goeke-Morey, & Cummings, 2002; Davies, Winter, & Cicchetti, 2006) argues that children interpret the occurrence of conflict in the home and conclude that the situation is deteriorating. The child experiences insecurity and distress.

Legal Intervention in Cases of Psychological Maltreatment

The law of every state defines child maltreatment and authorizes intervention by CPS and juvenile courts. It is relatively easy to define PA, sexual abuse, and physical neglect with the degree of precision that is necessary for legal intervention. PM, on the other hand, is challenging to define with the specificity required by law. Despite the difficulty, state laws attempt to define PM. Some laws require evidence of serious psychological injury or the likelihood of such injury before CPS may intervene. A few laws specify that the child's age, development, and culture should be considered. Some laws are very broad, allowing intervention whenever adults fail to provide for a child's mental or emotional needs. Florida's law specifies "isolation" as a form of PM. Hawaii includes "extreme mental distress" and "gross degradation." Vermont law requires a pattern of malicious behavior that results in a child's impaired psychological growth and development.

Every year, thousands of child maltreatment cases are commenced in juvenile courts. These cases accuse parents of physical neglect, PA, and sexual abuse. Very seldom are cases filed in which parents are accused *only* of PM. Despite the fact that PM is widespread and has consequences that can be just as serious as other types of maltreatment, very few juvenile court cases allege only PM. The government attorney who files the case nearly always accuses the parent(s) of some form of maltreatment *in addition* to PM. Attorneys are reluctant to allege only PM because this form of maltreatment can be difficult to prove in court. Thus, to increase the probability that the judge will approve intervention, the attorney alleges a type of maltreatment that is "easier" to prove. PM can "tag along" with the other form of maltreatment. Once intervention is approved, the judge has authority to order programs to reduce PM.

Despite the fact that PM seldom forms the sole basis for legal intervention, it is vital that child welfare attorneys and juvenile court judges receive training on the devastating effects of PM.

Investigation of Suspected Psychological Maltreatment

Investigation of suspected PM is complicated. The conclusion that a child has been psychologically maltreated requires a comprehensive investigation. General principles of investigation are discussed in Chapter 19. There is no psychological test that detects or diagnoses PM. Although there are self-report, collateral report, record review, and observational measures with good reliability and validity, these measures are not designed specifically for PM (for a review, see Brassard & Donovan, 2006). Clinical expertise is useful in the assessment of PM but is not always essential. APSAC (1995) published a framework for professionals evaluating children for the possibility of PM. The APSAC guidelines assist in case planning, legal decision making, and treatment planning.

PM is typically embedded in other forms of child abuse and neglect. Professionals are urged to look for signs of PM when investigating other forms of maltreatment (Trickett et al., 2009).

The professional conducting an investigation for PM takes numerous steps, including the following: (1) gather relevant information about what has been experienced, seen, heard, and reported about the suspected PM; (2) consult multiple sources (e.g., child, family, neighbors, relatives, school personnel); (3) utilize appropriate measures (e.g., interview, questionnaire, rating scale, observation, records review); (4) confer with other experts as needed; and (5) develop a comprehensive report describing the investigation and reaching conclusions.

Interventions With Child Victims and Maltreating Families

The past decade witnessed the development of a number of evidence-based psychological treatments for children and families affected by maltreatment and violence. Unfortunately, few evidence-based treatment programs directly address PM, and the few that do do so only tangentially. Yet, because PM is often embedded in other types of maltreatment, evidence-based treatments for other forms of maltreatment are sometimes useful with PM. Treatments that are relevant to PM often focus on disciplining effectively, managing problematic behavior, talking and playing with children, and building positive parent-child relations.

Parent-Child Interaction Therapy (PCIT) (Hembree-Kigin & McNeil, 1995) is a program in which parents receive step-by-step education on how to interact and play with their child. Coaching of the parent takes place by means of an electronic "bug in the ear." The parent is in one room with the child while the therapist/coach watches through a one-way mirror from an adjoining room. The therapist coaches the parent as the parent interacts with the child. Oftentimes psychologically maltreating caregivers' interactions with their children involve derogatory name-calling, ignoring, criticizing, threatening verbally, etc. PCIT assists parents in responding to their children with warmth, nurturance, and support through the techniques of reflective listening, prosocial interactions, and reduced criticism. PCIT teaches parents how to provide consistent consequences and contingencies for children's behavior. PCIT is described in Chapter 12.

Although including parents in the treatment of maltreated youth is important in changing behavior, there are times when including parents is contraindicated. Several treatment programs target externalizing symptoms in children and adolescents in individual or group modalities. As mentioned earlier, PM is associated with various externalizing behaviors including noncompliance and poor impulse control. A treatment program that helps with such behaviors is the Incredible Years Teacher Training Series. The series provides modules for teachers and for students, emphasizing prosocial behaviors and improved behavior management skills. The series has been effective in decreasing disruptive behavior at home and in the classroom, increasing the child's sense of empathy, and improving academic engagement. The series stresses positive reinforcement in the classroom and strengthening teacher–student relationships (Webster-Stratton, 2001). The series is designed on various levels of intervention whereby mental health professionals (e.g., psychologists, social workers, school counselors) choose the topics, participants, and types of behaviors to address in weekly sessions.

The Dina Dinosaur Social Skills and Problem-Solving curriculum is part of the Incredible Years Training Series. Dina Dinosaur uses a group or classroom format to promote positive peer interactions, conflict resolution skills, and social competence (Webster-Stratton, 1991).

Several programs target internalizing behaviors observed in psychologically maltreated youth. Treatment is designed to provide children with trusting compensatory relationships that model mutual respect and that teach the behavioral skills necessary to relate to others. The Primary Mental Health Project (Cowen et al., 1996) develops a positive relationship between children and a trained paraprofessional. The program targets internalizing behaviors common in maltreated children and focuses on building trust and mutual respect. The project has contributed to improved self-confidence, social problems solving, and a reduction in behavioral difficulties and shyness (Meller, LaBoy, Rothwax, Fritton, & Mangual, 1994).

Conclusion

Three subjects have arisen in the last few years, which could change the face of child protection and the manner in which PM is conceptualized and addressed. First is the ascendance of child well-being, development, and health as major purposes of child protection (Bennett, Hart, & Svevo-Cianci, 2009; International Institute for Child Rights and Development, 2008). Second is the emerging recognition of the need to infuse a child rights approach in child protection (Bennett et al., 2009; Hart, Cook, Madrid, & Svevo-Cianci, 2008). Third are the implications of genetic research, neuroscience, and social intelligence relative to psychosocial experience and development (Caspi et al., 2002; Davidson et al., 2003; Goleman, 1995, 2006; Kaufman et al., 2006; Kilpatrick et al., 2007; Mayer, Salovey, & Caruso, 2008; Rush et al., 2006). If these three topics are vigorously pursued in a coherent manner, they hold promise for moving child protection beyond its historically narrow focus on intervention to protect children. There is reason to hope that emerging biological, neurological, and psychosocial knowledge will advance respect for the child's holistic short- and long-term well-being and development. Such advancement would result in greater attention and support for preventing PM and promoting psychological well-being.

References

Ainsworth, M. D. S. (1969). Object relations, dependency, and attachment: A theoretical review of the infant-mother relationship. *Child Development, 40,* 969–1025.

Ainsworth, M. D. S. (1989). Attachments beyond infancy. *American Psychologist, 44,* 709–716.

Ainsworth, M. D. S., Blehar, M. C., Waters, E., & Wall, S. (1978). *Patterns of attachment: A psychological study of the strange situation*. Hillsdale, NJ: Erlbaum.

American Professional Society on the Abuse of Children (APSAC). (1995). *Guidelines for psychosocial evaluation of suspected psychological maltreatment of children and adolescents*. Elmhurst, IL: Author.

Baily, T. F., & Baily, W. H. (1986). *Operational definitions of child emotional maltreatment: Final report*. National Center on Child Abuse and Neglect (DHHD 90-CA-0956). Washington, DC: U.S. Government Printing Office.

Baker, A. J. L. (2009). Adult recall of childhood psychological maltreatment: Definitional strategies and challenges. *Children and Youth Services Review, 31*, 703–714.

Barnett, D., Manly, J. T., & Cicchetti, D. (1991). Continuing toward an operational definition of psychological maltreatment. *Development and Psychopathology, 3*, 19–29.

Belsky, J., Rovine, M., & Taylor, D. G. (1984). The Pennsylvania Infant and Family Development Project III: The origins of individual differences in infant-mother attachment: Maternal and infant contributions. *Child Development, 55*, 718–728.

Benedek, E. P. (1985). Children and psychic trauma: A brief review of contemporary thinking. In S. Eth & R. S. Pynoos (Eds.), *Posttraumatic stress disorder in children* (pp. 1–16). Washington, DC: American Psychiatric Association.

Bennett, S., Hart, S. N., & Svevo-Cianci, K. (2009). The need for a general comment for Article 19 of the UN Convention on the Rights of the Child: Toward enlightenment and progress for child protection. *Child Abuse and Neglect, 33*(11), 783–790.

Bilbro, T., Boni, M., Johnson, B., & Roe, S. (1979). *The relationship of parental acceptance-rejection to the development of moral reasoning*. Unpublished manuscript, University of Connecticut, Center for the Study of Parental Acceptance-Rejection.

Binggeli, N. J., Hart, S. N., & Brassard, M. R. (2000). *Psychological maltreatment: A study guide*. Thousand Oaks, CA: Sage.

Bowlby, J. (1951). Maternal care and mental health. *Bulletin of the World Health Organization, 31*, 355–533.

Bowlby, J. (1973). *Attachment and loss: Vol. 2. Separation: Anxiety and anger*. New York: Basic Books.

Bowlby, J. (1980). *Attachment and loss: Vol. 3. Loss*. New York: Basic Books.

Bowlby, J. (1982). *Attachment and loss: Vol. 1. Attachment* (2nd ed.). New York: Basic Books.

Bowlby, J. (1988). *A secure base: Clinical applications of attachment theory*. London: Routledge.

Brassard, M. R., & Donovan, K. L. (2006). Defining psychological maltreatment. In M. M. Feerick, J. F. Knutson, P. K. Trickett, & S. M. Flanzer (Eds.), *Child abuse and neglect: Definitions, classifications, and a framework for research* (pp. 151–197). Baltimore: Paul H. Brookes.

Brassard, M. R., Hart, S. N., & Hardy, D. B. (1993). The psychological maltreatment rating scales. *Child Abuse and Neglect, 17*, 715–729.

Braver, M., Bumberry, J., Green, K., & Rawson, R. (1992). Childhood abuse and current psychological functioning in a university counseling center population. *Journal of Counseling Psychology, 39*(2), 252–257.

Briere, J., & Runtz, M. (1988). Multivariate correlates of childhood psychological and physical maltreatment among university women. *Child Abuse and Neglect, 12*, 331–341.

Briere, J., & Runtz, M. (1990). Differential adult symptomatology associated with three types of child abuse histories. *Child Abuse and Neglect, 14*, 357–364.

Brown, S. E. (1984). Social class, child maltreatment, and delinquent behavior. *Criminology, 22*, 259–278.

Burlingham, D., & Freud, A. (1944). *Infants without families*. London: Allen & Unwin.

Burnett, B. B. (1993). The psychological abuse of latency age children: A survey. *Child Abuse and Neglect, 17*, 441–454.

Caples, H. S., & Barrera, M. (2006). Conflict, support and coping as mediators of the relation between degrading parenting and adolescent adjustment. *Journal of Youth and Adolescence, 35*(4), 603–615.

Caspi, A., McClay, J., Moffitt, T. E., Mill, J., Martin, J., Craig, I. W., et al. (2002, August 2). Role of genotype in the cycle of violence in maltreated children. *Science, 297*(5582), 851.

Chan, J. (1981). Correlates of parent-child interaction and certain psychological variables among adolescents in Hong Kong. In J. L. M. Dawson et al. (Eds.), *Perspectives in Asian Psychology*. Lisse: Swets & Zeitlinger.

Claussen, A. H., & Crittenden, P. M. (1991). Physical and psychological maltreatment: Relations among types of maltreatment. *Child Abuse and Neglect, 15*, 5–18.

Coleman, R. W., & Provence, S. (1957). Environmental retardation (hospitalism) in infants living in families. *Pediatrics, 19*(2), 285–292.

Cowen, E. L., Hightower, A. D., Pedro-Carroll, J. L., Work, W., Wyman, P. A., & Haffey, W. G. (1996). *School-based prevention for children at risk: The Primary Mental Health Project*. Washington, DC: American Psychological Association.

Crittenden, P. M., & Ainsworth, M. D. (1989). Child maltreatment and attachment theory. In D. Cicchetti & V. Carlson (Eds.), *Child maltreatment: Theory and research on the causes and consequences of child abuse and neglect* (pp. 432–463). New York: Cambridge University Press.

Crittenden, P. M., Claussen, A. H., & Sugarman, D. B. (1994). Physical and psychological maltreatment in middle childhood and adolescence. *Development and Psychopathology, 6*, 145–164.

Davidson, R. J., Kabat-Zinn, J., Schumacher, J., Rosenkranz, M., Muller, D., Santorelli, S. F., et al. (2003). Alterations in brain and immune function produced by mindfulness meditation. *Psychosomatic Medicine, 65*, 564–570.

Davies, P. T., Harold, G. T., Goeke-Morey, M. C., & Cummings, E. M. (2002). Child emotional security and interparental conflict. *Monographs of the Society for Research in Child Development, 67*(3), vii–viii. Chicago: University of Chicago Press.

Davies, P. T., Winter, M. A., & Cicchetti, D. (2006). The implications of emotional security theory for understanding and treating childhood psychopathology. *Development and Psychopathology, 18*(3), 707–735.

Egeland, B., & Erickson, M. (1987). Psychologically unavailable caregiving. In M. R. Brassard, R. Germain, & S. N. Hart (Eds.), *Psychological maltreatment of children and youth* (pp. 110–120). New York: Pergamon.

Engels, M. L., & Moisan, D. (1994). The psychological maltreatment inventory: Development of a measure of psychological maltreatment in childhood for use in adult clinical settings. *Psychological Reports, 74*, 595–604.

English, D. G., & LONGSCAN Investigators. (1997). Modified Maltreatment Classification System (MMCS). Available at: http://www.iprc.unc.edu/longscan/

Erickson, M. F., Egeland, B., & Pianta, R. (1989). The effects of maltreatment on the development of young children. In D. Cicchetti & V. Carlson (Eds.), *Child maltreatment: Theory and research on the causes and consequences of child abuse and neglect* (pp. 647–684). New York: Cambridge University Press.

Erikson, E. H. (1959). Identity and the life cycle: Selected papers. *Psychological Issue Monograph Series*, I (No. 1). New York: International Universities Press.

Finkelhor, D. (2008). *Childhood victimization: Violence, crime, and abuse in the lives of young people*. New York: Oxford University Press.

Finkelhor, D., Ormrod, R. K., & Turner, H. A. (2007). Re-victimization patterns in a national longitudinal sample of children and youth. *Child Abuse and Neglect, 31*(5), 479–502.

Finzi, R., Ram, A., Har-Even, D., Shnit, D., & Weizman, A. (2001). Attachment styles and aggression in physically abused and neglected children. *Journal of Youth and Adolescence, 30*(4), 769–786.

Finzi-Dottan, R., & Karu, T. (2006). From emotional abuse in childhood to psychopathology in adulthood: A path mediated by immature defense mechanisms and self-esteem. *Journal of Nervous and Mental Disease, 194*(8), 616–621.

Garbarino, J., Guttmann, E., & Seeley, J. W. (1986). *Psychologically battered child: Strategies for identification, assessment, and intervention*. San Francisco: Jossey-Bass.

Garno, J. L., Goldberg, J. F., Ramirez, P. M., & Ritzler, B. A. (2005). Impact of childhood abuse on the clinical course of bipolar disorder. *British Journal of Psychiatry, 186* (2), 121–125.

Garrison, E. G. (1987). Psychological maltreatment of children: An emerging focus for inquiry and concern. *American Psychologist, 42*(2), 157–159.

George, C., & Main, M. (1979). Social interactions of young abused children: Approach, avoidance, and aggression. *Child Development, 50*, 306–318.

Gibb, B. E., Chelminski, I., & Zimmerman, M. (2007). Childhood emotional, physical, and sexual abuse, and diagnoses of depressive and anxiety disorders in adult psychiatric patients. *Depression and Anxiety, 24*, 256–263.

Glaser, D. (2002). Emotional abuse and neglect (psychological maltreatment): A conceptual framework. *Child Abuse and Neglect, 26*, 697–714.

Glueck, S., & Glueck, E. (1950). *Unraveling juvenile delinquency*. New York: Harper & Row.

Goldberg, S., Perrota, M., Minde, K., & Corter, C. (1986). Maternal behavior and attachment in low birthweight twins and singletons. *Child Development, 57*, 34–46.

Goldfarb, W. (1945). Psychological privation in infancy and subsequent adjustment. *American Journal of Orthopsychiatry, 102*, 247–255.

Goleman, D. (1995). *Emotional intelligence: Why it can matter more than IQ*. New York: Bantam Books.

Goleman, D. (2006). *Social intelligence: The revolutionary new science of human relations*. New York: Bantam Books.

Greenbaum, J., Dubowitz, H., Lutzker, J. R., Johnson, K. D., Orn, K., Kenniston, J., et al. (2008). *Practice guidelines: Challenges in the evaluation of child neglect*. Elmhurst, IL: American Professional Society on the Abuse of Children.

Gross, A. B., & Keller, H. R. (1992). Long-term consequences of childhood physical and psychological maltreatment. *Aggressive Behavior, 18*, 171–185.

Grossman, K., & Grossman, K. E. (1985). Maternal sensitivity and newborns' orientation responses as related to the quality of attachment in northern Germany. In I. Bretherton & E. Waters (Eds.), Growing points in attachment theory and research (pp. 233–256). *Monographs of the Society for Research in Child Development, 209* (50, Parts 1 & 2).

Hart, S. N., Binggeli, N. J., & Brassard, M. R. (1998). Evidence of the effects of psychological maltreatment. *Journal of Emotional Abuse, 1*(1), 27–58.

Hart, S. N., & Brassard, M. R. (1986). *Developing and validating operationally defined measures of emotional maltreatment: A multimodal study of the relationship between caretaker behaviors and children characteristics across three developmental levels* (Grant No. DHHS90CA1216). Washington, DC: DHHS and NCCAN.

Hart, S. N., & Brassard, M. R. (1989–1991). Final report (stages 1 and 2). *Developing and validating operationally defined measures of emotional maltreatment: A multimodal study of the relationship between caretaker behaviors and children characteristics across three developmental levels* (Grant No. DHHS90CA1216). Washington, DC: DHHS and NCCAN.

Hart, S. N., & Brassard, M. R. (1991). Psychological maltreatment: Progress achieved. *Development and Psychopathology, 3,* 61–70.

Hart, S. N., & Brassard, M. R. (1991, 2001). *Definition of psychological maltreatment.* Indianapolis: Office for the Study of the Psychological Rights of the Child, Indiana University School of Education.

Hart, S. N., Brassard, M. R., & Karlson, H. C. (1996). Psychological maltreatment. In J. Briere, L. Berliner, J. A. Bulkley, C. Jenny, & T. Reid (Eds.), *The APSAC handbook on child maltreatment.* Thousand Oaks, CA: Sage.

Hart, S. N., Cook, P., Madrid, B., & Svevo-Cianci, K. A. (2008). *A child rights approach to child protection: The way forward to protect and promote child well-being, health and development.* Outline for position paper presented to the ISPCAN XV11 CONGRESS–Hong Kong September 10, 2008. Victoria, BC: IICRD.

Hart, S. N., Germain, R. B., & Brassard, M. (1987). The challenge: To better understand and combat psychological maltreatment of children and youth. In M. R. Brassard, R. Germain, & S. N. Hart (Eds.), *Psychological maltreatment of children and youth* (pp. 3–24). New York: Pergamon.

Hembree-Kigin, T. L., & McNeil, C. B. (1995). *Parent-child interaction therapy.* New York: Plenum Press.

Herrenkohl, R. C., Egolf, B. P., & Herrenkohl, E. C. (1997). Preschool age antecedents of adolescents' assaultive behavior: Results from a longitudinal study. *American Journal of Orthopsychiatry, 67*(3), 422–432.

Herrenkohl, R. C., Herrenkohl, E. C., & Egolf, B. P. (1983). Circumstances surrounding the occurrence of child maltreatment. *Journal of Consulting and Clinical Psychology, 51,* 424–431.

Herrenkohl, R. C., Herrenkohl, E. C., Egolf, V., & Wu, P. (1991). The developmental consequences of child abuse: The Lehigh longitudinal study. In R. H. Starr & D. A. Wolfe (Eds.), *The effects of child abuse and neglect: Issues and research* (pp. 57–80). New York: Guilford Press.

Herrenkohl, E. C., Herrenkohl, R. C., Toedter, L., & Yanushefski, A. M. (1984). Parent-child interactions in abusive and nonabusive families. *Journal of the American Academy of Child Psychiatry, 23*(6), 641–648.

Hoffman, M. L. (1970). Moral development. In P. H. Mussen (Ed.), *Carmichael's manual of child psychology* (Vol. 2). New York: Wiley.

Hughes, H. M. (1992). Impact of spouse abuse on children of battered women. *Violence Update, 2,* 8–11.

Hughes, H. M., & Graham-Bermann, S. A. (1998). Children of battered women: Impact of emotional abuse on adjustment and development. *Journal of Emotional Abuse, 1*(2), 23–50.

International Institute for Child Rights and Development. (2008). *Report of the International Child Protection and Rights Symposium, University of California–Davis, 9–11, March 2008.* British Columbia, Canada: IICRD–University of Victoria.

Jacobs, M., Spilken, A., & Noeman, M. (1972). Perception of faulty parent-child relationships and illness behavior. *Journal of Consulting and Clinical Psychology, 39,* 49–55.

Kairys, S. W., Johnson, C. F., & the Committee on Child Abuse and Neglect (2002). *The psychological maltreatment of children—Technical report.* Chicago: American Academy of Pediatrics, *109*(4), e68. Available at: www.pediatrics.org/cgi/

Kaufman, J., Yang, B., Douglas-Palumberi, H., Grasso, D., Lipschitz, D., Houshyar, S., et al. (2006). Brain-derived neurotrophic factor–5-HTTLPR gene interactions and environmental modifiers of depression in children. *Biological Psychiatry, 59*(8), 673–680.

Kilpatrick, D. G, Koenen, K. C., Ruggiero, K. J., Acierno, R., Galea, S., Resnick, H. S., et al. (2007). The serotonin transporter genotype and social support and moderation of posttraumatic stress disorder and depression in hurricane-exposed adults. *American Journal of Psychiatry, 164*(11), 1693–1699.

Krugman, R. D., & Krugman, M. K. (1984). Emotional abuse in the classroom. *American Journal of Diseases of Children, 138,* 284–286.

Lefkowitz, M., Eron, L., Walder, L., & Huesman, L. (1977). *Growing up to be violent: A longitudinal study of the development of aggression.* New York: Pergamon.

Loeber, R., & Stouthamer-Loeber, M. (1986). Family factors as correlates and predictors of juvenile conduct problems and delinquency. In M. Tonry & N. Morris (Eds.), *Crime and justice, an annual review of the research, 7,* 29–149. Chicago: University of Chicago Press.

Main, M. (1996). Introduction to the special issue on attachment and psychopathology: 2. Overview of the field of attachment. *Journal of Consulting and Clinical Psychology, 64*(2), 237–243.

Main, M., & George, C. (1985). Responses of abused and disadvantaged toddlers to distress in agemates: A study in the day care setting. *Developmental Psychology, 21*(3), 407–412.

Main, M., & Goldwyn, R. (1984). Predicting rejection of her infant from mother's representation of her own experience: Implications for the abuse-abusing intergenerational cycle. *Child Abuse and Neglect, 8,* 203–217.

Manley, R. (1977). Parental warmth and hostility as related to sex differences in children's achievement orientation. *Psychology of Women Quarterly, 1,* 229–246.

Maslow, A. H. (1970). *A theory of human motivation.* New York: Harper & Row.

Mayer, F. D., Salovey, P., & Caruso, D. R. (2008). Emotional intelligence: New ability or eclectic traits? *American Psychologist, 63*(6), 503–517.

McCord, J. (1983). A forty year perspective on effects of child abuse and neglect. *Child Abuse and Neglect, 7,* 265–270.

McGee, R. A., Wolfe, D. A., Yuen, S. A., Wilson, S. K., & Carnochan, J. (1995). The measurement of maltreatment: A comparison of approaches. *Child Abuse and Neglect, 19,* 233–249.

McGinn, N. F. (1963). Perception of parents and blood pressure. *Dissertation Abstracts, 24,* 872.

McLewin, L. A., & Muller, R. T. (2006). Attachment and social support in the prediction of psychopathology among young adults with and without a history of physical maltreatment. *Child Abuse and Neglect, 30*(2), 171–191.

Meller, P. J., LaBoy, W., Rothwax, Y., Fritton, J., & Mangual, J. (1994). *Community School District Four: Primary mental health project, 1990–1994.* New York: Community School District Four.

Miller, H., & Baruch, D. W. (1948). Psychosomatic studies of children with allergic manifestations: I, maternal rejection: A study of 63 cases. *Psychosomatic Medicine, 10,* 275–278.

Mullen, P. E., Martin, J. L., Anderson, J. C., Romans, S. E., & Herbison, G. P. (1996). The long-term impact of the physical, emotional, and sexual abuse of children: A community study. *Child Abuse and Neglect, 20*(1), 7–21.

Ney, P. G., Fung, T., & Wickett, A. R. (1994). The worst combinations of child abuse and neglect. *Child Abuse and Neglect, 18*(9), 705–714.

O'Leary, K. D., & Maiuro, R. D. (Eds.) (2001). *Psychological abuse in violent domestic relations.* New York: Springer.

Patterson, G. R. (1982). *Coercive family process.* Eugene, OR: Castalia.

Patterson, G. R. (1986). Performance models for antisocial boys. *American Psychologist, 41,* 432–444.

Pearce, J. W., & Pezzot-Pearce, T. D. (1994). Attachment theory and its implications for psychotherapy with maltreated children. *Child Abuse and Neglect, 18*(5), 425–438.

Portwood, S. G. (1999). Coming to terms with a consensual definition of child maltreatment. *Child Maltreatment, 4,* (1), 56–68.

Proceedings Summary of the International Conference on Psychological Abuse of Children and Youth. (1983, August). Indianapolis: Office for the Study of the Psychological Rights of the Child, Indiana University.

Prugh, D. G., & Harlow, R. G. (1962). Masked deprivation in infants and young children. In J. Bowlby (Ed.), *Deprivation of maternal care: A reassessment of its effects* (pp. 201–221). Geneva: World Health Organization.

Puckering, C., Pickles, A., Skuse, D., Heptinstall, E., Dowdney, L., & Zur-Szpiro, S. (1995). Mother-child interaction in the cognitive and behavioural development of 4 year old children with poor growth. *Journal of Child Psychology and Psychiatry and the Allied Disciplines, 36*(4), 573–595.

Rohner, R. P., & Rohner, E. C. (1980). Antecedents and consequences of parental rejection: A theory of emotional abuse. *Child Abuse and Neglect, 4,* 189–198.

Rorty, M., Yager, J., & Rossotto, E. (1994). Childhood sexual, physical, and psychological abuse in bulimia nervosa. *American Journal of Psychiatry, 151*(8), 1122–1126.

Rush, A. J., Karemer, H. C., Sackeim, H. A., Trivedi, M. H., Frank, E., Ninan, P. T., et al. (2006). Report of the ACNP Task Force on response and remission in major depressive disorder. *Neuropsychopharmacology, 31,* 1841–1853.

Sachs-Ericsson, N., Verona, E., Joiner, T., & Preacher, K. J. (2006). Parental verbal abuse and the mediating role of self-criticism in adult internalizing disorders. *Journal of Affective Disorders, 93*(1–3), 71–78.

Sheintuch, G., & Lewin, G. (1981). Parents' attitudes and children's deprivation: Child rearing attitudes of parents as a key to the advantaged-disadvantaged distinction in pre-school children. *International Journal of Behavioral Development, 4,* 125, 142.

Sroufe, L. A. (1979). The coherence of individual development: Early care, attachment, and subsequent developmental issues. *American Psychologist, 34,* 834–841.

Spitz, R. A. (1945). Hospitalism: An inquiry into the genesis of psychiatric conditions in early childhood. *The Psychoanalytic Study of the Child, 1*, 53–74.

Starkey, S. L. (1980). The relationship between parental acceptance-rejection and the academic performance of fourth and fifth graders. *Behavior Science Research, 15*, 67–80.

Steinberg, J. A., Gibb, B. E., Alloy, L. B., & Abramson, L. Y. (2003). Childhood emotional maltreatment, cognitive vulnerability to depression, and self-referent information processing in adulthood: Reciprocal relations. *Journal of Cognitive Psychotherapy, 17*(4), 347–358.

Trickett, P. K., Mennen, F. E., Kim, K., & Sang, J. (2009). Emotional abuse in a sample of multiply maltreated, urban young adolescents: Issue of definition and identification. *Child Abuse and Neglect, 33*, 27–35.

Turgi, P., & Hart, S. N. (1988). Psychological maltreatment: Meaning and prevention. In O. C. S. Tzeng & J. J. Jacobsen (Eds.), *Sourcebook for child abuse and neglect* (pp. 287–317). Springfield, IL: Charles C Thomas.

U.S. Department of Health and Human Services. (2008). *Child maltreatment 2006.* Washington, DC: U.S. Government Printing Office.

Vissing, Y. M., Straus, M. A., Gelles, R. J., & Harrop, J. W. (1991). Verbal aggression by parents and psychosocial problems of children. *Child Abuse and Neglect, 15*, 223–238.

Webster-Stratton, C. (1991). *Dinosaur social skills and problem-solving training manual.* Seattle: Incredible Years.

Webster-Stratton, C. (2001). *The Incredible Years: Parents, teachers, and children training series.* Seattle: Incredible Years.

Wright, M. O. (Ed.). (2008). *Childhood emotional abuse: Mediating and moderating processes affecting long-term impact.* Binghamton, NY: Haworth.

9 Neglect of Children's Health Care

Howard Dubowitz

Professionals concerned about maltreatment of children have focused on child physical and sexual abuse, paying less attention to child neglect (Wolock & Horowitz, 1984). There are several reasons why neglect has not received the attention it deserves (Dubowitz, 1994). First, the typically vague definitions of neglect make it an amorphous phenomenon (Greenbaum et al., 2008). Many professionals are understandably unclear about what constitutes neglect, how to identify neglect, and what course of action is appropriate and effective. Second, the strong association between child neglect and poverty (Giovannoni & Becerra, 1979) often evokes a sense of hopelessness among professionals, deterring them from becoming involved in the complex issues underpinning neglect situations. Thirdly, neglect does not evoke the horror and outrage of abuse. However, more than half of the reports for child maltreatment made in the United States each year are for neglect, and the morbidity and mortality associated with neglect are as severe as with abuse (e.g., Dong et al., 2004; Dubowitz, 2007; Teicher et al., 2004). This chapter focuses on one major form of neglect—neglect of children's health care. The chapter addresses the following: (1) definitional issues concerning neglected health care, (2) incidence, (3) etiology, (4) major manifestations, and (5) general principles for evaluation and (6) for intervention.

Legal aspects of neglect of children's health care are discussed in Chapter 22.

Defining Neglected Health

Neglect of health care occurs when children's basic health care needs are not met. This broad definition focuses on basic needs of children rather than on parental omissions in care (Dubowitz, Black, Starr, & Zuravin, 1993; Greenbaum et al., 2008). A basic health care need is a need that when it is not met jeopardizes or harms a child's health in a significant way (e.g., death of a child with diabetes due to lack of attention to medical recommendations)

(Geffken, Johnson, Silverstein, & Rosenbloom, 1992). Many situations do not, however, rise to the level of actual or potential harm (e.g., a missed follow-up appointment for an ear infection in a healthy child).

Implicit in the definition of neglect of health care is the likelihood that treatment will significantly benefit the child. If the benefit of treatment is uncertain (e.g., an experimental treatment for cancer), not receiving the treatment should not be construed as neglect.

The definition of neglect used in this chapter is based on a child's unmet needs, irrespective of what specific factors may contribute to the neglect. From the child's perspective, not receiving necessary care is neglect regardless of the reasons why such care is not provided. Contributing factors, however, are important for planning a response.

The broad definition of neglect of children's health care used here, with its focus on the child, differs from most legal definitions of neglect, which focus on parental failure to obtain medical care for their child. Child protective services (CPS) generally confine its involvement to such legal definitions, with its focus on parental failure.

The broad child-focused definition of neglect has several advantages over the narrow legal approach. The broad definition encourages us to consider the full array of possible contributory factors. Although parents are primarily responsible for their children's care, responsibility extends beyond parents to professionals, community agencies, and social policies, all of which influence children's health. In focusing on a child's needs rather than parental omissions, the broad definition is less blaming and more constructive.

There are several other important dimensions of neglect of children's health care: actual versus potential harm, short-term versus long-term harm, concern with physical and psychological outcomes, and a continuum of care. The following case helps illustrate many of these dimensions:

> Amy is a 6-year-old girl with severe asthma. She has been hospitalized four times in the past 2 years, twice in the intensive care unit. She was discharged from the hospital a week ago and given prescriptions for two medications. She comes to the office for follow-up and appears to be doing well. However, the prescriptions are not filled, and Amy has not received the recommended medications. Amy's mother explains that she is waiting to get her paycheck to fill the prescription. Amy is an only child who lives with her mother. After school, Amy's grandmother cares for her until her mother returns from work. There has been no contact with Amy's father in the past 3 years, and he makes no financial contribution to Amy or to her mother.

Actual Versus Potential Harm

Does there need to be actual harm for there to be neglect, or is the risk of harm sufficient? Most state laws include potential harm in their definitions of child abuse and neglect. CPS agencies, however, overwhelmed by the number of reports, often prioritize the more serious cases, and actual harm is usually viewed as more serious than potential harm. Excluding cases of potential harm is problematic, however, because the sequelae of neglect are often not immediate. In Amy's case, even though Amy appears to be healthy, her history of severe asthma indicates her vulnerability. Without the prescribed medications, her risk for recurrent asthmatic attacks is substantial. Severe asthma can be lethal. In Amy's case, not receiving the recommended medications constitutes neglect. The purpose of defining neglect is to ensure that children's health care needs are met. If we are interested in preventing neglect, a focus on actual harm risks being too narrow, too late.

Short-Term Versus Long-Term Harm

As stated above, the impact of neglect may not be immediately apparent, instead manifesting in the long term. Amy may be doing well today, but persistent failures in following recommendations jeopardizes her health and safety.

Physical and Psychological Outcomes

Our concern with children's health and well-being is a broad one. Accordingly, medical, dental, and mental health are all important aspects of health. Thus, a child is experiencing neglect if she has a history of hospitalizations due to severe dental or psychological problems and is not receiving prescribed medication or treatment. There could well be psychological problems related to Amy's asthma being inadequately treated.

A Continuum of Care

We artificially categorize cases as "neglect" or "not neglect" when the reality is that adequacy of care for basic needs falls on a continuum from optimal to grossly inadequate. The child welfare system is most often involved when we encounter situations that cross a threshold into "grossly inadequate." For example, few pediatricians would report Amy to CPS for neglect if the lapse in treatment occurred once or twice. More typically, neglect comes into focus when there is a pattern of repeated episodes that persist despite efforts to help and when harm results or is very likely to result.

Operationalizing the Definition
of Neglect of Children's Health Care

There are challenges to implementing the previous conceptual framework of neglect. How do we determine that a child's health is being neglected? Determining the adequacy of basic needs being met is at the core of assessing whether neglect exists. Epidemiological data guide us in some instances. For example, the risks associated with not wearing a bike helmet have been determined (Wesson, Spence, Hu, & Parkin, 2000), justifying a safety standard that children should wear helmets. Not doing so can be construed as neglect. In some cases, the child's history is informative, such as Amy's repeated hospitalizations for severe asthma, partly due to her not receiving prescribed medications. Finally, in some areas, common sense indicates that children's needs are being neglected (e.g., homelessness, hunger, lack of health insurance, and young children left alone).

There are instances when it is difficult to determine whether care is adequate (e.g., emotional support). The quality of care can be judged, but it is difficult to specify the threshold of adequacy. In general, neglect is considered only when there are serious inadequacies.

Although intermediate inadequacies may not meet a neglect threshold, they may nevertheless call for intervention. For example, the family of a child who has repeated hospitalizations for asthma may benefit from specific recommendations regarding strategies to maintain a smoke-free environment and identify early warning signs of asthma attacks.

Neglect should be considered when a child's condition can reasonably be attributed to a basic need not being met. For example, a child may have problems with diabetes control despite careful adherence to treatment. The disease may be inherently difficult to manage. Another issue concerns our knowledge (or lack thereof) as to what constitutes adequate care. For example, missing some doses of a course of antibiotics can still be adequate; 80% adherence to treatment for a streptococcal sore throat appears adequate to eradicate the infection (Olson, Zimmerman, & Reyes de la Rocha, 1985). Assessing neglect becomes still more complex when we recognize the variability among children and their needs. For example, one 10-year-old may be mature enough to be left alone briefly, but another may not.

How Do We Determine That a Child's Health Is Being Neglected?

Determining whether basic needs are met is at the core of assessing whether neglect exists. This section discusses factors that are relevant to this determination.

Severity

Severity is generally rated in terms of the actual or estimated potential harm as well as the degree of harm involved. For example, Amy's untreated asthma that results in admission to the intensive care unit would be rated as most severe, a regular hospital admission less so, a visit to the emergency department still less so, followed by mild symptoms not requiring professional attention, and, finally, no symptoms. Regarding potential harm, some risks entail only minor consequences, but others might be life threatening. Consideration of severity includes assessing the number of times the condition has occurred and its duration.

Likelihood of Harm

The likelihood of the harm occurring is important to consider. Missing a follow-up appointment for a child with eczema is very different from not seeking care for an infant who has been vomiting and had diarrhea for days. Both the potential medical and psychological ramifications should be considered. Although longitudinal research may help estimate the likelihood and nature of long-term outcomes associated with specific lapses in care (e.g., prenatal drug exposure), many neglectful situations are complicated by ongoing environmental challenges such as poverty.

Frequency/Chronicity

Neglect is usually inferred when there is a pattern of unmet needs. A dilemma arises regarding single or rare incidents that may constitute neglect. In some instances, omissions in care are unlikely to be harmful unless they are recurrent. For example, there may be serious risks for a child with a seizure disorder who repeatedly does not get medication but not if there is only an occasional lapse. However, an infant left unattended in a bath once, briefly, could drown. Thus, this single lapse could be construed as neglect. The intervention is likely to be different if there is a pattern of neglect.

Measuring the frequency or chronicity of a problem is difficult. In some instances, medical or pharmacy records show appointments not kept or prescriptions not filled. At times, parents or children may disclose how long they have had food shortages or problems accessing health care. In sum, neglect can be defined as occurring when a child's basic need is not met. Actual and potential harm are both of concern.

Incidence/Prevalence

It is difficult to estimate the extent of neglected health care. Health care providers do not identify many cases of health care neglect, and they may not report identified cases to CPS. In 2008, 71% of the 772,000 substantiated CPS reports were for neglect, <1% for medical neglect, 16% for physical abuse (PA), 9% for sexual abuse, and 7.3% for psychological maltreatment (PM). It should be noted that most states do not separately record medical neglect.

In 2008, it is estimated that 39.7% of fatalities were caused by multiple forms of maltreatment. Neglect was responsible for nearly 32% of fatalities

(U.S. Department of Health and Human Services, 2010). Most fatalities attributable to neglect were caused by lapses in supervision. One study documented 172 known deaths of children in the United States in which medical care was withheld on religious grounds; in most cases medical care would likely have saved their lives (Asser & Swan, 1998).

There is also research that focuses on societal neglect—that is, circumstances where children's basic needs are not adequately met due largely to gaps in services and inadequate policies and programs. For example, children's mental health needs are often not met (U.S. Department of Health and Human Services, 1999). One study of youth between ages 9 and 17 years found that only 38% to 44% of children meeting stringent criteria for a psychiatric diagnosis in the prior 6 months had had a mental health contact in the previous year (Leaf et al., 1996). Neglected dental care is widespread. For example, a study of preschoolers found that 49% of 4-year-olds had cavities, and fewer than 10% were fully treated. Another study found that 8.6% of kindergarteners needed urgent dental care (Tang et al., 1997). Neglected health care is not rare. If access to health care and health insurance is viewed as a basic need, then 8.7 million children experienced this form of neglect in 2006 (Cover the Uninsured, 2009).

Etiology

There is no single cause of child neglect. Belsky (1980) proposed an ecological theory of multiple and interacting factors at the individual (parent and child), familial, community, and societal levels. A toddler with a chronic, toxic blood lead level illustrates this theory. This child's health is being neglected by a lack of protection from lead and a lack of satisfactory treatment. Contributory factors may include the parents' unwillingness to allow treatment, the parents' inability to move to a lead-free home, a landlord's refusal to have the home deleaded, a city's inability to ensure an adequate lead abatement program, and society's limited investment in low-income housing. Understanding a neglectful situation requires an appreciation of all contributory factors so we can intervene optimally. Regardless of which contributory factors are responsible, a child with a high lead level experiences neglect.

Context—Society and Community

Context refers to the environment in which children live, including poverty, culture, and religion, as well as the community. The context shapes the attitude, knowledge, and behavior of parents and the quality of health care children receive. Poverty has been strongly associated with neglect: Neglect was identified 44 times more often in families with annual incomes under $15,000 compared with those earning above $30,000 (Sedlak &

Broadhurst, 1996). It should be noted, however, that most children raised in poor families do not experience neglect. They do, however, experience the adverse effects of poverty, arguably a form of societal neglect (Black & Krishnakumar, 1999).

Another aspect of context concerns culture and religion. Different cultures differ in their beliefs regarding health care. For example, children from Southeast Asia may receive the folkloric remedy of *Cao Gio* for a fever (Yeatman & Dang, 1980). A hard object is vigorously rubbed over the chest and may cause bruising. It is unclear whether this practice results in any benefit or significant harm, but there is the risk of not receiving appropriate care for a serious illness (e.g., meningitis). Some cultural differences are less dramatic, such as segments of the population that have little interest in psychotherapy. Variations in beliefs pose sensitive dilemmas as health care professionals strive to avoid an ethnocentric approach ("My way is right") and to respect cultural relativism (cultures differ and all should be accepted) (Korbin & Spilsbury, 1999). When a practice clearly harms children, and when good alternatives exist, society should ensure that children's needs for health care are adequately met.

Some parents hold religious views that are antithetical to Western medicine, believing in alternative approaches to health. For example, sick children may receive prayer from a Christian Scientist faith healer. Many illnesses (e.g., colds) are self-limiting, and satisfactory outcomes result regardless of treatment; other illnesses, however, can lead to serious harm without effective health care.

The community and its resources influence parent-child relationships and are strongly associated with maltreatment (Garbarino & Crouter, 1978). A community with a rich array of services such as parenting groups, child care, and good public transportation enhances the ability of families to nurture and protect children. Informal support networks, safety, and recreational facilities are important in supporting healthy family functioning. Families in a high-risk environment are less able to give and share and might be mistrustful of neighborly exchanges (Garbarino & Sherman, 1980). Neglect is strongly associated with social isolation (Polansky, Ammons, & Gaudin, 1985). In one large study, mothers of neglected children perceived themselves as isolated and as living in unfriendly neighborhoods (Polansky, Gaudin, Ammons, & Davis, 1985). In summary, communities can either offer valuable support to families or add to the stresses families experience.

Family

Disorganization of the home is characteristic of families of neglected children. Kadushin (1988) described chaotic families of neglected children, with impulsive mothers who repeatedly showed poor planning. Deficient problem-solving skills, poor parenting skills, and inadequate knowledge of children's needs are associated with neglect (Azar, Robinson, Hekemian, &

Twentyman, 1984; Herrenkohl, Herrenkohl, & Egolf, 1983; Jones & McNeely, 1980). The absence of fathers or their limited involvement in their children's lives may be factors in neglect (Dubowitz et al., 2001). Several studies have found more negative interactions between mothers and their young children in families of neglected children (e.g., Crittenden, 1988). Some cases of failure to thrive (FTT) are rooted in "a poor fit" between mother and child (Black, Feigelman, & Cureton, 1999). A child's passive or lively temperament may displease a parent. In addition, family problems such as spousal violence or lack of social support may contribute to a difficult parent–child relationship (Polansky et al., 1985; Wolock & Horowitz, 1979). In contrast, a supportive family can buffer the stresses that impair parenting, illustrating the importance of considering both risk and protective factors in assessing families for possible neglect.

Stress also has been associated with child maltreatment. One study found the highest level of stress—concerning unemployment, illness, eviction, and arrest—among families of neglected children, compared with abusive and control families (Gaines, Sangrund, Green, & Power, 1978). Lapp (1983) found stress to be frequent among parents reported to CPS for neglect, particularly regarding family relationships and financial and health problems.

Parents

Many of the characteristics of mothers of neglected children may contribute to children's health care needs not being met. Mothers' emotional problems, intellectual deficits, and substance abuse are associated with neglect. Emotional disturbances, especially depression, are found among mothers of neglected children (e.g., Polansky, Chalmers, Williams, & Buttenwieser, 1981). Intellectual impairment including mental retardation and a lack of education is associated with neglect (Kadushin, 1988; Martin & Walters, 1982; Wolock & Horowitz, 1979). High rates of substance abuse are found among families of neglected children (Ondersma, 2002). Maternal drug use during pregnancy has become a pervasive problem (Singer, 1999). Most illicit drugs pose definite risks to the fetus and child (Accornero et al., 2007). The compromised caregiving abilities of drug-abusing parents are a major concern.

Most decisions regarding children's health care are made by parents, including when to seek professional care. Crittenden's (1993) model helps refine our understanding of parental difficulties by considering four steps: (1) perception of the child's problem, (2) interpretation of the problem, (3) response, and (4) implementation. Difficulties at any of these steps may lead to unmet health care needs. The parent first needs to perceive the problem. Subtle signs such as decreased urination may go undetected. Inadequate knowledge about children and health and inappropriate expectations contribute to neglect. At times, parents may be in denial about a child's condition. Parents of neglected children are less knowledgeable about developmental milestones (Twentyman & Plotkin, 1982) and have limited knowledge about parenting, poor skills, and low motivation to be a good parent (Herrenkohl et al., 1983).

Parents may perceive the problem but interpret it incorrectly. For example, based on the parent's prior experience, a child's poor growth may seem normal. A parent may believe moodiness is common in children, unaware that children can be depressed. Popular interpretations of a symptom such as an infant crying because "he's spoiled" may lead to a problem being missed. Again, parents with limited cognitive abilities or emotional problems may have difficulty interpreting their child's cues, determining the care needed, and understanding and implementing the treatment plan.

After recognizing and interpreting the problem, parents choose their response. Initially, they may hope the problem will resolve spontaneously or with a home remedy. For example, parents may hope a small burn will heal without professional care—a reasonable assumption. If the condition deteriorates, only then may it be clear that medical care is needed. Such delays have been viewed suspiciously, but it is important not to misjudge reasonable delays. In considering delay, the context should be considered. If care was obtained at a point when a reasonable layperson could be expected to have recognized the need for professional help then it is not a neglectful situation. An inappropriate response, including delay, may result from inadequate knowledge, parental distress, and cultural or religious beliefs. For example, a depressed youngster may not receive psychotherapy if the parents hold such treatment in disdain.

Finally, the problem may be with implementing recommendations the family has received from health care providers. A parent's inaction may occur because the parent is distracted by other priorities (e.g., an eviction notice, obtaining drugs), depression, or difficulty accessing health care.

Other influences on parents' behavior may be useful for professionals to consider. Confidence in the remedy or in one's ability to implement the treatment is important (Liptak, 1996). Thus, a parent's belief that a medicine works enhances compliance. Motivation to address a health problem is important and may be influenced by the chronicity of the problem. With chronic problems, some parents become complacent. For all families, there is a need to balance many needs and to prioritize. For example, paying an electricity bill before filling a prescription may be appropriate in some circumstances. In other circumstances, however, such as Amy's asthma, the decision to delay implementing recommended treatment may place the child at risk, thereby constituting neglect.

Child

Children may contribute to their own neglect, directly and indirectly. A direct example is an adolescent's denial of diabetes, refusing to adhere to the treatment plan despite excellent efforts by caring parents. Some children give no or few cues that they need help. Children's age may influence perceptions of their vulnerability, with more concern directed to younger children. The unmet needs of adolescents may not evoke the same level of concern.

Belsky and Vondra (1989) described how children's health status could affect their parents' ability to provide care. For example, premature infants may require extended care in neonatal intensive care units, which may impair bonding and the baby's attachment to the parents. Caring for a child born with low birth weight can be challenging, and studies have found low birth weight to be a risk factor for neglect (Brayden, Altemeier, Tucker, Dietrich, & Vietze, 1992; Kotch et al., 1989).

Children with chronic health problems or disabilities have special needs that place them at added risk (Klerman, 1985). Many parents of such children are dedicated caregivers; others may be so stressed that they are unable to provide adequate care. Diamond and Jaudes (1983) found cerebral palsy to be a risk factor for neglect, but another study found no increase in maltreatment among 500 moderately to profoundly mentally retarded children (Benedict, White, Wulff, & Hall, 1990). Sullivan and Knutson (2000) found in a population-based study that disabled children were 3.4 times more likely to be identified as maltreated than nondisabled peers (9% vs. 31%). Families of children with special health care needs are often involved with multiple professionals, and increased surveillance may bias reports of neglect. A study found that children with mental health problems were at higher risk for maltreatment but not those children with developmental disabilities (Jaudes & Mackey-Bilaver, 2008). Overall, it appears that the special health care needs of children with disabilities may overwhelm some caring and competent parents, thus contributing to neglect (Klerman, 1985; Sullivan & Knutson, 2000).

The Disorder and the Treatment

The nature of the disorder may influence children's and parents' responses to recommendations or treatment (e.g., Liptak, 1996). For example, a disorder that is highly visible (e.g., an ugly rash) often evokes more of a response than a disorder that is not visible (e.g., lead poisoning). Children and parents who do not perceive that the disorder is serious or do not have confidence in the treatment are less likely to adhere to recommendations. Professionals can prevent neglect by ensuring that children and families are well informed about the disorder and the effectiveness of treatment.

The severity of symptoms makes a difference. Chronic health problems may be accepted without much alarm. For example, Amy's mother may accept that her daughter is a severe asthmatic who will periodically need to be hospitalized. This may be a valuable coping strategy, but undue complacency may result. Alternatively, a chronic and severe disease may evoke great distress that contributes to denial, such as is sometimes seen in adolescents with diabetes.

Neglect is also more likely to occur if the goals of treatment are not consistent with the goals of the child or family. For example, improving pulmonary function tests (a health professional's goal) may mean little to Amy, compared with being able to play sports (a child's goal). Thus, communication about the goals of the child and family and the impact of the disorder and treatment on those goals should help professionals frame the reasons for the treatment in a way that resonates with the goals of the child and family.

Concerns about side effects of treatment or doubts of its effectiveness may dissuade a parent from seeking care. Obesity is an example in which a parent may recognize the problem but be reluctant to engage in treatment that they see as burdensome. In addition to questions about the treatment, families may doubt their ability to implement recommended treatments. For example, the likelihood of neglect may be increased if a parent is anxious about injecting a child who has insulin-dependent diabetes. Professionals should help ensure that parents have both the competence and confidence to follow through with treatment.

The cost of treatment may contribute to the likelihood of neglect. For example, Amy's mother did not fill the prescriptions because she was waiting to receive her paycheck. Sensitive questioning is necessary to determine if a family is able to purchase recommended medications or to implement recommendations. When financial resources are a problem, professionals may consider less expensive options or look for strategies to minimize costs.

Poor communication may be a problem, with the treatment not being clearly conveyed or understood. Finally, simply remembering to take a medication several times in a busy day may be a challenge contributing to neglect. Working with families to help them incorporate recommended treatment into their daily routine helps families adhere to recommendations and avoid neglect.

The nature of health care includes the relationship between a professional and family (Gorski, 2000). Ideally, there is a relationship of mutual trust and respect. Families are more likely to follow recommendations if they have confidence that the recommendations are sound, will be beneficial, and are possible to implement. Without a trusting relationship, families may be discouraged from seeking help or from following recommendations. Ideally, pediatric primary care professionals focus on prevention to avoid serious health problems, including neglect. However, primary care professionals often have many issues to cover and not enough time, compromising their ability to offer comprehensive care. If the clinic or office is not perceived as friendly and supportive, families may feel discouraged from seeking care.

Manifestations of Neglected Health Care

This section discusses the more common forms of neglected health care.

Nonadherence (Noncompliance) With Health Care Recommendations

The most common form of neglected health care involves a lack of adherence with health care appointments, treatment, or recommendations, resulting in actual or potential harm (e.g., Amy not getting prescribed treatment).

Nonadherence with medical recommendations is common. For example, one study found that half of adolescents were nonadherent with medical regimens (Litt & Cuskey, 1980). Another study found only 25% of parents of children with attention deficit disorder adhered to the treatment plan; fewer than 10% consulted the physician before stopping medication (Firestone & Witt, 1982). The pervasiveness of noncompliance does not minimize its importance.

Noncompliance is not restricted to patients. Researchers have studied how well physicians manage medical conditions that have clear guidelines for treatment. Studies reveal that between 48% and 72% of doctors occasionally fail to adhere to treatment guidelines (Meichenbaum, 1989).

Failure or Delay in Seeking Health Care

Delay in seeking medical care for a child sometimes constitutes neglect. Consider this situation:

> Joe is a 10-month-old infant brought to the emergency department following 4 days of vomiting, diarrhea, decreased appetite, lethargy, and fever. On the second day, his father spoke with their pediatrician, who recommended an electrolyte solution, fever management, and follow-up if Joe's condition should worsen. The pediatrician mentioned that he would be leaving town for the holiday weekend, but a partner would be on call. Joe had had this problem once before, and it resolved after a few days. The emergency department staff found Joe to be at least 10% dehydrated and in need of admission to the intensive care unit. The staff were concerned that medical care had not been obtained earlier, raising a question of neglect.

Parents generally decide on the appropriate care for minor problems (e.g., a scrape, a cold, sadness at the death of a pet). As conditions become more serious, the need for professional care increases, and parents are responsible for seeking such care. Neglect occurs when necessary health care is not received or when delay is so significant that a child's health is harmed or jeopardized (e.g., Joe). The challenge for professionals is to understand what may be contributing to delay in seeking health care.

Joe's case highlights the importance of clear communication between professionals and caregivers. Although Joe's father contacted the pediatrician on the second day of his son's symptoms, Joe's prior recovery from similar symptoms, together with the holiday weekend, may have led to the decision to recommend home management without an office visit. Daily phone contact may have alerted the pediatrician to Joe's worsening condition prior to his need for hospitalization. Thus, Joe did not receive optimal care, although the family responded reasonably. The "system" was at fault.

Religiously Motivated Medical Neglect

Medical neglect can occur when parents actively refuse medical treatment. In some cases, parents believe an alternative treatment is preferable, perhaps because the treatment recommended by doctors is prohibited by their religion. For example, Jehovah's Witnesses, with their prohibition of blood transfusions, routinely refuse surgery when the need for transfusions is anticipated. Other religions, such as Christian Scientists, rely on faith healers and reject Western medicine.

Situations involving religious beliefs and children's health care can be difficult. How do we balance civil liberties, parental rights, and respect for religious belief against the medical needs of children? The principle of *parens patriae* establishes the state's authority to protect its young citizens. If a child's parents cannot or will not provide adequate care, the state must do so. However, 30 states have religious exemptions from their child abuse statutes. Such exemptions state, for example, "A child is not to be deemed abused or neglected merely because he or she is receiving treatment by spiritual means, through prayer according to the tenets of a recognized religion" (American Academy of Pediatrics, 1988, p. 169). These exemptions are based on the arguments of religious groups that the U.S. Constitution guarantees the protection of religious practice. This interpretation of the Constitution is challenged by court rulings prohibiting parents from martyring their children based on parental beliefs (*Prince v. Massachusetts*, 1944) and from denying them essential medical care (*Jehovah's Witnesses of Washington v. King County Hospital*, 1968). The American Academy of Pediatrics (AAP) has strongly opposed religious exemptions, arguing that the

> opportunity to grow and develop safe from physical harm with the protection of our society is a fundamental right of every child. . . . The basic moral principles of justice and of protection of children as vulnerable citizens require that all parents and caretakers must be treated equally by the laws and regulations that have been enacted by State and Federal governments to protect children. (American Academy of Pediatrics, 1988, pp. 169–171)

See Chapter 22 for discussion of the legal aspects of medical neglect.

Inadequate Food

Inadequate food may manifest as repeated hunger and may place a child at risk for impaired growth, including FTT. Although food insufficiency is related to poverty, more than half of food-insufficient individuals live in employed families. Hunger remains prevalent in the United States and may adversely affect children's growth and development. Inadequate food constitutes a serious form of neglect, and professionals should screen for food insufficiency by asking families if they have adequate food for their children.

FTT can result from inadequate nutrition. The etiology of FTT is multifactorial. The traditional classification of "organic" (i.e., medical) and "nonorganic" (i.e., psychosocial) FTT has limited usefulness; more often, there is a mixed etiology. Children with medical explanations for poor growth (e.g., celiac disease) often experience discomfort while eating and develop feeding problems. A psychosocial contribution should be considered regardless of the presence of a medical condition. In addition, psychosocial conditions should be implicated based on evidence, not simply by excluding medical causes (Black, Feigelman, & Cureton, 1999). Inadequate food in a context of psychosocial problems jeopardizes children's health and development (Mackner, Starr, & Black, 1997).

Obesity

Pediatric obesity has dramatically increased. Over 17% of American children have a body mass index (BMI) above the 95th percentile. There is a long list of complications of obesity during childhood and adulthood.

There are multiple contributors to obesity including genetic factors. Because environmental and family factors often contribute, some cases of morbid obesity may be a form of neglect in that the child's need for healthful food and physical activity is not being met. Not addressing the concern of obesity can constitute neglect, especially when a suitable program is available. In a 10-year study, children who were neglected (received little parent support) were sevenfold more likely to become obese as young adults than were children who were not neglected (Lissau & Sorensen, 1994).

Exposure to Environmental Hazards

The health risks associated with environmental hazards are firmly established. Hence, exposure to these hazards inside or outside the home is a form of neglect. Examples inside the home include poisonous substances and dangerous objects within easy reach of young children, smoking around children with pulmonary conditions (Gergen, Fowler, Maurer, Davis, & Overpeck, 1998), exposure to domestic violence (Sternberg, 1998) (see Chapter 10), and access to a loaded gun. Hazards outside the home include riding a bike without a helmet (Wesson et al., 2000), failure to use a car seat or seat belt (Stewart, 1997), and neighborhood violence (Osofsky, 1999). Exposure to lead may be a problem both in and out of the home (Tong, von Schirnding, & Prapamontol, 2000).

Drug-Exposed Newborns and Older Children

The prevalence of maternal drug use during pregnancy as well as high rates of substance abuse among families of neglected children were mentioned earlier.

In addition, use of illicit drugs and being raised in a drug-using environment jeopardize children's health and development.

The response to prenatal drug exposure varies. Chasnoff and Lowder (1999) describe responses ranging from inducements to engage in drug treatment all the way to criminal prosecution.

The use of legal but dangerous substances (e.g., tobacco, alcohol) during pregnancy also raises an important issue: Is such use neglect? Given our knowledge of the risks involved, it is probably not helpful to label use of these substances as neglect. At the same time, their use should be discouraged during pregnancy. Regarding older children, the risk of secondhand smoke, especially for children with pulmonary problems, is clear.

General Principles for Assessing Possible Neglect of Children's Health Care

The heterogeneity of neglect precludes specific recommendations for assessing all cases. The following general principles are intended to help guide assessment. Given the complexity and possible ramifications of determining whether a child is being neglected, an interdisciplinary assessment is ideal, including input from all professionals involved with the family.

1. Verbal children should be interviewed. Possible questions include: "Who do you go to if you're feeling sad?" "Who helps you if you have a problem?" "What happens when you feel sick?"

2. Do the circumstances indicate that the child's need(s) is not being adequately met? Is there evidence of actual harm? Is there evidence of potential harm and on what basis?

3. What is the nature of the neglect? Is it medical, mental health, dental, or inadequate food?

4. Is there a pattern of neglect? Are there indications of other forms of neglect or abuse? Has there been prior CPS involvement?

5. A child's safety is the paramount concern. What is the risk of imminent harm and of what severity?

6. What is contributing to the neglect?

7. What strengths/resources are there? Identifying strengths is as important as identifying problems.

8. What interventions have been tried and with what results?

9. Are other children in the household also being neglected?

10. What is the prognosis? Is the family motivated to improve the circumstances and accept help, or is there resistance? Are suitable resources, formal and informal, available?

General Principles for
Addressing Neglected Health Care

This section summarizes general principles for helping in cases of neglected health care.

1. Convey concerns to the family kindly but forthrightly. Avoid blaming. A positive relationship is critical for effective intervention.

2. Be empathic and state an interest in helping.

3. Address contributory factors, prioritizing those most important and amenable to being remedied (e.g., recommending treatment for a mother's depression). Parents may need *their* problems addressed before they can adequately care for their children.

4. Begin with the least intrusive approach, usually not CPS. For example, when faced with a child failing to thrive, an initial strategy might be to provide guidance on feeding and a suitable diet while closely monitoring the child's growth.

5. Consider the need to involve CPS, particularly when moderate or serious harm is involved and when less intrusive interventions have failed. If CPS is to be involved, present this fact to the parents as a necessary step to clarify what is occurring and what might be needed and as a way to get help for the child and the family.

6. Establish specific objectives (e.g., diabetes will be adequately controlled) with measurable outcomes (e.g., urine dipsticks, hemoglobin A1c). Similarly, advice should be specific and limited to a few reasonable steps. A written contract with parents can be helpful.

7. Engage the family in developing the plan; solicit their input and agreement.

8. Build on strengths. There are always strengths that provide a valuable hook to engage parents.

9. Encourage positive family functioning. Videka-Sherman (1988) described the need to focus on building positive family experiences, "not just controlling or decreasing negative interaction."

10. Encourage informal supports (e.g., family, friends, and fathers to participate in office visits). Informal supports are where most people get their support, not from professionals.

11. Consider support available through a family's religious affiliation.

12. Consider the need for concrete services (e.g., Medical Assistance, Temporary Assistance to Needy Families [TANF], Food Stamps) (Saudia, 1981).

13. Consider children's specific needs given what is known about the possible outcomes of neglect. Too often maltreated children do not receive direct services.

14. Be knowledgeable about community resources, and facilitate appropriate referrals.

15. Provide support, follow up, review progress, and adjust the plan as needed.

16. Recognize that neglect often requires long-term intervention with ongoing support and monitoring.

Advocacy Is Much Needed

Returning to the context in which neglect occurs, advocacy is needed at different levels: the individual child, parent, family, community, and society. Helping parents improve their children's treatment is advocacy on behalf of children who are unable to express or meet their own needs. Acknowledging the stress a parent feels and facilitating help are also advocacy. Professionals are often in a position to recognize service gaps in the community. By partnering with advocacy groups, professionals can work to secure additional resources for families to reduce the likelihood of neglect or provide services for children who have experienced neglect. Efforts to strengthen families and support the development of community resources are also forms of advocacy. Enhancing access to health care illustrates advocacy at the broadest level. Each of these levels of advocacy is valuable in addressing the problems underpinning the neglect of children's health care. In summary, professionals can play a pivotal role in ensuring children receive adequate health care and that they do not experience neglect.

Conclusion

Medical neglect can be a serious threat to children's well-being. Professionals have an opportunity to collaborate with families and with other professionals and agencies to ensure that children receive adequate care. Preventing neglect by educating families about children's health care needs and working with them to develop strategies for meeting those needs are critical roles for professionals.

References

Accornero, V. H., Amado, A. J., Morrow, C. E., Xue, L., Anthony, J. C., & Bandstra, E. S. (2007). Impact of prenatal cocaine exposure on attention and response inhibition as assessed by continuous performance tests. *Journal of Developmental and Behavioral Pediatrics, 28,* 195–205.

American Academy of Pediatrics (AAP). (1988). Religious exemptions from child abuse statutes. *Pediatrics, 81,* 169–171.

Asser, S., & Swan, R. (1998). Child fatalities from religion-motivated medical neglect. *Pediatrics, 101,* 625–629.

Azar, S., Robinson, D., Hekemian, E., & Twentyman, C. (1984). Unrealistic expectations and problem solving ability in maltreating and comparison mothers. *Journal of Consulting and Clinical Psychology, 52,* 687–691.

Belsky, J. (1980). Child maltreatment: An ecological integration. *American Psychologist, 35,* 320–335.

Belsky, J., & Vondra, J. (1989). Lessons from child abuse: The determinants of parenting. In D. Cicchetti & V. Carlson (Eds.), *Child maltreatment: Theory and research on the causes and consequences of child abuse and neglect* (pp. 153–202). New York: Cambridge University Press.

Benedict, M. I., White, R. B., Wulff, L. M., & Hall, B. J. (1990). Reported maltreatment in children with multiple disabilities. *Child Abuse and Neglect, 14,* 207–217.

Black, M. M., Feigelman, S., & Cureton, P. (1999). Evaluation and treatment of children with failure to thrive: An interdisciplinary perspective. *Journal of Clinical Outcomes Management, 6,* 60–73.

Black, M. M., & Krishnakumar, A. (1999). Predicting height and weight longitudinal growth curves using ecological factors among children with and without early growth deficiency. *Journal of Nutrition, 129,* 539S–543S.

Brayden, R., Altemeier, W., Tucker, D., Dietrich, M., & Vietze, P. (1992). Antecedents of child neglect in the first two years of life. *Journal of Pediatrics, 120,* 426–429.

Chasnoff, I. J., & Lowder, L. A. (1999). Prenatal alcohol and drug use and risk for child maltreatment. A timely approach to intervention. In H. Dubowitz (Ed.), *Neglected children: Research, practice, and policy* (pp. 132–155). Thousand Oaks, CA: Sage.

Child Welfare Information Gateway. (2009). *Child abuse and neglect fatalities: Statistics and interventions.* Available at: http://www.childwelfare.gov/pubs/fact sheets/fatality.cfm#children.

Cover the Uninsured. (2009). Available at: www.covertheuninsured.org.

Crittenden, P. M. (1988). Family and dyadic patterns of functioning in maltreating families. In K. Browne, C. Davies, & P. Stratton (Eds.), *Early prediction and prevention of child abuse* (pp. 161–189). London: Wiley.

Crittenden, P. M. (1993). Characteristics of neglectful parents: An information processing approach. *Criminal Justice and Behavior, 20,* 27–48.

Diamond, L. J., & Jaudes, P. K. (1983). Child abuse and the cerebral palsied patient. *Developmental Medicine and Child Neurology, 25,* 169–174.

Dong, M., Giles, W. H., Felitti, V. J., Dube, S. R., Williams, J. E., Chapman, D. P., et al. (2004). Insights into causal pathways for ischemic heart disease: Adverse childhood experiences study. *Circulation, 110,* 1761–1766.

Dubowitz, H. (1994). Neglecting the neglect of neglect. *Journal of Interpersonal Violence, 9,* 556–560.

Dubowitz, H. (2007). Fatal child neglect. In R. Alexander (Ed.), *Child fatality review.* St. Louis, MO: G.W. Publishers.

Dubowitz, H., Black, M., Starr, R., & Zuravin, S. (1993). A conceptual definition of child neglect. *Criminal Justice and Psychology, 20,* 8–26.

Dubowitz, H., Black, M. M., Cox, C. E., Kerr, M. A., Litrownik, A. J., Radhakrishna, A., et al. (2001). Father involvement and children's functioning at age 6: A multi-site study. *Child Maltreatment, 6,* 300–309.

Firestone, P., & Witt, J. E. (1982). Characteristics of families completing and prematurely discontinuing a behavioral parent-training program. *General Pediatric Psychology, 7,* 209–222.

Gaines, R., Sangrund, A., Green, A. H., & Power, E. (1978). Etiological factors in child maltreatment: A multivariate study of abusing, neglecting, and normal mothers. *Journal of Abnormal Psychology, 87,* 531–540.

Garbarino, J., & Crouter, A. (1978). Defining the community context of parent-child relations. *Child Development, 49,* 604–616.

Garbarino, J., & Sherman, D. (1980). High-risk neighborhoods and high-risk families: The human ecology of child maltreatment. *Child Development, 51,* 188–198.

Geffken, G., Johnson, S. B., Silverstein, J., & Rosenbloom, A. (1992). The death of a child with diabetes from neglect: A case study. *Clinical Pediatrics, 31,* 325–330.

Gergen, P. J., Fowler, J. A., Maurer, K. R., Davis, W. W., & Overpeck, M. D. (1998). The burden of environmental tobacco smoke exposure on the respiratory health of children 2 months through 5 years of age in the United States: Third National Health and Nutrition Examination Survey, 1988 to 1994. *Pediatrics, 101,* e8.

Giovannoni, J. M., & Becerra, R. M. (1979). *Defining child abuse.* New York: Free Press.

Gorski, P. A. (2000). Caring relationships: An investment in health? *Public Health Reports, 115,* 144–150.

Greenbaum, J., Dubowitz, H., Lutzker, J. R., Johnson, K. D., Orn, K., Kenniston, J., et al. (2008). *Practice guidelines: Challenges in the evaluation of child neglect.* Elmhurst, IL: American Professional Society on the Abuse of Children.

Herrenkohl, R., Herrenkohl, E., & Egolf, B. (1983). Circumstances surrounding the occurrence of child maltreatment. *Journal of Consulting and Clinical Psychology, 51,* 424–431.

Jaudes, P. K., & Mackey-Bilaver, L. (2008). Do chronic conditions increase young children's risk of being maltreated? *Child Abuse and Neglect, 32,* 671–681.

Jehovah's Witnesses of Washington v. King County Hospital, 278 F. Supp. 488 (Washington, DC, 1967), aff'd per curiam 390 US 598 (1968).

Jones, J. M., & McNeely, R. L. (1980). Mothers who neglect and those who do not: A comparative study. *Social Casework, 61,* 559–567.

Kadushin, A. (1988). Neglect in families. In E. W. Nunnally, C. S. Chilman, & F. M. Cox (Eds.), *Mental illness, delinquency, addictions, and neglect* (pp. 147–166). Newbury Park, CA: Sage.

Klerman, L. V. (1985). Interprofessional issues in delivering services to chronically ill children and their families. In N. Hobbs & J. M. Perrin (Eds.), *Issues in the care of children with chronic illness: A sourcebook on problems, services, and policies* (pp. 420–440). San Francisco: Jossey-Bass.

Korbin, J. E., & Spilsbury, J. C. (1999). Cultural competence and child neglect. In H. Dubowitz (Ed.), *Neglected children: Research, practice, and policy* (pp. 69–88). Thousand Oaks, CA: Sage.

Kotch, J., Browne, D., Symons, M., Ringwalt, C., Bentz, W., Evans, G., et al. (1989). *Stress, social support, and abuse and neglect in high risk infants.* Springfield, VA: U.S. Department of Commerce, National Technical Information Service.

Lapp, J. (1983). A profile of officially reported child neglect. In C. M. Trainer (Ed.), *The dilemma of child neglect: Identification and treatment.* Denver, CO: American Humane Association.

Leaf, P. J., Alegria, M., Cohen, P., Goodman, S. H., Horwitz, S. M., Hoven, C. W., et al. (1996). Mental health service use in the community and schools: Results from the four-community MACA Study. *Journal of the American Academy of Child and Adolescent Psychiatry, 35,* 889–897.

Liptak, G. S. (1996). Enhancing patient compliance in pediatrics. *Pediatrics in Review, 17,* 128–134.

Lissau, I., & Sorensen T. I. (1994) Parental neglect during childhood and increased risk of obesity in young adulthood. *Lancet, 343,* 324–327.

Litt, I. E., & Cuskey, W. R. (1980). Compliance with medical regimens during adolescence. *Pediatric Clinics of North America, 27,* 3–15.

Mackner, L. M., Starr, R. H., & Black, M. M. (1997). The cumulative effect of neglect and failure to thrive on cognitive functioning. *Child Abuse and Neglect, 21,* 691–700.

Martin, M., & Walters, S. (1982). Familial correlates of selected types of child abuse and neglect. *Journal of Marriage and the Family, 44,* 267–275.

Meichenbaum, D. (1989). Non-compliance. *Feelings and Their Medical Significance, 31,* 4–8.

Olson, R. A., Zimmerman, J., & Reyes de la Rocha, S. (1985). Medical adherence in pediatric populations. In N. Arziener, D. Bendel, & C. E. Walker (Eds.), *Health psychology treatment and research issues.* New York: Plenum.

Ondersma, S. J. (2002). Predictors of neglect within low socioeconomic status families: The importance of substance abuse. *American Journal of Orthopsychiatry, 72,* 383–391.

Osofsky, J. (1999). The impact of violence on children. *Future Child, 9,* 33–49.

Polansky, N., Ammons, P. W., & Gaudin, J. M., Jr. (1985). Loneliness and isolation in child neglect. *Social Casework, 66,* 38–47.

Polansky, N., Chalmers, M. E., Williams, D., & Buttenwieser, E. (1981). *Damaged parents: An anatomy of child neglect.* Chicago: University of Chicago Press.

Polansky, N., Gaudin, J. M., Jr., Ammons, P. W., & Davis, K. B. (1985). The psychological ecology of the neglectful mother. *Child Abuse and Neglect, 9,* 265–275.

Prince v. Massachusetts, 321 U.S. 158 (1944).

Saudia, C. (1981). What services do abusive families need? In L. Pelton (Ed.), *The social context of child abuse and neglect.* New York: Human Sciences Press.

Sedlak, A. J., & Broadhurst, D. D. (1996). *Third national incidence study/child abuse and neglect: Final report.* Washington, DC: National Center on Child Abuse and Neglect.

Singer, L. T. (1999). Advances and redirections in understanding effects of fetal drug exposure. *Journal of Drug Issues, 29,* 253–262.

Sternberg, K. J. (1998). Violent families. In M. E. Lamb (Ed.), *Parenting and child development in "nontraditional" families.* Mahwah, NJ: Lawrence Erlbaum.

Stewart, D. (1997). Motor vehicle occupant protection for children. *Injury Prevention, 3,* 312.

Sullivan, P. M., & Knutson, J. E. (2000). Maltreatment and disabilities: A population-based epidemiological study. *Child Abuse and Neglect, 24,* 1257–1273.

Tang, J., Altman, D., Robertson, D., O'Sullivan, D., Douglass, J., & Tinanoff, N. (1997). Dental carries prevalence and treatment levels in Arizona preschool children. *Public Health Reports, 112,* 319–331.

Teicher, M. H., Dumont, N. L., Ito, Y., Vaituzis, C., Giedd, J. N., & Andersen, S. L. (2004). Childhood neglect is associated with reduced corpus callosum area. *Biological Psychology, 56,* 80–85.

Tong, S., von Schirnding, Y. E., & Prapamontol, T. (2000). Environmental lead exposure: A public health problem of global dimensions. *Bulletin of the World Health Organization, 78*, 1068–1077.

Twentyman, C., & Plotkin, R. (1982). Unrealistic expectations of parents who maltreat their children: An educational deficit that pertains to child development. *Journal of Clinical Psychology, 38*, 497–503.

U.S. Department of Health and Human Services. (1999). *Mental health: A report of the surgeon general—executive summary*. U.S. Department of Health and Human Services, Substance Abuse and Mental Health Services Administration, Center for Mental Health Services, National Institutes of Health, National Institute of Mental Health, Rockville, MD.

U.S. Department of Health and Human Services. (2010). *Child maltreatment 2008*. Washington, DC: U.S. Government Printing Office.

Videka-Sherman L. (1988). Intervention for child neglect: The empirical knowledge base. In. A. Cowan (Ed.), *Current research on child neglect*. Rockville, MD: Aspen Systems Corporation.

Wesson, D., Spence, L., Hu, X., & Parkin, P. (2000). Trends in bicycling-related head injuries in children after implementation of a community-based bike helmet campaign. *Journal of Pediatric Surgery, 35*, 688–689.

Wolock, I., & Horowitz, H. (1979). Child maltreatment and maternal deprivation among AFDC recipient families. *Social Services Resource, 53*, 175–194.

Wolock, I., & Horowitz, H. (1984). Child maltreatment as a social problem: The neglect of neglect. *American Journal of Orthopsychiatry, 54*, 530–543.

Yeatman, G. W., & Dang, V. V. (1980). Cao Gia (coin rubbing): Vietnamese attitudes toward health care. *Journal of the American Medical Association, 244*, 2748–2749.

Child Maltreatment in the Context of Intimate Partner Violence

10

Sandra A. Graham-Bermann and Kathryn H. Howell

A significant number of children are exposed to violence in the home, including intimate partner violence (IPV), child abuse, corporal punishment, and violence in a relationship with a sibling (Carpenter & Stacks, 2009; Finkelhor, 2008). Historically, researchers in the areas of child abuse and IPV occupied different spheres of inquiry, used disparate sources of data, received funding from different agencies, reported results at different conferences, and published their work in different journals (see Graham-Bermann & Edleson, 2001). There is mandated reporting of suspected child maltreatment but not of IPV. Statistics on child abuse are collected in all 50 states, whereas states do not routinely document the number of IPV cases. Despite differences, researchers are paying increasing attention to the overlapping problems of child maltreatment and IPV.

Defining Exposure of Children to IPV

In the past, IPV has been used interchangeably with partner abuse, domestic violence, wife abuse, family violence, and interpersonal violence (Holden, 2003; Graham-Bermann & Brescoll, 2000; Jouriles, McDonald, Norwood, & Ezell, 2001). In this chapter, IPV refers to a pattern of assaulting and coercive behaviors that adults use against their intimate partners.

How do we define exposure of children to IPV? This is not a simple matter because exposure encompasses many experiences, not just direct observation of violence. Moreover, it is sometimes difficult to distinguish abuse of the mother from abuse of the child. Holden (2003) described several forms of childhood exposure to IPV: (1) prenatal violence, (2) a child's intervening in violence in an effort to stop it, (3) being directly victimized during violence against the mother, (4) participating in the assault on the mother, (5) being an eyewitness to violence, (6) overhearing violence, (7) observing the initial effects of violence, (8) experiencing the aftermath of violence, and (9) learning about a violent event.

Severe physical violence against women rarely occurs in isolation (Graham-Bermann, 1998; Straus, Hamby, Boney-McCoy, & Sugarman, 1995). Such violence is often accompanied by other forms of maltreatment of the woman, to which children may be exposed. Most children are exposed to more than one form of IPV. Further, children may be abused themselves when they try to stop the abuse of their mother.

Another definitional issue is whether exposing a child to IPV is itself a form of child maltreatment. Juvenile court judges agree that exposing children to IPV can constitute neglect (Myers, 2005). In a Florida neglect case, for example, a father exposed his children to IPV perpetrated against their mother (*D.W.G. v. Department of Children and Families*, 2002). The father argued that to constitute neglect, a child must actually see IPV. The Florida Court of Appeal disagreed, writing, "Children may be affected by domestic violence and may be aware of the violence, even if they do not see it occur with their own eyes" (*D.W.G. v. Department of Children and Families*, 2002, p. 242). In a few cases, men who exposed children to IPV were prosecuted for the crime of endangering the welfare of a minor (e.g., *People v. Johnson*, 2000). In Utah, it is a crime to commit "an act of domestic violence in the presence of a child" (Utah Criminal Code § 76-5-109.1[2][c]). Edleson (2004) articulates an argument against criminalizing exposure to IPV.

Exposure to IPV can constitute emotional child abuse (Trocmé & Wolfe, 2001). Emotional maltreatment is discussed in Chapters 7 and 8. Children coping with IPV often develop feelings of inadequacy, powerlessness, and helplessness (Wekerle & Wolfe, 2003). In one study, 52% of emotionally abused children who witnessed IPV developed posttraumatic stress disorder (PTSD).

Because of the overlapping nature of child maltreatment and IPV, it is important for child protection services workers (CPS) to safeguard children without stigmatizing or further endangering victimized women (Postmus & Ortega, 2005). In particular, CPS workers must understand that a woman's decision to disclose IPV can lead to further violence against her or the children.

Intentionality of Violence
That Is Observed or Experienced _____

It is clear that perpetrators of violence toward women intend to harm their victims. It is less clear whether abusers of adults intend to victimize the children who witness their violence. Regardless of intent, many children who observe IPV are injured on purpose or by accident during violent episodes. In a study of 221 children of abused women, 12% of the children were injured (Graham-Bermann, 2000). In some cases, batterers use children to manipulate the abused woman during the violent episode (Graham-Bermann, 2000; Jaffe, Poisson, & Cunningham, 2001).

Prevalence and Incidence of Co-occurring IPV and Child Abuse

In their groundbreaking epidemiological survey in 1975, Straus, Gelles, and Steinmetz (1980) disclosed the extent of violence in American homes, challenging the myth that the family is a haven of safety. Straus and his colleagues reported that people are more likely to be assaulted, beaten, or killed by their own family members than by outsiders. This disturbing fact is particularly true for children.

Surveys indicate that as many as 15.5 million children are exposed to IPV every year. Upwards of 7 million children are exposed to severe violence, meaning they witness a parent being beaten up, threatened with a gun or knife, stabbed, or shot (see McDonald, Jouriles, Ramisetty-Mikler, Caetano & Green, 2006). Young children appear to be disproportionately at risk for witnessing severe violence (Fantuzzo, Boruch, Beriama, Atkins, & Markus, 1997; Fantuzzo & Fusco, 2007).

When IPV occurs, children are eyewitness to most of it. Several studies documented that children were at home and present during IPV assaults 75% of the time (Hutchison & Hirschel, 2001). In one study of children exposed to IPV, mothers reported that their children witnessed all of the incidents of threats and mild violence. The children witnessed 78% of incidents of severe violence (Graham-Bermann, Gruber, Girz, & Howell, 2009).

Research from the last 20 years highlights the overlap between IPV and child maltreatment. Studies show a 30% to 60% co-occurrence between these two forms of family violence (Daro, Edleson, & Pinderhughes, 2004). Children who witness IPV in the home are 15 times more likely to be abused as compared to the national average (Osofsky, 2003). In a study of Head Start preschoolers, 50% of families experiencing IPV also experienced child abuse (Graham-Bermann, Habarth, & Howell, 2009).

The Evolution of Child Abuse in the Context of Intimate Partner Violence

Little is known about the development and timing of child abuse in the context of IPV. Stark and Flitcraft (1996) found that IPV usually predates abuse of the child. Stark and Flitcraft identified conditions associated with an abuser's concomitant maltreatment of the child to include dissolution of the marriage, separation, or a husband committed to dominance and control over family members (see Bowker, Arbitell, & McFerron, 1988).

Risk Factors for Co-occurring IPV and Child Abuse

Intergenerational Risk

One factor influencing the co-occurrence of child abuse and IPV is the mother's personal history of childhood abuse. Research shows that early physical abuse (PA) is related to higher levels of violence in the families of adult victims (Korbanka & McKay, 2000). One study compared the co-occurrence of child abuse and IPV, as well as the prevalence of child abuse and the parent's childhood history of abuse. Researchers analyzed data on 537 families who came to a community-based child abuse agency and found that 48.9% had experienced both child abuse and IPV. Further, 66.3% of parents had a childhood history of abuse and were also currently experiencing issues of abuse with their own children, highlighting the intergenerational transmission of violence (Folsom, Christensen, Avery, & Moore, 2003).

Researchers typically find an intergenerational transmission rate of 30%. The evidence shows that children from violent homes may become violent adults or may become the victims of violence in their adult relationships (Gelles & Cavanaugh, 2005). Longitudinal data reveal the astonishing statistic that children who are exposed to family violence are 189% more likely to experience violence in their own adult relationships (Amato, 2000).

Intrafamilial Risk

In addition to intergenerational risk factors influencing co-occurrence, research has examined characteristics of families that experience both IPV and child abuse. Families with co-occurrence of IPV and child abuse are more likely to be single-parent households, have fewer fathers biologically related to all of the children in the home, older mothers and older children, and more mothers with a history of alcohol and drug problems (Hartley, 2002).

Longitudinal research contributes to the understanding of familial factors associated with the co-occurrence of IPV and child abuse. Such research shows that IPV may impact a parent's cognitions about their child, which in turn may increase the likelihood of child abuse. To illustrate, McGuigan, Vuchinich, and Pratt (2000) evaluated 181 couples with firstborn infants and found that parents who experienced IPV in their child's first year of life developed significantly more negative cognitions about their child. These negative cognitions were experienced by both the women and the batterers. Such negative views of the child contributed to a significant increase in the likelihood of child abuse.

A final familial risk factor for co-occurrence of IPV and child abuse is substance abuse. Parental substance abuse or dependence is associated with increased risk for child abuse (Dore, Doris, & Wright, 1995). Although many perpetrators of IPV assault their partners without using alcohol, the temporal relationship between IPV and alcohol abuse has been amply demonstrated (Hartley, 2002). Less is known about the relationship between illicit drug use and IPV. In one study, the substance abuse of batterers was reported by women who received emergency treatment. Sixty-five percent of the batterers used both cocaine and alcohol at the time of the assault (Gondolf, 1993).

Environmental Risk

Beyond variables associated with the family unit, risk factors related to the co-occurrence of abuse and IPV exist in the broader environment (Tajima, 2004). Such factors include poverty, unemployment, neighborhood crime, financial stress, poor community health, and a lack of education (Herrenkohl, Sousa, Tajima, Herrenkohl, & Moylan, 2008; Tajima, 2004). Poor children of all ages are disproportionately affected by violence. General neighborhood disadvantage and community violence are particularly influential variables that have been connected with increased family violence (Margolin & Gordis, 2000).

Families from disadvantaged environments face particular challenges, including the difficulties of providing for children, managing child care, and negotiating public assistance hurdles (Heath & Orthner, 1999; Tigges, Browne, & Green, 1998). Such issues create significant stress within the home, often resulting in more emotional and physical violence. Taken together, adults who contend with risk factors within their home and their community are more likely to abuse each other and their children.

Age

Exposure to IPV and child abuse do not occur uniformly across the lifespan. Pregnancy is a time of heightened risk for IPV (Campbell & Parker, 1999). Abused women who are pregnant report that the target of violence is frequently the abdomen and, hence, the fetus (Seng et al., 2001). Upwards of 50% of abused women report being assaulted during pregnancy. Physical violence against pregnant women has been calculated at 154 of every 1,000 pregnant women up to the fourth month and 170 of every 1,000 pregnant women from the fifth to ninth months (Seng et al., 2001).

Young children are at greater risk for exposure to IPV than older children (Wolak & Finkelhor, 2001). To gather a broad base of data, the Spouse Assault Replication Program collected data from five cities from police officers and 2,402 female victims of misdemeanor IPV (Fantuzzo et al., 1997). When compared with census data from the same cities, IPV occurred disproportionately in households with children under age 5. Young children also were more likely to be exposed to multiple incidents of woman abuse and substance abuse than were children in older age groups. Younger age at the time of exposure to IPV is associated with more deleterious outcomes such as behavior problems in the clinical range and a higher prevalence of PTSD symptoms (Holden, Stein, Ritchey, Harris, & Jouriles, 1998; Lehmann, 1997).

A meta-analytic study by Sternberg, Baradaran, Abbott, Lamb, and Guterman (2006) reported that age moderated the effects of witnessing violence on children's externalizing behavior problems, with older children at greater risk for externalizing problems than younger children; however, children's age did not moderate the negative effects of IPV on internalizing problems. The authors suggested that older children may have more capacity to reflect on the meaning of violence and perhaps feel more anger or self-blame, which could account for the variations across different ages.

Gender

Are men or women more abusive toward children in the context of IPV? Research finds that male batterers abuse their children twice as often as abused women (Jouriles & Norwood, 1995). Furthermore, the severity of abuse to the woman is linked to the severity of abuse to the child (Straus & Gelles, 1990).

There is little evidence for gender differences in children's exposure to or reactions to IPV (Jaffe, Moffitt, Caspi, Taylor, & Arsenault, 2002; Sternberg et al., 2006). Boys from violent families have a higher risk of using abusive tactics in their teenage and young adult relationships (Pelcovitz et al., 1994). Girls who witness violence in the home are more likely to exhibit "internalized" behavior problems, including withdrawal and depression (Cummings, Pepler, & Moore, 1999; Fosco, DeBoard, & Grych, 2007). Both males and females are at risk for learning that violence is normal and as a result may be more likely to accept violence within their future families (Fantuzzo et al., 1991; Graham-Bermann, Lynch, Banyard, DeVoe, & Halabu, 2007; Grych, Jouriles, Swank, McDonald, & Norwood, 2000).

Outcomes Associated With
Co-occurring IPV and Child Abuse

IPV and child abuse are stressors on their own. When they combine, children experience multiple traumas. This is particularly concerning because as the number of adverse events accumulate, the risk for psychological problems grows. Such difficulties include mood and behavioral problems, bouts of intense fear, prolonged temper tantrums, sleep and eating problems, as well as regression in developmental achievements (Gewirtz & Edleson, 2007; Lieberman & Knorr, 2007). A meta-analysis of studies of the effects of children's exposure to IPV indicates that approximately 40% to 60% of school-age children exposed to IPV are in the clinical range on internalizing and externalizing behavioral problems such as anxiety, depression, and aggression (Wolfe, Crooks, Lee,

McIntyre-Smith, & Jaffe, 2003). Although there are fewer studies of young children and IPV, there is evidence associating IPV with decrements in preschoolers' development in areas of social behavior, academic performance, and physical and mental health (Graham-Bermann & Seng, 2005; McDonald, Jouriles, Briggs-Gowan, Rosenfield, & Carter, 2007).

Children growing up in violent homes show evidence of low self-esteem and difficulties in school (Graham-Bermann et al., 2009; Jaffe, Wolfe, & Wilson, 1990). These children also experience problems in interpersonal relationships, including heightened fears and worries about those in the home and difficulty establishing or maintaining friendships outside the home (Graham-Bermann, 1996). Of particular concern is the development of PTSD (Kilpatrick et al., 2003; Stover & Berkowitz, 2005). The prevalence of the disorders previously described is high, but the likelihood of experiencing subclinical symptoms and psychological distress is even higher (Levendosky & Graham-Bermann, 2000; Graham-Bermann et al., 2008).

Children respond differently to similar traumatic events. For example, although approximately 50% to 60% of preschool children exposed to IPV are found to be in the clinical range on internalizing and externalizing behavioral problems such as anxiety, depression, and aggression, many children do not show evidence of psychopathology at the time of assessment (Howell, Graham-Bermann, Czyz, & Lilly, in press). Whether children who appear unaffected will become symptomatic later—the so-called "sleeper effect"—is unknown.

Resilient Functioning

Despite the negative outcomes associated with witnessing IPV, upwards of 40% of children exposed to such violence are doing as well or better than children not exposed. Research on children who experience IPV shows that despite the experience, some children exhibit competent functioning and positive adjustment (Haskett, Nears, Ward, & McPherson, 2006; Jaffe, Caspi, Moffitt, Polo-Tomas, & Taylor, 2007). One meta-analytic review evaluating both child abuse and children exposed to family violence found that 37% of children who witnessed or personally experienced abuse fared as well as or better than children who were not exposed to such trauma (Kitzmann, Gaylord, Holt, & Kenny, 2003). Resilient children typically have less violence exposure, fewer fears and worries, and mothers with better mental health and parenting skills (Howell et al., in press; Graham-Bermann et al., 2009).

Interventions for Children Exposed to IPV

Programs have been designed to allay the negative effects of family violence on children, whether or not the child was directly assaulted. Many communities offer education, support, or intervention programs for children and abused women. Until recently, however, there has been little empirical evidence that these interventions help (National Research Council, 1998). Rigorous intervention studies are just beginning to be reported. Some of these studies show promising, if preliminary, results in improving the social, cognitive, and emotional functioning of children who experience violence.

The Kid's Club: A Preventive Intervention Program

The Kid's Club program was designed for children exposed to family violence (Graham-Bermann, 1992; Graham-Bermann et al., 2007). The Kid's Club is a 10-session intervention targeting 6- to 12-year-old children's knowledge about family violence, their attitudes and beliefs about families and family violence, their emotional adjustment, and their social behavior in a small group setting.

A parenting component empowers mothers to discuss the impact of violence on various areas of the child's development, build parenting competence, provide a safe place to discuss fears and worries, and build self-esteem in the context of a supportive group (Graham-Bermann & Levendosky, 1994). The intervention was designed to improve parenting skills, including discipline strategies, as well as enhance social and emotional adjustment.

A study of 221 families participating in The Kid's Club program represents the largest intervention evaluation to date for children of abused women (see Graham-Bermann, 2000). Preintervention and postintervention and 8-month follow-up assessments were made with regard to several areas of child functioning. Children exposed to high levels of IPV were randomly assigned to participate in a child-only intervention, a child-plus-mother intervention, or a comparison group that received "normal" services for 10 weeks.

For children who received the intervention, significant change from baseline was found in knowledge about violence, safety planning, social skills, emotion regulation, and emotional/behavioral domains (internalizing and externalizing behaviors). When mothers and children both received the intervention, effects in all areas were greater than when only the children were the focus of intervention. Children who received the intervention made more progress than did children in the control group (Graham-Bermann, 1998).

Interventions That Focus on Parenting

Two other programs address parenting, with an emphasis on managing the child's aggressive behavior (Jouriles et al., 1998). Jouriles and colleagues (1998) implemented a home-based program modeled on the work of Patterson (1986). The intervention was designed for abused women leaving shelters and their young children with high levels of conduct problems. Prescreening was used to identify children with clinical levels of aggression. Support and training were provided to the mother (e.g., problem-solving skills, parenting practices), and mentoring and support were given to the child. Outcome data for

18 families with 8-month follow-up indicated success in reducing conduct problems and enhancing mothers' parenting skills and coping.

Lieberman, Van Horn, and Ippen (2005) designed and tested a 50-week psychotherapy program for abused women and their preschool-age children. The aims of the program were to reduce traumatic stress and improve behavior for these children. Results showed that the program significantly reduced children's adjustment problems.

Community Detection and Prevention

Many different community agencies are involved in detecting and preventing IPV and child abuse, including CPS, law enforcement, the court system, domestic violence agencies, and medicine. Ideally, these providers coordinate to offer comprehensive services to victimized families.

Family physicians are often at the front line in identification of child trauma, including exposure to IPV and child abuse. Yet, many general practice doctors do not routinely inquire about both IPV and child maltreatment. Pediatricians may be in the best position to identify these stressors at an early stage and refer families to treatment resources. Pediatricians can coordinate with mental health providers to offer responsive services to families who experience violence in the home (Lieberman & Knorr, 2007).

CPS workers understand the co-occurrence of IPV and child abuse. Although social workers are aware of the issue, only about half say they perform systematic screenings for IPV in all cases of child abuse (Bourassa, Lavergne, Damant, Lessard, & Turcotte, 2006). The main obstacles to IPV detection include the abused woman's denial, lack of evidence, large caseloads, and failure of cooperation between service providers and victims.

Researchers in New York City implemented an IPV questionnaire for use with families reporting child abuse (Magen, Conroy, Hess, Panciera, & Simon, 2001). When the questionnaire was used, twice as many battered women were identified.

The Greenbook Project (Edleson & Malik, 2008) identifies interventions designed to create safety, increase well-being, and offer stability for families exposed to violence in the home. The Greenbook Project's focus is on coordinating services through child protection agencies, IPV prevention services, and juvenile/family courts. Once a child is identified as exposed to IPV, the Greenbook Project recommends: (1) keeping the child in the care of the non-offending parent, (2) developing a community service system with professionals trained to respond quickly and respectfully, and (3) providing a flexible response that covers the diverse range of family experiences (Edleson & Malik, 2008).

Conclusion

Greater funding is needed to establish a variety of interventions for children exposed to co-occurring IPV and child abuse. Comparative and longitudinal studies should be undertaken to establish the efficacy of interventions in different settings (e.g., shelters for abused women, community mental health programs, and schools) and for different groups of children. For example, children who are harmed by exposure to these potentially traumatic events require interventions that are different from interventions for children who show greater resilience. Yet, even resilient children may benefit from programs designed to prevent symptoms from appearing at a later date.

It is evident that programs targeted at preventing both IPV and child abuse must be developed and funded. If violence can be reduced, we can lessen the need for services. As communities work to identify families at risk and to provide education and screening for frontline workers, we hope children can escape the negative outcomes associated with dual victimization.

References

Amato, P. R. (2000). The consequences of divorce for adults and children. *Journal of Marriage and the Family, 62*, 1269–1287.

Bourassa, C., Lavergne, C., Damant, D., Lessard, G., & Turcotte, P. (2006). Awareness and detection of the co-occurrence of interparental violence and child abuse: Child welfare worker's perspective. *Children and Youth Services Review, 28*, 1312–1328.

Bowker, L. H., Arbitell, M., & McFerron, J. R. (1988). On the relationship between wife beating and child abuse. In K. Yllö & M. Bograd (Eds.), *Perspectives on wife abuse* (pp. 158–174). Newbury Park, CA: Sage.

Campbell, J., & Parker, B. (1999). Clinical nursing research on battered women and their children: A review. In A. S. Hinshaw, S. Feetham, & J. Shaver (Eds.), *Handbook of clinical nursing research* (pp. 535–559). Thousand Oaks, CA: Sage.

Carpenter, G. L., & Stacks, A. M. (2009). Developmental effects of exposure to intimate partner violence in early childhood: A review of the literature. *Children and Youth Services Review, 31*, 831–839.

Cummings, E. M., Pepler, D. J., & Moore, T. E. (1999). Behavior problems in children exposed to wife abuse: Gender differences. *Journal of Family Violence, 14*, 133–156.

D.W.G. v. Department of Children and Families, 833 So.2d 238 (Fla. Ct. App. 2002).

Daro, D., Edleson, J. L., & Pinderhughes, H. (2004). Finding common ground in the study of child maltreatment, youth violence, and adult domestic violence. *Journal of Interpersonal Violence, 19*, 282–298.

Dore, M. M., Doris, J., & Wright, P. (1995). Identifying substance abuse in maltreating families: A child welfare challenge. *Child Abuse and Neglect, 19*, 531–543.

Edleson, J. L. (2004). Should childhood exposure to adult domestic violence be defined as child maltreatment under the law? In P. G. Jaffe, L. L. Baker, & A. J. Cunningham (Eds.), *Protecting children from domestic violence: Strategies for community intervention* (pp. 8–29). New York: Guilford Press.

Edleson, J. L., & Malik, N. M. (2008). Collaborating for family safety: Results from the Greenbook multisite evaluation. *Journal of Interpersonal Violence, 23*(7), 871–875.

Fantuzzo, J. W., Boruch, R., Beriama, A., Atkins, M., & Marcus, S. (1997). Domestic violence and children: Prevalence and risk in five major cities. *Journal of the American Academy of Child and Adolescent Psychiatry, 36*(1), 116–122.

Fantuzzo, J. W., DePaola, L. M., Lambert, L., Martino, T., Anderson, G., & Sutton, S. (1991). Effects of interparental violence on the psychological adjustment & competencies of young children. *Journal of Consulting and Clinical Psychology, 59,* 258–265.

Fantuzzo, J., & Fusco, R. (2007). Children's direct sensory exposure to substantiated domestic violence crimes. *Violence and Victims, 22,* 158–171.

Finkelhor, D. (2008). *Childhood victimization: Violence, crime, and abuse in the lives of young people.* New York: Oxford University Press.

Folsom, W. S., Christensen, M. L., Avery, L., & Moore, C. (2003). The co-occurrence of child abuse and domestic violence: An issue of service delivery for social service professionals. *Child and Adolescent Social Work Journal, 20*(5), 375–387.

Fosco, G. M., DeBoard, R. L., & Grych, J. H. (2007). Making sense of family violence: Implications of children's appraisals of interparental aggression for their short- and long-term functioning. *European Psychologist, 12*(1), 6–16.

Gelles, R. J., & Cavanaugh, M. M. (2005). Violence, abuse, and neglect in families and intimate relationships. In P. C. McHenry & S. J. Price (Eds.), *Families & change: Coping with stressful events and transitions* (3rd ed., pp. 129–154). Thousand Oaks, CA: Sage.

Gewirtz, A. H., & Edleson, J. L. (2007). Young children's exposure to intimate partner violence: Towards a developmental risk and resilience framework for research and intervention. *Journal of Family Violence, 22,* 151–163.

Gondolf, E. (1993). Treating the batterer. In M. Hansen & M. Harway (Eds.), *Battering and family therapy: A feminist perspective* (pp. 105–118). Newbury Park, CA: Sage.

Graham-Bermann, S. A. (1992). *The Kid's Club: A preventive intervention program for children of battered women.* Ann Arbor: Department of Psychology, University of Michigan.

Graham-Bermann, S. A. (1996). Family worries: The assessment of interpersonal anxiety in children from violent and nonviolent families. *Journal of Clinical Child Psychology, 25*(3), 280–287.

Graham-Bermann, S. A. (1998). The impact of woman abuse on children's social development. In G. W. Holden, R. Geffner, & E. N. Jouriles (Eds.), *Children and marital violence: Theory, research, and intervention* (pp. 21–54). Washington, DC: American Psychological Association.

Graham-Bermann, S. A. (2000). Evaluating interventions for children exposed to family violence. *Journal of Aggression, Maltreatment & Trauma, 4,* 191–216.

Graham-Bermann, S. A., & Brescoll, V. (2000). Gender, power, and violence: Assessing the family stereotypes of the children of batterers. *Journal of Family Psychology, 14*(4), 600–612.

Graham-Bermann, S. A., & Edleson, J. (Eds.). (2001). *Domestic violence in the lives of children: The future of research, intervention, and social policy.* Washington, DC: American Psychological Association.

Graham-Bermann, S. A., Gruber, G., Girz, L., & Howell, K. H. (2009). Ecological factors discriminating among profiles of resiliency and psychopathology in children exposed to intimate partner violence. *Child Abuse and Neglect, 33*(9), 648–660.

Graham-Bermann, S. A., Habarth, J., & Howell, K. H. (2009, April). *Longitudinal contributions of corporal punishment, child abuse, and domestic violence to child adjustment.* Paper presented at the meeting of the Society for Research on Child Development, Denver, CO.

Graham-Bermann, S. A., Howell, K., Habarth, J., Krishnan, S., Loree, A., & Bermann, E. (2008). Toward assessing traumatic events and stress symptoms in preschool children from low-income families. *American Journal of Orthopsychiatry, 78*(2), 220–228.

Graham-Bermann, S. A., & Levendosky, A. A. (1994). *The Moms' Group: A parenting support and intervention program for battered women who are mothers.* Unpublished manuscript, University of Michigan.

Graham-Bermann, S. A., Lynch, S., Banyard, V., DeVoe, E., & Halabu, H. (2007). Community-based intervention for children exposed to intimate partner violence. *Journal of Consulting and Clinical Psychology, 75*(2), 199–209.

Graham-Bermann, S. A., & Seng. J. S. (2005). Violence exposure and traumatic stress symptoms as additional predictors of health problems in high-risk children. *The Journal of Pediatrics, 146*, 349–354.

Grych, J. H., Jouriles, E. N., Swank, P. R., McDonald, R., & Norwood, W. D. (2000). Patterns of adjustment among children of battered women. *Journal of Consulting and Clinical Psychology, 68*, 84–94.

Hartley, C. C. (2002). The co-occurrence of child maltreatment and domestic violence: Examining both neglect and child physical abuse. *Child Maltreatment, 7*(4), 349–358.

Haskett, M. E., Nears, K., Ward, C. S., & McPherson, A. V. (2006). Diversity in adjustment of maltreated children: Factors associated with resilient functioning. *Clinical Psychology Review, 26*, 796–812.

Heath, D. T., & Orthner, D. (1999). Stress and adaptation among male and female single parents. *Journal of Family Issues, 20*, 557–565.

Herrenkohl, T. I., Sousa, C., Tajima, E. A., Herrenkohl, R. C., & Moylan, C. A. (2008). Intersection of child abuse and children's exposure to domestic violence. *Trauma, Violence, & Abuse, 9*(2), 84–99.

Holden, G. W. (2003). Children exposed to domestic violence and child abuse: Terminology and taxonomy. *Clinical Child and Family Psychology Review, 6*, 151–160.

Holden, G. W., Stein, J. D., Ritchey, K. L., Harris, S. D., & Jouriles, E. N. (1998). Parenting behaviors and beliefs of battered women. In G. W. Holden (Ed.), *Children exposed to marital violence: Theory, research, and applied issues* (pp. 289–334). Washington, DC: American Psychological Association.

Howell, K. H., Graham-Bermann, S. A., Czyz, E., & Lilly, M. (in press). Assessing resilience in preschool children exposed to intimate partner violence. *Violence and Victims.*

Hutchison, I. W., & Hirschel, J. D. (2001). The effects of children's presence on woman abuse. *Violence and Victims, 16*, 3–17.

Jaffe, P., Poisson, S., & Cunningham, A. (2001). Domestic violence and high conflict divorce: Developing a new generation of research for children. In S. A. Graham-Bermann & J. L. Edleson (Eds.), *Domestic violence in the lives of children: The future of research, intervention, and social policy* (pp. 189–202). Washington, DC: American Psychological Association.

Jaffe, P., Wolfe, D., & Wilson, D. (1990). *Children of battered women.* Newbury Park, CA: Sage.

Jaffe, S. R., Caspi, A., Moffitt, T. E., Polo-Tomas, M., & Taylor, A. (2007). Individual, family, and neighborhood factors distinguish resilient from non-resilient maltreated children: A cumulative stressors model. *Child Abuse and Neglect, 31*, 231–253.

Jaffe, S. R., Moffitt, T. E., Caspi, A., Taylor, A., & Arsenault, L. (2002). Influence of adult domestic violence on children's internalizing and externalizing problems: An environmentally informed twin study. *Journal of the American Academy of Child and Adolescent Psychiatry, 41*(9), 1095–1103.

Jouriles, E. N., McDonald, R., Norwood, W. D., & Ezell, E. (2001). Issues and controversies in documenting the prevalence of children's exposure to domestic violence. In S. A. Graham-Bermann & J. L. Edleson (Eds.), *Domestic violence in the lives of children: The future of research, intervention, and social policy* (pp. 13–34). Washington, DC: American Psychological Association.

Jouriles, E. N., McDonald, R., Stephens, N., Norwood, W., Spiller, L. C., & Ware, H. S. (1998). Breaking the cycle of violence: Helping families departing from battered women's shelters. In G. W. Holden, R. Geffner, & E. N. Jouriles (Eds.), *Children exposed to marital violence: Theory, research, and applied issues* (pp. 337–370). Washington, DC: American Psychological Association.

Jouriles, E. N., & Norwood, W. D. (1995). Physical aggression toward boys and girls in families characterized by the battering of women. *Journal of Family Psychology, 9,* 69–78.

Kilpatrick, D. G., Ruggiero, K. J., Acierno, R. E., Saunders, B. E., Resnick, H. S., & Best, C. L. (2003).Violence and risk of PTSD, major depression, substance abuse/dependence, and comorbidity: Results from the National Survey of Adolescents. *Journal of Consulting and Clinical Psychology, 71,* 692–700.

Kitzmann, K. M., Gaylord, N. K., Holt, A. R., & Kenny, E. D. (2003). Child witnesses to domestic violence: A meta-analytic review. *Journal of Consulting and Clinical Psychology, 71*(2), 339–352.

Korbanka, J. E., & McKay, M. (2000). An MMPI-2 scale to identify history of physical abuse. *Journal of Interpersonal Violence, 15*(11), 1131–1139.

Lehmann, P. (1997). The development of posttraumatic stress disorder in a sample of child witnesses to mother assault. *Journal of Family Violence, 12,* 241–257.

Levendosky, A. A., & Graham-Bermann, S. A. (2000). Behavioral observations of parenting in battered women. *Journal of Family Psychology, 14,* 115.

Lieberman, A. F., & Knorr, K. (2007). The impact of trauma: A developmental framework for infancy and early childhood. *Psychiatric Annals, 37*(6), 416–422.

Lieberman, A. F., Van Horn, P., & Ippen, C. G. (2005). Toward evidence-based treatment: Child-parent psychotherapy with preschoolers exposed to marital violence. *Journal of the American Academy of Child and Adolescent Psychiatry, 44,* 1241–1248.

Magen, R. H., Conroy, K., Hess, P. M., Panciera, A., & Simon, B. L. (2001). Identifying domestic violence in child abuse and neglect interventions. *Journal of Interpersonal Violence, 16*(6), 580–601.

Margolin, G., & Gordis, E. B. (2000). The effects of family and community violence on children. *Annual Review of Psychology, 51,* 455–479.

McDonald, R., Jouriles, E. N., Briggs-Gowan, M. J., Rosenfield, D., & Carter, A. S. (2007). Violence toward a family member, angry adult conflict, and child adjustment difficulties: Relations in families with 1- to 3-year-old children. *Journal of Family Psychology, 21*(2), 176–184.

McDonald, R., Jouriles, E. N., Ramisetty-Mikler, S., Caetano, R., & Green, C. E. (2006). Estimating the number of American children living in partner-violent families. *Journal of Family Psychology, 20,* 137–142.

McGuigan, W. M., Vuchinich, S., & Pratt, C. C. (2000). Domestic violence, parents' view of their infant, and risk for child abuse. *Journal of Family Psychology, 14*(4), 613–624.

Myers, J. E. B. (2005). *Myers on evidence in child, domestic and elder abuse cases.* New York: Aspen.

National Research Council, Institute of Medicine. (1998). *Violence in families: Assessing prevention and treatment programs.* Washington; DC: National Academy of Sciences.

Osofsky, J. D. (2003). Prevalence of children's exposure to domestic violence and child maltreatment: Implications for prevention and intervention. *Clinical Child and Family Psychology Review*, 6, 161–170.

Patterson, G. R. (1986). The contribution of siblings to training for fighting: A microsocial and analysis. In D. Olweus, J. Block, &. M. Radke-Yarrow (Eds.), *Development of antisocial and prosocial behavior* (pp. 235–261). New York: Academic Press.

Pelcovitz, D., Kaplan, S., Goldenberg, B., Mandel, F., Lehane, J., & Guarrera, J. V. (1994). Post-traumatic stress disorder in physically abused adolescents. *Journal of the American Academy of Child and Adolescent Psychiatry*, 33(3), 305–312.

People v. Johnson, 740 N.E.2d 1075 (N.Y. 2000).

Postmus, J. L., & Ortega, D. (2005). Serving two masters: When domestic violence and child abuse overlap. *Families in Society*, 86(4), 483–490.

Seng, J. S., Oakley, D. J., Sampselle, C. M., Killion, C., Graham-Bermann, S., & Liberzon, I. (2001). Posttraumatic stress disorder and pregnancy complications. *Journal of Obstetrics and Gynecology*, 97, 17–22.

Stark, E., & Flitcraft, A. (1996). *Women at risk: Domestic violence and women's health*. Thousand Oaks, CA: Sage.

Sternberg, K. J., Baradaran, L. P., Abbott, C. B., Lamb, M. E., & Guterman, E. (2006). Type of violence, age, and gender differences in the effects of family violence on children's behavior problems: A mega-analysis. *Developmental Review*, 26, 89–112.

Stover, C. S., & Berkowitz, S. (2005). Assessing violence exposure and trauma symptoms in young children: A critical review of measures. *Journal of Traumatic Stress*, 18(6), 707–717.

Straus, M. A., & Gelles, R. J. (1990). *Physical violence in American families*. New Brunswick, NJ: Transaction.

Straus, M. A., Gelles, R. J., & Steinmetz, S. (1980). *Behind closed doors: Violence in the American family*. Garden City, NY: Anchor.

Straus, M. A., Hamby, S. L., Boney-McCoy, S., & Sugarman, D. (1995). *The revised conflict tactics scales (C7S2)*. Durham, NH: Family Research Laboratory.

Tajima, E. A. (2004). Correlates of the co-occurrence of wife abuse and child abuse among a representative sample. *Journal of Family Violence*, 19(6), 399–410.

Tigges, L. M., Browne, I., & Green, G. P. (1998). Social isolation of the urban poor: Race, class, and neighborhood effects on social resources. *Sociological Quarterly*, 39, 53–77.

Trocmé, N., & Wolfe, D. (2001).The Canadian incidence study of reported child abuse and neglect. In G. Phaneuf (Ed.), *Family violence in Canada: A statistical profile 2001* (pp. 85–224). Ottawa, ON: Statistics Canada.

Utah Criminal Codes 76-5-109.1(2)(c). (1997). *Commission of domestic violence in the presence of a child*.

Wekerle, C., & Wolfe, D. A. (2003). Dating violence in mid-adolescence: Theory, significance, and emerging prevention initiatives. *Clinical Psychological Review*, 19(4), 435–456.

Wolak, J., & Finkelhor, D. (2001). Children exposed to partner violence. In J. L. Jasinski & L. M. Williams (Eds.), *Partner violence: A comprehensive review of 20 years of research*. Thousand Oaks, CA: Sage.

Wolfe, D. A., Crooks, C. V., Lee, V., McIntyre-Smith, A., & Jaffe, P. G. (2003). The effects of children's exposure to domestic violence: A meta-analysis and critique. *Clinical Child and Family Psychology Review*, 6(3), 171–187.

PART III

Physical Abuse

Part III of the *APSAC Handbook on Child Maltreatment* addresses physical child abuse. Chapter 11 discusses medical evidence of physical abuse (PA). Chapter 12 describes mental health interventions for physically abused children and for adults who inflict such abuse.

11

Medical Evaluation of Physical Abuse

Robert M. Reece

Physical abuse (PA) can be defined as nonaccidental physical injury inflicted upon a child. PA may consist of hitting, pinching, kicking, shaking, burning, beating, cutting, or torturing. This chapter discusses medical evidence of PA.

Prevalence of Physical Child Abuse

In 2008, an estimated 772,000 children in the United States were victims of abuse or neglect (U.S. Department of Health and Human Services, 2010). Of this number, 16.1% were physically abused. Children in the age group birth to 1 year had the highest rate of PA victimization. In 2008, an estimated 1,740 children died due to abuse or neglect.

Accident or Abuse?

Physicians are asked to decide whether a child's injuries were the result of accident or abuse. To reach a decision, the doctor takes into account all relevant factors, including the following (Reece, 2004):

1. Social context where the child was injured.

2. Likely biases and motives of witnesses.

3. Physical examination of the child.

4. Probability the injuries could be accidental. The doctor considers nonabusive medical conditions (differential diagnosis) that might explain the injuries.

5. Investigations conducted by law enforcement or social services, including details of the exact place and circumstances where injuries occurred (e.g., bed or crib, bedding, furniture, distance to floor if caretaker claims child fell).

6. Use of selected laboratory and imaging modalities (blood tests, X-ray, CT scan, MRI).

7. Age and developmental status of the child. Knowledge of the developmental capabilities of children at particular ages helps determine what kinds of injuries are likely to be within the normal range for accidental injury.

8. The child's medical history as provided by the parents or caretakers. The medical history includes information about the pregnancy, labor and delivery, and neonatal course of the child. Inquiry into the presence of familial diseases is important, paying attention to bleeding and clotting disorders, neurological diseases, metabolic and bone disease, or other genetic conditions. The doctor asks about previous injuries, illnesses, and hospitalizations. Once the history is obtained, the physician asks, "In light of the medical history and the child's injuries, does the caretaker's explanation make medical and physical sense?" Caretakers who abuse children often provide implausible explanations for a child's serious or fatal injuries. Often the injury is explained as resulting from a fall (e.g., child fell off couch onto carpeted floor). A large literature discounts falls from short distances as being responsible for serious injuries. Sometimes the caretaker says, "I have no idea what happened," and this statement may or may not raise suspicions.

9. Does the history provided by caretakers change over time? If caretakers are lying, they may have difficulty maintaining a consistent lie over time.

10. Do different caretakers tell different stories when interviewed separately?

Abusive Head Injury

More fatalities and long-term morbidity are due to abusive head injury than any other form of PA (Reece, 2004; Reece & Christian, 2009). Children younger than 1 year of age are at highest risk for inflicted traumatic brain injury (Rorke-Adams, Duhaime, Jenny, & Smith, 2009). Studies estimate the rate of inflicted head injuries from 7.1 to 24.6 per 100,000 children (Reece & Christian, 2009).

Violent shaking of a baby or young child can cause serious injury or death (Christian, Block, & Committee on Child Abuse and Neglect, 2009). Shaken baby syndrome (SBS) is often used to describe head injuries when shaking is the likely explanation. Another widely used term is "shaken impact syndrome," which denotes a child shaken and slammed against a hard surface. SBS and shaken impact syndrome are slowly being replaced with the following terms: abusive head trauma, inflicted traumatic brain injury, inflicted childhood neurotrauma, nonaccidental head injury, and inflicted head injury.

Symptoms of abusive head trauma may include poor feeding, vomiting, lethargy, irritability, seizures, apnea or respiratory distress, or unresponsiveness. Seizures are common, being reported in about half of cases. Poor breathing patterns or cessation of breathing is reported in more than half. Hypothermia is common in head-injured children, with body temperatures as low as 95 degrees Fahrenheit.

A complete physical examination of the head-injured child is necessary because the child may have other injuries, including bleeding from injuries to organs in the abdomen. The child's neck is inspected for signs of injury such as finger marks seen with strangulation or other imprints of abuse. The doctor notes the presence of bruises on a child's back, thighs, or stomach. All observable injuries should be photographed.

Anatomy of the Infant Head

Understanding the anatomy of the infant's head is central to grasping the concepts of injury to this structure. In its most simple terms, the structures can be viewed as a series of layers, each consisting of different types of tissues. Each layer has unique properties, and they differ from each other in major ways. Because of this, each layer reacts to trauma in a different manner, leading to differing manifestations of injury.

The outermost layer—the scalp—consists of the skin covering the skull, subcutaneous tissue, and underlying fascia called the galea. The subgaleal space (also called the subscalpular space) between the scalp and skull is not truly a space. It is a potential space until blood or other material separates the scalp from the skull, filling the space.

Inside the skull, the brain is covered by three thin membranes: the dura mater, the arachnoid, and the pia mater. These membranes function as protective envelopes for the brain. The membranes also provide a matrix for blood vessels that supply blood to the brain. The dura mater is a structure consisting of dense fibrous tissue attached to the inner surface of the skull. The arachnoid membrane is a delicate, lacy, spiderweb-like membrane that lies inside of and adheres to the dura mater. Cerebrospinal fluid (CSF) is found in the subarachnoid space. CSF circulates throughout the central nervous system—brain and spine—and has important nutritional and elimination functions. The pia mater is adjacent to the surface of the brain and spinal cord and follows the convolutions (gyri and sulci) of the brain.

Running from front to back in the midline along the top of the brain within the dura mater is the superior sagittal sinus, a large venous channel carrying blood from the brain toward the heart. The superior sagittal sinus receives blood from 15 to 18 small bridging veins arranged from front to back on each side of the surface of the two hemispheres of the brain. These bridging veins arise from the surface of the brain and course through the pia and arachnoid membranes as well as the subarachnoid and subdural potential spaces, ending in the superior sagittal sinus of the dura mater. One end of each bridging vein is attached to the brain and the other end to the superior sagittal sinus of the dura. Because of this attachment, the bridging veins have limited mobility. This limited mobility accounts for their vulnerability to shearing and breakage if the brain is set in motion by violent shaking or impact.

The epidural space is a potential space inside the skull between the skull and the dura mater. If blood seeps into this space, the result is an epidural or extradural hematoma. A hematoma is a localized accumulation of blood. The subdural space, another potential space, lies beneath the dura mater. If blood flows into the subdural space, the result is a subdural hematoma.

The brain itself (parenchyma) lies beneath the subarachnoid space. The brain is made up of millions of neurons, the basic cell of the nervous system. Each neuron has one axon and several dendrites. Axons carry efferent (outgoing) nerve impulses, and dendrites carry afferent (incoming) impulses. The axons are gathered into nerve bundles and tracts going to the various parts of the body. The gray matter of the brain consists of the neuron cell bodies. The white matter consists primarily of the nerve bundles and tracts. Blood vessels (arterioles, venules, and capillaries) are everywhere within the brain substance.

A protein-rich material called myelin is laid down around the components of the central nervous system over the first 18 months of life. Myelin makes the brain of older children and adults firmer than the brain of an infant or young child. In addition to a relative lack of myelin, the infant brain contains approximately 25% more water than the brain of older children and adults. Pathologists describe the infant brain as being "gelatinous" in consistency. As a result, the infant brain is probably more vulnerable to trauma, although this has not been proven definitively.

The injuries in abusive head trauma can include scalp bruising (both visible and invisible), bleeding under the scalp but outside the skull (subscalpular hematoma), skull fractures, subdural and/or subarachnoid bleeding, cerebral edema (edema is extra fluid in the tissues), white matter injuries, hypoxic brain injury due to deprivation of oxygen, tears and contusions (bruises) of the brain itself, and injuries to the nerve roots of the cervical spinal cord. In rare cases, there is injury to the cervical (upper) spinal cord.

Skull fractures may be simple or complex. Simple fractures are linear and do not cross suture lines. Suture lines are the edges of the bony plates that make up the skull. In an infant, the sutures are not completely joined at the diamond-shaped "soft spot" on top of the baby's head. Complex fractures may also be linear, but they cross suture lines. Complex fractures include branching or stellate fractures, comminuted (isolated fragments of bone), depressed, compound (lacerations of the scalp caused by pieces of skull), and diastatic (growing).

Simple fractures imply less force, whereas complex fractures usually imply more force. For example, a depressed skull fracture is produced by a focal force (hammer), whereas a simple linear fracture may be caused by a short fall in which the forces are more diffuse or widely distributed.

Retinal Hemorrhages

The doctor examines the child's eyes, especially the retina. The retina is the surface that lines the interior of the globe of the eye. The retina is composed of 10 separate layers of tissue, richly supplied with blood vessels. Bleeding within these layers produces blots of blood or flame-shaped blood leakages that are known as retinal hemorrhages. Up to 90% of children with abusive head trauma have retinal hemorrhages—that is, bleeding from burst blood vessels in the retina.

Retinal hemorrhages seen in abusive head trauma have three features that distinguish them from retinal hemorrhages from disease conditions: First, with abuse there typically are many retinal hemorrhages (20 to 30). Second, retinal hemorrhage secondary to abuse involves multiple layers of the retina. Third, in abuse, retinal hemorrhages are typically extensive, spreading all the way out to the ora serrata (near the lens in the front of the globe). Retinal hemorrhages unrelated to maltreatment are usually closer to the surface of the retina (so-called preretinal hemorrhages), are most often confined to the posterior pole of the globe, and resolve quickly.

Although retinal hemorrhages are not diagnostic of inflicted head trauma, they are present in a high percentage of abuse cases and are not present in most accidental trauma. Cardiopulmonary resuscitation does not cause retinal hemorrhage in children. Seizures do not produce retinal hemorrhages.

Shaking and Impact as Mechanisms of Injury

There has been much debate among physicians about shaking versus shaking plus impact as the mechanism for the production of the lesions seen in some cases of abusive head trauma. This debate is unresolved, with adherents on both sides. Some researchers cite the absence of evidence of impact in a substantial number of reported cases as a reason to question the role of impact, while acknowledging that impact plays a role in some cases, especially severe or fatal cases.

Accurate data do not exist about the magnitude of forces required to injure the infant brain. This is because experimental evidence cannot be obtained on living infants that would measure the forces required to produce damage. Without such information, the debate over whether shaking alone is sufficient to cause massive injury cannot be resolved. We do know, as Rorke-Adams and colleagues (2009) state, that the head and brain can be injured by direct contact forces with damage at the point of contact.

In summary, shaking and the sudden deceleration of the head at the end of a shaking arc or at the time of impact do several things: First, bridging veins inside the skull are stretched and tear, causing subdural hematoma or sub-arachnoid hemorrhage. Second, the brain and the brainstem tissue are trau-matized by movement within the skull. Third, during shaking, the infant does not breathe, creating poor oxygen supply to the brain. This oxygen depriva-tion can continue after the shaking stops due to damage to the respiratory center of the brain. Fourth, as with all tissue damage, injured brain tissue swells and this leads to compression of the blood vessels supplying oxygen to the brain. Fifth, dying brain cells release the contents of their cells as the cell walls break down, releasing cellular enzymes that cause further oxygen depri-vation and destruction of adjacent brain cells. This damage to the brain causes the clinical picture that is recognized as abusive head trauma.

What Triggers Abuse?

Crying in infancy hits a peak at approximately the same time as the high-est incidence of abusive head trauma, suggesting a correlation between crying and abuse. Perpetrators who confess often cite inconsolable crying as the trig-ger that set off the abuse (Starling, Holden, & Jenny, 1995).

Frustrated by futile attempts to console the baby, the perpetrator loses control and grabs the infant by the chest under the arms, by the arms, or by the neck and violently shakes the baby. Some perpetrators describe shaking alone. Others describe shaking plus impact. A few offenders abuse the child further with punches, kicks or stomping on the infant after inflicting head trauma. When perpetrators are asked how long they abused the baby, esti-mates range from a few seconds to 15 seconds.

Long-Term Outcome for
Patients With Abusive Head Trauma

There are few long-term outcome studies of children with abusive head trauma. Existing research shows an early mortality rate of 15% to 25%. Of victims who survive, 80% to 90% are left with varying degrees of compro-mise ranging from severe learning disabilities, tetraplegia (paralysis of all four limbs), blindness, chronic seizure disorders, and, in the most severe cases, per-sistent vegetative state (Bonnier, Nassagne, & Evrard, 1995). A significant number of early survivors die later.

Abdominal Injuries _____

Injuries to the abdomen are the second most common cause of fatal child abuse (Cooper et al., 1988; Ledbetter, Hatch, Feldman, Fligner, & Tapper, 1988). Fatality rates for inflicted abdominal injuries are between 40% and 50%.

Ledbetter and colleagues (1988) described features that distinguish acci-dental from abusive abdominal injuries. In their study, abusive abdominal injuries: (1) were more common in younger children (median age 2.6 versus 7.8 years in accidental); (2) had vague histories accounting for the abusive abdominal injuries, whereas 70% of the injuries in the accidental group were due to motor vehicle accidents and 20% due to falls from significant heights; (3) had delayed medical care in contrast to the accident group, where care was prompt; (4) for the most part involved injuries to hollow organs (e.g., small intestine), whereas a solid organ (e.g., liver, spleen) was injured more often in the accidental group; and (5) had a higher mortality rate (53%) as compared to 21% in the accident cases.

Most inflicted abdominal injuries are caused by punching or kicking. The blow crushes organs against the spine or chest wall. The trauma may shear the blood vessels that nourish abdominal organs, causing internal bleeding. The intestines may be lacerated, spilling their contents into the abdominal cavity and causing peritonitis (infection). Mortality is due to severe blood loss or sepsis.

The signs and symptoms of traumatic abdominal injury—whether accidental or inflicted—are many. For some children, vomiting is the presenting symptom. Abdominal tenderness and distention may be the predominant sign. The absence of bowel sounds when the doctor listens with a stethoscope indicates the bowel is not functioning normally. Fever may be present, especially if there has been perforation of the intestine with resulting infection. External bruising is not always found, but if there are bruises, this usually indicates severe trauma. Neurologic impairment, a low red blood count, blood in the urine, or shock may be present.

Throat Injuries

The pharynx is the area between the mouth and what a layperson calls the back of the throat. The back of the throat connects to the trachea and the esophagus. Abusive injuries at the back of the throat are rare but are serious when present.

Vomiting of blood, coughing, gagging, poor feeding, respiratory distress, cyanosis, and fever are observed. Such injuries result from traumatic insertion of utensils or, in some cases, fingernails, which penetrate the thin posterior membranes and muscular layer at the back of the throat.

Thoracic Injuries (Injuries to the Chest)

Injuries to the thoracic cavity are described in approximately 12% of abused children, compared to about 5% of the general pediatric trauma population (Nance & Cooper, 2009). Rib fractures account for the majority of these injuries, although injuries to the heart and lungs are reported. *Commotio cordis*, a condition in which a blow to the front of the chest causes an interruption in the electrical conduction in the heart leading to cessation of heartbeat, is a rare form of child abuse. Cardiac lacerations and cardiac rupture can result from a direct blow to the chest over the heart. Lung contusions (bruises) and pneumothorax (collapsed lung) have also been seen in conjunction with direct blows to the chest.

Abusive rib fractures are often bilateral and near the child's spine. The fractures are often caused when the abusive adult grabs the child's chest under the arms and squeezes the chest with the fingers. Rib fractures are sometimes difficult to detect with a normal X-ray. A special imaging technique called bone scanning (bone scintigraphy) is sometimes used to detect fresh rib fractures. There is no reason to believe that rib fractures in a child are caused by cardiopulmonary resuscitation (CPR) (Price, Rush, Perper, & Bell, 2000).

Skeletal Injuries: Fractures

Active, playful children who are old enough to move around on their own sometimes break bones accidentally. Thus, the physician must distinguish accidental from inflicted fractures. It is estimated that abuse accounts for between 11% and 55% of fractures. In children under 1 year of age, the rate of abusive fractures may be as high as 70% because children so young are not highly mobile. Leventhal and colleagues (1993) reported that nearly a quarter of 350 fractures in children less than 3 years of age were due to abuse.

The fracture that is most specific for abuse is the classic metaphyseal lesion (CML) of long bones (arms and legs). The CML fracture is also called a "corner fracture," or a "bucket handle fracture." The CML is a splitting off of a disc of bone at the end of a long bone caused by flailing of the limb during abuse or due to a sharp jerk in the long axis of the bone. A CML fracture is particularly suspicious in a child less than 2 years of age (Kleinman, Marks, Richmond, & Blackbourne, 1995).

Certain factors increase concern that fractures may be due to abuse: (1) absence of a credible history explaining the fracture, (2) very young age of the patient, (3) children with abusive injuries in addition to the fractures, (4) delay in seeking medical care, and (5) caretakers provide an explanation for the fracture that does not make medical or physical sense.

The following fractures raise concerns about possible abuse: (1) multiple fractures, especially on both sides of the body (bilateral); (2) repetitive fractures; (3) fracture of hands or feet; (4) posterior (rear) rib fractures; (5) certain fractures of the collar bone (clavicle); (6) fracture of the shoulder blade (scapula); (7) fracture of the spine; (8) fracture of the breast bone (sternum); (9) fractures in various stages of healing; and (10) fractures of the skull (Cooperman & Merten, 2009).

When a doctor evaluates fractures for possible abuse, the doctor considers possible nonabusive explanations. In particular, the doctor considers: (1) accidental trauma; (2) obstetric trauma; (3) prematurity leading to abnormally low bone mass (osteopenia); (4) nutritional deficiencies such as rickets or scurvy; (5) metabolic disorders such as Menke's syndrome secondary hypoparathyroidism; (6) T-cell disease; (7) drug toxicity such as methotrexate, prostaglandin therapy, hypervitaminosis A; (8) infections such as osteomyelitis or syphilis; (9) neuromuscular disorders; (10) skeletal abnormality (dysplasia); (11) neoplasms; (12) genetic bone disease; and (13) osteogenesis imperfecta (OI), which is a generalized disorder of connective tissue with a broad spectrum of clinical expression. When OI is confused with inflicted skeletal trauma, the OI is almost always Type I or Type IV.

So-called temporary brittle bone disease (TBBD) is sometimes offered in court as the explanation for a child's fractures. There is no scientific foundation for TBBD, and TBBD has been discredited as an explanation for fractures.

Skin Injuries Due to Abuse

Human skin is made up of three layers. Outermost is the epidermis. This thin layer contains no blood vessels and receives nutrition from the layers below it. Underneath the epidermis is the dermis, which contains blood vessels and nerve cells. Below the dermis is the subcutaneous fat layer, which also contains blood vessels and nerves. The skin is a complex and amazing organ.

Skin injuries are the most common manifestation of child abuse and include bruises, abrasions, lacerations, petechiae (tiny bleeding points), burns, and bites. In determining whether skin lesions are accidental or inflicted, it is important to consider the location and pattern of injuries.

Bruises

Bruises result from bleeding into the dermis or subcutaneous tissues due to disruption of capillaries or deeper blood vessels by blunt force. Swelling of a bruise occurs because of the inflammatory response to the trauma. Swelling resolves as serum is reabsorbed over the first 2 to 3 days. Color changes in a bruise occur as the hemoglobin from the blood is broken down and metabolized. Table 11.1 indicates bruises that are more or less likely to be caused by abuse.

Table 11.1   Distinguishing Abusive Bruises From Accidental Bruises

Location of Bruises	
Likely Inflicted	**Likely Accidental**
Upper arms	Shins
Trunk	Hips (iliac crest)
Upper anterior legs	Lower arms
Sides of face	Prominences of spine
Ears and neck	Forehead
Genitalia and buttocks	Under chin

Patterns of Abusive Skin Injuries

When an instrument (e.g., belt, paddle) is used to hit a child, the instrument may leave a bruise that resembles the instrument. For example, a bruise produced by a looped electric cord may appear elliptical. A belt, belt buckle, or wire coat hanger leaves bruises conforming to the shape. The human hand may leave parallel lines showing the spaces between fingers and resembling a human hand (slap marks).

A ligature is a device that is tied around a body part or blood vessel. Ligatures tied to wrists or ankles in order to restrain a child leave burns or pressure lines. Lesions around the neck suggest ropes or strings.

Bruises of the upper arms or in the rib cage suggest encirclement bruises resulting from hard pressure applied during shaking or violent handling (Pascoe, Hildebrandt, Tarrier, & Murphy, 1979).

Can a doctor tell how new or old a bruise is by examining its color and shape? Dating bruises is an imperfect art due to the variability of skin color, healing characteristics, location of bruises, and varying age groups of children. It is difficult even to determine the age of bruises that seem to be in different stages of healing. It is best to rely on the patterns and location of bruises rather than their age to ascertain whether or not they are abusive or accidental.

Bites

A human bite inflicted by an adult is a primitive behavior that is a red flag for the child's safety. The size of the mark left from a bite helps determine whether the perpetrator is an adult or a child. Bites leave characteristic lesions that can be measured and compared with the dentition of the alleged perpetrator. Photographs of the bite marks are valuable, and swabs can be taken to pick up saliva for DNA analysis.

Burns

More than 2,000 children die every year from burns due to all causes. Tap water scalds, contact burns, and hot grease burns are the most prevalent burns in children. Burns from chemicals, electrical appliances, and microwave ovens comprise a small percentage of burns requiring hospitalization.

Approximately 10% to 20% of burns in children under age 3 years are inflicted. It is estimated that burns represent approximately 10% of all PA cases. The peak age of all burn victims is from 13 to 24 months (Rosenberg & Marino, 1989).

Frustrated or angry adults sometimes immerse a child's hands or feet in hot water, as a form of punishment. Forced immersion scald burns are usually uniform in depth of burned tissue, with sharply demarcated borders separating burned from spared skin. Such burns are often called stocking or glove burns due to their appearance (Katcher, 1981).

Immersion burns to the buttocks, lower back, and perineum (area containing the genitals and anus) occur when a child's body is forcibly held under hot water. In some cases, areas of skin are spared from scalding if these areas are in contact with a relatively cooler surface such as the bottom of the bathtub. When spared tissue is surrounded by burned skin, the term "donut burn" is sometimes used.

How long does it take for skin to burn? This depends on several factors, including age. Adult skin takes longer to be injured than the skin of a child. The time required to produce burns at particular degrees of temperature is listed in Table 11.2 (Moritz & Henriques, 1947).

Table 11.2   Time It Takes to Burn Skin

Degrees Fahrenheit	Adult's Skin	Child's Skin
127°	60 seconds	No data
130°	30 seconds	10 seconds
140°	5 seconds .	1 second
150°	2 seconds	<1 second
158°	1 second	<1 second

Dry contact burns occur when a hot object is brought into contact with skin. Objects of all kinds—especially household appliances—cause contact burns. The most frequent appliances are irons, hair dryers, hair curlers, cigarette lighters, light bulbs, grills from stoves or heaters, and cigarettes. Fresh cigarette burns are circular and blistered. As they heal, cigarette burns appear crater-like, with hyperpigmented edges. Accidental cigarette burns occur but do not have the precise circular shape of an inflicted burn. Accidental cigarette burns appear ovoid, and the burn is usually superficial. Little children are sometimes burned when they come in contact with the metal frame of a car seat, seat belt buckle, baby carrier, stroller, playpen, or other baby equipment.

Conclusion

PA often has serious and even fatal consequences. Physicians play a key role in detecting and diagnosing PA so that children can be protected and offenders held accountable.

References

Bonnier, C., Nassagne, M. C., & Evrard, P. (1995). Outcome and prognosis of whiplash shaken infant syndrome: Late consequences after a symptom-free interval. *Developmental Medicine and Child Neurology, 37*, 943–956.

Christian, C. W., Block, R., & Committee on Child Abuse and Neglect. (2009). Abusive head trauma in infants and children. *Pediatrics, 123*, 1409–1411.

Cooper, A., Floyd, T., Barlow, B., Niemirska, M., Ludwig, S., Seidl, T., et al. (1988). Major blunt abdominal trauma due to child abuse. *Journal of Trauma, 28*, 1483.

Cooperman, D. R., & Merten, D. F. (2009) Skeletal manifestations of child abuse. In R. M. Reece & C. W. Christian (Eds.), *Child abuse: Medical diagnosis and management* (3rd ed.). Elk Grove Village, IL: American Academy of Pediatrics.

Katcher, M. L. (1981). Scald burns from hot tap water. *Journal of the American Medical Association, 246*, 1219.

Kleinman, P. K., Marks, S. C., Jr., Richmond, J. M., & Blackbourne, B. D. (1995). Inflicted skeletal injury: A post mortem radiologic-histopathologic study. *American Journal of Roentgenology, 165*, 647–650.

Ledbetter, D. J., Hatch, E. I., Jr., Feldman, K. W., Fligner, K. L., & Tapper, D. (1988). Diagnostic and surgical implications of child abuse. *Archives of Surgery, 123*, 1101–1105.

Leventhal, J. M., Thomas, S. A., Rosenfeld, N. S., & Markowitz, R. I. (1993). Fractures in young children. Distinguishing child abuse from unintentional injuries. *American Journal of Diseases of Childhood, 147*, 87–92.

Moritz, A. R., & Henriques, F. C. (1947). Studies of thermal injury: The relative importance of time and surface temperature in the causation of cutaneous burns. *American Journal of Pathology, 23*, 695–720.

Nance, M. L., & Cooper, A. (2009). Visceral manifestations of child physical abuse. In R. M. Reece & C. W. Christian (Eds.), *Child abuse: Medical diagnosis and management* (3rd ed., pp. 172–187). Elk Grove Village, IL: American Academy of Pediatrics.

Pascoe, J. M., Hildebrandt, H. M., Tarrier, A., & Murphy, M. (1979). Patterns of skin injury in non-accidental and accidental injury. *Pediatrics, 64*, 245.

Price, E. A., Rush, L. R., Perper, J. A., & Bell, M. D. (2000). Cardiopulmonary resuscitation-related injuries and homicidal blunt abdominal trauma in children. *American Journal of Forensic Medical Pathology, 21*, 307–310.

Reece, R. M. (2004). Child abuse. In R. M. Kleigman, L. A. Greenbaum, & P. S. Lye (Eds.), *Practical strategies in pediatric diagnosis and therapy* (2nd ed.). Philadelphia: Elsevier.

Reece, R. M., & Christian, C. W. (Eds.). (2009). *Child abuse: Medical diagnosis and management.* (3rd ed.). Elk Grove Village, IL: American Academy of Pediatrics.

Rorke-Adams, L., Duhaime, A. C., Jenny, C., & Smith, W. L. (2009). Head trauma. In R. M. Reece & C. W. Christian (Eds.), *Child abuse: Medical diagnosis and management.* Elk Grove Village, IL: American Academy of Pediatrics.

Rosenberg, N. M., & Marino, D. (1989). Frequency of suspected abuse/neglect in burn patients. *Pediatric Emergency Care, 5*, 219–221.

Starling, S. P., Holden, J. R., & Jenny, C. (1995) Abusive head trauma: The relationship of perpetrators to their victims. *Pediatrics, 95*, 259–262.

U.S. Department of Health and Human Services. (2010). *Child maltreatment 2008: Summary.* Washington, DC: U.S. Government Printing Office.

12

Child Physical Abuse

Interventions for Parents Who Engage in Coercive Parenting Practices and Their Children

Melissa K. Runyon and Anthony J. Urquiza

This chapter describes mental health treatments that have an evidence base to support their use with children who have been physically abused and their parents who engage in coercive and/or physically abusive parenting practices.

Characteristics of Parents Who Physically Abuse Their Children

Parents who physically abuse their children engage in less effective and more negative parenting strategies and use more physical discipline than nonabusive parents (Chaffin et al., 2004; Lahey, Conger, Atkeson, & Treiber, 1984; Monroe & Schellenbach, 1989). Child physical abuse (PA) incidents often occur within the context of perceived child noncompliance, suggesting that parents who physically abuse their children have limited parenting skills. Milner (2000, 2003) reported that parents who are physically abusive possess attributional biases related to the activities of parenting and distorted perceptions of their children's behavior. These biases and distortions include hypervigilance to child noncompliance (and concurrent limited awareness of positive child behaviors), errors in accurately interpreting child emotional expressions, negative interpretations of child behaviors, greater than normal physiological responsivity to stressful stimuli, and preexisting negative schemata (which may impair appropriate responses to child behavior). Parents who engage in child PA have difficulty with affective expression and regulation leading to problems with irritability, hostility, and difficulty controlling anger (Mammen, Kolko, & Pilkonis, 2003; Patterson, DeBaryshe, & Ramsey, 1989; Simons, Whitbeck, Conger, & Chyi-in, 1991). A pattern of coercive parent-child interactions has been identified in parent-child dyads in which abuse occurs (Azar, 1997; Clausen & Crittenden, 1991; Fantuzzo, 1990; Milner, 2000).

Impact of Child Physical Abuse on Children

Children who experience PA have a range of emotional and behavioral difficulties. One third of children who are physically abused develop posttraumatic stress disorder (PTSD) (Saunders, Berliner, & Hanson, 2004). Physically abused children exhibit a wide array of externalizing and internalizing behaviors including aggression, noncompliance, and depression (Kolko, 2002; Kolko & Swenson, 2002; Wolfe, 1987). It is likely that certain family characteristics (e.g., domestic violence, inconsistent parenting, parental mental health problems) contribute to children's behavioral problems.

Approaches to Treatment

A variety of treatment approaches are employed to help parents who are at risk for PA and to help children who are affected by PA. In-home services (Fraser, Walton, Lewis, Pecora, & Walton, 1996), trauma-focused play therapy (Gil, 1996), and family therapy approaches (Ralston & Swenson, 1996; Saunders & Meinig, 2000) are described in the literature through case examples and other written accounts but to date have no controlled trials evaluating their efficacy. Other treatment approaches include therapeutic day care, which is associated with positive outcomes for children experiencing various forms of maltreatment (Moore, Armsden, & Gogerty, 1998). The in-home program known as SAFECARE targets health care, home safety, and parent-child interaction skills in families at risk for maltreatment and is associated with improvements in these areas (Gershater-Molko, Lutzker, & Wesch, 2003). A study examining the utility of an ecobehavioral approach demonstrated that families who received in-home services were less likely to reinjure or neglect their children than families who received other services in the community (Lutzker & Rice, 1987).

Coercive parent-child interactions involve characteristics of the parent, the child, and transactional aspects of the parent-child relationship. Parents and children alter their behavior in the process of establishing a coregulated system (Fogel, 1993; Patterson, 1982). Urquiza and McNeil (1996) assert that an ongoing negative, hostile, and coercive relationship sets the stage for PA. They, along with others, argue that to make meaningful changes in the relationship it is essential to involve both the parent and the child in the treatment process.

Given the characteristics of coercive relationships, effective treatment needs to address: (1) parenting skills, (2) distorted cognitions/attributions, (3) development of adaptive and nonviolent coping strategies, and (4) development of greater affective regulation. Three empirically tested interventions that incorporate all four of these elements, involve the parent *and* the child, and draw upon the principles of behavioral therapy or cognitive behavioral therapy (CBT) have been published in the literature and are described in the following order: (a) Parent-Child Interaction Therapy (PCIT); (b) Alternatives for Families: A Cognitive-Behavioral Therapy (AF-CBT) (formerly known as Abuse-Focused CBT); (c) Combined Parent-Child Cognitive Behavioral Therapy (CPC-CBT). A fourth cognitive behavioral–based intervention, Prevention of Adverse Reactions to Negative Events and Related Stress–Child Physical Abuse (PARTNERS-CPA), shows promise but has yet to appear in the literature (Brown, 2005). Interventions based on CBT or behavioral principles have a track record of rigorous, controlled treatment trials (Chaffin et al., 2004; Kolko, 1996b; Runyon, Deblinger, & Steer, in press).

Parent-Child Interaction Therapy

PCIT was developed for treatment of a broad range of childhood disorders (Eyberg & Robinson, 1983). It is a parent training program founded on social learning principles and contains an intensive positive interaction training component that incorporates both parents and children within the treatment session and relies on live coaching to change the dysfunctional parent-child relationship.

In traditional PCIT, families receive 14 weekly 1-hour sessions. Treatment guidelines are carefully followed to avoid divergence from treatment protocols and to ensure treatment integrity. PCIT is conducted in two phases: (1) child-directed interaction and (2) parent-directed interaction. Both phases of treatment are conducted within the context of an initial didactic training followed by therapist coaching in dyadic (primary caregiver–child) play situations. The coaching is conducted from an adjacent observation room using a "bug-in-the-ear" device. Parents are taught and then practice specific skills of communication and behavior management with their children.

In the child-directed interaction portion (typically seven sessions), parents are taught to allow their children to lead the play activity. Parents are instructed to describe, imitate, and praise their children's appropriate behavior and to reflect appropriate child talk. Parents learn not to criticize their children and to avoid using commands and leading questions that make it difficult for their children to lead the play. The major goal of the child-directed interaction portion is to create or strengthen a positive and mutually rewarding relationship between parents and children (Hembree-Kigin & McNeil, 1995).

In the parent-directed interaction portion (typically seven sessions that follow the child-directed sessions), parents are taught how to direct their children's activity and behavior. Parents are instructed in the use of clear, positively stated, direct commands and consistent consequences for behavior (i.e., praise for compliance, time-out in a chair for noncompliance). The major goal of the parent-directed interaction portion is to provide specific and effective parenting skills for parents to use in managing their children's behavior. Parents learn to establish and enforce "house rules" and to manage their children's behavior at home and in public places (Hembree-Kigin & McNeil, 1995). The parent-directed portion is used to decrease problematic behaviors while increasing low-rate prosocial behaviors (Eyberg & Boggs, 1998).

There have been numerous studies demonstrating the efficacy of PCIT for reducing child behavior problems (Eisenstadt, Eyberg, McNeil, Newcomb, & Funderburk, 1993; Eyberg, 1988; Eyberg & Robinson, 1982). In addition, treatment effects have been shown to generalize to the home (Boggs, Eyberg, & Reynolds, 1990), to school settings (McNeil, Eyberg, Eisenstadt, Newcomb, & Funderburk, 1991), and to untreated siblings (Eyberg & Robinson, 1983). Although portions of PCIT may be applicable to many different types of behavioral problems and can be implemented with children of varying ages, PCIT has been most effective with children who are aggressive and/or who have behavioral problems (e.g., oppositional behavior, defiance, and noncompliance), and children between the ages of 2 and 8 years.

Researchers have applied PCIT to the treatment of child PA (Chaffin et al., 2004; Timmer, Urquiza, Zebell, & McGrath, 2005). In a controlled comparison study examining the efficacy of PCIT with parents who engaged in abusive behavior, parent-child dyads were randomly assigned to one of three groups: PCIT, PCIT plus individualized enhanced services, or a community parenting group (Chaffin et al., 2004). For those assigned to the PCIT condition, there were significantly fewer rereports of PA and a relative improvement in parent-child interactions compared to those in the community condition. There were no differences between groups on other measures of child PA risk factors such as parental distress, social support, parental attitudes, or parental perception of children's behaviors. Another study found that PCIT was associated with improved compliance and reduced problem behaviors among children (Timmer et al., 2005). Researchers have examined the application of PCIT with abused children and their foster parents, finding significant reductions in child behavior problems and improvements in parenting skills and parent functioning (decreased parenting stress) (Borrego, Timmer, Urquiza, & Follette, 2004; Borrego, Urquiza, Rasmussen, & Zebell, 1999; Timmer, Borrego, & Urquiza, 2002; Timmer, Urquiza, & Zebell, 2006).

As mentioned earlier, one third of children who have been physically abused develop PTSD (Saunders et al., 2004). In one study, 81% of physically abused children presented partial PTSD symptoms (Runyon, Deblinger, & Schroeder, 2009), while children enrolled in another study reported at least four PTSD symptoms on the Kiddie-Schedule for Affective Disorders and Schizophrenia-PL (KSADS-PL; Kaufman et al., 1996), ranging from 4 to 11 symptoms with a mode of 7 symptoms (Runyon et al., in press). Thus, an important part of treatment is helping children to overcome the trauma associated with their abusive experiences and to cope with their distress.

PCIT emphasizes parent-child interactions but does not directly address the child's emotional distress. The ability of PCIT to improve parent-child interactions may indirectly lower the child's emotional distress, but in many cases it is important to deal directly with the child's distress (Runyon et al., 2009; Runyon et al., in press). PCIT can be supplemented with treatment strategies to ameliorate PTSD and similar issues.

CBT-based treatment models that directly address children's emotional distress (as opposed to PCIT, which is primarily a behavioral intervention and indirectly addresses the child's emotional distress) have many similarities and have data to support their utility with families at risk for child PA (Brown, 2005; Kolko, 1996b, Runyon et al., 2009; Runyon et al., in press). The treatments use CBT and social learning theory to conceptualize the development, maintenance, and treatment of child PA by parents and the emotional and behavioral difficulties exhibited by children. These treatment models utilize methods that directly address the behaviors, cognitions, and affective processes of children and parents. The treatment techniques build on one another, flow from session to session, and teach skills through modeling, coaching, behavioral rehearsal, praise, and corrective feedback. Three CBT-based treatments are described next.

Alternatives for Families: A Cognitive-Behavioral Therapy

There are three phases of AF-CBT treatment: (1) psychoeducation and engagement, (2) individual and family skills training, and (3) family applications that are conducted over the course of 12 to 24 one-hour sessions. The treatment includes child-directed, parent-directed, and family-directed components. Child-directed components include training in affect identification, expression and management, healthy coping, and social/interpersonal skills as well as cognitive processing related to coercive and/or abusive experiences. Essential components for the parent-directed portion of treatment involve engagement and rapport building as well as an examination of the reason for referral and causes of the coercive behavior amongst family members. Cognitive strategies involve examining the parent's beliefs about coercion and violence and unrealistic developmental child expectations that may contribute to aggressive parent-child interactions. Parents are offered affect regulation and parenting skills training to promote more positive parenting strategies. The family-directed components of treatment include PA psychoeducation;

abuse clarification, including the development of a safety plan; communication skills training; and nonviolent problem solving skills training.

Kolko (1996b) randomly assigned children and parents to one of three treatment conditions: individual AF-CBT for child and parent, family therapy, or general community treatment services. When compared to participants who received community treatment, parents and children receiving both individual AF-CBT and family therapy had greater improvements on measures of child externalizing behavior problems, parental distress, abuse risk, and family conflict and cohesion. Children in both conditions exhibited relative improvements in depression and anxiety. AF-CBT was more effective than family therapy in reducing parental anger and use of physical punishment (Kolko, 1996a). Official records revealed PA recidivism rates of 5% and 6% for the individual AF-CBT and family therapy conditions and 30% for those who received the community treatment.

Combined Parent-Child Cognitive Behavioral Therapy

CPC-CBT sessions consist of 16 ninety-minute sessions where the therapist meets separately and jointly with the parent and the child. Group CPC-CBT sessions consist of 16 two-hour sessions with a similar structure. Initial joint parent-child sessions are brief with more time allotted based on needs as treatment progresses.

The initial stages of CPC-CBT treatment involve: (1) engagement strategies and motivational interviewing/consequence review (Donohue, Miller, Van Hasselt & Hersen, 1998) to engage parents to participate in treatment; (2) abuse psychoeducation, including education about different types of violence, the continuum of coercive behavior, and the impact of violent behavior on children, for both parents and children; (3) education for parents about child development and realistic expectations for children's behavior; and (4) emotional expression skills training for children.

During the middle stages of CPC-CBT treatment, parents and children are taught adaptive coping skills (e.g., assertiveness, anger management). These skills help parents remain calm while interacting with their children, develop nonviolent problem-solving skills related to child rearing, and build positive parenting skills.

During the last stage of treatment, when improvements have been reported in parent-child interactions and children's fear, the children develop a trauma narrative. Concurrently, the parents write a letter in which they take full responsibility for their abusive behavior and relieve their children of fear and self-blame for the abuse.

Throughout all stages of treatment, parents practice the implementation of communication, positive parenting, and behavior management skills with the therapist then with their children. The therapist coaches parents and offers positive reinforcement and corrective feedback to enhance these skills. Parents and children rehearse the implementation of a family safety plan and communicate openly about the abuse.

A small pilot study was conducted that examined the feasibility of a group CBT model that incorporated the child into the offending parent's treatment. After their participation in 16 weeks of group CPC-CBT, parents and children reported statistically significant pre- to post-treatment reductions in the use of physical punishment, reductions in parental anger toward their children, reduced PTSD symptoms and behavioral problems in the children, and increased consistency in parenting (Runyon et al., 2009).

In a controlled comparison of CPC-CBT (Runyon et al., in press), treatment type was randomly determined, with subjects participating in 16 weeks of group CBT that included both the parent and child or the parent only. Although there were pre- to post-changes associated with both treatments, subjects participating in CPC-CBT reported greater gains in children's PTSD symptoms as well as positive parenting. Subjects in the parent-only CBT condition reported greater reductions in the use of parent-reported corporal punishment. While the follow-up sample was too small to draw definitive conclusions, these differences were maintained at a 3-month follow-up.

Prevention of Adverse Reactions to Negative Events and Related Stress-Child Physical Abuse

PARTNERS-CPA is an intervention designed for children and their caregivers in cases of child PA (Brown, 2005). It consists of 16 sessions that involve separate meetings with the parent and child as well as joint parent-child sessions. Treatment for caregivers generally consists of three phases: (1) enhancement of adaptive coping skills in order to reduce parental stress and enhance ability to coach their children, (2) evidence-based parent training based on Forehand and McMahon's (1981) work, and (3) clarification and family problem solving.

The child treatment components are delivered across three phases. The first phase involves helping the child develop effective coping skills that prepare the child to develop a trauma narrative during the second phase. The third phase involves safety planning, clarification, and family problem solving.

To examine program outcomes, evaluations are conducted before and after each phase of treatment. Preliminary research indicates decreases in child distress and parent-to-child violence as reported by both children and caregivers (Brown, 2005).

Engaging Parents in Treatment

Any treatment program must begin by engaging the parents, many of whom are guarded and hesitant. Some parents who engage in child PA are not receptive to mental health interventions, which results in a high dropout rate amongst this population. Barriers to treatment include: insufficient time, stigma associated with counseling, lack of transportation, inaccessible locations, low income, lack of information regarding available services, the child not wanting to attend, and unresponsive service providers (Acosta, 1980; Boyd-Franklin, 1993; McKay, Harrison, Gonzales, Kim, & Quintana, 2002). To address barriers, McKay developed empirically validated engagement strategies. Studies show that telephone and in-person engagement strategies address barriers and increase attendance and completion rates (McKay, Stoewe, McCadam, & Gonzales, 1998; Shivak & Sullivan, 1989; Szapocznik et al., 1988).

The therapist initially establishes a collaborative working relationship with parents by discussing their goals, emphasizing common objectives, identifying and eliminating barriers to treatment, and conducting problem solving around immediate concerns (Runyon et al., 2009; Runyon et al., in press). The therapist helps the parents understand the potential consequences of not following through with treatment (Donohue et al., 1998). Parents are encouraged to record and process consequences of their abusive behavior on themselves and their children (e.g., child protection report, child removed from home). The therapist acknowledges that it can be difficult to manage children's behavior and offers to work collaboratively with the parents to develop skills that decrease the likelihood of them experiencing these unpleasant consequences again. Parents are informed of the importance of their role in facilitating behavior change in their children and increasing positive parent-child interactions. Parents are provided with praise and corrective feedback for their participation and effort. The motivational procedures described here were incorporated in studies examining CPC-CBT (Runyon et al., 2009; Runyon et al., in press).

In their study of PCIT with abusive parents, Chaffin and colleagues (2004) incorporated a six-session motivational enhancement orientation group where parents viewed testimonials from program graduates and participated in other motivational techniques, including exercises to enhance their understanding of the potentially negative consequences of physical discipline. In the spirit of motivational interviewing, each participant was required to make a personal statement including their parenting beliefs, the effects of their parenting practices on themselves and others, and their goals for cognitive and behavior change.

To further enhance engagement, CBT models have attempted to increase the cultural sensitivity of the treatments and associated materials. For instance, the materials currently used in AF-CBT (Baumann & Kolko, 2005) have integrated the feedback from African American leaders, practitioners, and caregivers following a systematic series of projects designed to enhance its cultural relevance (Baumann & Kolko, 2005). Similarly, the initial outcome study examining CPC-CBT (Runyon et al., in press) included a sample comprised of 72% families that identified themselves as African American, Black, or Latino and culturally relevant materials were included based on feedback obtained from all participating consumers.

_____ Working With the Child and Parent Together

Although the amount of parent-child dyadic work varies among CBT and behavioral models, all of the models described here work with the parent and child together in order to teach parents noncoercive, nonviolent parenting skills and to improve parent-child interactions (Chaffin et al., 2004; Kolko, 1996b; Runyon et al., in press; Timmer et al., 2002). In addition to dyadic work and parenting skills, CBT models integrate a variety of affective, cognitive, and behavioral skills (i.e., cognitive coping, anger management, and relaxation) to assist parents in managing their emotions in order to remain calm and problem solve when faced with stressful situations, general or parenting related.

To integrate these skills, CBT and behavioral models examine the antecedents, behaviors, and consequences of parent-child interactions. The process allows parents to integrate effective parenting and coping skills into their repertoire, thereby increasing the generalizability of skills learned to everyday life. Parents examine dysfunctional beliefs, negative self-statements, and unrealistic expectations that contribute to and escalate their anger toward their children during a particular interaction. Parents learn to identify cues and triggers that signal their anger is escalating. They are given positive feedback for the use of adaptive coping skills and effective noncoercive parenting skills. Parents examine how they can do things differently to prevent situations that make them angry. By practicing these skills, parents learn to integrate what once may have seemed like abstract ideas into their daily interactions with their children.

Along with the acquisition of parenting skills, CBT models teach children a variety of adaptive coping skills including emotional expression, cognitive coping, anger management, assertiveness, relaxation, problem solving, role perspective taking, and social skills in an effort to assist them in coping with the abuse experienced and coping with general life stressors (Brown, 2005; Kolko, 1996b; Runyon et al., 2009). With regard to CPC-CBT and PARTNERS-CPA, these skills also prepare children to begin working on their trauma narratives (Deblinger & Runyon, 2005).

CBT models involve children and family members working together to develop a family safety plan (Kolko & Swenson, 2002; Runyon et al., 2009). The following variables are considered to evaluate a family's readiness for safety planning: (1) parent demonstrates an ability to control his/her anger, (2) child can identify a parent's anger cues, (3) child and parent report that the parent is using noncoercive parenting strategies, and (4) child and parent report improvements in parent-child interactions (positive parenting skills). The safety plan is then negotiated between the parent and the child. Family members identify a code word that allows all members of the family to use the safety plan if they believe a situation is escalating or perceive an interaction with a family member as threatening (e.g., child recognizes parent's anger cues).

When the code word is used, all family members retreat to preidentified locations in the home for a specified period of time so the family member who is angry can calm down. After the "cool off period" family members return to a preidentified location in the home (i.e., kitchen, living room) to continue with the previous discussion or interaction. If a parent was in the process of disciplining the child when the safety plan was triggered, the parent can continue the discipline in a calm manner.

After the safety plan is developed, family members rehearse the plan during treatment sessions. They are then asked to practice it at home each week. Parents and children are asked if they used the plan and whether it was effective.

CPC-CBT and PARTNERS-CPA focus special attention on PTSD symptoms in children given that studies examining these models have included PTSD symptoms in children as inclusionary criteria. CPC-CBT and PARTNERS-CPA borrow principles of gradual exposure from Trauma-Focused Cognitive Behavioral Therapy (TF-CBT) to target PTSD symptoms (Cohen, Deblinger, Mannarino, & Steer, 2004; Deblinger & Heflin, 1996; Deblinger, Lippmann, & Steer, 1996). The therapist gradually encourages the child to create a narrative about the details of the abuse experience, including abuse-related feelings, thoughts, and bodily sensations. Reliving the experience not only gradually exposes the child to the feared stimuli in an effort to reduce anxiety but also provides an opportunity for dysfunctional abuse-related thoughts to surface that may not otherwise surface during discussion about the abuse. It is notable that AF-CBT includes a separate but brief child and parent disclosure procedure.

In working with parents who have physically abused their children, there are a number of things to consider before having the child develop a trauma narrative. The child is encouraged to develop a trauma narrative during the later phases of treatment, not the initial stages of treatment. In cases where the child is having ongoing contact with the parent, it is critical to assess: (1) the degree to which parent and child are reporting an increase in positive parent-child interactions, (2) the degree to which the child feels safe in the home, (3) whether or not there is evidence that the parent is utilizing coping skills and parenting skills, and (4) whether or not there are ongoing reports of PA.

To address children's distorted beliefs about abuse and to heal the parent-child relationship, CBT models incorporate an abuse clarification process (Deblinger & Runyon, 2005; Kolko & Swenson, 2002; Lipovsky, Swenson, Ralston, & Saunders, 1998; Runyon et al., 2009) whereby the parent prepares a letter to the child that illustrates parental responsibility for the abusive behavior and attempts to alleviate the child's fear and self-blame. CPC-CBT is the only CBT model that incorporates the child's trauma narrative into the clarification process, thus giving the parent an opportunity to respond to the child's distorted cognitions and concerns about the abuse. These distortions may be related to shame, trauma symptoms, and depression.

Case Study of CBT With a School-Age Boy and His Mother

The case of 9-year-old James and his mother Jane, who physically abused him, demonstrates how CBT addresses the multifaceted needs of families in which coercive parent-child interactions occur. As described earlier, there are four treatment models based on CBT. This short chapter does not allow a complete description of how each CBT model could be used to help James and his mother. The case study described here employs a treatment program that incorporates various components of CBT.

Since James was in first grade, Jane, a single parent, had difficulty getting him to complete his homework. James's teachers said he was capable of completing his work but had a bad attitude. Initially, Jane threatened to spank James if he failed to complete his homework. At first the threats worked, but soon Jane found it necessary to carry out the threats. Despite spankings, homework went uncompleted, and James did poorly in school. Jane was extremely frustrated with what she referred to as James's lazy behavior. Her frustration led to more frequent spankings, once with a clothes hanger.

A teacher noticed that James was having trouble sitting at his desk. James was sent to the school nurse, who observed bruises on James's butt, thighs, and lower back. James told the nurse his mother hit him with a clothes hanger. The nurse filed a report with child protective services (CPS). Following an investigation, CPS substantiated PA. The CPS worker decided that James could remain at home as long as Jane agreed to enter therapy. The worker monitored the situation with home visits.

The CPS worker referred Jane and James to an agency that specialized in the treatment of child abuse and child trauma. An assessment prior to initiating treatment revealed that Jane had a moderate level of depression and a significant degree of anger related to James's behavior. Jane and James reported frequent use of physical punishment over the past year. James met full criteria for PTSD in conjunction with depressive symptoms including suicidal thoughts, which he indicated he would not act upon. James also reported getting frustrated easily, which sometimes resulted in him lashing out at others. He reported he had been in a few fights at school. According to James, Jane engaged in very few positive parenting practices. In fact, James could not remember anything his mother did that he liked in the past few months.

Therapy sessions involved working with Jane and James separately and together. Initially, Jane was hesitant to discuss her personal business with the therapist. The therapist empathized with Jane and encouraged her to work through a motivational procedure examining the consequences she experienced as a result of hitting James with the clothes hanger. Jane shared the following consequences and ranked them from most to least aversive: (1) James being fearful of her, (2) change in her relationship with James, (3) loss of privacy due to the CPS worker making unannounced visits, and (4) being negatively perceived by her friends and family as "a child abuser" and "a bad mother." The therapist motivated Jane to consider alternative forms of discipline in order to avoid these consequences in the future.

The therapist assessed Jane's goals for her son and for herself over the course of treatment. Jane said she wanted James to be respectful, to listen to her, and to perform well in school so he could attend college and have a "better life" than she was able to provide for him. The therapist praised Jane for her desire to instill strong values in James. The therapist discussed therapeutic techniques that would be used in treatment to help James attain these goals. Jane was asked to sign a written commitment that she would try to avoid using physical punishment with James.

During initial sessions with James, the therapist established rapport by talking about his love of football, his favorite cartoon, riding his bike with friends, and playing video games. James lamented that he was no longer on the football team because he had to miss practices to attend therapy. He said, "Mom said it is my fault because I told the nurse and the social worker what happened." The therapist explained that all families who come to the agency were there for help because someone hurt a child. James looked surprised and said, "Like my mom hurt me?" He told the therapist that he felt sad when his mom hit him and that he hid from her most of the time because he feared she would hit him again. He said he hoped his mom would stop hitting him. The therapist validated James's feelings and praised him for talking about it. She attempted to instill hope by explaining the treatment process and how his mother was learning alternatives to hitting.

In separate sessions, Jane and James received psychoeducation about abuse and violence. In one of her individual sessions, Jane was asked to identify abuse or violence that she and/or James had been exposed to in their home or community. She began with her own history and disclosed that she was severely beaten by her father. Jane reported numerous occasions when her father beat her with any object that was available (e.g., board, broomstick, belt, crutch). Jane reported that her father beat her with a board and then poured alcohol in the wounds. She thought she was going to die.

The therapist asked Jane about the impact of the abuse on her relationship with her father. Jane replied, "I hate him and haven't talked to him for years." Jane stated that when she was growing up she avoided her father as much as possible. With prompting from the therapist, Jane noted that James did not talk to her much and spent a lot of time in his room. At first, Jane did not think this was related to her treatment of him. Through a series of questions, however, Jane realized the parallels between her avoidance of her father when she was a child and James's avoidance of her. Jane told the therapist that she wanted a better relationship with her son than she had with her father. The therapist reassured Jane that during therapy she and James would spend time interacting in a positive manner that would strengthen their relationship.

In individual sessions, James learned to distinguish between physical discipline and PA. The therapist used a card game in which James earned points for providing correct answers. James enjoyed the game and did an excellent job providing examples of conduct that is abusive. When asked, "Who was responsible for the PA?" James initially stated his mom but then added, "She wouldn't have to hit me if I did what she told me to do." The therapist helped James understand that PA is never okay and that there are other ways his mom can safely and effectively address his noncompliant behavior.

The therapist helped James create a list of feelings that children may experience when they are physically abused. James shared a variety of emotions including fear, anger, self-blame, and sadness in response to his mother abusing him. The therapist praised James for knowing "many feeling words" and for sharing his feelings about what happened to him. The therapist helped James understand that his feelings were common given the abuse he had experienced.

In the middle stages of therapy, Jane worked to develop skills to control anger and to assist her in interacting calmly with James. Jane was asked to think about the first sign (anger cue) that she was getting angry. Jane indicated that she first noticed she was becoming angry when her voice got louder.

Jane and the therapist discussed a basic behavioral form of anger management: removing oneself from the situation. In addition, the therapist elicited strategies that Jane found helpful for calming herself when angry. Jane indicated that reading a book, walking around the block, and taking a bubble bath assisted her in remaining calm.

To further assist Jane in managing her anger, the therapist elicited Jane's beliefs about the causes of James's misbehavior. The therapist helped Jane understand the connections between her thoughts, feelings, and behaviors. Jane explained that she believed James was lazy. The therapist asked Jane to think about all the possible reasons for James not completing his homework. At first, Jane could only think of laziness. Gradually, she came up with other ideas—he did not understand the homework, he had trouble learning, or he needed assistance but was reluctant to ask.

Jane was not the only one to benefit from anger and emotion management training.

During individual sessions with James, the therapist offered cognitive coping, anger management, and assertiveness skills training. James rehearsed his new skills during anger-provoking situations on the playground. James identified people who he could approach for support (e.g., teacher, mom) and role-played with the therapist asking for help from these individuals.

All of the CBT and behavioral models discussed in this chapter use dyadic work as well as individual sessions to assist the parent in acquiring parenting skills. The goal in dyadic work is to enhance parent-child relationships and increase positive parenting strategies. In preparation for joint sessions, Jane was offered instruction in positive parenting skills such as praise, positive attention, differential attention, and active listening. Jane was given an opportunity to practice these skills with the therapist. Then, with the therapist available to coach her, Jane practiced each skill with James during joint sessions.

After practicing the new skills in therapy, Jane was encouraged to implement the skills at home. Jane was given specific weekly homework assignments. Jane was instructed to praise James for appropriate behavior, to give clear, direct instructions, and to provide consistent consequences for not okay behaviors. In addition, the therapist coached Jane in child-directed activities where Jane allowed James to direct games and fun activities. James told his mom that he had the most fun during their family game night when he got to pick the game they were going to play and make up his own rules for the game. Over time, Jane reported that James was increasingly responsive to her requests for him to do certain tasks (e.g., clean his room, complete homework). James reported an increase in positive experiences with his mother. He also reported that she yelled at him less and hit him less, which he described as "great!"

After Jane demonstrated an ability to use adaptive coping skills and remain calm while dealing with parenting situations, the therapist increased the time spent jointly with Jane and James. During these joint meetings, the therapist helped James and his mother develop a safety plan. When James or his mom noticed cues that the other was getting angry, they decided to use "stop sign" as their code to signal that it was time for Jane and James to go to their rooms to calm down.

In the final stage of therapy, the therapist helped Jane gain skills that would encourage James to communicate openly about his feelings surrounding the PA. Jane wrote a letter to her son apologizing for hitting him and assuring him that he did not deserve to be treated that way. Jane commented how happy she was that they talked more often and that she enjoyed the time they spent together.

Working with James, the therapist elicited details about the abuse with the clothes hanger. As James provided a poignant, emotional description of the incident, the therapist helped James process his abuse-related thoughts and feelings. Jane read James's description of the clothes hanger incident and was surprised at how traumatic it was for him. Jane reassured her son that she would use the skills she learned to remain calm and care for him in a kinder and gentler way.

By the end of therapy, James's symptoms of PTSD and depression had remitted. He reported that his mother was using positive parenting strategies including praise, active listening, and positive reinforcement. Jane said, "At first I was angry. I did not want anyone telling me how to parent my child. Now, I see how good things can be. I had no idea how this was going to impact my relationship with my son. We do so many things together now!" James thanked his mom for being kinder and not hitting him. At the graduation ceremony to celebrate their progress, James jumped into his mother's lap, hugged her, and said, "You are the best mom ever! I love you."

Jane tearfully hugged him and replied, "I love you, too."

Conclusion

The treatment models previously described—PCIT, AF-CBT, CPC-CBT, and PARTNERS-CPA—hold promise for addressing some of the fundamental difficulties within families who are at risk or in which PA has occurred. While these four interventions are each distinct in their approach to working with abusive families, they are interventions that focus on changing the parent-child relationship, which involves working with the parent and the child together. In addition, all of the programs focus on essential treatment needs: (1) enhancing parenting skills, (2) altering distorted parental cognitions/attributions, (3) developing adaptive and nonviolent coping strategies, and (4) developing greater affective regulation. Some of the treatments described also focus on assisting the child to heal from the traumatic experiences. While there may be additional treatments that gain research support, it is likely that they will also focus on these four essential treatment elements.

Researchers have just begun to identify treatments that are effective for addressing the multifaceted needs of families in which child PA occurs. Future research should examine potential moderating and mediating variables that may help illuminate who responds best to what type of treatment. Studies examining the outcomes associated with the dissemination of these evidence-based treatments to community agencies is also an important next step.

References

Acosta, F. X. (1980). Self-described reasons for premature termination of psychotherapy by Mexican American, Black American, and Anglo-American patients. *Psychological Reports, 47,* 435–443.

Azar, S. (1997). A cognitive behavioral approach to understanding and treating parents who physically abuse their children. In D. Wolfe, R.J. McMahon, & R.D. Peters (Eds.), *Child abuse: New directions in prevention and treatment across the lifespan.* Thousand Oaks, CA: Sage.

Baumann, B., & Kolko, D. J. (2005). *Improving the cultural relevancy of an evidence-based intervention for physically abusive families.* Pittsburgh: Center for Minority Health, University of Pittsburgh.

Boggs, S. R., Eyberg, S. M., & Reynolds, L. (1990). Concurrent validity of the Eyberg Child Behavior Inventory. *Journal of Clinical Child Psychology, 19,* 75–78.

Borrego, J., Timmer, S. G., Urquiza, A. J., & Follette, W. C. (2004). Physically abusive mothers' responses following episodes of child noncompliance and compliance. *Journal of Consulting & Clinical Psychology, 72,* 897–903.

Borrego, J., Urquiza, A. J., Rasmussen, R. A., & Zebell, N. (1999). Parent-child interaction therapy with a family at high risk for physical abuse. *Child Maltreatment, 4,* 331–342.

Boyd-Franklin, N. (1993). Race, class, and poverty. In F. Walsh (Ed.), *Normal family process* (pp. 361–376). New York: Guilford Press.

Brown, E. J. (2005). *Efficacy of a parent-child intervention for physically abused children and their caregivers.* Paper presented at the Annual Colloquium of the American Professional Society on the Abuse of Children, New Orleans, LA.

Chaffin, M., Silovsky, J. F., Funderburk, B., Valle, L., Brestan, E. V., Balachova, T., et al. (2004). Parent-child interaction therapy with physically abusive parents: Efficacy for reducing future abuse reports. *Journal of Consulting & Clinical Psychology, 72,* 500–510.

Clausen, A. H., & Crittenden, P. M. (1991). Physical and psychological maltreatment: Relations among types of maltreatment. *Child Abuse and Neglect, 15,* 5–8.

Cohen, J. A., Deblinger, E., Mannarino, A. P., & Steer, R. A. (2004). A multisite, randomized controlled trial for children with sexual abuse-related PTSD symptoms. *Journal of the American Academy of Child & Adolescent Psychiatry, 43,* 393–402.

Deblinger, E., & Heflin, A. (1996). *Treating sexually abused children and their nonof-fending parents: A cognitive-behavioral approach*. Thousand Oaks, CA: Sage.

Deblinger, E., Lippmann, J., & Steer, R. (1996). Sexually abused children suffering posttraumatic stress symptoms: Initial treatment outcome findings. *Child Maltreatment*, 1, 310–321.

Deblinger, E., & Runyon, M. K. (2005). Understanding and treating feelings of shame in children who have experienced maltreatment. *Child Maltreatment*, 10, 364–376.

Donohue, B., Miller, E., Van Hasselt, V. B., & Hersen, M. (1998). Ecological treat-ment of child abuse. In V.B. Van Hasselt & M. Hersen (Eds.), *Sourcebook of psychological treatment manuals for children and adolescents* (pp. 203–278). Hillsdale, NJ: Lawrence Erlbaum.

Eisenstadt, T. H., Eyberg, S., McNeil, C. B., Newcomb, K., & Funderburk, B. (1993). Parent-child interaction therapy with behavior problem children: Relative effectiveness of two stages and overall treatment outcome. *Journal of Clinical Child Psychology*, 22, 42–51.

Eyberg, S. M. (1988). Parent-child interaction therapy: Integration of traditional and behavioral concerns. *Child & Family Behavior Therapy*, 10, 33–46.

Eyberg, S. M., & Boggs, S. R. (1998). Parent-child interaction therapy for opposi-tional preschoolers. In C. E. Schaefer & J. M. Briesmeister (Eds.), *Handbook of parent training: Parents as co-therapists for children's behavior problems* (2nd ed., pp. 61–97). New York: Wiley.

Eyberg, S. M., & Robinson, E. A. (1982). Parent-child interaction training: Effects on family functioning. *Journal of Clinical Child Psychology*, 11, 130–137.

Eyberg, S. M., & Robinson, E. A. (1983). Conduct problem behavior: Standardization of a behavioral rating scale with adolescents. *Journal of Clinical Child Psychology*, 12, 347–357.

Fantuzzo, J. W. (1990). Behavioral treatment of the victims of child abuse and neglect. *Behavior Modification*, 14, 316–339.

Fogel, A. (1993). *Developing through relationships*. Chicago: University of Chicago Press.

Forehand, R. L., & McMahon, R. J. (1981). *Helping the noncompliant child: A clin-ician's guide to parent training*. New York: Guilford Press.

Fraser, M. W., Walton, E., Lewis, R. E., Pecora, P., & Walton, W. (1996). An exper-iment in family reunification: Correlates of outcomes at one year follow up. *Children and Youth Services Review*, 16, 335–361.

Gershater-Molko, R. M., Lutzker, J. R., & Wesch, D. (2003). Project SafeCare: Improving health, safety, and parenting skills in families reported for, and at-risk for child maltreatment. *Journal of Family Violence*, 18, 377–386.

Gil, E. (1996). *Treating abused adolescents*. New York: Guilford Press.

Hembree-Kigin, T., & McNeil, C. (1995). *Parent-child interaction therapy*. New York: Plenum.

Kaufman, J., Birmaher, B., Brent, D., Rao, U., Flynn, C., Moreci, P., et al., (1996). Schedule for affective disorders and schizophrenia for school-age children-present and lifetime version (K-SADS-PL): Initial reliability and validity data. *Journal of the American Academy of Child & Adolescent Psychiatry*, 36, 980–988.

Kolko, D. J. (1996a). Clinical monitoring of treatment course in child physical abuse: Psychometric characteristics and treatment comparisons. *Child Abuse and Neglect*, 20, 23–43.

Kolko, D. J. (1996b). Individual cognitive-behavioral treatment and family therapy for physically abused children and their offending parents: A comparison of clinical outcomes. *Child Maltreatment, 1,* 322–342.

Kolko, D. J. (2002). Child physical abuse. In J. E. B. Myers, L. Berliner, J. Briere, C. T. Hendrix, C. Jenny, & T. Reid (Eds.), *The APSAC handbook of child maltreatment* (2nd ed.). Thousand Oaks, CA: Sage.

Kolko, D. J., & Swenson, C. C. (2002). *Assessing and treating physically abused children and their families: A cognitive-behavioral approach.* Thousand Oaks, CA: Sage.

Lahey, B. B., Conger, R. D., Atkeson, B. M., & Treiber, F. A. (1984). Parenting status and emotional behavior of physically abusive mothers. *Journal of Consulting & Clinical Psychology, 52,* 1062–1071.

Lipovsky, J., Swenson, C. C., Ralston, M. E., & Saunders, B. E. (1998). The abuse clarification process in the treatment of intrafamilial child abuse. *Child Abuse and Neglect, 22,* 729–741.

Lutzker, J. R., & Rice, J. M. (1987). Using recidivism data to evaluate Project 12-Ways: An ecobehavioral approach to the treatment and prevention of child abuse and neglect. *Journal of Family Violence, 2,* 283–290.

Mammen, O., Kolko, D., & Pilkonis, P. (2003). Parental cognitions and satisfaction: Relationship to aggressive parental behavior in child physical abuse. *Child Maltreatment, 8,* 288–301.

McKay, M., Harrison, M., Gonzales, J., Kim, L., & Quintana, E. (2002). Multiple family groups for urban children with conduct difficulties and their families. *Psychiatric Services, 53,* 1467–1469.

McKay, M., Stoewe, J., McCadam, K., & Gonzales, J. (1998). Increasing access to child mental health services for urban children and their care givers. *Health and Social Work, 23,* 9–15.

McNeil, C., Eyberg, S., Eisenstadt, T., Newcomb, K., & Funderburk, B. (1991). Parent-child interaction therapy with behavior problem children: Generalization of treatment effects to the school setting. *Journal of Clinical Child Psychology, 20,* 140–151.

Milner, J. S. (2000). Social information processing and child physical abuse: Theory and research. In D. J. Hansen (Ed.), *Nebraska Symposium on Motivation* (Vol. 45, pp. 39–84). Lincoln: University of Nebraska Press.

Milner, J. S. (2003). Social information processing in high-risk and physically abusive parents. *Child Abuse and Neglect, 27,* 7–20.

Monroe, L. D., & Schellenbach, C. J. (1989). Relationship of child abuse potential inventory scores to parental responses: A construct validity study. *Child and Family Behavior, 12,* 39–58.

Moore, E., Armsden, G., & Gogerty, P. L. (1998). A twelve year follow up study of maltreated and at risk children who received early therapeutic care. *Child Maltreatment, 3,* 3–16.

Patterson, G. R. (1982). *Coercive family process.* Eugene, OR: Castalia.

Patterson, G. R., DeBaryshe, B. D., & Ramsey, E. (1989). A developmental perspective on antisocial behavior. *American Psychologist, 44,* 329–335.

Ralston, M. E., & Swenson, C. C. (1996). *The Charleston collaborative project: Intervention manual.* Charleston, SC: Author.

Runyon, M. K., Deblinger, E., & Schroeder, C. M. (2009). Pilot evaluation of outcomes of combined parent-child cognitive-behavioral group therapy for families at-risk for child physical abuse. *Cognitive Behavioral Practice, 16,* 101–118.

Runyon, M. K., Deblinger, E., & Steer, R. A. (in press). Comparison of combined parent-child and parent-only cognitive-behavioral treatments for offending parents and children in cases of child physical abuse. *Child and Family Behavior Therapy.*

Saunders, B. E., Berliner, L., & Hanson, R. F. (Eds.). (2004). *Child physical and sexual abuse: Guidelines for treatment (final report: January 15, 2004).* Charleston, SC: National Crime Victims Research and Treatment Center.

Saunders, B. E., & Meinig, M. B. (2000). Immediate issues affecting long term family resolution in cases of parent-child sexual abuse. In R. M. Reece (Ed.), *Treatment of child abuse: Common ground for mental health, medical, and legal practitioners* (pp. 36–53). Baltimore: The Johns Hopkins University Press.

Shivak, I. M., & Sullivan, C. W. (1989). Use of telephone prompts at an inner-city outpatient clinic. *Hospital & Community Psychiatry, 40,* 851–853.

Simons, R. L., Whitbeck, L. B., Conger, R. D., & Chyi-in, W. (1991). Intergenerational transmission of harsh parenting. *Developmental Psychology, 27,* 159–171.

Szapocznik, J., Perez-Vidal, A., Brickman, A. L., Foote, F. H., Santisteban, D., Hervis, O., et al. (1988). Engaging adolescent drug abusers and their families in treatment: A strategic structural systems approach. *Journal of Consulting & Clinical Psychology, 56,* 552–557.

Timmer, S. G., Borrego, J., & Urquiza, A. J. (2002). Antecedents of coercive interactions in physically abusive mother-child dyads. *Journal of Interpersonal Violence, 17,* 836–853.

Timmer, S. G., Urquiza, A. J., & Zebell, N. (2006). Challenging foster caregiver-maltreated child relationships: The effectiveness of Parent Child Interaction Therapy. *Child & Youth Services Review, 28,* 1–19.

Timmer, S., Urquiza, A. J., Zebell, N., & McGrath, J. (2005). Parent-child interaction therapy: Application to physically abusive and high-risk parent-child dyads. *Child Abuse and Neglect, 29,* 825–842.

Urquiza, A. J., & McNeil, C. B. (1996). Parent-child interaction therapy: An intensive dyadic intervention for physically abusive families. *Child Maltreatment, 1,* 134–144.

Wolfe, D. A. (1987). *Child abuse: Implications for child development and psychopathology.* Newbury Park, CA: Sage.

PART IV

Child Sexual Abuse

Part IV of the *APSAC Handbook on Child Maltreatment* analyzes child sexual abuse (CSA). Chapter 13 begins the analysis by defining CSA and describing the harmful consequences of this form of maltreatment. Children disclose sexual abuse in many ways, and disclosure is the subject of Chapter 14. Although most sexual abuse does not cause physical injury, it is important for children who may be sexually abused to receive a medical examination. The medical examination for sexual abuse is discussed in Chapter 15. CSA is psychologically damaging for many victims, and Chapter 16 describes mental health interventions designed to assist sexually abused children. Mental health treatment for adolescent and adult sex offenders is discussed in Chapter 17. Part IV ends with Chapter 18, which analyzes policies and laws that are intended to protect society from sex offenders.

13 Child Sexual Abuse

Definitions, Prevalence, and Consequences

Lucy Berliner

This chapter introduces Part IV of the book. The chapter defines child sexual abuse (CSA), discusses the prevalence of this form of maltreatment, and describes the harmful effects of sexual abuse.

Child Sexual Abuse Defined

Sexual abuse involves any sexual activity with a child below the legal age of consent, which is typically 14 to 18 years (Berliner, 2000; Finkelhor, 1979). Children below the age of consent are legally incapable of consenting to sexual activity. Sexual abuse includes sexual penetration, sexual touching, and noncontact sexual acts such as exposure or voyeurism. Sexual contact between a teenager or a child and a younger child can be abusive.

Unlike physical child abuse and neglect, in which the offender is typically a parent, sexual abuse includes abuse by *any* person. Most sexual abuse is not committed by parents. Fathers or stepfathers are the offenders in only 16% of cases, and even when all relatives are included, familial sexual abuse is a minority of cases (Hanson et al., 2006; Saunders, Kilpatrick, Hanson, Resnick, & Walker, 1999). The most common sexual abuser is an acquaintance or someone the child or family knows (Finkelhor, Ormrod, & Turner, 2009; Finkelhor, Ormrod, Turner, & Hamby, 2005; Saunders et al., 1999; Tjaden & Thoennes, 2000).

The Prevalence of Child Sexual Abuse

For many reasons, understanding the full scope of CSA is difficult. There are definitional differences across data sources concerning what behaviors constitute sexual abuse. Different sources use different data collection methods and often target specific age groups (e.g., adolescents) or subsets of the child population (e.g., only children abused by family members). Most incidents of sexual abuse are not reported to authorities, and many episodes are not revealed to professionals, friends, or family members (Finkelhor, Hotaling, Lewis, & Smith, 1990; Smith et al., 2000). Sexual abuse continues to be a stigmatizing and embarrassing experience. Consequently, some victims do not reveal past incidents even when sensitively asked. Disclosure of CSA is discussed in detail in Chapter 14. Thus, answering the seemingly simple question, "How common is sexual abuse?" turns out to be quite complicated.

There is no ongoing comprehensive national effort to document all incidents of CSA in the United States. The three most visible sources of national information offer an incomplete picture. First, official crime statistics capture only incidents of certain crimes that are detected by local law enforcement agencies and reported to the FBI Uniform Crime Reports program (U.S. Department of Justice, 2009). Crimes against children and youth are not broken out in the general crime statistics.

Second, the largest national survey of the annual incidence of crime in the United States, the National Criminal Victimization Survey (NCVS), assesses reports of crimes from a representative sample of the population but only asks about selected crimes that occur to people age 12 and older. Of course, many victims of CSA are below the age of 12. The NCVS has been criticized for its methodology in assessing sexual assault, and some critics argue that it underestimates the true incidence (Kilpatrick, 2004; Kilpatrick, McCauley, & Mattern, 2009).

Third, statistics derived from reports of suspected child maltreatment filed with child protection agencies and included in the National Child Abuse and Neglect Data System (NCANDS) describe only cases perpetrated by parents or caregivers (U.S. Department of Health and Human Services, 2010). Most CSA, however, is not perpetrated by parents or caregivers. The NCANDS report for 2008 indicated that approximately 3.3 million children were involved in reports to child protection agencies. An estimated 772,000 children were substantiated as victims of some form of child maltreatment. Of these, 9.1% were victims of sexual abuse.

Other important sources of information about the prevalence of CSA are surveys of community population samples. Survey studies either question adults about their history of sexual abuse as children or question children and/or adolescents about their experiences. Surveys can be very useful, particularly surveys that examine nationally representative samples. The results of such samples can be generalized to the full population.

Results from survey research often vary considerably due to differences in operational definitions of sexual abuse and research methods used

(Finkelhor, 1994). As well, surveys must overcome the stigma associated with CSA and the reluctance of some participants to divulge their experiences, even when reporting is anonymous. Even the best population surveys underestimate the true prevalence of sexual abuse.

Memory is another factor affecting estimates of abuse rates based on self-report. Two prospective longitudinal studies of adults with documented childhood sexual abuse histories found that more than 30% of the respondents did not report those early experiences when questioned (Widom & Morris, 1997; Williams, 1994). Although some of the nonreporting may be due to reluctance to reveal remembered abuse, Williams's (1994) analysis of the responses of women who did not report documented abuse cases suggests that they did not recall what had happened to them as children.

Two of the largest and most representative studies of childhood sexual assault are the National Women's Study (NWS) (Saunders et al., 1999) and the National Violence Against Women Survey (NVAWS) (Tjaden and Thoennes, 2000). The NWS used telephone interviews to assess a nationally representative sample of 4,008 adult women living in households in the United States. Three hundred thirty-nine of the women (8.5%) reported experiencing at least one completed rape prior to the age of 18. Lifetime prevalence rates of completed child rape did not differ significantly by the racial or ethnic identification of the woman. There was a significant age effect, with older age cohorts having substantially lower prevalence rates of rape than younger women. Average age at first child rape was 10.8 years and 60% of first child rapes occurred prior to age 13. The most common offender (39% of assaults) was a nonrelative known by the victim such as a neighbor, friend, peer, or coworker. Fathers or stepfathers committed 16% of the rapes, brothers 5%, boyfriends 9%, and 20% by other relatives. Strangers committed only 11% of all rapes. Of all the rapes, 42% were series rapes, meaning the same offender raped the child more than once. Only 12% of the rapes were reported to the authorities.

Tjaden and Thoennes (2000) used methods similar to the NWS to conduct the NVAWS, which also included men. The NVAWS surveyed a nationally representative sample of 8,005 adult men and 8,000 adult women living in households in the United States and found results similar to the NWS. Tjaden and Thoennes (2000) found that 9% of the women and 2% of the men reported a history of a completed rape prior to the age of 18.

Finkelhor (1994) reviewed retrospective prevalence surveys that were conducted with adults and concluded that at least 20% to 25% of women and between 5% to 15% of men experience some form of contact CSA. Many studies of the impact of sexual abuse in countries across the world find similar percentages (e.g, Fanslow, Robinson, Crengle, & Perese, 2007; Gilbert, Widom, Fergusson, Webb, & Janson, 2009; Johnson, 2004; Pereda, Guilera, Forns, & Gómez-Benito, 2009). As mentioned, differences in the reported rates of sexual abuse are likely accounted for by the types of screening questions asked, the research methodology, and perhaps cultural contexts as well as actual differences in prevalence among populations studied.

Recently, the general population telephone survey method has been extended to directly ask children and their parents about sexual abuse and other victimization experiences (Finkelhor, Turner, Ormrod, & Hamby, 2009; Finkelhor, Ormrod, et al., 2009; Finkelhor et al., 2005; Hanson et al., 2006). These surveys of nationally representative samples of children and youth find rates of approximately 6% annual incidence and 9% reported lifetime prevalence of sexual abuse. This methodology reduces the error associated with forgetting about abuse experiences but may result in underestimates of crimes committed by family members since the children are still living with their families. Few children in these surveys reported intrafamilial sexual abuse.

Sexual victimization of youth via the Internet is a newer form of sexual abuse. It can include unwanted sexual solicitations or exposure to pornography, inducement to engage in off-line sexual experiences with adults, and involvement in child pornography (Mitchell, Finkelhor, & Wolak, 2003). Rates of unwanted Internet sexual solicitations declined from 19% to 13%, but harassment (6% to 9%) and unwanted exposure to pornography (25% to 34%) increased from 2000 to 2005 (Mitchell, Wolak, & Finkelhor, 2007). However, a 2005 survey found that youth were more likely to report aggressive solicitations, and the rates of different forms of online sexual victimization decreased or increased with variations by age, gender, race, and household. There is little data on voluntary participation in illegal sexual activities or involvement in child pornography.

As reported retrospectively, nonclinical African American and Caucasian women have similar rates of CSA (Tjaden & Thoennes, 2000; Wyatt, 1985). The rate for Asian women is somewhat lower, and the rate for Native American women is somewhat higher (Tjaden & Thoennes, 2000). Hispanic women are at increased risk for incestuous abuse (Russell, 1984) and Latino adolescents report significantly higher rates of sexual abuse compared to youth of European descent (Newcomb, Munoz, & Carmona, 2009).

Reporting of sexual abuse increased significantly in the late 1980s and the early 1990s. Since the mid-1990s, however, there has been a significant decline in reports to child abuse authorities (Finkelhor, Turner, Ormrod, & Hamby, 2010; Jones, 2008; Jones, Finkelhor, & Kopiec, 2001; Sedlak et al., 2010). The reasons for the decline are likely complicated. It is possible that the decline is in part due to authorities becoming more stringent in the criteria applied to accepting reports. On the other hand, the decline in sexual abuse reports has occurred during the same time period as declines in virtually all other crime categories including homicide, physical abuse (PA) of children, rape, domestic violence, and other violent crime. The decline data for crimes against adults are derived from both official reports to the FBI's Uniform Crime Reports and self-reports of crime experiences in the NCVS. The decline of sexual abuse in the recently released findings from the NIS-4 report provide support for a true decline rather than change in reporting patterns (Sedlak et al., 2010). This study interviewed sentinel reporters to capture reporting behavior as well as actual reports. No evidence was found for a reluctance to report. This suggests that the decreases in sexual abuse reports represent real declines. These declines are likely at least in part attributable to the forces affecting the larger phenomenon of crime rates, such as decreased tolerance for abuse and crime.

Characteristics of Sexual Abuse Experiences

The characteristics of sexual abuse experiences vary depending on the data source. For example, child abuse reporting systems and clinical samples (i.e., subjects receiving mental health treatment) tend to overrepresent intrafamilial cases. Based on nonclinical, general population surveys (e.g., Finkelhor & Dziuba-Leatherman, 1994; Saunders et al., 1999), abuse by parent figures (parents and stepparents) constitutes between 6% and 16% of cases, and abuse by any relative comprises more than one third of cases. In nonclinical general population samples, teenagers represent up to 40% of offenders, and strangers account for a relatively small proportion (5% to 15%), with the remainder of cases involving individuals known to the child or family. In both clinical and nonclinical samples, the vast majority of offenders are male, although boys are more likely than girls to be abused by women (20% versus 5%) (Finkelhor & Russell, 1984).

Multiple episodes of sexual abuse are common, occurring in up to half of cases in nonclinical samples (e.g., Saunders et al., 1999) and in up to three fourths of children in clinical samples (Conte & Schuerman, 1987; Elliott & Briere, 1994; Ruggiero, McLeer, & Dixon, 2000). Completed or attempted oral, anal, or vaginal penetration occurs in about one fourth of nonclinical subjects (Finkelhor, 1994) and in half or more of clinical samples (Gomes-Schwartz, Horowitz, & Cardarelli, 1990; Ruggiero et al., 2000). The mean age for sexual abuse is approximately 9 years old, with a range from infancy to 18 years.

Compared to girls, boys are older at onset of victimization, more likely to be abused by nonfamily members, and more likely to be abused by women and by offenders who are known to have abused other children (e.g., Faller, 1989; Holmes & Slap, 1998).

In the few studies examining ethnicity, differences in the type and length of abuse experience, offender relationship to the victim, family characteristics, and family response are associated with ethnic background (Mennen, 1995; Rao, DiClemente, & Ponton, 1992). It is not clear what accounts for ethnic variations. Variation may be the result of reporting bias, differences in family configuration, cultural practices, or may simply be an artifact of the samples in these studies.

Families with a child who has been sexually abused are thought to have certain characteristics. Studies find that families of both incest and nonincest sexual abuse victims are less cohesive, more disorganized, and generally more dysfunctional than families of nonabused children (Elliott & Briere, 1994; Hoagwood & Stewart, 1989; Madonna, Van Scoyk, & Jones, 1991; Mannarino

& Cohen, 1996). The areas most often identified as problematic in incest cases are difficulties with communication, a lack of emotional closeness and flexibility, and social isolation (e.g., Dadds, Smith, Weber, & Robinson, 1991). Although it appears that families in which incest has occurred exhibit greater dysfunction, it is possible that the pathology is as much a result of the abuse as the cause (Briere & Elliott, 1993).

Some risk factors for sexual abuse have been identified. Girls are at higher risk for sexual abuse than boys. Both males and females are at increased risk if they have lived without one of their natural parents, have a mother who is unavailable, or perceive their family life as unhappy (Finkelhor & Baron, 1986; Finkelhor et al., 1990; Holmes & Slap, 1998). There is evidence that children who have a psychological or cognitive vulnerability may be at increased risk for sexual abuse (e.g., Tharinger, Horton, & Millea, 1990). The reported incidence of sexual abuse among children with a disability is 1.75 times the rate for children with no disability (National Center on Child Abuse and Neglect, 1993). There are insufficient data to confirm whether this is a reporting phenomenon or an actual increased vulnerability (Newman, Christopher, & Berry, 2000). Unlike other forms of child abuse, socioeconomic status does not appear to be related to sexual abuse.

Sexual abuse is perpetrated in a variety of ways. In some cases, even though the offender has a relationship with the child, the victimization occurs without warning. More typically, offenders engage in a gradual process of sexualizing the relationship over time (Berliner & Conte, 1990). Offenders may conceal the sexual nature of the activity by characterizing it as nonsexual (e.g., sex education, hygiene) or may encourage the child to consider the relationship as mutual. Repeat offenders generally calculate and plan their approach to victimizing children, often employing elaborate strategies to involve the children, maintain their cooperation, and prevent reporting (Conte, Wolfe, & Smith, 1989; Elliott, Browne, & Kilcoyne, 1995; Lang & Frenzel, 1988). In a substantial percentage of cases, offenders use force, threats, or fear (e.g., Elliott & Briere, 1994; Gomes-Schwartz et al., 1990; Saunders et al., 1999). The *modus operandi* (method of operating) of sex offenders is further described in Chapter 14.

Although most children experience sexual abuse as unwanted or aversive, this is not true of all victims. There is a group of adolescent victims who perceive the sexual experiences as consensual. These cases typically involve situations in which an adult such as a teacher, coach, youth leader, or other trusted person persuades the youth that the relationship is exceptional or a socially ostracized form of "true love." Sometimes there is no pretense of a special relationship but rather the youth agrees to participate in exchange for rewards such as money, access to illicit activities such as drinking or drugs, or simply for the experience. Lanning (1992) has described the youth in these situations as "compliant victims." Lanning (1992) emphasizes that in these cases the offenders are exploiting normal adolescent developmental processes that may make them especially vulnerable to participation in illegal sexual experiences.

Internet-based victimization cases often fit this characterization. Research has shown that sexual victimization via the Internet mostly involves adolescents who initiate or respond to sexual overtures and agree to meet in person with the offender (Wolak, Ybarra, Mitchell, & Finkelhor, 2007). Deception about age or the purpose of the encounter is rarely involved, and the youth do not usually see themselves as victims.

Effects of Child Sexual Abuse

Research conducted over the past 3 decades indicates that a wide range of psychological, health, and interpersonal problems are more prevalent among those who have been sexually abused in childhood compared to those who have not (e.g., Chartier, Walker, & Naimark, 2007; Maniglio, 2009; Widom & Morris, 1997). Sexual abuse during childhood is a significant risk factor for problems in adolescence (Hussey, Chang, & Kotch, 2006) and in adulthood (Dube et al., 2005). However, not all children exposed to sexual abuse develop detectable negative effects (Kendall-Tackett, Williams, & Finkelhor, 1993).

Recent developments in research on the impact of traumatic events help explain these results. The most important advance in studying the prevalence and impact of traumatic events has been the move away from focusing on a single type of trauma and toward assessing a range of victimization experiences and adversities (Dong et al., 2004; Finkelhor, 2008; Finkelhor, Ormrod, et al., 2009). It is now apparent that exposure to traumatic events is very common in the lives of children. For example, Finkelhor (Finkelhor et al., 2009) finds lifetime prevalence among children of 80% exposed to trauma, with 60% exposed each year.

Further, most children exposed to a potentially traumatic event have had other traumatic experiences as well. Finkelhor, Ormrod, and Turner (2009) describe a subsample comprising 22% of children who are "polyvictims" who have had an average of four victimizations. In a clinical sample recruited for a sexual abuse treatment study, Deblinger, Mannarino, Cohen, and Steer (2006) screened for other traumas and reported that the majority had experienced one or more additional traumas, including sudden loss of a loved one, witnessing domestic violence, PA, accident, or disaster.

Recognition that exposure to potentially traumatic events is common means that it is very likely that the human organism has developed methods of coping with difficult life experiences. Research on resilience and recovery in both children and adults supports this view. For example, Bonnano and Mancini (2008) found that the most common pathways for children exposed to potentially traumatic events is to recover without persisting negative effects.

At the same time, the results of these studies demonstrate that multiple abuse experiences and adversities is strongly associated with increased risk for negative outcomes (Dong et al., 2004; Turner, Finkelhor, & Ormrod, 2006).

As demonstrated in the Adverse Childhood Experiences Study (Dong et al., 2004), the probability of negative psychological and health outcomes increases with the number of adverse childhood experiences.

The fact that many children can recover naturally from trauma exposure—especially when they do not have multiple trauma experiences or other risk factors—does not mean that sexual abuse is a neutral experience. In the majority of sexual abuse cases, the contact is unwanted or forced. It is almost always upsetting and confusing, and in many cases it is painful, frightening, and shame inducing. Even when the experience does not produce persisting psychological difficulties, it has an effect on children because it is developmentally inappropriate, it alters the relationship within which it occurs, and it can lead to changes in children's perceptions of others and the safety in the world. Sexual abuse can affect life trajectory by increasing the risk for subsequent victimizations (Fargo, 2009) or impairing social and occupational functioning (Zielinski, 2009).

Risk Factors for Adverse Effects of Child Sexual Abuse

The primary finding with regard to risk factors for negative outcome of traumatic events including sexual abuse is that a child's "trauma burden" is a key factor in predicting outcome. The type of trauma is less important than the accumulation of a trauma history (Finkelhor, 2008). When adverse childhood events or traumas occur in addition to sexual abuse, the child's trauma burden is increased and is associated with more serious psychological and health outcomes (Dong et al., 2004).

Three main groups of factors contribute to risk of persistent harm from sexual abuse: (1) preabuse risk factors, (2) nature of the abuse as a risk factor, and (3) the response when a child discloses CSA.

1. *Preabuse Risk Factors.* The most important preabuse factors that increase risk of impact are a history of prior trauma and a history of prior psychological problems, particularly anxiety conditions. Children with preexisting anxiety disorders are at higher risk for developing posttraumatic stress disorder (PTSD), a finding that makes sense in view of the fact that PTSD is an anxiety disorder. Family characteristics such as parental psychopathology, illness, or domestic violence contribute to later psychosocial maladjustment (Fitzgerald et al., 2008). Children who already have had bad experiences, who have problems, or who live in families with impaired capacities would be expected to suffer disproportionately when they have a traumatic experience.

2. *Nature of the Abuse as a Risk Factor.* The nature of the abuse impacts risk in several ways. More serious abuse is associated with worse outcome. Abuse that involves violence or injury is more potentially harmful (Ruggerio et al., 2000). An important predictor of PTSD is perceived life threat, that is,

a subjective perception that one is in high danger or could be killed or seriously harmed (Saunders et al., 1999). Even abuse scenarios that do not involve violence or threat can produce this perception. Multiple episodes of abuse over time is a risk factor (Ruggerio et al., 2000). The number of victimizations may be less important than the effects of an extended period of time during which children believe they are at risk of abuse or are in danger.

3. *The Response When a Child Discloses CSA.* Postabuse factors related to harm include the response children receive when they report the abuse or when it becomes known. There is strong evidence that a negative response is associated with more harmful impact (Bernard-Bonnin, Hebert, Daignault, & Allard-Dansereau, 2008; Leifer, Shapiro, & Kassem, 1993; Mannarino & Cohen, 1997). Fortunately, most parents believe and support their children. When the offender is a family member, however, especially when the offender is the parent or paramour of the mother, belief and support for the child is sometimes compromised.

Nature of Abuse Effects

The negative effects of sexual abuse are the result of emotions and cognitions and their consequent behaviors associated with the abuse and its aftermath. The sexual abuse experience itself often produces intense negative emotions such as fear and shame. These emotions can become conditioned associations to memories of the abuse and can generalize to cues including specific circumstances or people that serve as reminders of the abuse. Avoidance of the memories and reminders is a common method of achieving temporary relief, but it can become maladaptive. Avoidance can take the form of active avoidance of situations and people, general numbing and restriction of emotions, active behaviors such as substance abuse, self-harming, or risky behavior. See Chapter 16 for discussion of mental health treatment of children who have been sexually abused.

Other negative emotional states such as depression and anger can result from sexual abuse. These emotions are usually the result of beliefs about the meaning of the abuse such as that it was unfair or that it represents the loss of a positive view of self and others. These emotional states are distressing to the child and can interfere with functioning. For example, even though it is accurate that abuse is unfair and some level of anger would be normal, anger that is not managed well can lead to behaviors that cause trouble in interpersonal relationships (Chaffin, Wherry, & Dykman, 1997).

As previously mentioned, sexual abuse can alter beliefs and assumptions about self, others, and the world in general. Some degree of changed beliefs is expected as a result of a significant negative experience. For example, one lesson of sexual abuse is that not everyone can be trusted. Even those who should be trustworthy sometimes are not. This altered belief, if not taken too far, could actually be protective for children in the sense that they learn that risk must be evaluated. On the other hand, beliefs such as that the abuse was deserved or was the child's fault, that being abused means that the child is ruined, that the child is unlovable, that no one can be trusted, and that the world is a dangerous place are unhelpful and associated with harm (Mannarino & Cohen, 1996; Daigneault, Tourigny, & Hebert, 2006; Fiering, Simon, & Cleland, 2009; Feiring, Miller-Johnson, & Cleland, 2007). Such beliefs can lead to behaviors that interfere with normal development and functioning.

Posttraumatic Stress

Posttraumatic stress (PTS) is the only abuse impact that is specific to the event itself. The symptoms include reexperiencing the event through unwanted and upsetting memories, avoidance of abuse memories or reminders, numbing of emotional response and hyperarousal reactions such as sleep problems, hypervigilance, irritability, and concentration problems (American Psychiatric Association, 2000). Sexually abused children consistently report high levels of these symptoms (Finkelhor, 2008; McLeer et al., 1998). More than one third of sexually abused children meet diagnostic criteria for PTSD (Dubner & Motta, 1999; Ruggiero, McLeer, & Dixon, 2000; Kilpatrick & Saunders, 1999), and a majority of sexually abused children exhibit some of the symptoms of PTSD (McLeer, Deblinger, Henry, & Orvaschel, 1992; McLeer et al., 1998; Wolfe, Gentile, & Wolfe, 1989). Sexually abused children have high rates of PTS or PTSD compared to children suffering other forms of maltreatment and compared to children exposed to nonabuse trauma (Deblinger, McLeer, Atkins, Ralphe, & Foa, 1989; Dubner & Motta, 1999).

Nonspecific Emotional Distress

Sexually abused children have more internalized distress than nonabused children (Boney-McCoy & Finkelhor, 1995; Gidycz & Koss, 1989; Mannarino & Cohen, 1996; McLeer et al., 1998; Stern, Lynch, Oates, O'Toole, & Cooney, 1995). Some sexually abused children have clinical levels of depression and anxiety, and these conditions frequently co-occur with PTSD (Deblinger et al., 2006). Sexual abuse is a risk factor for suicidal ideation and suicide attempts in children (Brodsky et al., 2008).

Behavior Problems

On standard measures of child behavioral problems, sexually abused children are reported by their parents to have more behavioral problems than nonabused children, although the problems do not always reach clinically significant levels (e.g., Einbender & Friedrich, 1989; Gomes-Schwartz et al., 1990; Mannarino & Cohen, 1996; Stern et al., 1995). Behavior problems following sexual abuse may arise as a function of emotional and cognitive responses to the abuse. Children who have intense negative emotional responses or heightened arousal may be unable to modulate these responses effectively and, as a result, act out through temper tantrums, outbursts, and overreactions to stimuli. Some children experience extreme anger related to the unfairness of abuse, being unprotected, the response to disclosure, family disruption, placement in foster care, or involvement as a witness in the criminal justice process.

The increase in behavior problems noted in sexually abused children may not be a direct effect of sexual abuse. Other reasons for behavior problems include inconsistent or harsh parenting and exposure to aggression and violence. Some parents of sexually abused children have compromised parenting capacities. In many sexual abuse cases, there is co-occurring PA or exposure to domestic or community violence that can produce behavior problems and aggression. In some cases, children's preexisting behavior problems may have put them at risk for sexual abuse.

Sexual Behavior

Not surprisingly, some sexually abused children have sexual behavior problems (e.g., Friedrich et al., 1992; Mannarino & Cohen, 1996). Again, not surprisingly, sexually abused children have more sexual behavior problems than children who are neglected, physically abused, or psychiatrically disturbed (Adams, McClellan, Douglass, McCurry, & Storck, 1995; Cosentino, Meyer-Bahlburg, Alpert, Weinberg, & Gains, 1995; Friedrich, Jaworski, Huxsahl, & Bengtson, 1997; Kendall-Tackett et al., 1993). At the same time, however, only about a third of sexually abused children exhibit sexual behavior problems (Friedrich, 1993).

Sexual behavior problems involve a range of sexual behaviors that are unusual or developmentally inappropriate (Friedrich, 2001). Age inappropriate sexual knowledge, interest, and curiosity can result in sexual preoccupation, sexualized interactions, poor boundaries, excessive masturbation, or involvement in sexual behavior with peers. Because sexually abused children have been exposed prematurely to adult sexuality, they may have sexual feelings that they are ill-equipped to manage. Some abused children learn that sexual touching is pleasurable and can serve as a form of self-soothing. Other children learn that sexual behavior is a powerful way of getting attention from peers or adults. Even negative attention can be reinforcing, especially for troubled children who have few other avenues or skills for meeting their needs.

Interestingly, aggressive sexual behavior in children is not directly linked to sexual abuse experiences. Friedrich and Luecke (1988) found that parental and family psychopathology were the primary predictors of this behavior. While sexual abuse experiences may lead to premature sexualization, other factors may be important or necessary to produce aggressive sexual behavior.

Sexual abuse can lead to an earlier sexual debut for some children or sexually risky behavior. For example, sexual abuse is associated with increased likelihood of multiple sexual partners, unhappy pregnancies, abortion, and sexually transmitted diseases (van Roode, Dickson, Herbison, & Paul, 2009). Sexual abuse places girls at increased risk for adolescent pregnancy (Noll, Shenk, & Putnam, 2009). This may be due to earlier onset of consensual sexual activity and therefore an increased period of risk (Boyer & Fine,1991). The pathway between CSA and adult revictimization is mediated by risky sexual behavior (Fargo, 2009).

Social Consequences

Sexually abused children tend to be less socially competent than nonabused children (Mannarino & Cohen, 1996; Stern et al., 1995). As a group, sexually abused children perceive themselves as different from others. Sexually abused youngsters tend to be less trusting of those in their immediate environment (Mannarino, Cohen, & Berman, 1994).

Short-Term Course of Symptoms

Over time, most sexually abused children's symptoms show a pattern of improvement (e.g., Kendall-Tackett et al., 1993). Between 10% and 24% of child victims either do not improve or deteriorate (Berliner & Saunders, 1996; Kendall-Tackett et al., 1993). Gomes-Schwartz and colleagues (1990) found that abused children who were initially least symptomatic had more problems at 18 months postabuse than did their initially more symptomatic peers. Friedrich and Reams (1987) observed in a series of case studies that symptoms tend to fluctuate over time rather than improve in linear fashion. In a longitudinal study of children in abuse-focused therapy, Lanktree and Briere (1995) found that symptoms subside at differential rates.

Conclusion _____

Sexual abuse is a relatively common experience in the lives of children. Many sexually abused children suffer psychological after-effects, and a history of childhood sexual abuse is a risk factor for problems in adulthood. The impact of CSA is quite varied, with some children exhibiting few deleterious consequences and others severely damaged. The good news is that resilience and recovery are common trajectories. Moreover, as discussed in Chapter 16, significant progress is being made to create and implement effective mental health treatments for sexually abused children and their nonoffending caretakers.

References

Adams, J., McClellan, J., Douglass, D., McCurry, C., & Storck, M. (1995). Sexually inappropriate behaviors in seriously mentally ill children and adolescents. *Child Abuse and Neglect, 19,* 555–568.

American Psychiatric Association (APA). (2000). *Diagnostic and statistical manual of mental disorders* (4th ed.). Washington, DC: Author.

Berliner, L. (2000). What is sexual abuse? In H. Dubowitz & D. DePanfilis (Eds.), *Handbook for child protection* (pp. 18–22). Thousand Oaks, CA: Sage.

Berliner, L., & Conte, J. (1990). The process of victimization: The victim's perspective. *Child Abuse and Neglect, 14,* 29–40.

Berliner, L., & Saunders, B. E. (1996). Treating fear and anxiety in sexually abused children: Results of a controlled 2-year follow-up study. *Child Maltreatment, 1,* 294–309.

Bernard-Bonnin, A.-C., Hebert, M., Daignault, I. V., & Allard-Dansereau, C. (2008). Disclosure of sexual abuse and personal and familial factors as predictors of post-traumatic stress disorder symptoms in school-aged girls. *Pediatrics and Child Health, 13,* 479–486.

Bonanno, G. A., & Mancini, A. D. (2008). The human capacity to thrive in the face of potential trauma. *Pediatrics, 121,* 369–375.

Boney-McCoy, S., & Finkelhor, D. (1995). Psychosocial sequelae of violent victimization in a national youth sample. *Journal of Consulting and Clinical Psychology, 63,* 726–736.

Boyer, D., & Fine, D. (1991). Sexual abuse as a factor in adolescent pregnancy and child maltreatment. *Family Planning Perspectives, 24,* 4–19.

Briere, J., & Elliott, D. M. (1993). Sexual abuse, family environment, and psychological symptoms: On the validity of statistical control. *Journal of Consulting and Clinical Psychology, 61,* 284–288.

Brodsky, B. S., Mann, J. J., Stanley, B., Tin, A. Oquendo, M., Birmaher, B., et al. (2008). Familial transmission of suicidal behavior: Factors mediating the relationship between childhood abuse and offspring suicide attempts. *Journal of Clinical Psychiatry, 69,* 584–596.

Chaffin, M., Wherry, J. N., & Dykman, R. (1997). School age children's coping with sexual abuse: Abuse stresses and symptoms associated with four coping strategies. *Child Abuse and Neglect, 21,* 227–240.

Chartier, M., Walker, J., & Naimark, B. (2007). Childhood abuse, adult health, and health care utilization: Results from a representative community sample. *American Journal of Epidemiology, 165*(9), 1031–1038.

Conte, J. R., & Schuerman, J. R. (1987). Factors associated with an increased impact of child sexual abuse. *Child Abuse and Neglect, 11,* 201–212.

Conte, J. R., Wolfe, S., & Smith, T. (1989). What sexual offenders tell us about prevention strategies. *Child Abuse and Neglect, 13,* 293–302.

Cosentino, C. E., Meyer-Bahlburg, H. F. L., Alpert, J. L., Weinberg, S. L., & Gaines, R. (1995). Sexual behavior problems and psychopathology symptoms in sexually abused girls. *Journal of the American Academy of Child and Adolescent Psychiatry, 34,* 1033–1042.

Dadds, M., Smith, M., Weber, Y., & Robinson, A. (1991). An exploration of family and individual profiles following father-daughter incest. *Child Abuse and Neglect, 15,* 575–586.

Daigneault, I., Tourigny, M., & Hebert, M. (2006). Self-attributions of blame in sexually abused adolescents: A mediational model. *Journal of Traumatic Stress*, *19*, 153–157.

Deblinger, E., Mannarino, A. P., Cohen, J. A., & Steer, R. A. (2006). A follow-up study of a multisite, randomized, controlled trial for children with sexual abuse-related PTSD symptoms. *Journal of the American Academy of Child and Adolescent Psychiatry*, *45*, 1474–1484.

Deblinger, E., McLeer, S. V., Atkins, M. S., Ralphe, D., & Foa, E. (1989). Posttraumatic stress in sexually abused, physically abused, and nonabused children. *Child Abuse and Neglect*, *13*, 403–408.

Dong, M., Anda, R. F., Felitti, V. J., Dube, S. R., Williamson, D. F., Thompson, T. J., et al. (2004). The interrelatedness of multiple forms of childhood abuse, neglect, and household dysfunction. *Child Abuse and Neglect*, *28*, 771–784.

Dube, S. R., Anda, R. F., Whitfield, C. L., Brown, D. W., Felitti, V. J., Dong, M., et al. (2005). Long-term consequences of childhood sexual abuse by gender of victim. *American Journal of Preventive Medicine*, *28*, 430–438.

Dubner, A. E., & Motta, R. W. (1999). Sexually and physically abused foster care children and posttraumatic stress disorder. *Journal of Consulting and Clinical Psychology*, *67*, 367–373.

Einbender, A. J., & Friedrich, W. N. (1989). Psychological functioning and behavior of sexually abused girls. *Journal of Consulting & Clinical Psychology*, *57*, 155–157.

Elliott, D. M., & Briere, J. (1994). Forensic sexual abuse evaluations of older children: Disclosures and symptomatology. *Behavioral Sciences and the Law*, *12*, 261–277.

Elliott, D., Browne, K., & Kilcoyne, J. (1995). Child sexual abuse prevention: What offenders tell us. *Child Abuse and Neglect*, *19*, 579–584.

Faller, K. C. (1989). Characteristics of a clinical sample of sexually abused children: How boy and girl victims differ. *Child Abuse and Neglect*, *13*, 281–291.

Fanslow, J. L., Robinson, E. M., Crengle, S., & Perese, L. (2007). Prevalence of child sexual abuse reported by a cross-sectional sample of New Zealand women. *Child Abuse and Neglect*, *31*, 935–945.

Fargo, J. D. (2009). Pathways to adult sexual revictimization: Direct and indirect behavioral risk factors across the lifespan. *Journal of Interpersonal Violence*, *24*, 1771–1791.

Feiring, C., Miller-Johnson, S., & Cleland, C. M. (2007). Potential pathways from stigmatization and internalizing symptoms to delinquency in sexually abused youth. *Child Maltreatment*, *12*, 220–232.

Feiring, C., Simon, V. A., & Cleland, C. M. (2009). Childhood sexual abuse, stigmatization, internalizing symptoms, and the development of sexual difficulties and dating aggression. *Journal of Consulting and Clinical Psychology*, *77*, 127–137.

Finkelhor, D. (1979). What's wrong with sex between adults and children? Ethics and the problem of sexual abuse. *American Journal of Orthopsychiatry*, *49*, 692–697.

Finkelhor, D. (1994). Current information on the scope and nature of child sexual abuse. *Future of Children*, *4*, 31–53.

Finkelhor, D. (2008). *Childhood victimization: Violence, crime, and abuse in the lives of young people*. New York: Oxford University Press.

Finkelhor, D., & Baron, L. (1986). High-risk children. In D. Finkelhor (Ed.), *A sourcebook on child sexual abuse* (pp. 60–88). Beverly Hills, CA: Sage.

Finkelhor, D., & Dziuba-Leatherman, J. (1994). Children as victims of violence: A national survey. *Pediatrics*, *94*, 413–420.

Finkelhor, D., Hotaling, G., Lewis, I. A., & Smith, C. (1990). Sexual abuse in a national survey of adult men and women: Prevalence, characteristics, and risk factors. *Child Abuse and Neglect, 14*, 19–28.

Finkelhor, D., Ormrod, R., & Turner, H. A. (2009). Lifetime assessment of poly-victimization in a national sample of children and youth. *Child Abuse and Neglect, 33*, 403–411.

Finkelhor, D., Ormrod, R., Turner, H., & Hamby, S. L. (2005). The victimization of children and youth: A comprehensive, national survey. *Child Maltreatment, 10*, 5–25.

Finkelhor, D., & Russell, D. E. H. (1984). Women as perpetrators: Review of the evidence. In D. Finkelhor (Ed.), *Child sexual abuse: New theory and research* (pp. 171–185). New York: Free Press.

Finkelhor, D., Turner, H., Ormrod, R., & Hamby, S. L. (2009). Violence, abuse, and crime exposure in a national sample of children and youth. *Pediatrics, 124*, 1411–1423.

Finkelhor, D., Turner, H., Ormrod, R., & Hamby, S. (2010). Trends in childhood violence and abuse exposure: Evidence from 2 national surveys. *Archives of Pediatric Adolescent Medicine, 164*, 238–242.

Fitzgerald, M. M., Schneider, R. A., Salstrom, S., Zinzow, H. M., Jackson, J., & Fossel, R. V. (2008). Child sexual abuse, early family risk, and childhood par-entification: Pathways to current psychosocial adjustment. *Journal of Family Psychology, 22*, 320–324.

Friedrich, W. N. (1993). Sexual victimization and sexual behavior in children: A review of recent literature. *Child Abuse and Neglect, 17*, 59–66.

Friedrich, W. N. (2001). *Psychological assessment of sexually abused children and their families.* Thousand Oaks, CA: Sage.

Friedrich, W. N., Grambsch, P., Damon, L., Hewitt, S. K., Koverola, C., Lang, R. A., et al. (1992). Child sexual behavior inventory: Normative and clinical compar-isons. *Psychological Assessment, 4*, 303–311.

Friedrich, W. N., Jaworski, T. M., Huxsahl, J. E., & Bengtson, B. S. (1997). Dissociative and sexual behaviors in children and adolescents with sexual abuse and psychiatric histories. *Journal of Interpersonal Violence, 12*, 155–171.

Friedrich, W. N., & Luecke, W. J. (1988). Young school-age sexually aggressive children. *Professional Psychology: Research and Practice, 19*, 155–164.

Friedrich, W. N., & Reams, R. A. (1987). Course of psychological symptoms in sex-ually abused young children. *Psychotherapy, 24*(2), 160–170.

Gidycz, C. A., & Koss, M. P. (1989). The impact of adolescent sexual victimization: Standardized measures of anxiety, depression and behavioral deviancy. *Violence & Victims, 4*, 139–149.

Gilbert, R., Widom, C. S., Fergusson, D., Webb, E., & Janson, S. (2009). Burden and consequences of child maltreatment in high-income countries. *Lancet, 373*, 68–81.

Gomes-Schwartz, B., Horowitz, J. M., & Cardarelli, A. P. (1990). *Child sexual abuse: The initial acts.* Newbury Park, CA: Sage.

Hanson, R. F., Self-Brown, S., Fricker-Elhai, A., Kilpatrick, D. G., Saunders, B. E., & Resnick, H. S. (2006). The relationship between family environment and vio-lence exposure among youth: Findings from the National Survey of Adolescents. *Child Maltreatment, 11*, 3–15.

Hoagwood, K., & Stewart, J. M. (1989). Sexually abused children's perceptions of family functioning. *Child & Adolescent Social Work, 6*, 139–149.

Holmes, W. G., & Slap, G. B. (1998). Sexual abuse of boys: Definition, prevalence, correlates, sequelae, and management. *Journal of the American Medical Association, 280*, 1855–1862.

Hussey, J. M., Chang, J. J., & Kotch, J. B. (2006). Child maltreatment in the United States: Prevalence, risk factors, and adolescent health consequences. *Pediatrics, 118*, 933–942.

Johnson, C. F. (2004). Child sexual abuse. *Lancet, 364*, 462–470.

Jones, L. (2008). Good news: Child victimization has been declining. Why? In D. Finkelhor, *Childhood victimization: Violence, crime, and abuse in the lives of young people* (pp. 122–147). New York: Oxford University Press.

Jones, L., Finkelhor, D., & Kopiec, K. (2001). Why is sexual abuse declining? A survey of state child protection administrators. *Child Abuse and Neglect, 25*(9), 1139–1158.

Kendall-Tackett, K. A., Williams, L. M., & Finkelhor, D. (1993). Impact of sexual abuse on children: A review and synthesis of recent empirical studies. *Psychological Bulletin, 113*, 164–180.

Kilpatrick, D. G. (2004). What is violence against women: Defining and measuring the problem. *Journal of Interpersonal Violence, 19*, 1209–1234.

Kilpatrick, D. G., McCauley, J., & Mattern, G. (2009, September). Understanding national rape statistics. *VAWnet Applied Research Forum.* Available at: http://www.vawnet.org/category/Documents.php?docid=2103&category_id=297

Kilpatrick, D. G., & Saunders, B. E. (1999). *Prevalence and consequences of child victimization: Results from the national survey of adolescents* (No. 93-IJ-CX-0023). Charleston: National Crime Victims Research & Treatment Center, Department of Psychiatry & Behavioral Sciences, Medical University of South Carolina.

Lang, R. A., & Frenzel, R. R. (1988). How sex offenders lure children. *Annals of Sex Research, 1*, 303–317.

Lanktree, C., & Briere, J. (1995). Outcome of therapy for sexually abused children: A repeated measures study. *Child Abuse and Neglect, 19*, 1145–1156.

Lanning, K. V. (1992). *Child molesters: A behavioral analysis for law enforcement officers investigating cases of child sexual exploitation.* Washington, DC: National Center for Missing and Exploited Children.

Leifer, M., Shapiro, J. P., & Kassem, L. (1993). The impact of maternal history and behavior upon foster placement and adjustment in sexually abused girls. *Child Abuse and Neglect, 17*, 755–766.

Madonna, P. G., Van Scoyk, S., & Jones, D. P. H. (1991). Family interactions within incest and nonincest families. *American Journal of Psychiatry, 148*, 46–49.

Maniglio, R. (2009). The impact of child sexual abuse on health: A systematic review of reviews. *Clinical Psychology Review, 29*, 647–657.

Mannarino, A. P., & Cohen, J. A. (1996). Abuse-related attributions and perceptions, general attributions, and locus of control in sexually abused girls. *Journal of Interpersonal Violence, 11*, 162–180.

Mannarino, A. P., & Cohen, J. A. (1997). Family-related variables and psychological symptom formation in sexually abused girls. *Journal of Child Sexual Abuse, 5*, 105–120.

Mannarino, A. P., Cohen, J. A., & Berman, S. R. (1994). The Children's Attributions and Perceptions Scale: A new measure of sexual abuse-related factors. *Journal of Clinical Child Psychology, 23*, 204–211.

McLeer, S. V., Deblinger, E., Henry, D., & Orvaschel, H. (1992). Sexually abused children at high risk for posttraumatic stress disorder. *Journal of the American Academy of Child and Adolescent Psychiatry, 31,* 875–879.

McLeer, S. V., Dixon, J. F., Henry, D., Ruggiero, K., Escovitz, K., Niedda, T., et al. (1998). Psychopathology in non-clinically referred sexually abused children. *Journal of the American Academy of Child and Adolescent Psychiatry, 37,* 1326–1333.

Mennen, F. E. (1995). The relationship of race/ethnicity to symptoms in childhood sexual abuse. *Child Abuse and Neglect, 19,* 115–124.

Mitchell, K. J., Finkelhor, D., & Wolak, J. (2003). Victimization of youths on the Internet. *Journal of Aggression, Maltreatment and Trauma, 8,* 1–39.

Mitchell, K. J., Wolak, J., & Finkelhor, D. (2007). Trends in youth reports of sexual solicitations, harassment and unwanted exposure to pornography on the internet. *Journal of Adolescent Health, 40,* 116–126.

National Center on Child Abuse and Neglect. (1993). *A report on the maltreatment of children with disabilities.* Washington, DC: U.S. Department of Health and Human Services.

Newcomb, M. D., Munoz, D. T., & Carmona, J. V. (2009). Child sexual abuse consequences in community samples of Latino and European American adolescents. *Child Abuse and Neglect, 33,* 533–544.

Newman, E., Christopher, R. S., & Berry, J. O. (2000). Developmental disabilities, trauma exposure, and posttraumatic stress disorder. *Trauma, Violence, and Abuse: A Review Journal, 1,* 154–170.

Noll, J. G., Shenk, C. E., & Putnam, K. T. (2009). Childhood sexual abuse and adolescent pregnancy: A meta-analytic update. *Journal of Pediatric Psychology, 34,* 366–378.

Pereda, N., Guilera, G., Forns, M., & Gómez-Benito, J. (2009). The international epidemiology of child sexual abuse: A continuation of Finkelhor (1994). *Child Abuse and Neglect, 33*(6), 331–342.

Rao, K., DiClemente, R. J., & Ponton, L. E. (1992). Child sexual abuse of Asians compared with other populations. *Journal of the American Academy of Child & Adolescent Psychiatry, 3,* 880–886.

Ruggiero, K. J., McLeer, S. V., & Dixon, J. F. (2000). Sexual abuse characteristics associated with survivor psychopathology. *Child Abuse and Neglect, 24,* 951–964.

Russell, D. E. H. (1984). *Sexual exploitation: Rape, child sexual abuse, and workplace harassment.* Beverly Hills, CA: Sage.

Saunders, B. E., Kilpatrick, D. G., Hanson, R. F., Resnick, H. S., & Walker, M. E. (1999). Prevalence, case characteristics, and long-term psychological correlates of child rape among women: A national survey. *Child Maltreatment, 4,* 187–200.

Sedlak, A. J., Mettenburg, J., Basena, M., Petta, I., McPherson, K., Greene, A., et al. (2010). *Fourth national incidence study of child abuse and neglect: Report to Congress.* Washington, DC: U.S. Department of Health and Human Services.

Smith, D. W., Letourneau, E. J., Saunders, B. E., Kilpatrick, D. G., Resnick, H. S., & Best, C. L. (2000). Delay in disclosure of childhood rape: Results from a national survey. *Child Abuse and Neglect, 24,* 273–287.

Stern, A. E., Lynch, D. L., Oates, R. K., O'Toole, B. I., & Cooney, G. (1995). Self-esteem, depression, behavior and family functioning in sexually abused children. *Journal of Child Psychology and Psychiatry, 36,* 1077–1089.

Tharinger, D., Horton, C. B., & Millea, S. (1990). Sexual abuse and exploitation of children and adults with mental retardation and other handicaps. *Child Abuse and Neglect, 14,* 301–312.

Tjaden, P., & Thoennes, N. (2000). *Full report of the prevalence, incidence, and consequences of violence against women: Findings from the National Violence Against Women Survey.* Washington, DC: U.S. Department of Justice, Office of Justice Programs, NCJ 183781.

Turner, H., Finkelhor, D., & Ormrod, R. (2006). The effect of lifetime victimization on the mental health of children and adolescents. *Social Science & Medicine, 62*(1), 13–27.

U.S. Department of Health and Human Services. (2010). *Child maltreatment 2008.* Washington, DC: U.S. Government Printing Office.

U.S. Department of Justice, Federal Bureau of Investigation. (2009, September). *Crime in the United States, 2008.* Available at: http://www.fbi.gov/ucr/cius2008/documents/aboutcius.pdf

van Roode, T., Dickson, N., Herbison, P., & Paul. C. (2009). Child sexual abuse and persistence of risky sexual behaviors and negative sexual outcomes over adulthood: Findings from a birth cohort. *Child Abuse and Neglect, 33,* 161–172.

Widom, C., & Morris, S. (1997). Accuracy of adult recollection of childhood victimization: Part 2. Childhood sexual abuse. *Psychological Assessment, 9,* 34–46.

Williams, L. (1994). Recall of childhood trauma: A prospective study of women's memories of child sexual abuse. *Journal of Consulting and Clinical Psychology, 62,* 1167–1176.

Wolak, J., Ybarra, M. L., Mitchell, K., & Finkelhor, D. (2007). Current research knowledge about adolescent victimization via the Internet. *Adolescent Medicine: State of the Art Reviews, 18,* 325.

Wolfe, V. V, Gentile, C., & Wolfe, D. A. (1989). The impact of sexual abuse on children: A PTSD formulation. *Behavior Therapy, 20,* 215–228.

Wyatt, G. E. (1985). The sexual abuse of Afro-American and white women in childhood. *Child Abuse and Neglect, 9,* 507–519.

Zielinski, D. S. (2009). Child maltreatment and adult socioeconomic well-being. *Child Abuse and Neglect, 33,* 666–678.

14

Disclosure of Child Sexual Abuse

Implications for Interviewing

Thomas D. Lyon and Elizabeth C. Ahern

W hether children are reluctant to disclose sexual abuse is an important issue. If children are reluctant, then abused children may deny and recant abuse. On the other hand, if abused children readily disclose, then denials and recantations may prove that an abuse allegation is false. If abused children are reluctant to disclose, then interviewers must look for means of reassuring children or otherwise overcoming their resistance. If abused children are forthcoming, then interviewers should focus on eliminating questions that might suggest abuse to a nonabused child. The truth lies somewhat in the middle. There is good evidence for reluctance, but there is also good evidence that most children who have previously disclosed abuse need not be asked leading questions to elicit their disclosure.

This chapter provides a synopsis of generally accepted facts about the disclosure of child sexual abuse (CSA). We review research on: (1) disclosure by children substantiated as sexually abused and (2) surveys of adults asking whether they were sexually abused as children. The research supports the proposition that CSA victims often delay disclosure or fail altogether to disclose abuse and that delays and nondisclosure are most common among children abused by a familiar person, especially a family member living in the child's household. The implications of the research are that inconsistencies

Authors' note: Preparation of this chapter was supported in part by National Institute of Child and Human Development Grant HD047290-01A2.

and recantations in children's reports may be due to reluctance rather than a false allegation.

We also review a literature that has been overlooked in discussions of abuse disclosure: research asking child sex offenders to describe their *modus operandi* (method of operating). Offenders describe methods for obtaining the acquiescence of children over time, often without physical violence and without fear of detection. The literature on offender *modus operandi* helps professionals understand the dynamics underlying children's failure to disclose abuse.

Child Studies and What They Tell Us About Disclosure

Professionals are familiar with Summit's paper on CSA accommodation (1983), which argues that sexually abused children's disclosures are delayed and inconsistent because of the dynamics of sexual abuse. It is important to be equally aware of a literature that criticizes accommodation and argues that accommodation is based on anecdote rather than scientific evidence (Bradley & Wood, 1996; *Gersten v. Senkowski*, 2004; Kovera & Borgida, 1997; London, Bruck, Ceci, & Shuman, 2005; Mason, 1995). Moreover, professionals should be alert to concerns that some of the research finding high rates of reluctance and recantation (e.g., Gonzalez, Waterman, Kelly, McCord, & Oliveri, 1993; Sorenson & Snow, 1991) was based on dubious claims of abuse (London et al., 2005).

London and colleagues reviewed the literature on children's disclosure of abuse and were critical of some components of accommodation but nevertheless concluded that delays in disclosure are common among victims of substantiated abuse (London et al., 2005). Furthermore, London's most recent review of the literature acknowledges that "a number of studies indicate that closer relationships are associated with longer delays and lower disclosure rates" (London, Bruck, Wright, & Ceci, 2008, p. 37). Specifically, London writes, "parentally abused children with low levels of family support" will exhibit lower disclosure rates and higher recantation rates than other abuse victims (London et al., 2008, p. 38; see Elliott & Briere, 1994; Lawson & Chaffin, 1992; Lippert, Cross, Jones, & Walsh, 2009; Malloy, Lyon, & Quas, 2007). The finding that abused children commonly delay disclosing abuse (if they disclose at all), and that this delay is attributable to the influence of adults close to the child, is consistent with other reviews of the literature on abuse disclosure (Lyon, 2002, 2007; Paine & Hansen, 2002).

Several studies with high rates of nondisclosure among children suspected of being abused found clear relations among delay, nondisclosure, and the child perpetrator relationship (Hershkowitz, 2006; Herskowitz, Horowitz, & Lamb, 2005; Pipe et al., 2007). Michael Lamb and his colleagues have conducted much of the recent research and emphasize the "motivational factors that make many children—more than a third of suspected victims and unknown numbers of children about whom no suspicions have been raised—reluctant to disclose abuse" (Lamb, Hershkowitz, Orbach, & Esplin, 2008, p. 17).

With respect to recantation, a study examining over 250 substantiated cases of sexual abuse in dependency court found that about a fourth of the children recanted at some point and that recantations were more likely if the child was abused by a member of his or her household, if the nonperpetrator parent expressed disbelief or was otherwise unsupportive of the allegation, and if the child was under 10 years of age (Malloy et al., 2007). If recantations are reasons to believe that the allegations are false, then the recantation rate should be lower among cases with other evidence of abuse. The authors tested for this possibility and did not find any evidence to support it. Although parental disbelief and the other factors influencing the rate of recantation vary widely across samples (London et al., 2008), the results demonstrate that recantation appears to follow the same dynamic as disclosure and that one should not assume that a recanting child who previously made a credible disclosure of abuse was not, in fact, abused.

Adult Surveys and What They Tell Us About Disclosure

There is consensus among researchers who survey representative groups of adults about their childhood sexual experiences that "failure to disclose is common among sexually abused children" (London et al., 2005; see Lyon, 2002, 2009; Paine & Hansen, 2002). Delayed disclosures are frequent, and a large percentage of adults across studies report never having told anyone about their abuse prior to the survey (Anderson, Martin, Mullen, Romans, & Herbison, 1993; Finkelhor, Hotaling, Lewis, & Smith, 1990; Fleming, 1997; Laumann, Gagnon, Michael, & Michaels, 1994; Smith et al., 2000; Wyatt, Loeb, Solis, Carmona, & Romero, 1999). For example, Laumann and colleagues (1994) surveyed over 3,400 adults in the United States and found that of those who stated they experienced contact sexual abuse before puberty, 74% of women and 78% of men did not tell anyone during their childhood. Because of the consistent findings, even critics of CSA accommodation conclude that "the overall pattern is that many children simply do not willingly tell" (London et al., 2008).

Surveys provide insight into factors that influence whether disclosure occurs. Four of the five representative surveys that tested for the effects of relationships on disclosure found that the relationship mattered, with closer relationships leading to lower rates of disclosure (Anderson et al., 1993; Kogan, 2004; Smith et al., 2000; Wyatt & Newcomb, 1990; but see Fleming, 1997). Moreover, a study examining the same sample as Smith et al. (2000) found that reporting to the police was more likely when the perpetrator was a stranger (Hanson, Resnick, Saunders, Kilpatrick, & Best, 1999). Three of the studies utilized statistical methods that enabled the researchers to control for case characteristics that might obscure the association between relationship and disclosure (Kogan, 2004; Smith et al., 2000; Wyatt & Newcomb, 1990).

Two of the nationally representative surveys asked respondents reporting abuse what factors deterred earlier disclosure. The most common reasons were embarrassment and shame (25% in Anderson et al., 1993; 46% in Fleming, 1997), expectations that the disclosure recipient would blame the child (29% in Anderson et al., 1993; 18% in Fleming, 1997) or that they would not be believed or not be helped (23% in Anderson et al., 1993; 23% in Fleming, 1997). Respondents in Anderson and colleagues' survey (1993) also mentioned concern for others: 24% stated that they did not want to upset anyone and 14% wanted to protect the abuser. In contrast, only 11% mentioned fear of the abuser. Finally, 18% stated that they were not bothered by the abuse.

Representative surveys have a number of advantages. First, they identify former victims who have never previously disclosed their abuse. Research on clinical samples, by contrast, enlists participants who already self-identified as former victims. Second, surveys are unlikely to include a large number of false allegations of abuse. Those who are skeptical of sexual abuse allegations have argued that parents and authorities pressure children to disclose abuse (Ceci & Bruck, 2006). However, fewer than 10% of respondents who acknowledge abuse in surveys state that their disclosure was reported to authorities (Mullen, Martin, Anderson, Romans, & Herbison, 1993; Russell, 1983; Smith et al., 2000). Therefore, respondent reports are unlikely to have been the product of having been suggestively questioned by biased adults.

Skeptics of sexual abuse allegations argue that therapists can create false allegations (Loftus & Ketcham, 1994). Yet only a very small percentage (2%) of women in surveys who acknowledge abuse report having remembered abuse with the help of a therapist (Wilsnack, Wonderlich, Kristjanson, Vogeltanz-Holm, & Wilsnack, 2002).

Although surveys identify large numbers of former abuse victims, there is good reason to believe that surveys underestimate the prevalence of abuse and exaggerate the likelihood that abuse is reported to authorities. The problem is simple: Former abuse victims may be reluctant to disclose abuse, even when questioned years after the abuse and when guaranteed anonymity by surveyors.

There are several lines of evidence suggesting that former victims remain reluctant to disclose abuse when questioned by surveyors, a problem called "survey reluctance" (Lyon, 2009). First, substantiated abuse is often subsequently denied by survey respondents. Reviewing the research on retrospective reports of childhood maltreatment, Hardt and Rutter (2004) concluded that "the universal finding [is] that, even with well-documented serious abuse or neglect, about a third of individuals do not report its occurrence when specifically asked about it in adult life." Second, more persistent questioning elicits more reports of abuse. In a nationally representative survey of American women, Wilsnack et al. (2002) found that the percentage of respondents reporting abuse doubled (from 15% to 31%) when researchers asked a greater number of specific questions about sexually abusive experiences. Several reviewers have noted that the most important determinant of prevalence rates in retrospective surveys appears to be the number of questions asked (Finkelhor, 1994; Hardt & Rutter, 2004), an observation formally confirmed in a meta-analysis by Bolen and Scannapieco (1999). Third, respondents surveyed more than once are often inconsistent in acknowledging that sexual abuse occurred. Fergusson and colleagues questioned a nationally representative group of adults about CSA when they were 18 and again when they were 21 (Fergusson, Horwood, & Woodward, 2000). Among the respondents who reported sexual abuse at 21, about half (45%) had failed to report abuse at 18 (37 out of 83), and among the respondents who reported sexual abuse at 18 years of age, more than half (54%) failed to report abuse at 21 (54 out of 100). In other words, over half of the respondents who reported abuse at some point did so in only one of the two interviews. Other studies have found similar inconsistencies in reporting across multiple interviews (Fry, Rozewicz, & Crisp, 1996; McGee, Wolfe, Yuen, Wilson, & Carnochan, 1995). The inconsistencies cannot be attributable to respondents' uncertainties about whether the reported behaviors were in fact sexual abuse, as some have claimed (London et al., 2005), because respondents were, if anything, less consistent in their reports of more serious abuse (Fergusson et al., 2000; Frye et al., 1996).

Why does it matter if many survey respondents fail to disclose childhood sexual abuse? Critics of sexual abuse accommodation acknowledge that surveys demonstrate that substantial numbers of abuse victims never disclose their abuse but claim that nondisclosure says nothing about whether victims would have disclosed had they been asked (London et al., 2008). Survey reluctance suggests that victims will deny abuse, even when directly asked and even if guaranteed anonymity and questioned long after the abuse occurred.

Furthermore, survey reluctance leads surveys to exaggerate the percentage of abuse that is disclosed to others (Lyon, 2009). This is a complex point and takes some explaining. The logic is that victims who never disclose as children are more likely to remain silent about their abuse in adulthood. This means that former victims who do disclose when surveyed will disproportionately be those who previously disclosed.

The effects of survey reluctance explain the common finding that younger respondents in surveys report *lower* rates of sexual abuse and *higher* rates of prior disclosure (Lyon, 2009). For example, Fergusson, Lynskey, and Horwood's (1996) survey of 18-year-olds found a lower prevalence rate than surveys of older adults and an unusually high rate of prior disclosure among those who acknowledged abuse (87%). The problem is that if many victims who had never told maintained their silence when questioned by the surveyor, the survey would both underestimate the prevalence of abuse and overestimate the likelihood that victims disclosed.[1]

In sum, surveys of adults tell us a great deal about disclosure of abuse. Most abuse victims who reveal abuse to surveyors never told anyone about their abuse while they were a child, and many had not revealed the abuse to anyone before the survey. Many abuse victims will fail to report abuse to surveyors or will report abuse inconsistently, evincing the difficulties victims have in disclosing abuse, even a long time after the abuse occurred. The likelihood of disclosure is affected by the closeness of the relationship between the victim and the perpetrator. Victims' failure to disclose is sometimes motivated by fear of the perpetrator but often includes self-blame or fears of being blamed by others.

The Modus Operandi of Child Sex Offenders and What It Tells Us About Victims' Secrecy

Across the adult and child literatures, a consistent factor is the importance of the relationship among the child, the alleged perpetrator, and other important people in the child's life, particularly the child's parents. These relationships hint at why a child would keep sexual abuse a secret. When the child is abused by a parent or close relative, the child is likely to refrain from disclosing as much from love as from fear—love for the perpetrator and for the other parent. Although disclosure may end the abuse, it will likely disrupt the child's relationships with some of the most important people in the child's life. Most sexual abuse is not perpetrated by parents, however, and delays in disclosure are not limited to parental abuse. How should we think about the dynamics of disclosure when the abuser is not related to the child?

One means of better understanding the dynamics of disclosure is to move from the victims' to the offenders' perspective. Research asking child sex offenders to describe their modus operandi dates back at least to the 1960s (Gebhard, Gagnon, Pomeroy, & Christensen, 1964), and a review published in 2009 surveyed the results of 19 studies (Leclerc, Proulx, & Beauregard, 2009). Research on offender modus operandi was largely motivated by the hope of improving prevention and treatment efforts (Salter, 2003). Here, we review the literature on modus operandi as a means of understanding the reasons why victims delay disclosure, fail to disclose abuse, or appear inconsistent in their disclosures. The research provides insight into the means by

---

[1]An alternative explanation for the high rates of reported prior disclosure among young respondents acknowledging abuse is that younger respondents are less likely to have forgotten that they disclosed abuse (London et al., 2008). But if the issue is forgetting, young adults should report as much abuse as older adults, and they should be highly consistent in reporting whether they were abused over time. The fact that they endorse less abuse and endorse abuse inconsistently is evidence that they are reluctant to disclose.

which sex offenders choose their prospective victims, obtain access to children, befriend children, desensitize children to sexual touch, progress to more serious sexual activities with children, and convince children to keep the abuse a secret.

Two common themes stand out. First, sex offenders emphasize the extent to which they seduce their victims over time rather than commit isolated assaults. Although it is probable that they understate the level of coercion and sometimes violence in their acts of molestation, a point discussed at greater length next, most child molestation includes attempts to obtain the assent and cooperation of victims. Of course, with this level of planning and preparation, offenders are unlikely to abuse a victim on only one occasion; at least two thirds of offenders maintain the same victim over time (Elliott, Browne, & Kilcoyne, 1995; Smallborne & Wortley, 2001).

Second, intrafamilial and extrafamilial sex offenders are similar. Although it was once believed that incest perpetrators are quite different than extrafamilial offenders (Becker, 1994), researchers have found that sex offenders often victimize children both within and outside their families (Abel, Becker, Cunningham-Rathner, Mittleman, & Rouleau, 1988), and the research on modus operandi finds more similarities than differences in approach. Because of their privileges and status with respect to children to whom they are related or who are under their care, intrafamilial sex offenders enjoy access that extrafamilial sex offenders lack. Extrafamilial sex offenders must overcome children's hesitancy to trust strangers and often seek to become "like family."

Only a minority of sex offenses against children are perpetrated by strangers. In Smallborne and Wortley's (2001) survey of 182 child sex offenders, "only 6.5 percent of offenders had their first sexual contact with a stranger" (p. 4). Rather, child sex offenders either seek out or take advantage of opportunities to molest children with whom they are familiar. In an analysis of the offense patterns of different types of sex offenders, Beauregard and colleagues (Beauregard, Proulx, Rossmo, Leclerc, & Allaire, 2007) described two types of interest: the "sophisticated rape track" who are offenders who work with or are involved with children and the "family infiltrator." Those in the sophisticated rape track,

> because of their position and status, may appear nonthreatening to their victims. They benefit from a context that affords them the opportunity to be in the presence of potential victims and, therefore, to establish intimate relationships with some of them through manipulative strategies (e.g., seduction, tricks, games). Moreover, they can easily create situations that allow them to be alone with potential victims (e.g., staying after school, camping trips, movies) not only to gain the victim's trust but also to provide a favorable context for sexual activity. (p. 1080)

Sullivan and Beech (2004) interviewed 41 perpetrators receiving treatment who molested children with whom they worked and found that 15%

chose their profession *exclusively* to provide access to victims; another 42% acknowledged that this partially motivated their job choice.

The family infiltrators "become acquainted with a family and offer different types of services, especially babysitting. Offenders specifically target women living alone with children" (Beauregard, Proulx, Rossmo, Leclerc, & Allaire, 2007, pp. 1080–1081).

In both types of cases, the child's parents are likely to view the offender favorably because of the offender's interest in the child. Indeed, in the family infiltrator scenario, the offender may appeal to the parent both as a surrogate father and as a friend or intimate partner.

Many sex offenders acknowledge that they choose victims on the basis of their apparent vulnerability. Interviewing a small sample of 20 child sex offenders, Conte, Wolf, and Smith (1989), found that offenders

> claimed a special ability to identify vulnerable children. Vulnerability was defined both in terms of children's status (e.g., living in a divorced home or being young) and in terms of emotional or psychological state (e.g., a needy, depressed, or unhappy child). (p. 299)

Forty-nine percent of the sex offenders interviewed by Elliott and colleagues (1995) stated that they targeted children who lacked self-confidence or self-esteem. Beauregard, Rossmo, & Proulx (2007) noted that child sex offenders often targeted "a child with family problems, without supervision, always on the street and in need of help" (p. 455).

The first step for the sex offender is to befriend the child, typically before any kind of physical contact is attempted. Leclerc and colleagues' review (2009) noted that child sex offenders adopt strategies "that are similar to prosocial behaviors which consist of demonstrating love, attention and appreciation" (p. 8). Both intrafamilial and extrafamilial sex offenders describe spending time with the child (Christiansen & Blake, 1990; Smallbone & Wortley, 2001) and giving the child gifts (Budin & Johnson, 1989; Christiansen & Blake, 1990; Kaufman et al., 1998), sometimes introducing the child to alcohol and pornography (Kaufman et al., 1998). Although the research sometimes finds differences in the rate with which intrafamilial and extrafamilial offenders endorse particular techniques, there is little consistency across studies. For example, Budin and Johnson (1989) found that extrafamilial offenders were more likely than incest offenders to bribe children with toys, whereas Kaufman and colleagues (1998) found that incest offenders were more likely to endorse buying the child gifts.

The first sexual contact often does not occur for a substantial period of time—particularly long given the speed with which children, especially young children, can form attachments to adults. In Smallbone and Wortley's (2001) study, 76% of the intrafamilial offenders, 28% of the extrafamilial offenders, and 39% of the mixed-type offenders knew the child more than a year before initiating abuse.

When the sexual abuser is the child's parent, the extra attention paid to the child not only has the effect of making the child feel special but isolates the child and the offending parent from other family members. Christiansen and Blake (1990) found that

> [p]otential victims become alienated from the mothers because these daughters are placed by their fathers in their mothers' traditional role of confidante, intimate friend, and sex partner. Alienation from siblings occurs because of the privileges and special favors potential victims receive. (p. 90)

The second step is to desensitize the child to sexual touch through progressively more invasive sexual touch and talk. Kaufman and colleagues (1998) found this to be the most often endorsed means of obtaining a child's compliance by both intrafamilal and extrafamilial child sex offenders (see also Lang & Frenzel, 1988). This approach has several purposes. The offender can test the child's willingness to consent (Christiansen & Blake, 1990) and the likelihood that the child will disclose (Kaufman, Hilliker, Lathrop, & Daleiden, 1988). If the child discloses at an early stage of the process, the offender can claim that the touch was merely affectionate, accidental, or otherwise nonsexual (Lang & Frenzel, 1988). As the abuse progresses, the offender can assure the child of the harmlessness and morality of the actions (Christiansen & Blake, 1990).

Third, the offender initiates overtly sexual acts. Offenders endorse a mixture of bribes and threats as a means of ensuring the victim's compliance, and the strategies are for the most part similar between intrafamilial and extrafamilial offenders (Kaufman et al., 1998; Lang & Frenzel, 1988). Kaufman and colleagues (1998) found that giving gifts was the most common form of bribery and that the most common threat, particularly among intrafamilial offenders, was to prey on children's helplessness by threatening to "tell on them about having sex with [the offender] or by making them feel as if there was nothing they could do to stop it" (p. 355). Researchers have speculated that the efficacy of such a threat is founded on the desensitization process: "victims' repeated acquiescence early in the grooming process (e.g., to nonsexual touch) may lead victims to believe that they have granted permission for more intrusive sexual contact" (Kaufman et al., 1998, p. 356; see also Conte et al., 1989).

If bribes or threats fail, many offenders are willing to resort to physical coercion. In Lang and Frenzel's (1988) sample, two thirds of the sex offenders "frightened the children in some way," and physical force was used in about the same proportion as bribery (p. 311). Most of the offenders in Elliott et al. (1995) claimed that if the child resisted they would stop and try to initiate contact later (61%), but a substantial minority (39%) stated that they would resort to threats or actual violence in order to complete the act. In Christiansen and Blake's (1990) sample of fathers who abused their daughters, less than one fourth acknowledged using threats or physical punishment. As we discuss next, these percentages may be understated by offenders.

To some extent, the power and status differences between adult offenders and the children they victimize make overt use of force unnecessary. Kaufman and colleagues (1998) noted that in comparing adolescent to adult offenders, they found that adult offenders endorsed fewer strategies overall, and in particular were less likely to have threatened the child with a weapon. They pointed out that adults' "greater physical sizes, statuses afforded by their age (i.e., 'When adults tell you to do something, you listen'), and greater perceived credibility may reduce the need for explicit threats to gain victim compliance in abusive sexual activity" (Kaufman et al., 1998, p. 356).

We have emphasized the extent to which nonphysically forceful means of molesting children are available both to intrafamilial and extrafamilial child sex offenders. Offenders who choose strangers as victims also sometimes employ nonforceful methods. Beauregard, Rossmo, and Proulx (2007) described the "hunting process" of 69 serial sex offenders who offended against strangers, and found that

> [t]hree methods are used by sexual offenders specifically against children: seduction/persuasion (13%), money/gift (16%), and games (9%). These methods help offenders make contact with the victims slowly and to gradually estimate their chance of succeeding in getting the victim involved in sexual activities. (p. 456)

Once the offender's acts are overtly sexual, the offender must confront the possibility that the child will disclose the abuse. The extent to which offenders reported asking or warning victims not to tell varies across studies, but the types of positive and negative inducements are similar. Offenders often refer to serious consequences from disclosure. Sixty-one percent of the offenders in Smallbone and Wortley (2001) threatened that they would go to jail or get in trouble. Forty-three percent of the incest offenders in Lang and Frenzel (1988) threatened that the family would split up. Twenty-four percent of the offenders in Elliott et al. (1995) used anger and the threat of physical force.

Offenders often describe the use of positive inducements or the ways in which disclosure will deprive children of the benefits of the abusive relationship. Kaufman and colleagues (1998) reported that offenders most often endorsed strategies involving giving or withdrawing benefits, in which offenders would give children special rewards or privileges, tell children that they would no longer love them or spend time with them if they disclosed, or tell children that their caregiver(s) would no longer love them. Similarly, Smallbone and Wortley (2001) found that offenders endorsed giving children special rewards or privileges (21%) and relied on children's fear that they would lose the offenders' affection (36%). In Elliott et al. (1995), 20% of offenders threatened loss of love or stated that the child was to blame. Lang and Frenzel (1988) found that these sorts of threats were more common among incest offenders than among extrafamilial offenders, in particular expressing love for the child, giving the child special favors, and avoiding punishing the child, perhaps because the threats implied the use of parental authority and control.

One problem with interviewing offenders is that they may misrepresent or misremember their behavior, particularly when it is inconsistent with how they prefer to view the abusive relationship. Sex offenders appear particularly likely to understate their use of threats in order to induce compliance and in order to convince the child not to disclose the abuse. The percentage of offenders who report ever specifically instructing the child not to tell varies widely across the studies, and in many studies, a majority of offenders deny uttering any threats to induce silence. In Budin and Johnson (1989), 25% acknowledged threats not to disclose. In Elliott et al. (1995), 33% acknowledged telling the child not to tell. In Lang and Frenzel (1988), 40% of extrafamilial offenders acknowledged telling the child not to tell, whereas 85% of incest offenders did so. These percentages inevitably increase if one consults other sources, either the sex offenders' therapists or the victims themselves. Kaufman and colleagues (1988) compared what child sex offenders admitted in interviews to what their therapists recalled from offenders' records (and prior admissions) and found that the sex offenders consistently underreported their use of threats both to induce compliance and to induce secrecy. Kaufman and colleagues (1988) found that the most underreporting involved threats to induce secrecy. Christiansen and Blake (1990) noted that "less than one-fourth of the perpetrators reported using threats or actual physical punishment [to induce compliance], yet almost half (45%) of the [incest] victims said that perpetrators did" (p. 96).

In sum, although child sex offenders clearly exaggerate the extent to which they seduced rather than forcibly assaulted their victims, it is clear that most child molestation is a process whereby the offender deliberately elicits the compliance and often the cooperation of the child victim. This process helps to explain why the child does not cry out at the first opportunity and both feels responsible for the abuse and fears being blamed should he or she disclose. In intrafamilial cases, the offender takes advantage of family loyalties. In extrafamilial cases, the offender takes steps to be "like family."

Implications of the Research for Interviewing Children

Professionals who work with sexual abuse victims understand that many victims are reluctant to disclose. As previously noted, surveys of adults consistently find that less than 10% of CSA was reported to authorities. At the same time, professionals realize that most of the children who come to official attention have disclosed their abuse. Because most victims do not disclose and are not recognized as victims, victims officially recognized as such are not recognized as victims in general.

This fact has two implications for practice. First, professionals must be careful before making assumptions about victims in general based on victims who disclose abuse. For example, some researchers argue that abused children will freely disclose abuse when questioned (Ceci, Kulkofsky, Klemfuss, Sweeney, & Bruck, 2007). These researchers base their argument on studies examining known cases of CSA seen by clinicians, social services, and law enforcement. The problem is that abuse is usually suspected because a child discloses. Victims who do not disclose generally are not questioned. Moreover, in the process of determining whether abuse occurred, professionals weed out cases in which children fail to disclose or in which the report is unconvincing. As a result, known cases are overwhelmingly cases in which disclosure occurred. These problems, which have been called "suspicion bias" (abuse is usually suspected because of disclosure) and "substantiation bias" (abuse is usually substantiated because of disclosure) (Lyon, 2007), have now been acknowledged by researchers who question whether abused children are reluctant to disclose (London et al., 2008).

The take-home point is that one cannot assume that denial of abuse, inconsistencies in an abuse report, or a recantation is compelling evidence that abuse did not occur. Substantiated cases contain few denials or recantations because denials or recantations reduce the likelihood of substantiation.

The second implication of the fact that victims coming to official attention are not representative of victims in general is the converse of the first. We cannot make assumptions about known victims based on victims in general. Many professionals once assumed (and some may still assume) that children suspected of being abused will deny abuse and that it is critical to use all necessary tools in order to extract disclosures. These professionals fail to realize that when suspicions are based on a prior disclosure, children have evinced a willingness to disclose and are likely to disclose again. Disclosure rates are high among children who previously disclosed (London et al., 2008).

If children questioned about abuse have disclosed previously, it should not be necessary to resort to suggestive techniques in order to elicit a disclosure. Researchers have uncovered a number of useful strategies for questioning children about abuse that increase informativeness without decreasing accuracy. Interview instructions teach child interviewees the virtues of admitting ignorance, asking for clarification, and correcting the interviewer (see Chapter 20). Narrative practice, in which children narrate a nonabusive event before being asked about abuse, has been found to increase the productivity of children's abuse reports (Sternberg et al., 1997) without evidence that accuracy is compromised (Roberts, Lamb, & Sternberg, 2004).

When interviewers use the National Institute of Child Health and Human Development (NICHD) investigative interview protocol, which utilizes both interview instructions and narrative practice, most disclosures are elicited with either "tell me why you are here" or through questions that referred to a prior disclosure without interviewers suggesting abuse (e.g., "I heard you talked to a policeman. Tell me what you talked about") (Sternberg, Lamb, Orbach, Esplin, & Mitchell, 2001). Of course, questions of this sort rely on the fact that most children questioned about suspicions of sexual abuse have made some sort of previous disclosure. Additional details are more productively elicited through open-ended questions such as "tell me more about [action mentioned by the child]" and "what happened next" than by closed-ended questions (Lamb et al., 2008). Children's reports are also more productive if the interviewer uses neutral encouragement (e.g., "You are doing very well") or addresses the child by name (Hershkowitz, 2009).

When suspicions of abuse arise for reasons other than disclosure, such as sexualized behavior, interviewers should be very cautious, because there is a good probability that the suspicions are unfounded. Although sexualized behavior may be much more common among abused children than among nonabused children (and therefore evidence that abuse should be suspected), the majority of children who behave sexually have not been abused (see Chapter 22). The problem with some techniques thought necessary for eliciting disclosures from reluctant children (such as asking a series of yes/no questions specifically inquiring about abuse) is that they risk increasing the likelihood of false allegations and, in a related way, make true reports difficult to distinguish from false reports. For example, by asking a direct yes/no question ("Did the man touch your vagina?") an interviewer guarantees that a true disclosure will look much like a false disclosure; in either case, a child is likely to simply say "yes" (see Chapter 20).

At the same time that professionals have a number of nonleading approaches to elicit disclosures, nondisclosure and recantation remain a major concern (Lyon, Lamb, & Myers, 2009), and children who are initially forthcoming about their abuse often become inconsistent or reluctant over the course of intervention (Malloy et al., 2007). Surprisingly little research has been conducted on effective and nonleading methods of eliciting disclosure from reluctant victims. One potentially useful technique is a promise to tell the truth, which has been found to increase honesty without increasing errors (Lyon & Dorado, 2008; Talwar, Lee, Bala, & Lindsay, 2002, 2004), even among maltreated children who have been coached to either falsely deny or falsely claim that events occurred (Lyon, Malloy, Quas, & Talwar, 2008). The extent to which this and other tools may reduce reluctance to disclose sexual abuse remains to be examined.

Interviewers should focus on the fact that when children do disclose, and thus are capable of and willing to describe their abuse, this provides a window of opportunity for eliciting convincing details of the abuse as well as facts that can explain predisclosure delays and postdisclosure inconsistencies and recantations. If a child subsequently recants abuse, the likelihood that the recantation is true or false can be assessed in light of the motivations and pressures that the child disclosed.

It may be possible to elicit details about the progression of abuse from non-sexual touching to sexual touching to more invasive acts. If the child narrates such a progression, this helps to explain why the child would delay disclosing abuse and why the child might blame himself or herself for the abuse and expect recipients of disclosure to blame the child as well ("I let him do it, so I can't complain").

Unfortunately, interviewers often ask children about multiple abusive events by asking "how many times" abuse occurred. Asking for a number rather than details of individual events makes it difficult for the interviewer to elicit evidence of the progression of abuse over time. The NICHD investigative interview protocol recommends that interviewers ask the child if the abuse occurred "one time or more than one time," and if the child responds that it occurred more than once, the interviewer asks the child to "tell me everything that happened the first time," "tell me everything that happened the last time," and "tell me everything that happened the time you remember the most" (Lamb et al., 2008).

Asking about individual acts is preferable to asking for numbers. Children have difficulty providing numerical estimates, particularly if the abuse occurred on multiple occasions over a long period of time. Indeed, even an adult would have difficulty answering such questions and would have to resort to estimation that is little more than an educated guess (Bradburn, 2000).

Asking children about individual acts often elicits details about idiosyncratic events such as interruptions of the abuse due to another person or another event (e.g. the perpetrator stopped because a parent was heard coming home). Reporting such events can lend credibility to the child's story because idiosyncratic details are unlikely to be the product of adult coaching or interview suggestiveness.

In order to understand the dynamics of abuse, including the alleged perpetrator's and the child's perspectives, interviewers need not ask leading or direct questions. Interviewers can elicit how the alleged perpetrator justified abuse by asking, "What did he tell you about what he was doing?" (Berliner & Conte, 1990) or "What did he say when/after he touched you?" In order to elicit the child's perspective, interviewers can ask the child, "How did you feel when he touched you?" and "How did you feel after he touched you?" If the "feelings questions" elicit physical feelings, the interviewer can then ask, "What did you think when/after. . . ?" questions. Conversely, if the interviewer seeks the child's physical reactions, he or she can follow up a feelings question with "How did your body feel. . . ?" These questions can be asked about individual abusive events as well as about abuse generally. For example, with respect to the first time sexual abuse occurred, children often disclose that they were confused by the perpetrator's actions or that they did not initially recognize that the actions were wrong (Berliner & Conte, 1990; Sas & Cunningham, 1995).

The interviewer can elicit useful information by asking the child to describe her feelings about the alleged perpetrator more generally (e.g., "How did you feel about him when you first knew him, before he touched you?"). Interviewers should not be surprised to elicit a mixture of negative and positive feelings (Berliner & Conte, 1990), which helps explain acquiescence to abuse, self-blame, initial reluctance to disclose, motives to recant, and the negative effects that abuse may have on children's sense of trust in adults. On the other hand, eliciting feelings about the perpetrator may also help determine if there were motivations to make a false report.

The interviewer can inquire into the child's prior disclosures and the child's reasons for disclosing (or for not disclosing sooner) (Hershkowitz, Lanes, & Lamb, 2007). This information may be elicited by asking, "What happened next?" subsequent to the child's description of the last act of abuse (Hershkowitz et al., 2007), or the interviewer can ask the child, "Who did you tell?" "What did you say to them?" and "When did you tell them?" Children have difficulty in reconstructing the time that they told, but a "when" question does not necessitate a reference to a specific time. "When" questions elicit information about what was happening before or at the time the child disclosed. In order to elicit the child's motivations, the interviewer can ask the child, "Why did you tell?" or "What kept you from telling?"

The responses of the people to whom a child disclosed are important. Children, particularly young children, are likely to disclose first to a parent. As discussed earlier, children are less likely to disclose and more likely to recant when nonoffending parents refuse to believe that abuse occurred or otherwise fail to support the child. On the other hand, children's reports are often doubted because of the assertion that a parent is influencing the child to make a false claim of abuse. Hence, the parent's reaction can play an important role in determining if the child's report is consistent over time. The interviewer can ask the child about the disclosure recipient's reactions ("What did she do/say when you told her?") and what the disclosure recipient told the child about talking to the interviewer ("What did your mom tell you about talking to me?"). The interviewer can ask the child what the parent and other interested adults have said about the alleged perpetrator ("What has x said about y?") and vice versa. This can reveal both pressures to accuse and pressures to deny that abuse occurred.

Finally, the child's current feelings are helpful in understanding the potential for future inconsistencies and recantation. The child can be asked, "How do you feel about [the alleged perpetrator] now?" "What happened to you since you told?" and "How do you feel about what has happened to you?" Children sometimes express regret that they disclosed abuse and unhappiness over the consequences of disclosing (Sas & Cunningham, 1995). These feelings can be useful in interpreting subsequent denials or recantations.

Although there is no research examining how recanting children can best be interviewed, our experience suggests that the same inquiries into the child's feelings and motivations and the motivations of others can be explored. The child can be asked why he or she originally alleged abuse and why he or she is retracting the allegations now. The child's reasons for making a false allegation can be assessed for their plausibility. The child can be asked open-ended questions designed to elicit as much detail as possible about the prior allegations.

Recanting children are likely to answer in one of two ways when asked about prior disclosures. Many children, particularly younger children, repeat the disclosures and may revert to discussing the abuse as if it really happened (e.g., they will answer "how do you know?" questions with "because I saw it"). Hence, a child will answer "no" if asked a direct question about abuse but if asked about prior disclosures, may repeat a credible narrative of abuse. Alternatively, children may simply deny prior disclosures. If those disclosures were made to impartial observers and adequately documented, this suggests that the child is feeling pressure to deny. Clearly, however, the best methods for interviewing recanting children have yet to be developed.

Conclusion

In sum, a good understanding of the dynamics of sexual abuse and the disclosure process can help interviewers do a better job when questioning children about alleged sexual abuse. Research clearly justifies concerns about nondisclosure and recantation of true allegations of abuse. At the same time, we still know very little about how to elicit disclosures from children who are unwilling to disclose. The optimum strategy is to do what we can with what we have: children who allege abuse and are brought to the attention of the authorities. Careful and thorough questioning of these children utilizing the most up-to-date interviewing approaches is the best we can do.

References

Abel, G., Becker, J., Cunningham-Rathner, J., Mittleman, M., & Rouleau, J. (1988). Multiple paraphilic diagnoses among sex offenders. *Bulletin of the American Academy of Psychiatry and the Law, 16*, 153–168.

Anderson, J., Martin, J., Mullen, P., Romans, S., & Herbison, P. (1993). Prevalence of childhood sexual abuse experiences in a community sample of women. *Journal of the American Academy of Child and Adolescent Psychiatry, 32*, 911–919.

Beauregard, E., Proulx, J., Rossmo, K., Leclerc, B., & Allaire, J. (2007). Script analysis of the hunting process of serial sex offenders. *Criminal Justice and Behavior, 34*, 1069–1084.

Beauregard, E., Rossmo, D. K., & Proulx, J. (2007). A descriptive model of the hunting process of serial sex offenders: A rational choice perspective. *Journal of Family Violence, 22*, 449–463.

Becker, J. (1994). Offenders: Characteristics and treatment. *Future of Children, 4*, 176–197.

Berliner, L., & Conte, J. (1990). The process of victimization: The victims' perspective. *Child Abuse and Neglect, 14*, 29–40.

Bolen, R. M., & Scannapieco, M. (1999). Prevalence of child sexual abuse: A corrective metanalysis. *Social Service Review, 73*, 281–313.

Bradburn, N. M. (2000). Temporal representation and event dating. In A. A. Stone et al. (Eds.), *The science of self-report: Implications for research and practice* (pp. 49–61). Mahwah, NJ: Lawrence Erlbaum.

Bradley, A. R., & Wood, J. M. (1996). How do children tell? The disclosure process in child sexual abuse. *Child Abuse and Neglect, 9*, 881–891.

Budin, L. E., & Johnson, C. F. (1989). Sex abuse prevention programs: Offenders' attitudes about their efficacy. *Child Abuse and Neglect, 13*, 77–87.

Ceci, S. J., & Bruck, M. (2006). Children's suggestibility: Characteristics and mechanisms. *Advances in Child Development & Behavior, 34*, 247–281.

Ceci, S. J., Kulkofsky, S., Klemfuss, Z., Sweeney, C. D., & Bruck, M. (2007). Unwarranted assumptions about children's testimonial accuracy. *Annual Review of Clinical Psychology, 3*, 311–328.

Christiansen, J. R., & Blake, R. H. (1990). The grooming process in father-daughter incest. In A. L. Horton, B. L. Johnson, L. M. Roundy, & D. Williams (Eds.), *The incest perpetrator: A family member no one wants to treat* (pp. 88–98). Newbury Park, CA: Sage.

Conte, J., Wolf, S., & Smith, T. (1989). What sexual offenders tell us about prevention strategies. *Child Abuse and Neglect, 13*, 293–301.

Elliott, D. M., & Briere, J. (1994). Forensic sexual abuse evaluations of older children: Disclosures and symptomatology. *Behavioral Sciences and the Law, 12*, 261–277.

Elliott, M., Browne, K., & Kilcoyne, J. (1995). Child sexual abuse prevention: What offenders tell us. *Child Abuse and Neglect, 19*, 579–594.

Fergusson, D. M., Horwood, L. J., & Woodward, L. J. (2000). The stability of child abuse reports: A longitudinal study of the reporting behaviour of young adults. *Psychological Medicine, 30*, 529–544.

Fergusson, D., Lynskey, M., & Horwood, L. J. (1996). Childhood sexual abuse and psychiatric disorder in young adulthood: I. Prevalence of sexual abuse and factors associated with sexual abuse. *Journal of the American Academy of Child & Adolescent Psychiatry, 35*, 1355–1364.

Finkelhor, D. (1994). Current information on the scope and nature of child sexual abuse. *Future of Children, 4*, 31–53.

Finkelhor, D., Hotaling, G., Lewis, I., & Smith, C. (1990). Sexual abuse in a national survey of adult men and women: Prevalence, characteristics, and risk factors. *Child Abuse and Neglect, 14*, 19–28.

Fleming, J. M. (1997). Prevalence of childhood sexual abuse in a community sample of Australian women. *Medical Journal of Australia, 166*, 65–68.

Fry, R. P. W., Rozewicz, L. M., & Crisp, A. H. (1996). Interviewing for sexual abuse: Reliability and effect of interviewer gender. *Child Abuse and Neglect, 20*, 725–729.

Gebhard, P. H., Gagnon, J. H., Pomeroy, W. B., & Christensen, C. V. (1964). *Sex offenders: An analysis of types.* New York: Harper & Row.

Gersten v. Senkowski, 299 F. Supp. 2d 84 (S.D.N.Y. 2004).

Gonzalez, L. S., Waterman, J., Kelly, R. J., McCord, J., & Oliveri, M. K. (1993). Children's patterns of disclosures and recantations of sexual and ritualistic abuse allegations in psychotherapy. *Child Abuse and Neglect, 17*, 281–289.

Hanson, R. F., Resnick, H. S., Saunders, B. E., Kilpatrick, D. G., & Best, C. (1999). Factors related to the reporting of childhood rape. *Child Abuse and Neglect, 23*, 559–569.

Hardt, J., & Rutter, M. (2004). Validity of adult retrospective reports of adverse childhood experiences: Review of the evidence. *Journal of Child Psychology and Psychiatry, 45*, 260–273.

Hershkowitz, I. (2006). Delayed disclosure of alleged child sexual abuse victims in Israel. *American Journal of Orthopsychiatry, 76*, 444–450.

Hershkowitz, I. (2009). Socioemotional factors in child sexual abuse investigations. *Child Maltreatment, 14*, 172–181.

Hershkowitz, I., Horowitz, D., & Lamb, M. E. (2005). Trends in children's disclosure of abuse in Israel: A national study. *Child Abuse and Neglect, 31*, 99–110.

Hershkowitz, I., Lanes, O., & Lamb, M. E. (2007). Exploring the disclosure of child sexual abuse with alleged victims and their parents. *Child Abuse and Neglect*, *31*, 111–123.

Kaufman, K. L., Hilliker, D. R., Lathrop, P., & Daleiden, E. L. (1988). Modus Operandi: Accuracy in self-reported use of threats and coercion. *Annals of Sex Research*, *6*, 213–229.

Kaufman, K. L., Holmberg, J. K, Orts, K. A., McCrady, F. E., Rotzien, A. L., Daleiden, E. L., et al. (1998). Factors influencing sexual offenders' modus operandi: An examination of victim-offender relatedness and age. *Child Maltreatment*, *3*, 349–361.

Kogan, S. M. (2004). Disclosing unwanted sexual experiences: Results from a national sample of adolescent women. *Child Abuse and Neglect*, *24*, 147–165.

Kovera, M. B., & Borgida, E. (1997). Expert testimony in child sexual abuse trials: The admissibility of psychological science. *Applied Cognitive Psychology*, *11*, S105–129.

Lamb, M. E., Hershkowitz, I., Orbach, Y., & Esplin, P. W. (2008). *Tell me what happened: Structured investigative interviews of child victims and witnesses.* London: Wiley.

Lang, R. A., & Frenzel, R. R. (1988). How sex offenders lure children. *Annals of Sex Research*, *1*, 303–331.

Laumann, E. O., Gagnon, J. H., Michael, R. T., & Michaels, S. (1994). *The social organization of sexuality: Sexual practices in the United States.* Chicago: University of Chicago Press.

Lawson, L., & Chaffin, M. (1992). False negatives in sexual abuse interviews. *Journal of Interpersonal Violence*, *7*, 532–542.

Leclerc, B., Proulx, J., & Beauregard, E. (2009). Examining the modus operandi of sexual offenders against children and its practical implications. *Aggression and Violent Behavior*, *14*, 5–12.

Lippert, T., Cross, T. P., Jones, L., & Walsh, W. (2009). Telling interviewers about sexual abuse: Predictors of child disclosure at forensic interviews. *Child Maltreatment*, *14*, 100–113.

Loftus, E. F., & Ketcham, K. (1994). *The myth of repressed memory.* New York: St. Martin's.

London, K., Bruck, M., Ceci, S. J., & Shuman, D. W. (2005). Disclosure of child sexual abuse: What does the research tell us about the ways that children tell? *Psychology, Public Policy, & Law*, *11*, 194–226.

London, K., Bruck, M., Wright, D., & Ceci, S. (2008). Review of the contemporary literature on how children report sexual abuse to others: Findings, methodological issues, and implication for forensic interviewers. *Memory, Special Issue: New insights into Trauma and Memory*, *16*, 29–47.

Lyon, T. D. (2002). Scientific support for expert testimony on child sexual abuse accommodation. In J. R. Conte (Ed.), *Critical issues in child sexual abuse* (pp. 107–138). Thousand Oaks, CA: Sage.

Lyon, T. D. (2007). False denials: Overcoming methodological biases in abuse disclosure research. In M.-E. Pipe, M. E. Lamb, Y. Orbach, & A. C. Cederborg (Eds.), *Disclosing abuse: Delays, denials, retractions and incomplete accounts* (pp. 41–62). Mahwah, NJ: Lawrence Erlbaum.

Lyon, T. D. (2009). Abuse disclosure: What adults can tell. In B. L. Bottoms, C. J. Najdowski, & G. S. Goodman (Eds.), *Children as victims, witnesses, and offenders: Psychological science and the law* (pp. 19–35). New York: Guilford Press.

Lyon, T. D., & Dorado, J. S. (2008). Truth induction in young maltreated children: The effects of oath-taking and reassurance on true and false disclosures. *Child Abuse and Neglect, 32*, 738–748.

Lyon, T. D., Lamb, M., & Myers, J. E. B. (2009). Author's response to Vieth (2008): Legal and psychological support for the NICHD interviewing protocol. *Child Abuse and Neglect, 33*, 71–74.

Lyon, T. D., Malloy, L. C., Quas, J. A., & Talwar, V. (2008). Coaching, truth induction, and young maltreated children's false allegations and false denials. *Child Development, 79*, 914–929.

Malloy, L. C., Lyon, T. D., & Quas, J. A. (2007). Filial dependency and recantation of child sexual abuse allegations. *Journal of the American Academy of Child and Adolescent Psychiatry, 46*, 162–170.

Mason, M. A. (1995). The child sex abuse syndrome: The other major issue in State of New Jersey v. Margaret Kelly Michaels. *Psychology, Public Policy, & Law, 1*, 399–410.

McGee, R. A., Wolfe, D. A., Yuen, S. A., Wilson, S. K., & Carnochan, J. (1995). The measurement of maltreatment: A comparison of approaches. *Child Abuse and Neglect, 19*, 233–249.

Mullen, P. E., Martin, J. L., Anderson, J. C., Romans, S. E., & Herbison, G. P. (1993). Childhood sexual abuse and mental health in adult life. *British Journal of Psychiatry, 163*, 721–732.

Paine, M. L., & Hansen, D. J. (2002). Factors influencing children to self-disclose sexual abuse. *Clinical Psychology Review, 22*, 271–295.

Pipe, M.-E., Lamb, M. E., Orbach, Y., Sternberg, K. J., Stewart, H., & Esplin, P. W. (2007). Factors associated with nondisclosure of suspected abuse during forensic interviews. In M.-E. Pipe, M. E. Lamb, Y. Orbach, & A. C. Cederborg (Eds.), *Child sexual abuse: Disclosure, delay and denial* (pp. 77–96). Mahwah, NJ: Lawrence Erlbaum.

Roberts, K. P., Lamb, M. E., & Sternberg, K. J. (2004). The effects of rapport-building style on children's reports of a staged event. *Applied Cognitive Psychology, 18*, 189–202.

Russell, D. E. H. (1983). The incidence and prevalence of intrafamilial and extrafamilial sexual abuse and female children. *Child Abuse and Neglect, 7*, 133–146.

Salter, A. C. (2003). *Predators: Pedophiles, rapists, and other sex offenders.* New York: Basic Books.

Sas, L. D., & Cunningham, A. H. (1995). *Tipping the balance to tell the secret: The public discovery of child sexual abuse.* London, Ontario, Canada: London Family Court Clinic.

Smallbone, S. W., & Wortley, R. K. (2001). Child sexual abuse: Offender characteristics and modus operandi. *Trends and Issues in Criminal Justice, 193*, 1–6.

Smith, D. W., Letourneau, E. J., Saunders, B. E., Kilpatrick, D. G., Resnick, H. S., & Best, C. L. (2000). Delay in disclosure of childhood rape: Results from a national survey. *Child Abuse and Neglect, 24*, 273–287.

Sorensen, T., & Snow, B. (1991). How children tell: The process of disclosure in child sexual abuse. *Child Welfare, 70*, 3–13.

Sternberg, K. J., Lamb, M. E., Hershkowitz, I., Yudilevitch, L., Orbach, Y., Esplin, P. W., et al. (1997). Effects of introductory style on children's abilities to describe experiences of sexual abuse. *Child Abuse and Neglect, 21*, 1133–1146.

Sternberg, K. J., Lamb, M. E., Orbach, Y., Esplin, P. W., & Mitchell, S. (2001). Use of a structured investigative protocol enhances young children's responses to free recall prompts in the course of forensic interviews. *Journal of Applied Psychology, 86,* 997–1005.

Sullivan, J., & Beech, A. (2004). A comparative study of demographic data relating to intra- and extra-familial child sexual abusers and professional perpetrators. *Journal of Sexual Aggression, 10,* 39–50.

Summit, R. (1983). The child sexual abuse accommodation syndrome. *Child Abuse and Neglect, 2,* 177–193.

Talwar, V., Lee, K., Bala, N., & Lindsay, R. C. L. (2002). Children's conceptual knowledge of lying and its relation to their actual behavior: Implications for court competence examinations. *Law and Human Behavior, 26,* 395–415.

Talwar, V., Lee, K., Bala, N., & Lindsay, R. C. L. (2004). Children's lie-telling to conceal a parent's transgression: Legal implications. *Law and Human Behavior, 28,* 411–435.

Wilsnack, S., Wonderlich, S. A., Kristjanson, A. F., Vogeltanz-Holm, N. D., & Wilsnack, R. W. (2002). Self-reports of forgetting and remembering childhood sexual abuse in a nationally representative sample of US women. *Child Abuse and Neglect, 26,* 139–147.

Wyatt, G. E., Loeb, T. M., Solis, B., Carmona, J. V., & Romero, G. (1999). The prevalence and circumstances of child sexual abuse: Changes across a decade. *Child Abuse and Neglect, 23,* 45–60.

Wyatt, G. E., & Newcomb, M. (1990). Internal and external mediators of women's sexual abuse in childhood. *Journal of Consulting and Clinical Psychology, 58,* 758–767.

15 Medical Issues in Child Sexual Abuse

Martin A. Finkel

Evaluating suspicions of child sexual abuse (CSA) is analogous to solving a complex puzzle. Unlike physical abuse (PA), where the child typically has physical injury that is apparent to the eye, sexually abused children seldom experience physical injury. The absence of readily apparent physical injury makes the sexual abuse puzzle especially challenging. This chapter discusses a key component to the evaluation of possible sexual abuse: the medical examination.

Should Children Receive a Medical Evaluation When Sexual Abuse Is Suspected?

Children who may have been sexually abused should have a comprehensive medical evaluation. Some child protective services (CPS) and law enforcement professionals believe children should only be referred for medical examination if there is a history of penetration or the potential to collect forensic evidence. On the contrary, medical examination is nearly always indicated. The examination is essential to diagnose and treat any effects from sexual contact. As well, the examination affords an opportunity to assure the child and concerned family members that the child is physically intact, or, as some would say "normal." Finally, the medical examination is an important step toward psychological healing. Sexually abused children often have questions about their experience, and medical professionals are well situated to answer questions and put children's minds at ease. For example, a 10-year-old wanted to know if she was going to get breast cancer because the offender put his mouth on her breast. A 9-year-old boy wanted to know if he was going to get "the dying disease": AIDS (Finkel, 2009b).

Except in unusual cases, children should experience only one medical examination. The best way to ensure that only one examination is necessary is to have the examination performed by a medical professional who is highly trained in such matters.

The Chief Complaint

In many ways, medical evaluation regarding possible sexual abuse is similar to evaluation of other medical conditions. The evaluation begins with the "presenting or chief complaint." Information regarding the chief complaint is provided by the child unless the child is too young or too traumatized to discuss what happened. With young children, the adult accompanying the child adds to information provided by the child. In many CSA cases, CPS and/or law enforcement provides information that is relevant to the medical evaluation.

The Medical History

Before diagnosing any medical condition, including sexual abuse, the clinician gathers a medical history. The professional asks questions about the child's medical, social, and family history. The professional asks about the child's genitourinary (GU) and gastrointestinal (GI) functioning. The professional finds out about any preexisting medical conditions that could provide an alternative diagnosis (Finkel, 2009b).

The professional asks about a range of issues, including: (1) the circumstances of the child's disclosure; (2) the alleged perpetrator's relationship to the child; (3) details of the alleged abuse; (4) efforts by the perpetrator or others to silence the child; (5) the child's worries and concerns; (6) the child's perception of what happened, especially the child's perception of penetration if penetration is suspected; (7) exposure to pornography; and (8) whether pictures were taken of the child.

Comprehensive Medical Examination

Most victims of CSA do not disclose immediately. For this reason, the medical examination usually does not have to be performed on an emergency basis. In the following circumstances, however, the examination should be conducted as quickly as possible: (1) the child complains of genital or anal discomfort; (2) there is a history of genital or anal bleeding; (3) the latest sexual contact was within 72 hours, increasing the likelihood that examination will discover fresh injury or biological products such as semen; (4) there is a need for medical treatment of possible pregnancy, sexually transmitted infection (STI), or injury; and (5) the emotional condition of the child or caretakers call for immediate examination (Adams et al., 2007;

Kellogg & American Academy of Pediatrics Committee on Child Abuse and Neglect, 2005).

The professional conducts a comprehensive, head to toe physical examination. Especially with young children, many doctors and nurses prefer to conduct the examination with the caretaker present. An adolescent patient may be asked whether they would like anyone to be in the room during the examination. Appropriate laboratory specimens are collected.

Following the examination, the professional meets with the child and the caretaker to explain the results of the examination and any prescribed treatments. The child and the caretaker are encouraged to ask questions. The professional communicates with CPS and/or law enforcement to describe findings and discuss next steps. A referral for a mental health evaluation and appropriate treatment should be made in most cases because the primary impact of sexual abuse is psychological.

The Importance of the Child's Words

The child's description of sexual abuse is often the most important and powerful evidence of the abuse. It is incumbent on medical professionals to know how to obtain children's statements in a manner that is nonsuggestive, empathetic, nonjudgmental, and facilitating. Rapport building, reassurance, and patience are essential for successful questioning.

Because of the nature of the medical setting, children's statements to medical professionals are sometimes qualitatively different than their statements to others, including CPS, law enforcement, and other adults. There is often a special relationship between a child and a nurse or doctor—a relationship of trust that prompts children to say, "I can tell you because you're a doctor" (Finkel, 2008).

What children say to medical professionals is often used in legal proceedings to prove abuse. Children's statements to professionals are hearsay, but states have an exception to the rule against hearsay that allows children's hearsay statements to medical professionals to be repeated in court. Hearsay and this exception are discussed in Chapter 22.

Genital and Anal Anatomy

Medical professionals are familiar with genital and anal anatomy, as well as variants of normal. It is important for nonmedical professionals to have a basic understanding of these matters so they can communicate with doctors and nurses and can understand medical reports. This section provides an introduction to genital and anal anatomy (Finkel, 2009b). See Figure 15.1.

Figure 15.1 | External Structures of the Female Genital Anatomy

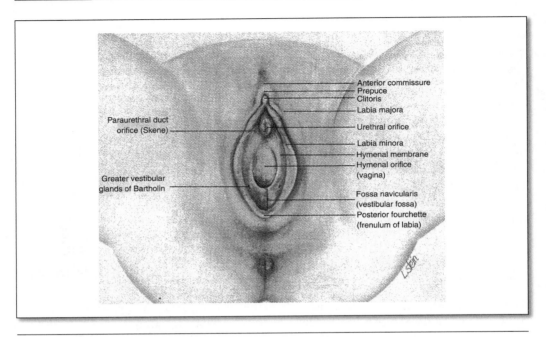

Source: Finkel, M. A., & Giardino, A. P. (2009). *Medical evaluation of child sexual abuse* (3rd ed.). Elk Grove Village, IL: American Academy of Pediatrics. Used with permission of the American Academy of Pediatrics.

Female Genitalia

Vulva. This term refers to all of the external genital structures of the female without acknowledging any specific component. As such it is a term that lacks specificity and is of little descriptive value. The external genital structures include: mons pubis, labia majora and labia minora, clitoral hood, posterior fourchette, fossa naviculars, and structures that form the vaginal vestibule.

Mons pubis. The mons pubis is the skin-covered mound of fatty tissue above the pubic symphysis (place where the left and right pubic bones join in front) and at the anterior (front) of the labia majora. In a newborn baby (neonate), maternal estrogen causes the mons pubis to appear plump. With the loss of maternal estrogen, the mons pubis loses its roundness. During late childhood, the mons pubis begins to thicken and assume a more adult form based on estrogen production. During puberty, the mons pubis becomes a site for pubic hair.

Labia majora. The labia majora are longitudinal folds of fatty and connective tissue that are covered by skin. This structure is analogous to the male scrotum. The labia majora are relatively large and thick at birth and remain so for several weeks to months following birth. Toward the front of the child's body, the folds are united by a commissure (a juncture). During puberty, the labia majora become covered with pubic hair.

Labia minora. The labia minora are thin folds of tissue. The external component of the labia minora is skin, while the inner component is mucosa similar to the lip of the mouth. The labia minora are protected by the labia majora. The labia minora join at the top to form the prepuce (fold of skin) surrounding the clitoris. At the bottom, the labia minora fuse to form the posterior fourchette. There are no hair follicles in the labia minora.

Clitoris. The clitoris is a cylindrical erectile structure that consists of a glans, prepuce, frenulum, and body. It is analogous to the penis of the male. In the neonate, the glans is disproportionately large. During growth and development, the clitoris grows at a slower pace than surrounding structures, and its relative size decreases. The glans is visible, whereas the body of the clitoris extends upward toward the pubis bone under the skin.

Urethral meatus. The urethra forms the outlet of the urinary system, and its opening forms the urethral meatus. The urethral meatus is surrounded by several mucoid secreting glands known as Skene's glands. A second set of secretory glands are the Greater Vestibular Glands of Bartholin, found more posteriorly. Neither set of glands or their respective ducts are generally visible to the naked eye.

Vaginal vestibule. The word *vestibule* means "entranceway." The vaginal vestibule is the space in front (outside) of the hymenal membrane and enclosed by the labia minora. The vestibule must be passed through for an object to enter the vagina. The vestibule is formed by the clitoral hood superiorly, the inner aspects of the labia minora laterally, the commissure/fourchette posteriorly, and the external surface of the hymenal membrane internally. The vaginal vestibule is lined by tissue called urogenital sinus epithelium.

Hymen. The hymen is a mucous membrane separating the external from the internal genital structures. The hymen is a recessed structure that sits inside the body at the entrance to the vagina. Except in rare circumstances, all girls have a hymen (Jenny, Kuhns, & Arakawa, 1987; Mor, Merlob, & Reisner, 1986). The hymen normally has an opening to allow genital secretions and menstrual blood to escape. The opening in the hymen is called the hymenal orifice or opening. The appearance of the hymenal membrane and the orifice changes with age and the degree of pubertal development (Berenson, 1993, 1995; Berenson & Grady, 2002; Heger, Ticson, Guerra et al., 2002; McCann, Wells, Simon, & Voris, 1990).

Assessment of the hymen includes the shape and size of the opening, degree of estrogen effects, and any acute or healed signs of injury (Ingram, Everett, & Ingram, 2001). The hymenal orifice edge is usually smooth and uninterrupted.

The membrane edge in the prepubertal child may have some translucency and can appear similar to the edge of a feather when the feather is held up to light.

When medical professionals describe the position of injury or irregularity of the hymen they usually refer to the face of a clock. With the child lying on her back, and the examiner standing at the child's feet, 12 o'clock refers to the top, while 6 o'clock refers to the bottom. Thus, an injury at the 5 o'clock position is toward the bottom and to the examiner's right (child's left).

Posterior fourchette. The posterior fourchette is the point at which the labia minora meet posteriorly. The structure is sometimes referred to as the frenulum of the labia. In the prepubertal child, the labia minora do not fuse, and the corresponding location is referred to as the posterior commissure.

Fossa navicularis. The fossa navicularis is a concave area between the posterior attachment of the hymen to the vaginal wall (6 o'clock) and the posterior fourchette.

Male Genitalia

Penis. The penis is a cylindrical, erectile structure composed of a glans, body, prepuce, and frenulum. The erectile bodies are covered by thin, loosely attached skin without fatty tissue or hair, except at the base. The prepuce is a fold of tissue that encircles the glans and has an opening that allows for retraction over the glans. The urethral meatus, or opening, is at the end of the glans.

In the uncircumcised male, the foreskin (prepuce) can be retracted over the glans by approximately 5 years of age. Circumcision removes the prepuce and the frenulum.

Scrotum. The scrotum is a saclike structure composed of skin, muscle, and connective tissue. It serves to protect the testicles and associated structures. The scrotal skin is thin and elastic and has obvious wrinkles (rugae). During puberty, the scrotum develops a thin covering of pubic hair and increased pigmentation.

Testes. The testes (testicles) are oval shaped structures inside the scrotum. In the normal male, both testes are descended. The right testis generally hangs lower than the left.

Epididymis. The epididymis is a long, narrow, tubelike structure that carries sperm from the testicles to the seminal vesicle. The epididymis may be felt through the thin skin of the scrotum until it enters the inguinal canal.

Anal Anatomy

The anus is the opening of the rectum through which feces passes. The opening is surrounded by both internal and external sphincter mechanisms that collectively make up the anal sphincter (see Figure 15.2). The tissue that

Figure 15.2   Anal Anatomy

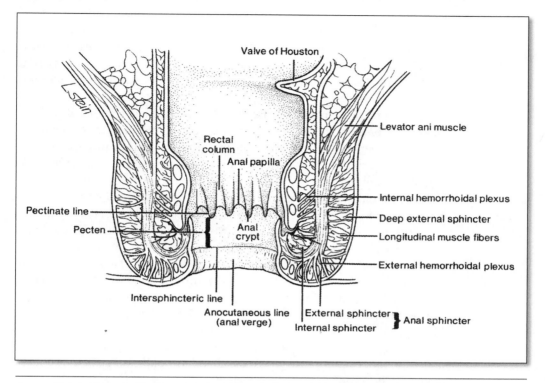

Source: Finkel, M. A., & Giardino, A. P. (2009). *Medical evaluation of child sexual abuse* (3rd ed.). Elk Grove Village, IL: American Academy of Pediatrics. Used with permission of the American Academy of Pediatrics.

overlies the external anal sphincter is the anal verge. The typical appearance of the external anus is that of a circumferentially symmetric, pigmented, puckered tissue (rugae) that has a natural tone and that reflexively tightens when the buttocks are separated (McCann, Wells, Simon, & Voris, 1989).

When the anus is examined with the child on their back with their legs flexed onto the belly or examined on their side with the legs flexed onto the belly (lateral decubitus position) for any extended period of time, it is possible for hemorrhoidal veins to fill up with blood (engorge), creating a purplish appearance that can take on a color similar to bruising. Differentiating bruising from venous engorgement can be done easily by changing the child's position.

Examination of the Genital and Anal Areas

In girls, examination of the external genital structures includes the mons pubis, labia majora, labia minora, clitoris, urethra, vaginal vestibule, hymen, Skene's and Bartholin's glands, posterior fourchette, and fossa navicularis. These external structures are referred to collectively as the vulva.

As previously mentioned, the dividing line between the external and internal genital structures is the hymenal membrane. Examination of the structures in the area of the vaginal vestibule usually can be accomplished without instrumentation or anesthesia. Examination of the innermost aspects of the vagina is generally reserved for pubertal children and requires use of a medical instrument called a speculum. In circumstances where it is necessary to examine the deeper vagina of a prepubertal child, the doctor typically uses anesthesia or sedation.

The genital examination of the prepubertal female is conducted with the child lying on her back with her legs relaxed out to the side or in stirrups (supine frog leg position). A supplemental position used to provide an additional view of the hymen is with the child lying on her belly with the buttocks placed in the air and the legs pulled up (prone knee chest position). The prone knee chest position is awkward for many children but is helpful when the child's hymen has a lot of loose (redundant) tissue. If examination in the supine frog leg position reveals evidence of sexual abuse, the child should be placed in the prone knee chest position to confirm the findings.

The examiner gently grasps the labia and separates them (labial separation) to allow observation of the vaginal vestibule. With slight pulling (labial traction), all aspects of the hymenal membrane and the tissue surrounding it can be visualized (Bays, Chewning, Keltner, Steinberg, & Thomas, 1990; McCann, Voris, Simon, & Wells, 1990). The use of a vaginal speculum to see the inner aspect of the vagina is not indicated in prepubertal children except under the rare circumstance where the child has significant genital trauma or there may be a foreign body in the vagina.

In the pubertal female, the knee chest position is not preferred. Rather, the child lies on her back with her legs out to the side, typically placed in stirrups. The examiner uses labial separation and labial traction to visualize the structures of the vaginal vestibule including the edge of the hymenal membrane. Because the hymenal membrane of the pubertal child is estrogenized, the tissue becomes redundant and elastic. To fully visualize the hymenal edge, and to differentiate initial observations that could be interpreted as abnormal, the edge is visualized completely, often with the aid of a saline moistened Q-tip.

With the pubertal female, the decision to use a vaginal speculum to examine the cervix and the posterior portion of the vagina is determined on a case by case basis. If the history suggests vaginal penetration in a pubertal child, speculum examination is generally warranted to provide a complete assessment and to check for an STI.

In boys, the genital examination includes the glans and frenulum (prepuce or foreskin if uncircumcised), shaft, scrotum, testicles and epididymis, inguinal region for adenopathy and hernias, and the perineum.

In girls and boys, anal examination includes the perianal region, which involves the tissues that surround the anal opening and the gluteal cleft, which is the groove between the buttocks, the anal verge (juncture between the anal canal and perianal skin) and, when indicated, the anorectal canal, which requires the use of an instrument called an anoscope.

The anal area in girls and boys is examined by asking the child to lie on their back and pull their legs up to their abdomen. Alternatively, the child lies on her or his side (lateral decubitus position) and pulls the legs up. The examiner manually separates the buttocks.

Anal sexual abuse may include penetration with a penis or a foreign object. Depending on the degree of force, the use of lubrication, and the "cooperativeness" of the victim, penetration may cause no damage or significant injury (McCann & Voris, 1993). Anal sexual abuse may cause frictional injury to tissues of the gluteal cleft caused by a penis rubbing between the buttocks.

The need to look inside the anus depends on the child's history. Anoscopy or sigmoidoscopy is most likely to be needed in acute cases when there is concern about possible internal trauma that extends beyond the external sphincter.

Fellatio typically causes no injury. If force is used, however, there may be tiny red dots called petechiae on the roof and back of the child's mouth. This injury results when capillaries are ruptured. Inside the upper and lower lip is a sliver of tissue called the frenulum that connects the lip to the gum. You can feel your frenulum by sticking your tongue up in front of your upper teeth. If a child's lip is forced away from the child's mouth, the frenulum can tear.

Less than 5% of sexually abused children have physical findings that provide definitive proof of abuse (Heger, Ticson, Velasquez, & Bernier, 2002). A higher percentage of children have physical findings that are nonspecific. DeLago and colleagues (2008) studied 161 sexually abused girls between 3 and 18 years of age. Sixty percent of the girls experienced one or more symptoms, with 53% complaining of genital pain, 37% experiencing painful urination (dysuria), and 11% bleeding following sexual contact. Forty-eight percent of girls who reported genital-to-genital contact had dysuria compared to 25% of girls who did not report genital-to-genital contact. Most injuries caused by sexual abuse are superficial and heal quickly. Mucosal injuries, for example, can disappear within 48 to 72 hours.

Acute findings of recent sexual abuse include active bleeding, bruising, and superficial abrasions and/or lacerations of genital or anal tissues. A complete interruption (transaction) of the hymenal membrane that extends to the base of the hymenal attachment is most likely explained by blunt force penetrating trauma. The presence of an STI or pregnancy in a pubertal child is diagnostic of sexual contact.

A number of medical conditions can be confused with trauma caused by sexual abuse (Frasier, 2009; Siegfried & Frasier, 1997). A skilled examiner is knowledgeable about such conditions and rules them out before reaching a diagnosis of sexual abuse.

In addition to ruling out benign medical conditions, the clinician considers the possibility of accidental trauma (Bond, Dowd, Landsman, & Rimsza, 1995; Dowd, Fitzmaurice, Knapp, & Mooney, 1994; Kadish, Schunk, & Britton, 1998; Spitzer et al., 2008). The most common accidental injury to the genital area is a straddle injury caused by falling onto the horizontal bar of a bicycle or playground equipment. The experienced examiner can usually distinguish a straddle injury from abuse.

A colposcope is a device similar to binoculars on a tripod. The clinician uses the colposcope to enhance visual examination of the genital and anal areas. The colposcope is equipped with a "red free" filter, which enhances the visualization of acute mucosal injuries as well as healed injuries. The colposcope is noninvasive and does not touch the child. Most colposcopes are equipped with a digital camera for still pictures and a video camera capable of recording the examination (Finkel, 1998; McCann, 1990).

Penetration

Some sex crimes require penetration. Rape, for example, is defined as sexual intercourse (penetration) by force and without the victim's consent. Penetration is the act of entering a space. In sexual abuse, an object may penetrate into the oral cavity, the vaginal vestibule, the vagina, and/or the anus. When thinking of the female genitalia, the depth of penetration can best be described if the genitalia are thought of as having two potential spaces to penetrate. The first space is the vaginal vestibule, which is the entrance to the vagina and is the space in front of the hymenal membrane that divides the external from the internal genital structures. When prepubertal children say that something was placed "in" them, the "in" often refers to penetration within the vestibule, not the vagina. The second and deeper space is the vagina.

In law, any penetration—however slight—is sufficient. With rape, for example, penetration past the hymen and into the vagina is *not* required. The slightest penetration of the labia majora is sufficient. In legal proceedings, penetration is often established with testimony from the victim and/or with expert medical testimony (Myers, 2005, 2010). Children, of course, are unaware of the legal definition of penetration. Moreover, children's descriptions of what happened to them and whether they were penetrated are not always accurate. Children describe their experiences and perceptions in their own age appropriate manner. Because children may not know if they were penetrated, it often falls to medical professionals to determine whether penetration occurred.

From a medical perspective, it is easier to determine if a child experienced penetration through the hymenal opening and in the vagina when the child is prepubertal. The relative lack of elasticity of the unestrogenized prepubertal hymen, coupled with a history of pain, bleeding, and observation of acute or healed(ing) trauma, supports the determination of vaginal penetration in the prepubertal child. Once a child enters puberty and the hymenal membrane is estrogenized, the hymenal membrane becomes more elastic, making it difficult to determine if vaginal penetration occurred unless examination reveals acute injuries to the hymen and/or the intravaginal area (Adams, Botash, & Kellogg, 2004; Berenson et al., 2002; Ingram et al., 2001).

Healed lacerations (transections) of the hymen in either the prepubertal or pubertal child are diagnostic of blunt force penetrating trauma. Acute and healed hymenal injuries are most commonly observed between the 4 o'clock and 8 o'clock position of the hymen with the child on her back (supine) (Adams

& Knudson, 1996; Heppenstall-Heger et al., 2003; McCann, 1998; McCann, Miyamoto, Boyle, & Rogers, 2007; McCann, Voris, & Simon, 1992).

Most injuries that prepubertal or pubertal children incur to their genitalia following penetration into the vestibule or the vagina are superficial and heal without any sign of trauma, even when the child describes pain and bleeding (Finkel, 1989). With genital fondling, as well as when a penis is placed between the labia and rubbed back and forth in the vestibule, there is the potential for superficial trauma to the mucosal surfaces. If injury occurs as a result of such contact, the child is likely to complain of pain, possibly bleeding, and to provide a history of burning with urination (dysuria) (DeLago et al., 2008).

Whenever injury occurs, force was used. Determining the degree of force required to inflict a particular injury is not possible beyond saying that sufficient force was used.

Injury can follow consensual sexual activity. Thus, the issue is not the degree of force but whether the child was able to consent to the activity they experienced. It is important to remember that the depth of penetration has no direct correlation to the seriousness of the psychological impact on the child.

Females and males may experience anal penetration. The anus, however, is designed to pass large diameter stools on a regular basis and therefore can allow introduction of foreign bodies such as a finger, penis, or object with either no residual or minimal residual trauma. In circumstances where lubrication is used to facilitate penetration, the potential for either acute or healed findings is reduced.

Sexually Transmitted Infection

When children experience inappropriate sexual contact, they are at risk for acquiring an STI (Girardet et al., 2009; Palusci & Reeves, 2003; Reading & Rannan-Eliya, 2007; Siegel, Schubert, Myers, & Shapiro, 1995). The spectrum of STIs includes Neisseria gonorrhoeae, Chlamydia trachomatis, Trichomonas vaginalis, herpes simplex virus (HSV), human papillomavirus (HPV), syphilis, hepatitis, and human immunodeficiency virus (HIV).

After the newborn period, when a child is present with an STI, the obvious implication is that the child came in contact with infected genital secretions. A popular but scientifically unsupported theory is that STIs are transmitted through innocent contact with infected secretions on inanimate objects such as toilet seats or washcloths. Medical professionals call such objects "fomites." More research is needed to determine whether STIs can be transmitted via contact with "dirty" fomites.

There is solid evidence that caretakers can innocently transmit HPV—responsible for the common hand wart—to the perianal area of a young child in the process of normal caretaking. When HPV is present in children who do not require genital/anal caretaking, the examiner considers alternatives (Stevens-Simon, Nelligan, Breese, Jenny, & Douglas, 2000).

In prepubertal sexually abused children, there is a low prevalence rate of STIs. As a general rule, prepubertal children are not routinely screened for STIs. Adolescents who are sexually active are at greater risk for acquiring an STI. As with prepubertal children, decisions about testing for STIs in the adolescent child are made on a case by case basis. When the offender is a stranger and the history suggests contact with potentially infected genital secretions, screening and treatment, including HIV prophylaxis, is often warranted.

Conclusion

This chapter provided an introduction to the medical assessment of possible CSA. Medical professionals are key players in society's effort to solve the puzzle of sexual exploitation. Balanced, objective, and well-documented medical opinions serve the best interests of children (Finkel, 2009a; Socolar, Champion, & Green, 1996). Along with colleagues from social work, law enforcement, and law, physicians and nurses strive to prevent sexual abuse and to ameliorate the suffering of children who are abused.

References

Adams, J. A., Botash, A. S., & Kellogg, N. (2004). Differences in hymenal morphology between adolescent girls with and without a history of consensual sexual intercourse. *Archives of Pediatric Adolescent Medicine, 158*, 280–285.

Adams, J. A., Kaplan, R. A., Starling, S. P., Mehta, N. H., Finkel, M. A., Botash, A.S., et al. (2007). Guidelines for medical care of children who may have been sexually abused. *Journal of Pediatric and Adolescent Gynecology, 20*, 163–172.

Adams, J. A., & Knudson, S. (1996). Genital findings in adolescent girls referred for suspected sexual abuse. *Archives of Pediatric and Adolescent Medicine, 150*, 850–857.

Bays, J., Chewning, M., Keltner, L. R., Steinberg, M., & Thomas, P. (1990). Changes in hymenal anatomy during examination of prepubertal girls for possible sexual abuse. *Adolescent Pediatric Gynecology, 3*, 34–46.

Berenson, A. B. (1993). Appearance of the hymen at birth and one year of age: A longitudinal study. *Pediatrics, 91*, 820–825.

Berenson, A. B. (1995). A longitudinal study of hymenal morphology in the first 3 years of life. *Pediatrics, 95*, 490–496.

Berenson, A. B., Chacko, M. R., Wiemann, C. M., Mishaw, C. O., Friedrich, W. N., & Grady, J. J. (2002). Use of hymenal measurements in the diagnosis of previous penetration. *Pediatrics, 109*, 228–235.

Berenson, A. B., & Grady, J. J. (2002). A longitudinal study of hymenal development from 3 to 9 years of age. *Journal of Pediatrics, 140*, 600–607.

Bond, G. R., Dowd, M. D., Landsman, I., & Rimsza, M. (1995). Unintentional perineal injury in prepubescent girls: A multicenter, prospective report of 56 girls. *Pediatrics, 95*, 628–631.

DeLago, C., Deblinger, E. D., Schroeder, C., & Finkel, M. A. (2008) Girls who disclose sexual abuse: Urogenital symptoms and signs following sexual contact. *Pediatrics, 122,* e221–e226.

Dowd, M. D., Fitzmaurice, L., Knapp, J. F., & Mooney, D. (1994). The interpretation of urogenital findings in children with straddle injuries. *Journal of Pediatric Surgery, 29,* 7–10.

Finkel, M. A. (1989). Anogenital trauma in sexually abused children. *Pediatrics, 84,* 317–322.

Finkel, M. A. (1998). Technical conduct of the child sexual abuse medical examination. *Child Abuse and Neglect, 22,* 555–566.

Finkel, M. A. (2008). "I can tell you because you're a doctor": Commentary on girls who disclose sexual abuse: Signs and symptoms following genital contact. The importance of the pediatricians detailed medical history when evaluating suspected child sexual abuse. *Pediatrics, 122,* 422.

Finkel, M. A. (2009a). Documentation, report formulation and conclusions. In M. A. Finkel & A. P. Giardino (Eds.), *Medical evaluation of child sexual abuse* (3rd ed., pp. 357–371). Elk Grove Village, IL: American Academy of Pediatrics.

Finkel, M. A. (2009b). Physical examination. In M. A. Finkel & A. P. Giardino (Eds.), *Medical evaluation of child sexual abuse* (3rd ed., pp. 53–104). Elk Grove Village, IL: American Academy of Pediatrics.

Finkel, M. A., & Giardino, A. P. (Eds.). (2009). *Medical evaluation of child sexual abuse: A practical guide* (3rd ed). Elk Grove Village, IL: American Academy of Pediatrics.

Frasier, L. (2009). The anogenital examination: Diagnostic dilemmas, mimics of abuse. In M. A. Finkel & A. P. Giardino (Eds.), *Medical evaluation of child sexual abuse* (3rd ed., pp. 211–235). Elk Grove Village, IL: American Academy of Pediatrics.

Girardet, R. G., Lahoti, S., Howard, L. A., Fajman, N. N., Sawyer, M. K., Driebe, E. M., et al. (2009). Epidemiology of sexually transmitted infections in suspected child victims of sexual assault. *Pediatrics, 124,* 79–86.

Heger, A. H., Ticson, L., Guerra, L., Lister, J., Zaragoza, T., McConnell, G., et al. (2002). Appearance of the genitalia in girls selected for nonabuse: Review of hymenal morphology and nonspecific findings. *Journal of Pediatric and Adolescent Synocology, 15,* 27–35.

Heger, A., Ticson, L., Velasquez, O., & Bernier, R. (2002). Children referred for possible sexual abuse: Medical findings in 2,384 children. *Child Abuse and Neglect, 26,* 645–659.

Heppenstall-Heger, A., McConnel, G., Ticson, L., Guerra, L., Lister, J., & Zaggagoza, T. (2003). Healing patterns in anogenital injuries: A longitudinal study of injuries associated with sexual abuse, accidental injuries, or genital surgery in the preadolescent child. *Pediatrics, 112,* 829–837.

Ingram, D. M., Everett, V. D., & Ingram, D. L. (2001). The relationship between the transverse hymenal orifice diameter by the separation technique and other possible markers of sexual abuse. *Child Abuse and Neglect, 25,* 1109–1120.

Jenny, C., Kuhns, M. L., & Arakawa, F. (1987). Hymens in newborn female infants. *Pediatrics, 80,* 399–400.

Kadish, H. A., Schunk, J. E., & Britton, H. (1998). Pediatric male rectal and genital trauma: Accidental and nonaccidental injuries. *Pediatric Emergency Care, 14,* 95–98.

Kellogg, N., & American Academy of Pediatrics Committee on Child Abuse and Neglect. (2005). The evaluation of sexual abuse in children. *Pediatrics, 116,* 506–512.

McCann, J. (1990). Use of the colposcope in childhood sexual abuse examinations. *Pediatric Clinics of North America, 37,* 863–880.

McCann, J. (1998). The appearance of acute, healing, and healed anogenital trauma. *Child Abuse and Neglect, 22,* 605–615.

McCann, J., Miyamoto, S., Boyle, C., & Rogers, K. (2007). Healing of hymenal injuries in prepubertal and adolescent girls: A descriptive study. *Pediatrics, 119,* e1094–e1106.

McCann, J., & Voris, J. (1993). Perianal injuries resulting from sexual abuse: A longitudinal study. *Pediatrics, 91,* 390–397.

McCann, J., Voris, J., & Simon, M. (1992). Genital injuries resulting from sexual abuse: A longitudinal study. *Pediatrics, 89,* 307–317.

McCann, J., Voris, J., Simon, M., & Wells, R. (1990). Comparison of genital examination techniques in prepubertal girls. *Pediatrics, 85,* 182–187.

McCann, J., Wells, R., Simon, M. A., & Voris, J. (1989). Perianal findings in prepubertal children selected for nonabuse: A descriptive study. *Child Abuse and Neglect, 13,* 179–193.

McCann, J., Wells, R., Simon, M. A., & Voris, J. (1990). Genital findings in prepubertal girls selected for nonabuse: A descriptive study. *Pediatrics, 86,* 428–439.

Mor, N., Merlob, P., & Reisner, S. H. (1986). Types of hymen in the newborn infant. *European Journal of Obstetrics, Gynecology, and Reproductive Biology, 22,* 225–228.

Myers, J. E. B. (2005). *Myers on evidence in child, domestic and elder abuse cases.* New York: Aspen Law and Business.

Myers, J. E. B. (2010). *Myers on evidence in child, domestic and elder abuse cases.* New York: Aspen Law and Business.

Palusci, V. J., & Reeves, M. J. (2003). Testing for genital gonorrhea infections in prepubertal girls with suspected sexual abuse. *Pediatric Infectious Disease Journal, 22,* 618–623.

Reading, R., & Rannan-Eliya, Y. (2007). Evidence for sexual transmission of genital herpes in children. *Archives of Diseases of Childhood, 92,* 608–613.

Siegel, R. M., Schubert, C. J., Myers, P. A., & Shapiro, R. A. (1995). The prevalence of sexually transmitted disease in children and adolescents evaluated for sexual abuse in Cincinnati: Rationale for limited STD testing in prepubertal girls. *Pediatrics. 96,* 1090–1094.

Siegfried, E. C., & Frasier, L. D. (1997). Anogenital skin diseases of childhood. *Pediatric Annals, 26,* 321–331.

Socolar, R. S., Champion, M., & Green, C. (1996). Physicians' documentation of sexual abuse of children. *Archives of Pediatric and Adolescent Medicine, 150,* 191–196.

Spitzer, R. F., Kives, S., Caccia, N., Ornstein, M., Goia, C., & Allen, L. M. (2008). Retrospective review of unintentional female genital trauma at a pediatric referral center. *Pediatric Emergency Care, 24,* 831–835.

Stevens-Simon, C., Nelligan, D., Breese, P., Jenny, C., & Douglas, J. M., Jr. (2000). The prevalence of genital human papillomavirus infections in abused and nonabused preadolescent girls. *Pediatrics, 106,* 645–649.

16

Mental Health Treatment for the Effects of Child Sexual Abuse

Elisabeth Pollio,
Esther Deblinger, and
Melissa K. Runyon

Child sexual abuse (CSA) remains a highly prevalent public health problem that negatively affects children, adolescents, and families across all ethnic groups, religious sects, socioeconomic classes, and regions of the world (Finkelhor & Ormrod, 2000). For many decades, researchers have documented the disruptive effects sexual abuse has on children's cognitive, emotional, social, and behavioral development. Recent research suggests abuse and its adverse effects may negatively impact brain development as well (Cohen, Perel, DeBellis, Friedman, & Putnam, 2002). It has been repeatedly found that survivors of sexual abuse are at increased risk for developing significant mental health disorders including posttraumatic stress disorder (PTSD), major depression, oppositional and conduct problems, as well as substance use disorders (e.g., Deblinger, McLeer, Atkins, Ralphe, & Foa, 1989; Kendall-Tackett, Williams, & Finkelhor, 1993; Spataro, Mullen, Burgess, Wells, & Moss, 2004). In addition, there is evidence that children who have been sexually abused may be at increased risk for suicide, medical difficulties, and interpersonal problems including revictimization experiences in adolescence or adulthood (Brown, Cohen, Johnson, & Smailes, 1999; Widom & Brzustowicz, 2006). Thus, while there is little question that some youngsters recover spontaneously from the effects of sexual abuse, many others require mental health treatment to prevent the development and ongoing debilitating effects of CSA.

Research on the impact of CSA has informed the development of treatments for this population. In addition, numerous studies have attempted to identify factors amenable to change that moderate the impact of CSA as well as mediate children's responses to treatment.

Parental Response

Parental response, support, and distress have proven to influence children's outcomes (Cohen & Mannarino, 1996, 1998; Deblinger, Lippmann, & Steer, 1996). One study found that children may experience feelings of shame following disclosure of sexual abuse, but their ability to overcome these feelings is often associated with the protection and support of others in the months following disclosure (Feiring & Taska, 2005). It is not surprising, therefore, that many interventions designed for this population include nonoffending caregivers in order to enhance the caregivers' ability to support their children and to assist them in coping with their own distress (Deblinger & Heflin, 1996). Many studies document that parents whose children have been sexually abused suffer a myriad of emotions including self-blame, anger, and depression. Furthermore, it has been found that mothers with a personal history of sexual abuse may be particularly vulnerable to distress and feeling alone in managing the crisis of discovering that their child has been sexually abused (Deblinger, Stauffer, & Landsberg, 1994). In addition, mothers whose children have been sexually abused by a parent, stepparent or partner, as opposed to another relative or nonrelative, are more likely to experience domestic violence, often by their child's abuser (Deblinger, Hathaway, Lippmann, & Steer, 1993). Thus, to optimally support a child's recovery from sexual abuse, it is important to assess parents' responses, their support resources, and their personal histories of abuse and/or trauma.

Children's Abuse-Related Attributions

Children's cognitive attributions and perceptions in relation to sexual abuse have been the focus of research. Studies demonstrate that children who experience higher levels of self-blame and feelings of shame are more likely to experience negative outcomes in the aftermath of CSA (Feiring, Taska, & Lewis, 1999; Cohen & Mannarino, 1997). Feiring and colleagues (1999) found that shame and self-blame related to abuse mediate the relationship between the number of abusive events and depression, self-esteem, and eroticism. A study examining treatment process with a sample of traumatized youth, many of whom had been sexually abused, found that youth who demonstrated more abuse-related processing in the context of therapy showed greater improvement on measures of PTSD and behavior problems (Hayes et al., 2009). Given these findings, it is not surprising that treatment goals across a variety of approaches include the uncovering and processing of abuse-related cognitive distortions that may be associated with children's symptoms, particularly PTSD and depression.

Sexual Behavior Problems

Survivors of sexual abuse experience a wide range of difficulties similar to individuals who have experienced other traumas. However, sexual behavior problems and dysfunctions have been found to be more commonly linked to the trauma of sexual abuse as compared to other traumas (Deblinger et al., 1989; Myers et al., 2002). The clinician working with this population must be prepared to address these difficulties because they not only have the potential to hinder social functioning but they can adversely affect other children if they lead to abusive sexual behavior. It is critical to involve nonoffending parents in treatment to develop behavior management strategies to manage these behaviors as well as address issues of monitoring and appropriate supervising of the child while they are interacting with other children. Without parental involvement, limited progress can be made to change behavior and enhance safety.

Recent treatment outcome research has documented the benefits of cognitive behavioral therapy (CBT) in helping children overcome sexual behavior problems (Cohen & Mannarino, 1996, 1997; Silovsky, Niec, Bard, & Hecht, 2007). A long-term follow-up study of children with sexual behavior problems (some of whom had a history of sexual abuse) documented significant long-term benefits of a short-term group CBT approach that involved children and their parents in reducing the likelihood of sexual offenses by these youngsters in adolescence and young adulthood (Carpentier, Silovsky, & Chaffin, 2006).

Risk of Revictimization

It is important to note that survivors of sexual abuse appear to be prone to sexual and/or physical revictimization in adolescence and adulthood (Arata, 2000). Thus, incorporating personal safety skills into treatment is critical. Moreover, research documents that body safety skills training that involves parents and utilizes behavior rehearsal for skill development leads to increased knowledge and personal safety skills among children who have experienced abuse (Cohen, Deblinger et al., 2004; Deblinger, Stauffer, & Steer, 2001; Runyon & Deblinger, 2008; Kenny, Capri, Thakkar-Kolar, Ryan, & Runyon, 2008). In addition, research suggests that this type of training appears to be associated with reduced risk of victimization in nonabused children as well (Finkelhor, Asdigian, & Dziuba-Leatherman, 1995; Finkelhor, Ormrod, & Turner, 2007).

Treatment Approaches

Different theoretical conceptualizations inform the development of treatments designed to address emotional and behavioral symptoms and to enhance the healing of children and adolescents who have experienced sexual abuse. Experts in this field have described a wide array of treatments designed to engage this population (Cohen, Mannarino, & Deblinger, 2006; Friedrich, 1990; Gil, 2006; James, 1989). Authors have described treatment approaches from distinct theoretical perspectives that reflect their appreciation for the crisis that unfolds in the aftermath of CSA. Authors generally have incorporated many similar elements designed to engage children and adolescents who have experienced sexual abuse.

With differing degrees of emphasis, most treatment approaches described in the literature recognize the importance of engaging children as well as their families, particularly nonoffending parents, in the treatment process. In addition, most therapies designed for this population incorporate creative methods to engage children and adolescents that involve play, art, games, and/or a combination of these methods. Moreover, most interventions are designed to not only reduce symptoms but also to restore and/or encourage feelings of mastery and strength in survivors of sexual abuse.

Although many of the treatment approaches share common threads, and most have clinical value, relatively few of the treatments described in the literature and utilized with this population have been empirically validated. Indeed, despite the well-documented negative psychosocial impact of CSA, it was not until the 1990s that empirical studies were published examining the efficacy of treatment for this population. Fortunately, empirical research is well underway to establish the benefits of different approaches involving individual, family, and group formats. Described next are some of the most commonly used treatment approaches developed for this population with a sampling of related research.

Play Therapy

Play therapy is widely used to address a variety of difficulties, including the sequelae of sexual abuse. Play therapy was one of the earliest treatments employed with children who had experienced sexual abuse. Play therapy is designed to reduce children's emotional distress through the symbolic communication of play as well as to remove obstacles that block the child's growth (Webb, 1999). The primary purpose is to "help troubled children express their conflicts and anxieties through the medium of play in the context of a therapeutic relationship" (Webb, 1999, p. 32). For victims of trauma, play therapy takes a corrective and reparative approach that allows the child to process the trauma in a manner that can be consciously understood and tolerated (Gil, 1996).

A few pre–post treatment studies have investigated the potential benefits of play therapy in treating children who have been sexually abused. These studies, however, often did not employ random assignment, comparison groups, or standardized treatments. One study of children ages 8 to 16 utilizing a pre–post design without a control group found significant decreases on measures of anxiety, depression, and PTSD over the 9-month course of therapy (Reyes & Asbrand, 2005). At posttreatment, however, several children reported significant scores on subscales related to sexual concerns, sexual preoccupation, and sexual distress, suggesting an approach that specifically addresses these concerns may need to be included in treatment. A study of children ages 3 to 9 investigated a 12-week program of individual client-centered play therapy in a pre–post design without a control group (Scott, Burlingame, Starling, Porter, & Lilly, 2003). Results indicated that children's self-reported sense of competency improved over time but no significant changes were found on parent-report measures related to the child's self-concept and behavior. Overall, the results for the play therapy approach used in this study were mixed.

There are a variety of play therapy approaches, generally falling into one of three categories: directive, nondirective, or an integration of the two. Directive play therapy can produce a fairly quick change in targeted symptoms, is of briefer duration, and may be manualized with standardized intervention protocols. "Manualized" means documented with clear guidelines for practice.

Strengths cited for nondirective play therapy include the creation of an environment that is comfortable for the child, a perception of increased control for the child, and allowing the child to set the pace and initiate trauma-related play (Shelby & Felix, 2005). There is concern, however, that nondirective play therapy in the absence of any directive work may not be applicable to children who have been sexually abused and that an active approach may be needed to assist sexually abused children process sexual abuse-related memories (James, 1989). In addition, a purely nondirective approach can be confusing to a child who has not been oriented to the purpose of therapy or who does not understand what is expected (Friedrich, 1990). A further concern is that the therapist may inadvertently reinforce a child's belief that the trauma is too overwhelming to address because there is no direct discussion of the trauma (James, 1989).

The integration of directive and nondirective approaches attempts to capitalize on the benefits of both. Gil (2006) describes an integrated treatment approach that seeks a balance in terms of trauma focus—not avoiding the topic of trauma while not overfocusing on it. Treatment goals include developing a therapeutic relationship of mutual trust and respect, assisting children with emotional expression and regulation, helping children enhance their feelings of competence, bringing trauma memories into awareness through directive and nondirective approaches, encouraging the integration of memories and creation of verbal or nonverbal trauma narratives, encouraging the releasing of energy and affect through symbolic expression, and processing the trauma experience within a family context.

Gil (2006) describes eliciting posttraumatic play—a child's "natural mechanism for gradual exposure"—through what she calls Trauma-Focused Play Therapy. The model involves selecting toys to be used as symbols of the trauma, directing children to play with the toys in cases where the toys are avoided for more than three sessions, observing and documenting the play, providing a verbal narrative, inviting the child to verbalize during play, observing the evolution in the play, encouraging dynamic movement, and, when the child's play is repetitive, noting the expression of affect and changing the sequence of play to create adaptive outcomes and provide a sense of mastery.

Given the widespread use of play therapy approaches with sexually abused children, further development and research is warranted. Trauma-Focused Play Therapy received a "promising and acceptable" rating in a review of 24 child abuse treatments funded by the Office for Victims of Crime (Saunders, Berliner, & Hanson, 2003). Gil (2006) described the integration of play therapy and evidence-based cognitive behavioral approaches. Although the integration of play therapy and CBT has yet to be empirically validated, randomized controlled trials examining their efficacy are underway.

Psychodynamic, Eclectic, and Family Treatment Approaches

Much has been written about the use of psychodynamic, eclectic, and family approaches with regard to treating sexually abused children. There has been limited research, however, on the efficacy of these approaches, and the studies that have been done generally do not employ random assignment, control groups, or standardized treatments. One study compared individual psychoanalytic and group psychoanalytic therapy formats with children ages 6 to 14 (Trowell et al., 2002). Results indicated a reduction in symptoms and improvement in functioning.

Another study investigated individual therapy alone compared with combined individual and group therapy (Nolan et al., 2002). Participants ages 6 to 17 were not randomly assigned to treatment condition, and there was no control group. The treatment, which was not standardized or manualized, represented current clinical practice in Ireland and integrated principles of psychodynamic, client-centered, and cognitive behavioral approaches. Both individual and combined individual and group treatments led to significant decreases in parent-reported behavior problems, significant improvements in child-reported depression and anger scores on a trauma symptom measure, and significant improvements on child-reported overall depression scores. Neither treatment led to significant changes on youth-reported internalizing or externalizing symptoms on a broader measure of functioning. There was one significant difference between the groups; combined individual and group therapy was significantly more effective at improving scores on the ineffectiveness subscale of a depression measure. Of note, however, more than twice as many children in the individual therapy-alone condition (46%) showed clinical improvement on a measure of overall behavioral adjustment as compared with the individual and group condition (20%). Results provide initial support for both treatment approaches, which did not differ significantly from each other overall. These results replicate other studies that suggest that more therapy services do not necessarily produce better results (Chaffin et al., 2004).

A repeated measures study of abuse-focused therapy, an eclectic model that incorporates "play therapy, cognitive behavioral treatment, and psychodynamic therapy," found symptom reduction among children ages 8 to 15 over the 1-year course of treatment, but the rate of reduction varied by symptom type (Lanktree, 1994, p. 58; Lanktree & Briere, 1995). More specifically, most symptoms responded by the 3-month assessment and showed a continued significant decrease at the 6-month assessment. Dissociative symptoms, however, which responded by the 3-month assessment did not decrease significantly from the 3-month to 6-month assessment. Conversely, sexual concerns did not respond by the 3-month assessment but showed significant decreases from the 3-month to 6-month assessment. Only anxiety and PTSD symptoms continued to decrease significantly from the 6-month to 9-month assessment, and anxiety, depression, and PTSD symptoms had decreased significantly at the 1-year assessment.

A family therapy approach to the treatment of CSA that combines individual and family sessions, referred to as a relational treatment model, highlights the importance of building family resilience, while also strengthening the child's protective relationships and the family's efforts to support the child's healing (Sheinberg & Fraenkel, 2001). A study comparing family therapy to "treatment as usual" for runaway adolescents with a history of physical or sexual abuse provides support for the theoretical framework guiding family systems therapy (Slesnick, Bartle-Haring, & Gangamma, 2006). The findings of this study indicate that improved family cohesion was linked to a reduction in substance use among teens. Moreover, the authors point out that the findings highlight the importance of focusing on increasing positive family communication and behavioral interactions as opposed to primarily focusing on eliminating problematic interactions.

The research described provides some promising initial results for various approaches to the treatment of sexual abuse. However, systematic empirical testing of the wide array of mental health services provided in the community is needed to rigorously evaluate effectiveness.

Cognitive Behavioral Therapy

CBT models are the most widely researched treatments for children who have been sexually abused. Building on the success of therapy for adults (Beck, 1976; Foa, Keane, & Friedman, 2000), CBT has been effectively adapted for children and adolescents. CBT treatment for this population typically incorporates activities that include education, skill development, gradual exposure of the child to sexual abuse memories and reminders, and safety skills training (Cohen, Mannarino, & Deblinger, 2006). Given the importance of including a caregiver in treatment, CBT models also often include nonoffending caregiver components to enhance caregiver coping skills, build on parent–child communication skills, and assist with behavioral management issues (Deblinger & Heflin, 1996; King et al., 2000). Although CBT requires therapists to actively structure sessions, engaging the child and caregiver in the therapeutic process in a collaborative manner is central to therapeutic success.

Studies of CBT with children who have been sexually abused using pre–post designs and randomized clinical trials demonstrate improvements in PTSD, other anxiety symptoms, depression, sexual behavior problems, and global functioning. Described next is a sampling of some of the CBT research.

A study utilizing random assignment compared two short-term treatments for children ages 8 to 13 years and their caregivers (Celano, Hazzard, Webb, & McCall, 1996). Treatment as usual (supportive, unstructured therapy) was compared with a treatment based on Finkelhor and Browne's (1985) theoretical model that utilized cognitive behavioral techniques. Both treatments produced significant decreases in child and caregiver-reported PTSD and parent-reported internalizing and externalizing symptoms, as well as significant improvements in clinician-rated overall functioning. Children in both conditions evidenced decreases in beliefs about self-blame and powerlessness. Caregivers in the CBT treatment condition reported greater decreases in self-blame and greater increases in caregiver support of the child and were more optimistic about the future.

Another study utilizing random assignment compared structured sexual abuse-specific group therapy with and without the addition of stress inoculation training and gradual exposure among children ages 4 to 13. Results indicated that both groups demonstrated significant reductions in symptoms of anxiety, depression, sexual behavior, internalizing and externalizing behavior, and some factors related to fear (but not fear total scores). However, there were no significant differences between the groups over time on measures of fear and anxiety, which may be attributed to the majority of participants not exhibiting clinically significant fear and anxiety at pretreatment (Berliner & Saunders, 1996).

To date, Trauma-Focused Cognitive Behavioral Therapy (TF-CBT) has the strongest evidence base of any treatment for CSA (Deblinger & Heflin, 1996; Cohen, Mannarino & Deblinger, 2006). TF-CBT has been rigorously researched, with seven pre–post or quasiexperimental studies and seven studies utilizing random assignment and comparison groups. TF-CBT was the only treatment to earn a "well-supported and efficacious" rating—the highest category—in the aforementioned review of 24 child abuse treatments funded by the Office for Victims of Crime (Saunders et al., 2003).

A Brief Summary of TF-CBT Research Involving Children Who Have Been Sexually Abused. In a preliminary pre–post study, Deblinger, McLeer, and Henry (1990) found no improvements during a baseline period but significant improvements in symptoms of PTSD, depression, anxiety, and, more broadly, internalizing and externalizing behaviors among children ages 3 to 16. In a randomized controlled trial, Cohen and Mannarino (1996) found that children ages 3 to 6 receiving TF-CBT had significantly greater symptom improvement than children receiving nondirective supportive therapy on measures assessing sexualized behavior, other behavioral difficulties, and internalizing symptoms. Treatment gains were maintained over a 1-year follow-up period (Cohen & Mannarino, 1997). A randomized dismantling study of TF-CBT with older children ages 7 to 13 compared a child-only TF-CBT intervention, a nonoffending parent-only TF-CBT intervention, a combined parent and child TF-CBT intervention, and a community referral condition. The results of this investigation document the critical importance of the child's direct involvement in TF-CBT with the therapist in overcoming PTSD symptoms, whereas the caregiver's involvement in TF-CBT seemed to be critical in alleviating children's behavior problems and depressive symptomatology. In addition to providing support for the efficacy of the TF-CBT model, the results of this study demonstrate that treatment gains from pre–post treatment were maintained over a 2-year follow-up period (Deblinger, Lippmann, & Steer, 1999). Another study involving random assignment of children within a similar age group (ages 7 to 14) found that children receiving TF-CBT made significantly greater improvements on measures of depression and social competence as compared to children receiving nondirective supportive counseling (Cohen & Mannarino, 1998). The TF-CBT model also showed promise with regard to sexually inappropriate behavior, as the number of children who had to be removed from the study due to these behaviors in the TF-CBT conditions (2 participants) as compared with the nondirective supportive condition (7 participants) approached statistical significance. Maintenance of treatment gains over a 1-year period were demonstrated in a follow-up study (Cohen, Mannarino, & Knudsen, 2005). In a two-site randomized controlled trial, TF-CBT was compared with Child-Centered Therapy (CCT) among children ages 8 to 14 (Cohen, Deblinger et al., 2004). Again, although children across both conditions showed significant improvements over time, children receiving TF-CBT exhibited significantly greater improvements on measures of PTSD, depression, and behavior problems, as well as improvements related to interpersonal trust, perceived credibility, and shame, as compared with children receiving CCT. Of note, more than twice as many CCT children continued to meet criteria for a diagnosis of PTSD as compared to children assigned to TF-CBT. Parents who received TF-CBT also reported significantly greater improvements in their own depression, abuse-related distress, parental support, and parenting practices, again emphasizing the importance of their inclusion in treatment. Treatment gains made by both children and parents were maintained over the 1-year follow-up period (Deblinger, Mannarino, Cohen, & Steer, 2006). A randomized controlled trial involving children ages 10 to 17 investigating TF-CBT plus the drug Sertraline compared with TF-CBT plus placebo provides further support for the TF-CBT model (Cohen, Mannarino, Perel, & Staron, 2007). Results indicate that youth assigned to both conditions improved significantly and equivalently on measures of PTSD, depression, anxiety, and behavior problems, as well as measures of parental distress.

A study conducted in Australia utilized random assignment to evaluate the treatment gains of a TF-CBT program for children ages 5 to 17 years, comparing a child-only condition, a family condition, and a wait-list control group (King et al., 2000). The results indicate that both CBT formats produced significant reductions in child and parent-reported PTSD symptoms and child-reported fear symptoms at posttreatment and follow-up, and in anxiety symptoms at follow-up, as compared with wait-list controls. The only significant difference found between the CBT treatment conditions was significantly greater improvement in fear symptoms at follow-up for the family CBT condition. The authors note that other differences may have emerged if the caregiver involvement in the family condition had not been confined solely to the problems of the child, as caregivers often reported their own symptoms of distress. There were only nine treatment completers in each condition, limiting the statistical power to detect differences.

Two studies have investigated the efficacy of TF-CBT in a group format. In a pre–post design involving children ages 2 to 6 and their nonoffending caregivers, Stauffer and Deblinger (1996) found significant decreases in children's symptoms as well as parental distress and significant improvement on a measure assessing parenting skills. Deblinger and colleagues (2001) conducted a randomized controlled trial comparing TF-CBT provided in a group format with a supportive educational therapy group involving children ages 2 to 8 and their nonoffending caregivers. Participation in either group yielded significant improvement; however, the TF-CBT group treatment demonstrated larger effect sizes than the supportive group treatment. More specifically, mothers in the TF-CBT group reported fewer intrusive thoughts and fewer negative emotional reactions related to the sexual abuse at posttreatment. In addition, children in the TF-CBT group showed significantly greater improvement in their knowledge of body safety skills as compared to those assigned to support groups.

It is important to note that the participants involved in the TF-CBT studies often experienced other traumas in addition to sexual abuse, suggesting the applicability of TF-CBT for treating the sequelae of other traumas. TF-CBT with some modifications has been used successfully with children who experienced a traumatic loss (e.g., Cohen, Mannarino, & Knudsen, 2004; Cohen, Mannarino, & Staron, 2006), children in foster care (Lyons, Weiner, & Scheider, 2006), as well as children suffering traumatic stress in the aftermath of 9/11 (Hoagwood et al., 2007) and Hurricane Katrina (Jaycox et al., in press). Regarding the research with children in foster care, results have shown that in addition to improving trauma symptoms, children treated with TF-CBT were significantly less likely to run away from their placement and significantly less likely to have placement disruptions (Lyons et al., 2006). Research applying TF-CBT to other traumatic experiences is underway.

Description of Trauma-Focused Cognitive Behavioral Therapy

TF-CBT is a components-based approach that incorporates individual child and caregiver sessions as well as conjoint sessions. The components of TF-CBT can be summarized by the acronym PPRACTICE (Cohen, Mannarino, & Deblinger, 2006).

Psychoeducation, which is interwoven throughout treatment, involves providing children and nonoffending caregivers with information about trauma and common reactions to normalize the experience and provide accurate information to combat distorted thinking.

Parenting Skills include praise, selective attention, time-out, and contingency reinforcement schedules. These skills are taught because even capable parents can be challenged in the wake of sexual abuse.

Relaxation Techniques are presented and practiced to reduce the physical manifestations of stress and trauma and to aid in coping with trauma reminders that may be triggered.

Affective Expression and Modulation involves building skills to help children express and manage their feelings more effectively, which is important given that children who are sexually abused often have a number of distressing feelings that may overwhelm them.

Cognitive Coping initially involves presenting the relationship between thoughts, feelings, and behaviors (the "cognitive triangle") and then identifying and challenging unhelpful and inaccurate thoughts that can lead to anxiety and depression. Children and caregivers learn to replace such thoughts with helpful, more accurate thoughts, which lead to more positive feelings and behaviors.

Trauma Narrative and Processing (i.e., gradual exposure) involves written, verbal, art and/or play activities that encourage the child in a graded manner to share and process abuse-related experience, including the associated abuse-related thoughts, feelings, and body sensations. These trauma-focused activities are based on the premise that repeated exposure to trauma reminders leads to a decrease in the distress associated with those reminders, thereby decreasing the need for avoidance strategies. Further, unhelpful or inaccurate thoughts that are identified through written narratives or discussions can be challenged and reframed.

In Vivo Mastery of Trauma Reminders involves gradual exposure to feared stimuli when the previous trauma-focused component is not sufficient to extinguish avoidant behaviors. Some children develop fears that generalize to innocuous stimuli—that is, feeling afraid when there is no actual danger. This feeling can lead a child to avoid any number of situations, interfering with daily functioning. It is important to develop a graduated plan for exposure to diminish the avoidance behavior in response to trauma cues such as darkness, bedtime, attending school, or other innocuous reminders of the abuse.

Conjoint Child-Parent Sessions are included to enhance communication between the child and caregiver, review educational information and skills, and read the child's narrative. It is important to prepare the child and caregiver for joint sessions, particularly sessions that involve hearing the child's narrative.

Enhancing Future Safety and Development involves teaching safety skills to help children feel empowered and enhance their ability to protect themselves as much as possible. Children learn ways of responding to potentially dangerous or uncomfortable situations, with an emphasis on communicating what occurred to trusted adults. This is often accomplished through role plays and behavior rehearsal.

In the final analysis, TF-CBT helps children and their caregivers review, integrate, and practice skills that not only help them cope with the trauma of sexual abuse but are intended to support their ability to manage the natural and unanticipated stressors of life they are likely to face in the future.

Among the treatment approaches reviewed in this chapter, cognitive behavioral interventions, and TF-CBT in particular, are the most rigorously tested and have the strongest evidence of efficacy. Several studies document the effectiveness of TF-CBT delivered in community settings with children who have experienced sexual abuse (Hayes et al., 2009; Lyons et al., 2006), as well as a wide array of other traumas.

A Case Study of TF-CBT With an Adolescent Female

To demonstrate how TF-CBT works in practice, we offer the following case composite from our clinical experience. A 15-year-old girl named Marlena (not her real name) and her mother were seen for counseling in the aftermath of the teenager's disclosure of sexual abuse by her maternal uncle. Marlena's mother had been widowed 10 years earlier. Since the death of her father, Marlena's uncle often babysat Marlena and her younger sister after school while their mother worked. Marlena disclosed the abuse to her mother when the mother arrived at the uncle's house to find Marlena and the uncle in a bedroom with the door closed. Marlena told her mother of repeated abuse over an extended period of time. Marlena's mother immediately took her to the police station where she was interviewed. Following a joint investigation by child protective services (CPS) and the police, the uncle was arrested and charged with sexual assault.

An assessment prior to initiating treatment revealed that Marlena met full criteria for PTSD and reported a clinically significant level of depression.

Marlena indicated she had thoughts of killing herself, but she would not act on them. When Marlena went for treatment, she rarely made eye contact. She hung her head, her long hair making her face barely visible. Rapport was established with Marlena by encouraging her to share her academic successes, her aspirations for college, and her love for nature. Despite her trauma and depressive symptoms, as well as her obvious feelings of shame and embarrassment related to her extensive sexual abuse, she was functioning well academically. Socially, however, Marlena tended to isolate herself. She reported very few close friends. She expressed considerable discomfort around boys and men. She also reported increasing conflict with her sister as well as her mother over issues relating to her choices of dress, her disregard for her personal hygiene, and her lack of responsibility for her chores.

To assess Marlena's expressive skills as well as abuse-related avoidance, a variation of the Sternberg and Lamb approach was used (Cohen, Mannarino, & Deblinger, 2006; Sternberg et al., 1993). Marlena was asked to describe a recent happy event (she chose a concert she attended at school). She was then asked to share everything she remembered about the concert, what she did, how she was feeling at the time, what she was saying to herself, and any sensations that her body felt. Marlena gave a very detailed account of the concert that was rich with thoughts and feelings. When reminded of these instructions and asked to tell the therapist what brought her to treatment, Marlena provided a brief description stating, "My uncle did bad things to me. He touched me and did other things. They tell me it's called sexual abuse." There was a great discrepancy between her ability to talk about the concert and her baseline for talking about the sexual abuse—her account was brief and devoid of thoughts, feelings, and specific details. Still, the therapist expressed appreciation for what Marlena shared. The therapist provided an overview of the treatment plan, highlighting the more neutral skill-building activities that might appeal to Marlena.

The beginning stages of treatment focused on separate psychoeducation and skill-building individual sessions designed to assist Marlena and her mother in coping with the myriad emotions they were experiencing. First, the therapist offered psychoeducation about CSA in an interactive manner including basic facts about the nature and prevalence of CSA, who sexually abuses children, why children do not disclose sexual abuse, etc. Marlena did an excellent job defining sexual abuse and provided many examples of what would be inappropriate sexual contact between a child and an adult including, but not limited to, kissing, touching breasts, oral sex, and sexual intercourse. The therapist helped Marlena understand that only a small percentage of children ever tell about their abuse. Marlena seemed shocked and relieved at the same time, stating, "I guess I did good by telling when I did."

In separate sessions, Marlena's mother similarly benefited from the educational information about CSA and was quite receptive to further developing her parenting skills in order to support her child's healing and healthy social development. It became clear that the mother was overprotecting and overindulging Marlena since the disclosure and needed support in actively encouraging her daughter to engage in independent and prosocial behaviors such as joining an after school club (i.e., jazz band), while also setting appropriate limits and consequences for problem behaviors (e.g., sibling conflicts).

Marlena's primary method of coping with her emotions appeared to be through the use of numbing and avoidance. To address these issues, the therapist assisted Marlena in developing positive coping skills. The therapist first focused on encouraging the use of various strategies for relaxing the mind and the body. Marlena was receptive to practicing progressive relaxation exercises in individual sessions. Her mother, on the other hand, insisted that her garden was her relaxation resource, though she explained to the therapist that lately even her garden did not distract her from her worries about her family's future. The therapist taught the mother some mindfulness activities that she could practice in her garden.

In individual sessions with Marlena, the therapist focused on affective expression and modulation as well as cognitive coping skills. After assessing Marlena's emotional vocabulary and her ability to appropriately express and manage her emotions, the therapist inspired a sense of fun and competition by asking Marlena and her mother in their individual sessions to record as long a list of emotions as possible so that they could determine who could come up with more feeling words. Marlena smiled as she worked hard to generate a handwritten list of more feeling words than her mother. However, Marlena indicated that although she knew many feeling words that she never used them in conversation. Thus, for homework, Marlena and her mother were encouraged to begin to share their positive and negative feelings on a daily basis. They reported back that this assignment turned into a playful exchange in the weeks that followed as well as at least one serious conversation in which Marlena shared feelings of disappointment and frustration. Marlena's mother reported that she tried to comfort her daughter and validate her feelings by utilizing the active listening skills the therapist practiced with her. The feelings lists Marlena and her mother developed became valuable tools when, later in the course of therapy, sessions focused more on the sexually abusive experiences.

In separate sessions, Marlena and her mother learned about the connections between thoughts, feelings, and behaviors and how replacing inaccurate, hurtful thoughts with helpful thoughts could help one cope and feel better about a situation.

Initially, Marlena resisted sharing her thoughts, but as she gained trust in the therapist, she began to understand that what we say to ourselves powerfully influences how we feel and behave and thus it is important to share internal monologues in therapy.

The therapist encouraged her to share what she would say to herself in situations where she tended to isolate herself from other teens. For example, when she entered the school cafeteria, Marlena often felt nervous and reported that she would say to herself, "I'll just sit by myself so I can get my studying done." When encouraged to dig a little deeper and catch the automatic thoughts that go by so fast that you hardly notice them, she paused a long time and eventually shared that she sometimes said to herself, "No one likes me. The boys think I'm creepy. They probably can tell I was sexually abused. I don't want to talk to anyone." She acknowledged that lunchtime was often her saddest and longest period of the day. She indicated that she knew she was different than other teens because she preferred math and science over lunchtime. Using this example, she began to understand how the things she was saying to herself were linked to her distressing feelings and her isolating behavior. Initially, the therapist simply praised Marlena's understanding of how her thoughts might be contributing to her distressing feelings, isolative behavior, and the nervous physical sensations she experienced during lunch. The therapist's praise and demonstrated understanding of her feelings about lunchtime seemed to be very comforting to Marlena. The therapist gently prodded Marlena to assess the accuracy of some of her self-talk by identifying thoughts that might be overgeneralized (e.g., "No one likes me") and then gently challenging these thoughts by having Marlena identify peers who liked her. As Marlena was able to identify and express her emotions and began to use more positive cognitive coping skills to regulate her emotions, she reported a decrease in suicidal thoughts.

By the middle stages of therapy (around session 5), Marlena began to develop a trauma narrative that started with a very positive introduction of herself including her age, grade, strengths, and favorite hobbies. The narrative also described her early positive relationship with her uncle and ultimately incorporated details and associated thoughts and feelings related to the sexual abuse. The therapist acted as a scribe to record the details as Marlena dictated them. At the beginning of each session, the therapist reviewed the narrative with the goal of gradually and repeatedly exposing Marlena to the memories of sexual abuse in order to decrease her feelings of anxiety while increasing her sense of mastery. Each week the therapist gave Marlena a choice of what she wanted to talk about (e.g., when she was interviewed by the police or the first time her uncle abused her). Using the feeling list developed earlier, Marlena was not only able to provide detailed accounts of abusive experiences but she was able to get in touch with and share the many feelings she experienced during the abusive episodes, as well as after she disclosed the sexual abuse and the feelings she presently felt while she was talking about the abuse. After completing the narrative, Marlena and her therapist worked on processing her thoughts and feelings related to these incidents. As she identified her feelings related to the abuse, she gradually provided additional details about her uncle sexually abusing her. She stated that she felt sad that he touched her vagina, that she would take showers after he left the room because she felt dirty, embarrassed that "she let him do that to her and that she did not tell someone sooner, that she was afraid that she could not have babies, and that he might do the same thing to her sister."

To assist her in coping with some of the dysfunctional thoughts about the abuse that were likely contributing to her feelings of shame and embarrassment, the therapist reviewed the psychoeducational and cognitive coping skills that had been taught earlier. The therapist used a best friend role-play in which Marlena played the best friend and attempted to convince her friend who had been sexually abused (the therapist) that she did nothing wrong, that her uncle was responsible for the abuse, and it was normal to trust her uncle because he was "family."

Each week, Marlena seemed a little brighter, and she increasingly made eye contact and began to hold her head higher. After providing a detailed narrative, rich with thoughts and feelings, the therapist asked Marlena to share the final episode or one episode that she thought she would never tell anyone about. Marlena responded with silence and eventually said, "I don't remember the last time." The therapist wondered if it was possible that she did not remember an incident that occurred only 4 months ago when she had so vividly recalled the first incident when she was 8 years old. The therapist was aware that Marlena had disclosed to the police that her uncle had vaginally and anally penetrated her. Marlena arrived at the next session with her head hung down and hair hiding her face. The therapist began upbeat and reminded Marlena what a wonderful job she had done talking about all the different types of sexual abuse and stated that they were going to revisit that topic. The therapist and Marlena sat on the office floor with a large piece of paper and markers, and the therapist encouraged Marlena to write down as many acts of sexual abuse as she could (e.g., mouth on penis, mouth on vagina, mouth on breasts, mouth on anus, penis in mouth, penis in vagina). When Marlena finished the list, the therapist read the list out loud and asked Marlena to circle all of the items on the list that her uncle did to her. Marlena circled a number of items, and the therapist replied, "I see a number of items on the list that we have talked about, but I also see something that we have not talked about." Marlena pointed to the penis in anus. The therapist acknowledged the difficulty Marlena was having in talking about and processing this incident, and Marlena disclosed that she was really scared that her uncle was going to hurt her. The therapist reassured Marlena that she was safe now and encouraged her to share what she could about that experience. Marlena provided an account of an incident where her uncle came into a bedroom at his home where she frequently stayed and made her take a shower. He then went into the bathroom and hit her so hard that she fell and ripped the shower curtain off. He jerked her up and forced her back into her bedroom and onto her bed where he vaginally and anally penetrated her. Marlena said that it hurt when she fell and that she felt dizzy. Marlena thought her uncle was really going to hurt her, even kill her. This was the first time her uncle had been physically violent and the first time he anally penetrated her, which was very shameful for Marlena. After the therapist assisted Marlena in processing her thoughts and feelings related to this incident, they spent the last few minutes engaged in a fun activity to help ground and orient the youngster. As they stood up, Marlena grabbed her therapist, hugged the therapist, and said, "Thank you." When the therapist asked, "For what?" Marlena made eye contact, smiled, and replied, "For helping me talk about this." During the next session, Marlena returned with head held high and her long hair pulled away from her face. There was a noticeable difference in her mood and demeanor.

In parallel sessions with Marlena's mother, the therapist helped the mother explore her thoughts and feelings about the abuse. With the therapist's help, the mother began to notice how often she berated herself for not knowing about the abuse. She learned to counter those thoughts with reminders about how she did not hesitate in going to the police and followed up to ensure that her daughter had all of the necessary medical and mental health services as soon as she became aware of the abuse. Still, Marlena's mother acknowledged that at times she felt very sorry for her brother and wondered if her daughter's beauty, pubertal development, and maybe even her flirting behavior caused her brother to lose control. With Marlena's consent, and in preparation for the conjoint sessions, the therapist encouraged the mother to read her daughter's narrative, which helped her fully appreciate how young her daughter was when the abuse began and how coercive her brother was in his abuse of Marlena. During these individual sessions, the therapist prepared the mother for conjoint sessions during which she and her daughter would review and discuss the narrative together.

The last stage of therapy included individual preparation sessions as well as conjoint sessions that focused on self-protection skills, education about healthy sexuality, and time for Marlena to share her trauma narrative with her mother. Her mother had been well prepared during her own individual sessions and responded in a slightly tearful, but very supportive, manner to Marlena's narrative. The parenting skills practiced throughout therapy, including praise and active listening, assisted Marlena's mother in responding positively during joint sessions as well as continuing to support her daughter after treatment ended.

After reviewing the narrative, mother and daughter were encouraged to share the praise that they prepared for each other. Marlena's mother reminded her daughter that the sexual abuse was not her fault and praised Marlena for telling and protecting her sister as well as working so hard in therapy to write such a courageous narrative. Marlena responded by thanking her mother for coming to therapy with her and helping her with "everyday things." The mother gushed with pride and reminded Marlena that she was so proud to be her mother and that as a family they could get through anything.

After 12 sessions, Marlena was reporting that she was no longer having intrusive thoughts or nightmares about the sexual abuse. In fact, based on a standardized assessment, Marlena's PTSD symptoms and depressed mood had remitted. Marlena's mother reported significant improvement in terms of Marlena's emotional and behavioral adjustment. However, despite cognitive coping and reassurance from the therapist and mother, Marlena continued to be concerned about whether or not she could have children because of the sexual abuse. The therapist encouraged Marlena to see the doctor who had seen her for a medical examination during the course of the CSA investigation and to obtain reassurance from the doctor. As Marlena had been avoidant of medical doctors in the past, it was suggested that she follow through with this appointment prior to their planned graduation as this would be an important aspect of her emotional healing. The doctor reassured

Marlena that she was "completely normal" and that when she grew up she would be able to have children.

Therapy ended with a graduation celebration during which the family shared the good report they had received from the physician. The therapist reviewed Marlena's and her mother's progress and presented them both with therapy graduation certificates. While the therapist expressed confidence that they both would continue to use the skills they learned in coping with everyday stressors and conflicts, Marlena and her mother were reminded that the door would always be open for them to return for booster sessions if they needed support in relation to significant stressors they might face in the future. Finally, Marlena's mother surprised Marlena with her favorite snacks, which they enjoyed while listening to music and celebrating their therapy accomplishments.

Conclusion

Early effective interventions like those that have been described are critical to short-circuit the highly disruptive effects CSA can have on the development and adjustment of children and families. Research not only enhances our understanding of the impact of CSA but informs the development and evaluation of efficacious treatments. Still, there is much progress to be made to ensure that treatments optimally address the diverse reactions to CSA exhibited by youth and their families. Research suggests the importance of cognitive and affective processing in overcoming PTSD and anxiety (Cohen, Mannarino, & Staron, 2006; Hayes et al., 2009). Parent training is critical to helping children overcome abuse-related behavior problems (Deblinger et al., 1996). Future research should focus on methods for optimizing outcomes by tailoring treatment to specifically address diverse issues. Moreover, gender, developmental, cultural, and familial characteristics should be further explored through research.

Treatment outcome research to date has primarily focused on children and adolescents seen in outpatient clinics in the aftermath of disclosing CSA. Future research should examine the benefits of sexual abuse-focused treatment for populations that exhibit high rates of CSA such as adjudicated females and youth in residential facilities. Unfortunately, many youth in these settings are not screened for trauma histories, and youngsters continue to suffer in silence from this pernicious problem. Moreover, some children, despite their disclosures, do not receive the sexual abuse-specific evidence-based treatments they need and deserve. Thus, greater efforts are needed to ensure that the diagnostic and therapeutic needs of children experiencing sexual abuse are identified and addressed and that families are educated and motivated to access such services. Finally, successfully identifying children and families who could benefit from treatment will not be sufficient if efficacious treatments are not available in community settings. Although several studies document the effective transportability of TF-CBT to community clinics (Hoagwood et al., 2007; Jaycox et al., in press; Lyons et al., 2006), more needs to be learned about optimal methods for disseminating training in evidence-based treatments for community therapists working with children who have experienced sexual abuse. In sum, while significant advances have been made in addressing the therapeutic needs of children who have experienced sexual abuse, continued research is critical to ensure that progress continues.

References

Arata, C. M. (2000). From child victim to adult victim: A model for predicting sexual revictimization. *Child Maltreatment, 5*, 28–38.

Beck, A. T. (1976). *Cognitive therapy and the emotional disorders.* New York: International Universities Press.

Berliner, L., & Saunders, B. E. (1996). Treating fear and anxiety in sexually abused children: Results of a controlled 2-year follow-up study. *Child Maltreatment, 1*, 294–309.

Brown, J., Cohen, P., Johnson, J. G., & Smailes, E. M. (1999). Childhood abuse and neglect: Specificity of effects on adolescents and young adult depression and suicidality. *Journal of the American Academy of Child & Adolescent Psychiatry, 38*, 1490–1496.

Carpentier, M. Y., Silovsky, J. F., & Chaffin, M. (2006). Randomized trial of treatment for children with sexual behavior problems: Ten-year follow-up. *Journal of Consulting and Clinical Psychology, 74*, 482–488.

Celano, M., Hazzard, A., Webb, C., & McCall, C. (1996). Treatment of traumagenic beliefs among sexually abused girls and their mothers: An evaluation study. *Journal of Abnormal Child Psychology, 24*, 1–17.

Chaffin, M., Silovsky, J. F., Funderbunk, B., Valle, L. A., Brestan, E. V., Balachova, T., et al. (2004). Parent-child interaction therapy with physically abused parents: Efficacy for reducing future abuse reports. *Journal of Consulting and Clinical Psychology, 72*, 500–510.

Cohen, J. A., Deblinger, E., Mannarino, A. P., & Steer, R. A. (2004). A multisite, randomized controlled trial for children with sexual abuse-related PTSD symptoms. *Journal of the American Academy of Child & Adolescent Psychiatry, 43*, 393–402.

Cohen, J. A., & Mannarino, A. P. (1996). A treatment outcome study for sexually abused preschool children: Initial findings. *Journal of the American Academy of Child & Adolescent Psychiatry, 35*, 42–50.

Cohen, J. A., & Mannarino, A. P. (1997). A treatment study for sexually abused preschool children: Outcome during a one-year follow-up. *Journal of the American Academy of Child & Adolescent Psychiatry, 36*, 1228–1235.

Cohen, J. A., & Mannarino, A. P. (1998). Interventions childhood traumatic grief: A pilot study. *Journal of the American Academy of Child & Adolescent Psychiatry, 43*, 1225–1233.

Cohen, J. A., Mannarino, A. P., & Deblinger, E. (2006). *Treating trauma and traumatic grief in children and adolescents.* New York: Guilford Press.

Cohen, J. A., Mannarino, A. P., & Knudsen, K. (2004). Treating childhood traumatic grief: A pilot study. *Journal of the American Academy of Child & Adolescent Psychiatry, 42*, 1225–1233.

Cohen, J. A., Mannarino, A. P., & Knudsen, K. (2005). Treating sexually abused children: One year follow-up of a randomized controlled trial. *Child Abuse and Neglect, 29*, 135–145.

Cohen, J. A., Mannarino, A. P., Perel, J. M., & Staron, V. (2007). A pilot randomized controlled trial of combined trauma-focused CBT and sertraline for childhood PTSD symptoms. *Journal of the American Academy of Child & Adolescent Psychiatry, 46*, 811–819.

Cohen, J. A., Mannarino, A. P., & Staron, V. R. (2006). A pilot study of modified cognitive-behavioral therapy for childhood traumatic grief (CBT-CTG). *Journal of the American Academy of Child & Adolescent Psychiatry, 45*, 1465–1473.

Cohen, J. A., Perel, J. M., DeBellis, M. D., Friedman, M. J., & Putnam, F. W. (2002). Treating traumatized children: Clinical implications of the psychobiology of posttraumatic stress disorder. *Trauma, Violence & Abuse, 3*, 91–108.

Deblinger, E., Hathaway, C. R., Lippmann, J., & Steer, R. (1993). Psychosocial characteristics and correlates of symptom distress in non-offending mothers of sexually abused children. *Journal of Interpersonal Violence, 8*, 155–168.

Deblinger, E., & Heflin, A. H. (1996). *Treating sexually abused children and their nonoffending parents*. Thousand Oaks, CA: Sage.

Deblinger, E., Lippmann, J., & Steer, R. (1996). Sexually abused children suffering posttraumatic stress symptoms: Initial treatment outcome findings. *Child Maltreatment, 1*, 310–321.

Deblinger, E., Lippmann, J., & Steer, R. (1999). Two-year follow-up study of cognitive behavioral therapy for sexually abused children suffering posttraumatic stress symptoms. *Child Abuse and Neglect, 23*, 1371–1378.

Deblinger, E., Mannarino, A. P., Cohen, J. A., & Steer, R. A. (2006). Follow-up study of a multisite, randomized, controlled trial for children with sexual abuse-related PTSD symptoms: Examining predictors of treatment response. *Journal of the American Academy of Child & Adolescent Psychiatry, 45*, 1474–1484.

Deblinger, E., McLeer, S., Atkins, M. S., Ralphe, D., & Foa, E. (1989). Post-traumatic stress in sexually abused, physically abused, and non-abused children. *Child Abuse and Neglect, 13*, 403–408.

Deblinger, E., McLeer, S. V., & Henry, D. E. (1990). Cognitive behavioral treatment for sexually abused children suffering post-traumatic stress: Preliminary findings. *Journal of the American Academy of Child & Adolescent Psychiatry, 29*, 747–752.

Deblinger, E., Stauffer, L., & Landsberg, C. (1994). The impact of a history of child sexual abuse on maternal response to allegations of sexual abuse concerning her child. *Journal of Child Sexual Abuse, 3*, 67–75.

Deblinger, E., Stauffer, L., & Steer, R. (2001). Comparative efficacies of supportive and cognitive behavioral group therapies for children who were sexually abused and their non-offending mothers. *Child Maltreatment, 6*, 332–343.

Feiring, C., & Taska, L. S. (2005). The persistence of shame following sexual abuse: A longitudinal look at risk and recovery. *Child Maltreatment, 10*, 337–349.

Feiring, C., Taska, L., & Lewis, M. (1999). Age and gender differences in children's and adolescents' adaptation to sexual abuse. *Child Abuse and Neglect, 23*, 115–128.

Finkelhor, D., Asdigian, N., & Dziuba-Leatherman, J. (1995). The effectiveness of victimization prevention instruction: An evaluation of children's responses to actual threats and assaults. *Child Abuse and Neglect, 19*, 141–153.

Finkelhor, D., & Browne, A. (1985). The traumatic impact of child sexual abuse: A conceptualization. *American Journal of Orthopsychiatry, 55*, 530–541.

Finkelhor, D., & Ormrod, R. (2000, June). Characteristics of crimes against juveniles. *Juvenile Justice Bulletin*, 1–12.

Finkelhor, D., Ormrod, R. K., & Turner, H. A. (2007). Poly-victimization: A neglected component in child victimization. *Child Abuse and Neglect, 31*, 7–26.

Foa, E. B., Keane, T. M., & Friedman, M. J. (Eds.). (2000). *Effective treatments for PTSD*. New York: Guilford Press.

Friedrich, W. N. (1990). Psychotherapy of sexually abused children and their families. New York: W.W. Norton & Company.

Gil, E. (1996). *Helping abused and traumatized children: Integrating directive and nondirective approaches*. New York: Guilford Press.

Gil, E. (2006). *Helping abused and traumatized children*. New York: Guilford Press.

Hayes, A. M., Webb, C., Grasso, D., Cummings, J. A., Vahlsing, J., & Helie, K. (2009). *Processes that inhibit and facilitate change in trauma-focused cognitive behavioral therapy for youth exposed to interpersonal trauma*. Manuscript submitted for publication.

Hoagwood, K. E., Vogel, J. M., Levitt, J. M., D'Amico, P. J., Paisner, W. I., & Kaplan S. J. (2007). Implementing an evidence-based trauma treatment in a state system after September 11th: The CATS project. *Journal of the American Academy of Child & Adolescent Psychiatry, 46*, 773–779.

James, B. (1989). *Treating traumatized children*. New York: Free Press.

Jaycox, L. H., Cohen, J. A., Mannarino, A. P., Walker, D. W., Langely, A. K., & Gegenheimer, K. L. (in press). *Children's mental health care following Hurricane Katrina within a randomized field trial of trauma-focused psychotherapy*. Manuscript submitted for publication.

Kendall-Tackett, K. A., Williams, L. M., & Finkelhor, D. (1993). Impact of sexual abuse on children: A review and synthesis of recent empirical studies. *Psychological Bulletin, 113*, 164–180.

Kenny, M. C., Capri, V., Thakkar-Kolar, R. R., Ryan, E., & Runyon, M. K. (2008). Child sexual abuse: From prevention to self-protection. *Child Abuse Review, 17*, 36–54.

King, N., Tonge, B. J., Mullen, P., Myerson, N., Heyne, D., Rollings, S., et al. (2000). Sexually abused children and post-traumatic stress disorder. *Counseling Psychology Quarterly, 13*, 365–375.

Lanktree, C. B. (1994). Treating child victims of sexual abuse. In J. Briere (Ed.), *Assessing and treating victims of violence* (pp. 55–66). San Francisco: Jossey-Bass.

Lanktree, C. B., & Briere, J. (1995). Outcome of therapy for sexually abused children: A repeated measures study. *Child Abuse and Neglect, 19*, 1145–1155.

Lyons, J. S., Weiner, D. A., & Scheider, A. (2006). *A field trial of three evidence-based practices for trauma with children in state custody*. Report to the Illinois Department of Children and Family Services.

Myers, J. E. B., Berliner, L., Briere, J., Hendrix, C. T., Jenny, C., & Reid, T. A. (Eds.). (2002). *The APSAC handbook on child maltreatment* (2nd ed.). Thousand Oaks, CA: Sage.

Nolan, M., Carr, A., Fitzpatrick, C., O'Flaherty, A., Keary, K., Turner, R., et al. (2002). A comparison of two programmes for victims of child sexual abuse: A treatment outcome study. *Child Abuse Review, 11*, 103–123.

Reyes, C. J., & Asbrand, J. P. (2005). A longitudinal study assessing trauma symptoms in sexually abused children engaged in play therapy. *International Journal of Play Therapy, 14*, 25–47.

Runyon, M. K., & Deblinger, E. (2008). Pediatrician's role in the treatment and prevention of child sexual abuse. In M. A. Finkel & A. P. Giardino (Eds.), *Medical evaluation of child sexual abuse: A practical guide*. (2nd ed.). Elk Grove Village, IL: American Academy of Pediatrics.

Saunders, B. E., Berliner, L., & Hanson, R. F. (Eds.). (2003). *Child physical and sexual abuse: Guidelines for treatment (Final report: January 15, 2003)*. Charleston, SC: National Crime Victims Research and Treatment Center.

Scott, T. A., Burlingame, G., Starling, M., Porter, C., & Lilly, J. P. (2003). Effects of individual client-centered play therapy on sexually abused children's mood, self-concept, and social competence. *International Journal of Play Therapy, 12*, 7–30.

Sheinberg, M., & Fraenkel, P. (2001). *The relational trauma of incest: A family-based approach to treatment*. New York: Guilford Press.

Shelby, J. S., & Felix, E. D. (2005). Posttraumatic play therapy: The need for an integrated model of directive and nondirective approaches. In L. A. Reddy, T. M. Files-Hall, & C. E. Schaefer (Eds.), *Empirically based play interventions for children* (pp.79–103). Washington, DC: American Psychological Association.

Silovsky, J., Niec, L., Bard, D., & Hecht, D. (2007). Treatment for preschool children with interpersonal sexual behavior problems: A pilot study. *Journal of Clinical Child & Adolescent Psychology, 36*, 378–391.

Slesnick, N., Bartle-Haring, S., & Gangamma, R. (2006). Predictors of substance use and family therapy outcome among physically and sexually abused runaway adolescents. *Journal of Marital and Family Therapy, 32*, 261–281.

Spataro, J., Mullen, P. E., Burgess, P. M., Wells, D. L., & Moss, S.A. (2004). Impact of child sexual abuse on mental health: Prospective study in males and females. *The British Journal of Psychiatry, 184*, 416–421.

Stauffer, L., & Deblinger, E. (1996). Cognitive behavioral groups for non-offending mothers and their young sexually abused children: A preliminary treatment outcome study. *Child Maltreatment, 1*, 65–76.

Sternberg, K. J., Lamb, M. E., Greenbaum, C., Cicchetti, D., Dawud, S., Cortes, R. M., et al. (1993). Effects of domestic violence on children's behavior problems and depression. *Developmental Psychology, 29*, 44–52.

Trowell, J., Kolvin, I., Weeramanthri, T., Sadowski, H., Berelowitz, M., Glasser, D., & Leitch, I. (2002). Psychotherapy for sexually abused girls: Psychopathological outcome findings and patterns of change. *The British Journal of Psychiatry, 180*, 234–247.

Webb, N. B. (1999). Play therapy crisis intervention with children. In N. B. Webb (Ed.), *Play therapy with children in crisis* (pp. 29–46). New York: Guilford Press.

Widom, C. S., & Brzustowicz, L. M. (2006). MAOA and the "cycle of violence": Childhood abuse and neglect, MAOA genotype, and risk for violent and anti-social behavior. *Biological Psychiatry, 60*, 684–689.

17 Treatment of Adolescent and Adult Sex Offenders

Laura G. Kirsch,
Amanda M. Fanniff, and
Judith V. Becker

Sexual offending constitutes a great problem in our society. In 2008, approximately 89,000 females were the victims of rape (U.S. Department of Justice, 2009), and in 2008, more than 70,000 children were the victims of sexual abuse (U.S. Department of Health and Human Services, 2010). It is widely believed that official records underestimate the actual incidence of sexual crimes (e.g., Abel et al., 1987; see Chapter 14). On a positive note, rates of child sexual abuse (CSA) have declined, although the reasons for the decline remain unclear (Finkelhor & Jones, 2004). What is clear is that there are too many victims of sexual assault. While prevention efforts hold promise for reducing victimization (see Chapter 2), prevention is not enough, however. In addition, treatment of known sex offenders also holds promise for decreasing sexual crime.

Approximately 1% to 2% of males will be convicted of a sexual offense in their lifetime (Marshall, 1997). Although the vast majority of sex offenders are adults, a significant proportion of sex crimes are committed by individuals under the age of 18. In 2008, juveniles accounted for more than 17% of arrests for sexual crimes (U.S. Department of Justice, 2009). Although sexual recidivism rates are generally low for adults (approximately 20% after 10 years; Harris & Hanson, 2004) and juveniles (approximately 13% after 5 years; Reitzel & Carbonell, 2006), there is obviously room for improvement. In addition to recent social control policies aimed at protecting society, such as sex offender registration, community notification, and involuntary civil commitment (see Chapter 18), another widely adopted strategy to reduce recidivism is sex offender treatment. Currently, most individuals convicted of sex crimes are required to participate in some form of sex offender treatment. Such treatment is offered in community settings and correctional and residential facilities (McGrath, Cumming, & Burchard, 2003). In this chapter, we discuss current practices with respect to the treatment of adult and adolescent sex offenders and review the literature regarding treatment effectiveness. Our discussion is specific to male offenders because females comprise only a small proportion of sexual arrests (approximately 6% in 2008; U.S. Department of Justice, 2009) and relatively little is known about female sexual offenders.

Of note, many people believe that all sex offenders are psychopaths. While there are a number of psychopathic sex offenders, particularly among rapists, the majority of individuals who commit sex offenses do not meet criteria for psychopathy (e.g., Porter et al., 2000). Psychopathy, however, is a significant predictor of sexual recidivism (e.g., Hanson & Morton-Bourgon, 2005), and should be taken into consideration when providing treatment (e.g., Seto & Barbaree, 1999).

Treatment of Adult Offenders

Current Treatment Programs

Current theories of the etiology of sexual offending are multidimensional and comprehensive. Theories integrate biological, psychological, developmental, and sociocultural explanations for the development of deviant sexual behavior (e.g., Beech & Ward, 2004; Finkelhor, 1984; Hall & Hirschman, 1991; Marshall & Barbaree, 1990a). Current sex offender treatment programs mirror these theories in terms of their comprehensiveness and multidimensionality.

Treatment programs for adult sex offenders typically employ multi-component cognitive behavioral therapy (CBT) within a relapse prevention (RP) framework (e.g., Marshall, 1999; McGrath et al., 2003). CBT is a psychotherapeutic approach that incorporates behavioral techniques with cognitive interventions to analyze and challenge distorted thinking in order to promote behavioral, thinking, and emotional change. Most treatment is conducted in a group format, and group members are typically heterogeneous with respect to criminal history and sexual offense patterns. Programs often incorporate a variety of treatment targets including deviant sexual arousal and the internal factors believed to be associated with increased risk for reoffending such as distorted cognitions, social skills deficits, empathy deficits, difficulties with impulse control and emotion regulation, poor interpersonal relationships, substance abuse, and pro-offending attitudes (Becker & Murphy, 1998).

Deviant sexual arousal is targeted using behavioral techniques that generally involve the pairing of aversive outcomes with sexually deviant fantasies in order to extinguish the conditioned association between sexual arousal and deviant sexual fantasy (e.g., McGuire, Carlisle, & Young, 1965). Aversive outcomes can include physical punishments such as noxious odors or painful electric shocks (which are used in aversion therapy) as well as mental representations of negative consequences resulting from deviant sexual acts (which are used in covert sensitization). In addition to reducing deviant arousal, behavioral techniques such as masturbatory reconditioning are used to help recondition sexual arousal to more appropriate sexual fantasies and behaviors. On occasion these techniques are supplemented with biological and pharmacological treatments designed to reduce sex drive such as antidepressants, anti-androgen medications, and, in rare cases, surgical castration.

Cognitive components of therapy focus on altering the cognitions that justify and maintain deviant sexual behavior. Therapy also works to enhance skills that are deficient in many sex offenders and that are believed to be essential for successful reintegration into the community (e.g., Geer, Estupinan, & Manguno-Mire, 2000; Marshall & Barbaree, 1990b). Cognitive techniques are employed to overcome denial and minimization of offending behaviors, challenge distorted attitudes and beliefs, and enhance victim empathy. Social competence is improved by providing training in social skills, communication skills, relationship skills, and problem-solving. Most treatment programs include sex education, anger management, emotion regulation, relaxation training, and substance abuse work.

In addition, most programs are designed within an RP framework, such that treatment is specifically designed to address the prevention of sexually deviant behaviors in the future. RP was first developed as an application of cognitive behavioral strategies for the treatment of addiction (Marlatt, 1982; Pithers, Marques, Gibat, & Marlatt, 1983). RP for sex offenders focuses on helping the offender analyze the chain of events preceding his prior offenses in order to identify the circumstances that lead to offending. Offenders are then provided with the skills needed to interrupt the chain and cope with high-risk situations that increase the probability of reoffense (Marques, Day, Nelson, & Miner, 1989).

Emerging Treatment Models

As previously stated, sex offender treatment programs use a CBT/RP treatment framework. Recently, however, supplementary approaches have emerged. The Good Lives Model was first proposed by Ward and Stewart (2003) and later developed by Ward and colleagues (e.g., Lindsay, Ward, Morgan & Wilson, 2007; Ward & Gannon, 2006). The Good Lives Model is a humanistic approach to the treatment of sexual offenders that stresses the importance of constructing a balanced, prosocial personal identity. This goal is achieved through the development of internal capabilities (i.e., skills, attitudes, and beliefs) and external conditions (i.e., support systems) in order to meet the offender's needs in adaptive, prosocial ways (Lindsay et al., 2007). The two primary aims of therapy are to reduce an offender's level of risk and equip the offender with the skills and resources necessary to lead a more prosocial life (Whitehead, Ward, & Collie, 2007). While this approach shows promise, there are currently little data to demonstrate its effectiveness.

Another promising approach is the multimodal self-regulation model (Stinson, Sales, & Becker, 2008). According to this approach, deficits in self-regulation shape the development of deviant sexual arousal. Treatment focuses on ensuring optimal outcomes in each of the major components of self-regulatory functioning: emotion, cognition, behavior, and interpersonal regulation (Stinson et al., 2008). Treatment targets include decreasing the use of maladaptive skills and developing adaptive and appropriate strategies, as well as enhancing the ability to monitor internal states.

Treatment Effectiveness

The goal of sex offender treatment is a reduction in sexual recidivism (Rice & Harris, 2003). Despite the widespread implementation of sex offender treatment programs, however, research demonstrating treatment effectiveness—reduced recidivism—is not yet conclusive. To be fair, it is very difficult to define and measure recidivism. The gold standard for evaluating therapy, the randomized clinical trial, is nearly impossible to implement in sex offender samples due to both ethical and logistical concerns. As for measurement, official police records underestimate reoffending (Abel et al., 1987; Weinrott & Saylor, 1991), and self-report measures of reoffending are questionable because sex offenders tend to deny and minimize their deviant behavior (e.g., Barbaree, 1991). Moreover, researchers disagree about the most appropriate aspects of recidivism to measure (i.e., any criminal activity? only violent crimes? all sexual offenses? specific sexual offenses? some combination of these?). Finally, the low base rate of reoffending necessitates a lengthy follow-up in order to detect treatment effects (Hanson, 2000). Follow-up periods of at least 4 years are required to adequately assess the effects of treatment on recidivism (Hall, 1995; Hanson & Bussiere, 1998; Marshall & Barbaree, 1990b). Given these challenges, most treatment outcome research measures the effectiveness of treatment by comparing official arrest and conviction records for general, sexual, and violent offenses for treated and nontreated sex offenders. The average follow-up period is approximately 5 years (Hanson et al., 2002).

Large-scale meta-analyses of treatment outcome research generally support the effectiveness of sex offender treatment, particularly CBT-based approaches. A meta-analysis including more than 9,000 offenders across 43 studies found significant reductions in both sexual and general recidivism for treated sex offenders (Hanson et al., 2002). Across all studies, the sexual recidivism rate for treated offenders was 12.3% compared to 16.8% for comparisons. When the analyses were limited to the more recent CBT-based treatment approaches, the results were more promising. Offenders treated in these programs demonstrated significantly lower sexual recidivism (9.9% treated, 17.4% comparison) and general recidivism (32% treated, 51% comparison) than comparison groups. Other researchers have also found evidence for the effectiveness of CBT for reducing recidivism in sexual offenders via both meta-analysis (Hall, 1995) and matched comparison research studies (e.g., Looman, Abracen, & Nicholaichuk, 2000; McGrath, Hoke, & Vojtisek, 1998).

Although research suggests that CBT/RP can be effective, there is also some evidence to the contrary (e.g., Furby, Weinrott, & Blackshaw, 1989; Quinsey, Khanna, & Malcolm, 1998). Marques and her colleagues conducted a methodologically rigorous controlled experimental study of sex offender treatment and did not find an overall treatment effect (Marques, Wiederanders, Day, Nelson, & van Ommeren, 2005). Sex offenders who were randomly assigned to receive a 2-year intensive cognitive behavioral inpatient treatment program within an RP framework followed by 1 year of community aftercare did not differ significantly from untreated offender controls with respect to sexual or violent recidivism over an 8-year follow-up period. Nevertheless, Marques and her colleagues did not conclude that their treatment was ineffective. Rather, they pointed out methodological weaknesses in the study that may have contributed to their results. For example, their treatment model was administered in the 1980s and used treatment methods that are far from today's state-of-the-art standards. Marques suggests while the study was informative in a number of areas, it does not provide support for the conclusion that treatment is ineffective for adult sex offenders.

Despite the paucity of methodologically sound well-controlled studies, and the null results from the Marques study, there is considerable evidence supporting the effectiveness of multicomponent CBT- and RP-based treatment for sex offenders. It is clear from the literature that these programs are currently the best treatments available, though more treatment outcome research is needed to replicate and extend existing findings.

Improving Sex Offender Treatment

It is possible that current treatment programs yield only modest reductions in recidivism because of limitations with both the etiological theories of sexual offending upon which the programs are based and the treatment methods used by most programs (Kirsch & Becker, 2006). It is likely that treatment effectiveness would be enhanced if treatment was individualized more effectively to meet each offender's needs and was specifically targeted to factors that are linked to sexual reoffending (e.g., antisocial orientation) (e.g., Hanson & Bussiere, 1998; Hanson & Morton-Bourgon, 2005).

It has been argued that for sex offender treatment to be optimized it must adhere to three main principles of effective treatment: risk, need, and responsivity (Andrews & Bonta, 2003). According to the risk principle, the intensity of treatment should correspond to an offender's level of risk, with the most intensive treatments reserved for high-risk offenders and little or no treatment offered to low-risk offenders (Harkins & Beech, 2007).

With sex offenders, risk is generally divided into two categories: static and dynamic. Static risk factors are fixed historical characteristics that have been proven to be associated with recidivism, including previous offense history, age at first offense, marital status, and victim characteristics. Commonly used static risk assessment instruments include the MnSOST-R (Epperson, Kaul, & Hesselton, 1998), VRAG (Quinsey, Harris, Rice, & Cormier, 1998), SORAG (Quinsey, Harris, et al., 1998), STATIC-99R (Hanson & Thornton, 1999), and RRASOR (Hanson, 1997). These instruments employ actuarial measures and have established reliability and validity for predicting sexual and nonsexual recidivism (e.g., Langton et al., 2007).

Dynamic risk factors are factors that have the potential to change and, when changed, are associated with increases or decreases in recidivism (Hanson & Harris, 2000). Dynamic factors are subdivided into stable and acute factors. Stable factors (also called criminogenic needs) have the potential for change but tend to be relatively stable over time, lasting weeks or months (i.e., substance abuse or dependence, deviant sexual interests, intimacy deficits). Acute factors are rapidly changing characteristics or states lasting hours or days that impact the timing of reoffense (i.e., mood state, intoxication).

Because static risk factors are relatively fixed and unchanging, it has been suggested that treatment should focus on stable dynamic factors, which are amenable to change (e.g., Hanson & Harris, 2000). Treatment should be tailored to an offender's criminogenic needs—stable dynamic factors that are related to an offender's risk for recidivism (Andrews & Bonta, 2003; Harkins & Beech, 2007).

The "responsivity" principle posits that treatment should be matched to an offender's learning style and abilities (Andrews & Bonta, 2003). Responsivity factors—those characteristics of an offender that influence his ability to benefit from treatment—determine what an offender's learning style will be. Such factors include psychopathy, motivation or readiness for treatment, intellectual functioning, hostility, and personality traits (Looman, Dickie, & Abracen, 2005).

Although current treatment programs are beginning to focus on risk, need, and responsivity, more effort should be directed toward individualizing treatment with these principles in mind. When treatment accounts for all three principles, positive outcomes increase (Andrews & Bonta, 2003).

Treatment effectiveness may also be enhanced by placing greater emphasis on therapeutic processes (Kirsch & Becker, 2006). For example, many sex offender therapists take a harsh and confrontational approach to treatment in order to overcome defensiveness and denial and to challenge sex offenders' deviant attitudes and beliefs (e.g., Salter, 1988). Research suggests, however, that a confrontational style may actually increase resistance and lead to decreased treatment gains (Fernandez, 2006). On the other hand, some research suggests that therapist warmth, support, and flexibility lead to greater client change and increased treatment effectiveness (e.g., Luborsky, McLellan, Diguer, Woody, & Seligman, 1997; Miller, 2000). Shifting toward a more supportive and less confrontational treatment style might be beneficial (Fernandez, 2006; Marshall et al., 2003). Other aspects of treatment that merit attention are group composition and environment (e.g., Harkins & Beech, 2007), increased collaboration with clients (Shingler & Mann, 2006), and greater emphasis on positivity and the use of goals (Fernandez, 2006).

Treatment for adult sex offenders has progressed significantly over the past 60 years. We are optimistic about the future of sex offender treatment and feel that if interventions continue to incorporate empirical findings like the ones just discussed, treatment will lead to significant reductions in sex offending.

Treatment of Adolescent Offenders

This section focuses on treatment for adolescent sexual offenders. It is important to note that despite early concerns that many juvenile offenders would become adult sex offenders, the majority of juvenile sex offenders are not arrested as an adult for a sexual offense, even when followed for 5 to 9 years (e.g., McCann & Lussier, 2008; Reitzel & Carbonell, 2006; Sipe, Jensen, & Everett, 1998). Please note: This chapter does not address young children with sexual behavior problems. For those interested in treatment of children with sexual behavior problems, we recommend the report of the Association for the Treatment of Sexual Abusers (ATSA) Task Force on Children with Sexual Behavior Problems (2006).

Current Treatment Programs

Research on adolescents who commit sex offenses has lagged behind research on adults. Though less is known regarding the etiology of sexual offending by adolescents, their offending behavior—like that of adults—is considered to be driven by the interaction of familial, environmental, psychological, and biological factors. Youth who commit sexual offenses often exhibit a variety of individual, family, peer, and school problems (e.g., Blaske, Borduin, Henggeler, & Mann, 1989; Ronis & Borduin, 2007; van Wijk et al., 2005). Research has begun to identify factors associated with juvenile sexual offending, including childhood maltreatment or observation of domestic violence (Daversa & Knight, 2007; Hunter, 2004; Johnson & Knight, 2000), substance abuse (Johnson & Knight, 2000), antisocial male role models (Hunter, 2004), sexual compulsivity (Johnson & Knight, 2000), and psychopathic traits (Daversa & Knight, 2007). Given the diversity of adolescent sex offenders, different subtypes likely follow different developmental trajectories to their offending behavior (e.g., Becker & Kaplan, 1988; Hunter, 2006).

Treatment for juvenile sex offenders is dominated by CBT, RP, and psychosocial educational models (McGrath et al., 2003). Current treatment programs offer predominantly group therapy, although individual and family treatment sessions are also offered. CBT components of treatment often include cognitive restructuring, victim awareness and empathy, anger management, social skills training, and sex education (McGrath et al., 2003). RP techniques are also used by most treatment programs (McGrath et al., 2003).

Although the majority of adolescent treatment is modeled after adult sex offender treatment, there are some important differences. In contrast to adult treatment programs, programs for adolescents seldom use behavioral sexual arousal control treatments such as odor aversion and masturbatory satiation (McGrath et al., 2003). Additionally, limited pharmacological interventions (e.g., SSRIs) are recommended for adolescent sex offenders given the unknown risks associated with prescribing antiandrogens (used with adults) to pubertal youth (Bradford & Fedoroff, 2006).

Multisystemic treatment (MST) has generated interest as a treatment for juvenile sex offenders. MST is a systems-based, social ecological approach to dealing with problem behaviors. In contrast to CBT/RP approaches that have been adapted from treatment for adult sex offenders, MST was developed for use with chronic juvenile delinquents and has been consistently demonstrated to be effective with this population (e.g., Borduin et al., 1995; Curtis, Ronan, & Borduin, 2004; Henggeler, Melton, & Smith, 1992). Services are intensive and delivered in the home and community rather than a therapist's office. Therapists intervene at the individual, family, peer, school, and community levels and rely on strengths within these systems to alter the youth's inappropriate behavior (Henggeler, Schoenwald, Borduin, Rowland, & Cunningham, 1998). Parents are provided the skills necessary to monitor and discipline their children in a consistent and effective manner. The therapist may incorporate cognitive behavioral elements and other traditional sex offender-specific interventions (Swenson, Henggeler, Schoenwald, Kaufman, & Randall, 1998).

Traditional CBT group therapy for adolescent sex offenders is not without critics. Hunter, Gilbertson, Vedros, and Morgan (2004), for example, question whether treatment should focus primarily on sexual-offending behaviors and whether changes seen in the therapist's office will generalize to real-world settings. In light of critiques of CBT group therapy, several new approaches that represent a shift away from this model have been described in the literature. Hunter and colleagues (2004), for example, describe two comprehensive community-based programs that share an emphasis on the integration of legal and clinical management, highly individualized service delivery, and the inclusion of family-focused interventions. The programs include some components of traditional sex offender CBT, but only as needed by particular youth, and always in the context of providing services for nonsexual problems. These programs have been well received by the communities in which they were implemented (Hunter et al., 2004).

Another new approach that may prove beneficial for adolescent offenders— as with adults—is the Good Lives Model. The model emphasizes the development of a positive self, which may be particularly important for adolescents who are struggling to establish a sense of identity (Thakker, Ward, & Tidmarsh, 2006). The positive nature of the therapeutic alliance in the Good Lives Model, and the importance placed on achieving realistic and positive goals, may motivate adolescents more effectively than traditional avoidance-based approaches, though outcome research needs to be conducted to determine if such claims are supported.

Treatment Effectiveness

Despite the methodological challenges involved in conducting outcome studies with adolescents, existing research suggests that treatment of juveniles is effective. A meta-analysis of nine studies including nearly 3,000 offenders found that adolescents who received treatment sexually recidivated at a significantly lower rate (7.4%) than those who did not receive any treatment (18.9%; Reitzel & Carbonell, 2006).

In addition to this meta-analysis, individual treatment outcome studies have demonstrated generally positive results for adolescent sex offender treatment as well. However, there are some significant methodological flaws with these studies. Specifically, many published studies regarding the effectiveness of CBT focus on deviant sexual arousal as an outcome measure rather than sexual recidivism (Becker, Kaplan, & Kavoussi, 1988; Hunter & Goodwin, 1992; Hunter & Santos, 1990; Kaplan, Morales, & Becker, 1993; Weinrott, Riggan, & Frothingham, 1997). Increasingly, the field is recognizing that deviant sexual arousal is not always (and possibly not usually) the motivation for offenses committed by adolescents (e.g., Chaffin, 2008), and research with adults has found that decreased deviant arousal is not associated with lower recidivism rates (Rice, Quinsey, & Harris, 1991). On a positive note, the only CBT/RP treatment study that utilized a comparison group and included recidivism as an outcome measure demonstrated that adolescents who completed a CBT/RP treatment program had lower sexual, violent, and nonviolent recidivism rates than a comparison group (Worling & Curwen, 2000). Although there are methodological concerns regarding this study as well (Letourneau, 2004), the results are still promising.

Three randomized, controlled trials of MST with juvenile sex offenders have demonstrated the effectiveness of this approach with this population (Borduin, Henggeler, Blaske, & Stein, 1990; Borduin & Schaeffer, 2001; Letourneau et al., 2009). These studies have shown reduced sexual and general recidivism (Borduin et al., 1990; Borduin & Schaeffer, 2001) as well as reductions in self-reported delinquency and problematic sexual behaviors (Letourneau et al., 2009).

There is reason to be optimistic about the treatment of juveniles who have committed sexual offenses. Despite the methodological flaws of the existing research, it appears that youth who receive some form of intervention are less likely to recidivate than those who do not receive treatment. While MST appears particularly promising, it is not yet clear that any approach is superior to another (Reitzel & Carbonell, 2006) or even that sex offender-specific treatments are more effective than nonspecific treatment (e.g., Lab, Shields, & Schondel, 1993).

Improving Adolescent Sex Offender Treatment

While the results of treatment outcome research with adolescents are generally positive, improvements to the types of treatment typically provided can be made. While CBT is still the dominant treatment modality in practice, innovative approaches are being implemented across jurisdictions (Hunter et al., 2004). Additionally, more than 30 states now have licensed MST therapists (Family Services Research Center, n.d.). We believe MST and the community-based programs described by Hunter and colleagues (2004) are likely to be more effective than traditional CBT. We also recommend that any new treatment approaches should follow these trends:

Decreased emphasis on deviant sexual interest. Given that many juvenile sex offenders may not have developed any deviant interests (e.g., Becker & Kaplan, 1988; Chaffin, 2008), and techniques targeting deviant interests may not be effective (Aylwin, Reddon, & Burke, 2005), the routine use of these techniques is unnecessary, though it may be useful for the small subsample of adolescent offenders who do demonstrate deviant sexual arousal.

Increased emphasis on treatment in the community. There are a number of potential benefits to treatment in the community. Keeping a youth in the community increases the likelihood of creating change in the youth's family, peer, and school environments. Additionally, community treatment can minimize adolescents' contact with other antisocial youth, which is believed to be associated with increased delinquency (McCord, Widom, & Crowell, 2001). Additionally, if our goal is to have adolescents develop healthy lives, removing them from the community to reside with other youth who have been labeled as deviant or disturbed is likely to be counterproductive.

Decreased reliance on group provision of treatment. While group treatment is cost-effective, groups of adolescent offenders can actually produce iatrogenic effects (e.g., Dishion, McCord, & Poulin, 1999). Many adolescents being treated for a sex offense have a history of committing other delinquent offenses (e.g., Fehrenbach, Smith, Monastersky, & Deisher, 1986; Ronis & Borduin, 2007); therefore, providers should be aware of the potential for negative effects and consider providing more individual therapy when possible and carefully composing groups when they must be utilized.

More informed by the treatment of delinquents. Given that juveniles who have committed sex offenses are often similar to other delinquents (e.g., Ronis & Borduin, 2007; van Wijk et al., 2005) and are more likely to reoffend nonsexually than sexually (e.g., Worling & Långström, 2006), the literature on the effective treatment of general delinquency should be seen as an excellent resource.

Increased reliance on risk, need, and responsivity principles. As with adults, focus on such principles may increase treatment effectiveness. While no risk assessment measure for adolescents has demonstrated predictive validity, a focus on general criminogenic needs is likely to be quite beneficial (O'Reilly & Carr, 2006). Such factors may include attitudes toward offending, peer relationships, and self-regulation skills (Longo, 2003). Additionally, if treatment for juveniles is to follow the responsivity principle, it must be developmentally sensitive. Thus the field needs to continue to move away from the "trickle-down" application of adult models to adolescents and children (Longo, 2003, p. 503). The application of adult models can lead to a focus on inappropriate treatment targets and the requirement that juveniles participate in lengthy treatment programs that may be unnecessary to create change in this population (Chaffin, 2008; Longo, 2003).

Conclusion

Sex offender specific treatment is effective for reducing sexual recidivism in both adult and adolescent offenders. We have yet to establish, however, the most effective and appropriate treatments for each population. Although CBT/RP-based programs have yielded some benefits with respect to recidivism reduction, the field has begun to recognize the merit of other approaches as well. Such approaches adhere to risk, need, and responsivity principles to a greater degree than traditional treatment models. Newer treatments such as Good Lives and MST also allow for greater individualization of treatment, which is likely to lead to greater reductions in recidivism (Andrews & Bonta, 2003). Hopefully, the field will continue to blend research findings with clinical practice, so that we can develop treatment programs that are maximally effective.

References

Abel, G. G., Becker, J. V., Mittelman, M., Cunningham-Rathner, J., Rouleau, J. L., & Murphy, W. D. (1987). Self-reported sex crimes of non-incarcerated paraphiliacs. *Journal of Interpersonal Violence*, 2, 3–25.

Andrews, D. A., & Bonta, J. (2003). *The psychology of criminal conduct* (3rd ed.). Cincinnati, OH: Anderson.

ATSA Task Force on Children with Sexual Behavior Problems. (2006). *Children with sexual behavior problems*. Beaverton, OR: Association for the Treatment of Sexual Abusers.

Aylwin, A. S., Reddon, J. R., & Burke, A. R. (2005). Sexual fantasies of adolescent male sex offenders in residential treatment: A descriptive study. *Archives of Sexual Behavior*, 34, 231–239.

Barbaree, H. E. (1991). Denial and minimization among sex offenders: Assessment and treatment outcome. *Forum on Corrections Research*, 3, 30–33.

Becker, J. V., & Kaplan, M. S. (1988). The assessment of adolescent sexual offenders. In R. Prinz (Ed.), *Advances in behavioral assessment of children and families* (Vol. 4, pp. 97–118). Greenwich, CT: JAI Press.

Becker, J. V., Kaplan, M. S., & Kavoussi, R. (1988). Measuring the effectiveness of treatment for the aggressive adolescent sexual offender. *Annals of the New York Academy of Sciences, 528,* 215–222.

Becker, J. V., & Murphy, W. D. (1998). What we know and do not know about assessing and treating sexual offenders. *Psychology, Public Policy, and Law, 4,* 116–137.

Beech, A. R., & Ward, T. (2004). The integration of etiology and risk in sexual offenders: A theoretical framework. *Aggression and Violent Behavior, 10,* 31–63.

Blaske, D. M., Borduin, C. M., Henggeler, S. W., & Mann, B. J. (1989). Individual, family, and peer characteristics of adolescent sex offenders and assaultive offenders. *Developmental Psychology, 25,* 846–855.

Borduin, C. M., Henggeler, S. W., Blaske, D. M., & Stein, R. J. (1990). Multisystemic treatment of adolescent sexual offenders. *International Journal of Offender Therapy and Comparative Criminology, 34,* 105–113.

Borduin, C. M., Mann, B. J., Cone, L. T., Henggeler, S. W., Fucci, B. R., Blaske, D. M., et al. (1995). Multisystemic treatment of serious juvenile offenders: Long term prevention of criminality and violence. *Journal of Consulting and Clinical Psychology, 63,* 569–578.

Borduin, C. M., & Schaeffer, C. M. (2001). Multisystemic treatment of juvenile sexual offenders: A progress report. *Journal of Psychology and Human Sexuality, 13*(3/4), 25–42.

Bradford, J. M. W., & Federoff, P. (2006). Pharmacological treatment of the juvenile sex offender. In H. E. Barbaree & W. L. Marshall (Eds.), *The juvenile sex offender* (2nd ed., pp. 358–382). New York: Guilford Press.

Chaffin, M. (2008). Our minds are made up don't confuse us with the facts: Commentary on policies concerning children with sexual behavior problems and juvenile sex offenders. *Child Maltreatment, 13,* 110–121.

Curtis, N. M., Ronan, K. R., & Borduin, C. M. (2004). Multisystemic treatment: A meta-analysis of outcome studies. *Journal of Family Psychology, 18,* 411–419.

Daversa, M. T., & Knight, R. A. (2007). A structural examination of the predictors of sexual coercion against children in adolescent sexual offenders. *Criminal Justice and Behavior, 34,* 1313–1333.

Dishion, T. J., McCord, J., & Poulin, F. (1999). When interventions harm: Peer groups and problem behavior. *American Psychologist, 54,* 755–764.

Epperson, D. L., Kaul, J. D., & Hesselton, D. (1998, October). *Final report of the development of the Minnesota Sex Offender Screening Tool-Revised (MnSOST-R).* Paper presented at the 17th Annual Research and Treatment Conference of the Association for the Treatment of Sexual Abusers, Vancouver, BC, Canada.

Family Services Research Center. (n.d.). Multisystemic Therapy (MST). Available at: http://academicdepartments.musc.edu/psychiatry/research/fsrc/subsites/mst.htm

Fehrenbach, P. A., Smith, W., Monastersky, C., & Deisher, R. W. (1986). Adolescent sexual offenders: Offender and offense characteristics. *American Journal of Orthopsychiatry, 56,* 225–233.

Fernandez, Y. M. (2006). Focusing on the positive and avoiding negativity in sexual offender treatment. In W. L. Marshall, Y. M. Fernandez, L. E. Marshall, & G. A. Serran (Eds.), *Sexual offender treatment: Controversial issues* (pp. 187–198). London: Wiley.

Finkelhor, D. (1984). *Child sexual abuse: New theory and research.* New York: Free Press.

Finkelhor, D., & Jones, L. M. (2004). *Explanations for the decline in child sexual abuse cases* [bulletin]. Washington, DC: U.S. Department of Justice, Office of Justice Programs, Office of Juvenile Justice and Delinquency Prevention.

Furby, L., Weinrott, M. R., & Blackshaw, L. (1989). Sex offender recidivism: A review. *Psychological Bulletin, 105,* 3–30.

Geer, J. H., Estupinan, L. A., & Manguno-Mire, G. M. (2000). Empathy, social skills, and other relevant cognitive processes in rapists and child molesters. *Aggression and Violent Behavior, 5,* 99–126.

Hall, G. C. N. (1995). Sexual offender recidivism revisited: A meta-analysis of recent treatment studies. *Journal of Consulting and Clinical Psychology, 63,* 802–809.

Hall, G. C. N., & Hirschman, R. (1991). Toward a theory of sexual aggression: A quadripartite model. *Journal of Consulting and Clinical Psychology, 59,* 662–669.

Hanson, R. K. (1997). *The development of a brief actuarial risk scale for sexual offense recidivism.* User Report 1997-04. Ottawa, Ontario, Canada: Department of the Solicitor General of Canada.

Hanson, R. K. (2000). Treatment outcome and evaluation problems (and solutions). In D. R. Laws, S. M. Hudson, & T. Ward (Eds.), *Remaking relapse prevention with sex offenders* (pp. 485–499). Thousand Oaks, CA: Sage.

Hanson, R. K., & Bussiere, M. T. (1998). Predicting relapse: A meta-analysis of sexual offender recidivism studies. *Journal of Counseling and Clinical Psychology, 66,* 348–362.

Hanson, R. K., Gordon, A., Harris, A. J. R., Marques, J. K., Murphy, W., Quinsey, V. L., et al. (2002). First report of the Collaborative Outcome Project on the effectiveness of psychological treatment for sex offenders. *Sexual Abuse: A Journal of Research and Treatment, 14,* 169–194.

Hanson, R. K., & Harris, A. J. R. (2000). Where should we intervene? Dynamic predictors of sexual offense recidivism. *Criminal Justice and Behavior, 27,* 6–35.

Hanson, R. K., & Morton-Bourgon, K. (2005). The characteristics of persistent sexual offenders: A meta-analysis of recidivism studies. *Journal of Consulting and Clinical Psychology, 73,* 1154–1163.

Hanson, R. K., & Thornton, D. (1999). *STATIC-99: Improving actuarial risk assessments for sex offenders.* Report No. 1999-02. Ottawa, Ontario, Canada: Office of the Solicitor General.

Harris, A. J. R., & Hanson, R. K. (2004). *Sex offender recidivism: A simple question.* Ottawa, Ontario, Canada: Public Safety and Emergency Preparedness Canada.

Harkins, L., & Beech, A. R. (2007). A review of the factors that can influence the effectiveness of sexual offender treatment: Risk, need, responsivity, and process issues. *Aggression and Violent Behavior, 12,* 615–627.

Henggeler, S. W., Melton, G. B., & Smith, L. A. (1992). Family preservation using multisystemic therapy: An effective alternative to incarcerating serious juvenile offenders. *Journal of Consulting and Clinical Psychology, 60,* 953–961.

Henggeler, S. W., Schoenwald, S. K., Borduin, C. M., Rowland, M. D., & Cunningham, P. B. (1998). *Multisystemic treatment of antisocial behavior in children and adolescents.* New York: Guilford Press.

Hunter, J. A. (2004). Developmental pathways in youth sexual aggression and delinquency: Risk factors and mediators. *Journal of Family Violence, 19,* 233–242.

Hunter, J. A. (2006). Understanding diversity in juvenile sexual offenders: Implications for assessment, treatment, and legal management. In R. E. Longo &

D. S. Prescott (Eds.), *Current perspectives: Working with sexually aggressive youth and youth with sexual behavior problem*s (pp. 63–77). Holyoke, MA: NEARI Press.

Hunter, J. A., Gilbertson, S. A., Vedros, D., & Morton, M. (2004). Strengthening community-based programming for juvenile sexual offenders: Key concepts and paradigm shifts. *Child Maltreatment, 9*, 177–189.

Hunter, J. A., & Goodwin, D. W. (1992). The clinical utility of satiation therapy with juvenile sexual offenders: Variations and efficacy. *Annals of Sex Research, 5*, 71–80.

Hunter, J. A., & Santos, D. (1990). The use of specialized cognitive-behavioral therapies in the treatment of adolescent sexual offenders. *International Journal of Offender Therapy and Comparative Criminology, 34*, 239–247.

Johnson, G. M., & Knight, R. A. (2000). Developmental antecedents of sexual coercion in juvenile sexual offenders. *Sexual Abuse: A Journal of Research and Treatment, 12*, 165–178.

Kaplan, M. S., Morales, M., & Becker, J. V. (1993). The impact of verbal satiation on adolescent sex offenders: A preliminary report. *Journal of Child Sexual Abuse, 2*, 81–88.

Kirsch, L. G., & Becker, J. V. (2006). Sexual offending: Theory of problem, theory of change, and implications for treatment effectiveness. *Aggression and Violent Behavior, 11*, 208–224.

Lab, S. P., Shields, G., & Schondel, C. (1993). Research note: An evaluation of juvenile sexual offender treatment. *Crime and Delinquency, 39*, 543–553.

Langton, C. M., Barbaree, H. E., Seto, M. C., Peacock, E. J., Harkins, L., & Hansen, K. T. (2007). Actuarial assessment of risk for reoffense among adult sex offenders: Evaluating the predictive accuracy of the Static-2002 and five other instruments. *Criminal Justice and Behavior, 34*, 37–59.

Letourneau, E. J. (2004). Letter to the editor: A comment on the first report. *Sexual Abuse: A Journal of Research and Treatment, 16*, 77–81.

Letourneau, E. J., Henggeler, S. W., Borduin, C. M., Schewe, P. A., McCart, M. R., Chapman, J. E., et al. (2009). Multisystemic therapy for juvenile sexual offenders: 1-year results from a randomized effectiveness trial. *Journal of Family Psychology, 23*, 89–102.

Lindsay, W. R., Ward, T., Morgan, T., & Wilson, I. (2007). Self-regulation of sex offending, future pathways and the Good Lives Model: Applications and problems. *Journal of Sexual Aggression, 13*, 37–50.

Longo, R. E. (2003). Emerging issues, policy changes, and the future of treating children with sexual behavior problems. *Annals of the New York Academy of Sciences, 989*, 502–514.

Looman, J., Abracen, J., & Nicholaichuk, T. P. (2000). Recidivism among treated sexual offenders and matched controls: Data from the Regional Treatment Centre (Ontario). *Journal of Interpersonal Violence, 15*, 279–290.

Looman, J., Dickie, I., & Abracen, J. (2005). Responsivity issues in the treatment of sexual offenders. *Trauma, Violence, & Abuse, 6*, 330–353.

Luborsky, L., McLellan, A. T., Diguer, L., Woody, G., & Seligman, D. A. (1997). The psychotherapist matters: Comparison of outcomes across twenty-two therapists and seven patient samples. *Clinical Psychology: Science and Practice, 4*, 53–65.

Marlatt, G. (1982). Relapse prevention: A self-control program for the treatment of addictive behaviors. In R. Stuart (Ed.), *Adherence, compliance, and generalization in behavioral medicine* (pp. 329–378). New York: Brunner/Mazel.

Marques, J. K., Day, D. M., Nelson, C., & Miner, M. H. (1989). The Sex Offender Treatment and Evaluation Project: California's relapse prevention program. In D. R. Laws (Ed.), *Relapse prevention with sex offenders* (pp. 247–267). New York: Guilford Press.

Marques, J. K., Wiederanders, M., Day, D. M., Nelson, C., & van Ommeren, A. (2005). Effects of a relapse prevention program on sexual recidivism: Final results from California's Sex Offender Treatment and Evaluation Project (SOTEP). *Sexual Abuse: A Journal of Research and Treatment, 17*, 79–107.

Marshall, P. (1997). *The prevalence of convictions for sexual offending.* Research Finding No. 55. Research and statistics directorate. London: Home Office.

Marshall, W. L. (1999). Current status of North American assessment and treatment programs for sexual offenders. *Journal of Interpersonal Violence, 14*, 221–239.

Marshall, W. L., & Barbaree, H. E. (1990a). An integrated theory of the etiology of sexual offending. In W. L. Marshall, D. R. Laws, & H. E. Barbaree (Eds.), *Handbook of sexual assault* (pp. 257–275). New York: Plenum.

Marshall, W. L., & Barbaree, H. E. (1990b). Outcome of comprehensive cognitive-behavioral treatment programs. In W. L. Marshall, D. R. Laws, & H. E. Barbaree (Eds.), *Handbook of sexual assault* (pp. 363–385). New York: Plenum.

Marshall, W. L., Fernandez, Y. M., Serran, G. A., Mullor, R., Thornton, D., Mann, R. E., et al. (2003). Process variables in the treatment of sexual offenders: A review of the relevant literature. *Aggression and Violent Behavior, 8*, 205–234.

McCann, K., & Lussier, P. (2008). Antisociality, sexual deviance, and sexual reoffending in juvenile sex offenders: A meta-analytical investigation. *Youth Violence and Juvenile Justice, 6*, 363–385.

McCord, J., Widom, C. S., & Crowell, N. A. (2001). The development of delinquency. In J. McCord, C. S. Widom, & N. A. Crowell (Eds.), *Juvenile crime, juvenile justice* (pp. 66–106). Washington, DC: National Academy Press.

McGrath, R. J., Cumming, G. F., & Burchard, B. L. (2003). *Current practices and trends in sexual abuser management: Safer Society 2002 nationwide survey.* Brandon, VT: Safer Society Press.

McGrath, R. J., Hoke, S. E., & Vojtisek, J. E. (1998). Cognitive-behavioral treatment of sex offenders: A treatment comparison and long-term follow-up study. *Criminal Justice and Behavior, 25*, 203–225.

McGuire, R. J., Carlisle, J. M., & Young, B. G. (1965). Sexual deviations as conditioned behavior: A hypothesis. *Behavior Research and Therapy, 2*, 185–190.

Miller, W. R. (2000). Rediscovering fire: Small interventions, large effects. *Psychology of Addictive Behaviors, 14*, 6–18.

O'Reilly, G., & Carr, A. (2006). Assessment and treatment of criminogenic needs. In H. E. Barbaree & W. L. Marshall (Eds.), *The juvenile sex offender* (2nd ed., pp. 189–218). New York: Guilford Press.

Pithers, W. D., Marques, J. K., Gibat, C. C., & Marlatt, G. A. (1983). Relapse prevention with sexual aggressives: A self-control model of treatment and the maintenance of change. In J. G. Greer & I. R. Stuart (Eds.), *The sexual aggressor* (pp. 214–234). New York: Van Nostrand Reinhold.

Porter, S., Fairweather, D., Drugge, J., Herve, H., Birt, A., & Boer, D. P. (2000). Profiles of psychopathy in incarcerated sex offenders. *Criminal Justice and Behavior, 27*, 216–233.

Quinsey, V. L., Harris, G. T., Rice, M. E., & Cormier, C. A. (1998). *Violent offenders: Appraising and managing risk.* Washington, DC: American Psychological Association.

Quinsey, V. L., Khanna, A., & Malcolm, P. B. (1998). A retrospective evaluation of the Regional Treatment Centre sex offender treatment program. *Journal of Interpersonal Violence, 13,* 621–644.

Reitzel, L. R., & Carbonell, J. L. (2006). The effectiveness of sexual offender treatment for juveniles as measured by recidivism: A meta-analysis. *Sexual Abuse: A Journal of Research and Treatment, 18,* 401–421.

Rice, M. E., & Harris, G. T. (2003). What we know and don't know about treating adult sex offenders. In B. J. Winick & J. Q. LaFond (Eds.), *Protecting society from sexually dangerous offenders: Law, justice, and therapy* (pp. 101–117). Washington, DC: American Psychological Association.

Rice, M. E., Quinsey, V. L., & Harris, G. T. (1991). Sexual recidivism among child molesters released from a maximum security psychiatric institution. *Journal of Consulting and Clinical Psychology, 59,* 381–386.

Ronis, S. T., & Borduin, C. M. (2007). Individual, family, peer, and academic characteristics of male juvenile sexual offenders. *Journal of Abnormal Child Psychology, 35,* 153–163.

Salter, A. C. (1988). *Treating child sex offenders and victims: A practical guide.* Newbury Park, CA: Sage.

Seto, M. C., & Barbaree, H. E. (1999). Psychopathy, treatment behavior, and sex offender recidivism. *Journal of Interpersonal Violence, 14,* 1235–1248.

Shingler, J., & Mann, R. E. (2006). Collaboration in clinical work with sexual offenders: Treatment and risk assessment. In W. L. Marshall, Y. M. Fernandez, L. E. Marshall, & G. A. Serran (Eds.), *Sexual offender treatment: Controversial issues* (pp. 225–239). London: Wiley.

Sipe, R., Jensen, E. L., & Everett, R. S. (1998). Adolescent sexual offenders grown up: Recidivism in young adulthood. *Criminal Justice and Behavior, 25,* 109–124.

Stinson, J. D., Sales, B. D., & Becker, J. V. (2008). *Sex offending: Causal theories to inform research, prevention, and treatment.* Washington, DC: American Psychological Association.

Swenson, C. C., Henggeler, S. W., Schoenwald, S. K., Kaufman, K. L., & Randall, J. (1998). Changing the social ecologies of adolescent sexual offenders: Implication of the success of multisystemic therapy in treating serious antisocial behavior in adolescents. *Child Maltreatment, 3,* 330–338.

Thakker, J., Ward, T., & Tidmarsh, P. (2006). A reevaluation of relapse prevention with adolescents who sexually offend: A Good-Lives Model. In H. E. Barbaree & W. L. Marshall (Eds.), *The juvenile sex offender* (2nd ed., pp. 313–335). New York: Guilford Press.

U.S. Department of Health and Human Services. (2010). *Child maltreatment 2008.* Washington, DC: U.S. Government Printing Office.

U. S. Department of Justice. (2009). *Crime in the United States, 2008.* Washington, DC: U.S. Government Printing Office.

van Wijk, A., Loeber, R., Vermeiren, R., Pardini, D., Bullens, R., & Doreleijers, T. (2005). Violent juvenile sex offenders compared with violent juvenile nonsex offenders: Explorative findings from the Pittsburgh Youth Study. *Sexual Abuse: A Journal of Research and Treatment, 17,* 333–352.

Ward, T., & Gannon, T. A. (2006). Rehabilitation, etiology, and self-regulation: The comprehensive Good Lives Model of treatment for sexual offenders. *Aggression and Violent Behavior, 11,* 77–94.

Ward, T., & Stewart, C. A. (2003). The treatment of sex offenders: Risk management and good lives. *Professional Psychology: Research and Practice, 34,* 353–360.

Weinrott, M. R., Riggan, M., & Frothingham, S. (1997). Reducing deviant arousal in juvenile sex offenders using vicarious sensitization. *Journal of Interpersonal Violence, 12,* 704–728.

Weinrott, M. R., & Saylor, M. (1991). Self-report of crimes committed by sex offenders. *Journal of Interpersonal Violence, 6,* 286–300.

Whitehead, P. R., Ward, T., & Collie, R. M. (2007). Time for a change: Applying the Good Lives Model of rehabilitation to a high-risk violent offender. *International Journal of Offender Therapy and Comparative Criminology, 51,* 578–598.

Worling, J. R., & Curwen, T. (2000). Adolescent sexual recidivism: Success of specialized treatment and implications for risk prediction. *Child Abuse and Neglect, 24,* 965–982.

Worling, J. R., & Långström, N. (2006). Risk of sexual recidivism in juveniles who sexually offend: Correlates and assessment. In H. E. Barbaree & W. L. Marshall (Eds.), *The juvenile sex offender* (2nd ed., pp. 219–247). New York: Guilford Press.

18

Preventing Sexual Abuse

Community Protection Policies and Practice

Elizabeth J. Letourneau and Jill S. Levenson

There are few thoughts more harrowing for parents than the prospect of a child being sexually abused. For many people, the most disturbing case is the horrific crime of a previously convicted sex offender kidnapping, raping, and murdering a child. Although such cases are rare, they draw tremendous public attention and outrage. In response to such cases, lawmakers pass tougher laws designed to prevent repeat offending. Readers of this book understand that much more common than abduction by a stranger is sexual abuse of children by people they know, including parents, relatives, and caretakers.

Protecting children from sexual predators has become a priority for lawmakers. To monitor known sex offenders and to prevent reoffending, a multitude of federal, state, and local laws have been enacted in the United States. In 2007 and 2008 alone, state legislatures considered at least 1,500 bills related to sex offenders, and 275 became law (Vandervort-Clark, 2009). Anyone convicted of a sexual crime is required to register with law enforcement authorities so that the offender's whereabouts are known. Registration information is available on publicly accessible Internet sites, allowing parents and concerned citizens to determine if registered sex offenders live nearby. Many jurisdictions forbid known sex offenders from living or working near places where children congregate. Increasingly, convicted sex offenders living in the community are required to wear global positioning devices that allow probation officers to determine their exact whereabouts. Approximately 20 states have laws allowing dangerous sex offenders to be involuntarily civilly committed to institutions. The laws previously described are among the most popular and widespread crime prevention strategies in America. But do they work?

This chapter begins with a brief review of historical trends regarding sex offender laws. Next, the chapter examines empirical research regarding the effectiveness of these laws. Particular attention is devoted to juvenile sex offenders. The chapter ends with suggestions for integrating policy responses with research and best practice.

History of Sex Offender Laws

Today's legislative focus on sex offenders was predated by two earlier waves of sex offender legislation. In some ways, today's "new" laws are merely modern versions of previous policies. For example, indefinite institutionalization of sex offenders was legalized in the early 1900s and revisited in the 1930s. In current form, civil commitment laws allow post-prison sentence institutionalization of "sexually violent predators." Most recent sex offender laws, however, focus on the management of offenders in the community, and this chapter focuses on these community protection policies.

There are several theories about why legal policies targeting sex offenders cycled in and out of popularity during the past century. One theory suggests that the first wave of legislation, in which sex offenders, other criminals, and the mentally ill or incapacitated were subjected to indefinite institutionalization and sterilization, was influenced by the intersection of sexology and eugenics (Ordover, 2003). Sexology was an emerging area of medical expertise in the late 1800s that held that sexual misbehavior of any type was indicative of increased risk for sexual murder or other violent crime (Jenkins, 1998; Laws & Marshall, 2003). During that time, the theory of eugenics gained acceptance, particularly among the upper classes that were fearful of poor inner-city residents and eager to embrace a scientific rationale that justified the stark economic discrepancies between classes (Ordover, 2003). Sexologists and eugenicists agreed that criminal tendencies were heritable and resistant to change, justifying extreme interventions that removed "sexual perverts" from society (via institutionalization) and prevented their procreation (via sterilization).

The second wave of sex offender legislation occurred from approximately 1930 to 1960 (LaFond, 2005). During this wave, 27 states permitted the indefinite commitment of "sexual psychopaths." Sexual psychopath laws typically specified indefinite commitment at inpatient treatment centers until such time as the treatment provider recommended release. Sutherland (1950) argued that sexual psychopath laws followed from three factors: intense newspaper coverage of sensational sex crimes, an emerging sociological shift in which sex criminals were viewed as needing treatment rather than punishment, and the desire of psychiatrists to ensure that sexual psychopaths were diagnosed and treated by members of their profession. Other theories suggest that the liberalization of female sexuality might have played a role by focusing public fear onto the most deviant sexual behaviors while traditionally proscribed behaviors became more acceptable (Freedman, 1987). Interest in sexual psychopathy waned in the 1960s. States repealed their sexual psychopath laws amid concerns that the laws were based on inaccurate predictions of dangerousness and that effective treatments were unavailable (Slovenko, 2002).

The third wave of sex offender legislation began approximately in 1990 and continues today. A likely contributor to the current wave of interest in community protection policies is the revolution in communication technologies that expanded tremendously in the 1990s with the Internet and 24-hour news coverage. Today, coverage of sensational sex crimes reaches instantly around the globe and is covered in detail on television and the Internet.

Rising crime rates throughout the 1980s created fear of "superpredators" and helped spark the "tough on crime" stance popularized by President Ronald Reagan that remains popular today (Lynch, 2002). Sexual criminals are thought of as particularly dangerous, prone to reoffending and beyond rehabilitation. These beliefs are reflected in public perception surveys in which citizens report that they are very much in favor of community protection laws (Levenson, Brannon, Fortney, & Baker, 2007; Lieb & Nunlist, 2008; Mears, Mancini, Gertz, & Bratton, 2008). Legislators often describe sex offenders as perverted, sick, compulsive, and untreatable. Many lawmakers believe sex criminals inevitably reoffend (Sample & Kadleck, 2008).

Recidivism

As previously stated, sex offenders are believed by many lawmakers, policy makers, and the public to have high recidivism rates. One often sees this statement: "The average sex offender has over 100 victims." This statistic comes from a 1987 study in which immunity was granted to sex offenders to encourage honest disclosure about their offenses (Abel et al., 1987). The mean (average) number of reported victims for pedophiles who molest boys was 150; the average for pedophiles with girl victims was 20. However, the median (midpoint) number of victims was 4.4 boys and 1.3 girls. The "average" incestuous offender had fewer than two victims. The authors explained that some individuals in the study engaged in a very large number of abusive acts, skewing the mean, and that the median values better approximate the typical behavior of sexual abusers. In other words, the majority of sex offenses are committed by a small number of predatory or pedophilic offenders.

The belief that most sex offenders reoffend is not supported by research (see Chapter 17). According to the U.S. Department of Justice, 5.3% of sex offenders released from prison were rearrested for a new sex crime within 3 years (Bureau of Justice Statistics, 2003). As follow-up periods get longer, the number of recidivists grows, but the chance that a convicted offender will recidivate decreases with more time spent offense-free in the community (Hanson, Morton, & Harris, 2003). Over 4 to 6 years, about 14% of over

20,000 sex offenders in an international sample were rearrested for a new sex offense (Hanson & Bussiere, 1998; Hanson & Morton-Bourgon, 2005). A 24% recidivism rate was observed over 15 years (Harris & Hanson, 2004) and 27% were rearrested over 20 years (Hanson et al., 2003). Available research suggests that after 2 decades the majority of convicted sex offenders have not recidivated. Of course, arrest data are not always accurate. Many crimes go undetected. Giving full credit to weaknesses in the data, however, research does not support the belief that most sex offenders recidivate.

Sex Offender Registration and Notification

Registration is the practice of requiring convicted sex offenders to register with law enforcement and periodically check in to provide information about their residence, employment, and other details. The aim of registration laws is to provide law enforcement with a database of information on sex offenders to help monitor known offenders and to aid in the investigation of new allegations.

Community notification is the practice of releasing registration information to citizens. The aim of public notification is to arm citizens with information to protect themselves and their children from sexual predators.

The federal government plays a leading role in shaping sex offender policy. The federal Jacob Wetterling Act of 1994 (see Appendix A) mandated that all states develop and maintain sex offender registries. The federal Megan's Law of 1996 (see Appendix A) required states to develop strategies for releasing information about convicted sex offenders to the public. The federal Pam Lychner Sexual Offender Tracking and Identification Act of 1996 (see Appendix A) required the development of a nationwide registry to prevent offenders from escaping registration requirements by moving from state to state. The federal Prosecutorial Remedies and Other Tools to End the Exploitation of Children Today (PROTECT) Act of 2003 (see Appendix A) mandated states to develop publicly accessible Internet sex offender registries.

Early versions of the federal laws previously mentioned gave states substantial leeway to implement registration and notification laws. For instance, states could choose which sex offenders would be publicly identified and which strategies would be utilized to do so. About half the states opted to release information only about sex offenders deemed to pose a high risk to public safety. Some states, such as Minnesota, Colorado, New Jersey, and California, developed risk assessment procedures and classified offenders into categories based on empirically derived risk factors or actuarial risk instruments. Higher risk offenders were subjected to more comprehensive community notification. Other states established criteria for releasing information about repeat offenders and offenders who committed predatory sexual violence against strangers. Some states, such as Florida and South Carolina, opted to release information about all convicted sex offenders regardless of their threat for future offending. In the early days of public notification, procedures included distribution of flyers, newspaper ads with photos of registered sex offenders, door-to-door warnings by police, and community meetings (Matson & Lieb, 1996). Today, the Internet provides the primary method of community notification.

The federal Adam Walsh Child Protection and Safety Act of 2006 (see Appendix A) standardized registration and notification procedures across states and removed much of the discretion previously allowed by federal law. For example, the Adam Walsh Act identified more sex crimes as requiring registration, lengthened the duration of registration above many state levels, and greatly increased the amount and type of information to be collected from registrants (e.g., all e-mail addresses used by a registrant). Additionally, the Adam Walsh Act requires that all registered offenders be included on publicly accessible Web-based notification sites for the duration of their registration period. Furthermore, the Adam Walsh Act requires that registration and notification be implemented on the basis of conviction, without consideration of recidivism risk. Indeed, states are prohibited from using risk assessment instruments to modify sex offender registration and notification requirements (U.S. Department of Justice, 2008). The Adam Walsh Act requires registration and notification for juveniles as young as 14 who commit certain sex crimes. Previous federal law did not target juveniles adjudicated in juvenile or family court.

_____ Residential Restrictions on Sex Offenders

As public awareness of sex offenders living in communities increased, so did efforts to prevent registered sex offenders from living near schools and places children play. Currently at least 30 states have laws designating where sex offenders can live (Meloy, Miller, & Curtis, 2008). Buffer zones generally span 1,000 to 2,000 feet around protected settings such as schools, parks, playgrounds, and day care centers. Some laws include other facilities such as arcades, amusement parks, movie theaters, youth sports facilities, school bus stops, and libraries (Meloy et al., 2008).

Too numerous to review are housing ordinances passed by local jurisdictions (cities, towns, and counties). These ordinances are typically modeled after zoning laws that prohibit adult establishments (e.g., strip clubs and adult bookstores) from operating within a certain distance from schools. Local ordinances often exceed state laws and expand restricted areas to 2,500 feet (almost a half mile). Over 130 municipal ordinances exist in Florida alone. Local sex offender zoning laws can be found in most states. When one city or county enacts such a law, a domino effect results as surrounding towns and counties pass similar laws in an attempt to prevent sex offenders from migrating to their communities (Levenson, Zgoba, & Tewksbury, 2007).

Effectiveness of Community Protection Laws in Preventing Child Sexual Abuse

A small but growing body of research examines the intended goals and unintended effects of sex offender laws. Some studies examine how stakeholders, including offenders, citizens, and others, view these laws. Research examines whether registration and notification are associated with prevention of sex crimes. There is research on the effects of sex offender laws on judicial decision making. A few studies examine the effects of residence restrictions.

Research on stakeholder views of registration and notification reveals consistency within and discrepancies between groups. Nonoffending citizens and policymakers are very supportive of registration and public notification (Levenson, Brannon, et al., 2007; Lieb & Nunlist, 2008; Mears et al., 2008; Sample & Kadleck, 2008), going so far as to indicate continued support even if policies show no evidence of reducing recidivism (Levenson, Brannon, et al., 2007). Judges, law enforcement, and parole/probation officers generally support these laws, while expressing concern about insufficient funding to implement the laws (Lawson & Savell, 2003; Zevitz & Farkas, 2000b), increased workload (Zevitz & Farkas, 2000a), and removal of judicial discretion (Bumby & Maddox, 1999). Some mental health professionals express skepticism about whether sex offender registration and notification laws prevent child sexual abuse (CSA). These professionals are concerned about obstacles these laws create for successful offender reintegration as well as their potential for creating a false sense of security for parents (Malesky & Keim, 2001).

Not surprisingly, sex offenders and their family members find the laws both onerous and harmful. Offenders report that the laws interfere with their ability to establish and/or maintain jobs, homes, and social ties. The laws lead to verbal and physical harassment (Burchfield & Mingus, 2008; Farkas & Miller, 2007; Levenson & Cotter, 2005; Levenson, D'Amora, & Hern, 2007; Mercado, Alvarez, & Levenson, 2008; Tewksbury, 2005; Tewksbury & Lees, 2006; Zevitz & Farkas, 2000c). Family members of registered sex offenders state that they, too, are impacted by the laws (Farkas & Miller, 2007; Levenson & Tewksbury, 2009). Employment problems experienced by offenders and resulting financial hardship are viewed as the most pressing issue by family members. In addition, family members living with a registered sex offender say they experience threats and harassment by neighbors. Children of registered sex offenders report stigmatization and differential treatment by teachers and classmates.

Research has generally failed to establish that sex offender registration and notification laws reduce recidivism (Adkins, Huff, & Stageberg, 2000; Letourneau, Levenson, Bandyopadhyay, Sinha, & Armstrong, in press; Sandler, Freeman, & Socia, 2008; Schram & Milloy, 1995; Zevitz, 2006; Zgoba, Witt, Dalessandro, & Veysey, 2009). A number of researchers focused on data from individual states and found no significant relationships between registration and notification laws and reduced recidivism. Zgoba et al. (2009) cautioned that the high costs of sex offender registration and notification laws may not be justified given their negligible impact on public safety. On the other hand, three studies report that registration and/or notification was associated with reduced sex crime recidivism (Duwe & Donnay, 2008; Prescott & Rockoff, 2008; Washington State Institute for Public Policy, 2005). Obviously, more research is needed.

There appears to be no relationship between sexual recidivism and the distance an offender lives from schools or day care centers. Even considering other relevant risk factors (e.g., prior arrests, age, marital status, predator status), residential proximity does not appear to predict recidivism (Zandbergen, Levenson, & Hart, in press). In Colorado, sex offense recidivists and nonrecidivists lived randomly throughout the geographical area with no pattern emerging of recidivists living closer to schools and day care centers (Colorado Department of Public Safety, 2004). An analysis of 224 recidivistic sex offenses in Minnesota concluded that residential restriction laws would not have prevented any repeat sex crimes (Duwe, Donnay, & Tewksbury, 2008).

Apart from recidivism, other aspects of registration and notification laws have received research scrutiny. The impact of sex offender registration and notification laws on judicial decision making was examined in one study, which found that South Carolina's registration and notification policy was associated with statistically significant increases in plea bargains to nonsex crimes and a significant decrease in final guilty determinations for cases involving adult defendants (Letourneau, Levenson, Bandyopadhyay, Armstrong, & Sinha, in press). Thus, registration and notification was associated with unintended effects on judicial decision making.

Scholars have studied whether failure to register is associated with increased risk for sexual recidivism. Results from three studies indicate that failure to register is associated with general recidivism but not sexual recidivism (Duwe & Donnay, in press; Levenson, Letourneau, Armstrong, & Zgoba, in press; Washington State Institute for Public Policy, 2005). These results suggest that failure to register is more indicative of general criminality and defiance of rules than sexually deviant intentions.

In summary, there is little evidence that sex offender registration and notification laws achieve the intended goal of preventing known sex offenders from repeating their crimes. There are unintended consequences of these laws that interfere with an offender's rehabilitation and reintegration in the community, creating instability, psychosocial stress, unemployment, and transience—all of which are associated with increased risk for general if not sexual recidivism.

Application of Registration and Notification Laws to Juveniles

The fear of so-called superpredators in the 1980s quickly spread to juvenile offenders. Many state laws, and now the federal Adam Walsh Act, specifically target juveniles who commit sex offenses. The Adam Walsh Act requires registration of juveniles adjudicated for offenses "comparable to or more severe than aggravated sexual abuse" (U.S. Department of Justice, 2008, p. 83). Juvenile sex offenders often are subjected to the same registration and public notification policies as adults—and occasionally to harsher penalties. For example, although the minimum registration duration permitted by the Adam Walsh Act is 15 years, juvenile offenses that qualify for registration require registration durations of 25 years or life (Chaffin, 2008). Registration can impact a young person's employment, academic opportunities, and, in many states, residential location.

As with adults, the justification for juvenile registration and notification relies on misperceptions regarding recidivism. Despite research demonstrating that juvenile sex offenders are unlikely to commit future sexually violent acts (Caldwell, 2002; Reitzel & Carbonell, 2006), the executive director of the organization Parents for Megan's Law told the *Houston Chronicle* in 2009, "Once a juvenile introduces violence into sexual behavior, it's hard to rehabilitate. . . . They are worthy of registration." Likewise, a former official of the U.S. Department of Justice defended juvenile registration and notification requirements, telling ABC News, "We're talking about teens who committed incredibly horrific sex crimes."

Research has examined the effects of registration and notification on juveniles. In a survey of family court judges, many judges indicated that registration and notification were inappropriate for juveniles and unlikely to be helpful (Bumby & Maddox, 1999). Registration and notification was not associated with deterrence of sexual or nonsexual violent recidivism for registered youth in South Carolina (Letourneau & Armstrong, 2008; Letourneau, Bandyopadhyay, Sinha, & Armstrong, 2009b). There was evidence of increased risk of nonperson offense charges, which the authors attributed to a law enforcement surveillance effect on registered youth (Letourneau et al., 2009b).

Letourneau and her colleagues examined the effects of registration and notification on juvenile justice decision making and found that prosecutors were less likely to move forward on juvenile sex crime cases following implementation of South Carolina's lifetime registration policy (Letourneau, Bandyopadhyay, Sinha, & Armstrong, 2009a).

Residence restrictions are especially detrimental for young offenders. In Florida and Indiana, young registered sex offenders experienced more transience and homelessness than older offenders, probably as a result of being unable to live with their families in residential neighborhoods (Levenson, 2008; Levenson & Hern, 2007). Because teens and young adults are still dependent on their parents financially and psychologically, housing restrictions may be uniquely problematic for these offenders. Youth with sexual behavior problems are prohibited from living with their families just when they most need support and structure. Registration, notification, and residence restrictions may aggravate rather than mitigate risk of recidivism for younger offenders.

While formal surveys of registered youth have not been conducted, anecdotal reports indicate that youths publicly identified by registration and notification laws suffer physical and emotional harm, ostracism from peers and adults in their communities, and interrupted schooling, among other negative consequences (Brown, cited in Michels, 2007; Human Rights Watch, 2007; Jones, 2007; Trivits & Reppucci, 2002). Requiring youth to register as sex offenders and find themselves listed as such on the Internet is not without cost. Apart from the immediate negative experiences reported by registered youth, research on general delinquency indicates that being labeled "deviant" can diminish a youth's social bonds and increase the likelihood of participating in criminal behavior (Paternoster & Iovanni, 1989; Triplett & Jarjoura, 1994). Being labeled a deviant increases the likelihood that juveniles will become or remain involved with delinquent peers, thus maintaining delinquent behavior over time (Hayes, 1997).

The intention of registration, notification, and related policies (e.g., residence restriction) is to improve community safety, deter sex crimes, and provide law enforcement with tools for more comprehensive and coordinated approaches to sex crime investigations. As noted, however, the application of these laws to juveniles seems unlikely to achieve these aims. Rather, application of registration and notification laws to children (as occurs in some states, such as South Carolina) and adolescents (as now federally mandated by the Adam Walsh Act) ignores the developmental differences between adult and juvenile offenders, ignores the rehabilitative potential of youth, and does little to address the multiple determinants of juvenile offending in a manner that is responsive to these youths' developmental needs (Letourneau & Miner, 2005).

Juvenile sex offenses cannot and should not be ignored. At the same time, commission of a sex offense should not cause a youth to be permanently labeled a sex offender. Policies that promote youths' concepts of themselves as sex offenders by requiring long-term registration and public notification are likely to interrupt the development of a positive self-identity (Letourneau & Miner, 2005). Many people believe sex offenders deserve whatever happens to them. It is well to remember, however, that many juveniles who sexually offend were victims themselves. Moreover, don't we believe that minors—even minors who commit crimes—can be helped?

Conclusion

Laws targeting sex offenders cycle in and out of popularity and typically are crafted without serious consideration of theory or evidence. Rather, these laws represent lawmakers' responses to citizens' demands that they "do something!" to address the sexual victimization of children. Based as they are on misguided assumptions, it is not surprising that modern-day community protection laws are not supported by the bulk of available research. If the laws were neutral, causing neither harm nor good, they could be left well enough alone. However, both theory and research suggest that community protection laws either cause harm or are likely to do so. For instance, the rapidly growing number of registered sex offenders dilutes the public's ability to identify truly dangerous individuals. The vast resources required for sex offender tracking limits funding available for victim services. The barriers erected by these laws prevent many adult offenders from successfully reintegrating into their communities and place offenders' innocent family members at risk of financial hardship, harassment, and stigmatization.

The effects of modern sex offender laws on juveniles, although less thoroughly studied, are likely to be worse that the effects on adults. Youth labeled sex offenders transition to adulthood with limited opportunities for employment, education, and housing. With the majority of scientific studies *not* finding a relationship between registration and public notification and reduced recidivism, the justification for these laws weakens, and unintended consequences may outweigh the best of intentions.

Although efforts to inform citizens about potential threats to children enjoy considerable public support, a case management team working with known offenders seems to offer greater hope for reduced recidivism, successful community reintegration, and improved safety. With this in mind, we offer the following suggestions for revising existing community protection policies.

Community protection policies are likely to be most effective when used in a discriminating and targeted manner rather than broadly applied to all sex offenders. Broadly inclusive policies imply that all sex offenders pose a severe and equal threat to communities. In particular, offense-based categories such as those prescribed by the Adam Walsh Act are likely to inflate risk in many cases but simultaneously underestimate the risk of offenders who succeeded in pleading guilty to some less serious nonsexual offense. As well, overly inclusive registries exacerbate the stigma and collateral consequences of registration for lower risk offenders. With these facts in mind, registration and notification requirements should be based on formal risk assessment and should be limited to higher risk offenders. In recognition of the fact that even high risk offenders do not always recidivate, offenders subjected to registration and notification requirements should be provided an opportunity to be released from registration after a reasonable period of law-abiding behavior in the community. Residence restrictions should be eliminated. There is no evidence supporting these policies, and they seem uniquely suited to impede the successful reintegration of offenders into their communities or to even meet basic human needs.

In addition to revising existing community protection laws, we believe that substantially increased resources should be devoted to collaborative risk management approaches that evaluate offender risks and needs, reinforce offender strengths, and facilitate support systems (English, Pullen, & Jones 1996, 1998; Ward & Brown, 2004). By working together, clinicians, parole officers, and child protection workers can apply restrictions, safety plans, and interventions relevant to a particular offender's patterns and risk factors.

Public education and awareness campaigns should highlight the likelihood that children are much more likely to be abused by someone they know and trust than by a stranger lurking in the park. Parents should be made aware of the signs and symptoms of CSA and the common types of grooming patterns used by perpetrators who gain access to victims via their positions of trust or authority.

When it comes to juvenile offenders, several changes would improve the current approach (see Letourneau et al., 2009a). First, registration requirements should be based on objective measures of recidivism risk posed by an individual youth rather than on a youth's conviction offense. Only high-risk youth should be subjected to registration. Second, for those high-risk youth subjected to registration, the duration of registration should be limited to reflect the developmental stage of the youth. Opportunities for removal from the registry should be available in the absence of new sex crime convictions. Third, registration information on youth should be accessible only by law enforcement personnel and should not be made public. Protecting juveniles from public notification requirements would reduce the shaming aspect of notification without compromising public safety. Fourth, residency restrictions should never be applied to juveniles. Fifth, other policies triggered by registration (e.g., prohibitions from public school grounds) should not apply to juveniles. Adoption of these recommendations would help to align community protection polices with the aim of rehabilitation.

References

Abel, G. G., Becker, J. V., Cunningham-Rathner, J., Mittelman, M. S., Murphy, M. S., & Rouleau, J. L. (1987). Self-reported crimes of nonincarcerated paraphiliacs. *Journal of Interpersonal Violence, 2,* 3–25.

Adkins, G., Huff, D., & Stageberg, P. (2000). *The Iowa sex offender registry and recidivism.* Des Moines: Iowa Department of Human Rights.

Bumby, K. M., & Maddox, M. C. (1999). Judges' knowledge about sexual offenders, difficulties presiding over sexual offense cases, and opinions on sentencing, treatment, and legislation. *Sexual Abuse: A Journal of Research & Treatment, 11*(4), 305–316.

Burchfield, K. B., & Mingus, W. (2008). Not in my neighborhood: Assessing registered sex offenders' experiences with local social capital and social control. *Criminal Justice and Behavior, 35,* 356–374.

Bureau of Justice Statistics. (2003). *Recidivism of sex offenders released from prison in 1994* (No. NCJ 198281). Washington, DC: U.S. Department of Justice.

Caldwell, M. F. (2002). What we do not know about juvenile sexual reoffense risk. *Child Maltreatment, 7,* 291–302.

Chaffin, M. (2008). Our minds are made up—Don't confuse us with the facts: Commentary on policies concerning children with sexual behavior problems and juvenile sex offenders. *Child Maltreatment, 13,* 110–121.

Colorado Department of Public Safety. (2004). *Report on safety issues raised by living arrangements for and location of sex offenders in the community.* Denver, CO: Sex Offender Management Board.

Duwe, G., & Donnay, W. (2008). The impact of Megan's Law on sex offender recidivism: The Minnesota experience. *Criminology, 46,* 411–446.

Duwe, G., & Donnay, W. (in press). The effects of failure to register on sex offender recidivism. *Criminal Justice and Behavior.*

Duwe, G., Donnay, W., & Tewksbury, R. (2008). Does residential proximity matter? A geographic analysis of sex offense recidivism. *Criminal Justice and Behavior, 35*(4), 484–504.

English, K., Pullen, S., & Jones, L. (1996). *Managing adult sex offenders: A containment approach.* Lexington, KY: American Probation and Parole Association.

English, K., Pullen, S., & Jones, L. (1998). The containment approach: An aggressive strategy for community management of adult sex offenders. *Psychology, Public Policy, and Law, 4*(1/2), 218–235.

Farkas, M. A., & Miller, G. (2007). Reentry and reintegration: Challenges faced by the families of convicted sex offenders. *Federal Sentencing Reporter, 20*(2), 88–92.

Freedman, E. B. (1987). "Uncontrolled desires": The response to the sexual psychopath, 1920–1960. *The Journal of American History, 74,* 83–106.

Hanson, R. K., & Bussiere, M. T. (1998). Predicting relapse: A meta-analysis of sexual offender recidivism studies. *Journal of Consulting and Clinical Psychology, 66*(2), 348–362.

Hanson, R. K., & Morton-Bourgon, K. (2005). The characteristics of persistent sexual offenders: A meta-analysis of recidivism studies. *Journal of Consulting and Clinical Psychology, 73*(6), 1154–1163.

Hanson, R. K., Morton, K. E., & Harris, A. J. R. (2003). Sexual offender recidivism risk: What we know and what we need to know. *Annals of New York Academy of Sciences, 989,* 154–166.

Harris, A. J. R., & Hanson, R. K. (2004). *Sex offender recidivism: A simple question* (No. 2004-03). Ottawa, Ontario, Canada: Public Safety and Emergency Preparedness Canada.

Hayes, H. D. (1997). Using integrated theory to explain the movement into juvenile delinquency. *Deviant Behavior: An Interdisciplinary Journal, 18,* 161–184.

Human Rights Watch. (2007). *No easy answers: Sex offender laws in the United States.* Available at: http://www.hrw.org/reports/2007/us0907/

Jenkins, P. (1998). *Moral panic: Changing concepts of the child molester in modern America.* New Haven, CT: Yale University Press.

Jones, M. (2007, July 22). The case of the juvenile sex offender: Is he a criminal marked forever or a kid whose behavior can be changed? *New York Times Magazine,* 33–39, 56, 58–59.

LaFond, J. Q. (2005). *Preventing sexual violence: How society should cope with sex offenders.* Washington, DC: American Psychological Association.

Laws, D. R., & Marshall, W. L. (2003). A brief history of behavioral and cognitive behavioral approaches to sexual offenders: Part 1. Early developments. *Sexual Abuse: A Journal of Research and Treatment, 15,* 75–92.

Lawson, L., & Savell, S. (2003). Law enforcement perspective on sex offender registration and community notification. *APSAC Advisor, 15*(1), 9–12.

Letourneau, E. J., & Armstrong, K. S. (2008). Recidivism rates for registered and nonregistered juvenile sexual offenders. *Sexual Abuse: A Journal of Research and Treatment, 20,* 393–408.

Letourneau, E. J., Bandyopadhyay, D., Sinha, D., & Armstrong, K. S. (2009a). The effects of sex offender registration policies on juvenile justice decision making. *Sexual Abuse: A Journal of Research and Treatment, 21,* 149–165.

Letourneau, E. J., Bandyopadhyay, D., Sinha, D., & Armstrong, K. S. (2009b). The influence of sex offender registration on juvenile sexual recidivism. *Criminal Justice Policy Review, 20,* 136–153.

Letourneau, E., Levenson, J. S., Bandyopadhyay, D., Armstrong, K., & Sinha, D. (in press). The effects of public registration on judicial decisions. *Criminal Justice Policy Review.*

Letourneau, E. J., Levenson, J. S., Bandyopadhyay, D., Sinha, D., & Armstrong, K. S. (in press). Effects of South Carolina's sex offender registration and notification policy on adult recidivism. *Criminal Justice Policy Review.*

Letourneau, E., & Miner, M. H. (2005). Juvenile sex offenders: A case against the legal and clinical status quo. *Sexual Abuse: A Journal of Research and Treatment, 17*(3), 293–312.

Levenson, J. S. (2008). Collateral consequences of sex offender residence restrictions. *Criminal Justice Studies, 21*(2), 153–166.

Levenson, J. S., Brannon, Y., Fortney, T., & Baker, J. (2007). Public perceptions about sex offenders and community protection policies. *Analyses of Social Issues and Public Policy, 7*(1), 1–25.

Levenson, J. S., & Cotter, L. P. (2005). The effect of Megan's Law on sex offender reintegration. *Journal of Contemporary Criminal Justice, 21*(1), 49–66.

Levenson, J. S., D'Amora, D. A., & Hern, A. (2007). Megan's Law and its impact on community re-entry for sex offenders. *Behavioral Sciences & the Law, 25,* 587–602.

Levenson, J. S., & Hern, A. (2007). Sex offender residence restrictions: Unintended consequences and community re-entry. *Justice Research and Policy, 9*(1), 59–73.

Levenson, J. S., Letourneau, E., Armstrong, K., & Zgoba, K. (in press). Failure to register as a sex offender: Is it associated with recidivism? *Justice Quarterly.*

Levenson, J. S., & Tewksbury, R. (2009). Collateral damage: Family members of registered sex offenders. *American Journal of Criminal Justice, 34*(1), 54–68.

Levenson, J. S., Zgoba, K., & Tewksbury, R. (2007). Sex offender residence restrictions: Sensible crime policy or flawed logic? *Federal Probation, 71*(3), 2–9.

Lieb, R., & Nunlist, C. (2008). *Community notification as viewed by Washington's citizens: A ten-year follow-up* (No. 08-03-1101). Olympia: Washington State Institute for Public Policy.

Lynch, M. (2002). Pedophiles and cyber-predators as contaminating forces: The language of disgust, pollution, and boundary invasions in federal debates on sex offender legislation. *Law and Social Inquiry, 27,* 529–566.

Malesky, A., & Keim, J. (2001). Mental health professionals' perspectives on sex offender registry web sites. *Sexual Abuse: A Journal of Research & Treatment, 13*(1), 53–63.

Matson, S., & Lieb, R. (1996). *Sex offender community notification: A review of laws in 32 states.* Olympia: Washington State Institute for Public Policy.

Mears, D. P., Mancini, C., Gertz, M., & Bratton, J. (2008). Sex crimes, children, and pornography: Public views and public policy. *Crime & Delinquency, 54,* 532–650.

Meloy, M. L., Miller, S. L., & Curtis, K. M. (2008). Making sense out of nonsense: The deconstruction of state-level sex offender residence restrictions. *American Journal of Criminal Justice, 33*(2), 209–222.

Mercado, C. C., Alvarez, S., & Levenson, J. S. (2008). The impact of specialized sex offender legislation on community re-entry. *Sexual Abuse: A Journal of Research & Treatment, 20*(2), 188–205.

Michels, S. (2007, August 16). Should 14-year-olds have to register as sex offenders? *ABC News*. Available at: http://abcnews.go./TheLaw/story?id=3483364&page=1

Ordover, M. (2003). *American eugenics: Race, queer anatomy, and the science of nationalism*. Minneapolis: University of Minnesota Press.

Paternoster, R., & Iovanni, L. (1989). The labeling perspective and delinquency: An elaboration of the theory and assessment of the evidence. *Justice Quarterly, 6,* 359–394.

Prescott, J. J., & Rockoff, J. E. (2008). *Do sex offender registration and notification laws affect criminal behavior?* Available at: http://ssrn.com/abstract=1100663

Reitzel, L. R., & Carbonell, J. L. (2006). The effectiveness of sex offender treatment for juveniles as measured by recidivism: A meta-analysis. *Sexual Abuse: A Journal of Research and Treatment, 18,* 401–421.

Sample, L. L., & Kadleck, C. (2008). Sex offender laws: Legislators' accounts of the need for policy. *Criminal Justice Policy Review, 19*(1), 40–62.

Sandler, J. C., Freeman, N. J., & Socia, K. M. (2008). Does a watched pot boil? A time-series analysis of New York State's sex offender registration and notification law. *Psychology, Public Policy and Law, 14*(4), 284–302.

Schram, D., & Milloy, C. D. (1995). *Community notification: A study of offender characteristics and recidivism*. Olympia, WA: Washington Institute for Public Policy.

Slovenko, R. (2002). *Psychiatry in law: Law in psychiatry*. New York: Brunner-Routledge.

Sutherland, E. H. (1950). The sexual psychopath laws. *Journal of Criminal Law and Criminology, 40*(5), 543–554.

Tewksbury, R. (2005). Collateral consequences of sex offender registration. *Journal of Contemporary Criminal Justice, 21*(1), 67–82.

Tewksbury, R., & Lees, M. (2006). Consequences of sex offender registration: Collateral consequences and community experiences. *Sociological Spectrum, 26*(3), 309–334.

Triplett, R. J., & Jarjoura, G. R. (1994). Deterrence or labeling: The effects of informal sanctions. *Journal of Quantitative Criminology, 10,* 43–64.

Trivits, L. C., & Reppucci, N. D. (2002). Application of Megan's Law to juveniles. *American Psychologist, 57,* 690–704.

U.S. Department of Justice. (2008). *The national guidelines for sex offender registration and notification: Final guidelines* [Electronic version]. Available at: http://www.ojp.usdoj.gov/smart/pdfs/final_sornaguidelines.pdf

Vandervort-Clark, A. (2009, September 30). *Legislating sex offender management: Trends in state legislation 2007-2008*. Paper presented at the 28th Annual ATSA Research and Treatment Conference, Dallas, TX.

Ward, T., & Brown, M. (2004). The good lives model and conceptual issues in offender rehabilitation. *Psychology, Crime & Law, 10*(3), 243–257.

Washington State Institute for Public Policy. (2005). *Sex offender sentencing in Washington State: Failure to register as a sex offender—revised*. Olympia, WA: Author.

Zandbergen, P. A., Levenson, J. S., & Hart, T. (in press). Residential proximity to schools and daycares: An empirical analysis of sex offense recidivism. *Criminal Justice and Behavior*.

Zevitz, R. G. (2006). Sex offender community notification: Its role in recidivism and offender reintegration. *Criminal Justice Studies, 19*(2), 193–208.

Zevitz, R. G., & Farkas, M. A. (2000a). The impact of sex offender community noti-
fication on probation/parole in Wisconsin. *International Journal of Offender Therapy and Comparative Criminology*, 44(1), 8–21.

Zevitz, R. G., & Farkas, M. A. (2000b). *Sex offender community notification: Assessing the impact in Wisconsin.* Washington, DC: U.S. Department of Justice.

Zevitz, R. G., & Farkas, M. A. (2000c). Sex offender community notification: Examining the importance of neighborhood meetings. *Behavioral Sciences and the Law*, 18, 393–408.

Zgoba, K., Witt, P., Dalessandro, M., & Veysey, B. (2009). *Megan's Law: Assessing the practical and monetary efficacy* [Electronic version]. Available at: http://www.ncjrs.gov/pdffiles1/nij/grants/225370.pdf

Appendix A: Web Addresses for Full Text of Federal Statutes Referenced in This Chapter

Adam Walsh Child Protection and Safety Act of 2006

- Original policy: http://www.govtrack.us/congress/billtext.xpd?bill=h109-4472
- Final guidelines: http://www.ojp.usdoj.gov/smart/pdfs/final_sornaguidelines.pdf

Jacob Wetterling Act of 1994

- http://www.law.cornell.edu/uscode/42/usc_sec_42_00014071----000-.html

Megan's Law of 1996

- http://www.personal-injury-info.net/megans-law-text.htm

Pam Lychner Sexual Offender Tracking and Identification Act of 1996

- http://www.sexoffendersusa.com/html/sxo_pam_lychner_act.html

Prosecutorial Remedies and Other Tools to End the Exploitation of Children Today (PROTECT) Act of 2003

- http://www.glin.gov/view.action?glinID=173594

PART V

Investigation and Substantiation of Neglect and Abuse

Part V of the *APSAC Handbook on Child Maltreatment* describes the means used to investigate and prove child abuse and neglect. Part V begins with Chapter 19, which discusses the investigation of maltreatment. Interviewing children about the possibility of abuse is a difficult task requiring skill and patience. Interviewing is described in Chapter 20. The law plays a significant role in responding to child abuse and neglect, and Chapter 21 describes a number of legal issues, including the duty of professionals to report suspected abuse and neglect, the role of confidentiality in professional practice with abused and neglected children, and testifying in court. Chapter 22 brings Part V and the handbook to a close by addressing the complicated issue of proving abuse and neglect in court.

19 Child Abuse and Neglect Investigation

Donna M. Pence

The term *investigation* has a clear meaning: There is a suspicion that a child has been abused or neglected, and information is gathered to confirm or disconfirm the suspicion. Investigation is the process of gathering information to establish facts. The investigative questions are: Did maltreatment occur? If so, who is responsible for the maltreatment? What evidence is there to support the conclusion maltreatment occurred? Does the evidence meet the requirements of the law to prove maltreatment in court? What are the weaknesses in the evidence? What is missing? (see Chapters 21 and 22 for analysis of proving maltreatment). What must be done to protect the child?

Law enforcement personnel are comfortable with the word *investigation*. Social workers sometimes prefer the term *assessment*. In this chapter, the term *investigation* is used regardless of the discipline of the investigator.

Two governmental systems have legal responsibility to investigate reports of child maltreatment: law enforcement and child protective services (CPS). In many cases, law enforcement and CPS coordinate their investigations. In appropriate cases, particularly when criminal maltreatment is *not* suspected, CPS investigates alone. In cases where the alleged perpetrator is not residing with the child or has no access to the child, law enforcement may investigate alone.

Whether an investigation is conducted by CPS or law enforcement, critical steps are involved. First, the investigator determines the pertinent individuals who should be contacted. Second, information is gathered and evaluated for accuracy and completeness. Third, the investigator consults with supervisors and/or other individuals who are knowledgeable in the area under investigation. This consultation provides the investigator an opportunity to articulate the initial hypothesis and preliminary findings, identify additional areas for inquiry, and tap into the knowledge and experience of someone who has experience with similar cases. Fourth, decisions are made as to whether maltreatment occurred. Fifth, if maltreatment occurred, does the maltreatment require intervention? From a CPS perspective, does the child or other children need protection? Is juvenile court intervention needed? From a criminal justice point of view, is there a person or persons who should be arrested and prosecuted for the maltreatment?

Not all professionals are "cut out" to be child maltreatment investigators. The types of abuse and the detailed descriptions of injuries and indignities perpetrated on children can be distressing. Cases involving child sexual abuse (CSA) and child fatalities can be especially troubling for professionals who investigate these cases on a regular basis. Investigators may experience vicarious trauma and/or memories of their own past traumatic experiences. Care should be taken to monitor one's reactions. Support should be sought if distressing emotions linger.

There is a specialized and evolving body of knowledge that is necessary for effective investigation. Knowledge of child development and the dynamics of all forms of child maltreatment are necessary. The competent investigator possesses the ability to plan the investigation and carefully gather, organize, and synthesize large quantities of information. The investigator begins each case with an open mind, accepting all possible conclusions, including the possibility that maltreatment did *not* occur. The investigator is sensitive to cultural issues that can affect perception. The investigator is a painstaking and objective documentarian, keeping careful notes and writing complete, objective, and accurate reports. Finally, the investigator is prepared to participate in legal proceedings, including testifying in court.

A number of agencies around the country conduct investigations without the benefit of a multidisciplinary team (MDT) process. Moreover, some forms of child maltreatment (e.g., nonfatal neglect, psychological abuse, and "minor" physical abuse [PA]) are typically investigated by CPS alone, without involvement from law enforcement or an MDT. Yet, the emerging consensus among experts on investigation is that the "best practice" for most cases is an MDT that uses an investigative protocol that sets out the roles and responsibilities of all involved professionals. Depending on the type of case, the MDT may include professionals from law enforcement, CPS, prosecution, legal counsel for CPS, medicine, mental health, and victim services.

The MDT approach can reduce the level of secondary trauma child victims may experience if they are exposed to repeated and uncoordinated questioning by numerous professionals. As well, the MDT reduces the risk of cases "falling through the cracks." The MDT's wealth of training, experience, and perspectives leads to increased accuracy in decision making, better evidence collection, and stronger accountability for offenders (Faller & Henry, 2000; Pence & Wilson, 1992, 1994; Staller & Faller, 2010).

Pitfalls to Successful Investigation _____

This section describes three potential pitfalls to successful investigation.

Turf Battles and Differing Perspectives

Professionals from social work and law enforcement approach their work from different perspectives and have different legal mandates. The primary mission of law enforcement is crime prevention and, when prevention fails, apprehension of lawbreakers. Social workers focus their energies on a broad range of social problems. Social workers in child protection are concerned with preventing maltreatment, protecting maltreated children and securing their safety, assisting struggling parents, reuniting families, creating new permanent families for children who cannot go home, enhancing children's well-being, and securing their futures.

There is no denying that police officers and social workers sometimes see things differently. Yet, despite differences, these professionals can understand their shared goals and appreciate that neither profession has all the answers. Both professions share the goals of protecting children, determining whether maltreatment occurred, and holding perpetrators accountable. The divergence between police and social workers often revolves around strategies and priorities.

Confirmation Bias

When an investigator first considers a report of possible maltreatment, the investigator draws on experience to construct a working hypothesis about what might have happened. The initial hypothesis gives the investigator a starting place for the investigation. A working hypothesis creates no problems unless the investigator consciously or unconsciously conducts the investigation so as to confirm the hypothesis, ignoring or discounting evidence that points away from the hypothesis. Investigators go astray when they mold the evidence to conform to their biases. Thus, an investigator who approaches each case with the mind-set of "abuse happened, and my job is to prove it," lacks an open mind, is biased, and will find it very difficult to conduct competent investigations. This investigator is likely to overlook or downplay evidence that casts doubt on the investigator's biases.

As stated earlier, the competent investigator approaches every case with an open mind and seeks to determine what, *if anything*, happened. Suppose, for example, that a 3-year-old girl whose parents are divorced comes home from a visit with her father and tells her mother, "Daddy hurt my tee-tee." The mother reports the father for suspected CSA. When the child is interviewed, she says the "hurting" happened in the bathroom at Daddy's house before he put her to bed. What are the possibilities? CSA is one possibility. Reasonable, benign alternatives include the possibility that the child urinated on herself and the father scrubbed too hard while bathing or wiping her. All reasonable nonabuse alternatives must be explored.

Source Monitoring

Source monitoring is the process of determining the source of one's memories. In the context of investigation, source monitoring focuses on how a person sharing information with an investigator came to "know" the information they report. Did the person actually experience what is described? Or is the person's description based not on personal experience but on what the person was told or infers, perhaps during a suggestive interview? Investigators must be careful to evaluate the source of a person's memories.

A 10-year-old boy was being interviewed following his removal from a "religious" compound. Thirteen other boys were also removed. The 10-year-old informed the investigator that he (the boy) gave "massages" to the adult male leader of the compound. The child's disclosure was corroborated when the child demonstrated how he "massaged" the leader. The child drew pictures during the investigative interview, which elaborated on his verbal description. He provided a great deal of specific information in response to open-ended questions. The investigator asked the child whether any of the other boys visited the leader's residence. The child said, "Yes." When the child was asked if he knew whether anything happened between the other boys and the leader, the child confidently stated, "The same as me. They massaged him." When asked how he knew the other boys massaged the leader, the child responded, "I just know." The investigator pressed the child with further questions, and he finally said that none of the other boys had ever talked about their visits to the residence and what happened there. The child had never actually seen any "massaging" activity between the leader and other boys. The child inferred from his own experience what had happened to the other boys. As it turned out, his inference was accurate for some of the other boys, who later disclosed abuse, but not for all of the boys. The investigator must always be concerned about the source of a person's memories and ask questions to determine how the person knows what they describe.

This is also true in interviewing adults. Frequently, adults will provide information with confidence, and the investigator assumes firsthand knowledge and accuracy. Detailed questioning as to the circumstances surrounding the interviewee's source of the information may elicit the information that they are making guesses, deductions, or interpreting what they saw or heard based on their background, experiences, or biases.

Cultural Issues in Investigation

Investigators must be aware of how culture impacts their perceptions of others and of themselves. Awareness of cultural variables allows the investigator to know how to approach the child and family, establish rapport, obtain valid information, arrive at an accurate determination, and formulate meaningful intervention.

The investigator should understand what subjects are considered taboo in the family. Neither children nor adults may be open to discussing issues they consider inappropriate to talk about with persons outside the family or with a person of the opposite gender. How does culture impact adult–child communication style? What are the belief systems in this family? For example, a family may believe abuse was the result of fate—that abuse was destined to happen and there was nothing anyone could do to prevent it. Such a belief is critical when assessing the family's ability to protect the child from further abuse (Fontes, 2005, p. 143).

Does this family have particular beliefs about virginity? If virginity is revered, a sexually abused child might be considered "damaged goods" with reduced prospects for marriage. Consider, for example, the father whose 10-year-old daughter was gang-raped, and who told social workers, "It was her fault. Do not bring her back. She has shamed the whole family."

How is maltreatment viewed in this culture and this family? A 9-year-old girl is left in charge of three younger siblings while the parents work. In the family's culture, a girl of 9 is considered mature enough to contribute to maintaining the household and to supporting the parents' labor. The parents do not see this as neglect.

How do members of this culture view government officials? The investigator should consider any previous contacts the child or the family has had with government agencies in this country or in the country of origin. Keep in mind that in some countries there is no equivalent to CPS. Moreover, in some societies, cooperation with government agencies, including police, is dangerous.

All professionals working in child protection must keep in mind that ethnic minority groups too often suffer discrimination and conflict with the majority culture. These unpleasant truths can influence the reception an investigator receives. Individuals who have negative experiences with government systems may be very sensitive to nuances of language and behavior from investigators. Overcoming years of distrust is not likely to occur in a single interview (Bell, 2007).

Components of the Investigation

Investigation does not occur in a vacuum. Investigation is a process driven by knowledge, experience, policy, procedure, law, and the expectations of agencies and the community. All investigations should receive the same level of thoroughness. Although most investigations do not result in legal proceedings in court, the wise investigator—whether law enforcement or CPS—approaches every case as though it could result in litigation. It is better to have covered all the bases during the investigation than to play catch-up months down the road when the case goes to court and attorneys ask difficult questions about why something was not done earlier or why it was not done according to procedure.

The following steps are standard for most investigations: First, the agency receives and prioritizes the report. Agencies have varying criteria to determine whether a report meets the threshold for investigation and its relative priority. If the threshold is met, agency policy dictates the response time for investigation to begin. Second, in appropriate cases the agency that receives the report cross-reports to other investigative agencies. Cross-reporting may trigger multi-disciplinary investigation. Third, the investigator assigned to the case gathers background information. The more comprehensive the background information, the easier it is to determine the safety of the child, the urgency of a response, and the appropriate roles for CPS workers, police officers, and other professionals. The investigator gathers information on the nature and frequency of the families' past involvement with governmental or community social service agencies, including any history of CPS and/or law enforcement reports.

Interview the Person Who Made the Report

In most cases, the investigator interviews the person who made the report. The investigator gathers information in addition to what was provided to the child abuse hotline or the agency receiving the report. A face-to-face meeting with the reporter helps the investigator assess the credibility and motives of the reporter. Although most people report maltreatment for the "right" reasons, false or questionable accusations occur.

The investigator asks the reporter about the details of what allegedly occurred. How did the reporter become aware of the situation? If the child disclosed to the reporter, exactly what did the child say? Exactly what questions elicited the disclosure? Were there other witnesses to the disclosure? What were the circumstances of the disclosure? (Children's disclosures are hearsay, and hearsay is discussed in Chapter 22.) What does the reporter know about the child and the family? How do they know it? Are there immediate concerns about the child's safety or the safety of others? Did the reporter contact other agencies or individuals? Is this the first time the reporter suspected abuse or made a report about this child? Can the reporter shed any light on the motives or intent of the adult who maltreated the child?

Interview the Child

Many communities have a child advocacy center (CAC) where children are interviewed by highly trained forensic interviewers. Such communities have established protocols about who interviews children. First responders—police officers and emergency response CPS workers—are trained to minimize questioning of the child and to leave formal forensic interviewing to the CAC. In communities without CACs, children may be interviewed repetitively, causing unnecessary stress and increasing the likelihood children will make inconsistent statements that can undermine their credibility as witnesses in court. (For detailed information on interviewing, see Chapter 20.)

Although first responders often keep interviewing to a minimum, these frontline professionals play a key role in the investigation. It is often first responders who are positioned to gather the most important evidence, including spontaneous disclosures from children and incriminating statements from offenders. First responders make sure the child is safe and the situation is stabilized. The responding police officer secures the scene to make sure no one destroys or tampers with evidence. If a CPS worker believes a crime may have occurred, and that evidence is available, the worker promptly informs the police.

Interview Witnesses and Collateral Sources

Interviews of witnesses and collateral sources are a normal part of the investigative process. Investigators prefer multiple types of information from multiple sources. The investigator interviews family members and persons acquainted with the child and the family. Neighbors and other children, including friends of the victim, sometimes provide valuable information. The investigator contacts professionals who know the child and family. The investigator looks for facts concerning the victim, including the victim's behaviors and statements. The investigator uncovers information about the suspect and the abuse itself.

The objectivity and motives of everyone who is interviewed is assessed. This is true whether the information supports or contradicts the child's statements. As noted by Pence and Wilson (1992), "discounting information that contradicts a child's statement during the investigation may result in an unpleasant surprise in court" (p. 99). Accepting *any* information without scrutinizing it carefully is a red flag for confirmation bias.

Potential witnesses should be interviewed separately. If a parent is suspected, interviews of the suspect and the nonoffending parent should occur separately.

Medical personnel frequently have information critical to decision making concerning whether injuries are inflicted or have other, nonabusive causes. They are important in the collection and documentation of medical findings. Utilizing physicians who specialize in child abuse is always preferred.

Interview the Nonoffending Parent

A *nonoffending* parent or caregiver is a primary parent or caretaker for a suspected child maltreatment victim who is believed not to have had overt knowledge of the maltreatment or taken part in the alleged maltreatment.

When abuse is perpetrated by someone outside the family, both parents are generally considered nonoffending. When one parent is the suspect, the other parent is generally nonoffending. In some cases, both parents are suspects.

The nonoffending parent is a vital source of information and should be interviewed as soon as possible. Nonoffending parents can be highly emotional—angry, frightened, and confused. They may have conflicting emotions and loyalties. They may fear for the safety of their child and for their own safety. If the offender is arrested, the nonoffending parent may be penniless. Some nonoffending parents are so distraught they cannot answer questions. Experienced investigators understand how to calm the nonoffending parent while simultaneously gathering evidence. For example, nonoffending parents appreciate knowing the steps of the investigative process and what is likely to happen next.

The investigator asks questions concerning the child, their normal behaviors and activities, medical history, social history, and events going on in the child's life such as family conflict, bullying at school, developmental and educational issues, and involvement with school or community groups and activities. In PA cases, the investigator learns when injuries were inflicted and when the nonoffending parent first noticed injuries, changes in the child's behavior, and shifts in family relationships. When CSA is suspected, it is important to determine whether a young child may have witnessed consensual sexual activity between parents or others and whether the child has been exposed to pornography. With adolescents, the investigator asks about drug and alcohol use as well as "consensual" sexual activity by the child with the child's boyfriend or girlfriend.

If the child disclosed to the nonoffending parent, the investigator documents the child's words and the circumstances of the disclosure. The investigator asks the nonoffending parent about previous abuse of the child or other children. The investigator asks whether the nonoffending parent is him- or herself a victim of violence. It is important to determine whether the nonoffending parent believes the child or whether the parent is aligned with the suspect.

The investigator asks the nonoffending parent about the alleged perpetrator. Sometimes this is the most difficult portion of the interview. For a parent who had no suspicion that their spouse or partner was abusing their child, the shock of discovery can be overwhelming. Nevertheless, questions must be asked about possible physical evidence such as clothing that might contain DNA, explicit photographs, instruments used to inflict pattern injuries, and more. The investigator asks about the suspect's behavior, habits, relationship with the child and other children, relationship with the nonoffending parent, role and responsibilities in caretaking, prior interaction with law enforcement or CPS, and anything the suspect may have told the nonoffending parent that could be relevant.

The investigator endeavors to find out how the suspect gained or maintained access to the child in the absence of the nonoffending parent or other witnesses. The suspect's level of control over the home and the family goes a long way toward explaining how a nonoffending parent might have been kept in the dark or "failed" to protect the child from abuse.

Child abuse often coexists with intimate partner violence (IPV), substance abuse, and, occasionally, parental mental illness. These factors may influence the child or the nonoffending parent's willingness to speak up about the abuse. It is important to discover the suspect's beliefs about what is "correct" or "normal" parenting, discipline, or personal boundaries. The suspect's history, as provided by the nonoffending parent, can provide clues to other victims or criminal behavior, which may lead to additional evidence. The investigator discusses with the nonoffending parent the possibility that more than one person may have had access to the child at crucial times.

Search and Seizure of Evidence by Law Enforcement

A search by law enforcement of the place where a child was abused may uncover evidence to support the allegation. Sometimes the search reveals evidence of other crimes. The search can document details of the "crime scene" that corroborate the child's description of the maltreatment. Thus, the search may document clothing, decor, and items in the room that dovetail with the child's description. Consider the case of a 16-year-old girl from an intact family who alleged that her father sexually abused her for 3 years. The father flatly denied the abuse, and at first the victim's mother sided with the father. During an interview, the victim described the sexual activity, including a washcloth her father laid on her abdomen to catch his semen as he masturbated. The victim also described a sexual self-help book for women that her father had shown her on several occasions. Finally, the victim described a vibrator that her father used on her. A search of the home located a washcloth fitting the description the girl provided, as well as the self-help book and the vibrator, both of which were hidden in the parents' bedroom. The victim's mother identified the book and vibrator as hers and stated that her daughter should not have known about them. This evidence, which supported her daughter's disclosure, convinced the mother her child was telling the truth.

Documentation of the scene should occur as soon as possible. Photographic documentation is preferred. The greater the delay in documenting the scene, the greater the likelihood the scene will be altered either intentionally or through the course of normal activity. In one case, an infant with a swollen and painful leg was brought by her parents to the emergency room. The mother stated that the father was removing the baby from an infant seat when the child's foot got caught in the leg opening. The father "tugged" on the child because he did not realize the child was stuck. Afterward, the infant cried whenever the leg was touched so the parents brought the child to the hospital. The baby had a fractured femur. The injury did not make sense in light of the parents' explanation, and a report of possible abuse was filed. A law enforcement investigator responded immediately and asked to see the infant seat. The investigator measured the size of the leg openings, and it became apparent that the opening was much larger than the baby's foot. The investigator confronted the father with this fact, and the father confessed that he had lost his temper while changing the baby's diaper and had yanked and twisted the child's leg. The father immediately realized he had injured the infant and invented the story of the infant seat to deflect responsibility. If the officer had not responded quickly, the infant seat might have been destroyed or hidden.

A CPS worker's role in the collection of physical evidence of abuse or neglect is generally limited to noting the existence of possible items of evidence and documenting the observations. As previously mentioned, the worker should notify law enforcement about physical evidence.

Interview the Suspect

The interview of a suspect requires as much thought as the interview of a child or a nonoffending parent. Interviewing suspects is an art practiced by experienced police officers. In cases where law enforcement is not part of the investigation, child protection workers interview the suspect. Child protection workers need prior training on interviewing persons suspected of maltreatment.

Focusing here on law enforcement interviews, it is often best to interview the suspect after evidence has been collected and witnesses interviewed. The more the investigator knows, the more effective the interview. Typically the investigator chooses a location where the conversation can take place with an illusion of privacy. The investigator introduces herself or himself and describes the investigator's role. The experienced interviewer typically begins by building rapport. There are occasions when an authoritarian, forceful style is necessary. In most cases, however, the investigator makes more progress with a businesslike but cordial approach. The investigator tells the suspect, "What we are looking for is simply the truth" or "There are two sides to every situation, and I'd like to give you this opportunity to share your side with me."

It is important for the suspect to have the opportunity to explain his or her perception of the situation. The investigator needs the suspect's own version (however distorted) of their relationship with the child; their normal interactions with the child; parenting activities; and events before, during, and after the alleged maltreatment. The suspect is given an opportunity to provide an alternative explanation for the child's injuries or statements. Quite often an abusive adult's explanation is inconsistent with the child's injuries and actually serves to incriminate the adult. In some cases, the suspect is provided a doll and asked to reenact what happened. Such reenactments often point toward guilt rather than away from it.

If the suspect denies the abuse or neglect, the investigator decides whether to confront the suspect with previously gathered evidence, including the child's disclosure statement. It is common for offenders to blame abuse on others, including the child. The offender may claim that the abuse was caused by stress at work, by the child's provocative behavior, or by alcohol. The suspect's excuses are often so flimsy and unconvincing that they point clearly to guilt.

At the conclusion of the interview, it is often wise to comment on the positive aspects of cooperating with authorities. Unless the suspect is going to be arrested at that time, the interviewer allows the suspect to leave the room on a positive note. The interviewer thanks the suspect for taking the time to talk, and the interviewer lets the suspect know they will be in touch if they need further information.

Case Synthesis and Decision Making

After the information gathering and evidence collection portion of the investigation is complete, the investigator "puts the puzzle together." An investigator with a law enforcement perspective asks whether maltreatment occurred and, if so, whether the evidence is sufficient to support an arrest and criminal charges. An investigator from CPS is equally interested in whether maltreatment occurred but, in addition, must make critical decisions about child safety and family functioning.

Conclusion

Investigating child abuse and neglect is challenging and important work. Done well, investigation protects children and holds offenders accountable.

References

Bell, C. C. (2007, June 11). *Evidence-based practice and cultural sensitivity.* Paper presented at the Evidence-based Practice and Cultural Competence in Child Welfare Invitational Forum, conference presentation. St. Paul, MN. Available at: http://www.cehd.umn.edu/ssw/G-S/m3edia/CarlBellTranscript.pdf

Faller, K. C., & Henry, J. (2000). Child sexual abuse: A case study community collaboration. *Child Abuse and Neglect, 24,* 1215–1225.

Faller, K. C., & Palusci, V. J. (2007). Children's advocacy centers: Do they lead to positive case outcomes? *Child Abuse and Neglect, 31,* 1021–1029.

Fontes, L. A. (2005). *Child abuse and culture: Working with diverse families.* New York: Guilford.

Jones, L. M., Cross, T. P., Walsh, W. A., & Simone, M. (2007). Do children's advocacy centers improve families' experiences of child sexual abuse investigations? *Child Abuse and Neglect, 31,* 1069–1085.

Kuehnle, K., & Connell, M. (2009). *The evaluation of child sexual abuse allegations: A guide to assessment and testimony.* Hoboken, NJ: John Wiley.

Newman, B. S., Dannenfelser, P. L., & Pendleton, D. (2005). Child abuse investigations: Reasons for using child advocacy centers and suggestions for improvement. *Child and Adolescent Social Work Journal, 22,* 165–181.

Pence, D., & Wilson, C. (1992). *The role of law enforcement in the response to child abuse and neglect.* Washington, DC: National Center on Child Abuse and Neglect.

Pence, D., & Wilson, C. (1994). *Team investigation of child sexual abuse: The uneasy alliance.* Thousand Oaks, CA: Sage.

Staller, K. M., & Fuller, K. (Eds.). (2010). *Seeking justice in child sexual abuse: Shifting burdens and sharing responsibilities.* New York: Columbia University Press.

Walsh, W. A., Lippert, T., Cross, T. P., Maurice, D. M., & Davison, K. S. (2008). How long to prosecute child sexual abuse for a community using a children's advocacy center and two comparison communities? *Child Maltreatment, 13,* 3–13.

20

Interviewing Children

Karen J. Saywitz,
Thomas D. Lyon, and
Gail S. Goodman

Interviewing children about child maltreatment is both challenging and rewarding. It is a little like dancing with a partner who has not yet mastered the steps and is unfamiliar with the music. In the beginning, there are awkward moments trying to make sense of the intentions and expectations of the other. A tentative interaction pattern is established with each turn of the conversation. The interview dance has a structure, yet it is a fluid process. It demands a certain level of flexibility to pursue specific information from children without stepping on their toes. It can be problematic if the interviewer is viewed as leading the child's movements too much. Success depends on the interviewer's ability to design a dance that elicits accurate and relevant information without tainting children's reports. When it works, it is a rewarding waltz.

Thankfully, interviewers are not left out on the dance floor alone to choreograph each interview anew. The past 25 years of empirical research have produced a sufficient evidence base to establish consensus on basic child forensic interview strategies—that is, on the basic steps of the dance. In this chapter, we highlight principles based on the best available science, understanding that such principles keep changing as new evidence accumulates and that there are gaps in the knowledge base where guidance is limited. Interviewers, like dancers and professionals in any field, need to stay abreast of new steps and developments.

First, we describe the database from which these steps derive. Then we discuss features of the interview about which there is sufficient empirical evidence and consensus to begin to build guidelines. These include the interview structure, setting, interviewer demeanor, children's reluctance and suggestibility, rapport development, narrative practice, introducing the topic of abuse, avoiding concepts that confuse children, instructions to children, phrasing of questions, evidence-based strategies for eliciting details, and multiple interviews.

Throughout, we demonstrate how to use these evidence-based strategies to interview children about possible maltreatment.

The Evidence Base

We draw our conclusions from a number of sources. These include studies of child witnesses in the field, laboratory analogue studies of children's recall of staged and fictitious events, guidelines developed by professional organizations such as the American Academy of Child and Adolescent Psychiatry (AACAP), the American Academy of Pediatrics (AAP), the American Professional Society on the Abuse of Children (APSAC), the American Psychological Association (APA), and protocols that have been empirically tested, the most well researched being the National Institute of Child Health and Human Development (NICHD) Investigative Interview Protocol (Lamb, Hershkowitz, Orbach, & Esplin, 2008) and the Cognitive Interview (CI) (Fisher & Geiselman, 1992; Saywitz, Geiselman, & Bornstein, 1992). Other protocols used in the field, such as Finding Words (Holmes & Vieth, 2003), also utilize some of the principles derived from the empirical literature, although there is limited research examining the behavior of interviewers trained in these approaches (Fairley, 2005; Lyon, Lamb, & Myers, 2009). Next, we present a brief overview of the scientific methods used to develop the database, and we describe some key findings.

Recent studies using field methodology provide important information about the eyewitness memory of victims of child sexual abuse (CSA). For example, in several field studies, researchers investigated the accuracy of child victims' memory when perpetrators recorded (e.g., videotaped) their sexual assaults, inadvertently providing researchers with objective documentation of the incidents against which to evaluate the children's later reports (see Paz-Alonso, Ogle, & Goodman, 2009, for review). In one such field study, Leander, Christianson, and Granhag (2007) examined eight children aged 3 to 10 years who were sexually abused by a single individual (a stranger). The perpetrator took photographs of the sex crimes he committed. He would abduct a child, take the child to a building or other location, and sexually assault the victim (e.g., attempted penetration). In addition to the photographs, the perpetrator confessed. The children provided accounts of the abuse to police. The children's disclosures occurred from 1 day to 5 years after the assaults. The children's accounts were compared to the photographs and the perpetrator's confession. The children provided accurate information describing events that preceded the sexual assaults, indicating they remembered the incident. Five children, however, failed to provide any sexual information. Only two of the eight children gave detailed reports of the sexual acts. Despite limited completeness, what children did report was quite accurate. Results from this and other field studies strongly suggest that children are able to provide accurate testimony about sexual abuse. Child victims' feelings of fear, shame, embarrassment, and/or guilt have been suggested as explanations for the finding that children omitted a considerably greater amount of sexual compared to neutral information (e.g., Leander et al., 2007).

In addition to field studies, which are relatively few in number, valuable information about forensic interviewing can be gleaned from analogue research in the laboratory. Analogue studies permit researchers to examine issues that cannot be addressed in field studies. To date, hundreds of analogue studies have been conducted. Overall, they show that memory is multiply determined, depending, for example, on characteristics of the child and the settings in which memory retrieval occurs (for review see Bottoms, Nadjowski, & Goodman, 2009).

With analogue research, memory for sexual abuse is not examined. Instead, memory for mundane experiences (e.g., playing games with a researcher), fictitious experiences (events that were never experienced by the child), or naturally occurring stressful experiences (e.g., medical procedures) is investigated to determine the accuracy of children's reports and how best to interview children. One beauty of such research is that children's suggestibility and tendency to make false reports can be examined with scientific precision. For example, in a well-known study (dubbed the "Mr. Science" study) by Poole and Lindsay (2001), 3- to 8-year-olds viewed and participated in science demonstrations. Later, their parents read a story that described events not actually experienced during the science show. In other words, the parents provided the children with fictitious information about what had happened during the science events. The children were then questioned by the researchers in follow-up interviews. Regardless of age, a number of children described the fictitious events, even in response to the researchers' open-ended prompts. Accuracy declined further when children were asked direct questions, especially for the younger children. The older children retracted many of their false reports after receiving instructions that helped them monitor the source of the misinformation. Younger children, however, did not benefit from the instruction. Such research provides vital information about children's suggestibility and proneness to false reports. Analogue studies are also quite useful in validating interview tactics that bolster the accuracy of children's reports.

Eisen, Goodman, Qin, Davis, and Crayton (2007) tested the memory of more than 300 3- to 16-year-old children who had experienced abuse or neglect. For health reasons, the children underwent an anogenital examination and a venipuncture, and the researchers examined the children's memory for these routine medical procedures. Clear developmental differences were observed. Children 6 years old and older were more accurate about details of the medical procedures than younger children. Children who suffered sexual and/or physical abuse (PA) were more accurate than children who experienced neglect.

Research like that previously described has been combined with knowledge gained from thousands of interviews conducted by police, social workers, medical professionals, and clinicians to develop child forensic interview guidelines. Research has evaluated the effectiveness of scientifically based interview protocols. An example is research on the CI (Fisher, Brennan, & McCauley, 2002), which can be used with adults and older children to obtain extensive and accurate reports (see Koehnken, Milne, Memon, & Bull, 1999, for a meta-analysis). Based on basic principles of memory, cognition, and communication, the CI requires that interviewees (1) reconstruct mentally the personal and environmental context at the time of the crucial event; (2) report everything, including partial information even though it may be considered unimportant; and (3) recount the event in a variety of orders and from a variety of perspectives. Interviewees are given specific directions to facilitate the recall of details, conversations, and names. Research on the CI reveals advantages with adults (e.g., Fisher & Geiselman, 1992) and (in its modified form) with children (Hayes & Delamothe, 1997; Holliday, 2003; Larsson, Granhag, & Spjut, 2003; McCauley & Fisher, 1995; Milne & Bull, 2003).

The most extensively studied child forensic interview protocol is the NICHD Protocol developed by Michael Lamb and his colleagues (see Lamb et al., 2008). Using this protocol, field researchers have examined the quality of children's memory reports in relation to such factors as age, rapport building, open-ended questioning, use of drawings, and numerous other interview-relevant factors. Based on thousands of NICHD Protocol interviews conducted in Israel and other countries, Lamb and his colleagues have worked to pinpoint the interviewing techniques that produce the best quality of information from children.

Evidence-Based Interview Strategies

Interview Structure

Interviews differ from ordinary conversations in that they usually have a definite purpose, a question–answer format, and a well-defined goal. Interview structures vary along a continuum from unstructured (where interviewers follow the child's lead), to highly structured (where exact wording of questions is scripted). In between are semistructured formats where interviewers follow questioning guidelines and cover predetermined topics, selecting from a tool kit of strategies. Structured protocols help prevent defective interviewing, and standardization increases adherence to evidence-based practices. Semistructured approaches afford more flexibility but also more room for error. Studies suggest that in the forensic context, totally unstructured interviews are ill advised. Even when interviewers are well trained, it is difficult for them to abide by best practice recommendations without following a structured or semistructured format.

Most protocols use a phased approach. Typically, this includes an initial preparatory phase (e.g., introductions, rapport development, promise to tell the truth, narrative practice, instructions), a second phase for information gathering (e.g., invitation for free recall "What happened?" followed by more focused questions to gather details), and finally a third phase of closure (e.g., recomposure if the child is upset, time for the child to ask questions). Phases vary in level of empirical support, with a great deal more research conducted on question types than on rapport development or closure.

Setting

Most guidelines recommend an age-appropriate, private, child-friendly setting with minimal distraction. Studies confirm that distractions require children to divide their attention, often with adverse affects on their ability to focus on the interview (e.g., Tun & Wingfield, 1993). Private interviews are recommended to eliminate the possibility of contamination from parents or others who may have a vested interest in the outcome. Even without overt pressure, children may be reticent in the presence of another person. Studies show that children are reluctant to accuse adults of wrongdoing in the adults' presence (Flin, Stevenson, & Davies, 1989; Peters, 1991, Experiment 4; but see Talwar, Lee, Bala, & Lindsay, 2004), or to accuse a peer of wrongdoing in the presence of an innocent peer (Harari & McDavid, 1969). Moreover, it should not be assumed that a parent's presence will decrease stress. Whether a child will experience a particular person's presence as supportive depends on the nature of the relationship between the child, the person offering support, and the kind of support provided (e.g., Goodman, Quas, Batterman-Faunce, Riddlesberger, & Kuhn, 1994, 1997).

Of course, there are cases in which children protest, refuse, and cannot be reassured (e.g., Goodman et al., 1998). Interviewers will want to consider taking precautions when they decide support persons are necessary during the interview, such as instructing the support person to sit behind the child and to redirect the child back to the interviewer if the child has questions. Many protocols recommend asking the adult to leave once the child is comfortable but before substantive questioning begins.

Interviewer Demeanor

There is scientific evidence suggesting that interviewers are more successful when they provide a supportive yet nonsuggestive atmosphere. Social support in the form of eye contact, relaxed body posture, smiling, and warm intonation has been shown to help children be more resistant to misleading questions and to improve interview performance without contaminating their accounts of nonabusive events (see Bottoms, Quas, & Davis, 2007 for review).

Obviously, it is critical that supportiveness not become selective reinforcement of responses that fit the interviewer's a priori beliefs. Interviewer bias has been linked with distortions of children's accounts, underscoring the need for objectivity and neutrality (Ceci & Bruck, 2006). In experimental studies, when interviewers are provided with biasing information about false events prior to the interview—and are allowed to script their own questions—they tend to ask repeated yes/no questions about the suggested events (Gilstrap, 2004), increasing error (White, Leichtman, & Ceci, 1997; but see Goodman, Sharma, Thomas, & Considine, 1995). If combined with selective reinforcement of desired responses, these questions can dramatically increase young children's errors (Garven, Wood, & Malpass, 2000; Garven, Wood, Malpass, & Shaw, 1998). Interviewers should strive to remain objective and neutral regarding the veracity of the allegations. Interviewers should explore alternative hypotheses and keep biases in check.

Children's Reluctance

Studies are clear that interviewers should refrain from pressuring reluctant children. Assuming the child is interviewed relatively soon after an initial disclosure, interviewers should use nonleading means of eliciting information. The goal is to provide an opportunity for disclosure of abuse without creating a false report.

Many abused children are ambivalent about disclosing and are subject to pressures to recant if they have previously disclosed (see Chapter 14). A child might have freely disclosed to a parent or a trusted adult but not be comfortable talking to a stranger. Moreover, very young children may need more guidance not just to overcome reluctance but to overcome their verbal and memory limitations. Dealing with nakedness and genital touch is potentially embarrassing (Saywitz, Goodman, Nicholas, & Moan, 1991)—even more so if the child recognizes that the touching was wrong.

Some sexual abusers warn victims not to tell (Smith & Elstein, 1993). Even without warnings, the secrecy surrounding abuse teaches the child not to tell. Sexual abusers may threaten violence toward the child, the child's mother, pets, or others, reinforcing reluctance to disclose (Sas & Cunningham, 1995). Perpetrators may seduce their victim, making the child reluctant to tell due to a sense of guilt. If family members have positive feelings about the abuser (e.g., uncle, mother's boyfriend), the child may be reluctant to get the adult in trouble (Sauzier, 1989).

Another reason to avoid pressuring reluctant children is that pressure may taint truly abused children's reports, undermine their credibility, or create avoidable inconsistencies in their reports. Even if the interviewer's leading questions do not in fact adversely influence the child's report (e.g., Quas et al., 2007), the presence of the questions may subject the interview to attack in court. See Chapter 22 for discussion of the courtroom strategy of attacking forensic interviews.

Studies do not suggest that it is necessary to avoid any questions that could be characterized as suggestive. Thus, interviewers are not limited to a simple, "Is there something you want to tell me?" and nothing more. Interviewers strive for a middle ground between suggestive questions and completely nonsuggestive open-ended invitations to speak. Finding the right balance requires skill, training, and experience.

Children's Suggestibility

Interviewers do not know ahead of time if a child has in fact been abused. Interviewers do know, however, that pressure on a nonabused child may lead to a false allegation (Ceci & Bruck, 2006). Researchers have demonstrated that a number of coercive interviewing techniques can produce false reports, particularly in preschool children. These techniques include selective reinforcement (rewarding desired responses and punishing undesired responses; Garven et al., 1998, 2000), stereotype induction (telling the child that the suspect is a bad person; Leichtman & Ceci, 1995), the use of authority (telling the child what the parent has said or what the interviewer believes; Ceci, Loftus, Leichtman, & Bruck, 1994), and the use and repetition of suggestive questions (Cassel, Roebers, & Bjorklund, 1996; but see Goodman & Quas, 2008; Quas et al., 2007).

Although individual differences in suggestibility proneness exist at every age, overall young children are particularly likely to fall sway to suggestive pressures. During the preschool years, children develop an understanding of the means by which knowledge is acquired and the possibility that beliefs could be false. They become better able to distinguish between events they have personally experienced and events about which they have been told, or heard, or imagined—a process known as source monitoring. Researchers have identified links between age trends in suggestibility and the acquisition of source monitoring abilities (Robinson & Whitcombe, 2003; Welch-Ross, 2000). Young children are inclined to assume that adults are knowledgeable, which increases their vulnerability to suggestion. Preschool children are more suggestible when questioned by an adult than when questioned by a child (Ceci, Ross, & Toglia, 1987), and susceptibility to the status of adults as questioners diminishes with age (Kwock & Winer, 1986). These studies highlight the importance of avoiding leading techniques and taking precautions to avoid suggestion.

Rapport Development

It is not uncommon for a young child to experience trepidation about leaving familiar caretakers to talk privately with an unfamiliar adult for an unknown purpose. Most guidelines mention that interviewers need to spend time establishing rapport. Yet, there is little scientific data available on the best methods for developing rapport with children. At least one study suggests maltreated children have more difficulty establishing rapport with professionals than nonmaltreated children with mental health problems (Eltz, Shirk, & Sarlin, 1995). Yet, little is known about how children decide whom to trust. Social support provided by the interviewer, as described earlier, should facilitate rapport. Studies of children's limited knowledge of the legal system suggest introductions and developmentally sensitive explanations that demystify the legal context might reduce children's uncertainty about interviewer intentions and improve their productivity (e.g., Nathanson & Saywitz, 2003).

Early verbal interactions during rapport building can be used to demonstrate that the child will be expected to provide as much detail as possible in his or her own words with minimal prompting. To this end, interviewers can rely on open-ended questions that call for multiword responses as opposed to questions that can be answered yes or no. Time spent in narrative practice, as described in the next section, may also serve the goal of furthering rapport.

Narrative Practice

Numerous studies have demonstrated the benefits of practice exercises prior to the substantive portion of the interview to create a template for later questioning patterns. Practice often consists of children answering open-ended questions about innocuous events during the introductory phase of the interview. Studies of the NICHD, CI, and Narrative Elaboration (NE) Protocols demonstrate that practice answering questions yields greater amounts of information in field studies and greater accuracy of recall in laboratory studies (e.g., Saywitz et al., 1992; Sternberg et al., 1997). In the field, Sternberg et al. (1997) found that when interviewers used open-ended prompts rather than option-posing questions in the beginning phase of the interview, children provided longer and richer responses to the first substantive question about abuse and longer responses to free recall questions throughout the interview. In the laboratory, NE and CIs involving similar procedures elicited more information that was accurate than did standard interviews. The optimal length of practice appears to vary by child, but 5 minutes is often sufficient. Observational research cautions against unduly lengthy narrative practice (Davies, Westcott, & Horan, 2000; Hershkowitz, 2009), and experimental work with 10 to 15 minutes of narrative practice has produced mixed results, possibly due to fatigue (Holliday & Albon, 2004; Roberts, Lamb, & Sternberg, 2004).

Various procedures for conducting narrative practice have been studied. In the NICHD Protocol, children are asked about a recent event (such as a birthday celebration) and prompted with "tell me more about the [detail provided by child]" and "what happened next" questions. Similarly, in the NE Protocol, interviewers ask school-age children to narrate a recent event: "Tell me what you did this morning from the time you got up until the time you got here" and follow up by asking, "Tell me more" or "What happened next?" (Saywitz, Snyder, & Nathanson, 1999). In the NE Protocol, preschoolers are asked to describe the interview room or to describe a storybook picture presented by the interviewer ("Tell me what's happening in this picture") to minimize the demands on memory while modeling questioning format (Dorado & Saywitz, 2001). In the CI modified for children, interviewers say, "Tell me what happens when you brush your teeth" (McCauley & Fisher, 1995). In all of these studies, interviewers taught children what to expect by modeling open-ended prompts ("What happened next? Tell me more. . . .") to help children practice elaborating on their descriptions in their own words without the use of leading or specific questions.

Introducing Topic of Interest

Children should be given the opportunity to provide a spontaneous report in response to open-ended questions. If children do not spontaneously mention abuse, introducing the topic is a sensitive and pivotal moment in the interview. Further research is needed to find ways that are nonleading and productive. However, research on the NICHD Protocol provides guidance for introducing the topic of abuse in an investigative interview when children have previously disclosed abuse to someone else. Interviewers open the conversation by saying, "Tell me why you came to talk to me." Researchers have found that most children in their studies who already disclosed abuse to someone else understood the purpose of the investigative interview and were ready to disclose (Sternberg, Lamb, Orbach, Esplin, & Mitchell, 2001). If the child does not mention abuse, the interviewer says, "It is important for me to understand why you came to talk to me." If the child remains unresponsive, the interviewer works through a series of increasingly focused questions, which are based on the child's previous disclosure (or the reason abuse is suspected) but avoids directly suggesting that a particular suspect has performed a specific act. For example, "I heard that you saw a policeman (or social worker, doctor, etc.) last week (or yesterday). Tell me what you talked about." Or, "I told you, my job is to talk to kids about things that might have happened to them. It's very important that I understand why you are here. Tell me why you think your mom (or your dad, etc.) brought you here today."

At the point that a child alleges abuse, most guidelines and protocols recommend that the interviewer say to the child the following: "Tell me everything that happened." The interviewer encourages the child to provide a narrative of the abuse, using questions such as "Tell me more about [action or detail mentioned by the child]" and "What happened next?" The CI instructs children to "tell everything that happened, even the little things that you might not think are very important." This permits the interviewer, rather than the child, to judge forensic relevance. The NE Protocol uses nonleading prompts to help children elaborate on participants, setting, actions, conversations, and emotions.

Research findings support beginning with very general prompts, but when these do not elicit a disclosure, protocols recommend that alternative strategies for engaging in a conversation about points of potential forensic relevance be conducted in the least leading fashion possible. However, there is little research testing the independent contribution of various strategies. Experts tend to recommend more indirect approaches. Faller (1996), for example, recommends asking about different people in the child's life and what the child likes and does not like about each individual. If the interviewer asks about a number of people other than the perpetrator, questions about the perpetrator would not be unduly leading.

The Finding Words approach uses anatomical drawings or dolls as an introductory tool (Holmes & Vieth, 2003; Vieth, 2006). Although dolls and drawings can be used nonsuggestively, evidence suggests that actual practice is often problematic (e.g., Everson & Boat, 2002; Thierry, Lamb, Orbach, & Pipe, 2005). Several researchers have raised concerns about the risks associated with anatomical drawings and dolls, particularly when used in interviews with preschool children (Bruck, Ceci, Francoeur, & Renick, 1995; Steward et al., 1996). Brown, Pipe, Lewis, Lamb, and Orbach (2007) found that encouraging children to provide verbal descriptions of abuse was superior to pointing to body parts on a drawing. Further research is needed to examine how interviewers trained by Finding Words use interviewing aids in the field and the impact on children's reports (Lyon et al., 2009).

Phrasing Questions in Language Children Understand

Numerous studies demonstrate the value of phrasing questions in grammar and vocabulary children can understand. Unfortunately, questions asked of child witnesses are routinely beyond their level of comprehension. Communication breakdowns occur when young children are asked long, overloaded questions using complex grammar and sophisticated vocabulary (Brennan & Brennan, 1988; Carter, Bottoms, & Levine, 1996; Perry, McAuliff, Tan, & Claycomb, 1995; Saywitz, Jaenicke, & Camparo, 1990). Interviewers are encouraged to simplify their language, for example, by clarifying terms in advance, asking children to tell the interviewer what they think a word means ("Tell me what allegation means") rather than asking whether children know what a word means ("Do you know what an allegation is?") because children are likely to answer "yes" even when thinking about a different word (e.g., "alligator"). To simplify language, use short sentences and simple grammar, devoid of embedded clauses and double negatives. Replace pronouns ("he" and "she") and deictics ("that" or "there") with proper names (e.g., replace "he" with "Steve") and specific locations (e.g., replace "there" with "in the garage"; see Saywitz & Camparo, 1998; Walker, 1999).

Avoiding Concepts That Are Difficult for Children to Understand

Interviewers should avoid questions with cognitive demands that exceed a child's knowledge and reasoning skills. For example, number and time are concepts common in investigative interviewing that develop gradually and are difficult for young children to understand and use accurately in verbal conversation.

Number

It can be problematic to ask a young child how many times an event occurred. The child is likely to pick an arbitrary number (a million; 38). As well, the number may change from interview to interview. A moment's reflection highlights what a difficult task it is to estimate how many times something

occurred. Either one imagines each event and mentally counts, or one estimates the number (Bradburn, 2000).

It is easy to misjudge a child's ability to estimate. Children can often recite
numbers before they know how to count and can count objects before they
can count events in memory (Wynn, 1990, 1992). What constitutes an event
is also open to question. Does the child enumerate abuse by reflecting on particular acts or on times when a series of acts occurred?

To approach questions regarding number, many experts recommend an
approach incorporated into the NICHD Protocol: After the child has first
disclosed abuse and described an episode, the interviewer asks, "Did this
happen one time or more than one time?" If the child says, "More than one
time," the interviewer then inquires about the last time the abuse occurred,
the first time the abuse occurred, and the time the child remembers the
most. The interviewer follows up by asking if there are any other times the
child remembers.

Time

Similar to children's understanding of numbers, children's understanding of time develops gradually. Children learn how to tell time on a clock
before they can estimate what time an event occurred. Unless one looks at
a watch or calendar during an event, subsequent recall of the time requires
inferential skills (e.g., "It was shortly before New Year's, so it probably
was December"; Friedman, 1993). Many children fail to make such inferences. The interviewer can often elicit information from the child about
contemporaneous events, which enables the interviewer to estimate the
time. For example, a child may state where other people were at the time
of the abuse (e.g., "My mother was at church"), or what the child was
doing (e.g., asleep at night, taking a nap after school). Legally, exact
dates and times are not necessary, particularly if the abuser had frequent
access to the child and the abuse occurred on multiple occasions over a
period of time (Myers, 2005).

Some temporal terms can be confusing for young children. "Yesterday"
and "today" are difficult for young children, in part because of their shifting
meaning (today is tomorrow's yesterday). For the young child, yesterday
often refers to anything in the past, and tomorrow refers to anything in the
future (Harner, 1982). Obviously, the interviewer should not assume that a
young child understands weeks and months or that the child can estimate
time using these intervals.

When questioning children about a sequence of events, interviewers
need to be cautious in using the terms *next*, *before*, and *after* because
younger children often describe events in the order in which they occurred
regardless of whether one asks about what happened before or after
another event (Carni & French, 1984). The safest course is to ask, "What
happened next?"

Instructions to Improve Children's Performance

Young children are accustomed to speaking to authoritative adults (teachers, parents) who already know the answers to many of their questions. Given a strongly worded question, children may agree not because of what they believe but because of their desire to please the interviewer and because of their reluctance to appear ignorant. It may be possible to reduce misconceptions children have about interviews through instructions. Researchers have examined instructions that increase children's willingness to say, "I don't know" or "I don't understand," reduce children's tendencies to defer to authoritative interviewers, and increase children's willingness to disclose negative experiences.

Giving permission to say "I don't know." Children are often reluctant to say "I don't know," particularly when asked yes/no questions (e.g., Poole & Lindsay, 2001) or specific Wh- questions (e.g., Memon & Vartoukian, 1996). A number of studies have found that instructing children that "I don't know" answers are acceptable reduces children's suggestibility to misleading questions (Cordon, Goodman, & Saetermoe, 2005; Endres, Poggenpohl, & Erben, 1999; Gee, Gregory, & Pipe, 1999; Saywitz & Moan-Hardie, 1994; Walker, Lunning, & Eilts, 1996; Warren, Hulse-Trotter, & Tubbs, 1991). Several studies include helping the child practice saying, "I don't know" by asking a few unanswerable questions, such as "If I ask you a question and you don't know the answer, then just say 'I don't know.' So, if I ask you the question 'What is my dog's name?', what do you say? OK, because you don't know. But what if I ask you 'Do you have a dog?' OK, because you do know."

Interviewers are cautioned to provide the child examples because a simple "It's OK to say I don't know" is likely to be ineffective (Geddie, Fradin, & Beer, 2000; Memon & Vartoukian, 1996; Moston, 1987). Furthermore, interviewers should reinforce giving an answer when one *does* know, so children don't overuse the "I don't know" response (Gee et al., 1999; Saywitz & Moan-Hardie, 1994).

Giving permission to say "I don't understand." Children rarely ask for clarification of questions they do not understand (Carter et al., 1996; Perry et al., 1995; Saywitz et al., 1999). Children are less adept than adults at monitoring their comprehension. Even if they recognize incomprehension, they are reluctant to let the interviewer know. Telling children that it is permissible to say they do not understand and that doing so will lead the interviewer to reword the question reduces the likelihood that grade school children will attempt to answer incomprehensible questions (Saywitz et al., 1999). Practice on a few incomprehensible questions improves school age children's performance still further (Saywitz et al., 1999) and even has some positive effect with preschool children (Peters & Nunez, 1998).

Different protocols use different variations on this instruction. In experimental studies, Saywitz and colleagues (1999) told children,

I am going to ask you some questions. Some of the questions will be easy to understand, and some questions will be hard to understand. When you hear a question you do not understand, tell me that you do not understand the question. Say, "I don't understand," "I don't know what you mean," or "I don't get it." (p. 61)

In addition, very young children were told to "put out your hand like a police officer stopping traffic to stop the question" (Saywitz et al., p. 61). In the NICHD Protocol, children are told,

If I ask you a question and you don't know what I mean or what I am saying, you can say, "I don't know what you mean." I will ask it in a different way. So, if I ask you, "What is your gender?" what do you say? Good, because "gender" is a big word. So, then I would ask, "Are you a boy or a girl?" OK, because boy or girl is an easier way to say gender. (Lamb et al., 2008, p. 86)

Warning children about misleading questions. Two studies have found positive effects from warning children that questions might mislead them and then giving permission for them to correct the interviewer (Saywitz & Moan-Hardie, 1994; Warren et al., 1991). Saywitz and Moan-Hardie (1994) included the following instruction as part of their intervention to reduce suggestibility:

Sometimes I may put my guess into a question or I may make a mistake. You should tell me if I am wrong. I was not there, and I could not know what happened. It is important for you to tell me if I make a mistake. I want you to correct me.

Telling children you don't know what happened and cannot help them answer questions. Children often assume that interviewers are knowledgeable, even though the interviewer did not witness the event (Saywitz & Nathanson, 1993). Children are more suggestible when they believe the interviewer knows what occurred (Ceci et al., 1987; Kwock & Winer, 1986; Lampinen & Smith, 1995; Toglia, Ross, Ceci, & Hembrooke, 1992). Informing children that one doesn't know has been shown to reduce suggestibility to misleading questions (Mulder & Vrij, 1996). Saywitz and Moan-Hardie (1994) found positive results with the following instruction: "I was not there. I could not know what happened. I will not be able to help you answer the questions." Similarly, Mulder and Vrij (1996) informed children, "I don't know what's happened to you. I won't be able to tell you the answers to my questions."

Eliciting a promise to tell the truth. Although children are unlikely to understand adult versions of the oath, by grade school children recognize the significance of promises, and still younger children understand that when one says one will do something, one is likely to do it (Lyon, 2000). Research with both maltreated and nonmaltreated children has found that eliciting a promise to tell the truth increases children's honesty (Lyon & Dorado, 2008; Lyon, Malloy, Quas, & Talwar, 2008; Talwar, Lee, Bala, & Lindsay, 2002, 2004). Lyon and his colleagues (2008) found positive effects from asking the child, "Do you promise that you will tell me the truth? Are you going to tell me any lies?"

In sum, interview instructions are easy to administer and improve the performance of many children. However, instructions are not a panacea. Highly leading questions will still elicit high rates of error (e.g., Mulder & Vrij, 1996), and children will underutilize the options provided them (e.g., to express incomprehension; Peters & Nunez, 1999; Saywitz et al., 1999). Although some research has found that preschool children benefit from instructions (Cordon et al., 2005; Peters & Nunez, 1998), younger children are likely to benefit less than older children because of their difficulties in understanding why and how one knows or doesn't know (Welch-Ross, 2000) and in detecting their incomprehension (Cosgrove & Patterson, 1977). Given the limitations of instructions, the optimal solution is to ask simple nonleading questions. The best way to improve children's performance is to improve the questions we ask.

Eliciting Additional Details Without Leading Questions

Interviewers should avoid suggestive techniques that mislead, introduce bias, reinforce interviewer expectations, apply peer pressure, stereotype the accused as a bad person, and invite children to pretend or speculate (Ceci & Bruck, 2006). Most interviewers know that they should not ask children leading questions, but few agree about what a leading question is. Data support the notion that questions lie along a continuum of impact. On one end of the continuum (the more leading end), the interviewer supplies details, and on the other end of the continuum (the more nonleading end) the child supplies details. Consider the distinction between free recall and recognition (recognition is sometimes called "option posing"). With free recall, the interviewer simply asks, "What happened?" and the child supplies the details. With recognition, the interviewer provides choices, and the child picks the correct choice. Hence, the interviewer supplies details that the child merely affirms or denies. Recognition questions tend to begin with "did," "was," and "were." Recognition questions often limit the child's response to a single word.

It is easy to understand why questions that move toward interviewer-supplied details increase the dangers of suggestibility. If the interviewer supplies details, many of the details are likely to be incorrect—the product of the interviewer's presuppositions or biases. And if children are susceptible to suggestion because they wish to please the interviewer or because they doubt their own memory, interviewer-supplied details may taint the child's report and possibly the child's memory for the event (Ceci & Bruck, 2006). Moreover, because children are inclined to guess, it is easier for them to guess in response to questions with interviewer-supplied details (Waterman, Blades, & Spencer, 2001).

Question Types

Elaboration prompts. Fortunately, there are questions that lie between free recall and recognition. To elicit additional detail in the child's own words, studies suggest interviewers refer to details mentioned by the child previously and follow up with a request for elaboration like "Tell me more about . . . " (e.g., "You said he put some cream on his finger. Tell me more about that"; Dorado & Saywitz, 2001; Lamb et al., 2008). In order to encourage the child to continue to provide narrative information, interviewers should make liberal use of "What happened next?" questions (Lamb et al., 2008).

Wh- questions. Wh- questions typically begin with "What," "Where," "When," "Who," "Why," or "How." Wh- questions can be either general or specific. As Wh- questions become more specific, the interviewer supplies more of the details. Compare "What was the man wearing?" (more general) with "What color were the man's shoes?" (more specific). In comparison to free recall prompts like "What happened?" specific Wh- questions focus on particular aspects of the to-be-remembered event. This is helpful to the child who has difficulty self-generating details. However, as Wh- questions become more specific, two dangers increase. One danger is that the interviewer's beliefs about the event will affect the child's report (e.g., the interviewer assumes the man was wearing shoes). Another danger is that a child who is inclined to guess will come up with a plausible response—one that is incorporated into the child's report.

Yet, exceedingly general questions can become so vague or abstract that they sail over children's heads. A helpful guide to balance the general and the specific is to try to use concepts that are concrete and easy to visualize, rather than speaking in generalities, without introducing leading information not already mentioned by the child. One can follow up on answers to general questions to be certain the interviewer accurately understands the child's answer with prompts that ask children to explain their answer in their own words (e.g., "Tell me more about. . . ." or "What makes you think so?").

When compared to the forced-choice questions described next, Wh- questions are often the least leading form of follow-up question to elicit elaboration. For example, when questioning children about sexual abuse, it is tempting to ask, "Were your clothes on or off?" because this detail helps clarify that the touching was sexual and affects the seriousness of the abuse. However, because the question is forced choice (recognition), children will often simply choose one of the options. In contrast, the interviewer who asks, "Where were your clothes?" will discover that children often describe their clothes such that they were neither on nor off (e.g., "around my knees"). If the child had simply chosen one of the options ("on" or "off"), the interviewer would have formed an inaccurate picture of the event. Similarly, interviewers will often ask, "Did he hit you?" which can be less leadingly asked in Wh- form as "What did he do with his hands?"

Exploring event details with Wh- questions. The NE Protocol provides guidance on using Wh- questions to explore five basic characteristics of incidents: (1) participants (e.g., "Who was there?" "What did the person [or name of person identified by child] look like?"); (2) location (e.g., "Where were you?" "What did the place look like?"); (3) specific actions (e.g., "What did the person [or name of person previously identified by child] do?"); (4) conversations (e.g., "What did the person [or name of person identified by child] say or tell you?"); and (5) emotional states of participants (e.g., "How did you feel when. . . ." "What did the person do or say to make you think he was [insert name of emotion suggested by child] . . . ?"). These categories are derived from a rich body of research on children's event knowledge and narrative skills (Nelson, 1986; Stein & Glenn, 1978).

Another element of elaboration is to prompt children to justify their answers with "What makes you think so?" Or "What made him do that?" (Saywitz & Snyder, 1996; Saywitz, Snyder, & Lamphear, 1996). For example, when a child said someone was mad, a request from the interviewer for clarification elicited from the child the behaviors the child observed that led to the impression of anger, "He yelled at my sister to get out when she walked in on us."

A Wh- question is not only a way to avoid the dangers of suggestibility but it is also a means of eliciting details that an interviewer would not elicit were he or she limited to recognition questions. If an interviewer asks a series of yes/no questions, the interviewer is likely to receive a series of yes/no answers, and the information obtained will only be as good as the interviewer's ability to imagine the details. If the interviewer asks Wh- questions that require multiword responses, children will often mention idiosyncratic details of the abuse that lend their reports credibility. Moreover, the likelihood of logically inconsistent responses is reduced if questions are Wh- rather than yes/no.

Yes/no questions. Recognition questions can vary in how leading they are. The simplest sort of recognition question is a yes/no question. Like Wh- questions, yes/no questions can be either general ("Did he say anything?") or specific ("Did he tell you to keep a secret?"). Yes/no questions are not highly leading but can be problematic if a child has a response-bias (a tendency to answer questions yes or no) or is reluctant to answer. The research is mixed on whether young children do indeed exhibit a "yes" bias to yes/no questions (cf. Greenhoot, Ornstein, Gordon, & Baker-Ward, 1999 [yes-bias not detected] with Peterson, Dowden, & Tobin, 1999 [yes-bias detected]). However, there is good evidence that young children are reluctant to answer "I don't know" to yes/no questions (Poole & Lindsay, 2001; Walker et al., 1996). Moreover, in laboratory studies, children's responses to yes/no questions are less accurate than their responses to open-ended questions (Baker-Ward, Gordon, Ornstein, Larus, & Clubb, 1993).

Yes/no questions can be made more leading by turning them into negative term questions (e.g., the negative form of "Did he tell you to keep a secret?" is "Didn't he tell you to keep a secret?"; Whipple, 1915) or tag questions (e.g., "He told you to keep a secret, didn't he?"; Greenstock & Pipe, 1996). Negative term questions and tag questions are particularly likely to affect the responses of preschool children, who are more vulnerable to interviewer pressure. Fortunately, these two question types are not difficult to avoid.

Most guidelines recommend that when yes/no questions are necessary, they are followed by open-ended prompts to elaborate. For example, if an interviewer asks a specific yes/no or forced-choice question, the interviewer follows up with an open-ended question to minimize the suggestiveness of the specific question (Sternberg, Lamb, Esplin, Orbach, & Hershkowitz, 2002). If a child answers, "Yes" to "Did he say what would happen if you told anyone?" the interviewer follows up with "What did he say?"

Forced choice/multiple choice questions. Another kind of recognition question that is potentially problematic is the forced-choice question in which the interviewer gives the child a series of choices from which the child chooses the "correct" response (e.g., "Was his shirt red or blue?"). Like yes/no questions, forced-choice questions assist the child in generating details but may also supply erroneous information. Because of their reluctance to answer "I don't know" to recognition questions, young children may feel compelled to choose one of the options even if they don't know the correct answer, and even if neither answer is correct. When children choose randomly, they tend to choose the last option (Walker et al., 1996).

It is often difficult to interpret the meaning of a child's response to a forced choice question. Interviewers often make the mistake of rephrasing Wh- questions as yes/no questions, by prefacing the Wh- question with "Can you tell me. . . ?" or "Do you know. . . ?" Although one could argue that prefacing Wh- questions in this way reduces the likelihood that a child will guess a detail (because she can instead answer "no"), "No" responses are ambiguous. For example, if one asks "Do you know if he said anything?" it is unclear if a "No" response means "No, I don't know," or "No, he didn't say anything."

In summary, eliciting additional detail requires attention to the phrasing of questions in the least leading format. Avoid complex grammar, sophisticated vocabulary, and difficult concepts. Questions that allow children to describe event details in their own words, such as Wh- questions about observable information that require multi-word responses followed by open-ended prompts to explore basic event categories, are preferable to questions that elicit one-word answers such as yes/no, tag, negative insertion, and multiple choice questions.

Multiple Interviews

Excessive interviewing of young children using suggestive techniques can be detrimental to the accuracy of their reports (e.g., Ceci et al., 1994; but see Quas et al., 2007). However, repeated nonleading interviewing tends to uncover new details (Hershkowitz & Terner, 2007; see reviews in LaRooy, Katz, Malloy, & Lamb, in press, and LaRooy, Lamb, & Pipe, 2009). Researchers have not found a detrimental effect of repeating open-ended

Wh- questions (who, what, where, when, how). Repetition of yes/no questions, however, can be problematic, especially those with embedded information that came from sources outside the child (see review in Lyon, 2002).

Conclusion

Much has been learned from scientific research on forensic interviewing of children. Although challenges remain, research provides important insights into choreographing child forensic interviewing into a successful "dance"—one that is informed by science. Guidelines and protocols help teach both the interviewer and the child the appropriate steps—steps that promote accurate and complete reports. In this way, there is less stepping on each others' toes, and the interviewer is less likely to be accused of inappropriately leading the child's performance. Research helps the interviewer design a dance that optimizes the chances of eliciting accurate and credible information. This dance benefits all.

References

Baker-Ward, L., Gordon, B. N., Ornstein, P. A., Larus, D. M., & Clubb, P. A. (1993). Young children's long-term retention of a pediatric examination. *Child Development*, *64*, 1519–1533.

Bottoms, B. L., Nadjowski, C. J., & Goodman, G. S. (Eds.). (2009). *Children as victims, witnesses, and offenders*. New York: Guilford Press.

Bottoms, B. L., Quas, J. A., & Davis, S. L. (2007). The influence of interviewer-provided social support on children's suggestibility, memory, and disclosures. In M.-E. Pipe, M. E., Lamb, Y. Orbach, & A-C. Cederborg (Eds.), *Child sexual abuse: Disclosure, delay, and denial* (pp. 135–158). Mahwah, NJ: Lawrence Erlbaum.

Bradburn, N. M. (2000). Temporal representation and event dating. In A. A. Stone et al. (Eds.), *The science of self-report: Implications for research and practice* (pp. 49–61). Mahwah, NJ: Lawrence Erlbaum.

Brennan, M., & Brennan, R. (1988). *Strange language: Child victims under cross examination*. Riverina, Australia: Charles Stuart University.

Brown, D. A., Pipe, M.-E., Lewis, C., Lamb, M. E., & Orbach, Y. (2007). Supportive or suggestive: Do human figure drawings help 5- to 7-year-old children to report touch? *Journal of Consulting and Clinical Psychology*, *75*, 33–42.

Bruck, M., Ceci, S. J., Francoeur, E., & Renick, A. (1995). Anatomically detailed dolls do not facilitate preschoolers' reports of a pediatric examination involving genital touching. *Journal of Experimental Psychology: Applied*, *1*, 95–109.

Carni, E., & French, L. A. (1984). The acquisition of before and after reconsidered: What develops? *Journal of Experimental Child Psychology*, *37*, 394–403.

Carter, C., Bottoms, B. L., & Levine, M. (1996). Linguistic and socio-emotional influences on the accuracy of children's reports. *Law and Human Behavior*, *20*, 335–358.

Cassel, W. S., Roebers, C. E. M., & Bjorklund, D. F. (1996). Developmental patterns of eyewitness responses to repeated and increasingly suggested questions. *Journal of Experimental Child Psychology*, *61*, 116–133.

Ceci, S. J., & Bruck, M. (2006). Children's suggestibility: Characteristics and mechanisms. *Advances in Child Development & Behavior, 34,* 247–281.

Ceci, S. J., Loftus, E. F., Leichtman, M. D., & Bruck, M. (1994). The possible role of source misattributions in the creation of false beliefs among preschoolers. *International Journal of Clinical and Experimental Hypnosis, 42,* 304–320.

Ceci, S. J., Ross, D. F., & Toglia, M. P. (1987). Age differences in suggestibility: Narrowing the uncertainties. In S. J. Ceci, M. P. Toglia, & D. F. Ross (Eds.), *Children's eyewitness memory.* New York: Springer.

Cordon, I. M., Goodman, G. S., & Saetermoe, C. L. (2005). Facilitating children's accurate responses: Conversational rules and interview style. *Applied Cognitive Psychology, 19,* 249–266.

Cosgrove, J. M., & Patterson, C. J. (1977). Plans and the development of listener skills. *Developmental Psychology, 13,* 557–564.

Davies, G. M., Westcott, H. L., & Horan, N. (2000). The impact of questioning style on the content of investigative interviews with suspected child sexual abuse victims. *Psychology, Crime and Law, 6,* 81–97.

Dorado, J., & Saywitz, K. (2001). Interviewing preschoolers from low and middle income communities: A test of the narrative elaboration recall improvement technique. *Journal of Clinical Child Psychology, 30,* 566–578.

Eisen, M. L., Goodman, G. S., Qin, J. J., Davis, S., & Crayton, J. (2007). Maltreated children's memory: Accuracy, suggestibility, and psychopathology. *Developmental Psychology, 43,* 1275–1294.

Eltz, M. J., Shirk, S. R., & Sarlin, N. (1995). Alliance formation and treatment outcome among maltreated adolescents. *Child Abuse and Neglect, 19,* 419–431.

Endres, J., Poggenpohl, C., & Erben, C. (1999). Repetitions, warnings, and video: Cognitive and motivational components in preschool children's suggestibility. *Legal & Criminological Psychology, 4,* 129–146.

Everson, M. D., & Boat, B. W. (2002). The utility of anatomical dolls and drawing in child forensic interviews. In M. L. Eisen, J. A. Quas, & G. S. Goodman (Eds.), *Memory and suggestibility in the forensic interview* (pp. 383–408). Mahwah, NJ: Lawrence Erlbaum.

Fairley, C. L. (2005). *Semi-structured versus non-structured interview protocols in the assessment of child abuse: Does it really matter?* Unpublished doctoral dissertation, University of South Carolina.

Faller, K. C. (1996). *Evaluating children suspected of having been sexually abused.* Thousand Oaks, CA: Sage.

Fisher, R., Brennan, K. H., & McCauley, M. (2002). The Cognitive Interview method to enhance eyewitness recall. In M. L. Eisen, J. A. Quas, & G. S. Goodman (Eds.), *Memory and suggestibility in the forensic interview* (pp. 265–286). Mahwah, NJ: Lawrence Erlbaum.

Fisher, R. P., & Geiselman, R. E. (1992). *Memory-enhancing techniques for investigative interviewing: The cognitive interview.* Springfield, IL: Charles C Thomas.

Flin, R., Stevenson, Y., & Davies, G. M. (1989). Children's knowledge of court proceedings. *British Journal of Psychology, 80,* 285–297.

Friedman, W. J. (1993). Memory of the time of past events. *Psychological Bulletin, 113,* 44–66.

Garven, S., Wood, J. M., & Malpass, R. S. (2000). Allegations of wrongdoing: The effects of reinforcement on children's mundane and fantastic claims. *Journal of Applied Psychology, 85,* 38–49.

Garven, S., Wood, J. M., Malpass, R. S., & Shaw, J. S. (1998). More than suggestion: The effect of interviewing techniques from the McMartin Preschool case. *Journal of Applied Psychology, 83,* 347–359.

Geddie, L., Fradin, S., & Beer, J. (2000). Child characteristics which impact accuracy of recall and suggestibility in preschoolers: Is age the best predictor? *Child Abuse and Neglect, 24,* 223–235.

Gee, S., Gregory, M., & Pipe, M.-E. (1999). "What colour is your pet dinosaur?" The impact of preinterview training and question type on children's answers. *Legal & Criminological Psychology, 4,* 111–128.

Gilstrap, L. L. (2004). A missing link in suggestibility research: The behavior of field interviewers in unstructured interviews with young children. *Journal of Experimental Psychology: Applied, 10,* 13–24.

Goodman, G. S., & Quas, J. (2008). Repeated interviews in children's memory. *New Directions in Psychological Science, 17*(6), 386–389.

Goodman, G., Quas, J., Batterman-Faunce, J., Riddlesberger, M., & Kuhn, J. (1994). Predictors of accurate and inaccurate memories of traumatic events experienced in childhood. In K. Pezdek & W. Banks (Eds.), *False memory debate* (pp. 3–28). San Diego, CA: Academic Press.

Goodman, G., Quas, J., Batterman-Faunce, J., Riddlesberger, M., & Kuhn, J. (1997). Children's reactions to and memory for a stressful event: Influences of age, anatomical dolls, knowledge, and parental attachment. *Applied Developmental Science, 1,* 54–75.

Goodman, G. S., Sharma, A., Thomas, S. F., & Considine, M. G. (1995). Mother knows best: Effects of relationship status and interviewer bias on children's memory. *Journal of Experimental Child Psychology, 60,* 195–228.

Goodman, G. S., Tobey, A., Batterman-Faunce, J., Orcutt, H., Thomas, S., Shapiro, C., et al. (1998). Face-to-face confrontation: Effects of closed-circuit technology on children's eyewitness testimony and jurors' decisions. *Law and Human Behavior, 22,* 165–203.

Greenhoot, A. F., Ornstein, P. A., Gordon, B. N., & Baker-Ward, L. (1999). Acting out the details of a pediatric check-up: The impact of interview condition and behavioral style on children's memory reports. *Child Development, 70,* 363–380.

Greenstock, G., & Pipe, M.-E. (1996). Interviewing children about past events: The influence of peer support and misleading questions. *Child Abuse and Neglect, 20,* 69–80.

Harari, H., & McDavid, J. W. (1969). Situational influence on moral justice: A study of 'finking.' *Journal of Personality and Social Psychology, 11,* 240–244.

Harner, L. (1982). Talking about the past and the future. In W. J. Friedman (Ed.), *The developmental psychology of time* (pp. 141–169). New York: Academic Press.

Hayes, B. K., & Delamothe, K. (1997). Cognitive interviewing procedures and suggestibility in children's recall. *Journal of Applied Psychology, 82,* 562–577.

Hershkowitz, I. (2009). Socioemotional factors in child sexual abuse investigations. *Child Maltreatment, 14,* 172–181.

Hershkowitz, I., & Terner, A. (2007). The effects of repeated interviewing on children's forensic statements of sexual abuse. *Applied Cognitive Psychology, 21,* 1131–1143.

Holliday, R. E. (2003). The effect of a prior cognitive interview on children's acceptance of misinformation. *Applied Cognitive Psychology, 17,* 443–457.

Holliday, R. E., & Albon, A. J. (2004). Minimising misinformation effects in young children with cognitive interview mnemonics. *Applied Cognitive Psychology*, *18*, 263–281.

Holmes, L. S., & Vieth, V. (2003). Finding Words/Half a Nation: The forensic interview training program of CornerHouse and APRI's National Center for Prosecution of Child Abuse. *The APSAC Advisor*, *15*, 4–8.

Koehnken, G., Milne, R., Memon, A., & Bull, R. (1999). The cognitive interview: A meta-analysis. *Psychology, Crime & Law*, *5*, 3–27.

Kwock, M. S., & Winer, G. A. (1986). Overcoming leading questions: Effects of psychosocial task variables. *Journal of Educational Psychology*, *78*, 289–293.

Lamb, M. E., Hershkowitz, I., Orbach, Y., & Esplin, P. W. (2008). *Tell me what happened: Structured investigative interviews of child victims and witnesses*. London: Wiley.

Lampinen, J. M., & Smith, V. L. (1995). The incredible (and sometimes incredulous) child witness: Child eyewitnesses' sensitivity to source credibility cues. *Journal of Applied Psychology*, *80*, 621–627.

LaRooy, D., Katz, C., Malloy, L. C., & Lamb, M. E. (in press). Do we need to rethink guidance on repeated interviews? *Psychology, Public Policy, and Law*.

LaRooy, D., Lamb, M. E., & Pipe, M.-E. (2009). Repeated interviewing: A critical evaluation of the risks and potential benefits. In K. Kuehnle & M. Connell (Eds.), *The evaluation of child sexual abuse allegations* (pp. 327–361). New York: Wiley.

Larsson, A. S., Granhag, P. A., & Spjut, E. (2003). Children's recall and the Cognitive Interview: Do the positive effects hold over time? *Applied Cognitive Psychology*, *17*, 203–214.

Leander, L., Christianson, S. Å., & Granhag, P. A. (2007). A sexual abuse case study: Children's memories and reports. *Psychiatry, Psychology, and Law*, *14*(1), 120–129.

Leichtman, M. D., & Ceci, S. J. (1995). The effects of stereotypes and suggestions on preschoolers' reports. *Developmental Psychology*, *31*, 568–578.

Lyon, T. D. (2000). Child witnesses and the oath: Empirical evidence. *Southern California Law Review*, *73*, 1017–1074.

Lyon, T. D. (2002). Applying suggestibility research to the real world: The case of repeated questions. *Law & Contemporary Problems*, *65*, 97–126.

Lyon, T. D., & Dorado, J. (2008). Truth induction in young maltreated children: The effects of oath-taking and reassurance on true and false disclosures. *Child Abuse and Neglect*, *32*, 738–748.

Lyon, T. D., Lamb, M. E., & Myers, J. E. B. (2009). Author's response to Vieth (2008). *Child Abuse and Neglect*, *33*, 71–74.

Lyon, T. D., Malloy, L. C., Quas, J. A., & Talwar, V. (2008). Coaching, truth induction, and young maltreated children's false allegations and false denials. *Child Development*, *79*, 914–929.

McCauley, M. R., & Fisher, R. P. (1995). Facilitating children's eyewitness recall with the revised cognitive interview. *Journal of Applied Psychology*, *80*, 510–516.

Memon, A., & Vartoukian, R. (1996). The effects of repeated questioning on young children's eyewitness testimony. *British Journal of Psychology*, *87*, 403–415.

Milne, R., & Bull, R. (2003). Does the cognitive interview help children to resist the effects of suggestive questioning? *Legal & Criminological Psychology*, *8*, 21–38.

Moston, S. (1987). The suggestibility of children in interview studies. *First Language, 7*, 67–78.

Mulder, M., & Vrij, A. (1996). Explaining conversation rules to children: An intervention study to facilitate children's accurate responses. *Child Abuse and Neglect, 10*, 623–631.

Myers, J. E. B. (2005). *Myers on evidence in child, domestic, and elder abuse cases.* New York: Aspen.

Nathanson, R., & Saywitz, K. J. (2003). The effects of the courtroom context on children's memory and anxiety. *The Journal of Psychiatry and Law, 31*, 67–98.

Nelson, K. (1986). *Event knowledge: Structure and function in development.* Hillsdale, NJ: Lawrence Erlbaum.

Paz-Alonso, K., Ogle, C. M., & Goodman, G. S. (2009). Children's memory and testimony in "scientific case studies" of child sexual abuse: A review. In B. Cooper, M. Ternes, & D. Griesel (Eds.), *Issues in investigative interviewing, eyewitness memory, and credibility assessment: Festschrift for John Yuille.* New York: Springer.

Perry, N., McAuliff, B., Tan, P., & Claycomb, C. (1995). When lawyers serve children: Is justice served? *Law and Human Behavior, 19*, 609–629.

Peters, D. P. (1991). The influence of stress and arousal on the child witness. In J. Doris (Ed.), *The suggestibility of children's recollections* (pp. 60–76). Washington, DC: American Psychological Association.

Peters, W. W., & Nunez, N. (1998, March). *Lawyerese and comprehension monitoring: Teaching child witnesses to recognize linguistic confusion.* Paper presented at the American Psychology-Law Society Meeting, Redondo Beach, CA.

Peterson, C., Dowden, C., & Tobin, J. (1999). Interviewing preschoolers: Comparisons of yes/no and wh- questions. *Law and Human Behavior, 23*, 539–555.

Poole, D. A., & Lindsay, D. S. (2001). Children's eyewitness reports after exposure to misinformation from parents. *Journal of Experimental Psychology: Applied, 7*, 27–50.

Quas, J. A., Malloy, L. C., Melinder, A., Goodman, G. S., D'Mello, M., & Schaaf, J. (2007). Developmental differences in the effects of repeated interviews and interviewer bias on young children's event memory and false reports. *Developmental Psychology, 43*(4), 823–837.

Roberts, K. P., Lamb, M. E., & Sternberg, K. J. (2004). The effects of rapport-building style on children's reports of a staged event. *Applied Cognitive Psychology, 18*, 189–202.

Robinson, E. J., & Whitcombe, E. C. (2003). Children's suggestibility in relation to their understanding about sources of knowledge. *Child Development, 74*, 48–62.

Sas, L. D., & Cunningham, A. H. (1995). *Tipping the balance to tell the secret: The public discovery of child sexual abuse.* London, Ontario, Canada: London Family Court Clinic.

Sauzier, M. (1989). Disclosure of child sexual abuse: For better or for worse. *Psychiatric Clinics of North America, 12*, 455–469.

Saywitz, K. J., & Camparo, L. (1998). Interviewing child witnesses: A developmental perspective. *Child Abuse and Neglect, 22*, 825–843.

Saywitz, K. J., Geiselman, R. E., & Bornstein, G. K. (1992). Effects of cognitive interviewing and practice on children's recall performance. *Journal of Applied Psychology, 77*, 744–756.

Saywitz, K. J., Goodman, G. S., Nicholas, E., & Moan, S. (1991). Children's memories of a physical examination involving genital touch: Implications for reports of child sexual abuse. *Journal of Consulting and Clinical Psychology, 59*, 682–691.

Saywitz, K. J., Jaenicke, C., & Camparo, L. (1990). Children's knowledge of legal terminology. *Law and Human Behavior*, 14(6), 523–535.

Saywitz, K. J., & Moan-Hardie, S. (1994). Reducing the potential for distortion of childhood memories. *Consciousness and Cognition*, 3, 257–293.

Saywitz, K. J., & Nathanson, R. (1993). Children's testimony and their perceptions of stress in and out of the courtroom. *Child Abuse and Neglect*, 17, 613–622.

Saywitz, K. J., & Snyder, L. (1996). Narrative elaboration: Test of a new procedure for interviewing children. *Journal of Consulting and Clinical Psychology*, 64, 1347–1357.

Saywitz, K. J., Snyder, L., & Lamphear, V. (1996). Helping children tell what happened: Follow up study of the narrative elaboration procedure. *Child Maltreatment*, 1, 200–212.

Saywitz, K. J., Snyder, L., & Nathanson, R. (1999). Facilitating the communicative competence of the child witness. *Applied Developmental Science*, 3, 58–68.

Smith, B. E., & Elstein, S. G. (1993). *The prosecution of child sexual and physical abuse cases: Final report.* Washington, DC: National Center on Child Abuse and Neglect.

Stein, N., & Glenn, C. (1978). *The role of temporal organization in story comprehension* (Tech. Rep. No. 71). Urbana: University of Illinois, Center for Study of Reading.

Sternberg, K. J., Lamb, M. E., Esplin, P. W., Orbach, Y., & Hershkowitz, I. (2002). Using a structured protocol to improve the quality of investigative interviews. In M. L. Eisen, J. A. Quas, & G. S. Goodman (Eds.), *Memory and suggestibility in the forensic interview* (pp. 409–436). Mahwah, NJ: Lawrence Erlbaum.

Sternberg, K. J., Lamb, M. E., Hershkowitz, I., Yudilevitch, L., Orbach, Y., Esplin, P. W., et al. (1997). Effects of introductory style on children's abilities to describe experiences of sexual abuse. *Child Abuse and Neglect*, 21, 1133–1146.

Sternberg, K. J., Lamb, M. E., Orbach, Y., Esplin, P. W., & Mitchell, S. (2001). Use of a structured investigative protocol enhances young children's responses to free-recall prompts in the course of forensic interviews. *Journal of Applied Psychology*, 86, 997–1005.

Steward, M. S., Steward, D. S., Farquhar, L., Myers, J. E. B., Reinhart, M., Welker, J., et al. (1996). Interviewing young children about body touch and handling. *Monographs of the Society for Research in Child Development*, 61, 4–5 (Serial No. 248).

Talwar, V., Lee, K., Bala, N., & Lindsay, R. C. L. (2002). Children's conceptual knowledge of lying and its relation to their actual behaviors: Implications for court competence examinations. *Law and Human Behavior*, 26, 395–415.

Talwar, V., Lee, K., Bala, N., & Lindsay, R. C. L. (2004). Children's lie-telling to conceal a parent's transgression: Legal implications. *Law and Human Behavior*, 28, 411–435.

Thierry, K. L., Lamb, M. E., Orbach, Y., & Pipe, M.-E. (2005). Developmental differences in the function and use of anatomical dolls during interviews with alleged sexual abuse victims. *Journal of Consulting and Clinical Psychology*, 73, 1134–1135.

Toglia, M. P., Ross, D. F., Ceci, S. J., & Hembrooke, H. (1992). The suggestibility of memory: A social-psychological and cognitive interpretation. In M. L. Howe, C. J. Brainerd, & V. F. Reyna (Eds.), *Development of long term retention* (pp. 217–241). New York: Springer.

Tun, P., & Wingfield, A. (1993). Is speech special? Perception and recall of spoken language in complex environments. In J. Cerella, J. Rybash, W. Hayer, & M. Commons (Eds.), *Adult information processing: Limits on loss* (pp. 425–457). San Diego, CA: Academic Press, Inc.

Vieth, V. (2006). Finding words in court: The forensic interviewer as expert witness. *Reasonable Efforts, 3*(2), 1–2. Available at: http://www.ncptc.org/vertical/Sites/%7B8634A6E1-FAD2-4381-9C0D-5DC7E93C9410%7D/uploads/%7BA0A23136-2DCD-4D02-8A2D-DDDDF6906FB1%7D.PDF

Walker, A. G. (1999). *Handbook on questioning children: A linguistic perspective* (2nd ed.).Washington, DC: ABA Center on Children and the Law.

Walker, N. E., Lunning, S., & Eilts, J. L. (1996, June). *Do children respond accurately to forced choice questions? Yes or no.* Paper presented at the Recollections of Trauma: Scientific Research and Clinical Practice Conference, Port de Bourgenay, France.

Warren, A., Hulse-Trotter, K., & Tubbs, E. (1991). Inducing resistance to suggestibility in children. *Law and Human Behavior, 15,* 273–285.

Waterman, A. H., Blades, M., & Spencer, C. P. (2001). Interviewing children and adults: The effect of question format on the tendency to speculate. *Applied Cognitive Psychology, 15,* 1–11.

Welch-Ross, M. (2000). A mental-state reasoning model of suggestibility and memory source monitoring. In K. P. Roberts & M. Blades (Eds.), *Children's source monitoring* (pp. 227–255). Mahwah, NJ: Lawrence Erlbaum.

Whipple, G. M. (1915). *Manual of mental and physical tests: Part 2. Complex processes* (2nd ed.). Baltimore: Warwick & York.

White, T. L., Leichtman, M. D., & Ceci, S. J. (1997). The good, the bad, and the ugly: Accuracy, inaccuracy, and elaboration in preschoolers' reports about a past event. *Applied Cognitive Psychology, 11,* 37–54.

Wynn, K. (1990). Children's understanding of counting. *Cognition, 36,* 155–193.

Wynn, K. (1992). Children's acquisition of the number words and the counting system. *Cognitive Psychology, 24,* 220–251.

21 Legal Issues in Child Abuse and Neglect Practice

John E. B. Myers

Many legal issues arise in practice with abused and neglected children. Faller, Grabarek, and Vandervort (2009) observe, "Child welfare practice is perhaps the most legally intensive specialty within the social work profession" (p. 972). Chapter 6 discusses criminal prosecution of child maltreatment. Chapter 4 describes the role of the juvenile court in protecting children from maltreatment. The complexities of proving maltreatment in court are the subject of Chapter 22. The present chapter discusses three legal issues: the duty to report suspected maltreatment to authorities, confidentiality and privilege, and testifying in court.

Duty to Report Suspected Child Abuse and Neglect

Every state requires professionals who interact with children to report suspected child abuse and neglect. The reporting duty applies to social workers, physicians, dentists, nurses, psychologists, counselors, teachers, law enforcement officers, and child care professionals. Kalichman (1993) writes, "Across states, there are nearly 40 different professions specifically named in mandatory reporting laws" (p. 24).

The duty to report suspected maltreatment is triggered when a professional possesses the level of suspicion specified in the reporting law. Reporting laws differ slightly in the words used to describe the triggering level of suspicion. Common phrases include "cause to believe," "reasonable cause to believe," "known or suspected abuse," and "observation or examination that discloses evidence of abuse." Although the words differ, the basic thrust of reporting laws is the same across the United States: A report is required when a professional has information that would lead a competent professional to believe maltreatment is likely. Whether the triggering level of suspicion exists depends on the facts of the case interpreted through the lens of experience and judgment.

Although it is sometimes difficult to determine when the triggering level of suspicion exists, one thing is clear: The reporting law does not require the professional to be certain maltreatment occurred. Reporting is triggered by suspicion and not certainty. A professional who postpones reporting until all doubt is eliminated violates the reporting law. Moreover, a mandated reporter is required to report suspected maltreatment whether or not the professional believes reporting is wise. When maltreatment is suspected, reporting is mandatory and not discretionary.

The reporting law leaves final decisions about whether maltreatment occurred to investigating authorities and not reporters. Thus, Kalichman (1993) advises professionals "not to investigate the occurrence of child abuse by engaging in activities outside of ordinary professional roles" (p. 154). Zellman and Faller (1996) add that professionals should report suspicions and leave investigation to authorities. This is not to say that professionals ask no questions. Alternatives to maltreatment are considered. The point is that in-depth investigation and decision making about maltreatment is reserved for child protective services (CPS) or law enforcement—not the reporter. Once the triggering level of suspicion is reached, the reporter turns the matter over to the authorities.

Confidentiality and the Duty to Report

Professionals have ethical and legal duties to protect confidential information. Generally, a client must consent to release of confidential information. When the client is a child, parents or caretakers normally consent to release of confidential information. For mandated reporters, however, the child abuse reporting law supersedes confidentiality. A professional must report despite the fact that reporting requires release of confidential information to authorities. Even so, the reporting law does not completely abrogate confidentiality. Generally, disclosure is limited to information required by the reporting law. Confidential information that is not required by law to be disclosed is protected.

Liability of Reporters

Liability for failure to report. Intentional failure to report suspected child abuse or neglect is a crime. In addition to criminal liability, if a mandated reporter does not report suspected maltreatment—and the child is further abused or killed—the professional can be sued for malpractice (*Landeros v. Flood*, 1976). Several states have laws specifically authorizing lawsuits against professionals who willfully fail to report.

Liability for reporting. In a small number of cases, angry parents sued the professional who reported suspected maltreatment. Most such lawsuits are dismissed because the child abuse reporting law gives professionals immunity from civil liability.

Immunity from liability. Child abuse reporting laws provide immunity from civil liability for professionals who report suspected maltreatment. Professionals should understand, however, what immunity does and does not do. Immunity does not prohibit an angry parent from suing. Rather, immunity gives a professional a way out of a lawsuit after the suit is filed. Immunity is an escape hatch. If a lawsuit is filed, the judge decides whether immunity applies. If so, the professional escapes the lawsuit at an early stage, usually long before a trial.

Although immunity does not directly prohibit parents from suing, immunity often has the indirect effect of preventing lawsuits. The attorney advising the parents explains that immunity will probably defeat the lawsuit, and the parents decide not to sue.

Guidelines Regarding Reporting

Seth Kalichman (1993) is an expert on reporting laws. In his book on the subject, Kalichman advises

> Knowledge of state laws regarding requirements to report suspected child maltreatment is necessary for all mandated reporters. Treatment and research professionals need standard informed-consent procedures that detail clearly the conditions under which confidentiality is limited. Disclosures of child abuse can be interpreted as evidence of maltreatment and should surpass reporting thresholds. Suspicions of child maltreatment based on behavioral or physical indicators that do not appear to warrant reporting require close evaluation before reporting can be dismissed completely. Professionals operate within their areas of competence and defined professional roles and should not overstep their limitations to verify the occurrence of child abuse. Parents or guardians must be informed of a report before it is filed unless doing so would endanger the welfare of the child or children. Professionals should keep thorough and detailed records of information released in a report. Professionals are expected to follow up on reports to the child protection system. When professionals do not report suspected child maltreatment because they have caused a report to be filed by someone else, they must follow up on the case and verify that a report was filed with the child protection system. Cases of suspected child abuse that do not surpass reporting criteria should be discussed with a colleague to achieve some degree of objective reliability in reporting decisions. Training in recognizing signs of child maltreatment should be obtained by all human service professionals to the degree to which they have potential contact with abused children or abusive adults. (pp. 149–151)

See also Kalichman (1999).

Confidential Records and Privileged Communications

Abused and neglected children interact with many professionals. Each professional who comes in contact with the child documents the interaction. Much of this information is confidential and must be protected from inappropriate disclosure. Confidentiality arises from three sources: (1) the ethical duty to protect confidential information, (2) laws that make certain records confidential, and (3) privileges that apply in legal proceedings.

Ethical Duty to Safeguard Confidential Information

The ethical principles of social work, psychology, medicine, nursing, and other professions require professionals to safeguard confidential information revealed by clients. The *Code of Ethics* of the National Association of Social Workers (NASW) (1999) provides: "Social workers should protect the confidentiality of all information obtained in the course of professional service, except for compelling professional reasons" (Standard 1.07(c)). *The Ethical Principles of Psychologists and Code of Conduct* of the American Psychological Association (APA) (2002) provides: "Psychologists have a primary obligation and take reasonable precautions to protect confidential information" (Standard 4.01). The *Principles of Medical Ethics* of the American Medical Association (AMA) (2001) require physicians to "safeguard patient confidences within the constraints of the law." The *Code of Ethics for Nurses* of the American Nurses Association (ANA) (2001) states that nurses safeguard the patient's right to privacy by carefully protecting information of a confidential nature.

Laws That Make Patient Records Confidential

Every state has laws that make certain records confidential. Some of the laws pertain to records compiled by government agencies such as CPS, public hospitals, and courts. Other laws govern records created by professionals and institutions in private practice such as physicians, psychotherapists, and private hospitals. The federal Health Information Privacy Protection Act (HIPPA) also governs the confidentiality of records.

Privileged Communications

The ethical duty to protect confidential information applies in all settings: in the clinic, the cafeteria, the courtroom—everywhere. In the context of legal proceedings, however, certain professionals have an additional duty to protect confidential information. In legal proceedings, the law prohibits disclosure of confidential communications between certain professionals and their clients. These laws are called privileges.

Unlike the expansive ethical obligation to protect confidential client information, privileges apply only in legal proceedings. Privileges clearly apply when professionals testify in court and are asked to reveal privileged information. Privileges also apply during legal proceedings outside the courtroom. For example, in many civil cases and a few criminal cases, attorneys take pretrial depositions of witnesses. During a deposition, questions may be asked that call for disclosure of privileged information. If this occurs, the professional or one of the attorneys should raise the privilege issue.

Communication between a client and a professional is privileged when three requirements are fulfilled. First, the communication (oral or written) must be between a client and a professional with whom privileged communication is possible. All states have some form of physician–patient and psychotherapist–patient privilege. In most states, there is no social worker–client privilege unless the social worker is performing a clinical function and thus comes under the psychotherapist–client privilege. Similarly, in most states there is no nurse-patient privilege.

The second requirement for privilege is that the client must seek professional services. The client must consult the professional to obtain diagnosis, treatment, counseling, or advice.

The third requirement of privilege is that the client must intend to communicate in confidence with the professional. Privileges only cover communications that the client intends to be confidential. The privilege covers confidential statements from the client to the professional as well as statements from the professional to the client. Thus privilege is a two-way street. Privilege generally does not attach to communications the client intends to be released to other people.

In legal proceedings, the presence or absence of a privilege is important. In court, a professional may have to answer questions that require disclosure of information the professional is ethically bound to protect. By contrast, the professional generally does not have to answer questions that require disclosure of privileged information. Thus, in legal proceedings a privilege gives protection that is greater than the protection afforded by the ethical duty to protect confidential information.

The fact that a third person is present when a client discloses information may or may not eliminate the confidentiality required for privilege. The deciding factor usually is whether the third person is needed to assist the professional. For example, suppose a physician is conducting a physical examination and interview of a child. The presence of a nurse during the examination does not undermine the confidentiality of information revealed to the doctor. Furthermore, presence of a child's parents need not defeat privilege. The important factor is whether the third person is needed to assist the professional. A privilege is not destroyed when colleagues consult about cases.

Privileged communications remain privileged when the relationship with the client ends. In most situations, the client's death does not end the privilege.

The privilege belongs to the client—not the professional. In legal parlance, the client is the "holder" of the privilege. As the privilege holder, the client can prevent the professional from disclosing privileged information in legal proceedings. Suppose, for example, that a treating physician is subpoenaed to testify about a client. While the physician is on the witness stand, an attorney asks a question that calls for privileged information. At that point, the client's attorney should object. The client's attorney asserts the privilege on behalf of the privilege holder—the client. The judge then decides whether a privilege applies. If the client's attorney fails to object to a question calling for privileged information, or if the client is not represented by an attorney, the professional may assert the privilege on behalf of the client. Indeed, the professional has an ethical duty to assert the privilege if no one else does. The professional might address the judge and say, "Your Honor, I would rather not answer that question because answering would require disclosure of information I believe is privileged." When the judge learns that a privilege may exist, the judge decides whether the question should be answered.

Disclosure of Confidential and Privileged Information

This section discusses disclosure of confidential and privileged information.

Client consent. Client consent plays the central role in release of confidential or privileged information. Gutheil and Appelbaum (1982) observed, "With rare exceptions, identifiable data can be transmitted to third parties only with the patient's explicit consent" (p. 5). A competent adult may consent to release of confidential or privileged information to attorneys, courts, or anyone else. The client's consent must be informed and voluntary. The professional should explain any disadvantages of disclosing confidential or privileged information. For example, the client may not realize that disclosure may waive privileges that would otherwise apply.

A professional who discloses confidential or privileged information without client consent can be sued. With an eye toward such lawsuits, Gutheil and Appelbaum (1982) wrote,

> It is probably wise for therapists always to require the written consent of their patients before releasing information to third parties. Written consent is advisable for at least two reasons: (1) it makes clear to both parties involved that consent has, in fact, been given; (2) if the fact, nature or timing of the consent should ever be challenged, a documentary record exists. The consent should be made a part of the patient's permanent chart. (p. 6)

When the client is a child, parents or caretakers normally have authority to make decisions about release of confidential and privileged information. When a parent is accused of maltreatment, however, it may not be appropriate for the parent to make decisions regarding the child's confidential or privileged information. In the event of a conflict between the interests of the child and a parent, a judge may appoint someone else, such as a guardian ad litem, to make decisions about confidential and privileged information.

Subpoenas. A subpoena is issued by a court, typically at the request of an attorney. A subpoena is a court order and cannot be ignored. Disobedience of a subpoena can be punished as contempt of court. There are two types of subpoenas: (1) a subpoena requiring an individual to testify, called a sub-poena *ad testificandum*, and (2) a subpoena requiring a person to produce records or documents, called a subpoena *duces tecum*.

A subpoena does *not* override privileges such as the physician–patient and psychotherapist–patient privileges. A subpoena for testimony requires the professional to appear, but the subpoena does not mean the professional has to disclose privileged information. A judge decides whether a privilege applies and whether a professional has to answer questions or release records.

Before responding to a subpoena, the professional should contact the client or, in the case of a child, a responsible adult. The client may desire to release confidential or privileged information.

It is often useful, with the client's permission, to communicate with the attorney issuing the subpoena. In some cases, the conversation lets the attorney know the professional has nothing that can assist the attorney, and the attorney withdraws the subpoena. Even if the attorney insists on compliance with the subpoena, the conversation may clarify the limits of relevant information in the professional's possession. Care should be taken during such conversations to avoid disclosing confidential or privi-leged information.

If doubts exist concerning how to respond to a subpoena, consult an attorney. Legal advice should not be obtained from the attorney who issued the subpoena.

Reviewing client records before or during testimony. When a professional is asked to testify, relevant records are reviewed to refresh the profes-sional's memory. In some cases, the professional leaves the record at the office. In other cases, the record is taken to court. Generally, it is appro-priate to review pertinent records before testifying. Indeed, such review is often essential for accurate testimony. Professionals should be aware, how-ever, that reviewing records before or during testimony can impact confi-dentiality or privilege.

While a professional is on the witness stand, the attorney for the alleged perpetrator may ask whether the professional reviewed the child's record prior to coming to court. If the answer is yes, the attorney may ask the judge to order the record produced for the attorney's inspection. In most states, the judge has authority to order the record produced. If the professional takes the record to court and refers to it while testifying, the judge is likely to order the record disclosed to the attorney.

Child abuse reporting laws override confidentiality and privilege. Child abuse reporting laws require professionals to report suspected child abuse and neglect to authorities. As mentioned earlier, the reporting laws override the ethical duty to protect confidential client information. Additionally, the reporting requirement overrides privilege.

Although reporting laws abrogate confidentiality and privilege, abrogation usually is not complete. Professionals limit the information they report to the information required by law. Information that is not required to be reported remains confidential and/or privileged.

Emergencies. In emergencies, a professional may have little choice but to release confidential or privileged information without prior authorization from the client. The law allows release of such information in genuine emergencies.

Court-ordered medical and psychological examinations. A judge may order an individual to submit to a medical or psychological evaluation to help the judge decide the case. Because everyone knows from the outset that the professional's report will be shared with the judge and the attorneys, the obligation to protect confidential information is limited, and privileges generally do not attach.

Testifying in Court as an Expert Witness

This section discusses expert testimony.

Who Qualifies as an Expert Witness

Before a professional may testify as an expert witness, the judge must be persuaded that the professional possesses sufficient knowledge, skill, experience, training, and education to qualify as an expert. To provide the judge information on the professional's qualifications, the professional takes the witness stand and answers questions about the professional's education, specialized training, and relevant experience. Typically, the attorney who offers a professional's testimony asks all the questions related to qualifications. Occasionally, the judge asks questions. The opposing attorney has the right to question the professional in an effort to convince the judge that the professional should not be allowed to testify as an expert. Such questioning by opposing counsel is called *voir dire*. When the professional's qualifications are obvious, there usually is no *voir dire*.

Preparation for Expert Testimony

When a professional prepares to testify, it is important to meet with the attorney for whom the expert will testify. Pretrial conferences are ethically and legally proper. During preparation, the expert and the attorney discuss questions the attorney plans to ask as well as likely areas of cross-examination. Preparation includes review of relevant records, although professionals should keep in mind that reviewing records can compromise confidentiality.

Forms of Expert Testimony

Expert testimony usually takes one of three forms: (1) an opinion, (2) a lecture providing technical or clinical information for the judge or jury, or (3) an answer to a hypothetical question. It is not uncommon for expert testimony to take more than one form.

Opinion Testimony. The most common form of expert testimony is an opinion. Thus, a physician might opine that a child's history and the findings of a physical examination are consistent with child sexual abuse (CSA).

An expert must be reasonably confident that the opinion offered in court is correct. Lawyers use the term *reasonable certainty* to describe the necessary degree of confidence. Unfortunately, reasonable certainty is not well defined in law. It is clear that experts may not speculate or guess. It is equally clear that experts do not have to be 100% certain their opinion is correct. Thus, reasonable certainty lies somewhere between speculation and certainty—closer to the latter than the former.

A helpful way to self-assess the degree of certainty supporting expert opinion is to ask one's self the following questions: In formulating my opinion, did I consider all the relevant facts? Do I have a thorough understanding of the pertinent clinical and scientific principles? Did I use methods of diagnosis and assessment that are appropriate, reliable, and valid? Are my assumptions, inferences, and conclusions reasonable and supported by the data? Did I thoroughly consider and rule out all other explanations?

A lecture to educate the jury. Experts sometimes testify in the form of a lecture that provides the jury or judge with information on technical, clinical, or scientific issues. This form of expert testimony is used, for example, in some CSA cases when the defense attorney asserts that a child's delayed reporting, inconsistent disclosure, or recantation means the child cannot be believed. When the defense attacks a child's credibility this way, judges often allow an expert witness to inform the jury that it is not uncommon for sexually abused children to delay reporting, provide partial or piecemeal disclosures, or to recant. Equipped with this information, the jury is in a better position to evaluate the child's credibility.

The hypothetical question. In some cases, expert testimony is elicited in response to a hypothetical question. A hypothetical question asks the expert about a hypothetical set of facts that mirror the facts of the case on trial. Consider, for example, a fatal head injury case in which the expert is a physician. The attorney says, "Doctor, let me ask you to assume that the following facts are true." The attorney describes a hypothetical child victim, including the child's eating, feeding, and sleeping patterns; the time when the 911 call was placed; the child's condition when the paramedics arrived; the child's injuries; and observations made by emergency room doctors. The attorney ends by asking, "Doctor, I'm interested in your opinion about the timing of this hypothetical child's injuries. Based on the facts I have described to you, do you have an opinion, based on a reasonable degree of medical certainty, regarding the time when the child was injured in relation to the time the 911 call was placed?" Alternatively, the hypothetical question might be, "Doctor, assuming that the child was injured by shaking, how soon after the shaking would you expect the child to exhibit symptoms?"

Attorneys cross-examining expert witnesses often ask hypothetical questions. The cross-examiner may try to undermine the expert's opinion by presenting a hypothetical set of facts that differs from the facts described by the expert. The cross-examiner then asks, "Doctor, if the facts I have suggested to you turn out to be true, would that change your opinion?" Chadwick (1990) observes that it is "common to encounter hypothetical questions based on hypotheses that are extremely unlikely, and the witness may need to point out the unlikelihood" (p. 967). When an expert witness is cross-examined about a hypothetical set of facts, the expert should be reasonable but should stick to the original opinion. One possible response to the cross-examiner's hypothetical question is, "If the facts were as you suggest, my opinion might change. The facts you suggest, however, are not the facts of the case I evaluated."

Cross-Examination and Impeachment of Expert Witnesses

Testifying begins with direct examination. During direct examination, the expert witness answers questions from the attorney who asked the expert to testify. After direct examination, the opposing attorney has the right to cross-examine the expert. Cross-examination is sometimes followed by redirect examination. Redirect examination gives the expert an opportunity to clarify issues that were raised on cross-examination (see Brodsky, 2004; Stern, 1997).

Cross-examine positively and negatively. Cross-examination is of two types: positive and negative. With positive cross-examination, the cross-examining attorney does not attack the expert. Rather, the attorney questions the expert in a positive—even friendly—way, seeking agreement from the expert on certain facts or inferences that may be helpful to the attorney's client. With negative cross-examination, by contrast, the attorney seeks to undermine (impeach) the expert's testimony.

A cross-examining attorney who plans to use negative as well as positive cross-examination typically begins with positive questioning in the hope of eliciting favorable testimony from the expert. Negative cross-examination is postponed until positive cross-examination pans out.

Master the facts. The skilled cross-examiner masters the facts of the case and shapes questions to manipulate the witness into providing answers that favor the cross-examiner's client. To avoid being manipulated, the expert must know the facts at least as well as the cross-examiner.

Maintain a calm, professional demeanor. The experienced expert witness refuses to be cajoled or tricked into verbal sparring with the cross-examiner. The professional is at all times just that—professional. Given the aggression of some cross-examiners, it can be a challenge to maintain a calm, professional demeanor on the witness stand. Remember, however, that the jury is looking to you for guidance and wisdom. The jury wants a strong expert but not someone who fights with the cross-examiner. This does not mean, of course, that the expert cannot employ pointed responses during cross-examination. The expert should express confidence when challenged and should not vacillate or equivocate in the face of attack. On the other hand, the expert should concede weak points and acknowledge conflicting evidence. It is not a good idea to respond to a cross-examiner with sarcasm.

Ask for clarification. Do not answer a question unless you fully understand it. When in doubt, ask the attorney to clarify. Such a request does not show weakness. After all, if you do not understand a question, you can be sure the jury doesn't either. When a cross-examiner's question is really two or three questions in one, the other attorney may object that the question is "compound." Absent an objection, it is proper for the expert to ask the cross-examiner which of the several questions the attorney would like answered.

Ask leading questions during cross-examination. From the lawyer's perspective, the key to successful cross-examination is controlling what the witness says in response to the cross-examiner's questions. With the goal of "witness control" in mind, the cross-examiner asks leading—often highly leading—questions. Unlike the attorney conducting direct examination, who is not supposed to rely on leading questions, the cross-examiner has free reign to ask all the leading questions the examiner desires.

The cross-examiner seeks to control the expert with leading questions that require short, specific answers, preferably limited to "yes" or "no." The cross-examiner keeps the witness hemmed in with leading questions and seldom asks "why" or "how" something happened. "Why" and "how" questions relinquish control to the expert; the relinquishing control is precisely what the cross-examiner does not want.

When an expert attempts to explain an answer to a leading question, the cross-examiner may interrupt and say, "Please just answer yes or no." If the expert persists, the cross-examiner may ask the judge to admonish the expert to limit answers to the questions asked. Experts are understandably frustrated when an attorney thwarts efforts at clarification. It is sometimes proper to say, "Counsel, it is not possible for me to answer with a simple yes or no. May I explain myself?" Chadwick (1990) advises,

> When a question is posed in a strictly "yes or no" fashion, but the correct answer is "maybe," the witness should find a way to express the true answer. A direct appeal to the judge may be helpful in some cases. (p. 960)

Judges sometimes permit witnesses to amplify their opinion during cross-examination. Remember, too, that after cross-examination there is redirect examination during which the attorney who asked you to testify can ask clarifying questions.

Undermine the expert's facts, inferences, or conclusions. One of the most effective cross-examination techniques with expert witnesses is to get the expert to agree to the facts, inferences, and conclusions that support the expert's opinion and then dispute or undermine one or more of those facts, inferences, or conclusions. Consider a case where a physician testifies a child probably experienced vaginal penetration. The cross-examiner begins by committing the doctor to the facts and assumptions underlying the opinion. The attorney says, "So, doctor, your opinion is based exclusively on the history, the physical examination, and on what the child told you. Is that correct?" "And there is nothing else you relied on to form your opinion. Is that correct?" The cross-examiner commits the doctor to a specific set of facts and assumptions so that when the cross-examiner disputes those facts or assumptions, the doctor's opinion cannot be justified on some other basis.

Once the cross-examiner pins down the basis of the doctor's opinion, the cross-examiner attacks the opinion by disputing one or more of the facts, inferences, or conclusions that support it. The attorney might ask whether the doctor's opinion would change if certain facts were different (a hypothetical question). The attorney might press the doctor to acknowledge alternative explanations for the doctor's conclusion. The attorney might ask whether other experts might come to different conclusions based on the same facts.

Rather than attack the doctor's facts, inferences, or conclusions during cross-examination, the attorney may limit cross-examination to pinning the doctor down to a limited set of facts, inferences, and conclusions, and then, when the doctor has left the witness stand, offer another expert to contradict the doctor's testimony.

Utilize learned treatises. The cross-examiner may seek to undermine the expert's testimony by confronting the expert with books or articles (called learned treatises) that contradict the expert. The rules on cross-examination with learned treatises vary from state to state. There is agreement on one thing, however. When an expert is confronted with a sentence or a paragraph selected by an attorney from an article or chapter, the expert has the right to put the selected passage in context by reading surrounding material. The expert might say to the cross-examiner, "Counsel, I cannot comment on the sentence you have selected unless I first read the entire article. If you will permit me to read the article, I'll be happy to comment on the sentence that interests you."

Present the possibility of bias. The cross-examiner may raise the possibility that the expert is biased. For example, if the expert is part of a multidisciplinary team (MDT), the cross-examiner might proceed as follows:

Q: Now doctor, you are employed by Children's Hospital, isn't that correct?

A: Right.

Q: At the hospital, are you a member of the MDT that investigates allegations of child abuse?

A: The team performs medical examinations and interviews. We do not investigate. The police investigate. But yes, I am a member of the hospital's MDT.

Q: Your team regularly performs investigative examinations and interviews at the request of the prosecuting attorney's office, isn't that correct?

A: Yes.

Q: When you complete your investigation for the prosecutor, you prepare a report for the prosecutor, don't you?

A: A report and recommendation is prepared and placed in the child's medical record. On request, the team provides a copy of the report to the prosecutor and, I might add, to the defense.

Q: After your team prepares its report and provides a copy to the prosecutor, you often come to court to testify as an expert witness for the prosecution in child abuse cases, isn't that right, doctor?

A: Yes.

Q: Do you usually testify for the prosecution rather than the defense?

A: Correct.

Q: In fact, would I be correct in saying that you always testify for the prosecution and never for the defense?

A: I am willing to testify for the defense, but so far I have always testified for the prosecution.

Q: Thank you, doctor. I have no further questions.

The cross-examiner seeks to portray the doctor as biased in favor of the prosecution, but the cross-examiner does not ask, "Well then, doctor, isn't it a fact that because of your close working relationship with the prosecution, you are biased in favor of the prosecution?" The cross-examiner knows the answer is "No," so the cross-examiner simply plants seeds of doubt in the jurors' minds and then, when it is time for closing argument, the cross-examiner reminds the jury of the doctor's close working relationship with the prosecution.

Recall that cross-examination is followed by redirect examination. During redirect, the prosecutor might ask, "Doctor, in light of the defense attorney's questions about your responsibilities with the MDT, are you biased in favor of the prosecution?" The doctor can set the record straight.

Cross-examination causes considerable anxiety. Yet, with experience, professionals become more comfortable with the role of expert witness and with cross-examination.

Conclusion

Professionals from social work, mental health, medicine, nursing, and education are the key players in child protection. The law plays a supporting role. Hopefully, the legal material in this chapter will assist professionals in their important work with children and families.

References

American Medical Association (AMA). (2001). *Principles of medical ethics*. Chicago: Author.

American Nurses Association (ANA). (2001). *Code of ethics for nurses*. Silver Spring, MD: American Nurses Publishing.

American Psychological Association (APA). (2002). *The ethical principles of psychologists and code of conduct*. Washington, DC: Author.

Brodsky, S. L. (2004). *Coping with cross-examination*. Washington, DC: American Psychological Association.

Chadwick, D. L. (1990). Preparation for court testimony in child abuse cases. *Pediatric Clinics of North America, 37*, 955–970.

Faller, K. C., Grabarek, M., & Vandervort, F. (2009). Child welfare workers go to court: The impact of race, gender, and education on the comfort with legal issues. *Children and Youth Services Review, 31*, 972–977.

Gutheil, T. G., & Appelbaum, P. S. (1982). *Clinical handbook of psychiatry and the law*. New York: McGraw-Hill.

Kalichman, S. C. (1993). *Mandated reporting of suspected child abuse: Ethics, law & policy* (1st ed.). Washington, DC: American Psychological Association.

Kalichman, S. C. (1999). *Mandated reporting of suspected child abuse: Ethics, law & policy* (2nd ed.). Washington, DC: American Psychological Association.

Landeros v. Flood, 551 P.2d 389 (Cal. 1976).

National Association of Social Workers (NASW). (1999). *Code of ethics*. Washington, DC: National Association of Social Workers Press.

Stern, P. (1997). *Preparing and presenting expert testimony in child abuse litigation: A guide for expert witnesses and attorneys*. Thousand Oaks, CA: Sage.

Zellman, G. L., & Faller, K. C. (1996). Reporting of child maltreatment. In J. Briere, L. Berliner, J. A. Buckley, C. Jenny, & T. Reid (Eds.). *The APSAC handbook on child maltreatment*. Thousand Oaks, CA: Sage.

22 Proving Child Maltreatment in Court

John E. B. Myers

This chapter addresses the legal issue of proving child abuse and neglect in court. Criminal litigation was discussed in Chapter 6. Juvenile court protective proceedings were described in Chapter 4. Expert testimony was discussed in Chapters 11, 15, and 21.

The Rules of Evidence

When criminal or juvenile court litigation is commenced, there is always the possibility of a court trial. As explained in Chapter 6, most cases do not proceed all the way to trial. Cases that do go to trial are governed by a complex set of laws called rules of evidence. Every state has its own rules of evidence, and there are minor differences from state to state. For the most part, however, the rules of evidence are similar across the United States. The rules of evidence apply in civil as well as criminal trials, although some rules differ between criminal and civil cases.

Evidence consists of testimony of witnesses, documents, and objects such as guns and drugs. Testimony from experts is evidence, and expert testimony plays an important role in many child abuse and neglect cases.

To be admissible in court, evidence must be relevant. Evidence is relevant if it helps prove or disprove something that is important (material or of consequence) in the case. For example, a child's testimony describing how he was abused is relevant—so is the gun used in a holdup.

Relevant evidence can be excluded by the judge if the evidence is highly disturbing and likely to unfairly prejudice the jury against the defendant. In murder cases, for example, judges sometimes exclude gruesome autopsy photos of the victim. I hasten to add, however, that even gruesome photos are allowed if they help an expert witness explain a victim's injuries or the cause of death.

Hearsay Evidence

Hearsay evidence plays an important role in many child abuse cases. To understand hearsay, it is useful to begin with an example. Four-year-old Beth is being examined by a physician because she told a friend that her father gave her "bad touches." In response to a question from the doctor, Beth points to her genital area and says, "Daddy put his pee-pee in me down there. Then he took it out and shook it up and down and white stuff popped out and got all over me. It was yucky." Beth's words are powerful evidence of abuse. Criminal charges are filed against Beth's father, and the case goes to trial. The prosecutor calls the doctor as a witness and asks the doctor to repeat Beth's words and to describe her pointing gesture. Before the doctor can speak, however, the defense attorney objects that Beth's words and gesture are hearsay. The law in all states is that hearsay is inadmissible in court unless the hearsay meets the requirements of an exception to the rule against hearsay.

Hearsay Defined

Are Beth's words and gesture hearsay? Hearsay is an out-of-court assertion that is repeated in court to prove the truth of the matter asserted. To understand this definition, it is useful to divide it into three components. A child's words are hearsay when: (1) the child's words were intended by the child to describe something that happened (e.g., describe abuse), (2) the child's words were spoken before the court proceeding at which the words are repeated by someone who heard the child speak (words were out of court), and (3) the child's words are repeated in court to prove that what the child said actually happened (repeated to prove the truth of the matter asserted). A person who makes a hearsay statement is called a declarant.

Analysis of Beth's words reveals that they are hearsay. First, Beth intended to describe something that happened. Second, Beth made her statement before the court proceeding where the prosecutor asks the doctor to repeat Beth's words. Finally, the prosecutor offers Beth's words in court to prove that what Beth said actually happened—the truth of the matter asserted.

Beth's words are not the only hearsay. Her gesture pointing to her genital area also is hearsay. The gesture was nonverbal communication intended by Beth to describe abuse. The judge will sustain the defense attorney's hearsay objection unless the prosecutor persuades the judge that Beth's words and gesture meet the requirements of an exception to the rule against hearsay.

In Beth's case, as in many other child abuse cases, the prosecutor's ability to convince the judge that Beth's hearsay statement meets the requirements of an exception to the hearsay rule depends as much on the documentation of the professional to whom the child disclosed as on the expertise of the prosecutor. If the doctor knew what to document when Beth disclosed abuse, the prosecutor has a good chance of persuading the judge to allow the doctor to repeat Beth's words and gesture despite the fact that they are hearsay.

Exceptions to the Hearsay Rule

There are more than 30 exceptions to the rule against hearsay. Only a handful of exceptions, however, play a day-to-day role in child abuse litigation. The four most frequently used hearsay exceptions are discussed here.

1. Excited Utterance Exception

An excited utterance is a hearsay statement that relates to or describes a startling event. The statement must be made while the child is under the emotional stress caused by the startling event. The theory behind the excited utterance exception is that statements made under significant stress are likely to be true. All states have a version of the excited utterance exception. The factors listed below are considered by the judge in deciding whether a hearsay statement is an excited utterance:

Nature of the event. Some events are more startling than others, and the judge considers the likely impact a particular event would have on a child of a similar age and experience. In most cases, sexual abuse or physical abuse (PA) is sufficiently startling to satisfy the excited utterance exception.

Amount of time elapsed between the startling event and the child's statement relating to the event. The more time that passes between a startling event and a child's statement describing the event, the less likely a judge is to conclude that the statement is an excited utterance. Although passage of time is important, elapsed time is not the only factor judges consider. Judges have approved delays ranging from a few minutes to many hours. The professional should document as precisely as possible how much time passed between the abuse and the child's statement—minutes count.

Indications the child was emotionally upset when the child spoke. The judge considers whether the child was crying, frightened, or otherwise upset when the statement was made. If the child was injured or in pain, the judge is more likely to find an excited utterance.

Child's speech pattern. In some cases, the way a child speaks—e.g., pressured or hurried speech—indicates excitement.

Extent to which child's statement was spontaneous. Spontaneity is a key factor in the excited utterance exception. The more spontaneous the statement, the more likely it meets the requirements of the exception.

Questions used to elicit child's statement. Asking questions does not necessarily destroy the spontaneity required for the excited utterance exception.

As questions become suggestive, however, spontaneity may dissipate, undermining the exception.

First safe opportunity. In many abuse cases, children remain under the control of the abuser for hours or days after an abusive incident. When the child is finally released to a trusted adult, the child has the first safe opportunity to disclose what happened. A child's statement at the first safe opportunity may qualify as an excited utterance even though considerable time has elapsed since the abuse occurred.

Rekindled excitement. A startling event such as abuse may be followed by a period of calm during which excitement abates. If the child is later exposed to a stimulus that reminds the child of the startling event, the child's excitement may be rekindled. Rekindled excitement sometimes satisfies the excited utterance exception to the rule against hearsay.

Professionals should document the foregoing factors and any additional evidence that a child was distraught when describing maltreatment.

2. Medical Diagnosis or Treatment Exception

All states have a "diagnosis or treatment" exception to the hearsay rule for certain statements to professionals providing diagnostic or treatment services. The professional to whom the child speaks may be a physician, psychiatrist, psychologist, nurse, clinical social worker, paramedic, EMT, or medical technician. The diagnosis or treatment exception includes the child's statements describing medical history as well as statements describing present symptoms, pain, and other sensations. The exception includes the child's description of the cause of illness or injury. Unlike the excited utterance exception, the child does not have to be upset for the medical diagnosis or treatment exception to apply.

In many cases, the child is the one who makes the hearsay statements that are admissible under the diagnosis or treatment exception. Sometimes, however, an adult describes the child's history and symptoms to the professional. So long as the adult's motive is to obtain diagnosis or treatment for the child, the adult's statements are admissible under the exception.

The rationale for the diagnosis or treatment exception is that hearsay statements to professionals providing diagnostic or treatment services are reliable because the patient has an incentive to be truthful with the professional. This rationale is applicable for older children and adolescents. Some young children, however, may not understand the need for accuracy with health care providers. When a child does not understand that the child's own well-being may be affected by the accuracy of what is said, the rationale for the diagnosis or treatment exception evaporates, and the judge may rule that the child's hearsay statement does not satisfy the exception.

The diagnosis or treatment exception has its clearest application with children receiving traditional medical care in a hospital, clinic, or physician's office. Most children have at least some understanding of doctors and nurses and the importance of telling the clinician "what really happened." Judges are less certain about application of the diagnosis or treatment exception to mental health treatment, where the child may not understand the importance of accuracy. Yet, when there is evidence that a child understood the need for accuracy with a mental health professional, judges generally conclude that the diagnosis or treatment exception extends to hearsay statements during mental health treatment.

To increase the probability that a child's statements describing maltreatment satisfy the diagnosis or treatment exception to the rule against hearsay, professionals are encouraged to take the following steps:

a. Discuss with the child the clinical importance of providing accurate information and of being completely forthcoming. A physician might say, "Hello, I'm Dr. Jones. I'm a doctor, and I'm going to give you a checkup to make sure everything is OK. While you are here today, I'll ask you some questions so I can help you. It's important for you to listen carefully to my questions. When you answer my questions, be sure to tell me everything you know. Tell me only things that really happened. Don't pretend or make things up. Your answers to questions help me to do my job as a doctor, so it is important for you to tell me things that really happened."

b. The diagnosis or treatment exception only applies to statements that are pertinent to the professional's ability to diagnose or treat. Thus, it is important to document why information disclosed by a child is pertinent to diagnosis or treatment. For example, the professional might document that after questioning a child, the professional decided to test for a sexually transmitted infection (STI).

c. If the child identifies the perpetrator, the professional should document why knowing the identity of the perpetrator is pertinent to diagnosis or treatment. For example, knowing the identity of the perpetrator is important in deciding whether it is safe to send the child home. As well, the professional needs to know the perpetrator's identity if there is a possibility the child was exposed to an STI. The decision to refer a child for mental health services is influenced in some cases by the identity of the abuser, making identity pertinent.

3. Residual and Child Hearsay Exceptions

Most states have a hearsay exception known as a residual or catchall exception, which allows use in court of reliable hearsay statements that do not meet the requirements of one of the traditional exceptions (e.g., excited utterance, medical diagnosis or treatment). In addition to the residual exception, which applies in all kinds of cases, most states have a special hearsay exception for reliable statements by children in child abuse cases.

When a child's hearsay statement is offered under a residual or child hearsay exception, the most important question is whether the statement is reliable. Professionals who interview, examine, and treat children play a vital role in documenting the information judges consider to determine whether children's statements are sufficiently reliable to be admitted under residual or child hearsay exceptions. Professionals should document the following:

Spontaneity. The more spontaneous a child's statement, the more likely a judge is to find it reliable.

Statements elicited by questioning. The reliability of a child's statement may be influenced by the type of questions asked. When questions are suggestive or leading, the possibility increases that the questioner influenced the child's statement. It should be noted, however, that suggestive questions are sometimes necessary to elicit information from children, particularly when the information is embarrassing. The smaller the number of suggestive and leading questions, the more likely a judge is to conclude that a child's statement is reliable.

Consistent statements. Reliability may be enhanced if the child's description of abuse is consistent over time.

Child's affect and emotion when hearsay statement was made. When a child's emotions are consistent with the child's statement, the reliability of the statement may be enhanced.

Play or gestures that corroborate child's hearsay statement. The play or gestures of a young child may strengthen confidence in the child's statement. For example, a child's use of dolls may support the reliability of the child's statement.

Developmentally unusual sexual knowledge. A young child's developmentally unusual knowledge of sexual acts or anatomy supports the reliability of the child's statement.

Idiosyncratic detail. Presence in a child's statement of idiosyncratic details of sexual acts points to reliability. Jones (1992) wrote,

The interview can be examined for signs of unique or distinguishing detail. This may be found both within the account of the sexual encounter and/or in unrelated recollections. Examples include children who describe smells and tastes associated with rectal, vaginal, or oral sex. (p. 53)

Child's belief that disclosure might lead to punishment of the child. Children hesitate to make statements they believe may get them in trouble. If a child believed disclosing abuse could result in punishment, confidence in the child's statement may increase.

Child's or adult's motive to fabricate. Evidence that the child or an adult had or lacked a motive to fabricate affects reliability.

Medical evidence of abuse. The child's statement may be corroborated by medical evidence.

Changes in child's behavior. When a child's behavior alters in a way that corroborates the child's description of abuse, it may be appropriate to place increased confidence in the child's statement.

None of the foregoing factors is a litmus test for reliability. Judges consider the totality of circumstances to evaluate reliability, and professionals can assist the legal system by documenting anything that indicates the child was or was not telling the truth when describing abuse.

4. Fresh Complaint of Sexual Assault

A child's initial disclosure of sexual abuse may be admissible in court under an ancient legal doctrine called fresh complaint of rape or sexual assault. In most states, a child's fresh complaint is not, technically speaking, hearsay. The law of fresh complaint varies considerably across the country. Suffice to say that in most states a child's initial disclosure of sexual abuse may be admissible as evidence of fresh complaint, or, as it is called in some states, "outcry."

Impact of the U.S. Constitution on Hearsay

There are two sources of law that govern hearsay. First, the rule against hearsay, previously discussed, which is part of the law of evidence. Hearsay exceptions (e.g., excited utterance, medical diagnosis or treatment) are part of evidence law. Second, in addition to the law of evidence, with its hearsay rule and exceptions, the U.S. Constitution places limits on the use of hearsay in criminal cases. The Constitution's Sixth Amendment contains the so-called Confrontation Clause, which provides, "In all criminal prosecutions, the accused shall enjoy the right . . . to be confronted with the witnesses against him." The U.S. Supreme Court has interpreted the Confrontation Clause to limit the types of hearsay that can be used against defendants in criminal cases. To be admissible against the defendant in a criminal trial, hearsay must satisfy *both* the Confrontation Clause *and* an exception to the rule against hearsay. In some situations, hearsay that fits an exception is inadmissible in court because it violates the Confrontation Clause.

Three decisions of the U.S. Supreme Court—*Crawford v. Washington* (2004), *Davis v. Washington* (2006), and *Melendez-Diaz v. Massachusetts* (2009)—define the impact of the Confrontation Clause on the admission of hearsay in criminal cases. Before discussing these cases, it is important to mention two subsidiary principles. First, if the child who made a hearsay statement (the declarant) is able to testify in court and be cross-examined by the defense attorney about the hearsay, then the Confrontation Clause is satisfied, and the child's hearsay can be admitted without affront to the Confrontation Clause. Of course, the child's hearsay still has to meet the requirements of an exception to the rule against hearsay.

The second subsidiary principle is that the constitutional limits on hearsay apply only in criminal cases. Thus, the Confrontation Clause does not apply in civil proceedings such as child protection proceedings in juvenile court and litigation to terminate parental rights.

In a criminal prosecution, when the prosecutor offers hearsay against the defendant, the Confrontation Clause as interpreted in *Crawford v. Washington* (2004), *Davis v. Washington* (2006), and *Melendez-Diaz v. Massachusetts* (2009) comes into play. As stated earlier, if the child can testify and be cross-examined about the hearsay, the Confrontation Clause is satisfied. However, when the child is unable to testify in court, the question under *Crawford v. Washington* (2004), *Davis v. Washington* (2006), and *Melendez-Diaz v. Massachusetts* (2009) is whether the child's hearsay statement was "testimonial" when it was made. If the child's hearsay was testimonial, then it cannot be admitted against the defendant. On the other hand, if the child's statement was nontestimonial, then the Confrontation Clause places no limit on use of the statement against the defendant.

Under *Crawford v. Washington* (2004), *Davis v. Washington* (2006), and *Melendez-Diaz v. Massachusetts* (2009), the word *testimonial* is a term of art. A hearsay statement can be testimonial even though it bears no resemblance to testimony in court. Hearsay is testimonial when a reasonable person in the position of the declarant would understand that the statement could be used in later criminal proceedings. For example, a person's answers to questions during formal police interrogation at a police station are testimonial because a reasonable person in that situation understands the police are gathering evidence for possible use in court.

Children's hearsay statements to parents, relatives, teachers, friends, foster parents, and babysitters are nontestimonial. Statements to child protection workers conducting investigations are usually testimonial. Children's statements during formal forensic interviews at child advocacy centers are testimonial.

Hearsay statements to physicians, nurses, and other medical professionals are nontestimonial when the professional's primary motive for questioning the child is clinical. The fact that the professional is aware of the forensic implications of communicating with children about maltreatment does not alter this conclusion. On the other hand, when a medical professional questions a child primarily for legal reasons, the child's statements are likely testimonial.

Although many statements to police officers are testimonial, some are not. The answer depends on the circumstances in which the officer questions the child. Statements to police are most likely to be nontestimonial when the police ask questions in the context of an ongoing emergency. Thus, a child's answer to a police officer's question, "What happened?" shortly after the officer arrives in response to a 911 call is typically nontestimonial because the question is intended to assess the situation, see whether medical help is necessary, and determine whether the victim and the officer are safe. As the initial emergency abates—and the officer's questions shift to gathering evidence—statements become testimonial.

In deciding whether statements to police officers are testimonial, judges consider: (1) Was there an ongoing emergency? (2) Was the child safe or in danger? (3) Was medical assistance necessary? (4) Was the child alone or protected by others? (5) Was the child seeking help? (6) Was the child describing events that were happening? Or was the child describing past events? (7) How much time elapsed since the abuse occurred? (8) What was the level of formality of the questioning?

Importance of Documentation

Professionals are in an excellent position to document children's hearsay statements. Without careful documentation of exactly what questions were asked and exactly what children said, the professional will not likely remember months or years later when the professional is called as a witness and asked to repeat what the child said. Documentation is needed not only to preserve the child's words but also to preserve a record of the many factors indicating whether the child's hearsay statements meet the requirements of an exception to the hearsay rule and whether the statements are testimonial.

Proof of Physical Abuse

PA is defined as nonaccidental physical injury (see Chapter 11). To prove PA, attorneys rely on expert testimony from pediatricians, radiologists, pathologists, and other physicians. Judges permit doctors to describe a child's injuries and offer an opinion that the injuries were not accidental. A physician may describe the means used to inflict injury and the degree of force required. A physician may opine on cause of death. Abusive adults often provide implausible explanations for a child's serious or fatal injuries (e.g., child fell off couch onto carpeted floor), and a physician may testify that the caretaker's explanation is not consistent with the child's injuries.

A physician may describe bruises on a child's body. As explained in Chapter 11, it is not possible to date bruises with precision. In many cases, however, an expert can distinguish accidental from inflicted bruises. A doctor may describe fractures, internal injuries, bites, burns, and other injuries. Battered child syndrome (BCS) was described by Kempe and his colleagues (1962). BCS is diagnostic of nonaccidental injury, and a physician may testify that a child has BCS.

Head injury is one of the most dangerous and deadly forms of nonaccidental injury. Inflicted head injury is particularly common in very young children and babies. Injuries to the skull and/or brain are caused by inflicting direct blows to the head, slamming the child against an object, and shaking. As explained in Chapter 11, there is some controversy over whether shaking alone can cause massive brain injury and death. Judges allow physicians to describe head injury, including shaken baby syndrome (SBS).

When a young child or baby is brought to the hospital with massive head injuries, caretakers often say the child fell a relatively short distance. Falls—even short falls—can injure. For the most part, however, falls of less than four feet seldom result in serious or fatal injury.

The majority of American parents believe in corporal punishment (Flynn, 1996; Garbarino, 2005). The law permits parents to use "reasonable" corporal punishment. Unfortunately, a great deal of PA—including fatal abuse—is the result of corporal punishment that got out of control (Myers, 2006). When a parent is on trial for PA, the parent may defend by stating that they were using reasonable corporal punishment. To determine whether corporal punishment was reasonable, judges consider the child's age and size, the means used to inflict discipline (e.g., open hand versus closed fist or belt), the place on the child's body that was hit (bottom versus head), how much pain or injury occurred, and whether there was a single questionable incident of excessive punishment or a history of brutality (Myers, 2005).

In addition to expert medical testimony, proof of PA is assisted by a thorough investigation by police or child protective services (CPS). Investigators examine the place where the child was injured. Photographs are taken, and evidence is preserved. Investigators interview witnesses and the adult suspected of hurting the child. See Chapter 19 for discussion of investigation.

Rob Parrish (2005, 2006), an experienced prosecutor, notes that it can be very challenging to prove serious PA and child homicide. Parrish observes that these cases are often hotly contested, with both sides presenting expert medical testimony. Even if the prosecutor succeeds in proving abuse, Parrish explains that it is sometimes difficult to prove who injured or killed the child.

Proof of Neglect

Neglect occurs when parents or caretakers fail to provide a child with basic food, clothing, shelter, or medical care. Neglect is defined and described in Chapter 7. The juvenile court's role in protecting neglected children is addressed in Chapter 4. Occasionally, neglect is so severe that it constitutes a crime and is prosecuted in criminal court (see Chapter 6). Psychological neglect is the subject of Chapters 7 and 8.

The key to proving neglect in court—as with other forms of maltreatment—is thorough investigation (Greenbaum et al., 2008). Investigation is discussed in Chapter 19. Neglect investigation is typically the bailiwick of child protection workers. In juvenile court, the investigating CPS worker is normally the key witness, describing the investigation and making treatment and placement recommendations. Testimony from the CPS worker may be supplemented by testimony from physicians, psychologists, or psychiatrists.

Medical neglect occurs when parents refuse to provide their child with essential medical treatment. The medical and psychological dimensions of medical neglect are analyzed in Chapter 9. The focus here is law. When parents refuse recommended medical, dental, or psychiatric treatment, the treating physician endeavors to change their minds. If the parents persist in refusing and the physician believes treatment is critical, the physician has to decide whether to file a report of medical neglect with CPS. If a report is filed, CPS workers investigate, and in appropriate circumstances they commence proceedings in juvenile court seeking a court order overriding the parents' refusal.

The judge in a medical neglect case conducts a difficult balancing act. The judge balances (1) the right of parents to make medical decisions for their children, (2) the government's interest in the child's well-being, and (3) the child's interests. Each medical neglect case is unique, and no two balancing processes are the same. Yet, there is a pattern in judicial decision making. If medical treatment is essential to save a child's life and the treatment is likely to be effective and without serious or painful side effects, the judge is likely to overrule the parents and authorize treatment. On the other hand, if the lifesaving treatment is experimental or has a relatively low probability of curing the child's condition, the judge is likely to defer to parents.

In non–life-and-death cases, where treatment is important but not essential to preserve life, it is difficult to predict how a judge will rule. The judge considers the seriousness of the medical condition and the likelihood the proposed treatment will be effective. The result turns on the facts of the case, with the odds favoring the parents.

In most medical neglect cases, the parents' decision to refuse medical care for their child is based on the parents' religious beliefs. Parents have the right to raise their children in a particular religious tradition. This does not mean, however, that parents have unlimited authority to deny essential medical care to their children in the name of religion. The U.S. Supreme Court observed,

> The family itself is not beyond regulation in the public interest, as against a claim of religious liberty. . . . The right to practice religion freely does not include liberty to expose the community or the child to communicable disease or the latter to ill health or death. . . . Parents may be free to become martyrs themselves. But it does not follow they are free, in identical circumstances, to make martyrs of their children. (*Prince v. Massachusetts*, 1944, pp. 167, 170)

In a similar vein, the Arizona Supreme Court wrote, "If there is a direct collision of a child's right to good health and a parent's religious beliefs, the parents' rights must give way" (*In re Appeal in Cochise County*, 1982, p. 465).

Proof of Sexual Abuse

Child sexual abuse (CSA) is often difficult to prove. Sexual abuse occurs in secret, and there seldom are eyewitnesses other than the child. The U.S. Supreme Court observed, "Child abuse is one of the most difficult crimes to detect and prosecute, in large part because there are no witnesses except the victim" (*Pennsylvania v. Ritchie*, 1987, p. 60). As discussed in Chapter 15, most sexual abuse causes no injury that can be detected by a medical professional. In the majority of sexual abuse trials, the child testifies, and the outcome of the case rises or falls on the child's shoulders. Although most children are effective witnesses, some children are too young, too shy, or too traumatized to testify.

In the effort to prove sexual abuse, attorneys sometimes turn to medical and mental health professionals for expert testimony. The remainder of this chapter describes medical and psychological evidence of CSA.

Medical Evidence of Child Sexual Abuse

As mentioned earlier and described in detail in Chapter 15, most forms of sexual abuse do not cause physical injury. In the unusual case where medical evidence is found, the evidence can be used in court to help prove abuse (see Berkoff et al., 2008).

Psychological Evidence of Child Sexual Abuse

CSA causes psychological symptoms in many but not all victims. See Chapters 13 and 16. Does the presence of psychological symptoms that are observed in sexually abused children provide evidence of sexual abuse? This seemingly simple question is the source of controversy.

1. Psychological Sequelae of Child Sexual Abuse

At its core, sexual abuse is psychological abuse; a fundamental betrayal of trust. Adults are supposed to protect children—not exploit them. Some sexually abused children feel the abuse is their fault and that they are unworthy, unlovable damaged goods. Sexual abuse causes stress-related symptoms, including nightmares, regression to earlier stages of development (e.g., bedwetting or soiling in potty-trained children), depression, poor self-concept, misbehavior at home and at school, somatic problems such as headaches and stomachaches, anxiety, hypervigilance, and fear. Many sexually abused children have some of the symptoms of posttraumatic stress disorder (PTSD), and roughly a third of sexually abused children meet the full diagnostic criteria for PTSD (see Chapters 13 and 16).

2. Stress-Related Psychological Symptoms Are Seen in Nonabused as Well as Abused Children

Stress-related symptoms are not unique to sexual abuse. Witnessing domestic violence, for example, causes symptoms in some children (see Chapter 10). Children who are physically abused or neglected but not sexually abused may have mental health issues. Family disorganization, poverty, and substance/alcohol abuse are stressful for children. Some children growing up in "normal" homes are anxious and symptomatic, and some psychological symptoms (e.g., nightmares) are so common among nonmaltreated children that they are a normal part of growing up.

3. Do Psychological Symptoms Seen in Sexually Abused Children and Nonabused Children Provide Evidence of Sexual Abuse?

No one disputes that sexual abuse causes stress-related psychological symptoms in some children. Difficulties arise, however, when we ask, Does the presence of psychological symptoms seen in sexually abused children provide evidence of sexual abuse? If a symptom were seen *only* in sexually abused children then the answer would be yes. The symptom would be diagnostic of sexual abuse or, as some say it, pathognomonic for sexual abuse. Unfortunately, there is no psychological symptom or group of symptoms that is found only among sexually abused children. Moreover, there is no psychological syndrome that diagnoses sexual abuse. Finally, there is no psychological test that can tell whether a child was abused.

All of the stress-related symptoms observed in sexually abused children are seen to a greater or lesser extent in nonabused children. To rephrase the question from the preceding paragraph: Does the presence of psychological symptoms observed in sexually abused *and* nonabused children provide evidence of sexual abuse? In some cases the answer is yes, but arriving at that answer requires understanding of two issues: (a) How often is the symptom observed in sexually abused *and* nonabused children? (b) What are the populations of sexually abused *and* nonabused children?

a. *How often is the symptom observed in sexually abused* and *nonabused children?* If a symptom is seen more often in abused than nonabused children, the symptom may have some tendency to prove abuse (Lyon & Koehler, 1996). The more often the symptom is observed in abused children and the less often in nonabused children, the greater the probative value. This conclusion is complicated, however, by the fact that little comparative data is available on the prevalence of various symptoms among abused and nonabused children. Moreover, quite a few sexually abused children have no detectable symptoms.

b. *What are the populations of sexually abused* and *nonabused children?* The fact that a symptom is seen more often in sexually abused than nonabused children is not enough to conclude that the symptom is probative of abuse. One must also consider the fact that the population of nonabused children is much larger than the population of abused children. Even though a symptom is observed more often in sexually abused children, because there are more nonabused than abused children, most children with the symptom will be nonabused.

Consider the imaginary city of Dillville. Ten thousand female children between 3 and 10 years of age live in Dillville. Twenty percent of Dillville's girls are sexually abused—a number that finds support in the literature. There are 2,000 sexually abused 3- to 10-year-old girls in Dillville and 8,000 nonabused girls. A 5-year-old Dillville girl started wetting the bed at night, and medical reasons for the bed-wetting are ruled out. Sexual abuse causes some potty-trained children to wet the bed. Does this child's bed-wetting tend to prove sexual abuse? Assume bed-wetting in potty-trained children is observed in 20% of sexually abused children and 5% of nonabused children. We would expect to find 400 sexually abused bed-wetters among Dillville girls. Yet, because 5% of nonabused children wet the bed, and because there are many more nonabused than abused children, we find an equal number of bed-wetters—400—among the nonabused Dillvillers. If all we know about a child is that she wets the bed, she is just as likely to be nonabused as abused.

Tinkering with the numbers reinforces the point that psychological symptoms seen in abused as well as nonabused children say little about sexual abuse. Suppose 10% of sexually abused and 5% of the nonabused girls wet the bed. Now 200 sexually abused Dillville girls wet the bed and 400 nonabused girls do so. A bed-wetter is twice as likely to be nonabused as abused.

4. As Symptoms Add Up, Does Probative Value Increase?

Does the fact that a child has multiple stress-related symptoms increase the likelihood the child was sexually abused? The more stress-related symptoms a child has, the more likely the child experienced *some* stress-inducing event, but sexual abuse is not the only possibility. The statistical impact of population sizes remains.

5. Posttraumatic Stress Disorder

As mentioned earlier, up to a third of sexually abused children meet the diagnostic criteria for PTSD. Is a diagnosis of PTSD evidence of sexual abuse? Should an expert witness testify that because a child was diagnosed with

PTSD the child was probably sexually abused? This raises two issues. The first issue relates to the statistical matters previously discussed: What is the prevalence of PTSD in abused *and* nonabused children? And what are the populations of sexually abused *and* nonabused children? Only when these questions are answered can we determine whether a diagnosis of PTSD tends to prove sexual abuse. In all likelihood, a diagnosis of PTSD says little about sexual abuse because some nonabused children have PTSD and because the population of nonabused children is much larger than the population of abused children.

The second issue raised by a diagnosis of PTSD as evidence of sexual abuse relates to the diagnostic criteria for PTSD as defined by the *Diagnostic and Statistical Manual of Mental Disorders* (DSM-IV) (American Psychiatric Association, 2000). The DSM-IV criteria provide in part: "The person has been exposed to a traumatic event. . . ." (American Psychiatric Association, 2000, p. 467). Thus, a clinician considering a diagnosis of PTSD must accept as given that the client experienced a traumatic event. Yet, if the diagnosis assumes that a traumatic event occurred, how can the diagnosis prove that very event? The answer is that it cannot. A diagnosis of PTSD is not useful to prove sexual abuse. DSM-IV is careful to remind us "that a diagnosis does not carry any necessary implications regarding the causes of the individual's mental disorder or its associated impairments" (American Psychiatric Association, 2000, p. xxxiii).

A diagnosis of PTSD is very useful in clinical settings. When it comes to evidence in court, however, the diagnosis should not be mentioned, and the witness should focus on the child's symptoms. Of course, if these symptoms are also observed in nonabused children—and they are—then we are back to the twin issues of symptom frequency in abused and nonabused children and population sizes.

6. Symptoms That Have a Relatively Strong Connection to Sexual Abuse

Stress-related symptoms seen in sexually abused and nonabused children say little about sexual abuse. With children younger than 10 or so, however, symptoms of a sexual nature have a strong connection to sexual knowledge, and sexual knowledge is sometimes rooted in sexual abuse. Particularly concerning are (1) aggressive sexuality in young children, (2) imitation by young children of adult sexual acts, and (3) sexual knowledge that is unusual for a child of that age (Friedrich, Grambasch, Broughton, Kuipers, & Beilke, 1991).

Children are not asexual. Yet, developmentally inappropriate sexual knowledge or behavior in a young child indicates sexual knowledge. Consider a 4-year-old who says, "Joey's pee-pee was big and hard, and he made me lick it, and white stuff popped out and tasted really yucky." This child has seen a pornographic video, been coached, or been sexually abused. A sexually naive 4-year-old could no more make this up than a coffee-naive child could describe the process and product of an espresso machine. If pornography is ruled out—pornography is unlikely to be the explanation when a child describes the taste and feel of seminal fluid—that leaves coaching or abuse. Could a 4-year-old be coached to provide such a graphic description of abuse and ejaculation? Anything is possible, but coaching seems unlikely. That leaves abuse. In sum, graphic descriptions of sexual abuse from young children—"His pee-pee spit on me"—often provide strong evidence of sexual abuse.

In addition to words, the following behaviors indicate developmentally inappropriate sexual knowledge: attempting to engage in explicit sex acts, inserting objects in the child's or someone else's vagina or anus, initiating French kissing, masturbating excessively, masturbating with an object, and imitating sexual intercourse (Brilleslijper-Kater, Friedrich, & Corwin, 2004). Again, one must rule out benign explanations before attributing such behavior to sexual abuse. Moreover, although sexual behavior is uncommon in nonabused children, it does occur, reviving the conundrum of population sizes. The fact that sexual behavior is much more frequent in sexually abused than nonabused young children does not eliminate the fact that the population of nonabused children is much larger than the population of abused children (Melton, Petrila, Poythress, & Slobogin, 2007). Giving proper respect to population sizes and benign alternatives, developmentally unusual sexual knowledge often provides evidence of sexual abuse.

7. Can Mental Health Professionals Reliably Diagnose Child Sexual Abuse?

Mental health professionals providing treatment routinely consider the symptoms described earlier to make treatment decisions. But is the degree of certainty required to diagnose sexual abuse in the clinic sufficient to provide expert testimony in court? Put another way, can mental health professionals diagnose sexual abuse with sufficient reliability to make their testimony useful in litigation?

This question divides experts on CSA. Some experts, notably Gary Melton, argue mental health professionals cannot reliably detect sexual abuse (Melton & Limber, 1989; Melton et al., 2007). Melton asserts that evaluating symptoms observed in abused and nonabused children is a matter of common sense and that mental health professionals have little to add. Moreover, Melton argues that when mental health professionals make decisions about sexual abuse they rely so heavily on the child's words that a diagnosis of sexual abuse is little more than a thinly veiled opinion the child told the truth. The law makes clear that expert witnesses are not allowed to opine that a child was truthful or that sexually abused children generally tell the truth (Myers, 2005). Melton concludes judges should not permit mental health professionals to testify a child was sexually abused. Indeed, Melton argues professionals who offer such testimony act unethically.

Herman (2005, 2009) reviewed empirical research on the accuracy of clinical judgments about sexual abuse and concluded along with Melton that such judgments lack reliability. Similar skepticism is expressed by Faust, Bridges and Ahern (2009), who conclude that clinical judgments about sexual abuse are based on unverified methods and speculation. Other experts agree (Horner, Guyer, & Kalter, 1993).

Garb (1998) is an authority on the accuracy of clinical judgments by mental health professionals. Garb's research indicates that when it comes to evaluating causation—e.g., was this child sexually abused?—mental health professionals fare poorly.

On the other side of the debate, many mental health professionals believe it is possible in some cases for experts to conclude that sexual abuse is the most likely explanation for a child's symptoms and statements (Sgroi, Porter, & Blick, 1983). Faller (2002) concludes this is the majority position in the United States.

How do judges react to expert mental health testimony that a child was sexually abused? Although some judges allow such testimony, the majority of appellate courts rule that mental health professionals may not testify that a child was sexually abused.

8. Can Mental Health Professionals Testify That a Child's Symptoms Are Consistent With Sexual Abuse?

Although the majority position among appellate courts is that mental health professionals may not testify that a particular child was sexually abused, most courts do allow mental health professionals to testify that a child's symptoms are "consistent with" sexual abuse. Yet, there are two problems with "consistent with" testimony. First, although testimony that a child's symptoms are consistent with sexual abuse is not an opinion in so many words that a child was sexually abused, the testimony is offered in court precisely for that purpose. The testimony invites the following reasoning: Because the child has symptoms consistent with sexual abuse, the child was sexually abused. Thus, "consistent with" testimony is really an opinion the child was abused. As previously discussed, however, most appellate courts reject expert mental health testimony that a child was sexually abused. Moreover, as we have seen, there is considerable controversy among mental health professionals about the reliability of such testimony. "Consistent with" testimony effectively hides the controversy behind the innocuous term *consistent with*. If testimony in the form of a direct opinion on sexual abuse is excluded, the same should probably be true for testimony that a child's symptoms are consistent with sexual abuse.

A second concern about "consistent with" testimony is that many symptoms that are consistent with sexual abuse are also consistent with nonabuse. Nightmares are consistent with sexual abuse but are also consistent with a host of issues that have nothing to do with sexual abuse. Indeed, nightmares are consistent with *normal* child development. "Consistent with" testimony masks the twin issues of symptom frequency and population size, discussed earlier. When an expert testifies that a child's symptoms are consistent with sexual abuse, the jury or judge takes the testimony as proof the child was sexually abused. A jury or judge is unlikely to appreciate the complexity of symptom frequencies in abused and nonabused children, along with population sizes.

Given the problems with "consistent with" testimony, one can argue that such testimony should not be allowed in court unless the expert who provides the testimony addresses two issues. First, it is not enough for the expert to testify that a child's symptoms are consistent with sexual abuse. The expert should explain *why* the symptoms tend to *prove* sexual abuse. Second, the expert should explain the impact of symptom frequency and population size on probative value. Only when symptom frequency and population size are added to "consistent with" testimony is the jury or judge equipped with the information needed to give "consistent with" testimony its proper weight. Absent this information, "consistent with" testimony is inherently misleading (see Myers, 2010).

9. Summary

Mental health testimony offered to prove sexual abuse is complex and controversial. If such testimony is admissible in court at all, it should be offered only by highly qualified experts. The professional should have a thorough grasp of child development, including memory and suggestibility, normal sexual development, the impact of sexual abuse, normal and abnormal psychology, medical evidence of sexual abuse, the process by which children disclose sexual abuse, proper and improper interview methods, prevalence rates in abused and nonabused children, the impact of population sizes, and the strengths and weaknesses of clinical judgment. The professional should be conversant with the debate regarding the reliability of expert testimony offered to prove sexual abuse. Only a handful of mental health professionals working with sexually abused children possess this depth of knowledge. Professionals who lack this expertise should not provide expert testimony that a child was sexually abused or has symptoms consistent with sexual abuse.

Psychological Testimony to Rehabilitate a Child's Credibility

A common defense strategy in CSA cases is to undermine the child's credibility by pointing out that the child delayed reporting, gave inconsistent versions of the abuse over time, or recanted. When the defense adopts this strategy, most judges allow the prosecutor to rehabilitate the child's credibility with expert testimony that it is not uncommon for sexually abused children to delay reporting, be inconsistent, or recant (Myers, 2005).

This is an appropriate place to mention Child Sexual Abuse Accommodation Syndrome (CSAAS). This much misunderstood "syndrome" was described by Roland Summit (1983). Summit's goal was to help mental health professionals understand the psychological dynamics of sexual abuse, particularly incest. Summit explained that many sexually abused children delay reporting. The child feels trapped and struggles to make the best of a bad situation—she accommodates. When disclosure finally comes, it may be halting and piecemeal. Following disclosure, some children feel compelled to recant.

Summit never intended CSAAS as a test for sexual abuse. The syndrome neither detects nor diagnoses sexual abuse. Thus, CSAAS does not prove sexual abuse. Rather, CSAAS assumes abuse occurred and explains how children respond. Although CSAAS should not be offered in court to prove abuse, the syndrome plays a useful role in rehabilitating children's credibility. CSAAS helps the jury understand delayed reporting, halting and inconsistent disclosure, and recantation.

Expert Testimony Attacking and Defending Interviews

In most CSA trials, the child testifies. In addition, the child's hearsay is often admitted. The child's credibility is the centerpiece of the prosecution's case and the bull's-eye for the defense attorney. The defense must shake the jury or judge's confidence in the child. With the child's credibility in mind, this section addresses expert testimony focused on how children are interviewed.

To the end of undermining a child's credibility, a common defense strategy is to offer expert testimony critiquing interviews of children. Judges are receptive to such testimony. In *State v. Wigg* (2005), the Vermont Supreme Court outlined permissible uses of expert testimony on interviewing. First, the court approved expert testimony on proper and improper methods of interviewing. Second, the court ruled that an expert may comment on whether the interviews in the case on trial comply with accepted practice. Third, the court rejected expert testimony that interviewing undermined a particular child's credibility. The court's rejection of expert testimony that interviewing undermined a child's credibility is in line with the rule that expert witnesses may not testify that a child was telling the truth.

When the defense offers expert testimony attacking interviews of the child, the prosecution can cross-examine the expert and offer expert testimony of its own. In the final analysis, the best defense against the attack on the interviewer is to ensure that professionals who interview children are competent. Competent interviewing defends itself.

Conclusion

Child maltreatment takes an enormous toll on children and society. The legal system plays a key role in protecting children and holding accountable those who harm them.

References

American Psychiatric Association (APA). (2000). *Diagnostic and statistical manual of mental disorders* (4th ed.). Washington, DC: Author.

Berkoff, M. C., Zolotor, A. J., Makoroff, K. L., Thackerary, J. D., Shapiro, R. A., & Runyan, D. K. (2008). Has this prepubertal girl been sexually abused? *Journal of the American Medical Association, 300*, 2779–2792.

Brilleslijper-Kater, S. N., Friedrich, W. N., & Corwin, D. L. (2004). Sexual knowledge and emotional reaction as indicators of sexual abuse in young children: Theory and research challenges. *Child Abuse and Neglect, 28*, 1007–1017.

Crawford v. Washington, 541 U.S. 36 (2004).

Davis v. Washington, 547 U.S. 813 (2006).

Faller, K. C. (2002). *Understanding and assessing child sexual maltreatment* (2nd ed.). Thousand Oaks, CA: Sage.

Faust, D., Bridges, A. J., & Ahern, D. C. (2009). Methods for the identification of sexually abused children: Issues and needed features for abuse indicators. In K. Kuehnle & M. Connell (Eds.), *The evaluation of child sexual abuse allegations* (pp. 3–19). New York: Wiley.

Flynn, C. P. (1996). Regional differences in spanking experiences and attitudes: A comparison of Northeastern and Southern college students. *Journal of Interpersonal Violence, 11*, 59–80.

Friedrich, W. N., Grambasch, P., Broughton, D., Kuipers, J., & Beilke, W. L. (1991). Normative sexual behavior in children. *Pediatrics, 88*, 456–464.

Garb, H. N. (1998). *Studying the clinician: Judgment research and psychological assessment.* Washington, DC: American Psychological Association.

Garbarino, J. (2005). Corporal punishment in perspective. In M. Donnelly & M. A. Straus (Eds.), *Corporal punishment of children in theoretical perspective* (pp. 8–18). New Haven, CT: Yale.

Greenbaum, J., Dubowitz, H., Lutzker, J. R., Johnson, K. D., Orn, K., Kenniston, J., et al. (2008). *Practice guidelines: Challenges in the evaluation of child neglect.* Elmhurst, IL: American Professional Society on the Abuse of Children.

Herman, S. (2005). Improving decision making in forensic child sexual abuse evaluations. *Law and Human Behavior, 29*, 87–120.

Herman, S. (2009). Child sexual abuse evaluations. In K. Kuehnle & M. Connell (Eds.), *The evaluation of child sexual abuse allegations* (pp. 247–266). New York: Wiley.

Horner, T. M., Guyer, M. J., & Kalter, N. M. (1993). The biases of child abuse experts. Believing is seeing. *Bulletin of the American Academy of Psychiatry and Law, 21*, 281–292.

In re Appeal in Cochise County, 650 P.2d 459 (Ariz. 1982).

Jones, D. P. H. (1992). *Interviewing the sexually abused children: Investigation of suspected abuse*. London: Royal College of Psychiatrists.

Kempe, C. H., Silverman, F. N., Steele, B. F., Droegmueller, W., & Silver, H. K. (1962). The battered-child syndrome. *Journal of the American Medical Association, 181*, 17–24.

Lyon, T. D., & Koehler, J. J. (1996). The relevance ratio: Evaluating the probative value of expert testimony in child sexual abuse cases. *Cornell Law Review, 82*, 43–78.

Melendez-Diaz v. Massachusetts, 129 S. Ct. 2527 (2009).

Melton, G. B., & Limber S. (1989). Psychologists' involvement in cases of child maltreatment. *American Psychologist, 44*, 1225–1233.

Melton, G. B., Petrila, J., Poythress, N. G., & Slobogin, C. (2007). *Psychological evaluations for the court: A handbook for mental health professionals and lawyers* (3rd ed.). New York: Guilford Press.

Myers, J. E. B. (2005). *Myers on evidence in child, domestic and elder abuse cases*. New York: Aspen.

Myers, J. E. B. (2006). *Child protection in America: Past, present and future*. New York: Oxford University Press.

Myers, J. E. B. (2010). Expert testimony in child sexual abuse litigation: Consensus and confusion. *UC Davis Journal of Juvenile Law & Policy, 14*, 1–57.

Parrish, R. (2005). Preparing a case for court. In A. P. Giardino & R. Alexander (Eds.), *Child maltreatment* (3rd ed). St. Louis, MO: G.W. Medical Publishing.

Parrish, R. (2006). Prosecuting a case. In L. Frasier, K. Rauth-Farley, R. Alexander, & R. Parrish (Eds.), *Abusive head trauma in infants and children* (pp. 393–420). St. Louis, MO: G.W. Medical Publishing.

Pennsylvania v. Ritchie, 480 U.S. 39 (1987).

Prince v. Massachusetts, 321 U.S. 158 (1944).

Sgroi, S. M., Porter, F. S., & Blick, L. C. (1983). Validation of child sexual abuse. In S. M. Sgroi (Ed.), *Handbook of clinical intervention in child sexual abuse*. Lanham, MD: Lexington Books.

State v. Wigg, 889 A.2d 233 (2005).

Summit, R. C. (1983). The child sexual abuse accommodation syndrome. *Child Abuse and Neglect, 7*, 177–193.

Author Index

Chang, J. J., 221
Chapman, D. P., 145
Chapman, J. E., 297
Chartier, M., 221
Chasnoff, I. J., 159
Chelminski, I., 131
Chen, L., 28
Cheng, V. K., 118
Chewning, M., 260
Christensen, C. V., 238
Christensen, M. L., 170
Christian, C. W., 184
Christiansen, J. R., 240, 241, 243
Christianson, S. Å., 338, 339
Christopher, R. S., 220
Chyi-in, W., 196
Cicchetti, D., 19, 113, 114, 115, 116, 132, 279
Clausen, A. H., 104, 131, 132, 196
Claycomb, C., 346, 348
Cleland, C. M., 224
Clubb, P. A., 352
Cohen, J. A., 204, 220, 221, 223, 224, 225, 226, 267, 268, 269, 270, 273, 274, 275, 276, 277, 279, 284, 285
Cohen, N. E., 5
Cohen, P., 150
Cohn Donnelly, A., 20
Cohyen, P., 267
Cole, R., 28, 117
Coleman, R. W., 132
Collie, R. M., 292
Collins, A., 108, 110, 111, 112, 113
Collmer, C. W., 116
Cone, L. T., 296
Conger, R. D., 114, 115, 195, 196
Conroy, K., 175
Considine, M. G., 341
Conte, J. R., 219, 220, 240, 241, 246
Conway, E. F., 106
Conway, J., 22
Cook, P., 137
Cook, S. J., 115
Cooney, G., 224, 225, 226
Cooper, A., 188, 189
Cooperman, D. R., 190
Cordon, I. M., 348, 350
Cormier, C. A., 294
Corter, C., 133
Cortes, R. M., 279
Corwin, D. L., 392
Cosentino, C. E., 225

Cosgrove, J. M., 350
Cotter, L. P., 312
Courtney, M. E., 69
Cowen, E. L., 137
Cox, C. E., 152
Craig, I. W., 137
Crayton, J., 339
Crengle, S., 217
Crichton, L., 115
Crisp, A. H., 237
Crittenden, P. M., 104, 106, 131, 132, 133, 152, 196
Crooks, C. V., 172
Crosby, A., 27
Cross, T. P., 234
Crouter, A., 151
Crowell, N. A., 298
Cumming, G. F., 290, 295, 296
Cummings, E. M., 134, 172
Cummings, J. A., 268, 278, 284
Cunningham, A. H., 169, 246, 247, 342
Cunningham, P. B., 296
Cunningham-Rathner, J., 239, 289, 292, 309
Cureton, P., 152, 158
Curtis, K. M., 311
Curtis, N. M., 296
Curwen, T., 297
Cuskey, W. R., 156
Czyz, E., 173

Dadds, M., 28, 220
Daignault, I. V., 223
Daigneault, I., 224
Daleiden, E. L., 240, 241, 243
Dalessandro, M., 312
Damant, D., 175
D'Amico, P. J., 276, 284
Damon, L., 225
D'Amora, D. A., 312
Dang, V. V., 151
Daro, D., 18, 21, 23, 24, 25, 26, 28, 29, 32, 169
Daversa, M. T., 295
Davidson, R. J., 137
Davies, G. M., 341, 344
Davies, P. T., 134
Davis, K. B., 151, 152
Davis, S. L., 339, 341
Davis, W. W., 158
Dawud, S., 279
Day, D. M., 291, 293

Subject Index

About the Editor _____

John E. B. Myers, JD, is a distinguished professor and scholar at the University of the Pacific McGeorge School of Law. He is the author or editor of eight books and more than 100 articles and chapters on child maltreatment. His writing has been cited by more than 140 courts, including the U.S. Supreme Court. He is a frequent speaker at conferences, having made more than 400 presentations around the world.

About the Contributors

Elizabeth C. Ahern, BA, is a developmental psychology PhD student at the University of Southern California (USC). Her research interests include children's disclosure of maltreatment and the emergence of early lying ability. She is also a child forensic interviewer at the Center for Assault Treatment Services in Van Nuys, California, and at the Edelman Children's Court in Monterey Park, California.

Judith V. Becker, PhD, is professor of psychology and psychiatry as well as acting director of the Psychology, Policy, and Law Program at the University of Arizona. She has been conducting clinical research in the area of sexual abuse/aggression for over 30 years. She is the past president of the Association for the Treatment of Sexual Abusers. She has published over 100 scholarly articles and chapters on the topic of sexual abuse/aggression. She also consults on clinical and forensic cases.

Lucy Berliner, MSW, is the director of the Harborview Center for Sexual Assault and Traumatic Stress in Seattle. She is a clinical associate professor at the University of Washington School of Social Work and the University of Washington Department of Psychiatry and Behavioral Sciences. Her activities include clinical practice with child and adult victims of trauma and crime, research on the impact of trauma and the effectiveness of clinical and societal interventions, and participation in local and national social policy initiatives to promote the interests of trauma and crime victims.

Nelson Binggeli, PhD, earned his doctorate in Counseling Psychology from Georgia State University and is currently a staff psychologist at the Georgia Institute of Technology Counseling Center. His special interests include mind-body approaches to stress management, cognitive-behavioral therapy for mood and anxiety disorders, psychological assessment, and helping people to overcome the effects of unsupportive environments and traumatic experiences.

Marla R. Brassard, PhD, is a professor in the School Psychology Program at Teachers College, Columbia University. She focuses her research on psychological maltreatment of children—its assessment, the emotional/behavioral injuries that result, and contextual factors that moderate the effects of maltreatment (particularly the role of schools, teachers, and peer relationships). She also studies psychological aggression in teacher-student and peer relationships. She has published four books, numerous articles and chapters, cochaired the task force that wrote the *Guidelines for the Psychosocial Evaluation of Suspected Psychological Maltreatment* (1995), and coauthored the Psychological Maltreatment Rating Scales.

Deborah Daro, PhD, is a research fellow at Chapin Hall at the University of Chicago. Prior to joining Chapin Hall in 1999, she served as the director of the National Center on Child Abuse Prevention Research, a program of the National Committee to Prevent Child Abuse. Most recently, her research and written work has focused on developing reform strategies that embed individualized, targeted prevention efforts within more universal efforts to alter normative standards and community context.

Howard A. Davidson, JD, is the director of the American Bar Association Center on Children and the Law in Washington, D.C. He has been actively involved with the legal aspects of child protection for 35 years. He has directed the center since its 1978 establishment. He served as chair of the U.S. Advisory Board on Child Abuse and Neglect, is a founding board member of the National Center for Missing and Exploited Children, is on the board of End Child Prostitution and Trafficking/USA (ECPAT/USA), and is a member of the Maryland Children's Justice Task Force. He was named by the mayor of Philadelphia to a Department of Human Services Community Oversight Board to help guide improvements in that city's child protection system. Howard has authored many articles, including "Federal Law and State Intervention When Parents Fail: Has National Guidance of Our Child Welfare System Been Successful?" published in 2008 in the *Family Law Quarterly*.

Esther Deblinger, PhD, is a professor of psychiatry and the codirector of the Child Abuse Research and Services Institute (CARES) of the University of Medicine and Dentistry of New Jersey (UMDNJ)–School of Osteopathic Medicine. Her collaborative research funded by the National Institute of Mental Health (NIMH) led to the development of Trauma-Focused Cognitive Behavioral Therapy (TF-CBT), a well-established treatment approach for youth and their families recognized by the U.S. Department of Health and Human Services as a "model program." She has coauthored two professional books on the treatment of child sexual abuse and other traumas as well as several children's books on body safety.

Diane DePanfilis, PhD, MSW, is professor and associate dean for research and the director of the Ruth H. Young Center for Families and Children at the University of Maryland School of Social Work. She has worked in the field of child maltreatment for over 37 years in direct practice as a caseworker, supervisor, and manager of child protective services (CPS); as a national trainer and consultant; and as a researcher and scholar. Her current work emphasizes the intersection between research, policy, and practice particularly related to families and children. She has conducted extensive studies related to the delivery of child welfare services, the prevention of child maltreatment, and the implementation of policies and community service programs.

Vielka Diaz, EdM, is a bilingual school psychologist with the New York City Department of Education. She is a graduate of Teachers College, Columbia University, where she continues to assist in research focusing on psychological maltreatment. She is currently pursuing a specialty in school neuropsychology.

Howard Dubowitz, MD, MS, is a professor of pediatrics and director of the Center for Families at the University of Maryland School of Medicine. He is on the Council of the International Society for the Prevention of Child Abuse and Neglect and is a board member of Prevent Child Abuse America (PCA America). He is a clinician, researcher, and educator, and he is active in the policy arena. His main interests are in child neglect and prevention. He edited *Neglected Children: Research, Practice and Policy* (1999), coedited the *Handbook for Child Protection Practice* (2000), and has written over 140 publications.

Byron Egeland, PhD, is the Irving B. Harris Professor of Child Development at the University of Minnesota. He is a coprincipal investigator of the Minnesota Longitudinal Study of Parents and Children, a 33-year longitudinal study of high-risk children and their families. The 2005 book *The Development of the Person: The Minnesota Study of Risk and Adaptation from Birth to Adulthood* (Egeland and colleagues) received the American Psychological Association's (APA) Eleanor Maccoby Book Award in Developmental Psychology. He received the Distinguished Research Career Award from the American Professional Society on Abuse of Children (APSAC) and is a fellow in the APA, the American Psychological Society (APS), and the American Association of Applied and Preventive Psychology (AAAPP).

Martha Farrell Erickson, PhD, served as founding director of the Children, Youth and Family Consortium (CYFC) and director of the Irving B. Harris Programs in infant and early childhood mental health at the University of Minnesota. Since retiring from the university in 2008, she has continued to speak and consult extensively throughout the United States and abroad, with an emphasis on evidence-based preventive intervention with young children and families in high-risk circumstances. She also appears regularly on TV and radio in the Twin Cities and, with her daughter, hosts the weekly talk show *Good Enough Moms.*

Amanda M. Fanniff, PhD, is a postdoctoral fellow in the Department of Mental Health Law and Policy at the University of South Florida. She completed her doctorate in clinical psychology with a secondary emphasis in psychology, policy, and law at the University of Arizona, and completed her clinical internship at Western Psychiatric Institute and Clinic. Her primary research interest is the study and development of age-appropriate assessment, treatment, and policy regarding juvenile offenders in two contexts: (1) juveniles adjudicated for sexual offenses and (2) juveniles who may be incompetent to stand trial.

Martin A. Finkel, DO, is a professor of pediatrics and the medical director and cofounder of the CARES Institute at the University of Medicine and Dentistry of New Jersey–School of Osteopathic Medicine. He is an internationally recognized authority and pioneer on the medical evaluation and treatment of children alleged to have been sexually abused. He has published numerous articles, authored chapters, and is the coeditor of the 3rd edition of the textbook *Medical Evaluation of the Sexually Abused Child: A Practical Guide* (2009).

Gail S. Goodman, PhD, is distinguished professor of psychology and director of the Center for Public Policy Research at the University of California, Davis (UC Davis). Her research concerns memory development, child maltreatment, trauma and memory, and children in the legal system. She has received many awards for her research, including the 2008 Urie Bronfenbrenner Award for Lifetime Contribution to Developmental Psychology in the Service of Science and Society, and two Distinguished Contributions awards in 2005 from the APA (the Distinguished Contributions to Research in Public Policy Award and the Distinguished Professional Contributions to Applied Research Award).

Sandra A. Graham-Bermann, PhD, is a professor in the Department of Psychology at the University of Michigan. She studies different forms of violence that contribute to children's social and emotional dysfunction, with a special interest in the role of traumatic stress. She has developed and tested intervention programs designed to help children ages 4 to 13 and their mothers. In addition to published studies, she is coeditor of *Domestic Violence in the Lives of Children: The Future of Research, Intervention, and Social Policy* (2001) and *How Intimate Partner Violence Affects Children: Developmental Research, Case Studies, and Evidence-Based Treatment* (in press).

Stuart N. Hart, PhD, is deputy director of the International Institute for Child Rights and Development, Centre for Global Studies, University of Victoria, British Columbia. He is the founding director of the Office for the Study of the Psychological Rights of the Child and professor emeritus of the School of Education, Indiana University–Purdue University Indianapolis (IUPUI). He codirected with Marla Brassard, of Columbia University, a national study that produced the operational definitions for psychological maltreatment of children now used in many parts of the world. He has presented and published extensively on psychological maltreatment of children and on children's rights. He was a member of the NGO Advisory Panel for the UN Secretary General's Study on Violence Against Children, and he is on the editorial boards of *Child Abuse and Neglect—The International Journal* and *School Psychology International*. He is cochair of the Working Group to develop a draft General Comment for Article 19 of the UN Convention on the Rights of the Child for the UN Committee on the Rights of the Child.

Kathryn H. Howell, MS, is a doctoral student in clinical psychology at the University of Michigan. Her research centers on preschool children exposed to intimate partner violence (IPV), specifically examining resilience and coping mechanisms in this population. In addition to presenting research at national and international conferences, she coauthored a chapter on resiliency, risk, and protective factors and has published results of a study assessing traumatic events and stress symptoms in preschool age children from low income families.

Laura G. Kirsch, PhD, completed her clinical internship with the Federal Bureau of Prisons in Los Angeles, and is now a postdoctoral fellow in the Law and Psychiatry Program at the University of Massachusetts Medical School. Her research interests include examining the affective capacities of psychopaths, as well as studying the etiology, treatment, and management of sexual offenders. Clinically, she is interested in conducting forensic evaluations for criminal and civil referral questions.

Elizabeth J. Letourneau, PhD, is an associate professor in the Department of Psychiatry and Behavioral Sciences, Medical University of South Carolina. She has conducted clinical and policy research on adult and juvenile sexual offending since 1989. Currently, her research focuses on treatment effectiveness for juveniles who have sexually offended and the effects of legal policies such as registration and notification. She has numerous publications and serves as principal investigator for several grant-funded projects in these research areas. She is an active member of the Association for the Treatment of Sexual Abusers.

Jill S. Levenson, PhD, is an associate professor of human services at Lynn University, as well as a licensed clinical social worker with over 20 years of experience treating sexual abuse victims, survivors, perpetrators, and nonoffending parents. Her numerous publications include studies investigating the impact and effectiveness of social policies designed to prevent sexual violence. She is a coinvestigator on two grants funded by the National Institute of Justice investigating the effectiveness of sex offender registration and notification in reducing recidivism. She has published over 50 articles and book chapters and has coauthored three books on the treatment of sex offenders and their families.

Thomas D. Lyon, JD, PhD, is the Judge Edward J. and Ruey L. Guiardo Chair in law and psychology at USC. His research interests include child abuse and neglect, child witnesses, and domestic violence. He is the past president of the APA's Section on Child Maltreatment (Division 37) and a former member of the Board of Directors of APSAC. His work has been supported by the National Institutes of Health (NIH), the National Science Foundation, the U.S. Department of Justice, the National Child Abuse and Neglect Data System (NCANDS), the California Endowment, and the Haynes Foundation.

Donna M. Pence, BS, is a training and curriculum specialist at the Academy for Professional Excellence of the Public Child Welfare Training Academy, School of Social Work, San Diego State University Foundation. She was the first female special agent for the Tennessee Bureau of Investigation (TBI), appointed in 1976. For 2 years prior to her bureau employment, she was a patrol officer for the Metro Nashville Park Police. During her 25 years with the TBI, her assignments included undercover agent, homicide, sex crimes investigations, and child abuse investigations. She supervised the TBI's Drug Enforcement Unit and the Training and Recruitment Unit. Since 1985, she has lectured at state, national, and international levels on the investigation of child maltreatment and child death. She is a member of the FBI National Academy Associates (125th Session), a former board member of APSAC, and cochair of APSAC's task force on the guidelines on investigative interviewing of child victims. She has authored, coauthored, or contributed chapters in numerous publications on child abuse investigations, including *Team Investigation of Child Sexual Abuse: The Uneasy Alliance,* with Charles Wilson.

Elisabeth Pollio, PhD, is the mental health director of the Foster Care Program at the CARES Institute, UMDNJ–School of Osteopathic Medicine. She has provided mental health screenings to children entering foster care, psychological evaluations to children who have experienced maltreatment, and TF-CBT in a group format to children who have been sexually abused. She is also the coordinator of the postdoctoral fellowship program at the CARES Institute.

Robert M. Reece, MD, is clinical professor of pediatrics at Tufts University. He is the editor of two textbooks on child abuse as well as editor of *The Quarterly Update.* He was section chair of the American Academy of Pediatrics (AAP) and served on several boards of child abuse organizations.

Erin Rivelis, PhD, is a psychologist at a juvenile detention center in Westchester, New York, and an adjunct assistant professor of psychology and education at Teachers College, Columbia University. Her research focuses on the relationship between parental psychological maltreatment, psychological control, and the adverse impact on a youth's development and behavior. Clinically, she has worked in juvenile detention and residential treatment with children and adolescents who have behavioral and emotional difficulties including trauma histories and maltreatment.

Melissa K. Runyon, PhD, is treatment services director of the CARES Institute and associate professor of psychiatry at the UMDNJ–School of Osteopathic Medicine. Through federally funded grants, she and her colleagues have developed an evidence-based practice, Combined Parent-Child Cognitive Behavioral Treatment (CPC-CBT), for children and families at risk for child physical abuse. She has also collaborated with colleagues on research funded by NIMH to examine TF-CBT with children who have been sexually abused. She disseminates CPC-CBT nationally and internationally, has multiple publications in the area of child maltreatment, and has coauthored a therapeutic children's book for children who have been physically abused.

Karen J. Saywitz, PhD, is a professor at the University of California, Los Angeles (UCLA), School of Medicine, Department of Psychiatry and associate director of UCLA TIES for Families in the Department of Pediatrics, a program that provides multidisciplinary services to families adopting children with special needs from the foster care system. For 20 years, she has directed programs at UCLA providing mental health services to children and families in the public sector and trained students in medicine, psychology, social work, nursing, and law to do the same. Her research focuses on the capabilities, limitations, needs, and recovery of children involved in the legal system due to adverse early experiences, such as abuse or neglect. She has published widely in the areas of forensic child interviewing, court preparation, and child mental health services.

Anthony J. Urquiza, PhD, is a clinical psychologist and director of Mental Health Services and Clinical Research at UC Davis Children's Hospital, Department of Pediatrics, CAARE Center. His primary clinical research interest and publications address all types of violence with an emphasis on interventions for high-risk families. He has been active in developing and disseminating Parent-Child Interaction Therapy (PCIT). As director of the PCIT Training Center, he has been responsible for training more than 100 community mental health agencies throughout the United States and several other countries.

Supporting researchers for more than 40 years

Research methods have always been at the core of SAGE's publishing program. Founder Sara Miller McCune published SAGE's first methods book, *Public Policy Evaluation*, in 1970. Soon after, she launched the *Quantitative Applications in the Social Sciences* series—affectionately known as the "little green books."

Always at the forefront of developing and supporting new approaches in methods, SAGE published early groundbreaking texts and journals in the fields of qualitative methods and evaluation.

Today, more than 40 years and two million little green books later, SAGE continues to push the boundaries with a growing list of more than 1,200 research methods books, journals, and reference works across the social, behavioral, and health sciences. Its imprints—Pine Forge Press, home of innovative textbooks in sociology, and Corwin, publisher of PreK–12 resources for teachers and administrators—broaden SAGE's range of offerings in methods. SAGE further extended its impact in 2008 when it acquired CQ Press and its best-selling and highly respected political science research methods list.

From qualitative, quantitative, and mixed methods to evaluation, SAGE is the essential resource for academics and practitioners looking for the latest methods by leading scholars.

For more information, visit **www.sagepub.com**.